Everybody Belongs

WITHDRAWN

CRITICAL EDUCATION PRACTICE

SHIRLEY R. STEINBERG AND JOE L. KINCHELOE, *SERIES EDITORS*

BECOMING A STUDENT OF TEACHING
Methodologies for Exploring
Self and School Context
by Robert V. Bullough, Jr.
and Andrew D. Gitlin

OCCUPIED READING
Critical Foundations for
an Ecological Theory
by Alan A. Block

DEMOCRACY, MULTICULTURALISM,
AND THE COMMUNITY COLLEGE
A Critical Perspective
by Robert A. Rhoads
and James R. Valadez

ANATOMY OF A COLLABORATION
Study of a College of Education/
Public School Partnership
by Judith J. Slater

TEACHING MATHEMATICS
Toward a Sound Alternative
by Brent Davis

INNER-CITY SCHOOLS,
MULTICULTURALISM,
AND TEACHER EDUCATION
A Professional Journey
by Frederick L. Yeo

RETHINKING LANGUAGE ARTS
Passion and Practice
by Nina Zaragoza

EDUCATIONAL REFORM
A Deweyan Perspective
by Douglas J. Simpson
and Michael J. B. Jackson

LIBERATION THEOLOGY
AND CRITICAL PEDAGOGY
IN TODAY'S CATHOLIC SCHOOLS
Social Justice in Action
by Thomas Oldenski

CURRICULUM
Toward New Identities
edited by William F. Pinar

WRITING EDUCATIONAL BIOGRAPHY
Explorations in
Qualitative Research
edited by Craig Kridel

EVERYBODY BELONGS
Changing Negative Attitudes
Toward Classmates with Disabilities
by Arthur Shapiro

TEACHING FROM UNDERSTANDING
Teacher As Interpretive Inquirer
edited by Julia L. Ellis

PEDAGOGY AND THE POLITICS
OF THE BODY
A Critical Praxis
by Sherry Shapiro

CRITICAL ART PEDAGOGY
Foundations for
Postmodern Art Education
by Richard Cary

EVERYBODY BELONGS
CHANGING NEGATIVE ATTITUDES TOWARD CLASSMATES WITH DISABILITIES

ARTHUR SHAPIRO

ROUTLEDGEFALMER
A MEMBER OF THE TAYLOR & FRANCIS GROUP
NEW YORK AND LONDON

First paperback edition published in 2000 by
RoutledgeFalmer
29 West 35th Street
New York, NY 10001

Published in Great Britain by
RoutledgeFalmer
11 New Fetter Lane
London EC4P 4EE

RoutledgeFalmer is an imprint of the Taylor & Francis Group.

10 9 8 7 6 5 4 3 2 1

Library of Congress Cataloging-in-Publication Data

Shapiro, Arthur H., 1938–
      Everybody belongs : changing negative attitudes toward classmates with dis-
abilities / by Arthur Shapiro.
          p.   cm. — (Garland reference library of social science ; v. 882. Critical
education practice ; v. 14)
      Includes bibliographical references (p.   ) and index.
      ISBN 0-8153-1179-6 (alk. paper)
      ISBN 0-8153-3960-7 (pbk)
      1. Inclusive education—United States.   2. Toleration—Study and teaching (El-
ementary)—United States.   3. Discrimination against the handicapped—United
States.   4. Disabled students—United States—Social conditions.   5. Students—
United States—Attitudes.   6. Teachers—United States—Attitudes.   I. Title.   II.
Series: Garland reference library of social science ; v. 882.   III. Series: Garland
reference library of social science.   Critical education practice ; vol. 14.
LC1201.S53   1999
306.43'2—dc21   98–46202
                                                                                CIP

Printed on acid-free, 250-year-life paper
Manufactured in the United States of America

For Elly,
for Mindy and Matthew,
for Erik, Rochelle, Yitzchak and Shoshana

What's been important to my understanding of myself and others is the fact that each one of us is so much more than any one thing. A sick child is much more than his or her sickness. A person with a disability is much more than a handicap. (Fred Rogers in *You are Special*, p. 9)

Table of Contents

Acknowledgments   ix

Chapter One   3
   Why Change Attitudes?

Chapter Two   37
   Issues of Language and Terminology

Chapter Three   81
   The Minority Group and Medical Model Paradigms

Chapter Four   145
   Early Attitudes and Their Legacies

Chapter Five   267
   Disabilities and Common Sense Approaches

Chapter Six   341
   Critical Educational Practices for Changing
   Negative Attitudes

Some Final Thoughts About this Book   445

Appendix One   447
   Resources

Bibliography   491

Index   539

Acknowledgments

This book is the result of the help and support I received from several persons. With genuine gratitude and appreciation I would like to identify and publicly thank these individuals: Shirley Steinberg and Joe Kincheloe, friends and editors who provided continuous guidance and encouragement; Harvey Kaye, David Spelkoman, Howard Margolis, Elizabeth Barton, Roslyn Simon, Ina White, Robin Zimenoff, Coleen Fraser and Robert Shanberg for providing input and furnishing ideas; Doug Biklen, Bob Bogdan and Bob Burgdorf for providing much of the "philosophical anchoring" of this book; Joe Shapiro and Mary Johnson for their encouragement; Elly Shapiro, whose love, help, encouragement, understanding and meticulous proofreading helped make the completion of this book possible; and a special thanks to John Swinton, my editor, who so greatly improved my writing.

To all of these individuals I will always be grateful. It is with sincere humility that I acknowledge these friends that have enabled me to fulfill an ambitious dream.

EVERYBODY BELONGS

CHAPTER ONE

Why Change Attitudes?

Attitudes and Images Learned Early in Life

The evil prosthesis of Captain Hook, the sinister hump of Richard III, the pitiable crutch of Tiny Tim, the blind bumbling antics of Mr. Magoo, the comical speech of Porky Pig, even the pathetic pleas of poster children in their wheelchairs—these are six examples of negative disability images deeply ingrained in our culture. Because the influence of such images so often works subliminally, most of us remain unaware of how we internalize them or how they affect, in particular, childrens' attitudes and their accompanying behaviors. Forming attitudes regarding disability from such images is like basing assumptions about African culture on old Tarzan movies.

We learn negative attitudes toward disability early in life from such strong cultural influences as school, the media, our language and literature. Many first encounters with literature, for example, include stereotyped characters like the childish dwarfs and hump-backed wicked witch in *Snow White*, the *Little Lame Prince*, the evil giant in *Jack and the Beanstalk*, or the sly deformed dwarf, *Rumpelstiltskin*. Franks (1996) found that many various disabilities are used symbolically in fairy tales. For example, in Grimm's Fairy Tales (1945/1995), the story of *Cinderella* ends with her stepsisters having their eyes picked out by doves. The final line reads, "And so, for their wickedness and falseness they were punished with blindness for the rest of their days" (p. 161). Similarly, the prince who climbs up Rapunzel's hair to get into the tower loses his sight by having his eyes "scratched out by the thorns among which he fell" and is forced to "wander about blind in the wood [with] nothing but roots and berries to eat" (p. 132).

Such images impress on young minds that people with physical or mental differences are to be feared, pitied, trivialized, or ridiculed. Children learn early from these stories that physical beauty symbolizes goodness and disability symbolizes evil. Furthermore, the evil disabled ones are always out to ravage the attractive ones. "Our memories of these and other characters often become indelible, impervious to any experiences we may have with disabled individuals in real life" (Bowe, 1978, p. 109).

Childrens' reading matter regularly reinforces such images. Weinberg and Santana (1978), for example, found that individuals with disabilities in comic books are often characterized as evil. One only need to recall the villains of Dick Tracy (even named for their physical differences) including Prune Face, Brow, BB Eyes, Flat Top, Mumbles, Itchy Oliver, Ugly Christine, Pouch and even a female named Lispy who spoke with a speech disorder (Crouch, 1987).

Biklen, Ford and Ferguson (1989) stressed the importance of examining the meanings of disability in culture so as to understand the issues of disability and schooling. Attitudes are acquired through "observational learning" whereby a child observes surrounding behaviors and influences. Unfortunately, many negative influences in our culture teach children early in life to accept the idea that certain human qualities like physical "wholeness," good looks, high intelligence, and clear speech, are valued and identified with high status individuals, whereas the qualities of others are demeaned, stigmatized, ridiculed, feared and degraded. Youngsters learn to assume that people with disabilities are more "different from" than "similar to" persons without them, and those differences lessen them and set them apart. The consequences of such beliefs result in segregation and isolation which, in turn, reinforce negative attitudes.

Studies conducted by Gerber (1977); Goodman, Gottlieb and Harrison (1977); and Horne (1985) reveal that non-disabled students often demonstrate negative attitudes toward their disabled peers making them feel rejected and less accepted. Unfortunately, many youngsters enter school with stereotypic views and attitudes toward those perceived as different (Salend, 1994). According to Baum and Wells (1985),

> The devaluing of human differences appears to be acculturized in children as they grow and develop. [Y]ounger children show more acceptance of their handicapped peers than older children do. Their awareness of handicapping conditions at about four is followed by beginning negativism by about five years of age (p. 282).

Brodkin (1993) found that

Children are not born biased, but they notice differences at a young age. By age five, children begin to absorb society's messages and fears. Between the ages of seven and nine, children's awareness of differences may be transformed into full-blown prejudice (p. 75).

James (1975) related some of the consequences of such prejudice. He found that

Life can be a living hell for children who are different. Deviance, even in its minor forms, is seldom tolerated in our society. Almost any sensitive person who spends a few hours on a busy playground or in the halls of an elementary or junior high school will find more than one child being teased because he is fat, thin, crippled, ugly, retarded, or otherwise different (p. 16).

Such prejudice must be directly addressed in the schools. Simply integrating youngsters with disabilities into the mainstream without pedagogically dealing with attitudes is meaningless and, in some cases, increases negative attitudes. Schools need this information because they are mandated to deal with the successful integration of their pupils who have educational handicaps. Morrison and Ursprung (1990), for example, found a definite need for educational programs directed at altering children's attitudes toward disabled individuals:

There is considerable evidence suggesting that such an undertaking is important and would be beneficial. Classroom teachers, counselors, and other people working to implement such projects know these endeavors must be based on the assumption that the dissemination of accurate information about disabilities will lead to increased positive attitudes and reduction of social rejection, stigmatization, and prejudice (p. 183).

Legislation like the *Education for All Handicapped Children Act (PL 94-142,* 1975 as amended by IDEA), *Section 504 of the Rehabilitation Act* (1973) and the *Americans With Disabilities Act* (1990) all mandate that persons with disabilities receive the opportunity to function in "normalized," "least restrictive" environments. The primary outcome of this federal legislation is the increased inclusion and mainstreaming of students with educational handicaps in the public schools, resulting in greater interaction between disabled and non-disabled peers (Bookbinder, 1978; Carlberg and Kavale, 1980). Jones and

Guskin (1986), however, found that if the laws and service persons providing equal educational opportunities for children with disabilities are
to be effective, school environments must be made increasingly receptive to those who make up this population. Both the courts and Congress
appear to have recognized that full integration into communities and
schools would improve our traditional views of persons with disabilities. But such improvement appears to be possible only through a better
understanding of the attitudes that determine status and treatment of
such people in our schools and other social institutions. The effectiveness of new laws and service patterns is inherently related to
changes in the attitudes of communities, professionals, and persons with
disabilities and their families. Despite recognition, then, that full integration into communities and schools will alter traditional views toward
persons with disabilities, the achievement of this full integration
appears to be possible only through face to face interaction and a better
elucidation of our current attitudes toward them and attitude change in
general.

Even the perception of what constitutes "positive attitudes" differs
between persons with disabilities and those without them. For example,
Makas (1990) found that

> [D]isabled people and non-disabled people differ significantly in their
> perceptions of what constitutes "the most positive attitudes toward
> persons with disabilities." For the disabled respondents, "positive atti-
> tudes" would mean either dispensing with the special category of dis-
> ability entirely, or promoting attitudes that defend the civil and social
> rights of disabled persons. For the non-disabled respondents, "posi-
> tive attitudes" reflect a desire to be nice, helpful, and ultimately place
> the disabled person in a needy situation. Non-disabled individuals
> may actually be perceived by disabled people, therefore, as express-
> ing negative attitudes when, in fact, the non-disabled persons are try-
> ing hard to express what they consider to be positive attitudes. . . .
> Thus the paradox of well-intentioned liberalism is that the recipient
> frequently experiences the interaction as offensive (p. 30).

The Importance of a
Multidimensional-Experiential Approach

Unfortunately, positive social interaction has yet to prove a natural outcome of mainstreaming as an integrative process (Dewer, 1982).
Teachers in the regular grades that include mainstreamed youngsters
classified as handicapped are most often given assistance and training to

address "cognitive" rather than "affective" needs. They are more apt to receive help with teaching approaches for various subjects rather than help with learning to nurture friendship-building and social integration (Guinagh, 1980).

Salend (1984) found that typical or regular classroom students can play a significant role in determining the success or failure of integration. He found that the process can be greatly facilitated when non-disabled students interact positively with their peers classified as handicapped, particularly when they serve as role models, peer tutors and friends. But he noted further that, "the ability and willingness of regular education students to help make mainstreaming successful may be influenced by their attitudes toward their mainstreamed peers" (p. 161).

Thus, to facilitate genuine social integration, it is critical to train regular teachers to become actively involved in the preparation of their non-disabled students in understanding and developing positive attitudes toward their peers with disabilities. Changing negative attitudes, however, can be difficult. It requires a great deal of planning and a multidimensional process that includes a knowledge of how attitudes develop and a variety of experiential techniques. Derman-Sparks (1989) noted,

[F]ostering anti-bias attitudes toward disability and empowering children with disabilities requires much more than being together in the classroom. Children with disabilities need to see themselves reflected in the world around them, in pictures, in toys, in books, in role models. They need acceptance for who they are and in an environment that fosters their autonomy and the development of alternative modes of interaction with the world. Nondisabled children need to gain information, ask questions, and express their feelings about disabilities. Contact by itself does not necessarily reduce nondisabled children's fears—it may even intensify them—unless adults take active steps to promote children's learning about each other. . . . Anti-bias teaching about disabilities also requires that teachers become aware of their own deep-seated attitudes (pp. 39-40).

Researchers like Schroedel (1979) and Watts (1984) found the most effective components of such a multi-dimensional process for altering negative attitudes toward persons with disabilities included experiential (active participation) techniques. The use of social gaming (for example, role-playing and simulation activities always followed by discussion); value confrontation; interaction with persons with disabilities (for example, cooperative learning and interactions with guest speakers with disabilities); providing applicable information through books, articles, and a wide variety of audio and visual media, (for example, movies, slides, audio and videotapes, and compact disks); exposing students to assistive technology, adaptive devices, aids and appliances and the use of puppets to depict vignettes and lead discussion. Such Multi-dimensional and experiential methods were found successful for changing negative attitudes by Donaldson (1980); Israelson (1980); Jones, Sowell, Jones, and Butler (1981); Dewer (1982); Popp (1983); Kilburn (1984); Bergantino (1984); Bauer (1985); Binkard (1985); Raschke and Dedrick (1986); Riester and Bessette (1986); and Fiedler and Simpson (1987). All concluded that planned programs using such "multi-dimensional" and "experiential" methods to teach peers acceptance of classmates with disabilities result in positive gains in student acceptance and facilitate positive perceptions of youngsters with disabilities. Donaldson (1980) suggested the following categories: (a) direct and indirect contact with, or exposure to, disabled persons; (b) information about disabilities; (c) persuasive messages; (d) analysis of the dynamics of prejudice; (e) disability simulation; and (f) group discussions. Similarly, Morrison and Ursprung (1990) stressed that the material developed for any program needs to be organized for various methods of presentation including (1) actual experiences with disabled persons of equal or valued status who represent non-stereotypic images of disabilities, who should convey information about what it is like to be disabled and how they want non-disabled persons to relate to them; (2) exposure to individuals with disabilities who have successfully adjusted to their disability and who can display their confidence and independence; (3) exposure to various methods of presentation that will keep the children's interest including simulations of disability, puppet shows, and films. Each of these elements receives a thorough analysis in Chapter VI. First we must examine attitudes themselves.

The Nature of Attitudes

An attitude is the general tendency of an individual to act in a certain way under special conditions. This general tendency can be displayed in two kinds of action: what the individual does and what the individual says. In other words, an attitude is defined as "a favorable or unfavorable evaluative reaction toward something or someone, exhibited in one's beliefs, feelings or intended behavior" (Meyers, 1987). It is, therefore, the tendency for an individual to act or react positively or negatively to his or her world based on the values, beliefs, and paradigms rooted in his or her social experiences. An attitude may be viewed as a positive or negative emotional reaction to a person or object accompanied by specific beliefs that tend to cause its holder to behave in specific ways toward its object.

While definitions of attitude may vary slightly, most include three interrelated basic elements: (1) a belief or "cognitive" component, (2) an emotional or "affective" component, and (3) an action or "behavioral" component. The components are interrelated because positive and complimentary beliefs are accompanied by liking and positive feelings while uncomplimentary and negative beliefs are accompanied by dislike and negative feelings. These beliefs and feelings, in turn, represent a tendency to act. As Yuker (1977) stated,

> If the beliefs and feelings are positive, there will be a tendency to move toward the object of the attitude, and to say and do nice things. If the beliefs and feelings are negative there will be a tendency to avoid the object, or to say or do negative things. If the beliefs and feelings are ambivalent, the person's actions will vacillate, sometimes they will be positive, other times they will be negative (p. 93).

Liebert (1975) suggested that the three components of attitude often form from observational learning—that is, the kind of learning where the behavior of one person is changed simply by observing the behavior of others—like the face to face interaction between students without disabilities and students with disabilities. Bowe (1978) stated that

> Attitudes appear to be heavily dependent upon contact with information about what attitudes concern. People who have had extensive contact with disabled people tend to regard them more favorably and to recognize more fully than do people with less contact and that they differ greatly among themselves (p. 112).

Unfortunately, the schools through their model of labeling and segregation, often provide the basis of negative attitudes. Students viewed as different are banished, denied access, and receive negatively loaded labels which, in turn, causes guilt, pain, and shame, not only for them but for their parents as well. Once labeled, they are treated as being somehow less than the others. Such negative attitudes, in turn, affect the youngsters' self-images.

Characteristics of Attitudes

Jones and Guskin's (1986) studies of attitudes and attitude change in special education revealed that college students, especially teachers in training, are the most common subjects for studies of attitudes toward physical disability and mental retardation. These studies often focus on characteristics that are easy to measure, such as experience with disabled individuals and major fields of study. A frequently used measure in their study is the social distance scale in which subjects are asked to indicate how close they are willing to get to persons with different types of disabilities. Their results generally reveal a greater avoidance toward the most severely disabled person and a preference for physically disabled persons over those labeled as mentally retarded. They state that a few attempts have been reported of systematic efforts to modify attitudes by exposure to handicapped persons or other specific educational efforts. Their results have not been consistent.

Theories of Attitude Change

Various theories exist on changing attitudes toward persons with disabilities and several are based on Lewin's theory of attitude change. Lewin (1948) identified two forces that affect the modification of attitudes: restraining forces (factors which inhibit any change), and driving forces (factors which promote existing opinion or behavior). In analyzing Lewin's theory, Evans (1976) emphasized that

> Attitude for opinion modification must be thought of as a result of either the reduction in restraining forces or an increase in driving forces surrounding an opinion or behavior. Attitudes are a quasi-stationary equilibrium when driving and restraining forces are equal. Attitude modification thus necessitates an unbalancing or unfreezing of the present attitude by either reducing a restraining force or increasing a driving force (p. 573).

Thus, Evans (1976) identified the uneasiness and inhibitions non-disabled persons felt when interacting with disabled persons as a restraining force. This force may be reduced by having disabled persons express their feelings about their disability and the attitudes of others during interviews. By reducing the discomfort (the restraining force) of the non-disabled person, attitudes may change more positively. Should the experience accentuate the discomfort, a negative attitude could take place.

In developing her theory of information presentation, Donaldson (1980) approached the driving force rather than the restraining force. She indicated that the use of live or media presentations could unfreeze currently held beliefs. Credible presenters who represent nonstereotypic images of disabled persons may result in positive attitude changes but the possibility of negative change exists if the individual receives information that confirms or presents a negative stereotype of disabled persons. Further, Donaldson advised those involved in changing attitudes to follow some model that incorporates the ideas that opinion or attitude modification be thought of as a result of either the reduction in restraining forces or an increase in driving forces surrounding an opinion or behavior. For example, when discussing individuals with disabilities, one can seek to reduce the discomfort that occurs when non-disabled persons interact with disabled individuals by presenting a message sufficiently powerful enough to unfreeze a currently held belief.

Negative Attitudes and the Concept of Self
As Brodkin (1993) stated, "A child who is the victim of prejudice experiences not only emotional pain and social and economic barriers, but also permanent damage to his or her confidence and sense of self-worth" (p. 75). Self-concept plays a critical role in the development of personality. Rogers (1951) defined the self-concept as

> an organized configuration of perceptions of the self which are admissible to awareness. It is composed of such elements as the perceptions of one's characteristics and abilities; the value qualities which are perceived as associated with experiences and objects; and goals and ideals which are perceived as having positive or negative valence (pp. 136-137).

In other words, the self-concept is the total way in which people perceive themselves. It includes their abilities, characteristics, and especially the positive and negative evaluations placed on them. One's self-concept is both learned and changeable with each new experience. It is often referred to as both the "image" and the "process" of change:

> The individual reflects his experiences against his self-concept; in turn, his self-concept influences what he will learn from his experiences. Therefore the formation of a self-concept is a process in which the individual is constantly changing his awareness of himself and the way he perceives the world (Kokaska & Brolin, 1985, p. 131).

Thus, one's sense of "self" is influenced largely by one's interactions and encounters with others, particularly "significant others"—that is to say, teachers, parents, siblings, classmates and friends who comprise various circles of affinity around the individual. The most influential circle includes the disabled child's friends and peers. The attitudes of these groups affect both the development of the disabled child's self-concept, and the socialization of that youngster into typical community activities.

The next attitudinal circle includes the relationships of the disabled youngster and the rehabilitation professionals with whom he or she comes into contact: teachers, social workers, counselors, psychologists, physicians, nurses and clergy. In these roles, the educators and rehabilitation practitioners provide information, services and stability. Their attitudes can have enormous impact on both the medical and psychosocial processes of adjustment to disability the disabled youngster experiences. The attitudes of these professionals can strongly influence the attitudes of members of the first social circle, mainly family and peers, as well as the attitudes exhibited within the larger third circle, society at large (Antonak, 1988).

The third and outermost circle includes the attitudes of the general public. Society's negative attitudes toward disabled individuals in general erect obstacles to the fulfillment and attainment of life goals. Such detrimental attitudes are often covert, but may be detected in the use of media stereotypes, derogatory labels and prejudicial beliefs (Antonak & Livneh, 1988).

It is easy to see how a youngster's disability and self-image are closely connected. As Umbreit and Baker (1983) stated,

> A disability's full effect on a child is likely to extend far beyond the immediate physical or mental limitations. Whether as a direct result of frustrations emanating from the disability itself or as a function of socialization, the disabled child's self-concept is bound to be affected (Jones, 1983, p. 1).

Meyerowitz (1962) earlier noted this connection between self-image and disability:

> Both the awareness of differences and awareness of being segregated from those who are not different can negatively affect the child's atti-

tude toward himself, his self-concept and self-esteem (Safford, 1978, p. 291).

Morris (1991) asserted that "prejudice lies at the heart of the segregation which many disabled people experience both as children and adults" (p. 18). Mayen and Skrtic (1988) further stated that "the essence of discrimination is segregation" (p. 475). Since attitudes shape, direct and underlie actions, prejudice (a thought), often becomes discrimination (an act), making those to whom it is directed the recipients of segregation, exclusion, patronization, negative social policy and biased cruel treatment. For instance, when students with educational handicaps are placed into separate programs, the message for the typical student becomes "Look what happens if you don't measure up—banishment." For the student classified as handicapped, the message from the school system connotes, "There is something wrong with you; you don't fit in." Such negative treatment contributes to the destruction of a youngster's concept of self, which plays a critical role in the development of personality.

Thus, an individual's sense of "self" is influenced largely from one's interactions and encounters with teachers, classmates, friends and even influences like the media. How can a child develop a positive self concept if he or she constantly receives messages he or she interprets as "You are laughable, pitiable, sad, abnormal, unfortunate and valueless?" As Wahl (1995) explained,

> [B]eing routinely confronted with unfavorable media images of oneself, along with the experience and anticipation of the negative public attitudes illustrated by such depictions, likely contributes to lowered self-esteem. People who are bombarded with unfavorable information about themselves, social scientists have established, begin to internalize such images, to doubt themselves, to conceive of themselves in the same distorted and demeaning ways that others appear to (p. 106).

Shea and Bauer (1997) stressed the importance of providing role models:

> For learners with disabilities to succeed in a world where norms of the majority prevail, they must first have a strong sense of self and their identity as an individual with a disability. They should be given access to role models, individuals with disabilities who can challenge them and instill confidence that barriers can be overcome. This contributes

to the positive development of the individual's self-concept and affects their outlook on life (pp. 444-445).

Schools themselves cause negative self-esteem for students classified as handicapped by officially giving them negatively loaded labels like "mentally retarded," "emotionally disturbed," "chronically ill," "neurologically impaired," and "socially maladjusted." One can readily see how such terms might damage a child's self esteem, and since prevailing attitudes like these devalue the worth of youngsters with disabilities, they often encourage those children to hold themselves in low regard. Once labeled, they are usually placed in segregated settings thereby reinforcing the already powerful message that they are less than others and not good enough to attend school with them. Cohen (1974/1977) stated, "Studies of the effects of being labeled 'mentally retarded' (and then placed in a special class for 'retarded' children) appear to indicate that such labeling is a detriment to the child's self-esteem and social acceptance" (p. 118). The disability becomes a "learned inferiority." Unfortunately, once such inferiority is internalized within the individual, it becomes a cue for other persons' judgments. Yuker (1979) wrote of the importance of placing one's disability in perspective with one's abilities:

> The way people see themselves is very often a major factor in the way other people see them. I think you can characterize disabled people in terms of the percentage of the time they think of themselves as being disabled. Some people are aware of their disability 100 percent of the time. Others, who are equally severely disabled, are only aware of the disability 5 to 10 percent of the time. Such people are very different from one another. I am quite convinced that the percentage of time you think of yourself as disabled influences the percentage of time *other* people think of you as disabled. Self-concept, again, is critical, and it influences others. . . . The disabled individual is also "able." One has to ask at any given time, is it my abilities that are more important or my disabilities? I have both. . . . It is a matter of the balance of the two. That balance is reflected in self-concept. The balance influences the way you interact with others, and the way other people perceive you (pp. 47-48).

Attitudes of acceptance evinced by the schools, in general, and typical classroom students, in particular, can greatly influence the successful integration of their peers classified as handicapped into regular educational settings. Once positive attitudes are established, typical classmates can provide support and encouragement in educational and social settings (Salend, 1994). But, the example the school sets is critical. Students with disabilities may have difficulty interpreting cues that may affect their self concepts because of the ways such youngsters perceive themselves within their environments. If one has a disability that limits sensory reception (for example, blindness or deafness), one will have difficulty gaining accurate information about one's self within one's environment. While blindness can limit the amount of input entering into one's information system (for example, a smile or a wink), deafness can limit the rules for processing information (for example, the learning of language).

The Importance of Teaching Tolerance

Schools have a responsibility to change negative attitudes that result in discrimination, prejudice and segregation. Because a central purpose of our education is the promotion of values and attitudes crucial to our pluralistic society and democratic form of government, it becomes especially important to address those beliefs and attitudes that lead to discrimination—the denial of certain members of society the right and opportunity to full social, educational, economic, and political participation. By definition, a democracy is government by the people. Educators, therefore, need to understand the importance of teaching future citizens to care about the rights of others (Lickona, 1991). Schools can play an important role in bringing about needed social change by preparing "each generation to examine and, when necessary, to alter existing social values, practices and beliefs" (Sadker & Sadker, 1991, p. 140). The challenge of bringing youngsters back into the mainstream of education who have been excluded on the basis of a handicapping condition is an "exciting, controversial and dynamic process for it challenges the basic assumptions of each of us and the same time introduces us to new ways of thinking and seeing" (Forest, 1989, p. 5).

A school is sometimes seen as a "melting pot or a kind of glue to hold the American fabric together" (Sadker & Sadker, 1991, p. 137) and therefore has a responsibility to help socialize and unify society. As Rubenfeld (1994) stated,

> School, of course, is one of the great defining experiences in our country. Almost more than family life, it is the Great Socializer. It is where we learn to juggle friends, enemies, and acquaintances, to cope

with real-world authority and to test the outside of the disciplinary
envelope, to work and play together, and from time to time to cut
loose in wonderful self-induced mass hysteria. In short, school is
where we learn to be functioning members of a culture, not just our
parents' kids. And it is this vital piece of learning that special education can never provide (pp. 235-236).

In addition, schools have a responsibility for encouraging diversity
and tolerance, eliminating discrimination, increasing among youngsters
an understanding of those perceived to be different, and respecting and
protecting the rights of all diverse populations within our pluralistic
society. Each individual child is the responsibility of the school and has
a right to attend without having to feel inferior. Schools must recognize
their responsibility to confront bigotry in all its *ism* forms. They can
reduce harmful attitudes by instilling helpful ones, "and make disability
a topic of investigation and discussion in the same way that some
schools explore the issues of sexism and racism" (Biklen, Ford &
Ferguson, 1989, p. 257).

"Disablism" (earlier termed "handicapism") is discrimination
toward persons with disabilities and is akin to racism and sexism. (The
concept is discussed in detail in Chapter III.) All such "isms" are forms
of discrimination based on outward personal appearance. The term
"handicapism" was coined by Bogdan and Biklen (1977), who referred
to it as "the stereotyping, prejudice, and discrimination practiced by
society against disabled people" (p. 14). As a form of prejudice, disablism is often based on negative stereotypical images most of which
operate subliminally (Shapiro & Spelkoman, 1979). The majority of
Americans are unaware these negative attitudes exist within us. In their
report for the United States Commission on Civil Rights, Bell and
Burgdorf (1983) found that

> Most people do not harbor conscious prejudices against handicapped
> people or even realize that such prejudice is a serious problem in
> American society. Many perceive handicapped people's disadvan-
> taged social and economic status as resulting from innate limitations
> caused by handicaps. Authorities from every branch of government
> have concluded, however, that prejudice and discrimination are major
> causes of the disadvantages confronting handicapped people (p. 17).

When asked to draw a picture of a person with blindness, many
grade schoolers will most likely portray a sad individual with dark

glasses, a cane, and a tin cup for begging. Ordinarily, children's life experiences provide few real interactions with persons with visual impairments. Stereotyped images persist without exposure and interaction to help offset them (Salend, 1994).

The Rise of Prejudice and Discrimination in the Schools
Contrary to common belief, considerable prejudice exists among school-aged youngsters and tends to increase and become more rigid as they progress through the grades. Baskin and Harris (1977) found youngsters classified as handicapped often to be rejected and ostracized by their peers. In high-density, potentially explosive situations like lunchrooms or playgrounds, they were particularly subject to social abuse. "Simply put, students with disabilities are not often chosen as friends" (Rowley-Kelly & Reigel, 1993, p. 245). "While some studies suggest that students view their mainstreamed peers positively. . . the majority of studies indicate that students who do not have disabilities demonstrate negative attitudes toward their peers that do" (Salend, 1994, p. 162). It is not surprising then, that Lickona (1991) cited peer cruelty as among the frightening trends in schools, along with a marked increase in violence and vandalism, disrespect for authority, bigotry, bad language, and declining civic responsibility.

An extreme example of such peer cruelty appeared in the famous Glen Ridge case where on March 1, 1989, five high school football players in that affluent North Jersey community enjoyed an afternoon of fun and games by taking turns inserting a broom handle, a stick, and a baseball bat into the vagina of a seventeen-year old girl with mental retardation, while eight others stood by. Three of the four boys brought to trial were found guilty of aggravated sexual assault and, with the other, of conspiracy to commit aggravated sexual assault. While some of the original thirteen boys present left at the outset of the attack on the girl, not one made an effort to protect her.

Although this was a one-time incident, some youngsters perceived as different by their peers face ridicule and teasing on an ongoing basis. Van Etten (1988) described how she had to face constant cruel teasing as a student with dwarfism:

> The day is clear in my mind, when a group of kids saw me walking
> onto the school grounds. I was alone and there were about six or
> seven of them. One child noticed me and made sure the rest didn't
> miss seeing me. She pointed at me, and they all jumped up and down

laughing and making fun of me in their excitement. Most times, I would have just ignored them, but this day it was impossible. Their message was loud and clear—I looked funny. I couldn't take it and tears spilled out as I walked passed them and heard their jeers behind me (p. 35).

Some youngsters do not limit their expressions of cruel behavior to their school age peers. Ellis (1990), a disability rights advocate with cerebral palsy, reported this personal frightening experience while driving:

> I was stuck in traffic on Route 1. A bus carrying a high school athletic team was stalled next to me. One of the guys on the bus saw me through the window. He pointed me out to his buddies. They crowded to the window, mimicking my awkwardness. The muscles in my neck and face tightened, further distorting my body. I couldn't escape them. Finally, the traffic began to move (B 3).

Unfortunately, cruel terms like "tard cart," "mental rental," and "banana wagon" are commonly heard from school-aged youngsters describing the small yellow vans that often transport their classified as handicapped schoolmates to special education programs. Safford (1978) believed that such intolerance is more a reflection of adult prejudices and of adult-imposed segregation than innate cruelty. He observed, "The name-calling may not reveal imitation of adult behavior so much as identification with adult attitudes" (p. 292).

The Rationale For Teaching Disability Awareness
The preceding examples illustrate the need to incorporate disability awareness into the overall curriculum within our schools. Because research suggests that many children enter schools with prejudiced and stereotypical views of those perceived as different, and particularly of their peers with disabilities, schools need to focus more on bringing diverse populations together amicably (Gerber, 1977; Goodman, Gottlieb & Harrison, 1977; Horne, 1985; Salend, 1994). Research also suggests a need for educators to become especially sensitized to the effects of disablism and the development of accepting attitudes. For example, Schroedel (1979) and Jones (1984) compiled studies that repeatedly demonstrated that children easily accept negative subliminal attitudes learned early in life from influences like the mass media,

comic books, literature, language, and common fairy tales. Schroedel (1979) reviewed more than 100 studies on attitudes toward persons with disabilities leading him to conclude that

> Modifying attitudes toward and among Americans who are disabled is an important business. The thoughts and feelings which compose attitudes influence the behaviors of both those who perceive and are perceived. . . . Once individuals understand these effects of their attitudes, this awareness can create the desire for change (p. 15).

According to Salend (1994), primary among the factors that shape the development of negative attitudes are the media, which tend to portray persons with disabilities negatively. Bowe (1978) stressed that as long as society fears persons with disabilities it will continue to treat them in separate out-of-way hospitals, institutions and schools. He wrote, "As long as we pity disabled people, we will continue to see them as objects of charity rather than as equals deserving a say in their own destinies" (p. 111).

A Matter of Right and Rights
The world of persons with disabilities has begun to change rapidly, both in the area of technology, and in the new challenges to physical and attitudinal barriers. The terms "handicapped" and "disabled," themselves, are now challenged as is the medical paradigm traditionally used as the lens for viewing the issues of disabilities and special education. On all fronts, persons with disabilities are entering the mainstream. Institutions are being closed. Ramps and reserved parking places are now evident. The public has begun to become aware of concepts like "least restrictive environment," "normalization," "deinstitutionalization," "integration," "inclusion," "independent living," "supported employment," and "reasonable accommodation."

Overcoming prejudices learned at an early age, however, can be problematic. Educators need special skills to recognize and counter stereotypical negative images and their sources. Their role is critical for the success of full inclusion and acceptance of disabled individuals into our schools and society, which is now a matter of rights as well as a matter of right. People with disabilities are now forging their own civil rights movement (J. Shapiro, 1993), and persons with disabilities have recently emerged, along with other minorities, as a vocal political force—no longer willing to be "done to" and not satisfied with being "done for" (Safford, 1978, p. 291).

The Americans With Disabilities Act (1992) now guarantees persons with disabilities the right to equal access to promote their integration into all aspects of society including public accommodations, transportation, communications, employment, recreation and education. In addition, the *Education for All Handicapped Children Act* (PL 94-142 as amended by *The Individuals with Disabilities Education Act IDEA*) requires all educationally handicapped students between the ages of three and twenty-one to receive a free and appropriate education in the least restrictive setting possible to meet their unique needs. The role of the school in the development of positive attitudes has now become particularly significant, and to a degree legally mandated.

A meaningful result of this legislation has been the increasing integration of youngsters with disabilities into so-called "regular education" in the public schools, resulting in their increased interaction with their non-disabled peers. Instruction in segregated settings is now viewed as restrictive because it deprives youngsters both with and without disabilities the learning experiences essential for the fullest development of their humanness, attitudes of acceptance being a critical ingredient for the successful integration of any oppressed group. All educators must fully understand how least restrictive environments require welcoming attitudes (Safford, 1978).

The Three R's: Recognition, Respect, and Responsibility

The recognition of full inclusion of students with disabilities as a moral value represents a momentous trend in educational thinking (Biklen, Ferguson & Ford, 1989). Inclusion both benefits youngsters with disabilities, and reinforces the moral values of recognition, respect and responsibility for non-handicapped youngsters as well.

Recognition refers to the degree of attention a person or a group receives. Before one can be respected, one's existence must be recognized. For example, African-Americans were really not recognized on television before the 1960's. Although at that time approximately 13 percent of the American population was African-American, foreign viewers estimated the African-American population to be about 1 percent, based on what they viewed on American television. Black Americans were simply not recognized as a people. On television, no

African-Americans played judges, lawyers, doctors, bankers, professors, or teachers. In fact, they never appeared in commercials or on quiz shows. One can judge the degree of respect they received by the stereotyped roles in which they were portrayed, like Amos 'n' Andy. Sometimes they were chauffeurs named after cities like Jack Benny's Rochester and Charley Chan's Birmingham (Liebert,1975). Today's young television viewers who are used to seeing African-Americans in professional roles, in commercials and on quiz shows, have a different paradigm regarding African-Americans. Television has recognized them as part of the American whole. Just as African Americans and women have received the recognition they deserved, persons with disabilities are becoming less hidden. For example, chain stores like Nordstrom and Kids R Us now employ models with disabilities in their advertising. Commercials for McDonald's, AT&T and Levi Jeans all feature persons with disabilities. Since 1986, nine Academy Award nominees in the Best Actor or Actress categories played characters with mental or physical disabilities (*In Case You Didn't Know*, 1994). Persons with various disabilities were depicted without stereotypes in such films as *Coming Home* (1978), (paraplegia); *The Elephant Man* (1980), (disfigurement); *Children of a Lesser God* (1987), (deafness); *Gaby: A True Story* (1987) (cerebral palsy); *Rain Man* (1988), (autism); *Born on the Fourth of July* (1989), (paraplegia); *My Left Foot* (1989) (cerebral palsy); *Scent of a Woman* (1993), (blindness); *The Piano* (1993) (muteness), and *Forrest Gump* (1995), (mental retardation). Chris Burke, a young man with Down Syndrome, had a starring role in his own television show, *Life Goes On.* Stand up comics with disabilities like Geri Jewell, Kathy Buckley, Alex Valdez, Henry Holden and Chris Fonseca are becoming more and more common (Meyer, 1995). Miss America of 1995, Heather Whitestone, has deafness. There is little doubt that persons with disabilities are finally beginning to be *recognized* as an integral part of our population.

Respect refers to the means by which someone demonstrates regard for the worth of someone else. Respect for others requires one to treat all people as having dignity and rights commensurate with one's own.

Responsibility is an extension of respect. In Licona's (1992) formula, if we learn to respect persons with disabilities, we value them. If we value them, we feel some responsibility for their welfare. The behavior in that Glen Ridge basement demonstrated a lack of respect for both females and persons with mental retardation. Consequently, no one took responsibility for the young woman's well-being.

Integration, Mainstreaming, Normalization,
Least Restrictive Environment, and Inclusion

Educators and legislators freely acknowledge the benefits of integrating educationally handicapped youngsters with their non-handicapped peers. Before discussing such educational and social benefits, however, we need some clarification of terms. The concept of "integration" implies several terms producing confusion among those unaware of their definitional nuances. The most common of these terms are (1) "least restrictive environment" (or alternative), (2) "normalization," (3) "mainstreaming," and (4) "inclusion."

Integration refers simply the concept of group homogeneity. It is the direct opposite of segregation, particularly as related to such homogenized environments as segregated schools, segregated institutions, segregated classes and segregated services. (Albright, Brown., Vandeventer & Jorgensen, 1989).

Least Restrictive Environment is a term included within *The Education for All Handicapped Children* Act (P.L. 94-142 as amended by *IDEA*):

> [To] the maximum extent appropriate, handicapped children. . . are educated with children who are not handicapped, and that special classes, special schooling, or other removal of handicapped children from the regular educational environment occurs only when the nature or the severity of the handicap is such that education in regular classes with the use of supplementary aids and services cannot be achieved satisfactorily (20 *U.S.C. Sec.* 1412[5]).

Normalization is a principle that developed largely as an answer to the philosophy of segregating developmentally disabled individuals by institutionalization. Wolfensberger (1972) defined it as the

> Utilization of means which are as culturally normative as possible, in order to establish and/or maintain personal behaviors and characteristics which are as culturally normative as possible (p. 28).

Individuals placed in institutions often lived segregated and structured lives. Institutionalized clients were traditionally told when to go to bed, when to get up, when to brush their teeth, when to eat, when to use the toilet, when to engage in recreation and when to go to work or school. They often resided, worked, and carried out educational and recreational activities all within the confines of the institution. Normalization means that individuals with disabilities live their lives with normal routines, and make such personal decisions as choosing when to go to bed or get up, when to eat, and how to use their personal time. It also means experiencing such normal routines of life as living at one location and going to school or work at another. It further means enjoying the right to participate in leisure activities in a variety of situations, learning to cope with unpredicted unstructured situations, taking risks, and having age-appropriate experiences without being treated like juveniles. Normalization also means living in a sexually integrated society and in a normal physical facility.

Mainstreaming commonly refers to the process of returning some students with disabilities to general education while maintaining a separate system of special classes, services and programs for others. Absent from state and federal law, the term has been defined over the years in various ways including these five:

1. the temporal, instructional, and social integration of eligible exceptional children with normal peers based on an ongoing, individually determined, educational planning programming process, and requiring clarification of responsibility among regular and special education administrative, instructional, and supportive personnel (Kauffman, Gottlieb, Agard & Kukic, 1975, p. 9);

2. maximum integration in the regular class combined with concrete assistance for the regular class teacher (Gearheart & Weishahn, 1984, p. 3);

3. providing special education and related services to exceptional children while they are attend regular classes and schools (Reynolds & Birch, 1988, p. 1);

4. the process of bringing exceptional children into daily contact with non-exceptional children in an educational setting (Kirk & Gallagher, 1989, p. 41); and

5. providing equal access to educational opportunities for students with disabilities; teaching all students how to appreciate differences among individuals; sharing resources, skills and time; sharing responsibilities for students with disabilities; providing a climate in which positive attitudes prevail; realizing that students

with disabilities belong in the regular class environment and
should receive support services as needed; creating change and
realizing that change will not occur instantly (Wood, 1993, p. 6);

One commonly accepted definition of "Supported Inclusive
Education" emerged from the PEAK Parent Information Center (1988):

Supported inclusive education refers to the educational option for all
students regardless of their disability to be educated in age-appropriate regular classes in their neighborhood school. All necessary supports are provided for students and educators to ensure meaningful
participation in the total school community (p. 2).

In addition, the Institute on Community Integration of the University of
Minnesota (n.d.) listed among the basic benefits of integrated school
communities the following six:

1. PREPARATION FOR ADULT LIVING—The goal of education is to prepare
individuals to be contributing members of society. Segregated settings
cannot prepare individuals to function in integrated community and
work environments because they do not afford those with or without
disabilities opportunities to develop the attitudes, values, and skills
required to get along with one another as interdependent members of
society. By attending their local schools, students with disabilities
receive instruction in the communities where they live, practicing skills
in the communities where they live, practicing skills in the actual community settings where they're needed, gaining familiarity with the
locale, and developing a sense of belonging.

2. IMPROVED LEARNING—Many types of learning occur best in integrated schools. Students with disabilities who are placed in regular classes
have an environment in which to grow socially and academically. Peers
are often the best models and teachers of many socially valued behaviors, and in integrated settings students with disabilities have opportunities to learn many things, including mobility and vocational, social,
and communication skills, from students without disabilities. Like all
children, those with disabilities need to encounter a variety of experiences and in integrated settings they're exposed to a wide range of
activities, people, environments, and ideas.

3. GROWTH FOR PEERS—Having students with disabilities in their schools and classes, peers without disabilities learn to develop skills in dealing with others who are different from themselves. As both adults and peers grow in their abilities to relate to students with disabilities, they serve as models for one another, supporting and reinforcing these new interaction skills. This experience often leads to growth in their self-esteem and interpersonal behaviors, paving the way for the formation of rewarding adult relationships with a variety of people in community, home, and workplace settings.

4. FRIENDSHIP DEVELOPMENT—Integration affords students with and without disabilities opportunities to become friends with one another. Peer relationships between students with disabilities and classmates without are important now and in the future and are essential to a successful and fulfilling life in the community. Some of the friends students with disabilities make in school today will be their co-workers and fellow community members as they reach adulthood.

5. ACCEPTANCE OF INDIVIDUAL DIFFERENCES—People in our society have many misconceptions about persons with disabilities. The best way to overcome these is by bringing people together in integrated settings. As students with and without disabilities interact as classmates and friends, their parents and teachers have the opportunity to witness successful integration in action. This new experience enables many adults to embrace the vision of a society that accepts and values the inclusion of persons with disabilities into all aspects of community life.

6. SUPPORT OF CIVIL RIGHTS—Like all students, those with disabilities have the right to attend regular school and regular classes, and to receive an appropriate education within those regular classes. Public Law 94-142 entitles all children with disabilities to a free and appropriate public education in the least restrictive environment possible. Their integration is also a civil rights issue. In a democratic society, every person is to be afforded equal opportunities; segregated settings symbolize society's rejection of one segment of the population. Through participation in integrated schools and communities, students with and without disabilities can experience the richness of a society that values and includes all citizens.

Moreover, Rubenfeld (1994) recently stressed the benefit of integration to the non-disabled child:

> Even non-disabled students suffer from this kind of segregation. Just as students with disabilities have no opportunity to use their hard-earned social skills outside their segregated classroom, so students without disabilities never have the experience of dealing with people who have disabilities on a day-to-day basis and learning that they are, in fact, fellow human beings. Segregated education fosters stereotypes at a time when students are both hungry for experience and highly impressionable. It may leave non-disabled students with a clearer picture of life in Chile or China than in that mysterious classroom down the hall with all the wheelchairs in it. Mystery provokes anxiety, and anxiety breeds a kind of easy contempt—*not* an attitude we want to encourage in children who will grow up to teach, provide services for, or make policy about a new generation of children with disabilities (pp. 236-237).

In fact, Voeltz (1980) went so far as to suggest that negative attitudes and behavior may actually represent a skill deficit in typical youngsters, since most miss the opportunity to acquire the social skills they need to engage in a positive interaction with their disabled classmates.

The Schools' Role

According to Biklen, Ford and Ferguson (1989), "Schools, like parents, can try to prevent bad attitudes by instilling positive ones" (p. 264). But before attempting to change attitudes through disability awareness, educators must understand some important basic principles. One of the most important is the idea that any plan for successfully including students with disabilities encompasses a great deal more than just teaching about disability awareness. Changing attitudes toward persons with disabilities should be viewed as more than just a one-time event; it must go on continually in the school. Educators need to understand that the attitude change strategies presented here can create problems if treated as quick fixes. How, when, and where the material is presented is extremely critical. Presenting the curriculum, exercises, and methods in this book as special events can discourage the integration and acceptance of youngsters with disabilities. The regular student body may interpret the effort as a series of superficial exercises emphasizing differences rather than encouraging an appreciation of uniqueness (Biklen, Ford and Ferguson, 1989). This book goes beyond the teaching of disability awareness and changing attitudes; it serves as a component of supported integration. According to Biklen, Ford and Ferguson (1989), successful integration is not

> a special event or episodic occurrence that can be added on to an otherwise segregated organizational structure. It cannot be achieved through annual involvement in Special Olympics, a week-long series of attitude change workshops, or a disability awareness day. Also, it would be wrong to think of integration as achievable merely through the introduction of a new curriculum concept. Rather, integration is a fundamental, constant, part of people's professional perspective, personal beliefs, and daily life (p. 266).

For a disability awareness program to become an integral part of the school ethos, teachers need to develop specific strategies to facilitate the successful inclusion of students with disabilities into general education classrooms. Neither teachers in regular classrooms nor teachers of special education want students with disabilities simply placed into general education classes without supports. Without supports, what results is commonly called "dumping." Successful inclusion does not occur without planned assistance (Salend, 1994).

In the past, as segregated special education students found themselves increasingly included and mainstreamed, educators tended to focus their efforts just on preparing them to enter their new less protected settings. The placement into these new environments, with their substantial social and academic risks, often offered as many dangers and disadvantages as opportunities. But it soon became apparent that for true integration to occur, the whole school had to address it, including typical youngsters, their regular teachers, administrators, boards of education, and parents because "integration is a fundamental, constant, part of people's professional prospective, personal beliefs, and daily life" (Biklen, Ford, & Ferguson, 1989, p. 266). Although everyone recognized the importance of teaching integrated special education students the skills and techniques to promote their adjustment to their new environment, the responsibility for making inclusion work rested with regular educators who would adjust those environments both to accept students with disabilities and to ensure them respect as equals. As Baskin and Harris (1984) observed,

The major barrier to successful mainstreaming lay in classrooms where attitudes of rejection left disabled youngsters isolated even while surrounded by their peers. Consequently, many in the educational community redirected their energies toward shaping the perceptions, beliefs, and behaviors of non-disabled students vis-a-vis the newcomers to the school. Addressing this aspect of the problem meant restructuring the mainstream to make it more hospitable and accepting. Years of segregation had insured that most pupils in regular schools would be unacquainted with persons sustaining serious sensory, intellectual, physiological, or behavioral deficits and predictably would be without appropriate strategies for interaction (pp. ix-x).

The New York State Board of Regents (1993) declared the importance of ongoing in-service education on attitude change a prerequisite to the success of educating youngsters classified as handicapped in the Least Restrictive Environment: "The ability to promote increased student outcomes for students with disabilities in a Least Restrictive Environment will depend, in a large part, on the skills and attitudes of general education and special education personnel" (p. 170). The board specifically recommended that the State Education Department require selected curriculum units to address the inclusion of special education students and the rights of persons with disabilities. "Prerequisite to full inclusion requires all students to be knowledgeable with both the legal and moral components of the rights of people with disabilities" (p. 168). Collins, Schneider and Kroeger (1995) stated that it was important for educators

to come to know and own our roles especially as regards the way our classrooms resist or replicate stereotypes about and stereotypic actions toward people with disabilities, and ways in which our classrooms might promote informed, accurate, and respectful ideas and practices (p. 13).

Although the need to educate youngsters by teaching disability awareness is important and perhaps even self-evident, Mortenson (1980) found that issues regarding prejudicial attitudes and behavior tend to receive low priority. He found only a few programs preparing classroom teachers to deal with "prejudice in terms of higher cognitive levels, intervention skills, the appropriate instructional materials, or teaching models" (p. iv). As Gallagher (1995) recently stated,

> Observational studies of children and adults interacting with disabled children in the familiar surroundings of home, neighborhood, and integrated schoolrooms indicate that these negative perceptions can be changed. Once the disabled person became known as a person, the importance of the disability, the burden of the stigma, faded into the background (p. 253).

According to Gallagher (1995), such hospitable circumstances shifted the focus of an associate's attention from the superficial characteristics of appearance to deeper, more important traits of personality and behavior. The participants responded less to a disabled or handicapped child and more "to Nick or Patrick or Libby, as persons, who, almost incidentally, had a physical disability" (p. 253).

Attitudes can be modified. As youngsters who exhibit prejudicial behavior become aware of the effects of their negative feelings, they can develop a desire to change. Since attitudes in youngsters are learned, theories of cognition can be applied to modify negative attitudes. As youngsters receive new ideas and stimuli, their prejudicial attitudes often fade: "Attitudes appear to be heavily dependent upon contact with and information about what attitudes concern," (Bowe, 1978, p. 112). But the settings of the contacts youngsters have with disabled persons are extremely critical. As Bowe explained, "If we see blind beggars rather than blind lawyers, our attitudes are more likely to be negative" (p. 114).

Attitude change does not occur simply because integration has taken place. Positive attitudes cannot be mandated; they must be taught. Nor can legislation guarantee "least restrictive attitudes." True integration can be achieved only through planned interaction. The influence on fostering positive attitudes with planned interaction was discussed by Staron (1996) who concluded, "[F]or both boys and girls, the more contact a sixth grade student had with individuals with disabilities, the more favorable attitudes he or she had toward other children with disabilities" (p. 230). Makas (1990a), earlier concluded that her research clearly supported the value of investigating the nature of the contact as well as the amount of contact which non-disabled people have had with disabilities.

Meanwhile, though the strategies of inclusion and mainstreaming have been underway for some time, positive social interaction has not always been the natural outcome. Teachers provided with some training to address cognitive rather than affective needs often find themselves unprepared to promote social integration and acceptance. Guingagh (1980) noted that most mainstreamed disabled children begin their regular classes with slight and unplanned social contact with their nondisabled peers. He also found teachers with little ability to promote friendships in their classes with both their disabled and non-disabled students: "[Helping] children become better friends," Guinagh noted, "is not central to instruction" (p. 2).

Importance of Planned Social Contact

The need for planned social contact and teacher training becomes imperative in light of research cited by Asher and Tailor (1982) that showed in peer nomination observations mainstreamed disabled children less accepted and more rejected than their nondisabled classmates. A little earlier, Johnson and Johnson (1980) found that placing students with disabilities into the mainstream without the proper support and preparation can be extremely harmful:

> Placing handicapped students in the regular classroom is the beginning of an opportunity. But, liked all opportunities, it carries the risk of making things worse as well as the possibility of making things better. If things go badly, handicapped students will be stigmatized, stereotyped, and rejected. Even worse, they may be ignored or treated with the paternalistic care one reserves for pets. If things go well, however, true friendships and positive relationships may develop between the nonhandicapped and handicapped students. . . . What is needed is an understanding of how the process of acceptance works in a classroom setting and an understanding of the specified teaching strategies that help to build positive relationships between handicapped and nonhandicapped students as they attend the regular classroom together (p. 10).

Critical to success is the preparation of the regular school for the child's inclusion. It begins with a clear understanding that, integration is a moral not a medical issue centered on the belief that until every student is regarded as a peer and equally valued, the education of all children is diminished. Integration also exemplifies the belief that youngsters with severe disabilities are as important, welcomed and valued as those who may be gifted or talented or star athletes.

When a youngster with a disability integrates into the regular school setting, all children benefit both by a more carefully taught curriculum and an opportunity to learn to accept and appreciate individual differences. Teaching methods like cooperative learning improve and enhance the typical youngster's academic abilities as well, since one must learn in order to teach.

It is an inherent part of public education's responsibility to help all youngsters learn to deal with the world in which they live—a world that now guarantees, through such laws as the *Americans With Disabilities Act*, the increasing full inclusion into society of disabled persons. The purpose of teaching about disablism is to help everyone, teachers and students alike, respond openly and empathetically to the 15 percent of the population with disabilities.

For example, when negative depictions of persons with physical and mental disabilities—or for that matter, discriminatory practices—appear in literature and the media, all educators, including administrators, regular teachers, pupil personnel service workers like school psychologists and guidance counselors, should address the wrong impressions and misinformation. Without banning or censoring, educators should learn how to use the symbolism as an object lesson on prejudice and negate its damaging messages. An English teacher, for example, when covering Shakespeare's plays, should include a discussion of sexism when teaching *The Taming of the Shrew*, anti-Semitism when teaching *The Merchant of Venice*, and disablism when teaching *Richard III*.

The Purposes of This Book

This book provides information and insights designed to change teachers' and students' negative attitudes, develop empathy for persons with disabilities, and support their inclusion in both school and society. Attitude changes and empathy development can help bridge the gap between persons with disabilities and those without them. The process begins by studying and gaining a full understanding of the paradigms regarding special education and disability, particularly the medical (deficit) model and the independence (disablism) model. Students and teachers need to learn that disablism focuses not on the personal medical causes or etiologies of disabilities, but on understanding the negative environmental, social, and civil rights effects of handicaps. Its overriding theme is that one can reduce handicapist thinking in our schools by eliminating negative attitudes and segregation that emanate largely from the medical paradigm. Blatt (1987) stressed that the conquest of mental retardation—that its elimination will not be achieved until youngsters learn to live with each other, and until segregation of all forms (especially that which occurs in our schools) is eliminated, and until schools not only believe but teach that all human beings are precious and valuable to society (p. 6). His words ring true for those who face all forms of disablism.

This book provides all teachers with information, insight and critical education practices to counteract the segregating and isolating forces in our schools and society by emphasizing peoples' commonalities rather than what separates them, stressing that persons with disabilities are different in degree, not kind, and expanding our growing tolerance of human variation. The book pursues these goals by addressing these three crucial questions:

1. How can the schools help change negative attitudes toward individuals with disabilities into positive attitudes, while our society constantly promotes attitudes and practices that demean them?

2. How can we influence the attitudes of school children so that they develop without prejudices and misconceptions about classmates with disabilities?

3. How can we encourage true integration by creating a climate in which students with disabilities find acceptance and respect as their non-disabled peers learn about the benefits, advantages and opportunities of living in a diverse and pluralistic society?

Meanwhile, in order to achieve empathy and true integration in their classes, teachers must learn

1. the major contributors toward negative attitudes, including language, history, culture, the media and education;

2. to appraise the impact of language and the meanings of concepts like "handicap," "disability," "disablism," "stereotype," "prejudice" and "discrimination";

3. methods of developing student awareness of disablism and its relationship to other forms of oppression, especially the similarities and differences between racism, sexism, and disablism;

4. specific methods that lead to successful integration;

5. methods that can be used to assess negative student attitudes so these attitudes can be changed;

6. strategies and methods—for example, simulations, role playing, classroom discussions, interacting with classroom speakers with disabilities and partaking in a media watch—for use in teaching students to accept individual differences;

7. specific teaching strategies and methods to dispel popular beliefs and myths about persons with disabilities—for example that such persons are sick, prefer and need segregation, need and seek sympathy, are similar within disability groups, are abnormal or are less valuable;

8. ways to sensitize students to understand and empathize with the frustrations and restrictions imposed by various sensory, physical or mental disabling conditions;

9. how to provide opportunities for both teachers and students to share experiences and feelings related to the condition of being disabled and handicapped in a supportive group environment;

10. how to provide an opportunities for youngsters to reflect on their own feelings when disabled or handicapped;

11. how to break down the invisible barriers of fear and curiosity that youngsters may have about people who have disabilities, particularly with classmates and guest speakers who have them;

12. how to help youngsters develop an awareness of and appreciation for what it means to have a disability;

13. how to help students understand the potentials and limitations of corrective devices used by persons with disabilities;

14. how to help youngsters see beyond the disability to others who in reality are more like them than different from them;

15. how to increase the comfort and ease with which both their students and they, themselves interact with people who seem different, no matter what those differences might be;

16. how to provide basic information on common disabilities needed for building empathy and developing a positive perspective for dealing with individuals with disabilities;

17. how to examine one's own thoughts about and feelings toward persons with disabilities;

18. how to make students understand that disablism denies humaneness to both non-disabled and disabled persons;

19. how to help students understand how the physical and social environment can be improved so that disabilities will not be handicapping;

20. how to provide students with varying subject matter perspectives and information on disabling conditions; and

21. how to help students understand the civil rights of persons with disabilities—for example *PL 94-142, IDEA, Section 504,* and *The Americans With Disabilities Act.*

By showing teachers how to present students with various experiential techniques and information about disabilities their students' attitudes toward persons who have them will be positively affected. As Bookbinder (1979) aptly stated,

> When ordinary children understand the causes, visible effects and consequences of disabilities, they will try to treat disabled children as they would anyone else (p. 3).

Attitudes can be changed by the development of cognitive sophistication through planned intervention based on an understanding of important established learning principles. Schools have the responsibility both to prepare disabled youngsters to enter the mainstream of school and society, and to prepare the mainstream to accept fully youngsters with disabilities without handicapping them through prejudicial attitudes. But, before discussing "how" to teach disability awareness, we need to examine "what" needs to be taught, specifically the language and terminology; the paradigms of handicap, disability, and disablism; the origins and history of attitudes toward persons with disabilities; information on specific disabilities; and common sense approaches to addressing them. Having examined the what we can then turn to the issue of how to change negative attitudes.

CHAPTER TWO

Issues of Language and Terminology

Hurtful Language

Handicapist attitudes toward people with disabilities are often embedded in language. Language, after all, is the architecture of our thoughts and a primary conveyer of a culture and its attitudes. It both expresses ideas and concepts and it shapes them. The words we choose communicate our thoughts and feelings and reflect our values and attitudes. Accordingly, Froschi, Colon, Rubin and Sprung (1984) asserted that we must eliminate words and expressions that stereotype persons with disabilities before we can fashion a truly inclusive environment.

Like sticks and stones, negative language hurts. It subtly denotes values, defines relationships, and, over time, prejudices views and directs behavior. As Burgdorf (1980) noted, "The power of words to affect people's lives by subtly influencing their conceptions of reality, emotional associations, and self-concepts should not be underestimated" (p. 48).

Vash (1981) explained how changes in language reflect changes in the status of minority group members:

> Words have the power to shape images of the referenced objects and their choice is important in building or breaking down stereotypes. A group is oppressed, hidden, stripped of power, and made to feel ashamed of the power of its being. Then social conditions shift in a way that permits the lid of oppression to be lifted a bit. A few of the stronger members climb out and hold the lid aside so that more can follow. Before you know it, you have a "movement" and one of the first orders of business is negotiating acceptable language by which to identify the members when it becomes necessary (p. 22).

How can words hurt on the personal level? Van Etten (1988), an attorney with dwarfism, wrote of the words used to refer to her that attempted to make her feel inferior. Words she found especially hurtful included "defect," "victim," "burden," "afflicted," "unfortunate," "restricted" and "abnormal." She stressed, "The only way I suffer any of these descriptions is by the mouth of people who insist on using these words to describe me" (p. 217).

Davies (1987) described her feelings of being labeled "cripple." The word first appeared in the Tenth Century Lindisfarne Gospel and is derived from the verb "creep" (Mairs, 1994). Davies wrote,

> "[C]rippled" is an ugly and stumbling word. There is no dignity there at all—only a picture of someone twisted, pitiful, poor, and not very bright. This is a personal prejudice that took hold long ago for reasons sunk deep into the subconscious. But I find when I use crippled, I am stressing the harshness and purely physical fact of paralysis. The word, in its darkest intensity, blots out the power and the hope of the spirit (p. 43).

Many cultures besides ours perpetuate misconceptions about people with disabilities with negative language. For example, *kasiru,* which means "stupid," is a common term used by Ugandan society to refer to persons with deafness (UNESCO, 1994). Among the Truk peoples of the East Central Carolines, persons with muteness and deafness are called *umes* and are also thought of as "crazy" (Maisel, 1953). [Please note that the definitions in quotes provided here are as they appeared in their original sources.] Japanese words like *mekura* ("blind"), *tenkan* ("epileptic"), *bikko* ("lame"), *kichigal* ("insane"), and *chimba* and *fugúsha* ("deformed") are all pejorative terms. Both in the United Kingdom and the United States *spastic* has become to mean someone who is clumsy, incapable or incompetent (UNESCO, 1994).

In addition, McBee (1995) listed the following demeaning terms found in other countries:

China	can fei ("disabled," "useless") and que zi ("cripple");
Denmark	krøbling ("cripple");
France	boiteux ("lame"), estropié ("maimed") infirme ("sick"), mutilé ("mutilated"), dé fecteaux ("faulty"), invalide ("invalid");
Germany	*krupel* ("cripple"), *lahme* ("lame"), *kranke* ("invalid");

Holland	kreuple ("cripple"), gebrekkige ("broken"), verminkte ("mutilated"), invalide ("invalid");
Italy	sciancato/storpio("crippled"),zoppo("wobbling"), mutilato ("mutilated");
Norway	krøpling ("cripple");
Poland	kaleka ("cripple"); kalawy ("lame"), inwalida ("invalid");
Portugal	aleijado ("cripple"), coxo ("lame"), o deixe-que-and Brazil enchuto ("one who limps");
Spain and Mexico	menos válido ("less valid"), mutilado ("mangled"), cojo/manco/mocho ("amputee"), chueco ("gimp"), Güilo ("moves poorly");
Sweden	krympling ("cripple"), lamsla ("lame") (p. 51).

Political Correctness

Demeaning terminology contributes to the negative self-image of persons with physical and mental differences or disabilities and perpetuates handicapist attitudes and practices (Biklen & Bogdan, 1977). Negative language increases the difficulty of people with disabilities to surmount deeply entrenched, often subtle and unconscious prejudice— prejudice that results in discrimination and interferes with their rights to receive an appropriate education or occupation, a home where they choose, and even in some instances, survival itself.

Even with the demonstrable hurt and damage to self-esteem such language causes, however, some still oppose what has been contemptuously called "politically correct" terminology. Fiedler (1996) for example, suggests that little is altered by "verbal changes" and "superficial relabeling":

It seems to me only an easy way of appeasing the guilt we cannot really allay over our instinctive responses to men and women with drastic difficulties in ambulation to stop calling them "gimps" or "cripples" and refer to them instead as the "handicapped" the "disabled"—or, in that ultimately idiotic euphemism adopted after a heart-searching discussions at the last Democratic Convention, as the "challenged." I will not presume to speculate about how the lame themselves regard such euphemisms, though I suspect in many different ways, depending on how they have learned to live in the impaired bodies they inhabit (p. 36).

Hughes (1993) in *The Culture of Complaint* went so far as to state that

We want to create a sort of linguistic Lourdes, where evil and misfortune are dispelled by a dip in the waters of euphemism. Does the "cripple" rise from his wheelchair, or feel better about being stuck in it, because someone in the Carter administration decided that, for official purposes he was "physically challenged?" (Garland, 1995, p. 4).

Francis (1985) reported similar sentiments by an anonymous letter writer to a disability rights advocate who had notified a newspaper about using "antiquated and derogatory" terminology:

Ms. Joseph:

So you are "outraged and offended" at the Manhattan Mercury's use of the terminology "wheelchair bound." I guarantee that you are *nowhere* as outraged and offended as I am by you bleeding hearts that think just because you are crippled, the whole world should revolve around you.

I speak for most people when I say that we are getting damn tired of this "politically correct" garbage. If you are a cripple or a retard, then that's what you are. Sugary sweet descriptions don't change a damn thing (p. 4).

But, the issue is less one of political correctness and more one of respect and the development of positive self-images. In their fight for rights, persons with disabilities have made inappropriate language a major issue and have become militant about insensitive terms applied to their persons (Burgdorf, 1980; J. Shapiro, 1993). Sutherland (1984) observed that "it is for people with disabilities to decide how we chose to define ourselves, and few of us choose to do so according to the prejudices of people who consider themselves able bodied" (p. 14). "In the wake of the American civil rights movement," Hirsch and Hirsch (1995) stated, "increasing numbers of oppressed groups are claiming their right to define who they are and what terms should be used to describe them" (p. 23).

Just as other minority groups have claimed the right to determine language used to refer to themselves (for example, Black rather than Negro or Colored, Asian rather than Oriental, Native American rather than Indian, or woman rather than chick, babe, gal, or broad), persons with disabilities no longer want to hear outdated or derogatory terminology like "lame," "unfortunate," "hunchback," "gimp," "deaf and dumb," "Mongoloid" or "having fits." Wahl (1995) listed some of the various common derogatory terms often used in the mass media to express mental illnesses or a person with one: "crazy," "lunatic," "insane," "madman," "psycho, "sick," "nut," "wacko," "weirdo," "screwy," "fruitcake," "cuckoo-bird," "kook," "crazoid," "loony" "deranged" and "demented" (pp. 19, 21-22). He observed that "the problem with these terms, as with slang terms for other groups is that they are fundamentally disrespectful, and, therefore, offensive" (p. 23). He also explained that

> Virtually all slang terms for mental illness have undertones of disapproval or negative judgment of some sort. In addition, many of the slang terms are residuals of past unflattering concepts of mental illness (for example "lunatic"), leftovers of a time when people with mental illness were seen as little more than insensate beasts, when they were chained in dungeons and treated as objects of amusement for nobles who paid to view them as if in a human zoo. Terms with such a history cannot help but convey a lack of sympathy and respect for people with mental illnesses (p. 22).

Padilla (1993), a parent who advocates the careful use of language, related how language used especially by professionals can be hurtful and offensive to disabled persons and their families:

> I can still recall vividly the paralyzing disbelief that struck me as the neurologist who gazed upon my baby daughter during her first seizure asked, "How long has she been having fits?" It was 1976. How could a specialized medical professional use such a term to describe my baby? Hadn't I read this word in some Shakespearean play? Didn't it mean a person possessed by the devil? Images of wild animals with foaming mouths flashed through my mind. Was my baby having a "fit"—an uncontrolled tantrum or a medieval attack? Or was my baby experiencing her first seizure? The neurologist who described my child's first seizure as a "fit" did so not because he was a callous, uncaring man. He did so because that was probably the language he

learned in his medical training and because he has never been the parent of a child having a seizure. If he were, he would become instantly and forever sensitized to the importance of selecting appropriate words to describe seizures. . . . Professionals must give considerable thought to the language they select when speaking to families. Their "patients" are our "children" (pp. 24-25).

Most persons with disabilities often view terms like "physically challenged," "differently abled," "able disabled" and "handi-capable" as patronizing euphemisms. Although they are commonly used to refute common stereotypes of incompetence, they are often considered defensive and reactive (Linton, 1998).

Perhaps the well-meaning term that persons with disabilities find most objectionable is "physically challenged" which implies that barriers are acceptable and that disability is really just a self-actualization test:

> The politically correct 'physically challenged' and all its preposterous associates, such as 'vertically challenged' for dwarfs and 'follicularly challenged' for the bald, bring their own cultural load and dispose us to regard those whom they denote in a selective way—as rising, or failing to rise, to the challenge of the physical world (Garland, 1995, p. 4).

Similarly, Linton (1998) stated the following regarding "physically challenged"

> Non-disabled people use it in conversation around disabled people with no hint of anxiety, suggesting that they believe it is a positive term. The phrase does not make much sense to me. To say that I am physically challenged is to state that the obstacles to my participation are physical, not social, and that the barrier is my own disability. Further, it separates those of us with mobility impairments from other disabled people, not a valid or useful partition for those interested in coalition building and social change. Various derivatives of the term *challenged* have been adopted as a description used in jokes. For instance, "vertically challenged" is considered a humorous way to say short, and "calorically challenged" to say fat. A review of the Broadway musical *Big* in the *New Yorker* said that the score is "melodically challenged" (p. 14).

Such terms condescend and imply a reluctance to accept people as they are. Most persons with physical impairments do not view barriers as challenges that will make them stronger, more courageous, or better citizens by overcoming them and pulling themselves up by their own bootstraps. Most of us see a challenge as something individuals can overcome and solve by themselves. Barriers are environmentally handicapping. As one person with a physical disability noted,

> Until you've made it your responsibility to get downtown, and discovered there are no buses with lifts running on that route, you may not fully comprehend that it isn't a personal *challenge* you're up against, but a system resistant to change (*The Problem with Challenge*, 1992, p. 23).

Zola (1982), wrote of environmental barriers he often encountered that he would not recognize as "challenging":

> Chairs without arms to push myself up from; unpadded seats which all too quickly produce sores; showers and toilets without handrails to maintain my balance; surfaces too slippery to walk on; staircases without banisters to help me hoist myself; buildings without ramps, making ascent exhausting if not dangerous; every curbstone a precipice; car, plane, and theater seats too cramped for my braced leg; and trousers too narrow for my leg brace to pass through (p. 208).

Thompson (1985), added "It is not fun to be disabled. Being disabled is not a 'challenge' we voluntarily undertake. Nor is it that we are merely 'differently abled.' We are 'disabled'; there are just some things that we can't do, at least as quickly or easily as other people" (p. 79).

It is interesting to note that not all persons with disabilities agree on the effects of negative language. Some, like Kriegel (1991), find uncharitable terms useful in calling attention to their situations and "wear" such terms as badges of honor:

> I am a man who has lived all but eleven of his years here on earth as a cripple, a word I prefer to the euphemistic "handicapped" or "disabled," each of which does little more than further society's illusions about illness and accident and the effects of illness and accident. For to be "disabled" or "handicapped" is to deny oneself the rage, anger, and pride of having managed to survive as a cripple in America. If I

know nothing else, I know that I have endured—and I know the price I have paid for that endurance (p. 61).

Zimmerman (1985/1990) too, had ambivalent feelings toward "handi-capped" and "disabled,"

> "Crippled" is out. "Disabled" is in—but I don't like it either. "Handicapped" is old fashioned, and I accept it easily when labels are necessary. Golfers desire handicaps, eagerly. You can give a horse a handicap, and it can still win the race. But you know what they do to disabled horses, don't you? Shoot them! Actually, the only label I will accept without qualification is "person" (p. 37).

Disability and Handicap

Before attitudes change, we need to reach an understanding of and agreement over fundamental concepts, terminology and language. A good place to start is with the basic terms "disability" and "handicap" whose definitions traditionally raise controversy and spread confusion (Burgdorf, 1980). As Vash (1981) noted, "To be disabled is one thing. To be handicapped is quite another" (p. 22). Although commonly used interchangeably, the terms disability and handicap are not synonymous. Understanding the difference is basic because it frames one's paradigm of the subject—as being viewed as medical, dealing with illness, or being viewed as social, dealing with civil rights.

Disability

"Disability" is currently the term preferred by professional and advoca-cy groups (Patton, Blackbourn & Fad, 1996). Basically, a disability relates to an actual, and in most cases a permanent, deviation or loss in physique or functioning that can often be objectively measured—for example, blindness in acuity loss, and deafness in decibel loss. It is an impairment or loss of function which can often be specified in objective physical biomedical terms. Limitations of visual or auditory acuity, muscle weakness or impaired control, the amputation of an extremity, epilepsy, autism, paraplegia, and quadriplegia, are examples of disabil-ities. "Disability" describes a reduction of one's activity or ability that results from an acute or chronic condition (Patton, Blackbourn & Fad, 1996; Shea & Bauer, 1997; Thomson, 1997). According to Ingstad and Whyte (1995), "We usually think of disability in contrast to an ideal of normal capacity to perform particular activities and to play one's role in social life" (p. 3).

Some writers—including Wright (1983), Johnson (1994) and Ingstad and Whyte (1995)—use a three-fold distinction between the terms "impairment," "disability" and "handicap." They define "impairment" as a difference in body structure, "disability" as including functional limitations and societal attitudes, and "handicap" as disadvantaged outcomes in physical or social environments. Wright (1983) defined the term "disability" as the "limitation of function that results directly from an impairment at the level of a specific organ or body system" (p. 11). For our purposes in this book, "disability" and "impairment" are interchangeable.

Handicap

An individual who is unable to perform certain activities because of his or her interaction with the environment is considered to be "handicapped." According to Patton, Blackbourn and Fad (1996), "'Handicap' refers to the additional negative burden placed by society on an individual through barriers affecting areas such as access, transportation, and attitude" (p. 6). Shea and Baluer (1997) viewed a handicap as being "a disadvantage resulting from a disability that limits or prevents fulfillment of a role" (p. 12). It is a disadvantage or difficulty that arises only in the pursuit of some specific goal. The inability to travel independently, communicate by telephone, drive an automobile, use a computer, read a newspaper, hear traffic sounds, enter a public building, or secure appropriate employment are examples of handicaps.

Actually, it is the environment itself that is handicapping—for example, money access machines, urinals, or pay telephones placed too high to be used by persons in wheelchairs or with dwarfism. In a sense, a handicap is the disadvantage imposed by the disability the person experiences in his or her particular environment. Different disabilities result in different handicaps. Blindness is a disability that commonly results in one's inability to get around and be mobile. Deafness is a disability that commonly results in one's inability to understand. Thus, while blindness handicaps an individual's mobility and transportation, deafness often handicaps an individual's communication. But both blindness and deafness often result in the handicap of being pitied, stigmatized, feared and considered less of a human being.

Handicaps, therefore, are the burdens imposed upon individuals by society and the environment in which they must function. They are by-products of the interaction between the deviation and the environment. B. Wright (1983) characterized handicaps as the "actual obstacles the person encounters in the pursuit of goals in real life, no matter what their source" (p. 11).

Thus, disabilities can be characterized as "personal" and handicaps as "environmental." As Yuker (1979) explained,

> To me a disability is a physical or mental condition. It is a characteristic of a person. People have disabilities. A handicap, from my point of view, is often a characteristic of the environment rather than the individual. The person may have the disability but the environment produces the handicap (p. 33).

Hale (1979) explained further that a physical disability, no matter how or by what it was caused, is a medically determined fact that can be described explicitly. The term handicap is, in effect, a concept that "is open to change as well as interpretation" (pp. 2-3). In addition, as we shall see, handicaps are situational and often bound by attitude and culture.

According to Burgdorf (1980), "When used generically, terms like 'handicapped persons,' 'handicapped children,' or 'the handicapped' have a narrower meaning, referring to a particular type of disadvantage—a mental, physical, or emotional disability or impairment" (p. 3). A person with a handicap, therefore, is one who has a mental, physical or emotional disability that makes achievement in some area of life functioning unusually difficult. Burgdorf (1980) stressed further that physical, mental, or emotional disabilities qualify as handicaps only if they hinder achievement. He stated that the term "unusually difficult" makes it clear that the hinderance must be substantial; a slight or inconsequential disability or impairment is not a handicap.

Disability as Normal Variation
Using the term "normal" to refer only to individuals without disabilities is to imply that those with disabilities are "abnormal" (Blaska, 1993). "Abnormal" has extreme negative implications. It is offensive and should not be used when referring to human beings. Educators need to accept the concept of all individuals, including those having disabilities, as being normal. In other words, all people should be perceived of as being within a greatly diverse group where all are normal and equally worthy. Davis (1995) recently stressed that

> [M]ost constructions of disability assume that the person with disabilities is in some sense damaged while the observer is undamaged. Furthermore, there is an assumption that society at large is intact, normal, setting a norm, undamaged. But the notion of an undamaged observer who is part of an undamaged society is certainly one that needs to be questioned (p. 24).

Davis (1995) further questioned the concept of normalcy and its construction:

> I would like to focus not so much on the construction of disability as on the construction of normalcy. I do this because the "problem" is not the persons with the disabilities; the problem is the way that normalcy is constructed to create the "problem" of the disabled person (pp. 23-24).

A basic concept educators need to stress to their able-bodied students is the idea that being different or having a disability does not make an individual wrong or abnormal. "Little people," for example, refer to persons without dwarfism as having "average" height, not "normal" height. They consider themselves to be normal, only "packaged differently."

Thus, as students with disabilities attempt to overcome their handicaps by dealing with their environments differently, their non-handicapped peers should not view their efforts as abnormal. For example, if a girl with deafness uses American Sign Language as a primary means of communication, it may not be normal for the rest of her class, but it is normal for her. If a boy with blindness uses Braille, it too may not be normal for the rest of the class, but it is normal for him. Students need to accept the idea that using a chair with wheels is just as normal for a student with a physical impairment as it is for the principal's secretary. Just because students with disabilities may cope with the environment differently to compensate for their physical and mental limitations, they should not be stigmatized and perceived as being abnormal or less valuable human beings.

Another important concept to stress is that non-handicapped students are more "like" than "unlike" their handicapped peers. Persons with disabilities are different in degree rather than different in kind. In fact, of all youngsters, those with disabilities are the least identifiable as a social group. As Keniston (1979) observed

> They share no common physical, psychological, or cultural charac-
> teristics: the blind child, the child with cerebral palsy, and the child
> with minimal brain damage are less like each other than each is like
> his or her able-bodied age mates. What distinguishes handicapped
> children is above all a *social* fact: they differ from the able-bodied
> norm, and for this reason are assigned a stigmatized and deviant
> social role (p. xiii).

Thus, an individual with blindness and an individual with deafness have
more in common with a non-disabled person than they do with each
other. Social barriers between children tend to fall when we emphasize
one's normality or similarity to others (Shapiro & Barton, 1991). As
Sutherland (1984) stated, "We have to recognize that disablement is not
merely the physical state of a small minority. It is the normal condition
of humanity" (p. 18).

Disability as a Separate Culture
A primary example of disability as a culture may be found in the area of
deafness. Although deafness is commonly perceived of as a disability,
many who have it do not recognize it as such. According to Turnbull,
Turnbull, Shank and Leal (1995), there is little agreement that exists on
how to refer to persons with deafness. While some persons with deafness
prefer emphasis on the disability first (Deaf person), others prefer emphasis on the person first (person with deafness). The issue to one who
does not understand may seem trivial but in reality it is not. The issue is
how deafness is perceived. To some, deafness is seen as a culture with
deaf persons, like those of other cultures, united by their common physical characteristics (deafness or hearing loss), their common language
(sign language), and their common needs (for accommodations in communication). Such individuals want the letter "D" capitalized when referring to themselves as a distinct subcultural population as in "Deaf people."
The individuals who prefer the people-first approach refer to themselves
as "persons who are deaf" or "persons who are hard of hearing."

    Davis (1995), too, recently discussed how members of the Deaf
community may not consider themselves "disabled":

> The Deaf reject this term, now seeing themselves as a linguistic sub-
> group like Latinos or Koreans. They feel that their culture, language,
> and community constitute them as a totally adequate, self-enclosed,
> and self-defining sub-nationality within the audist state. As such, the
> Deaf do not regard their absence of hearing as a disability, any more

than a Spanish-speaking person would regard the inability to speak English as a disability. . . . They see their state of being defined not medically but rather socially and politically (p. xiv).

How one views deafness often determines how one views deaf issues. For example, one of the most volatile issues involving Deaf culture is that regarding cochlear implants, hearing aid devices consisting of a microphone and a processor. The device allows the brain to "hear" by sending signals to electrodes implanted in the head stimulating the auditory nerve. It is estimated that well over half of the individuals who have them are then able, for the first time, to hear and understand speech without speech (lip) reading *(People in Motion,* 1995).

This invention causes great controversy, however, because much of the Deaf community views itself as part of a separate culture with its own language. Thus, not hearing is considered a "cultural difference" not a "medical loss." As Little People view themselves as being "differently packaged," with nothing wrong with themselves, the Deaf community rejects "the notion that deafness is a defect that needs to be fixed, that somehow deaf people are not whole," [and] "when parents emphasize changing the child to make him like other, more perfect children, the psyche is often scarred" *(People in Motion,* 1995, p. 7). The issue of cochlear implants is an interesting one that can inspire lively classroom discussions over cultural viewpoints.

Disability as Group Diversity

Who is considered disabled? Those commonly described as disabled constitute an extremely diverse heterogeneous group. Few people ever really consider the range of people to whom the term applies. In fact, identifying disabled persons and determining their number can be difficult because associations, states, laws, branches of government, and persons with disabilities themselves use different definitions.

Certain severe types of impairments—blindness, deafness, severe mental retardation, absence or paralysis of arms or legs—are almost always considered disabilities. Other impairments—partial hearing or vision loss, color or night blindness, the loss of a finger or toe—may not be considered disabilities at all.

In short, we have no true consensus of what constitutes a disability. J. Shapiro (1993) observed that the number of persons with disabilities varies depending on who does the counting and what disabilities are included. In the United States, the range generally runs between 35 million and 54 million, or about 17-20 percent of the population. During debate on the *Americans with Disabilities Act*, President Bush, disability advocates, and the media used 43 million. But even that large figure excluded those with learning disabilities, those who are HIV positive and those with other conditions like back problems covered under various civil rights laws. The same counting problem exists on the international level where the latest figures are estimated at about 245 million disabled people. One needs to keep in mind, however,

> Estimates depend on what counts as a disability (the first figures included malnutrition), on how severe an impairment must be before it is considered disabling, and how categories are implemented in actually gathering data. . . . [C]ultural factors are especially involved in attempts to count cases of disability (Ingstad & Whyte, 1995, p. 9).

The *Disability Statistics Abstract* (1991) stated that in 1989, an estimated 14.1 percent of all non-institutionalized United States' residents—34.2 million people—had an activity limitation attributable to a chronic condition. "Limitation of activity" refers to a long-term reduction in a person's capacity to perform activities that others the same age commonly accomplish. For youngsters under 5, the major activity is playing; for ages from 5 to 17, attending school; for persons from 18 to 69, working or keeping house; and for those over 70, the ability to live independently.

Individuals are identified as "disabled" for a variety of reasons. The diverse people who constitute this group include those who cannot walk, who learn at a slower rate than most others, who experience seizures, who are considered malformed or disfigured. Also included are those who speak differently or those who cannot hear or see. Some have reasoning and thought processes that do not function in conventional ways. Others have such learning disabilities, as attention deficit disorders, dyslexia or hyperactivity. Still others have had medical problems like kidney disease, arthritis, heart disease, diabetes, cancer, or seizures, from which they have recovered (United States Commission on Civil Rights, 1983, p. 4).

Further diversity described by J. Shapiro (1993) includes disabilities that are "congenital" (present at birth), and "adventitious" (acquired later in life). Some like muscular dystrophy, cystic fibrosis, and certain forms of vision and hearing loss are "progressive" in severity, while others, like an amputation, are not. Several disabilities, like seizure conditions, are "episodic." Also, conditions like multiple sclerosis are both episodic and progressive. Some disabilities are curable. Certain disabilities, like severe facial disfigurement, are immediately visible; others, like learning disabilities or diabetes are hidden. Compounding the diversity of the hundreds of types of disabilities is the fact that they each come in differing degrees of severity, and individuals can have them in combinations.

Legal definitions also add to the diversity of disability definitions. The *American's with Disabilities Act* (ADA), defines disability to include "those who may only be perceived as disabled"—like those with alcoholism or a drug dependency or obesity—which may not be disabling by themselves but create "handicapist" attitudes in others. Regarding the wide diversity of the use of the term, the New York Board of Regents (1993) stated that

> Although the term "disability" is widely used, there is no single widely accepted definition of what it means. To most people, the term is associated with people who use wheelchairs, have visual or hearing impairments, or who are mentally retarded. Yet the term might be construed broadly to include individuals with a much wider range of chronic physical and mental conditions, or even—as in the Americans with Disabilities Act (ADA)—to people who are believed to have such conditions. ADA refers to 43 million Americans with disabilities—depending on how one defines disability, one might count anywhere from 20 to 60 million (p. 38).

Disability as Culturebound

Ingstad and Whyte (1995) stressed that the public should resist taking the concept of disability for granted:

> In many cultures, one cannot be "disabled" for the simple reason that "disability" as a recognized category does not exist. There are blind people and lame people and "slow" people, but "the disabled" as a general term does not translate easily into many languages (p. 7).

Similarly, Edwards (1996) reported that in ancient Greece, there was no all-inclusive word for 'disability' until the Athenian political institution of the fifth century B.C.E., democracy, necessitated it. "Even then," according to Edwards, "a blind person and a persons with one leg—for example—would not have perceived themselves to be in the same category" (p. 29).

Disability as Developmental

"Developmental disability" refers to a group of conditions that appear during an individual's developmental period resulting in a serious limitation of one's ability to participate in major life activities. The term was incorporated in the federal law *PL 95-822*, The Developmental Disabilities Bill of Rights Act (1978)—and shifted emphasis from "medical etiology" to "functional limitations," thereby making an individual's eligibility for services not contingent on a specific medical diagnosis. Under this act, a developmental disability is attributable to a mental or physical impairment that begins before age 22, and is likely to continue indefinitely and results in substantial limitations in three or more areas of major life activity (American Association on Mental Retardation, 1992a). The state of New Jersey further defines a developmental disability as

> [A] severe chronic disability of a person which: (1) is attributable to a mental or physical impairment or combination of impairments; (2) is manifest before age 22; (3) is likely to continue indefinitely; (4) results in substantial functional limitations in three or more of the following areas of major life activity: self-care, receptive and expressive language, mobility, self-direction, and capacity for independent living or economic self-sufficiency; and (5) effects the need for a combination and sequence of special interdisciplinary care, treatment or other services which are of life-long or extended duration and are individually planned and coordinated (New Jersey Developmental Disabilities Council, 1993, p. 1).

Common developmental disabilities include autism, cerebral palsy, mental retardation, or spinal bifida. Impairments like severe head injury, blindness, deafness, or mental illness *may* be considered developmental disabilities if they meet the criteria just listed. One should have the idea that such definitions are beginning to focus on the functional abilities rather than medical disabilities.

Disability as Relative

Some persons with disabilities question any terms that separate people into disabled and able-bodied categories because they believe it perpetuates the "myth of the normal healthy body." In fact, Sutherland (1984) found there is no sharp dividing line between disability and non-disability. For example, at what point are persons considered blind?

Individuals with some vision are labeled "legally blind." In reality, no two distinct groups exist with those considered disabled constituting a smaller group within a larger group. As Sutherland noted, "[V]ery few people have bodies that work with 100 percent efficiency" (p. 17). For example, are those who wear glasses because of a slight refractive error like hyperopia (far-sightedness) or myopia (near-sightedness) considered disabled? These and other conditions, like hay fever allergies, are generally placed in the non-disability category. Sutherland (1984) aptly stated that

> These conditions do not reflect the degree to which an individual is incapacitated by the condition in question; they are made according to categories rather than individual cases. Thus, a person with severe hay fever may be greatly more incapacitated than a person who has mild or well-controlled epilepsy, but is still more readily accepted as normal (p. 17).

Handicap as Relative

"Handicap" is also a relative term. The severity of a handicap to an individual cannot be determined solely by the severity of the disability. Occupationally, the amputation of a leg may be much more of a handicap to a basketball player than to a computer operator. Severe acne may be more of a handicap to one youngster than congenital blindness to another. As Gallagher (1995) recently observed, "A condition such as poor eyesight is largely a trivial matter in a society where eyeglasses are readily available. In an Aboriginal hunting society, poor eyesight is a calamity" (p. 242).

A person might be handicapped for any number of reasons, one of which could be the presence of a disability. B. Wright (1983) asserted that with some impairments, like facial disfigurement, the handicapping factors are caused entirely by negative social and personal attitudes since the disfigurement involves no functional loss. She stressed that "a person with a disability may or may not be handicapped, and a person who is handicapped may or may not have a disability" (p. 11).

Scholl (1986) explained the influences of personal and societal attitudes and expectations that can make a person with a visual disability handicapped:

> A handicap results when an individual is placed at an actual or perceived disadvantage in the performance of normal life functions

because of personal and social expectations and attitudes toward the impairment. For example, if all jobs required reading fine print, all persons with visual impairments would be handicapped. All jobs do not require normal visual functioning but sometimes persons with visual impairments are not even allowed opportunities to demonstrate their competence. When this happens, they are handicapped because of societal attitudes (p. 26).

Handicap as a Negative Social Creation

A "handicap" is a phenomenon created by society, not an objective categorization. In fact, social judgment is one of the most important elements in delineating who is and who is not handicapped (Burgdorf, 1980). One becomes handicapped only as a result of receiving that label. In addition, by becoming aware of the large degree of artificiality and arbitrariness inherent in the concept of handicap, one can gain quite a different perspective on the process by which the "handicapped" label is applied as well as on the implications that follow its bestowal (Burgdorf, 1980).

Freidson (1965) described a handicap in social terms as an imputation of an "undesirable" difference. The individual is defined as handicapped simply because he or she deviates from what others believe to be "normal" or "appropriate." Bartel and Guskin (1980) further explained the process as a social group defining its standards that a particular individual can not meet and then treating that person as unacceptable or of lower status for failing to meet those standards.

In addition, society handicaps persons with disabilities by denying them opportunities. Lord (1981) described handicap as a social phenomenon engendering society's negative attitudes, economic deprivation, segregation, and denial of human rights.

Because handicaps are socially created this way, one can become handicapped without changing one's own characteristics, just one's environment. Suppose, for example, a hearing man with no background in deaf education found himself working at, or attending, a residential school where almost all of the students and all of the faculty and staff members had deafness and communicated by a combination of American Sign Language, finger spelling, Cued Speech, and speech reading—none of which the "hearing" man understood. Let us also suppose that the group took pride in their deafness and Deaf culture and, therefore, ardently encouraged the student body and faculty to take a strong political and social stand regarding the rights of persons with deafness—insisting, for example, that television programs be closed-captioned, that the president of the school have deafness, that actors with deafness receive preference for playing characters with deafness in the media, and that American Sign Language be taught in public schools with credit given as a foreign language. In that situation, the presence of hearing ability—not the absence of it—would be a handicap. In addition, if the Deaf community viewed the hearing person as occupying a lower status with less desirability and less ability, he might suffer poor self-esteem, poor social adjustment and stress, which might lead to a display of reduced competence.

Handicap as Situational
Persons are handicapped only in certain situations. While a person with deafness would tend to be more handicapped attending a concert than a silent movie, a person with blindness would tend to be more handicapped at the movie than at the concert. Reasonable accommodations like ramps, talking books, closed captioned television programs, classroom aides, assistive technology, or lowered urinals change the environment and eliminate the handicap.

Vash (1981) stressed that a because a handicap is defined in terms of social consequences and handicaps may vary greatly, depending on what the person is trying to do, "[I]t does not make sense to speak of a 'handicapped person' in a global way" (p. 23). "References to handicaps always should make clear in what pursuits the individual is handicapped" (p. 206). For example, a man weighing two-hundred and fifty pounds may be handicapped in his goal of wanting to be a thoroughbred jockey by his being too big. That same man, at that same weight, may be handicapped in his goal of wanting to be a sumo wrestler because of his being too small. In any case, he certainly would not be considered handicapped in all situations.

Handicap as Individually Created
Some handicaps appear to be created by the attitude of the individual himself or herself. Kennedy, Austin and Smith (1987) found that persons with a specific disability can convince themselves to become handicapped when they could, in fact, function perfectly well under the right conditions. Such handicapping behavior often results from a poor self-concept and low self-esteem.

Handicap as Community Defined

A community can determine whether a disability becomes a handicapping condition. Perhaps the most revealing research to illustrate the concept of community-defined handicap was conducted by Groce (1985), who investigated the social aspects of a high incidence of hereditary deafness on Martha's Vineyard. "In modern Western societies," she wrote, "'handicapped' individuals have been expected to adapt to the ways of the nonhandicapped. But the perception of a handicap, and of its associated physical and social limitations, may be tempered by the community in which it is found" (p. 50).

Deafness is often socially isolating because the hearing find it difficult to communicate with deaf individuals. But on Martha's Vineyard, an isolated island south of Cape Cod with a high incidence of deafness, hearing individuals were bilingual in English and the Vineyard sign language resulting in complete integration of deaf individuals into all aspects of society. Groce (1985) found that

> Unlike individuals similarly handicapped on the mainland, deaf Vineyarders were included in all of the community's work and play situations. They were free to marry either hearing or deaf persons. According to tax records, they generally earned an average or above average income (indeed several were wealthy), and were active in church affairs (p. 50).

Groce went on to observe that "One of the strongest indications that the deaf were completely integrated into all aspects of society is that in all the interviews I conducted, deaf Islanders were never thought of or referred to as a group or as 'the deaf.' Every one of the deaf people who is remembered today is thought of as a unique individual" (p. 4). To support this finding, Groce recalled a particular interview with a woman in her early nineties whom she asked,

> "Do you know anything similar about Isaiah and David?"
> "Oh yes," she replied, "they both were very good fishermen, very good indeed."
> "Weren't they both deaf?" I prodded.
> "Yes, come to think of it, I guess they both were," she replied.
> "I'd forgotten about that" (p. 4).

One person interviewed stated, "I didn't think about the deaf any more than you'd think about anybody with a different voice" (p. 5). Yet another said, "[T]hose people weren't handicapped. They were just deaf" (p. 5). Here are some more quotes from Vineyarders:

1. You'd never hardly know that they were deaf and dumb. People up there got so used to them that they didn't take hardly any notice of them (p. 51).

2. They were just like anybody else. I wouldn't be overly kind because they'd be sensitive to that. I'd just treat them the way I treated anybody (p. 51).

Groce (1985) found that most of her informants had never noticed anything unusual about the manner in which their deaf fellow citizens were integrated into their society and they were even truly puzzled by "an outsider's interest in the subject" (p. 51). She also came to the conclusion that a community can determine whom it considers handicapped. The community of Martha's Vineyard viewed deafness as something that just sometimes happened and that one's inability to hear "simply did not affect a person's status in the community" (p. 52). Nance (1975) came to the same conclusion after finding that the twenty-six members of the isolated Tasaday tribe of the Philippine Islands learned sign language to communicate with its two members with deafness (cited in Moores, 1996, p. 30).

Handicap as Attitude

Persons with disabilities often state that the greatest handicaps they face in their environments are not their physical or mental conditions but the attitudes of others. Because handicaps are not permanent but situational, they can be eliminated, if "reasonable accommodations" are provided and the environment is adjusted to compensate for and accept the disability. To accomplish this, however, educators need to start blaming the environment, not the victim. If a high school student with short stature can not reach a wall telephone, the fault lies with the telephone's placement, not with the youngster's height. Placing that telephone out of reach, however, indicates an "I don't care" attitude toward the needs of small persons. Non-handicapped students need to learn that they can play a critical role in helping their disabled peers overcome their handicaps.

Similarly, if a student is unable to read a page because he or she has a learning disability, the fault lies not in having the disability but in the nature or form of the reading material. As Safford (1978) explained,

A physically disabled child, for example, may have an educational handicap only to the extent that the educational system makes it so. The term "hyperactive" applied to a child may have no meaning whatsoever except in relationship to institutional standards and adult frustration levels. It is submitted that the restrictive attitude toward the handicapped of "blaming the victim" is pervasive in our society and that even advocates for the handicapped are not immune (p. 297).

Handicap as Culturebound

Culture, too, can play a significant role in determining who receives a handicapped label. A disability often affects the individual's culturally defined identity. Ingstad and Whyte (1995), for example, found that cultural assumptions about one's physique and personhood must be seen in the context of ordinary social interaction. Physical disabilities raise moral and metaphysical questions about personhood, responsibility, and how differences are defined and tolerated as well as about autonomy and dependence, capacity and identity, and the meaning of loss.

Disabilities or differences considered to be handicapping in one culture may be liberating in another. How a culture defines a handicap was illustrated by Conrad and Schneider (1992) who cited the example of the South American tribe that commonly acquired dyschromic spirochetosis, a disease that causes colored spots on the skin. The condition was so common that tribal members who did not have it were stigmatized, seen as deviant, and excluded from marriage. Likewise, among a present-day African tribe whose members have a condition known as "lobster-claw syndrome" possessing the regular five fingers is considered a "malformation" (Garland, 1995). Similarly, according to Conrad and Schneider (1992), among the Papago Native Americans in the Southwest, obesity has a prevalence of nearly 100 percent and is viewed as totally normal and certainly not seen as an illness.

In New Guinea, persons with albinism are regarded as blessed while in Senegal, they are considered to be ominous and threatening. The Bayaka, a Congolese tribe, exalts their blind members while ridiculing those with deafness. On the other hand, deaf members of an Amazonian tribe are not considered handicapped nor face stigmatization because the entire tribe communicates mostly in a sign language (Garland, 1995).

B. Wright (1983) recalled the Chinese custom of foot binding as a sign of nobility. As infants, the feet of ruling class females were wrapped so as to restrict growth. Each foot was folded downward and slowly crushed over a period of years until the toe and heel nearly met. The small feet were then covered with a petite silken coverlet called a lily. Upon reaching adulthood, the women, who then were unable to walk, were carried by servants as a sign of their elite status. Although such diminutive feet may be considered a physical impairment, they were certainly not regarded as a handicap. In fact, between the eleventh to the twentieth centuries such lily feet denoted high status in China *(Topics of the Times,* 1994, p. E-3).

In parts of Africa, an individual of pure Pygmy descent is viewed as a member of a distinct tribe with a distinct set of traits, not as a person with a form of dwarfism. The difference is viewed as one of culture not physical deviance (Gleidman & Roth, 1980). In fact, Devlieger (1994) noted that African concepts of disability and differentness are mostly holistic as opposed to scientific and tend to reflect relations between human beings, God and the environment. Questions regarding the root cause of the disability is based on terms of these relationships. In the Songye tribe of East Kasai, Zaire, for example, three categories of children are considered deviant: faulty children (baana ba bilema), ceremonial children (baana mishinga) and miserable children (baana ba malwa). Faulty children are treated as being born with a fault caused by God or by a faulty relationship with some family member or the environment. Because such physical disabilities cannot be removed, the youngsters are simply accepted by the Songye as "normal abnormalities" (Devlieger, 1994, p. 86.) Ceremonial children are born under unique circumstances or have special bodily characteristics at birth. This group includes twins, children born with teeth, children born with umbilical cords around their necks or children of breach births. Such children receive special ceremonies, are thought to have special powers, and have higher status than other children. Miserable children—for example, those born with conditions like albinism, dwarfism, or hydrocephaly—are considered supernatural beings who have touched the anti-world of sorcerers, will be in this world only a short time, and will soon return to their other world. Songye tribe members severely regulate and limit all interaction with them, and in earlier times practiced infanticide in the belief that having been sent by God, miserable children should be returned to God so He could then send back sound children. Devlieger (1994) noted that community elders were involved in this ritualized practice and the tribe never considered murder.

The idea, as in the Songye society, that disability does not always or necessarily lead to a stigmatized status can be found in cultures throughout the world. For example, when Van Ripper and Emerick (1984) met an entire family that stuttered on the South Pacific Island of Fiji, they found no penalty or stigma arising from the condition:

> As our guide and translator phrased it, "Mama kaka; papa kaka, and kaka, kaka, kaka, kaka." All six persons in that family showed marked repetitions and prolongations in their speech, but they were happy people, not at all troubled by their stuttering. It was just the way they talked. No hurry, no frustration, no stigma, indeed very little aware-ness. We could not help but contrast their attitudes and the simplicity of their stuttering with those which would have been shown by a sim-ilar family in our land, where the pace of living is so much faster, where defective communication is rejected, where stutterers get penalized all their lives (p. 5).

Many Native American cultures regarded people with disabilities or differences as spiritually special, assumed them to have healing powers, and gave them leadership roles (Saxton & Howe, 1987). Baskin and Harris (1977) found that the role of medicine man or healer was often held by a tribal member with a disability. For example, in Iroquois folk-lore, Hadui, a medicine man with a physical disability, was known to be an expert in the secrets of medicine and curative herbs: "The ancient role of storyteller was a powerful one and often held by the disabled" (p. 20). During severe inclement weather, especially during the harsh winters, Native Americans were often confined to their dwellings. During those times, individuals with physical disabilities or differences traveled from tribe to tribe, and received warm welcomes as advisors, trainers and entertainers. In fact, if such disabled Native Americans were too weak or impaired to walk, willing apprentices considered it an honor to carry them and gain an opportunity to memorize their tales they told, learn the games they led and copy the crafts they taught. Special regard for persons with disabilities or differences is a pervasive characteristic of Native American culture as is the belief that diminished ability, whether physical or mental, is more than compensated for by some special gift at storytelling, herbal curing, toolmaking, or orating (Thomas, Miller, White, Nabokov, & Deloria, 1993). Such cultural beliefs are repre-sented in Native American sacred images—for example Kokopelli, "the humpbacked flute player" whose frequent and widespread appearance on pottery and in pictographs suggest that he was a well-traveled and widely recognized deity of considerable potency" (Young, 1990, p. 1).

An identical disabling condition could, of course, be assigned totally opposite meanings in different cultures. Buscaglia (1983), for example, pointed out that while the Sem Ang people of Malaysia used persons with orthopedic impairments as wise men to settle tribal disputes,
the Balinese treated their tribal members with the same conditions as
"societal taboo" (p. 162). Such diversity of cultural attitudes is common
world wide. Maisel's search through the anthropological literature from
the Human Relations Area Files at Yale University (1953) for information regarding the ways various societies, and tribes treated their members with differences and disabilities revealed these interesting and varied responses:

1. Among the Siriono Indians sickness often led to abandonment and
   death.

2. Among the Azand tribe, children born with physical differences
   were totally loved and accepted by their parents. In fact, a supplementary fifth finger or first toe, surprisingly common in the tribe,
   was considered an enviable addition.

3. Among the Navajo tribe those with physical deviations were often
   the victims of sadistic humor by other tribe members who enjoyed
   mimicking, mocking and giving uncomplimentary names to them.

4. Among the Masai tribe, misshapen and weak children were killed
   immediately after birth.

5. The Dieri, a tribe of Australian aborigines, also practiced infanticide,
   killing deformed children and babies born to unmarried mothers.

6. The Chagga of East Africa believed that children born with physical disabilities propitiated evil spirits thereby allowing other tribal
   members to be normal. Thus, they had a fear of killing their "disfigured" children, including those with more or less than five
   fingers or those with more serious "deformities."

7. The Truk peoples of the East Central Carolines held only their
   strongest and healthiest members in great esteem. Elderly and disabled tribal members were considered "superfluous."

8. The Creek Native Americans greatly revered their elders. The aged infirm were killed only for humanitarian reasons, such as to keep them from falling into enemy hands.

9. The Daho of Western Africa select as their state constables persons with physical differences. Children born with physical disabilities are believed to be under the protection of special supernatural agents.

10. The Ponape of the Eastern Carolines treated their children with physical and mental disabilities like all other children.

11. The Witoto Indians of the Northwest Amazon submerged their newborn infants in the nearest stream with the hope that only the fittest would survive.

12. "Deformed" children of the Jukun in Sudan were left to perish in the bush or in a cave out of the fear that they had been begotten by an evil spirit.

13. In the Balinese tribe, sexual relations with "albinos," "idiots," "lepers," and the "sick" or "deformed" was strictly forbidden.

14. Among the Maori tribe of New Zealand, persons with disabilities were stigmatized and often received derisive uncomplimentary nicknames (cited in B. Wright, 1983, pp. 444-446).

Thus, as Garland (1995) recently found, "In plain language, different cultures react differently to different anomalies and with differing degrees of emotional intensity, even though no culture will ignore them altogether" (p. 2). Saxton and Howe (1987) described how arbitrary meanings of disability in culture become personalized:

> We are not bound by traditional definitions of what it means to be disabled. The more insight we gain, the more we realize that nearly everything the culture has told us about the experience of disability and illness (the burden, the tragedy, the suffering, the limits) is based on arbitrary sets of values. There is no evidence that our experiences are universally negative or bad (p. 106).

Thus, different cultures view disability in extremely divergent ways. There is little doubt that how a society's culture perceives and addresses a disability is a major factor in determining just how handicapping a disability will be to its possessor. In other words, the individual's culture defines how the disability affects his or her identity. It is culture that defines how biological impairments and differences relate to personhood (Ingstad & Whyte, 1995).

Origin of Handicap
Currently, the term "handicap" carries a negative connotation among most persons either with or without disabilities, and an explanation of its origins may help clarify its meaning. Aversion to the word is often rooted in the common misconception that it comes from "begging with one's cap-in-hand." Some believe that the term originated during the time of King Henry VII of England, when the law prohibiting street begging was rescinded for disabled veterans who could not obtain employment and, therefore, went into the streets to beg "cap in hand" for change from those passing by (Ola, 1995). No reliable documentation of that origin, however, can be found.

Etymologically, "handicap" was originally called "hand-in-cap," which referred to a trading lottery game in seventeenth century England. It was an old form of barter in which an umpire held the money in his hand in a cap for two people who wanted to make an exchange (Hourihan, 1980; Davis, 1995; Ingstad & Whyte, 1995). In the game of "hand-in-cap" one person would challenge an article that belonged to another and would then offer something of his own in exchange. The parties held a deposit of forfeit money in their hands concealed in a cap, pending the umpire's decision (Burgdorf, 1980; Davis, 1995). The umpire described the merchandise to be traded and set the additional amount the owner of the inferior article should pay to make the exchange fair. The two barterers withdrew their hands from the hat empty to signify their refusal of the umpire's decision, or full to signify their acceptance. If both hands were full, the exchange was made and the umpire kept the forfeit money. If both hands were empty, the umpire kept the forfeit money but no exchange took place. Otherwise, each barterer kept his own property, and the individual who had accepted the umpire's decision took the forfeit money as well.

According to Cohen (1977), a handicap later became a form of "contest" where difficulties were placed on superior competitors or advantages given to inferior competitors in order to equalize their chances of winning. In golf or bowling it is common to assign "handicaps" for example, a certain number of strokes or pins, in order to equalize a match involving players with different skill levels. As Ingstad and Whyte (1995) observed, "[T]he term came to be used in relations to competitions in which unequal competitors were weighted so as to make the match more equal" (p. 7). During the eighteenth century, the word was applied to the process of an umpire determining the extra weight to be carried by the faster horse in a "handicap race" with lots being drawn from a hat to see if the race were "on" or "off" (Davis, 1995). "Handicap" later took on the meaning of being any race or contest in which advantages or compensations were given to different contestants according to their varied abilities. By the nineteenth century, the negative implications—"to put at a disadvantage"—began to emerge. "It was only a very late sense that switched from the idea of a superior competitor being weighed down to a newer sense of an inferior unduly burdened with a disability" (Davis, 1995, p. xiii). As Hourihan (1980) observed, "From the idea of giving a certain number of strokes to a poorer player, it is easy to see how the word took on the meaning of 'deficiency,' especially an anatomical, physiological or mental deficiency that prevents or restricts normal achievement" (p. 2). Gradually, the past participle, "handicapped," became associated with individuals at a perceived physical disadvantage.

Handicap as Negative Educational Label

Who is considered "handicapped" in our society relies, as we have seen, on the social judgment of others. In addition, one becomes "handicapped" by becoming publicly labeled. Thus, "the handicapped" comprise an artificial grouping created by the labeling process (Burgdorf & Burgdorf, 1976). As Braginsky and Braginsky (1971) stated, "In our society a cost is exacted from the child whom we must maintain. The cost usually takes the form of labeling him 'mentally retarded' or 'mentally ill.' While imprisonment has a set period of time and cost, the label is a burden the child must carry throughout his life" (p. 161).

Barnes (1975) stated that behavior labeled as deviant occurs in situations where someone does something that upsets someone else. She found the principle particularly applicable in schools where the children who disturb are the children who get labeled:

> A lot of times we really need to look into the interactions between the
> labeler and the labeled, if we really want to talk about what handi-

capped means. A handicap is not something contained within the child, but it's something that's specifically involved in the setting the child is in, and the adult who is labeling that child (p. 69).

Evaluative labeling was described as early as 1946 by Johnson who wrote that labels

emphasize our common tendency to evaluate individuals and situations according to the names we apply to them. . . . [T]his is a way of saying that the way in which we classify something determines in a large measure the way in which we react to it. We classify largely by naming. Having named something, we tend to evaluate it and so react to it in terms of the name we have given it. We learn in our culture to evaluate names or labels, or words, quite independently of the actualities to which they might be applied (cited in Rollin, 1987, p. 113).

Patton, Blackbourn and Fad (1996) explained why such labels become noxious:

Of course, what is derogatory in a name is the social role, quality, deviancy, or conformity it suggests. In our society, the imagery conjured up by any label for a handicapping condition tends to be stigmatizing, not because of the label itself, but because of our archaic attitudes toward handicaps. The stigma of being exceptional will not go away, no matter what the label, until a handicap is no longer the reason for pity, mourning, disgust, humor, segregation, or reverence. When we can laugh, cry, teach, learn, struggle, and enjoy persons who have handicaps as we do with other individuals who share our human limitations, there will be no pain in the label (p. 34).

Unfortunately, youngsters with educational handicaps face such stigmas because the field of Special Education, as currently structured, is based on such labeling. In order to receive educational programs, services, and funding, youngsters are given such negatively loaded medical type labels as mentally retarded, emotionally disturbed, chronically ill, socially maladjusted, learning disabled, physically or neurologically or perceptually impaired, or communication, auditorialy, visually, physically or multiply handicapped. Granger and Granger (1986) called such labeling "an epidemic affecting some 12 percent of all children in public education" (p. 4).

Special education labels are officially called "classifications" and are often believed to be accurate descriptors of children. Unlike true medical labels that have standardized meanings, however, special education classifications vary from state to state in both their names and definitions. A student classified "perceptually impaired" in New Jersey may be "learning disabled" in New York with the criteria also varying.

Special educators often use classifications that are clearly inappropriate expressions of the "medical model," which characterizes students as "sick." At one time, New Jersey, for example, classified all pregnant students as "chronically ill." Medical labels and grouping may be justified for providing medical services to persons with similar medical problems—for example a coronary care unit in a hospital. While such groupings in a hospital setting are temporary, in school settings they become permanent. Such groupings, do not make sense when providing most special education services. As Gartner and Joe (1987) stated, "While an orthopedic handicap may be a basis for adapting the physical education program, it offers no basis—except for administrative convenience—for grouping students for spelling instruction" (p. 205). Similarly, if youngsters learn through observation and modeling, does it make sense to place youngsters classified as "communication handicapped" with other youngsters who can not communicate or to place youngsters classified as "emotionally disturbed" often as a result of being exposed to models of unacceptable behavior, with others in special class and even separate special schools where all exhibit unacceptable behavior?

But no matter what the state, such labels certify youngsters "defective," sending them the message that "something is wrong with them" rather than something is wrong in the environment. In addition, they also often get the message that they are unfit to be taught with "normal" children.

Blaming the victim takes place when the youngster, instead of being considered to "have" a handicap, is considered to "be" handicapped. He *is* mentally retarded, she *is* emotionally disturbed. One aspect of a child perceived by others as stigmatizing thus comes to be viewed as the whole person (Gartner & Joe, 1987). The effect on the self-image can be catastrophic.

Negative terms like "disturbed," "ill," "impaired" and "retarded," accentuate the negative and often cause great shame to both parents and youngsters (Shapiro & Margolis, 1986). This directly opposes the desire of parents and educators to bolster that youngster's self esteem. Biklen

(1989) stated that such classification labels take on an encompassing quality.

> A student who was having difficulties in learning becomes a mentally retarded student, a learning disabled student, an emotionally disturbed student, a blind student. The disability, once a suspected characteristic, then an identified quality, now becomes the defining factor of the student. With the label and a placement to go with it, disability achieves what sociologists call "master status." Those who interact with or observe the labeled person have trouble seeing a person; they see instead a disabled person and all of the stereotypes associated with that status (p. 13).

In fact, because the labels have such a negative connotation, their initials are often substituted for the words themselves. Youngsters are not referred to as being educable mentally retarded, emotionally disturbed, or neurologically impaired. Instead they become "EMR's," "ED's" and "NI's."

Labels often work against children and adults with disabilities by conjuring up distorted or diminished expectations and stereotyped images of what particular individuals are like. The label takes the place of the person's individuality, and it invites others to define the essence of the person with the disability. We view that person through the "lens" of the label and never get to know the individual behind the label. Thus, the person and the disability become one and the same, and the person often endures the effects of a "stigma spread" by being viewed as totally disabled—aptly illustrated by those who yell at persons with blindness or who treat persons with small stature or mental retardation as children. Smith and Neisworth (1975) noted that one devalued trait suggests another and persons behave differently toward others who are negatively labeled. Mullins (1979), too, cautioned against "assigning identity on the basis of one stereotyping negative characteristic" which concentrates attention on the disability and conceals the person's many other attributes. For example, the statement "Stevie Wonder, a singer who happens to have blindness" emphasizes singer; whereas "Stevie Wonder, the blind singer" makes blindness the prominent feature and trivializes singer.

Gartner and Lipsky (1987) wrote that "in a variety of ways, persons with disabilities are neither treated like nor viewed as 'normal people.' More often, they are treated 'specially' either for their own good or someone else's, but always according to an externally imposed standard" (p. 380). All educators need to understand that labeling causes the differentiation of people, stigmatizes them, and makes them less than human (Goffman, 1963; Blatt, 1987).

Person First Language—Concept of the Whole Person

For integration to be successful, schools need to build more favorable impressions of their classified handicapped pupils by encouraging a focus on them as "whole" individuals. As we have noted, the non-handicapped youngster often sees the disability as the most obviously different characteristic of a classified classmate. The youngster is viewed as a symbol or as a "disability with a person attached." Stressing the "whole person concept"—that is, understanding that one characteristic is not the most important aspect of any individual—helps the non-handicapped youngster learn the difference between the symbol and the individual. "The importance of preserving the personhood of the individual with a disability also leads us to reject any metaphors or descriptions of behavior suggestive of less than human status" (B. Wright, 1983, p. 9). Wahl (1995) stressed that terms referring to persons with mental illnesses as "schizophrenics" or "psychotics" subtly dehumanizes the person by "implying that the disorders *define* the individual rather than describe a fluctuating or temporary psychiatric condition" (p. 21).

With all of the variations of disabling types, categories, severity and causes, people with disabilities tend to be treated as a distinct class, different from the rest of society. They are categorized as "them" versus "us" (Bowe, 1978) and viewed as a group called, "The Disabled." Most people who have disabilities find the term "The Disabled" objectionable, feeling themselves depersonalized by the implication that one's disability is one's identity. Vash (1981) cautioned against using terms like "the handicapped" and "the disabled," although prized for their brevity, "carry the hidden cost of summarizing the individual(s) described as nothing more than one of their characteristics, one that conjures up a negative image in the minds of most" (p. 206).

B. Wright (1983) stressed the importance of using the verb "have" rather than "be" with disabilities. For example, when called an "epileptic" or "stutterer," rather than "a person who has epilepsy or a stutter," an entire human being is described by just one characteristic (Shapiro & Barton, 1991). Vash (1981) pointed out that such labels arouse social disapproval and cause socially destructive stereotyping—for example, an "alcoholic" is seen as more reprehensible than "a person with a drinking problem."

Thus, collective nouns like "The Disabled," "The Retarded," "The Mentally Ill" or "The Blind," evoke well established sets of assumptions and stereotypes. As Sutherland (1984) observed, "'The Disabled' are generally understood to be a small, clearly defined section of society, quite distinct from the public at large—poor dependent creatures, immediately recognizable as physically different from normal people" (p. 13). Wahl (1995) similarly emphasized that

> Just as terms like "a schizophrenic" or "a diabetic" identify individuals in terms of their illnesses as if that were their only and most important characteristic, these broad references to "the mentally ill" convey a similar lack of appreciation of the basic human character of *individuals* with psychiatric disorders. Such terminology also communicates that "the mentally ill" are a special and distinct group who are, unlike the rest of "us." Designation of those with mental illnesses as "the mentally ill" (or to people with other disabilities as "the disabled," to people without homes as "the homeless," and so forth), advocates argue, encourages others to view them in terms of their differences (p. 43).

Wahl (1995) also described how the mass media use psychiatric labels to refer to individuals rather than to their disorders:

> Even references to "a schizophrenic person," while preferable to "a schizophrenic," place the emphasis on the disorder rather than on the person. More appropriate designations would be "a person experiencing psychotic symptoms" or "an individual with schizophrenia." Although admittedly more awkward, these suggested references are consistent with our designations of other health conditions: people [with] cancer are unlikely to be referred to as "cancerous people" or "the cancerous" (p. 21).

Global phrases like "disabled person" or "invalid sister" categorize persons as totally disabled in contrast to phases like "person with a disability," which connotes that a person with many other attributes happens to have a disability. Terms like "person with blindness," "people with deafness," or "citizens with developmental disabilities" stress the common status of person-hood. The use of global labeling obscures complexity and individuality. B. Wright (1983) explained the incongruity:

Is a disabled person one who is unable to do anything? More accurately, then, a disabled person is also an able person. In fact, the person is typically more able than disabled. Why then, call the person disabled? It is precisely the perception of a person with a physical disability as a disabled person that reduces the person to the disabling aspect of his or her functioning (p. 8).

As Davis (1995) explained, "The term 'person with disabilities' is preferred by many to 'disabled person' since the former implies a quality added to someone's personhood rather than the second term's reduction of the person to the disability" (p. xiii). The use of such terms as "disabled person," implies that individuals within a disability are typically alike and that they form a distinct group that is different from the rest of society (Burgdorf, 1980). For example, there is no such thing as a "typical blind person." Within the group of persons with visual impairments, there are variations in severity and types of blindness, as well as other critical factors like "time of onset." Although two individuals may currently have identical losses in acuity, one born with blindness (congenitally blind) and one who became blind later in life (adventitiously blind), will have very different concepts of redness, the sunset, the height of the Empire State Building, or traveling ninety miles an hour. In addition, the individual born with blindness, having no memory of being a sighted person, or any identity as such, would consider his or her condition normal. In short, individuals with visual impairments can not be grouped into the category of "the blind." The variations are too numerous to allow for a typical case. This is true for all categories of disability.

Person-first language stresses the personhood of the subject. As Vash (1981) noted, "After that basic mental image has been set, the modifying adjectival clause 'with a disability' is less likely to dominate the conveyed concept of the person" (p. 206).

All educators must remember that the use of person-first language establishes an attitude of respect and acceptance of their students with individual differences. Of most importance is using person first language when professional colleagues, parents, and fellow classmates refer to individual children (Blaska, 1993).

Metaphors, Idioms and Figurative Language
Terms like, "turning a deaf ear" for someone not listening, "lame duck" for someone without power, or "blind" to describe someone who refus-

es to face facts, in reality, identify people "who are trying against huge cultural odds to maintain a shred of dignity in a society that uniformly denigrates [sic] them to worse than second-class status" (*Disability Rag*, March-April 1992, pp. 26-28). "In virtually every language context, the simile or metaphor used to describe an unpleasant or disagreeable situation is identical to or derivative of the words naming the disability itself" (Baskin & Harris, 1977, p. 8).

Nowhere is this more evident than in the words relating to little people. Feldman (1975) coined the work "heightism" and argued that considerable research supported the idea that height greatly influences one's career and job choices, one's social and romantic choices, one's political choices (for example, getting elected), and the development of one's self-esteem. According to Gillis (1982),

> Society is obsessed with height, and our language reflects that obsession. We call impractical people "short-sighted." Cheating at the cash register is described as "short changing" the customer. In commodities trading, when we sell what we don't have, we sell "short." When did a winner get the "short" end of the stick? Not enough food? Call it "short rations." (But whoever heard of "tall" rations or "long" rations?) Time after time our language, and presumably the thinking that is reflected by language, associates short with dishonesty, inadequacy, and other failings or shortcomings if you want to be consistent (p. 9).

In addition, we speak of someone with prejudice as having a "small mind." Unimportant communication is "small talk." Conversely, if a man is important we say he is a big man, who stands tall and probably has a big job which pays him big money. If he is kind, he has a big heart.

Gillis (1982) gave as a primary example of height bias in the English Language the use of the common synonym for height, the word "stature." Beside height, stature is defined as having a similar meaning to words like quality, caliber, merit, value, virtue, worth, prestige, standing, ability, capacity, competence, dignity, rank, and status. "Some language experts would say that this constant association between "status" and "stature" actually helps to cause heightism (p. 10). As Phifer (1979), a little person, stated,

> How short are you? That's what people really mean when they ask me "How tall are you?" But short, in our society, is an insult. Short is untall (p. 3).

Phifer (1979) stressed further that when we "look up" to someone, we respect them automatically. Conversely, when we "look down" on people, we question their abilities in every sense, both mental and physical. "In fact, the words 'look down' mean to disapprove" (p. 16). And, of course, those who do not meet our expectations do not "measure up."

Many other common words carry hidden negative connotations for people with disabilities. For example, a criminal is a *crook* (because he is "crooked" as opposed to "straight"); a villain is a "heavy;" someone who exhibits behavior that we do not like or that we think is odd is a "creep", a word that shares origins with "cripple." A tired individual is said to be "vegging out," a term derived from one's being a "vegetable."

Often, these negative terms take on moralistic implications. For example, Gallagher (1995) found that

> [I]n many languages the terms used to describe a disabling condition are often moral value words, heavy with implied meaning—something is "wrong" with his leg; he has a "bum" leg; his leg is "not right;" this is a "bad" leg; is it "good" to walk on? (p. 247).

We may be unaware of how such language strongly influences us because of its subtleness. But, teachers need to know how such language evolves.

The Evolution of Meanings

The stage for stereotypical images and self-fulfilling prophecies about well-being and achievement can also be set by institutional categorizing and legal labeling. The meanings assigned to negative labels often change and take on lives of their own. Respectable scientific terms used to evoke deprecating images soon become pejorative epithets, and as time goes by the original definitions become lost or forgotten. Burgdorf (1980) described the evolutionary pattern of the development of terminology applied to handicaps:

> New terms are selected, generally from medical or social science, to describe a particular condition; the innovative terminology is often acclaimed as the ultimate, precise, scientific name for the condition. The new term is introduced into the vocabulary of the leading professionals and gradually is absorbed into general usage. Over the course of many years, the term becomes associated with social stereotypes and acquires derogatory connotations. Eventually, it is replaced by a

new term, which does not yet have any such negative implications,
and the process begins all over again (p. 46).

Such labels as "idiot," "imbecile" and "moron" were once perfectly acceptable scientific clinical terms to describe levels of mental retardation ("feeble mindedness"), that later developed into prejudice-laden
pejoratives. "Moron," for example, is now used to belittle or poke fun
at people, as in the use of moron jokes or the recent headline, "The
Moron Movie Mogul—He makes short, bad movies by doing really
dumb things" (Polak, 1988, p. 9). By itself this headline does not
significantly harm those with mental retardation, except at a personal
level. When added to the countless other examples, however, the respect
society has for persons with mental retardation cannot help but dimin-
ish. One finds another example of how meanings change in the word
"monster", which originally meant someone with a physical difference;
today it has an evil connotation (Bogdan, 1988).

While the meaning of the word is in the process of change it may
still be considered respectable as it continues to appear in respectable
information sources. For example, while many persons with disabilities
consider the term "Mongoloid" both racist and handicapist (properly,
Down syndrome) dictionaries rarely classify it as pejorative or derisive.
Thus such terms continue to appear commonly in newspapers, as in the
human interest story: "Danny Whiteneck, a 400 pound Mongoloid victim of epilepsy and cerebral palsy, will be 45 years old Monday" (Will
there be a birthday card for Danny? 1981, p. A6). For comparison, technical terms like "cretin" are used in pejorative or uncomplimentary
ways, as in an interview in *The New York Times* (Norman, 1988, p. B4)
in which a distinguished English professor opined, "I've got some students of nearly equal intelligence, some of whom spell like cretins and
some like angels." No doubt the professor was well intentioned but
unaware of the message conveyed by his use of "cretin."

Negative Imagery

Thomas Dunn, the former Mayor of Elizabeth, New Jersey, while
attempting to insult a local newspaper, wrote, "The front page must be
set up by a moron shoved out of a State Institution that demands 'mainstreaming' of its patients" (1993, p. 3). Similarly, Rogers, an Arizona
Assistant Attorney General, was quoted as saying, "We're destroying
Arizona's reputation as the bastion of the lame, lazy, and incompetent"
(cited in Baskin & Harris, 1984, p. 15). Negative metaphors and pejo-

rative images like those used by Dunn and Rogers—both high public officials—is extremely distasteful to persons with disabilities. Is it any wonder that one of the largest barriers to persons with disabilities developing a strong self-image is the constant use of such negative metaphors? This type of figurative language, which is universally negative, reveals unconscious values and beliefs about others (Baskin & Harris, 1977).

Unfortunately, these images of disabilities can also be used intentionally to ridicule people. For example, *The Disability Rag* (March-April, 1987) reported that an arts and entertainment editor of the *Kansas City Star,* reviewing the film *Playing for Keeps* stated, "By now we're all used to lame teen comedies, but *Playing for Keeps* is so bad it's practically paraplegic" (p. 17). Baskin and Harris (1984) quoted the prestigious magazine, *Smithsonian,* as describing items on a menu for non-English speaking individuals as "a surprising phenomenon that brings relief to the famished foreigner who suddenly realizes that ordering a meal is possible even for the linguistically lame" (p. 15). In a similar fashion *The Toledo Journal,* while attempting to make its readers aware of personal racial biases, offered a Quotient Test introduced with the following question, "Are you a racial retard?" (cited in We wish we wouldn't see, *Disability Rag & Resources,* 1996, March-April, p. 24).

The language used by Walker, the Russian correspondent for the British publication *Guardian,* in his August 1991 report described the following scene:

> As we went along the path that leads across the tiny bridge to the cathedral we ran a gauntlet not just of beggars but of cripples and wheelchairs and other helpless mental patients, drooling and quivering and jerking palsied limbs. When I stopped to find some money the wheelchairs charged and crashed together. An ancient woman in a brown shawl who had been standing on her crutches, suddenly heaved forward, using a crutch to sweep away legs from under two of the pressing beggars and pinioned my arm, snatching at the handful of change. A heave of her buttock and a wheelchair was skidded aside. One of the droolers howled like a dog and began to have what looked like an epileptic fit. I backed away to the church, and left them snarling in this almost medieval scene (cited in Pointon & Davies, 1997, p. 9).

Johnson (1988) was correct in her assertion that "Language and the words used are probably our [persons with disabilities] biggest handicap, and the problem continues to be perpetuated by the media" (New Jersey Developmental Disabilities Council, p. 8). For example, a sports editor of the *Philadelphia Inquirer* (Dolson, 1988) wrote "Playing [basketball against] Kentucky at Rupp Arena with five midgets would be better than that." "Midget" categorically implied constitutional inferiority. Similarly, *Time Magazine* (Stacks, 1988) used the headline *Dwarf No More* about George Bush's primary victory over Bob Dole to show that Bush had overcome adversity, that he was now someone to be reckoned with and looked up to. Clearly *Time* chose "dwarf" to invoke the image of a loser, someone of no consequence in the previous primaries whose political substance and clout had been suspect. In these contexts the midget and dwarf metaphors perpetuate negative images of persons with differences.

Persons with disabilities trying to overcome disablism obviously resent labels like "victim," "afflicted" and "invalid." These terms reinforce images of pity, highlight limitations and detract from human worth. They perpetuate distorted, misleading images of persons with disabilities as consumed by their disability and completely dependent on others, instead of the more accurate image of multifaceted people with intact abilities in other areas. People with disabilities resent words that suggest they are sick, pitiful, childlike, dependent, or objects of admiration—words that, in effect, "convey the imagery of poster children and supercrips" (J. Shapiro, 1993, p. 332-33). It is important for educators to scrutinize these terms to understand why many persons with disabilities resent them.

Victim

Persons with disabilities often deeply resent the epithet "victim," which is used as a metaphor and projects an image of powerlessness. Journalists use it to sensationalize events. Those who are robbed, raped or murdered are said to have been intentionally victimized. A person may be a victim of such an act, but not of a natural condition like a cold or sore throat. It follows, therefore, that if a youngster can not be a victim of a cold or sore throat, he or she can not be a victim of multiple sclerosis, cerebral palsy, or muscular dystrophy.

Peters (1987) argued that diseases are not rational and subjective, nor do they have a will. Disabilities do not intentionally seek out and victimize someone the way a felon would. Use of the term evokes pity and deflects any awareness of a responsibility to assure equal acceptance. Peters observed, that using phrases like "victim of multiple scle-

rosis" puts the blame on the wrong party and obscures the concept that
the solution lies in social changes for access and rights (overcoming the
handicap) rather than curing the disability. She also believes that the
word's emotional overtones in the public ear correspond to the public
impression: "They believe we *are* victims—helpless, dependent, [and]
our victimizer a disease or bodily imperfection. The victimizer of disabled people isn't a disease; rather, the real 'victimizer' is discriminatory attitudes, lack of access, and lack of rights" (p. 22).

Affliction

When disability is associated with divine retribution for bad behavior, it
is a classic instance of "blaming the victim." According to Gallagher
(1995), "[M]ost people view disability as some sort of moral judgment"
(p. 247), apparently based on the belief that humans prefer to avoid a
world in which the innocent are punished along with the guilty:

> Man wants to believe that pain and illness—certainly terrible punish-
> ments—must be the consequences of evil doing. In such a simplistic
> world construct—life according to Disney—the good are rewarded
> and the bad are crippled and no good life is lived in vain. . . . This
> desire to blame the chronically ill and disabled for their condition, to
> hold them somehow guilty and punished for some undefined sin, per-
> haps, is caused by the degree of subconscious fear that the disabled
> arouse in the minds of most people. The non-disabled have a subcon-
> scious fear that the disabled person has perpetrated some evil act—or
> is about to perpetrate something evil—that has brought on punish-
> ment (Gallagher, 1995, p. 247).

Thus, the term "affliction" conveys punishment for immoral deeds
(mostly sexual) and is often used in mythology and the Bible regarding
blindness. Oedipus, who slept with his mother—one of the worst
taboos—had blindness "afflicted" on him as punishment. Samson, too,
lost his eyes for his misdeeds. Unfortunately many believe the false-
hood that blindness is an "affliction" caused by masturbation or sexually transmitted diseases like syphilis. The term "afflicted with AIDS," for
example, has strong implications of divine retribution for an individual's homosexual orientation or sexual promiscuity. Gallagher (1995)
further stated that

> This [belief] continues up to the present time—as seen, for instance,
> in the view that people with AIDS have brought the disease upon

themselves by their behavior as homosexuals. Even modern medicine, with its psychosomatic theory of illness, carries with it the implication that the sick are responsible for their sickness (p. 248).

Words like "affliction" and "misfortune" are often used synony-mously although they differ significantly from each other. For example, Stein (1984) in *The American College Dictionary*, defines misfortune as "ill luck;" "a mischance or mishap." In contrast, "affliction suggests not only misfortune but the emotional effect of this." *Webster's Third New International Dictionary (*unabridged; Grove, 1981) defines the adjec-tive "afflicted" as "grievously affected or troubled." "Affliction" is defined as self-mortification, a state of pain, distress, or grief." Thus the commonly used phrase "He is afflicted with blindness" may imper-ceptibly convey that blindness causes deep emotional scars and contin-ued grief when, in fact, the person may be as emotionally healthy and optimistic as anyone without a disability and may not be overly con-cerned about his or her blindness at all.

Such beliefs, however, persist today and continue to affect rela-tionships with persons with disabilities. As Buscaglia (1983) stated,

> It is possible that if we were to examine our own feelings regarding limitations such as blindness, deafness, cerebral palsy, epilepsy, crip-pling [sic] diseases, and others, we would find that we still believe, as did our ancestors, that their basic causes lie in the transgressions of parents, their lack of good judgment, or punishment for their sins (p. 63).

Invalid

The *Random House College Dictionary* (Stein, 1984) defines the noun "invalid" as "an infirm or sickly person, esp. one who is too sick, weak or old to care for himself." As an adjective, "invalid" means "not valid, without force or foundation, indefensible, deficient in substance or cogency; weak, void, without legal force." It is the same word; only the accent has changed. The examples include, "He was invalidated for life" and "His invalid sister." *The Random House Thesaurus* (Stein, 1984a) associates enfeebled person, incapable and powerless with "invalid." It offers the horrible example, "The invalid is confined to the wheelchair for life." Certainly the messages inherent in the label "invalid" devalue those to whom they refer by defining them almost exclusively in terms of their disability and ignoring their complexity and competence. Commonly the consequence of words like "victim," "invalid" and "crippled" is infantilizing paternalism bestowed by persons without disabilities and resentment from those being thought of as hopeless, weak, or of no force. These terms translate very readily, almost unconsciously, into "of no value, of no consequence."

Zola (1982) described how invalid and similar terms evolve from viewing persons with physical disabilities as sick:

> While most minority groups grow up in some special subculture and thus develop certain norms and expectations, the physically handicapped are not similarly prepared. Born for the most part into normal families, we are socialized into that world. The world of sickness is one we enter only later, poorly prepared and with all the prejudices of the normal. The very vocabulary we use to describe ourselves is borrowed from that society. We are de-formed, dis-eased, dis-abled, disordered, ab-normal, and, most telling of all, called an in-valid (p. 206).

More Strong Messages: Framing the Shot

"Written materials," Mullens (1979) noted, "can portray vivid images equally as well as photographs. Visualize the difference between a person 'confined to a wheelchair' compared to 'someone who uses a wheelchair.' Confinement implies 'restriction,' or 'imprisonment' or 'restraint' whereas use signifies 'control for a purpose' or 'extension of ability'" (p. 20). Yet many news stories routinely use terms like "wheelchair-bound" and "confined to a wheelchair" to describe persons with disabilities (see for example, Leach, 1988), leaving the impression that wheelchair users are glued to their transportation and "suffer" from confinement. Most wheelchair users see their wheelchairs as "unconfining." Vash (1981) referred to such terms like "person confined to a wheelchair" as "abjure passive constructions" and "person who uses a wheelchair" as an "active construction" (p. 207).

Although the difference in phraseology used to describe wheelchair users may sound trivial, its importance lies in the attitudes unknowingly projected. "Confined to a wheelchair" subtly perpetuates the stereotype that people with physical disabilities are helpless and pitiable whereas "uses a wheelchair" supports the more accurate image that with a wheelchair such persons have the opportunity and competence to do many things for themselves. As Vash (1981) observed,

> The former conveys an image of passive sitting and victimization. The latter suggests a person who is actively using a wheelchair as a tool for living life. The difference is that between the "helpless invalid" of fifty years ago and the "consumer activist" of today (p. 207).

The distinction between "can do" and "can't do" is important and emotionally charged for persons with disabilities, as was ironically illustrated in the same issue of *Time Magazine* (Brand, 1988), in which Gallaudet students explained why they demonstrated to demand the appointment of a *deaf* president and additional "deaf" board members: "This is the Selma of the deaf. Prejudice is believing that hearing people have to take care of deaf people."

The President of the CUNY Coalition of Students with Disabilities asserted that "Attitudes are the real disability" (*March is Women's Month*, 1988).

Change by Example

An article in *The New York Times* on racism and language by McClean (1988) concluded that "[W]hile we may not be in a position to change the English language, we can, as responsible adults, change our usage of the language" (p. 26). Fortunately, educators can do a great deal eliminate stereotypes, bias and discrimination. For example, they can teach their students to

1. Use language in more accurate and sensitive ways.

2. Sensitize students to how newspapers, the electric media, and literature employ language in ways that perpetuate disablism.

When we fail to help students use language to reflect an accurate reality, we inadvertently perpetuate disablism. Increasing awareness and reinforcing accurate, sensitive communication can go a long way toward eliminating social barriers that adversely affect persons with disabilities. Teachers have a crucial role in reducing the effects of negative language on the self image of handicapped students. The success of mainstreaming and inclusion relies on successful social integration. Thus, it becomes important for teachers to learn how to respond to and deal with incidents of scapegoating and name-calling as they occur.

CHAPTER THREE

The Minority Group and Medical Model Paradigms

To view disability issues solely as medical is analogous to viewing gender issues as gynecological or racial issues as dermatological. The actual medical losses of sight, hearing, intelligence, or limbs cause less heartache than the prejudice, discrimination and intolerance that so often follows and attends the loss (Glideman, 1979; Bell & Burgdorf, 1983; Hahn, 1987; Oliver, 1994; Mackelprang & Salsgiver, 1996; Rioux, 1996). "People with disabilities are handicapped mainly by society's mistaken beliefs about their abilities" (*About being sensitive,* 1995, p. 3). One needs to go beyond physiological or cognitive conditions to gain a full understanding of disability (Rioux, 1996). "Many people with disabilities believe that the obstacles they face are often as much the result of society's attitudes as they are any physical limitation of their bodies and their minds" (*People in Motion,* 1995, p. 2). How we define disability and respond to persons who have them, depends on our economic and social structures and central values (Oliver, 1990, p. xii).

Unfortunately, most existing ideas and policies regarding individuals with impairments "appear to be based on erroneous assumptions about the nature and meaning of disability" (Hahn, 1987, p. 181). In 1995, UNESCO reported that

> One of the commonest responses to impairment is to perceive it as an unmitigated personal and social disaster or tragedy; a loss or deficiency (some countries define disabled people by percentages, i.e. one can be 50 percent of a normal person). These powerful negatives elicit either fear, pity, or admiration, depending on how the disabled person copes (p. 30).

"There are many people within the disability community who are concerned that the medical model perpetuates a view that disabled people will not be normal unless or until they are cured of their disability" (People in Motion, 1995, p. 2). As Rioux (1996) stated,

> If there is a way to "fix" such people, then that reduces the social bur-
> den and "do-gooders" are willing to pay the price for habilitation and
> rehabilitation. The primary objective of the programs and services is
> then to fix the person so he or she can be like others without disabili-
> ties (p. 9).

Because the primary issues regarding disabilities and special education are matters of understanding and rights, not medical treatment, one understands them better through a social, minority group, independence paradigm—fighting disablism (handicapism)—rather than through the commonly used diagnostic-prescriptive medical paradigm —fighting disease. The medical paradigm views disability as a sickness to be cured. It defines the nature of disability in terms of individual deficiencies and biology, in particular the individual's biological inadequacies (Mackelprang & Salsgiver, 1996). As Rioux (1996) concluded, "Rehabilitation in itself, no matter how effective, will not lead to fulfilling the goals of human rights" (p. 9).

The minority group or independence paradigm views disability as a natural part of life with its challenge to make society and the environment accessible and user friendly. It considers the needs of persons with disabilities not as "individual" pathology but as "social" pathology. Its focus is not on charity but on an individual's right to be a participating citizen of one's country (Rioux, 1996). It permits a person with a disability to be perceived, less as an individual recipient of special education, medical services, or charity, and more as a member of an oppressed minority facing constant discrimination and segregation (Bogdan & Knoll, 1988). Jernigan (1983), for example, stressed that

> [Persons with blindness] are a minority, in the same way that Blacks
> or Jews are a minority. The condition is not so much limiting as it is
> unpopular. The restrictions and denials of basic freedoms experienced
> by the blind are motivated by good intentions, but the result is dis-
> crimination (p. 65).

Waxman (1992), describing the extent of the discrimination encountered, stated that

Disabled people face a pattern of oppressive societal treatment and hatred, much as women face misogyny, gay men and lesbians face homophobia, Jews face anti-Semitism and people of color face racism. [D]ata about rape, child sexual abuse, incest, sexual harassment, battery, neglect, defamation and other forms of violence directed at disabled people indicate that they are much more likely to be targeted for violence than their nondisabled cohorts. Ongoing research estimates that sexual violence directed at disabled people is one and a half times that directed at nondisabled people of the same sex and age (p. 5).

Hahn (1987) explained the importance of the minority group paradigm in erasing prejudice and discrimination:

This approach views prejudice and discrimination as the major issues confronting citizens with disabilities. Since the primary source of the problem can be traced to defects in what might be termed the attitudinal environment of society rather than to personal deficiencies, the solution can not be achieved solely by seeking continuous improvements in the functional and occupational capacities of disabled individuals. Instead, the eradication of bias and segregation requires extended effort to secure equal rights for disabled citizens and the rigorous enforcement of anti-discrimination measures (p. 184).

As Hahn (1987) further stated, "Viewing disability issues in terms of etiology rather than in terms of rights, focuses on the 'functional-internal' traits of individuals rather than on the 'external-environmental' problems, issues, and obstacles they commonly face" (p. 182).

Effects on Social Policy

The paradigm of disability we use determines not only our individual attitudes, but our social policies and legislation as well. As Liachowitz (1988) argued, "The medical-pathological paradigm of 'disability legislation' effected a shift from physical inferiority to social inferiority by forcing an emphasis on the handicapped individual, and by discouraging acknowledgment of socially created sources of deviance" (p. 11). The minority group paradigm is based on the link between equality and difference (Rioux, 1996). Hahn (1988) explained how the medical "functional-limitations" model presupposes inferiority:

Minority groups have been subjected to various forms of exploitation and oppression, and the sources of their treatment may be traced to pervasive social values of the dominant majority. A principal problem in establishing the concept of disabled persons as an oppressed group has been the prevalent assumptions of their biological inferiority. Whereas a major thrust of social science research on other minorities during the past century has been to refute such assumptions and to demonstrate that their unequal status stems primarily from prejudicial attitudes, many professionals as well as popular images of disabled individuals continue to harbor presuppositions of inferiority based on their functional incapacities. Consequently, it has been commonly overlooked that the origins of prejudice are based on wide-spread perceptions that disabled individuals violate important cultural norms and values, and that this fact permits them to be set apart from the remainder of the population (p. 119).

Instead of focusing on medical perspectives, the minority group approach concentrates attention on the extent to which "the environment is a product of collective decisions or non-decisions by the public and political leaders that have a different impact on members of society" (Hahn, 1987, p. 184). At the core of the "minority group paradigm" of disability is the acknowledgment that all aspects of the environment—including transportation, communication, architecture, and social organizations (especially education)—are shaped by public policy that reflect attitudes based on paradigms. Oliver (1990) observed that

As far as disability is concerned, if it is seen as tragedy, then disabled people will be treated as if they are victims of some tragedy or circumstance. This treatment will occur not just in everyday interactions but will be translated into social policies which will attempt to compensate these victims for the tragedy that has befallen them (pp. 2-3).

Unfortunately, such compensation may lead to preferential treatment which, in turn, conveys an image of pity. Gartner and Joe (1987) stressed the existence of a "pernicious reciprocal relationship" between image and policy. "In effect, preferential tax treatment or lowered bus fares on the basis of impairment. . . without reference to individual income, conveys an image of pathetic figures who need charity. Dignity seems a high price to pay for a cheap bus ticket" (p. 4). Oliver (1990) observed that

[I]f disability is defined as social oppression, then disabled people will be seen as the collective victims of an uncaring or unknowing society rather than as individual victims of circumstance. Such a view will be translated into social policies geared towards alleviating oppression rather than compensating individuals. It almost goes without saying that at present, the individual and tragic view of disability dominates both social interactions and social policy (pp. 2-3).

Hahn (1987) earlier elaborated on the limitations of the paradigm that defined disability almost exclusively from a medical viewpoint:

Disability was considered a "defect" or "deficiency" that could be located within the individual. From the clinical perspective of medicine, efforts to improve the functional capabilities of individuals were regarded as the exclusive solution to disability, and policy changes were essentially excluded from consideration as a possible remedy for the difficulties confronting the disabled (p. 181).

Similarly, Pope and Tarlov (1991) stressed,

The so-called medical model has influenced the development of most of the nation's disability-related programs. The model defines disabling conditions as principally the product of physical and mental problems that constrain performance. Influenced by this view, health and social agencies provide a mix of services that, for the most part, categorize affected individuals as permanently ill and incapable of meeting their own needs. Therefore, the problems that disability related programs seek to address are often viewed as inherent to the individual and as independent of society (p. 244).

Kirchner (1996) explained the focus of the minority group-civil rights-independence model and the importance of shifting away from the medical-functional limitations model:

The new paradigm focuses heavily on social context rather than individual impairment alone, and suggests that the most important policy issue is how to design and modify the environment—including attitudes and social arrangements—to permit access by all to the full range of valued roles. But many policy influentials, and probably most of the rest of the public—including, it is important to note, people who become disabled—still function within the old paradigm. They assume what others now see as fallacy: that biomedical impairment equates to disability, and that disability equates to dependence (p. 81).

As Covey (1989) wrote, "To try to change outward attitudes and behaviors does very little good in the long run if we fail to examine the basic paradigms from which these behaviors flow" (p. 28). But before paradigms can be shifted, they need to be understood.

Paradigms

The word "paradigm," as commonly used today, means a model, theory, perception, assumption or frame of reference. Generally, it is the way one perceives, understands or interprets a topic or issue; it is, in short, an explanation or model. Covey (1989) stated that individuals interpret (often unknowingly) everything they experience through such paradigms, frequently without questioning their accuracy. People simply assume the way they view things is the way they really are or the way they should be: "And our attitudes grow out of these assumptions. The way we see things is the source of the way we think and the way we act" (p. 24). Thus, paradigms are the source of our attitudes and behaviors. If, for example, we view persons with disabilities through a medical (deficit) paradigm, we see them as sickly patients in need of diagnosis, labeling and repair. Then we behave toward them as such. If we view persons with disabilities and youngsters in special education through a civil rights (independence) paradigm, we see them as members of a minority group faced with constant prejudice and discrimination. Then we behave toward them as such. Similarly, if we view special education through a medical paradigm with its diagnosis, labeling and prognosis attributes, the classified youngsters the paradigm is supposed to serve become patients rather than students. Unfortunately, most qualitative research in the field focuses on the aspects of methods rather than paradigms (Ferguson, Ferguson & Taylor, 1992). As Covey (1989) observed examining our paradigms is extremely important:

> The more aware we are of our basic paradigms, maps, or assumptions, and the extent to which we have been influenced by our experience, the more we can take responsibility for those paradigms. . . and be open to their perceptions, thereby getting a larger picture and a far more objective view (p. 29).

Thus, in order to change negative attitudes toward persons with disabilities, we need to shift paradigms, that is, find a new way of thinking about disability.

The Medical Paradigm

Hardman, Drew and Egan, (1996) explained the essence of the medical paradigm:

> The medical model has two dimensions: normal and pathological. Normal is defined as the absence of a biological problem. Pathological is defined as alterations in an organism caused by disease, which is a state of ill health that interferes with or destroys the organism. The medical model often referred to as the disease model, focuses primarily on biological problems and on defining the nature of the disease and its pathological effects on the individual. The model is universal and does not have values that are culturally relative. It is based on the premise that being healthy is better than being sick, regardless of the culture in which one lives (p. 18).

Medical definitions are, however, "partial and limited and fail to take into account wider aspects of disability" (Oliver, 1990, p. 5). Yet society's distorted images of persons with disabilities most often result from its understanding and interpreting the meaning of disability in a medical rather than a social-civil rights paradigm. For example, wheelchair users are often perceived as chronically ill or sickly. This association between wheelchair use and illness has probably emerged from the standard hospital practice of using wheelchairs to transport persons with illnesses. Someone may use a wheelchair for a variety of reasons that may have nothing to do with lingering sickness, but our perceptions link illness and wheelchair use.

Disability has often been perceived as a "health-related inability" that results in vocational limitations. Much of the social treatment and devaluation of persons with disabilities depend on society's negative perceptions toward what is believed to be their economic uselessness (Liachowitz, 1988). Mackelprang and Salsgiver (1996) recently found that one of the prevailing fundamental beliefs rooted in our culture is that

> [P]eople with disabilities can not and should not work or otherwise be productive. Contributing to the belief that people with disabilities should not work is the role of sick people in Western culture. People

with disabilities, whom society assumes are "sick," are expected to fill this role even when they are perfectly healthy. As with those who are sick, people with disabilities are to be taken care of and to be provided for. Their only obligation is to be grateful for the help given them, thus subjecting them to a form of benevolent oppression (p. 10).

Hahn (1987) stressed that focusing on the capacity to work almost at the expense of other life activities is a "unidimensional" approach that "makes some unwarranted and untenable assumptions about the linkage between impairments and productivity" (p. 182). Such an approach reinforces the stereotype of persons with disabilities as useless, costly and burdensome. Similarly, as Hirsch and Hirsch (1995) found,

> The medical model of disability, while useful and effective for the medical treatment of a disabling condition, usually helps perpetuate stigmatizing cultural conceptions of disability when applied to such other aspects of a disabled person's life as educational, professional, social, economic, recreational and civic activities and interests. Under the medical model, a disability remains a problem that is located solely in the person rather than in the interaction between the person and the environment. Also under this model, and mode of thinking a life with limited experiences seems to be the "natural" consequences for a person with a significant disability (p. 23).

According to Pope and Tarlov (1991),

> The independent-living and disability rights movements blame adherence to the medical model for the creation of disability-related programs that foster dependence rather than personal autonomy. Members of these movements correctly argue that disability is the result of a dynamic process involving complex interactions among biological, behavioral, psychological, social, and environmental factors. Some have called for the "demedicalization" of disability in order to reflect the broader view of society (p. 244).

Tessier (1995), a disability rights activist and former candidate for Congress, stressed how the medical model, with its emphasis on "cures," results in the persecution of persons with disabilities:

> The medical model is a trap. It defines us simply as physical limitations, medical conditions. It is what justifies the cures, the treatments, incarcerations until you're somehow whole again. And it makes it

impossible for us to be seen as full, rounded people. That's the core of our oppression (cited in *Thirteen: WNET*, p. 2).

Hevey (1992) explained how his paradigm shift away from the medical model liberated him:

I evidently saw epilepsy as my hidden cross. I cannot explain how significantly all this was turned around when I came into contact with the notion of the social model of disabilities, rather than the medical model which I had hitherto lived with. Over a matter of months, my discomfort with this secret beast of burden called epilepsy, and my festering hatred at the silencing of myself as a disabled person ("because I didn't look it") completely changed. I think I went through an almost evangelical conversion as I realized that my disability was not, in fact, the epilepsy, but the toxic drugs with their denied side-effects; the medical regime with its blaming the victim: the judgment through distance and silence of bus-stop crowds, barroom crowds, and dinner-table friends; the fear; and, not least, the employment problems. All this was the oppression, not the epileptic seizure at which I was hardly (consciously) present (pp. 1-2).

Our society tends to medicalize any form of deviance. As Conrad (1996) stressed, "The increasing medicalization of deviant behavior and the medical institution's role as an agent of social control has gained considerable notice (p. 69). He then defined medicalization as, "Defining a medical problem or illness and mandating or licensing the medical profession to provide some type of treatment for it" (p. 69).

As far back as 1851, a prominent physician in the pre-Civil War South published in a prestigious medical journal a description of the disease, drapetomania, "which only affected slaves and whose major symptom was running away from the plantations of their white masters" (Conrad & Schneider, 1992, p. 35).

Macionis (1989) explained how the growing influence of medicine within American society—particularly psychiatry—has resulted in the medicalization of deviance. In the recent past, pregnancy, childbirth, contraception, diet, exercise, alcoholism, other addictions, erratic behavior, hyperactive children and disability were not considered medical matters (Conrad & Schneider, 1992).

The American Psychiatric Association (1994a) in its Fourth Edition of the *Diagnostic and Statistical Manual of Mental Disorders (DSM-IV)* now includes diagnostic categories for disorders connected to "bereavement," "academic problems," "malingering," "occupational problems," "religious or spiritual problems," "problems with melancholic features," "pathological gambling disorders," and even "noncompliance with treatment." According to Herbert (1998), "[T]he current volume identifies more than 300 disorders, up from 106 just 18 years ago" (p. 63). In a similar way, when asking the Food and Drug Administration in 1995 to regulate tobacco as an addictive drug, President Clinton called cigarette smoking "a pediatric disease" (Stolberg, 1996, p. B3).

The medicalizaton of deviance changes behavior patterns previously understood in moral terms into medical matters. Therefore, labels used to designate normality or deviance change from moral terms like "bad" and "good" to medical terms like "sick" and "well." Such medicalization transformed deviance from "badness" to "sickness," with its social response becoming "therapeutic" rather than "punitive." When deviant behavior is seen as willful it tends to be defined as a crime; when it is perceived as unwillful it tends to be defined as sickness (Conrad & Schneider, 1992).

Analyzing the medical model is important because its view of deviance, which locates the source of such behavior within the individual, mandates intervention with a medical form of treatment considered morally neutral because it is scientifically based (Conrad & Schneider, 1992). In fact, the medical community has developed scientific mechanisms to measure such differences including IQ scores for mental retardation, decibel loss for hearing impairments, acuity loss for visual impairments, functional limitations scales, and "a host of other standardized testing mechanisms or classification schemes to measure the extent of incapacity" (Rioux, 1996, p. 4).

Linton, Mello and O'Neill (1995) found the underlying concept of the medical model view of disability to be a "personal medical condition, rather than a social issue; and individual plight rather than a political one" (p. 5). In their discussion of the medicalization of disability they stated,

> Medical, educational and social service personnel have wielded enormous power over people with disabilities using the tools of diagnosis, labeling, treatment, and institutionalization. It is often difficult to explain what is wrong with this arrangement. The seemingly benevolent impulses that drive these practices belie the paternalism and control these tools serve. The arrangement privileges the medical definitions of people's lives over the social and political definitions.

The solution to the "problem" of disability is seen as residing in the resources and facilities of the medical establishment, rather than in legislative bodies and social institutions. The arrangement buys into the assumption that people with disabilities are more concerned with cures than rights, more plagued with their conditions than with discrimination. It also assumes that all human variations labeled "disabilities" require a medical definition (p. 8).

Meanwhile, the medical establishment has traditionally portrayed disability to the rest of society (New York Board of Regents, 1993). But overcoming handicaps becomes difficult when society focuses on disabilities solely as medical matters. The sociological dimension of the problem becomes obscured by stressing disability as a disease-like medical condition relegating the individual to the role of a patient needing treatment (Gleidman & Roth, 1980). Handicapping conditions are more social constructs than objective situations (Bogdan & Knoll, 1988).

Persons in the disabilities rights movement are extremely sensitive to the medical issue. Most, for example, avoid terms like "care" which suggest they are sick and should be passive recipients of medical services like personal attendants: "Personal assistance, in the eyes of persons in the disability rights movement, is an item of social liberation—just like a lightweight wheelchair or a bus lift—not a form of medical care" (J. Shapiro, 1993, p. 254). If a man is disabled, the person paid to help him get dressed is called a *personal care attendant*; if a man is wealthy, the person paid to help him get dressed is called a *valet*.

Placed in the role of "permanent patient," one loses power and dignity. When Evan Kemp, a disability rights leader with quadriplegia and a wheelchair user, was invited in 1991, as Chairperson of the Federal Equal Employment Opportunity Commission, to make a speech in Jacksonville, Florida, city officials sent an ambulance rather than a van to pick him up. Kemp refused the transportation on the basis of not being sick and flew home (J. Shapiro, 1993).

The Role of Labeling

The use of labeling exacerbates the issue of medicalization. As Bart (1984) explained,

Labeling is an integral part of medical and behavioral management, since, without the definitional act of diagnosis, further intervention or treatment would be impossible. Defining or treating a child as disabled or deviant directs attention away from the social and structural, since it takes the individual as its unit of concern (p. 111).

The label "disabled" affects a person's whole identity, not just those aspects that may be considered medical (Blatt, 1987). As Rioux (1996) found,

> Classification schemes have led to the person being confused with the characteristics being classified when programs are designed and delivered so services are for those with some level of intellectual disability or for "quads" rather than for those who want to learn to cook. And classification schemes are used as the eligibility criteria for inclusion or exclusion rather than interest, aptitude or need (p. 6).

Labels may even influence parental treatment of children with disabilities. For example, Waxman (1992) found that "the literature on the incidence of intentional harm inflicted on disabled children shows any factor which advances the parent's perception of the child as 'different' or 'difficult' greatly increases the likelihood of abuse" (p. 5).

When Wolfensberger, Nirje, Olshansky, Perske and Roos (1972) examined the characteristics that tend to appear in service programs structured on the medical model, they found that such programs view individuals as patients with their conditions given labels requiring diagnosis and prognosis. Medical personnel, notably physicians, often make decisions about non-medical matters like school inclusion and discipline. Programs are viewed as treatment with school becoming "educational therapy." Daily schedules may revolve around medical matters—for example, the dispensing of medication. Additionally, physical or medical techniques tend to be used in the management of behavior. For example, Wolfensberger et al. (1972/1975) noted that negative behavior displayed by youngsters classified "emotionally disturbed" may be treated with medication rather than counseling:

> Labeling is an integral part of medical and behavioral management, since, without the definitional act of diagnosis, further intervention or treatment would be impossible. Defining or treating a child as disabled or deviant directs attention away from the social and structural, since it takes the individual as its unit of concern (p. 111).

Furthermore, labeling has been traditionally used to place individuals within a "hierarchy of inability" and then impose upon them an artificial limit on their capacities with the implication that persons with disabilities are static without the ability to change. Labeling and the medical model tend to view persons with a disabilities as being different in "kind" rather than "degree." That is, they are viewed not as having simple differences of degree on the scales of human variation, but having differences that make them a different type of human that require dissimilar treatment. As Rioux (1996) recently stated,

> [W]e hear about how people with disabilities can be treated with electric shock therapy because they have different ways of feeling and reacting to pain. We are told that people with disabilities prefer to be among others like themselves. We are swayed by claims that prevention is the single most important issue in the face of disability, thus "ability-cleansing" is legitimized even while "ethnic-cleansing" is condemned and denounced. We are led to believe that segregation, normally considered an undesirable circumstance, is preferable for the development and personal growth of those with disabilities (pp. 4-5).

Wahl (1995) asserted that labels like "psychotic," "schizophrenic" and "psychopathic" are often misused by the media to describe actual medical conditions with the consequence that individuals with those conditions are presented as fundamentally different from others in their nature, physical appearance and basic humanity.

The Sick Role

According to Clinard and Meier (1979), "The ambivalence that many people display toward forms of disability relates to their conception of the 'sick role'" (p. 528). Parsons (1951) described the "sick role" or "patient role" in terms of sets of exemptions. To Parsons, sickness did not simply refer to a biological illness; it was a type of deviant behavior which "was socialized in a kind of role" (Buxton, 1985, p. 85). Parsons' classic formulation of the sick role has five primary characteristics:

1.   The patient is expected to define the sick role as "undesirable";

2.   Illness exempts the patient from normal role obligations and responsibilities, and he or she is usually relieved of regular familial, occupational, and other duties;

3.   The patient is not held at fault for his or her condition; and

4.   The condition of being sick is considered legitimate *if*

5.   The patient does everything in his or her power to facilitate recovery (which means cooperating fully with medical professionals, especially physicians).

Another characteristic is the presumption that the sick role will be temporary (Gleidman & Roth, 1980). As Shontz (1975) observed, "The sick role requires passivity, dependence on medical authority, and submission to treatment regimens" (p. 132).

Considering disabilities as medical in nature invokes the huge prestige of the medical profession, and although genuinely humane in intention, "fatally obscures from view the disastrous psychological and sociological consequences that follow from expecting a handicapped person to fulfill permanently the role obligations expected of a good patient" (Gleidmen & Roth, 1980, p. 37). For example, the sick role Parsons described is considered to be reversible. One who is ill stays home from work so that he or she can later return cured. But for the most part, blindness, deafness, physical impairment, amputations or mental retardation are permanent conditions. The patient never gets better and as a result receives a permanent assignment to the subservient paternalistic role—for example, "Jerry's kids."

Liachowitz (1988) noted, regarding Parsons' model, that

> [S]ociety places persons whom it calls sick in an identifiable social role. According to his thesis, occupants of the sick role are expected to pay for public largesse either by recovering (and then beginning or resuming a contributing role) or by dying—an alternative engendering in society the gratification of having given without material return. Thus the many handicapped people whose physical disorder is permanent remain in position of indebtedness—a position that probably accounts for at least some portion of their socially deferred devaluation (pp. 10-11).

Gleidman (1979) stated that the sick role allows the individual no ability to live an adult life and that

> [T]he role of a patient in middle-class society is functionally very similar to that of a child. We expect the patient to be cheerful and

accepting, to obey doctors' orders, and, in general, devote all his energies to getting well. When an able bodied person falls sick, he ceases
to be judged as an adult; in return, he is expected to work actively to
get well. The area defined to his control shifts to the sickbed. But in
America a person labeled handicapped is assigned a specially destructive variant of the sick role. Not merely powerless because he is sick,
he is defined as doubly powerless because he cannot master the job of
"getting well." Unable to fill that role obligation, he is seen as socially powerless, deprived of a political identity—until he chooses to
assert one (p. 60).

Because the sick role is seen as a temporary shelter from normal obligations, the permanently disabled individual is invariably excluded
from normal opportunities and is not taken seriously when trying to
assert his or her social abilities. When a person with a disability refus-
es to behave like a good patient, the behaviors are often viewed as
"symptoms of maladjustment." In fact, refusal to cooperate actively
with the source of help to achieve recovery leads to the individual's loss
of personal rights and dignity. Society generally sees nothing wrong
with placing disabled individuals under the perpetual tutelage of those
experts who provide the help. In fact, society expects them constantly
to, "Subordinate their own interests and desires—which include leading
a normal social life—to the therapeutic goals and programs decreed by
the professional providing the help (Gleidman & Roth, 1980, pp. 42-
43). As Hirsch and Hirsch (1995) stated,

> The medical model of diagnosis, treatment, and cure that character-
> izes modern medicine, gives great authority to the medical and "help-
> ing" professionals while relegating the recipients of medical care to
> the "sick role" and similar states of disfranchisement (p. 22).

Mackelprang and Salsgiver (1996) similarly found,

> The medical model views physicians as treatment directors and nurs-
> es, therapists, social workers and other health care professionals as
> assistants who help direct patients' lives. Patients are passive recipi-
> ents of treatments that are dispensed by professionals who are experts.
> The experts make the decisions and inform patients of those deci-
> sions. If people with disabilities who use professional services
> attempt to become active consumers and control their care, they

become vulnerable to the withdrawal of help from providers who do not like having their authority questioned (p. 9).

An excellent example was provided by Starkloff (1992), a disability rights activist with quadriplegia, who related the following incident encountered upon his entering a nursing home for care:

> We had this terrible meal once, meat loaf and mashed potatoes floating in this watery stewed tomato sauce, so I complained to Brother Damian. He looked at me and said, "Max, after all we've done for you, you think you have a right to complain?" (cited in Nagler, 1993, p. 63).

Blumberg (1991) decried how persons with disabilities, especially children, lose their dignity by repaying their "debt" to the medical community by being used as teaching tools and submitting to "public stripping."

The Medical Model and Special Education
According to Shea and Bauer (1997),

> [T]he medical or deficit model has driven the eduction of learners with disabilities. This model contends that the disability should be diagnosed, prescriptive programs should be designed, and efforts should be made to remediate the disability (p. 423).

Historically, the first special educators were physicians like Jean-Marc-Gaspard Itard, Edouard Sequin and Maria Montessori who, according to Shea and Bauer (1997), unwittingly established a legacy of medical influence on special education practices that plagued, and continue to plague the profession of special education:

> Their emphasis on etiology (finding the cause or causes of a condition), symptomatology (identifying the cluster of symptoms or the symptom by which a condition is recognized), exclusionary diagnosis (differential diagnosis or a diagnosis that differentiates a condition from other conditions), and hospitalization for persons with mental retardation left special education, much like medicine, with an intervention system that was usually implemented only after symptoms became sufficiently severe to necessitate referral and extensive evaluation (p. 26).

Thus, the medical model continues to prevail in special education. "Even though special education doesn't rely solely on medical diagnosis, the field by definition forefronts the physical, cognitive and sensory impairments of individuals. The diagnoses and label become the major defining variable of learners, and the pedagogical practice is largely determined by these designations" (Linton, Mello and O'Neill, 1995, p. 7). Thus, classified handicapped students are often viewed as patients in need of remediation and cure, rather than as students who learn differently. For educational programming purposes, youngsters are given medical labels like "neurologically impaired" and "chronically ill." Individual education plans are referred to as "educational prescriptions." According to Biklen (1989), the deficiency is seen to be within the youngster, who is viewed as a "five cylinder car with one cylinder not functioning" rather than as a youngster "designed as a four cylinder car" needing remedial and special education "repairs":

> Students perceived as having problems, like something broken, are sent to resource rooms, special classes, even special schools or institutions, to be repaired and later returned. Unlike a real repair shop, however, in special education many students, indeed the preponderance of them (excluding those with speech impairments that are either cured or simply disappear by the time students reach secondary level) never escape the special label. They stay in the repair shop (p. 8).

Unfortunately, viewing the problem as medical often suggests that all other activities, including future planning, be suspended until the child is cured or remediated:

> And far from suspending normal activities to concentrate on a "cure," the child needs most of all to get on with the business of learning how to lead a full life (Keniston, 1979, p. xiv).

Schools may believe they are relieved of their obligations to teach students perceived as ill. The attitude may be, "He's mentally retarded or neurologically impaired; that's why he didn't learn." Barnes (1975) stressed that educators using the medical model often say the child "is" handicapped and has something "wrong" with him or her irrespective of the environment in which the child is reacting. Keniston (1979) found that

> Defining the situation as essentially medical relegates it to the realm of physiological defects and assigns central responsibility to a spe-

cialized group of professionals. What is omitted is everything that is most vital to the lives of the handicapped: the socially learned preconceptions and reactions of the able-bodied; the absence of societal place and provision for people like them; the socially communicated sense of stigma and doom; the socially generated expectation that handicapped children have no real future as adults. And, conveniently for the able-bodied, the medical paradigm absolves them of all responsibility (p. xiv).

As Biklen, Ford and Ferguson (1989) concluded,

> Assessment and classification, diagnosis and treatment, disorders and syndromes, therapy and intervention are all terms that bespeak the medicalization of special education. They represent the language of student-as-patient. . . . These words and the approach they represent imply that the purpose of special education is to fix students' problems. They suggest that difficulties in schooling belong to the student instead of being a product of school and student interaction (p. 262).

Sapon-Shevin (1989) stated the importance of shifting to a new paradigm this way:

> A new vision of schools must emerge from an understanding of school functions and practices that incorporate historical, political, economic, and professional frames of reference about both education and disability. The underlying notions that have guided special education must now be replaced by a totally new way of viewing children and their differences (p. 93).

The Minority Group-Independence-Disablism (Handicapism) Paradigm

A realization of the dependence forced on them by the medical model, coupled with the Civil Rights movement of the 1960's, has only recently led persons with disabilities to demand control of their lives and full access to mainstream society (Mackelprang & Salsgiver, 1996). This demand evolved into a paradigm of disability with various names including, the "minority group" paradigm, the "civil rights" paradigm, the "disablism" paradigm or the "independence" paradigm. For the purposes of this book they will be used interchangeably.

Examining the topic of disability through the minority group paradigm provides a lens through which we can gain a broader understanding of society and the significance of human variation. Such a lens helps to clarify a broad range of issues involving autonomy, competence, wholeness, independence, dependence, health, physical appearance, aesthetics, community and the notion of perfection (Linton, Mello and O'Neill, 1995). As Hirsch and Hirsch (1995) aptly stated, "The minority group model tends to locate the limitations associated with a disability in the built environment—such as physical barriers—and/or the social environment—such as limiting stereotypes and expectations" (pp. 23-24). Rioux (1996) stressed that the civil rights paradigm views

> [E]ligibility for an entitlement to a program or service is not treated as a social privilege to be distributed on a discretionary basis to a select target population that can establish personal "merit." Rather it becomes a matter of an individual social right guaranteed on the basis of clearly defined conditions or as an ethical imperative binding the state or community or non-governmental organizations to the individuals with needs (p. 6).

To comprehend the minority group paradigm of disability, one needs to understand the concept of disablism, and its consequences. The original term, "handicapism," was likened to racism and sexism when first coined by Bogdan and Biklen (1977) who defined it as "a set of assumptions and practices that promote the differential and unequal treatment of people because of apparent or assumed physical, mental, or behavioral differences" (p. 14). They also referred to it as "the stereotyping, prejudice and discrimination practiced by society against disabled people" (1977, p. 4). Because of the current discomfort with the term "handicap," the concept is gradually becoming revised as "disablism." Stevens (1995), in the United Kingdom, defined "disablism" as "the identification and treatment of people on the grounds of disability. Disablism operates in a similar way to sexism and racism, and can of course be considered as a problem of non-disabled people, in the way they relate to disabled people" (p. 281). In order to understand disablism fully, one should examine its three components: prejudice, stereotype and discrimination.

Prejudice

Prejudice comes from the word "prejudge" (Gersten & Bliss, 1974). Allport (1958) defined it as an "avertive or hostile attitude toward a person who belongs to a group, simply because he belongs to that group, and is therefore presumed to have the objectional qualities ascribed to that group" (p. 8). Bogdan and Knoll (1988) similarly defined it as a "grossly simplified belief about the characteristics of some group of people, which is uncritically generalized to all members of that group" (p. 466). Meyers (1987) defined the term simply as an "unjustifiable negative attitude toward a group and its individual members" (p. 483). According to Henderson and Bryan (1997) five most common forms of prejudice and beliefs toward people with disabilities include that they (1) are inferior, (2) are totally impaired, (3) are less intelligent, (4) need charity and (5) prefer the company of others with disabilities (pp. 70-75).

Allport (1958) argued that humans have a propensity to be prejudiced, a pernicious aspect of a normal and natural tendency to form generalizations, concepts and categories whose content represents an oversimplification of our world of experience (p. 26). He further believed that an adequate definition of prejudice contains two essential ingredients: an "attitude" related to an overgeneralized (and erroneous) "belief." Although prejudicial statements may sometimes express the attitudinal factor, and may sometimes express the belief factor, they most often go together.

Attitudinal prejudice is expressed in common statements like these:

- Seeing a person in a wheelchair upsets me.

- I wouldn't want a person with mental retardation living in my neighborhood.

- Watching a severely disabled person eat upsets me.

- Dwarfs makes me laugh.

- I pity deaf people.

- Thank God I'm not mentally retarded or physically disabled.

- I'd rather die than become blind or deaf.

- I can't help but adore children with Down syndrome.

- People with disabilities make me ill at ease.

- I fear people with mental illness.

- Stuttering is funny.

Some of the most common prejudicial belief statements sound like this:

- Persons with physical disabilities feel resentment and envy toward the able bodied.

- People in wheelchairs are sick and chronically ill.

- People with disabilities are naturally inferior.

- People with disabilities are different in kind, not degree.

- People with disabilities are more comfortable with "their own kind."

- People with disabilities have a distinct type of personality.

- People with blindness are sad and acquire a sixth sense.

- People with deafness are perpetually suspicious of others.

- People with mental retardation are unpredictable and can not control their sexual urges.

- People with mental illness are dangerous.

- People with disabilities are abnormal.

- People with disabilities are brave and courageous.

- All persons with deafness can read lips.

- People with disabilities lead lives that are different from others.

- People who stutter think like they talk.

- People with disabilities can never really accept their conditions.

Bogdan and Knoll (1988) hypothesized that such beliefs are "the essence of handicapism, because they provide the rationale for our actions toward disabled people" (p. 467).

Prejudice distorts social relationships by overemphasizing a particular characteristic like a disability. These differences should not be denied but considered in perspective. Allport (1954) called this overemphasized trait a "master status," which, in turn, galvanizes all manner of one's thoughts and feelings about persons in this group (p. 136).

Physical and mental differences exist among all people and awareness of individual differences and sensitivity to the actual needs and specific limitations of persons with disabilities are important parts of relating to them appropriately and positively. But as the United States Commission on Civil Rights (1983) pointed out, "[I]mputing more difference to a handicapped person than exists is a form of prejudice" (p. 22).

Prejudice toward persons with disabilities resembles other forms of prejudice and shares such common roots as the urge to classify and the tendency to form in-groups and out-groups (United States Commission On Civil Rights, 1983). "Over-categorization" according to Allport (1958), "is perhaps the commonest trick of the human mind; given a thimbleful of facts, we rush to make generalizations as large as a tub" (p. 9).

Studies like those conducted by English (1977) revealed that various forms of prejudice are connected and that persons who tend to be racist and sexist also tend to be handicapist. Bowe (1978) found that

> Attitudes toward disability exist not in a vacuum but in an entire constellation of other attitudes [and] attitudes toward one object tend to be related to and influenced by attitudes toward other objects that are seen as being similar in some way. The key factor seems to be one of differentness (pp. 120-121).

Gliedman and Roth (1980) found an important aspect of prejudice present in all "isms" is a discrepancy of power where persons are assigned roles based on superiority and inferiority.

Stereotype

"When prejudice takes on the form of a specific belief regarding a particular group, it is a stereotype" (Bogdan & Knoll, p. 467). Stereotypes are generalizations about a group of people that distinguish its members from others. According to Enteman (1996) the term comes from the trade of journalism:

> [T]he original stereotype was called a flong, which was a printing plate that facilitated reproduction of the same material. The typesetter could avoid recasting type by using the stereotype. Thus, a stereotype imposes a rigid mold on the subject and encourages repeated mechanical usage. . . . The purposes of the stereotype are the same as in the print history. They are grounded in laziness (p. 9).

According to Meyers (1987), "To stereotype is to generalize" (p 483). Believing, for example, that almost all persons with blindness have outstanding musical talent by selectively remembering the music of Ray Charles, Stevie Wonder, Diane Schuur, Jose Feliciano, Al Hibbler, George Shearing, and Ronnie Milsap is to form a stereotype.

To Allport (1958), a stereotype is an exaggerated belief associated with a category: "Its function is to justify (rationalize) our conduct in relation to that category" (p. 187). A stereotype, Allport explained, is not identical with a category but is, rather, a fixed idea that accompanies the category. For example, the category of "persons with blindness" can be held in mind simply as a neutral, factual, non-evaluative concept pertaining merely to the impairment of not being able to see. It becomes a stereotype when, and if, the initial category is weighted with pictures and judgments of persons with blindness as automatically having melancholia, clumsiness, a sixth sense or innate musical ability.

Jernigan (1983), an activist with blindness, stated that one of the most important problems people who acquire blindness must face is becoming aware of and learning to cope with such public attitudes and misconceptions about blindness "that go to the very root of our culture and permeate every aspect of social behavior and thinking":

> These misconceptions go back to the days when a blind person could not dodge a spear. In today's society, dodging a spear is not an essential ability but the stereotype of helplessness has remained intact, surrounded by a host of other stereotypes: The blind are simple, spiritual, musical; they have a special sixth sense; their other senses are more acute—in short, they are different and apart from the rest of society (pp. 58-59).

Sutherland (1981) asserted that stereotypes cause persons with visible disabilities to become very aware that they are seen as different from others in ways that go far beyond the facts of their disabilities:

> We are subjected to a whole range of false assumptions and hostile and depersonalising reactions based upon these assumptions. We are held to be visually repulsive; helpless; pathetic; dependent; too independent; plucky, brave and courageous; bitter, with chips on our shoulders; evil (the 'twisted mind in a twisted body'); mentally retarded; endowed with mystical powers; and much else. The fact that many of these characteristics are quite incompatible is an indication of how unreasoning such stereotypes are (p. 58).

Sutherland (1984) also asserted that stereotypes become "self-fulfilling prophecies," forcing the individual with the disability into a roll that can then be used to justify the original treatment. As he astutely noted, "Someone who is assumed to be stupid is unlikely to receive much intellectual stimulation" (p. 59).

Stereotypes also have a large influence on how groups think of themselves. As Medgyesi (1996) explained,

> Stereotypes are hard to shake. Even when those words and images evolve into a soft, more politically correct focus, they still pack a wallop in terms of how the world views a particular group. More insidiously, those stereotypes shape the way a particular group views itself within the context of the world-at-large (p. 44).

In analyzing children's attitudes toward their peers with mental retardation, Siperstein and Bok (1986) called stereotypes "perceiver characteristics." They explained that

> [S]tereotyping is fundamental to the way children process information regarding their mentally retarded peers. Children's stereotypes are beliefs about the characteristics of groups of targets, such as the mentally retarded. Although these stereotypes often may include a kernel of truth, there is usually much misinformation in them. Stereotypes obstruct the judgmental process that a child engages in because the stereotype provides a sense of absolutism. Within a stereotype there is a tendency to overstress the similarity among the members of the group—in this case the mentally retarded (p. 61).

Many variations of disability stereotypes exist; some overlap and some are even diametrically opposite—for example, the idea that persons with physical disabilities are "super good" like Tiny Tim or "super bad" like Captain Hook. Educators need to examine these images, their sources, and the attitudes they nourish. As the New York Board of Regents (1993) found,

> In the historical tapestry, people with disabilities have been woven in as a moral thread, a lesson to society of the living existence of corruptible or evil influences, or, as a panacea to society, of the redemptive qualities of charity. This moral construct has given rise to a number of inaccurate portrayals that serve as convenient fictional and nonfictional vehicles for the media (p. 160).

Wolfensberger, Nirje, Olshansky, Perske and Roos (1975) described the varieties of typical attitudes toward retarded persons. Such attitudes exist toward people with other disabilities as well. They enumerated typical ways in which persons with disabilities are viewed and their implications for institutional (for example, school) attitudes as well as personal attitudes. The next few pages discuss Wolfensberger's enumeration.

1. THE OBJECT OF PITY—THE DISEASED OR SICK PATIENT: This stereotype is often directly related to the medical model of viewing persons with disabilities as ill and needing to be fixed, healed or remediated. The implication for this model is that the problem is personally internal not environmentally interactional. Relying on this stereotype, a teacher with a classified child in class may never consider what effect the structure of the classroom has on the behavior of that youngster (p. 70).

Wolfensberger (et al.) listed five views persons have of individuals with mental retardation as objects of pity:

First, the person with mental retardation is seen as "suffering" from his or her condition, and shifting the emphasis to the alleviating of this suffering.

Second, although the person with mental retardation may be seen as "suffering" he or she may also be believed to be unaware of his or her deviancy.

Third, the person with mental retardation is seen as "an eternal child" who "never grows."

Fourth, being held blameless for his or her condition, the person is seen as not accountable for his or her behavior.

Fifth, the retarded individual is viewed with a "there but for the grace of God go I" attitude.

The stereotype of disabled persons as pitiable and pathetic leads to the perception of them as victims of misfortune and in need special attention and services. Others may see them as suffering from their conditions even though   such subjective perceptions   may   inaccurate. J. Shapiro (1993) related this story of disability activist Marylou Breslin:

> Awaiting her flight at the airport, the executive director of the Berkeley-based Disability Rights Education and Defense Fund (DREDF) was sitting in her battery-powered wheelchair, in her dressed-for-success businesswoman's outfit, sipping from a cup of coffee. A woman walked by, also wearing a business suit, and plunked a quarter into the plastic cup Breslin held in her hand. The coin sent the coffee flying, staining Breslin's blouse, and the well-meaning woman, embarrassed hurried on (p. 19).

Such stories circulate widely among wheelchair users.

This pitiable characterization is exemplified in literature by characters like the rich little "cripple," Clara, in Johanna Spyri's *Heidi* or Tiny Tim in *A Christmas Carol*. The stereotype is often used by authors as a devise for revealing another character's goodness and sensitivity. Biklen and Bogdan (1977) found that

> In such instances, the disabled persons seem to have been included primarily so that a main character can be seen showing love, kindness, and pity toward them. Pitiable and pathetic characters are often portrayed as having hearts of gold, which serves to elicit even greater feelings of pity (rather than genuine compassion) from audiences or readers (p. 6).

As Fiedler (1996) stated,

> If there is an archetypal image of the handicapped stronger, more obsessive even than that of the sinister *senex* with a hump or a hook, it is that of the pitiful *puer* embodied in the crippled boy forever perched on Bob Cratchit's shoulder. . . . It was his image that presid-

ed over the founding of charitable institutions. . . . to care for "crippled children" (45).

He stated further that the image of Tiny Tim is "as vulgarly cheerful-tearful and as commercially viable as the Easter seal cripple-of-the-year which descends directly from it" (p. 45).

2. THE SUB-HUMAN ORGANISM: Another common stereotype views persons with disabilities as subhuman. Although most of us consider this stereotype as thing of the past, examples continue to appear, as in a young boy's school record which stated "dangerous when cornered" (Barnes, 1975, p. 70), or the *New Jersey Administrative Code for Special Education* in the 1970's which listed as a symptom of perceptual impairment the "caged animal syndrome."

Persons referred to like this are obviously perceived as not fully human. As Wolfensberger (1972) stated, "[T]he retarded are particularly apt to be unconsciously perceived or even consciously labeled as subhuman, as animal-like, even as 'vegetables' or 'vegetative.'" He recalled the public statement of a state institution's superintendent who referred to some of the residents as "so called human beings below what we might call an animal level of functioning" (pp. 16-17).

This imagery is also subtly included in literature by writers like Steinbeck (1937) who, in his classic, *Of Mice and Men,* describes Lennie, a character with obvious mental retardation, as walking "heavily, dragging his feet a little, the way a bear drags his paws" (p. 10). Steinbeck then describes Lennie drinking from a stream "with long gulps, snorting into the water like a horse" (p. 10). The book ends with Lennie being "disposed of" by a shot to the back of his head similar to the way an old sick dog had been "disposed of" earlier in the story.

Wahl (1995), describing how the media and literature portray persons with mental illnesses as being "virtually inhuman," provided these examples: "The mentally ill killer in Rex Miller's *Slice* is many times referred to as less than human, as more like an animal than a human being" [and] as "having a laugh like a barking dog." He is also called "the thing," "the monster" and "a rare subspecies of humanity." Similarly, in *By Reason of Insanity,* Shane Stevens describes the villain with mental illness "a shrewd cunning animal" and "an authentic monster." In the childrens' book *How to Eat Fried Worms,* one of the youngsters states, "Don't let him see you're afraid. Crazy people are like dogs. If they see you're afraid, they attack" (pp. 45-46). According to Fiedler (1996),

[Not] until the late eighteenth century, with the rise of sentimentalism and the obsession with the excluded and marginal, which climaxed with the reign of Victoria, did the blind, the deaf, and the halt become major characters in books written by authors and intended for readers who, thinking of themselves as non-handicapped, were able to regard the handicapped as essentially alien, absolute others. In search of context, fellow human beings with drastically impaired perception, manipulation, and ambulation tend, of course, to be stereotyped, either negatively or positively but in any case rendered as something more or less than human (p. 34).

"Viewing youngsters with disabilities as subhuman," according to Barnes (1975), "turns schools into zoos and educators into caretakers implying that such youngsters need to be contained and controlled, not taught" (pp. 70-71). When schools perceive children as less than human or "second class citizens" they generally feel no obligation to teach them.

3. SINISTER OR EVIL—THE MENACE OR THE MONSTER: According to Wolfensberger (1975),

Unknown events or objects, if alien enough, tend to arouse negative feelings in both man and beast. Man's history consists mostly of his persecution of fellow men who were different in features, skin pigmentation, size, shape, language, customs, dress, etc., and it is apparent that man has been apt to see evil in deviancy. It is not surprising that one role perception prominent in the history of the field is that of the retarded individual as a menace (p. 13).

Longmore (1987) found that the most common association of disability is with malevolence. "Deformity of the body symbolizes deformity of the soul. Physical handicaps are made the emblems of evil" (p. 66). Fiedler (1996) similarly stated, "[I]n the throes of our paranoia and projection, we convince ourselves that the crippledness of the cripple is an outward and visible sign of an inward state" (p. 41). Bogdan, Biklen, Shapiro and Spelkoman (1982) maintained that this role commonly appears in the media (p. 32). McGinn (1997) explained the relationship of monstrosity and ugliness:

The monster has always been with us. Misshapen, deformed, hideous, terrifying—the monster prowls and lurks, bent on doing us unprecedented damage. He is strong, agile, determined. His nature is to be preternatural, yet he is generally mortal, not quite purely demonic. He uses no weapons, save those native to him. . . . The monster is a rich source of human anxiety. [Monsters] act as visible embodiments of evil, by way of the idea that evil is a form of ugliness. If the evil spirit were to become visible, this is how it would look—as "ugly as sin." Monsters exist, in effect, because of the psychic entrenchment of the aesthetic theory of virtue (p. 144).

Bogdan (1988) illustrated how such stereotypes are internalized. He described watching *Treasure Island* on television one evening with his ten year old son and his friend:

Near the beginning of the film my son's friend, Jeremy, who was confused about the plot asked: "Who's the bad guy?" My son replied: "If they look bad, they are bad" (p. vii).

Bogdan, struck by his son's insight, continued:

In the film, part of being bad is looking bad, and villains were marked by various disfigurements and disabilities, such as missing limbs and eyes. Horror film monsters are scarred, deformed, disproportionately built, hunched over, exceptionally large, exceptionally small, deaf, speech impaired, visually impaired, mentally ill, or mentally subnormal. In fact, the word monster is standard medical terminology for infants born with blatant defects (p. vii).

Kiger (1989) found the messages regarding disability in film are often derogatory, victimize or degrade persons with impairments, and add up over time to "establish distinct patterns of imagery" (p. 155).

Much of the media, of course, are simply reflecting images, attitudes, and stereotypes found in our culture. In fairy tales, the evil ones are most often giants, as in *Jack in the Beanstalk*, dwarfs like *Rumpelstiltskin*, or Quilp, "the monstrous dwarf who stalks 'Little Nell' through the pages of Charles Dickens's *The Old Curiosity Shop*" (Fiedler, 1996, p. 41). Often, they are also toothless witches with humps on their backs and eye patches. Remember the crooked man who lived in a crooked house? The relationship between outer physique and evilness is exemplified by the characterization of *Captain Hook,* named for his prothesis.

Unfortunately, the fact that such stereotypical portrayals appear in classical literature, gives them respectability and even prestige, making it difficult for those with real disabilities to overcome deeply entrenched, complex prejudices (Margolis & Shapiro, 1987). One of the most popular classical literary devices for conveying evil or disparagement is "the twisted mind in the twisted body" (Margolis & Shapiro, 1987). According to Baskin and Harris (1977), it is common for authors to use the device of the "deformed" outer body to reflect the "deformed" inner qualities of their characters. Similarly, Davis (1997) found, "If disability appears in a novel, it is rarely centrally represented. . . . [S]ufficient research has shown, more often than not villains tend to be physically abnormal, scarred, deformed or mutilated" (p. 19). As Thurer (1980) asserted, "The disabled have had a bad literary press. Physical deformity, and any outer defect has come to symbolize an inner defect" (p. 12).

Richard III provides an excellent example of this stereotype. According to Fiedler (1996), Richard provided "the prototype for the innumerable maimed villains who follow" (p. 41). Shakespeare exploited his audiences' negative perceptions of physical disability by distorting the appearance of the king, who in life was not disabled (Rogers, 1978) to accentuate the evil side of his personality. "Richard's deformity is inextricably tied to his malevolent lust" (Thurer, 1980, p. 13). Shakespeare describes Richard as a "subtle, false, murderer—even of children—to achieve his ends. His villainy and deformity are woven together at the very beginning of the play:

> I, that am curtail'd of this fair proportion,
> Cheated of feature by dissembling nature,
> Deform'd, unfinisht, sent before my time
> Into this breathing world, scarce half made up,
> And that so lamely and unfashionable
> That dogs bark at me as I halt by them
> Why, I, in this weak piping time of peace,
> Have no delight to pass away the time
> Unless to spy my shadow in the sun,
> And descant on mine own deformity:
> And therefore, since I cannot prove a lover,
> To entertain these fair well-spoken days,
> I am determined to prove a villain,
> And hate the idle pleasures of these days (Act I, Scene i).

Biklen and Bogdan (1977) describe the disability images found in Stevenson's classic, *Treasure Island.*

> In evoking the terror and suspense that mark this book's opening pages, the key elements are the disabled characters Black Dog and Blind Pew. The former is introduced as a "tallow-faced man, wanting two fingers." This minor disability sets a tone that is built up when the second man is described as that "hunched and eyeless creature," and it is the latter who hands Billy Bones the dread black spot. In addition, when Long John Silver is introduced as a good guy, there is only a casual mention of the fact that he has a wooden leg. Later, when his treachery is revealed, the references to his "timber" leg become ominous and foreboding (p. 7).

In a similar manner, Longmore (1987) recalled the TV adventure series *Wild Wild West* in which Michael Dunn, played the villain, Miguelito P. Loveless, a "hunchbacked dwarf" who consistently wants revenge on the able bodied world. Like Shakespeare's Richard, he displayed rage over his "affliction" by seeking retaliation against those perceived normal. In one episode he says to the story's hero, "I grow weary of you, Mr. West. Weary of the sight of your strong, straight body."

Melville, too, used disability to symbolize a warped personality. In *Moby Dick*, Ahab loses his mind over the white whale's destruction of his leg and sacrifices himself and his crew in a mad, obsessive pursuit of revenge. As Kriegel (1982) observed,

> Melville's Captain Ahab is not merely crippled—his leg torn from his body by the white whale—he is "crippled" in the deepest metaphysical sense. His injury became his self-hood (p. 18).

The reader's fear of Ahab is further heightened by the description of Ahab's scar, which begins under the hair of his head and extends to the length of his body (Margolis & Shapiro, 1987), and when Ishmael describes hearing Ahab's wooden leg tapping back and forth across the deck in the middle of the night (Biklen & Bogdan, 1977).

Wolfensberger et al. (1975) maintained that the person with a disability may be perceived as being an "individual menace," because of alleged propensities toward various crimes against persons or property, or as a "social menace" because of alleged contribution to social disorganization and genetic decline (pp. 19-20).

Unfortunately, this image reinforces three common prejudices against people with disabilities: disability is a punishment for evil, people with disabilities are embittered by their misfortunes, and disabled people resent people who are not disabled and would, if they could, destroy them (Longmore, 1987; the New York Board of Regents, 1993). The image of disabled persons as menaces to society includes the belief that they threaten our genetic pool. This familiar stereotype relies on a simplistic understanding of eugenics and social Darwinism and it leads to segregation, institutionalization and sterilization. Most repugnant here is the concept of the "social menace" as used by the Nazis toward all forms of differentness in their quest for "racial purification."

To focus more on American literature, John Steinbeck's Lennie in *Of Mice and Men* exemplifies the social menace contributing to genetic decline and social disorganization. Lennie kills small animals like pigeons and puppies and then finally a young woman, because he literally does not know his own strength (Bogdan & Biklen, 1977, and Margolis and Shapiro, 1987). Kanner (1964) captured the essence of this image. He noted that

> [In the early 1900's] mental defectives were viewed as a menace to civilization, incorrigible at home, burdens to the school, sexually promiscuous, breeders of feebleminded offspring, victims and spreaders of poverty, degeneracy, crime and disease (p. 88).

The President's Committee on Mental Retardation (1977) provided three interesting "articles of belief" from 1912 during the eugenics scare which guided practice in the treatment of "feebleminded" individuals during the early part of this century based on this stereotype:

> First, there is always danger of uncontrollable and impulsive brutality and dangerous aggressiveness, even in the most mild appearing mental defectives, especially as they reach adult age. They are of essentially violent nature.
>
> Second, the feebleminded are prone to crime and delinquency, contributing to a large proportion of the criminal population. Since they do not distinguish right from wrong, their behavior tends to be dominated by primitive anti-social drives.
>
> Third, feebleminded persons, especially females, have abnormally strong sex drives which they are unable to control. They tend, therefore, to be degenerate and prolific (pp. 138-139).

If these were the views and beliefs of professionals who worked with the "feebleminded" population, what positive attitudes could the public have had?

Unfortunately, schools still often view classified handicapped youngsters as "menaces," particularly those classified as emotionally disturbed or socially maladjusted. Many teachers and administrators fear acting-out older students. As with traditional menaces, such youngsters are believed to be out of control. The typical reaction of teachers and administrators is to control student behavior by psychotropic drugs or segregation into separate classes, separate schools, intermediate units, institutions or home instruction programs.

4. THE UNSPEAKABLE OBJECT OF DREAD: Closely related to the stereo-type of evilness is the "monster" or the "object of dread." Wolfensberger et al. (1975) described the perception of this individual as a "dreadful entity or event" (p. 20). This stereotype is often used in terms of retribution for sins, like the disabled child sent to its parents by God as punishment for their sins. Longmore (1987) described this character as monster or predator or "one reviled by society as repulsive to behold and dangerous to its well-being." The character also has a "violent loss of self-control, living in a moral vacuum where life holds little value" (p. 68). As Cohen (1996) observed,

> The monster is born only at this metaphoric crossroads, as an embod-iment of a certain cultural moment—of a time, a feeling, a place. The monster's body quite literally incorporates fear, desire, anxiety and fantasy (ataractic or incendiary), giving them life and an uncanny independence. The monstrous body is pure culture (p. 4).

This stereotype appears in classic horror stories like *The Phantom of the Opera, Dr. Jekyll and Mr. Hyde*, and *The Hunchback of Notre Dame*. Hugo's description of Quasimodo's physique leaves little to the reader's imagination:

> [A]nd God knows what intensity of ugliness his features could attain [and] we shall not attempt of give the reader any idea of that tetra-hedron nose, of that horseshoe mouth, of that little left eye stubbled up with an eyebrow of carroty bristles, while the right was complete-ly overwhelmed and buried by an enormous wart; of those irregular teeth, jagged here and there like the battlements of a fortress; of that horny lip, over which one of those teeth protruded, like the tusk of an

elephant; of that forked chin; and above all of the expression, of min-
gled malice, amazement and sadness (p. 15).

Hugo continued,

> [H]is body might have been described as a twisted grimace: his huge
> head bristled with stiff red hair; between his shoulders was an enor-
> mous hump which had a corresponding projection in front; his legs
> were so strangely made that they could touch only at the knees, like
> two sickles with their handles joined; his feet were immense and his
> hands were monstrous (p. 15).

Educators and students alike should realize that the image of persons with disabilities as evil, dangerous, monstrous and menacing has
had serious effects on our attitudes. By linking unattractiveness (which
is, after all, a value judgment) and physical and mental differences with
murder, terror, violence and evil, we create and perpetuate society's
prejudices—prejudices that produce fear and avoidance of persons with
disabilities, and ultimately their systematic, intentional exclusion from
society (Bogdan, Biklen, Shapiro & Spelkoman, 1982).

5. THE HOLY INNOCENT: In many and various cultures, individuals with
disabilities—particularly those with mental retardation—have been
viewed as the "special children of God."

> As such they are usually seen as incapable of committing evil volun-
> tarily, and consequently may be considered living saints. It may also
> be believed that they have been sent by God for some special purpose.
> The role of the retarded as holy or eternal innocents has been recog-
> nized in a number of cultures and eras. This role perception was
> reportedly prevalent among American Indians and in medieval
> Europe (Wolfensberger et al. 1975, pp. 14-15).

Disabled individuals seen as a holy innocents were generally considered
to be "harmless children" no matter their chronological ages. As a
result, special educators frequently acquire the "Albert Schweitzer" or
"Mother Theresa" syndrome, and the public often remarking they must
have "outstanding patience" and are "doing God's work." Barnes
(1975) believed that one implication of viewing special students as eternal children is that educators tend to overprotect them. Eternal children
are kept from growing or experiencing the "dignity of risk." Because a

"normal" life involves taking risks, overprotection prevents normalization. But risk-taking is necessary for normal growth and development. If students with disabilities are to succeed in the larger community, they need to learn how to function with people who are not handicapped. Youngsters assigned to classes for those classified as trainable mentally retarded may be safe and protected but they hopefully will be accepted as adults once they enter the outside world and therefore, should be prepared for that eventuality.

A major effect of the Holy Innocent stereotype is the juvenilization of adults with disabilities. For example, an adult named William with mental retardation is more apt to be called Billy or Willy than Bill. Such juvenilization is a nuisance often encountered by Little People. Van Etten (1988), a lawyer with dwarfism, related the following incident that took place aboard an airplane:

> The airline hostess began to plump my pillows to make me more comfortable. I was impressed with the personal service until I noticed this special treatment was not being given to other passengers. The offer of a glass of milk betrayed the attitude of the hostess—I was to be treated like a child. Her attitude toward me was paternal even though she knew I was traveling on an adult ticket (p. 127).

Beisser (1989), a physician who became quadriplegic from polio similarly related that

> Nurses and attendants often talked to me as if I were a baby. If I became soiled through no fault of my own, they were likely to say, "Naughty, naughty," or "You've been a bad boy" (p. 22).

An apt example of such juvenilization occurred on the television show, *Fantasy Island* where Herve Villechaize, an actor with dwarfism, played the part of Tattoo, Mr. Roarke's mystical right hand man. In her book on disability portrayals in television and film, Koblas (1988) described the role:

> Tattoo was often sympathetic to the guests but often caused trouble, as well as getting into pickles. He was never presented in a very serious light, providing instead, comic relief—although often at the expense of his own integrity. Tattoo had the judgment of a child and required chastising from Mr. Roarke quite often. However, in one

episode, he *did* reveal that people often treated him like a little boy instead of a man (p. 456).

6. THE OBJECT OF COMEDY, RIDICULE AND CURIOSITY: Throughout history people with disabilities have been viewed as funny, incompetent and odd, from the use of persons with cerebral palsy and dwarfism as court jesters to the exhibition of freaks to the spastic antics of Jerry Lewis. Fiedler (1978) traced the historical roots of this stereotype to traditions based on arguments of such philosophers as Aristotle, who viewed persons with physical anomalies as jokes of nature. "The tradition which derives from him, therefore, views such creatures as sources of amusement rather than of terror, thus, justifying showing them off for profit among the lowly, and keeping them for pets in the households of the wealthy" (p. 231). Fiedler (1996) wrote later,

> Yet there would seem always to have been a hunger in all of us, a need to behold in quasi-religious wonder our mysteriously anomalous brothers and sisters. For a long time, this need was satisfied in Courts for the privileged few, at fairs and sideshows for the general populace, by collecting and exhibiting Giants, Dwarfs, Intersexes, Joined Twins, Fat Ladies, and Living Skeletons. Consequently, even in a world that grew ever more secular and rational, we could still continue to be baffled, horrified, and moved by Freaks, as we were able to be by fewer and fewer other things once considered sacred and terrifying. Finally though, the Sideshow began to die, even as the rulers of the world learned to be ashamed of their taste for human "curiosities." By then, however, their images had been preserved in works of art, in which their implicit meanings are manifest (pp. 50-51).

The dramatic use of characters with disabilities "is a theatrical tradition rooted in antiquity" (Klobas, 1988, p. xi). Such humor has long been a part of Hollywood's history. In Buster Keaton's 1921 silent film, *The Playhouse*, two "one-armed" men sit side by side in a theater. Because one lacks his right arm and the other his left they applaud by clapping the other's hand as each act concludes. The system works well until they disagree on the caliber of one particular act. One of the duo sadistically then prevents the other from applauding by sitting on his own hand.

Disney's creation, Dopey Dwarf, with his multiple disabilities of dwarfism, muteness and Down syndrome features has amused generations of children and adults. His childlike treatment, common toward those with mental retardation, is heightened by the fact that he is the only one of the seven to wear a nightshirt rather than trousers, to have huge ears, and to display no beard.

The visually impaired Mr. Magoo is the "archetypal incompetent disabled person" in children's media (Barnes, Berrigan & Biklen, 1978, p. 59). Jernigan (1983) wrote of Magoo,

> Because he is almost blind he bumbles and blunders through a series of bloopers—walking into telephone poles and apologizing to them because he thinks they are people, patting the tops of fire plugs and speaking to them as children and walking up half-finished skyscrapers. The humor is based on the exaggeration of the stereotype; the public believes that blindness is somewhat like this but the overstatement is meant to remove it from the realm of cruel mockery (pp. 59-60).

Jernigan (1983) related that in 1974 and 1975, an agency providing service for persons with blindness made Mr. Magoo the center of their fund-raising campaign. When the National Federation of the Blind wrote in protest, the sighted agency president answered,

> The advertising message is especially directed at people who are *responsible* for the blind—not the blind themselves. We don't feel the blind person will tend to identify himself with Mr. Magoo necessarily; in fact, many may not even know who he is. If there is any kind of a negative aspect in the fact that Mr. Magoo has poor eyesight, it is all the more effective, just as a crippled child on a muscular dystrophy poster is more effective than a normal child (p. 60).

Portraying individuals with blindness as incompetent, clumsy, and inept hardly began with Mr. Magoo. The image has always been a Hollywood favorite. In the 1934 movie *It's a Gift* Charles Sellon, as Mr. Muckle, a character with blindness, totally demolishes W. C. Fields' store by plowing into the plate glass window with his cane, accidently smashing the goods on the shelves, shattering a pile of glass bulbs and stepping into a basket of eggs. As he leaves the store, he demolishes the front door with his white cane and then crosses a busy street where speeding cars and clanging fire engines miraculously miss him.

A similar image of blindness occurs in Max Sennett's short, *Skylarking*, where the hero, proudly showing off his shiny new car, stands horrified as a man with blindness systematically breaks the windows and lights with his tapping cane. Interestingly, the hero fails to intervene out of embarrassment.

Such negative depictions by Hollywood continue. In his history of physical disability in the movies, Norden (1994) described the "sheer bad taste" in the film, *See No Evil, Hear No Evil*, in which Gene Wilder played Dave, a actor with a hearing impairment who runs a Manhattan newsstand with Walt, a man with blindness played by Richard Pryor:

> *See No Evil, Hear No Evil* is an unending series of slapstick gags that trade on the characters' disabilities. Pryor as Wally drives a commandeered police car into a garbage barge and later has a shoot-out with a blind villain. Wally pretends to read newspapers (upside down ones, of course) as he rides the subway while the lip-reading Dave tries to fulfill his side of the conversation even while his back is turned. Created with astonishingly poor judgment, *See No Evil, Hear No Evil,* does little beyond dredging up the old imagery of disabled people as Comic Misadventurers (p. 292).

Today, such depictions are routinely challenged by disability rights groups. In 1991, members of the National Federation of the Blind protested outside of the ABC network offices around the country in objection to a character with blindness in the sitcom *Good and Evil*, who similarly destroys a chemistry laboratory by clumsily wielding his long white cane, and then attempts to solicit a date with a fur coat on a coat rack, mistaking it for a woman (J. Shapiro, 1993, p. 37). Similarly, in 1997, after learning that the Walt Disney Company was reviving Mr. Magoo for a film starring Leslie Nielsen, the National Federation passed a resolution to "take whatever action appropriate to protest" because, "The message is that lack of sight means incompetence" (Mr. Snafoo,1997, p. 21).

Ridicule of different speech is also ingrained in our culture. Porky Pig's classic clonic spasm stutter and Elmer Fudd's and Tweety Bird's articulation substitutions have long reinforced a youngster's right to laugh at persons with speech impairments. Carlisle (1985), who had difficulties with stuttering his entire life, underscored the fact that for thousands of years authors and actors have taken advantage of the notion that audiences find disabilities funny:

> It is difficult to understand how adults can derive entertainment from looking or listening to people with disabilities. Jokes that imply that handicapped people are stupid are in poor taste, and also somewhat

cowardly, since the target is seldom in a position to retaliate. Nonetheless, people should retaliate more. . . . If more people expressed their distaste, the media might get the message (pp. 189-190).

This is exactly what happened in 1988 when members of the National Stuttering Project protested Michael Palin's comical portrayal of Ken, a man who stuttered because of his repressed anger in *A Fish Called Wanda* (J. Shapiro, 1993).

7. THE BURDEN: Viewing persons with disabilities as burdens to society promotes the condition of disability as gloomy, pessimistic and unfortunate. Movies like *Whatever Happened to Baby Jane?*, *Sorry Wrong Number*, and *Lady Chatterly's Lover* reinforced this stereotype.

When children are regarded as burdens, the result is dependency, inequality and rights becoming privileges. Education becomes an act of generosity. School districts often regard their handicapped students as burdens usurping services, taking away resources from "regular" students and, therefore, deserving lesser experiences than their non-handicapped peers receive (Barnes, 1975).

Bogdan and Knoll (1988) stated that although different sets of stereotypes are often mutually contradictory, "they continue to be taken seriously and are used to justify particular modes of treatment" (p. 467). They further noted that regardless of how inaccurate or contradictory, stereotypes can be steadfastly maintained. Meyers (1987) explained the process this way:

Whenever a member of a group behaves as expected, the fact is duly noted; the prior belief is confirmed. When a member of the group behaves inconsistently with the observer's expectation, the behavior may be explained away as due to special circumstances; or it may be misinterpreted leaving the prior belief intact (p. 524).

Allport (1958) made the point that it is a bad idea to use censorship to protect people from stereotypes in literature and the media. Of such stereotypes, he stated, "Better to strengthen one's ability to differentiate among them, and handle their impact with critical power" (p. 196). He also believed that "from the point of view of the theory of prejudice the changeability of stereotypes is important. They wax and wane with the intensity and direction of prejudice" (p. 198).

It is important to note, in any case, that although stereotypes do bias our judgments of groups, we are often able to set them and our prejudices aside when we come to know a particular individual (Meyers, 1987, p. 527). The inclusion of youngsters with disabilities in mainstream education provides the opportunity for children to interact, thereby allowing them to get to know each other as persons first. Stereotypes and prejudices change when planned face to face interaction takes place.

Changing stereotyped images, however, is not an easy task. As Hockenberry (1995), a television reporter with paraplegia, stated,

> Each stereotype thrives in direct proportion to the distance from each class of persons it claims to describe. Get close to the real people and these pretend images begin to break up, but they don't go easily. Losing a stereotype is about being wrong retroactively. For a person to confront such assumptions they must admit an open-ended wrong for as long as those assumptions have been inside them. There is a temptation to hold on to why you believed those stereotypes."I was once frightened and disgusted by a person in a wheelchair." To relinquish such a stereotype is to lose face by giving up a mask (p. 89).

Discrimination

Discrimination is "the unjustifiable negative behavior toward a group and its members" (Meyers, 1987, 484). As prejudice and stereotyping are the cause of disablism, discrimination is the effect. Prejudice is a thought; discrimination is an act. According to Meyers, "Prejudice is negative attitude; discrimination is negative behavior" (p. 484). Bogdan and Biklen (1977) discussed this relationship:

> Prejudice and stereotype point to the cognitive and ideological substance of handicapism. The concept of discrimination provides the structural and behavioral aspect. Unfair and unequal treatment of individuals or group on the basis of prejudice and stereotypes translates into discrimination (p. 15).

Hahn (1989) stressed that

> The basic thrust of the "minority-group" model of disability asserts that disabled men and women have been subjected to the same forms of prejudice, discrimination, and segregation imposed upon other oppressed groups which are differentiated from the remainder of the

population on the basis of characteristics such as race, ethnicity, gender, and aging. Disabled persons not only have exhibited one of the highest rates of unemployment, welfare dependency, and poverty in the United States; but they also have experienced a more pervasive form of segregation in education, housing, transportation, and public accommodations than the most rigid policies enacted by racist governments (pp. 234-235).

As Clark (1954) stated, "Segregation is the way in which a society tells a group of human beings that they are inferior to other groups of human beings in the society (cited in Weicker, 1995, p. 163). Similarly, Weicker (1995) expressed,

[T]he history of society's formal methods for dealing with people with disabilities can be summed up in two words: segregation and inequality. As society, we have treated people with disabilities as inferiors and have made them unwelcome in many activities and opportunities generally available to other Americans. . . . The costs to our society of discrimination are much greater than the costs of eliminating such discrimination (p. 163).

Allport (1958) observed earlier that "discrimination comes about only when we deny to individuals or groups of people equality of treatment which they may wish" (p. 50). Five of the most common forms of discrimination encountered by persons with disabilities follow:

1. UNEQUAL RECOGNITION BEFORE THE LAW: This form of discrimination results in persons with retardation being sterilized, being prevented from voting, marrying, driving a car or holding public office. Vash (1981) stressed how becoming stigmatized and devalued can lead to oppressive legislation:

Disability leads to devaluation, which in turn leads to segregation and its ubiquitous companion, oppression. The person is seen as outside the law, too aberrant to be included under the constitutional or statutory protection. This leads to impoverished education and socialization, with resultant noncompetitive status. Poverty and powerlessness ensue, reinforcing both self-devaluation and devaluation by others (p. 127).

One of the best examples of such devaluation were "ugly laws" like the Chicago statute which stipulated that

No person who is diseased, maimed, mutilated or in any way deformed so as to be an unsightly or disgusting object or improper person to be allowed on the public ways or other public places in this city, shall therein or thereon expose himself to public view, under a penalty of not less than one dollar nor more than fifty dollars for each offense (*Chicago, Illinois Man. Code 6-34, 1966, repealed 1974*, cited in Burgdorf & Burgdorf, 1976, p. 863; see also Bowe, 1978, p. 186; and Pfeiffer 1989, p. 6).

Among the discriminatory laws cited by Pfeiffer (1989) was a New Jersey statute titled "An act to authorize and provide for the sterilization of the feeble-minded (including idiots, imbeciles and morons), epileptics, rapists, certain criminals, and other defectives" (p. 8, see also Burgdorf, 1980, p. 861), and a Washington act (26 Revised code 26.04.030), which prohibited the marriage of anyone who

is a common drunkard, habitual criminal, imbecile, feeble-minded person, idiot or insane person, or person who has theretofore been afflicted with hereditary insanity, unless it is established that procreation is not possible by the couple intending to marry (p. 9).

Another example of unequal recognition before the law can be found in the early decision of the Wisconsin Superior Court in *Beattie v. Board of Education* (1919) which ruled that although a physically disabled youngster constituted no threat, and was academically capable, he could not attend public school because his presence produced a "depressing and nauseating effect on the teachers and school children" (*Beattie v. Board of Education, 169 Wis. 231, 232, 172N.W. 153, 154,* as cited in L. Burrello and D. Sage, 1979, p. 37).

2. UNEQUAL EDUCATION: This form of discrimination results in segregated and substandard facilities—like classes held in the basement or next to the boiler room—lack of services, exclusion, lower standards and labeling. Shea and Bauer (1997) found that "As a group, persons with disabilities have far less education than other Americans" (p. 18).

3. UNEQUAL EMPLOYMENT: Shea and Bauer (1977) found that

even though persons with disabilities have demonstrated excellent job performance, and employing them appears to involve limited additional cost, companies have not employed persons with disabilities in large numbers.The acceptance of workers with disabilities in the workplace is marked with paradox. Though both co-workers and employers report comfort and willingness to work with individuals with disabilities, two-thirds of these individuals are not working (pp. 20-21).

A result of not finding employment is that persons with disabilities are poorer than other Americans (Shea & Bauer, 1997). The unemployed say they can work but are prevented from doing so because of a discriminatory hiring practices or lack of transportation (J. Shapiro, 1993, p. 27).

Perhaps one of the starkest examples of job discrimination based on physical differences can be found in the making of the film *The Wizard of Oz,* in which the actors with dwarfism, hired to play the Munchkins, were paid less than the dogs hired to play Toto (Cox, 1989).

4. UNEQUAL FREEDOM OF MOVEMENT: This form of discrimination results in large scale residential institutionalization: the systematic placement of persons with disabilities into substandard residential facilities where incidents of abuse by staff and other residents, dangerous physical conditions, gross understaffing, overuse of medication to control residents, medical experimentation, inadequate and unsanitary food, sexual abuses, use of solitary confinement and physical restraints, and other serious deficiencies and questionable practices have been exposed (United States Commission on Civil Rights, 1983, pp. 32-33).

5. LACK OF TRANSPORTATION: More than one million persons with physical disabilities, blindness or deafness, who live within a short walk of transit service cannot physically use it (United States Commission on Civil Rights, 1983, p. 39). Shea and Bauer (1997) stated that

> Persons with disabilities are generally unable to travel as they would like and have difficulty attending social events outside the home, such as theater, concerts, and sports events. They are less likely than persons without disabilities to go to the movies, eat in restaurants, grocery shop, or participate in general community life (p. 18).

How Stereotyping, Prejudice and Discrimination Develop
Educators and students must examine how disablism manifests itself and its ramifications on both the personal (individual) level and the

societal level (Bogdan & Biklen, 1977). According to Patton, Blackbourn and Fad (1996) stereotype, prejudice and discrimination develop into disablism in the following manner:

Stereotyping leads to viewing adults with mental retardation as child-like;

Prejudice leads to the belief that they are incapable of being responsible for their own behaviors; and

Discrimination results in these adults being denied library cards or similar privileges (p. 11).

Disablism Toward Women—A Special Dilemma

Any discussion of prejudice and discrimination toward persons with disabilities would be incomplete without including the special plight of disabled women. The special issues regarding women with disabilities have become more visible thanks to such books and publications as those by Deegan and Brooks (1985), Browne, Connors and Stern (1985), Fine and Asch (1988) and Rousso (1988). As the City of New York's Commission on the Status of Women (1979) noted,

In addition to the formidable barriers associated with their disabilities, disabled women must also contend with the vast range of obstacles that discourage women from full participation in society. Disabled women who want to join the workforce are regularly subjected to employers who feel that priority in job placement should be given to disabled men, and directors of rehabilitation and job training programs who do not only favor men but also direct women into sex-stereotyped employment. These attitudes are often accompanied by the more general assumption that disabled women prefer to remain dependent at home (p. 1).

Fine and Asch (1985) argued that "disability is a more severely handicapping condition for women than for men" (p. 6). They traced the differential experience to the more limited role choices and limited role models available to disabled women.

Whereas disabled men are obliged to fight the social stigma of disability, they can aspire to fill socially powerful male roles. Disabled women do not have this option. Disabled women are perceived as inadequate for economically productive roles (traditionally considered appropriate for males) and for the nurturing reproductive roles considered appropriate for females (p. 6).

Among the economic, social and psychological realities women with disabilities face, Fine and Asch (1985) found they are

- less likely to be employed than disabled men (It is estimated that 65 to 76 percent of all disabled women are unemployed);

- less likely than disabled men to receive training in vocational schools or on-the-job;

- less likely to be college educated than disabled men;

- once employed, liable to earn less than men with disabilities and women without disabilities;

- less likely to live in families with incomes above the poverty level than men with disabilities;

- liable to receive disproportionately lower levels of disability insurance benefits and coverage;

- less likely to marry, and liable to marry at a later age, and once married more likely to be divorced compared to women without disabilities;

- more apt to be deserted than men with disabilities (Fine and Asch noted that 90 percent of women with alcoholism are left by their husbands while 10 percent of men with alcoholism are left by their wives);

- often medically advised not to have children and are more liable than other women to be threatened with or become victims of involuntary sterilization;

- often viewed as asexual, nonsexual or inappropriate as sexual beings; and

• often overlooked when laws and programs are formulated regarding child custody, reproductive freedom and domestic violence.

An estimated six and one half million women with disabilities in the United States are victimized by this type of double discrimination. For example, the conditions under which they are abused are not widely known, but national experts estimate that as many as half of all developmentally disabled women have been sexually molested, primarily by those upon whom they rely for their most basic needs (Zola, 1986, p. 15). In short, the situation of women with disabilities requires constant attention and close examination.

Disablism, Racism and Sexism
Persons with disabilities often share problems with those who belong to other minority groups (B. Wright, 1983). In fact, disablism is closely akin to racism and sexism. For example, like ethnic minorities and women, persons with disabilities often find themselves pejoratively stereotyped and suffered prejudice and discrimination based on their physical appearance. In addition, women, ethnic groups and persons with disabilities have all been associated with lower socioeconomic status. In addition, persons with disabilities, like persons of certain ethnic groups are considered undesirable marriage partners by many so-called normal members of the larger society. Another similarity between minority groups, women and persons with disabilities is that all benefit now from social movements that fight to secure their equality and the civil rights (Lerner, 1987, p. 277).

Although all "isms" are forms of prejudice, stereotyping and discrimination, disablism, as a concept, has six unique differences:

1. DIVERSE GROUP MEMBERSHIP: Those discriminated against under the rubric of disablism comprise a much more diversified group than victims of racism and sexism. One thinks of the recipients of discrimination by sexism as primarily women and the recipients of racism as primarily African Americans, Latinos, Asians, or Native Americans. By contrast, hundreds of different disabilities exist, each with its own group advocating for its own issues. In fact, sometimes their agendas conflict. While wheelchair user activists fought for the establishment of sidewalk curb cuts, organizations of persons with visual impairments fought the concept; persons with blindness who tapped the curbs with their canes often use curbs for a sense of location (J. Shapiro, 1993). Some persons

with blindness believed that the absence of a curb at the end of each block would put them in greater peril of walking directly into the street and oncoming traffic.

In addition, the diverse groups that make up the category considered disabled are both numerous and small. Because real contact and interaction is so limited, the stereotypes tend to remain unaffected by first hand experiences. For example, if a male believes the stereotype of the "dumb blonde" he has a greater chance of dispelling the stereotype through frequent contact with blonde women. But if people believe that persons with blindness are funny and accident prone, they are liable to go on basing their attitudes on images like Mr. Magoo, not on real persons with visual impairments. That is a crucial reason for the need for personal contact, like that provided by including disabled students in the general student population.

2. LACK OF GROUP PRIDE, HERITAGE AND A COMMON POSITIVE IDENTITY: The experience of the "consciousness of kind" is different for persons with disabilities than for members of ethnic groups. Ethnic groups possess a common cultural heritage and shared history distinct from the rest of society (Lerner, 1987). Almost all African Americans are proud of their skin color and do not want to change it. They believe "Black is beautiful." Jews, Asians, Latinos, or Native Americans also take pride in the many characteristics unique to their group. This pride is, in fact, a sign of self-acceptance (B. Wright, 1983). But as Gleidman and Roth (1980) stated, "No one argues that mental retardation is good, blindness is beautiful, that doctors should stop research into the causes of cerebral palsy" (p. 23). Zola (1982) made this observation:

> As the melting pot theory of America was finally buried, people could once again say, even though they were three generations removed from the immigrants that they were proud to be Greek, Italian, Hungarian, or Polish. With the rise of Black power, a derogatory label became a rallying cry, Black is beautiful! And when female liberationists saw their strength in numbers, they shouted, Sisterhood is powerful! But what about the chronically ill and disabled? Can we yell, Long live cancer! Up with multiple sclerosis! I'm glad I had polio! Clearly a basis of a common positive identity is not readily available (p. 208).

Only recently have civil rights advocacy organizations like Little People of America taken the position that nothing is wrong with persons having dwarfism or other differences. In fact, Little People do not see themselves as a different kind of human being, only "differently packaged." Instead of feeling ashamed of who they are, they speak of "dwarf pride" (Ablon, 1984), and refer to persons without dwarfism as having "average" rather than "normal" height. Other members of disability organizations are also now beginning to take pride in their identity as persons with disabilities:

> For the first time, people with disabilities are defining themselves. They are saying that their existence is all right. Like homosexuals in the early 1970's, many disabled people are rejecting the stigma that there is something sad or to be ashamed of in their condition (J. Shapiro, 1993, p. 20).

3. ISOLATION: Unlike ethnic minorities, persons with disabilities do not constitute a group with a common descent. Group membership is not transmitted, for the most part, by either genetic or socially recognized rules of inheritance. By comparison, ethnic groups are based on family units and, as Learner (1987) stated, "Loyalty to the ethnic collectivity is easily nurtured as a part of the general socialization process. By contrast, the handicapped child is often forced to cope with his or her plight without similar sympathetic others" (p. 278). Because the situation of persons with disabilities differs from that of other groups in that their differences are not likely to be shared by other family members, they may develop feelings of isolation.

> Racial characteristics are genetically inherited and religious characteristics are often socially inherited; however, individuals with a disability are often the only ones in their family so affected. As children, they may even be unaware that there are others who have a similar disability and thus may feel no affiliation with any minority group (B. Wright, 1983, pp. 24-25).

4. THE DIFFERING GOALS OF EQUITY AND EQUALITY: The basic goal of the Feminist and the Civil Rights Movements is *equality*—the idea that persons are equal and should be treated so. The goal of the disablism movement is *equity*—the idea that each person gets the reasonable accommo-

dations he or she needs to become equal. As a popular disability awareness bumper sticker states, "At least Rosa Parks could get on the bus."

5. ADVENTITIOUS DISABILITIES: Many persons with disabilities who are the recipients of disablism were not born with their impairments but acquired them later in life. In contrast, ethnicity and gender are acquired at birth and are, therefore, "a much more perfectly ascribed status" (Lerner, 1987, p. 279). An individual who acquires a disability not only must learn to cope with the negative attitudes of others, but he or she also needs to confront his or her own negative attitudes held prior to the disability's occurrence.

6. MEDICAL MODEL INFLUENCES: A final difference between disablism and racism and sexism of course, is, of course, the large influence medical and psychiatric community plays in the lives of persons with disabilities. The extent of this influence needs to be carefully examined before one can fully understand disablism.

Personal Reactions to Disability

Cohen (1974/1977) related why persons without disabilities react in certain ways to persons who have them:

> We feel uncomfortable with persons who are disabled because we don't know how to act with them. We are afraid of saying the wrong thing, of not doing something we should, of doing something we shouldn't. When we happen to mention something about "seeing" in the presence of a blind person we feel uneasy, as if we had said a taboo word, as if blind people don't know that others can see. When a deaf person is present we almost shout our conversational communications. When we are with a person who has a problem with motor control, such as most cerebral palsied persons do, we may hover about him constantly trying to relieve him of all movement tasks or we may shrink from offering help altogether. We don't know what is appropriate, and we are afraid to ask. Our own ambivalent feelings toward the disabled make us afraid to ask (p. 12).

Because prejudice distorts social relationships by overemphasizing some characteristic like a disability, it often results in stereotyping. Common attitudes toward persons with disabilities resulting from this distortion are, "discomfort," "pity and patronization" and "stigmatization" (United States Commission On Civil Rights, 1983). Other common reactions include "stigma spread," "requirement for mourning," "expectation discrepancy," "blaming the victim" and "passing." Each of these reactions warrants analysis in the next eight sections:

Discomfort, Guilt, and Embarrassment

Research indicates that interaction with persons with disabilities—particularly those with visible disabilities—commonly produces feelings of discomfort and embarrassment in non-disabled people (Gleidman and Roth, 1980). These feelings occur especially among persons who lack the experience of interacting appropriately with persons who have impairments. No one likes to be in a position of not knowing how to act appropriately, and when one meets a physically different person, a "perceptual snap" occurs which often results in an uneasy situation causing discomfort and embarrassment. For example, do I extend my hand to a person with blindness or one whose right hand or arm has been amputated? How do I respond to someone with cerebral palsy whose speech is unintelligible? How do I deal with the person with a stutter who gets embarrassed because I'm embarrassed? Does the person with the disability know that I feel uncomfortable? Research indicates that in face-to-face contacts, both persons with and without disabilities typically display anxiety and strain about how each will perceive the other (Goffman, 1963; Bogdan & Biklen, 1977; B. Wright, 1983).

Hahn (1988) divided feelings of discomfort and guilt into two distinct sub categories, "existential anxiety" and "aesthetic anxiety." "Existential anxiety" refers to the threat of potential loss of functional capabilities by nondisabled persons:

> The existential anxiety triggered by disabilities occasionally may become the subject of conscious attention. Sometimes these concerns are evident in the silent thought that "there, but for the grace of God [or luck or fate or other fundamental beliefs], go I." At other times, these worries may be verbalized in statements such as, "I would rather be dead than live as a paraplegic [or as blind, deaf, or immobilized]." In fact, the threat of a permanent and debilitating disability with its resulting problems, can even outrank the fear of death, which is, after all, inevitable (p. 120).

Zola (1982) illustrated how such feelings evoke guilt in nondisabled individuals:

> When the able bodied confront the disabled they often think with a shudder, "I'm glad it's not me." But the relief is often followed by guilt for thinking such a thought, a guilt they'd just as soon not deal with either. The threat to be dispelled is the inevitability of one's own failure. The discomfort that many feel in the presence of the aged, the suffering, and the dying is the reality that it could just as well be them. All this, then, is the burden that we the physically handicapped carry. In every interaction, our baggage includes not only our own physical infirmity but the sense of infirmity we evoke in others and their consequent incapacity to deal with us (p. 202).

An individual with paraplegia asserted, "The disabled serve as a constant, visible reminder to the able-bodied that the society they live in is a counterfeit paradise, that they too are vulnerable. We present a fearsome possibility" (In J. Shapiro, 1993, p. 38). Cohen (1977) earlier stated, "The fear of becoming handicapped is strong, and handicapped people arouse in us an awareness of our own vulnerability, an awareness that we would rather push from our consciousness" (p. 6). Similar fears were stressed by Bell and Burgdorf (1983) who stated, "Psychologically, handicaps may be symbolic evidence of everyone's vulnerability to death, disease, and injury, which may force people to face 'unpleasant truths about themselves'" (p. 23).

Such fears must, however, be confronted if attitudes are to be changed. As Bowe (1978) stated, "[A]s long as we are anxious about disabilities and afraid of disabilities ourselves, we will resist attitude change toward disabled individuals" (p. 118).

Callahan (1989) sometimes meets this type of reaction to his quadriplegia with caustic sarcasm:

> Often I've found myself in a slow elevator with a crowd of people who first stare at me and then look away. I try to break the ice with a pleasant remark such as, "Damn! I knew I should have crawled up the stairs!" (p. 188).

"Aesthetic anxiety" has two major aspects according to Hahn (1988):

> First, the discrimination directed at disabled individuals is partly due to their being devalued because they do not present conventional images of human physique or behavior. Second, aesthetic anxiety may result in a tendency to place those who are perceived as different or strange in a subordinate role (pp. 120-121).

Thus, negative feelings occur most frequently among nondisabled people without a knowledge of how disabilities affect those who have them and how to respond properly. This uneasiness often results in both the nondisabled person and the person with the disability wanting to end the encounter quickly, thereby establishing a pattern of avoidance.

Patronization, Sympathy and Pity

Van Etten (1988) described how she felt being patronized because of her dwarfism:

> Patronization is another form of abuse. It is an insensitivity to my wish to be treated as any other person. It shows itself when people pat you on the head or take you by the hand when they walk alongside you. I find it especially frustrating, because often the person cannot be told that their behavior is offensive. Many times they are people in authority over you (p. 141).

Pity is probably the most common emotion expressed toward persons with disabilities (Hourihan, 1980) and it is linked to the medical view that they are sickly and in need of help to survive. In reality, pity (or its more acceptable synonym, "sympathy") means, "I feel sorry for you." The givers of sympathy consider themselves in a better position than the receivers. It puts them in a position of being better off, which in turn can negatively affect the self-esteem of the receiver who is put into a dependent role with its second class status. "Pity," according to Wright (1983), "presumes a status relationship in which the other person looks down upon the recipient; it involves devaluation even though the other person may wish to help the sufferer" (p. 318). Cohen (1974/1977) believed pity to be

> a reaction that was helpful to the disabled in the past when their survival depended upon the charity that came from it, and when the alternative to pity was rejection. The alternatives are no longer limited to pity or rejection. While there is still a place for compassion, the drive today is for the development of maximum competence, the recognition of rights, the provision of opportunities, and the willingness to relate to the disabled as individual human beings (pp. 16-17).

Rioux (1996) added, "Our notion of services has been tarnished by the notion that people with disabilities are unfortunate, pitiable people, so services have been designed to serve people for whom we felt sorry" (p. 8).

According to Wolfensberger et al. (1972/1975), "[T]his form of pity perception is benevolent and is accompanied by compassion and acceptance, although it may be devoid of respect for the [disabled] person" (p. 20). It is also overly solicitous. As Gliedman (1979) stated, "[T]he disabled must also cope with a kind of paternalism from their able-bodied allies that has long been discredited in race relations" (p. 59).

A prime example is the concept of big charity campaigns, especially the one for "Jerry's Kids." The stereotype of persons with disabilities as pitiable and in need of our mercy and sympathy is often reinforced by such charity campaigns, especially with their accompanying telethons. They often perpetuate the stereotype of persons with disabilities as needy by promoting images of disabled children as helpless, poor, pathetic individuals who need our donations to become human (Bowe, 1978). Although most persons with these disabilities are adults, children are used because they are more marketable and can present a horror story of a helpless, lonely life, bringing the tears and pity that equate to dollars, "getting to our purse strings by pulling on our heart strings." Many disability rights activists believe that by selling a message of dependence, charities portray a people as being totally needy. "The spectacle of Lewis, sweating and weeping, begging for the folks out there to save 'my kids' has long struck many observers as distasteful and demeaning" (Bennetts, 1993, p. 86).

Because non-disabled persons often feel and act on moral obligations to help disabled persons, many organizations and individuals spend a great deal of time, money and effort on staging telethons and benefit sporting contests to support research, services, and facilities for persons with disabilities and their families. "Charitable impulses, however, can become pity or patronization (United States Commission on Civil Rights, 1983, p. 24); and the recipients of such charity often receive compassion without respect. Wolfensberger (1972), described this form of 'benevolent paternalism.'"Usually, this form of pity perception is benevolent and is accompanied by compassion and acceptance, although it may be devoid of respect for the deviant person" (p. 20). Furthermore,

> Pity can be very hostile to the achievement of equality and respect. If you feel sorry for someone, you might pledge a donation, but you are

not likely to offer them a good job, or approve of them dating your sister (Hershey, 1992, p. 38).

Hershey went on to state her strong position on pity and telethons:

> Pity is a complex and deceptive emotion. It pretends to care, to have an interest in another human being. It seems to want to take away pain and suffering. But if you look at pity up close, you notice that it also wants to distance itself from its object. A woman calls in and boasts, "My two children are perfectly healthy, thank God!" Pity does not share another's reality, only remarks on it (p. 38).

Morris (1991) concluded that charities and the cultural representation of disabled people on which they rely constitute a "fundamental undermining of disabled people as autonomous human beings" (p. 108). She maintained that charities create a culture of dependency. They sell a message of dependence. In this situation, persons with disabilities become the recipients of other people's good will who also have the power to decide who is or who is not a deserving case. Waxman (1991) called this situation a "power differential" in which the lives of persons with disabilities are determined by others:

> I would argue that any reaction which creates separation and inequality between people—which pity certainly does, however benevolent it might appear—is destructive. People cannot live together in community, recognizing and respecting each other as human beings if one group feels superior to the others for any reason (p. 38).

Bennetts (1993) provided an additional example noting that Jerry Lewis considers the disability rights activists expressing negative views of the telethon a "handful of malcontent ingrates who are in chairs I bought them" (p. 86). Morris (1991) also asserted this form of dependency:

> Although charities collect money from the general population, they very rarely give disabled people money; this would be to give us too much power. Instead the help is in the form of equipment, holidays, and so on. Health and social services professionals play a key role in defining what we need (p. 108).

Morris (1991) also asserted that charity is actually about making non-disabled persons feel good about themselves:

> Charities need to present disability in such a way as to encourage peo-
> ple to part with their money. The portrayal of a strong disabled person
> going about his or her life and enjoying it, is not going to bring in any
> money. . . . It is an emotional reaction which charities are seeking, and
> the emotional reactions which provoke people to give money are
> those of pity and guilt (pp. 108-109).

Longmore (1996) similarly found that, "telethons are not primarily fund
raisers; they're cultural rituals to find out who's valid and who's not. In
other words, those who give, are; those who take aren't" (cited in
Medgyesi, pp. 46-47).

To heighten the emotions of pity and guilt, fund-raisers routinely
rely on images of children with physical disabilities. A poster child is an
image fund-raisers create for the sole purpose of evoking public pity to
obtain money. Although most individuals who have these disabilities
are adults, images of children are lucrative, representing horror stories
of helpless, lonely lives and undamming tears of pity that turn to dollars. J. Shapiro (1993) expressed this ironic view:

> The poster child is a sure-fire tug at our hearts. The children picked to
> represent charity fund-raising drives are brave, determined, and inspi-
> rational, the most innocent victims of the cruelest whims of life and
> health. Yet they smile through their unlucky fates—a condition that
> weakens muscles or cuts life expectancy to a brutish handful of years,
> a birth defect or childhood trauma. No other symbol of disability is
> more beloved by Americans than the cute and courageous poster
> child—or more loathed by people with disabilities themselves (p. 12).

Of most importance is a full understanding of the terms "sympathy" and "empathy." Sympathy (pity) is probably the most common
emotion youngsters express toward persons with disabilities. But most
persons with disabilities do not want the pity and sympathy their physical or mental conditions evoke. They want instead an understanding of
the problems they face when having to deal with an environment not
accommodating their needs. As early as 1981, Kemp wrote this in *The
New York Times*:

> The Jerry Lewis Muscular Dystrophy Telethon, with its pity approach
> to fund raising, has contributed to the prejudices which create vast
> frustration and anger among the 36 million disabled people in this
> country. For most of us who have one of the 40 neuromuscular dis-

eases for which the Muscular Dystrophy Association seeks cures, barriers to employment, transportation, housing and recreation can be more devastating and wasteful of our lives than the diseases from which we suffer. The very human desire for cures for these diseases can never justify a television show that reinforces a stigma against disabled people. These prejudices create stereotypes that offend our self-respect, harm our efforts to live independent lives and segregate us (September 3, Opinion Page).

Bennetts (1993) cited Longmore's comments asserting that telethons, with a combined audience of 250 million, are the single most powerful cultural mechanism defining the public identities of people with disabilities in our society today (p. 92). Longmore (1987) discussed the differing viewpoints of the money raisers and the disability rights activists:

The message of telethons is that whatever the condition people with disabilities have, that condition has essentially spoiled their lives, and the only way to correct that is to cure them. The message of the disability rights movement is that it's possible to be a whole person with a disability (p. 92).

Hevey (1992) described how charity drives purposefully add to the confusion of disabilities and handicaps:

Charity advertising is both the parasite which lives off this confusion and the public ordination of it. It represents the highest public validation of the isolation of disabled people. It presents a solution to the "problem" of disablement by a disguised blaming of the victim. It fails to find a solution because it is itself the problem. But what is missing from charity advertising is the center of this grand solution—the separating out of the impairment from the disablement (handicap), the medical view from the social view. The dominant form of impairment imagery, that of charity advertising, cannot demonstrate this struggle because the very essence of charities is to obstruct the making of this link (p. 51).

Hockenberry (1995), who found a positive side, wrote,

Doubtless, Jerry Lewis had no clue that his telethon provided a useful low-end benchmark for disability empowerment. For that reason alone it is useful far beyond the millions of dollars it raises for research and cures. Much of Jerry's money goes into investigating genetic screening to prevent people with MDA from even coming into the world. Jerry's kids are people in wheelchairs on television raising money to find a way to prevent their ever having been born. When crips watch the telethon, the words "bravery" and "courage" and "heroism" do not come to mind (p. 33).

The medical model causes a loss of power not only on the individual level but on the group level as well. An example of such a power loss was supported by empirical research in the United Kingdom by Drake (1996) who found that persons with disabilities were greatly under-represented in positions of authority within traditional charities (a situation found in the United States as well). He concluded that

The values, attitudes, and beliefs of those who govern traditional charities accord largely with the "personal tragedy" or medical model of disability, and a major consequence of this perspective is that disabled people are confined to roles in which they have little opportunity to exercise power in the traditional voluntary sector (p. 5).

Drake (1996) also stated on a positive note that

Although change is taking place, traditional charities continue to adhere to values and beliefs funded on the personal tragedy perspective of disability. . . . However, the hegemony of the medical paradigm is being increasingly challenged by disabled people whose views more closely accord with an understanding of disability fostered by the social model (p. 20).

Although most charity drives and telethons are based on public pity and sympathy, that is exactly what most persons with disabilities do not want. What they do want from the public is empathy. While sympathy expresses pity and sorrow, empathy is the ability to imagine oneself in the other person's situation and comprehend his or her feelings. Empathy means, "I understand." Sympathy can hurt a person's self-image because it reinforces dependency and second class status. Empathy engenders a positive self-image because the individual believes he or she is expressing a need that is being heard and understood. An understanding of empathy and sympathy is a valuable lesson for all students to learn (Shapiro, Barton & Barnhart, 1991). In a book written and illustrated entirely by children with disabilities (1984, H. Exley, ed.) several expressed these personal thoughts regarding pity:

- What I need from you is only my rights and not a lot of sympathy (p. 20).

- It's not the handicapped people who need rehabilitating but the rest of the world. Don't pat on the head, offer help, talk to the handicapped out of pity. Talk to them because you like them. Otherwise don't bother (p. 82).

- I hate people who feel sorry for me, because I don't feel sorry for myself (p. 83)

- It's not nice being handicapped, but I'm not unhappy with my situation as I could have been born a chicken or a duck (p. 59).

Stigma and Devaluation

Stigma and devaluation is the depreciation of the worth of an individual because of his or her disability or handicap. According to the United States Commission on Civil Rights (1983), "Perhaps the most significant attitude toward handicaps is that they are considered extremely negative characteristics" (p. 25). Handicapping conditions are frequently and illogically viewed as "blameworthy" characteristics. A disability is viewed as a "badge of disgrace" (Burgdorf, 1980). As Goffman (1963) stated,

> Such an attribute is a stigma, especially when its discrediting effect is very extensive; sometimes it is also called a failing, a shortcoming, a handicap. It constitutes a special discrepancy between virtual and actual social identity (p. 3).

Goffman also observed that the term "stigma" is a deeply discrediting attribute. Moreover, what we really need is a language of relationships, not attributes (pp. 4-5). As Shea and Bauer (1997) found,

> Acceptance is the primary problem confronting an individual with a stigma. In social situations in which an individual is perceived to have a stigma, categorizations that do not fit are usually applied and uneasiness is experienced by both parties (p. 28).

Goffman classified stigmas into three distinct types, depending on how they are perceived:

> First, *abominations of the body*, or the various physical *deformities*;
> Second, *blemishes of individual character* that is to say, those with weak wills, domineering or unnatural passions, treacherous and rigid beliefs, dishonesty, as well as those inferred from a record of, for example, a mental disorder, imprisonment, addiction, alcoholism, homosexuality, unemployment, suicidal attempts and radical political behavior; and
> Third, *tribal stigma*, or race, national, religion; or a stigma that can be transmitted through lineages and equally contaminate all members of a family (p. 4).

These classifications resemble those Allport (1958) listed earlier:

a. anatomical differences;
b. physiological differences;
c. differences in abilities;
d. "basic personality" of members of a given group;
e. cultural practices and beliefs (p. 94).

Stigma Spread

Hanna and Graff (1977) used the term "stigma spread" for the common tendency to perceive the person with a disability as disabled with respect to both physique and such other characteristics as personality, intelligence, and physical abilities beyond those affected (p. 73). Gallagher (1995) wrote that [this] spread describes the phenomenon which occurs when some or all attributes of a person's character are thought to be the function of a handicap" (p. 254). Wright (1983) referred to it as "the power of single characteristics to evoke inferences about a person" (p. 31). She added, "Not only are specific characteristics of the person inferred from physique, but the person as a whole is sometimes evaluated accordingly. The problem becomes especially harmful when global devaluation takes place so that the person as a person is felt to be less worthy, less valuable, less desirable" (p. 34). Much earlier Goffman (1963) stated, "We tend to impute a wide range of imperfections on the basis of the original one, and at the same time to impute some desirable but undesired attributes, often of a supernatural cast, such as sixth sense, or understanding" (p. 5). Examples of stigma spread include these four:

1. Speaking in an unusually loud voice to someone with blindness, or speaking about a person with a disability in his or her presence as if her or she were not there, for example, a waiter or waitress asking a nondisabled person in the presence of a disabled person for the disabled customer's order. As one youngster with cerebral palsy said,

> Some people think I can't understand them, so they will talk to my mother or brother instead of to me. Mom is great about letting them know that I am smart, and that it is always better when people talk to me rather than acting like I am not there (in Westridge Young Writers Workshop, 1994, p. 21);

2. Assuming someone with cerebral palsy is also mentally retarded;

3. Assuming a person with dwarfism is childlike;

4. Assuming that a person with a stutter thinks like he or she talks.

Noddin (1962) illustrated how stigma spread can affect an individual with blindness:

> I've heard people talking about me on buses and subways. They think you're deaf and dumb, [*sic*] too. Once I was out with my teacher, standing on a corner waiting to cross a street. A lady came by and asked him, "Why doesn't she cross the street?" He replied that there was a train going by. "Why, can she hear?" the lady asked. It makes me mad that people are so ignorant. One of my strong ambitions is to prove that I'm an individual (p. 152).

Diodati (1962) related a similar experience:

> It is not unusual for me to have to stand on a bus while people around me discuss my blindness. People quite often assume that if a person in blind he is also deaf. And many times we are treated as though we can't think clearly. Most blind people are especially glad to be able to hear and feel and think, and when people deny you these human faculties, you feel awfully discouraged. I know that blindness is different from vision, but there is a whole lot of a human being that stays the same when one sense fails (pp. 186-187).

Similarly, a woman dating a federal worker with blindness wrote the following to Jernigan (1983) during his tenure as President of the National Federation of the Blind:

> Jim and I made a trip to the hospital emergency room. He had got some poison ivy and it had spread to his eyes. The nurse on duty was horrible. She thought him to be blind, deaf, mute, stupid, and incapable of doing anything. She asked me, "What's his name? Where does he live? Do his eyes itch?" I was offended and said, "I think he can answer his own questions." Jim calmly told her what she wanted to know, but I could tell he was mad (p. 64).

Jernigan (1983) concluded,

> What is difficult to convey is the cumulative effect of these stereotyped attitudes. They are all pervasive in the experience of blind people; they make up the context of the society in which we live (p. 63). To put it simply, the experience of being blind is dominated not by the lack of sight but by the negative attitudes of the sighted public (p. 65).

This is true not only for persons with blindness, but for all persons with disabilities as well.

Position of Subject and Requirement for Mourning
Hanna and Graff (1977) defined "position of subject" as meaning "that people evaluate others in terms of their own physical equipment and abilities" (p. 74). They defined "requirement for mourning" as a "concept that says when physique is assigned a high status value and is seen as essential to personal security, people will tend to insist that the disabled person is unfortunate" (p. 75). Persons without disabilities tend, therefore, to mourn for the disabled individual and have exaggerated negative, and lowered expectations for them. Wright (1983), distinguished between three types of requirements for mourning: (1) "empathetic requirement for mourning"—that is, because disabilities are judged to be negative, unwanted, imposed and not chosen, there is an expectation of suffering; (2) "self-aggrandizing requirement for mourning," which allows nondisabled persons to preserve and elevate their own statuses by considering disabled persons "unfortunate sufferers" and, in turn, to recognize our status as superior; and "ought requirement for mourning," which "stems from the need to preserve codes of proper behavior. . . . Maintaining the ought standards of proper conduct and

connotes moral obligation. . . . The ought requirement of mourning can also reflect the belief that disability is a punishment for sin and therefore the person ought to suffer" (pp. 79-82).

Expectation Discrepancy

Expectation discrepancy occurs when the behavior and adjustment expected of disabled persons are inconsistent with what others have observed. This reaction occurs as a pronounced reaction of surprise that things are better than expected or worse than expected. Overly praising or showing surprise at a child with blindness who learns to read Braille, or a child with deafness who learns sign language conveys the message that such adaptations are unexpected. Showing pity toward such impairments may communicate the notion that the condition is "bad," not "different." Shea and Bauer (1997) found that the attitude that "disability is a thing to be overcome" nurtured an emergence of the "inspirational disabled person" image. They found that

> [T]he Disability Rights Movement discards the notion that people with disabilities should be courageous or heroic overachievers, since most individuals with disabilities simply are trying to lead their own lives, not inspire anyone. In fact, within the disabilities rights culture, the term *supercrip* has emerged for individuals who attempt extraordinary feats to demonstrate that their disabilities can be "overcome" (p. 19).

Blaming the Victim

A handicapping condition develops when an individual has a problem within the environment, in which case, one can blame either the individual or the environment. For example, if a man with dwarfism can not reach an automatic teller machine, a urinal or a telephone, it is not his height that is handicapping him; it's the height at which these objects were placed. A urinal or telephone can be made lower, an individual can not be forced to grow. Assigning a stigmatizing label to a youngster having a problem in a school environment and removing him or her from the regular classroom is most often a result of blaming the victim because the problem is seen as within the child rather than the school. Ryan (1971) enumerated a four stage formula for blaming the victim:

First, identify a social problem. Second, study those affected by the problem and discover in what ways they are different from the rest of us as a consequence of deprivation and injustice. Third, define the differences as the cause of the social problem itself. Finally, of course, assign a government bureaucrat to invent a humanitarian action program to correct the differences (p. 8).

Passing

Another personal reaction toward disability is "passing." However, it is different from the others because it is a reaction sometimes used by the person with a disability rather than toward him or her. Passing is a management technique used by a disabled person to hide the disability when possible for the purpose of avoiding the stress of being devalued. Of course, the success of the technique depends on the visibility of the disability (Clinard and Meier, 1979). As Hanna and Graff (1977) explained,

> The person tries to conceal the disability because it is viewed the same way the normal majority views it. If it is expected that a disability is something to be ashamed of, the obvious way to eliminate the shame is to eliminate the disability. Where this cannot be accomplished medically, repression allows the individual to attempt to experience the non-handicapped position again (p. 67).

Although persons who are passing may be perceived as able-bodied they, however, "often pay a high psychological price for their successful strategies of concealment" (Gleidman, 1979, p. 63). For example,

> The person cannot forget. . . when reality requires that the disability be taken into account. The vigilance required leads not only to physical strain, but also to problems with interpersonal relations. Considerable interpersonal distance must be maintained to guard against another's raising the topic of disability (Hanna and Graff, 1977, p. 67).

Conclusion

Increasingly, through litigation and legislation, society is taking a sociopolitical approach that considers disability "a product of the interaction between the individual and the environment" (Hahn, 1987, p. 182). Social policy and the time-honored tendency to view disability solely through the medical paradigm is slowly changing, possibly because of an increased interest in Disabilities Studies as an accepted academic field of study similar to Black Studies or Women's Studies. The political civil rights movement of persons with disabilities, which resulted in the passage of the Americans With Disabilities Act, also accounts for the heightened interest. But disability issues have been viewed through the civil rights and minority group paradigm only recently, and meaningful understanding of this paradigm shift away from the medical model must occur if further progress is to be made. As Hahn (1987) aptly stated, "Educational efforts that seek to explain and to clarify the analogies between the status of other minorities and the treatment of disabled citizens can contribute significantly to the struggle of the latter group for freedom and equality" (p. 185).

The public and especially the schools need to explore these issues because they daily address basic moral issues and values including humanness, segregation, freedom and liberty. As Rioux (1996) observed, "The particular condition of an individual may exacerbate his or her ability to function like the rest of us, but in a human rights framework difference is not an excuse to discriminate. It is a challenge to our creativity" (p. 9).

But changing paradigms, from the medical model the social rights model is difficult, and an exploration of some specific disability images and their effects on individuals can, at this point, promote understanding.

CHAPTER FOUR

Early Attitudes and Their Legacies

Examining the historical treatment toward persons with disabilities contributes insight into the origins of our current common attitudes, particularly fear, rejection, fascination, ridicule and pity. Because such attitudes do not arise in a vacuum—they emerge from the customs, laws and practices of the past—we need to examine their foundations in order to understand them fully. An historical perspective reveals an evolutionary progression and suggests how far our society has come in its acceptance, treatment and integration of persons with disabilities. It also reminds us how far we still have to go: "If society is to deal fairly and honorably with its disabled brothers and sisters, there must be a general understanding and awareness of what should constitute fairness and how society has failed to be fair in the past" (Gallagher, 1995, p. xiii). History can teach us some important comparative lessons.

Early attitudes and beliefs toward persons with disabilities and readily discernible differences have influenced greatly how disabilities, and the people who have them, are treated today. Writing on deformity and disability in the Greco-Roman world, Garland (1995) stated that

> [T]he study of history can never fruitfully be an end in itself. Rather, it forms part of a discourse between the past and the present, whose purpose is to measure cultural distance and difference, as well as to establish cultural similarity and identity (p. xii).

Throughout history, discriminatory treatment toward persons with disabilities has varied greatly from nation to nation and culture to culture, ranging from complete rejection and ostracism to semi-deification (Safilios-Rothchild, 1970; Mackelprang & Salsgiver, 1996). According to Barton (1996), "Disabled people have been the recipients of a range of offensive responses by other people. These include, horror, fear, anxiety, hostility, distrust, pity, over-protection and patronizing behavior (p. 8.).

However, such treatment of persons with disabilities has been one of increasing humanization, away from extermination, banishment and exclusion. We now move toward the as yet elusive goal of full acceptance, respect, civil rights and social inclusion. Funk (1987) defined such humanization as the "recognition that disabled people have human needs and characteristics, and public policy must be designed to reflect and further this human potential" (p. 8).

Blatt (1987) recalled that the severest form of punishment in ancient times was not execution but banishment. In a sense, the history of disability can be traced through various eras each reflecting different forms of banishment and segregation, each leaving its influence on modern attitudes. For instance, as Hitler initiated the Nazi policy of "euthanasia," a euphemism for murdering disabled children considered by the state as being "life unworthy of life," he paid tribute to the similar policy of ancient Sparta, where babies with disabilities were hurled to their deaths from cliffs for the betterment of the state.

The Importance of Context

Because handicaps are environmental, any society's treatment of persons with disabilities should be understood within the context of the "social environment" and cultural conditions of its own time. For instance, to comprehend the early Greek and Roman treatment of persons with disabilities, one must be aware of other predominant attitudes of their respective periods: the acceptance of poverty, misery, suffering and slavery as part of everyday life; the glorification of strength and beauty resulting in the rejection of infirmity and deformity; and religious practices that blunted sensitivity toward the value of life (Ross, 1978). Early Greek and Roman cultures included a narrow concept of what was physiologically normal or abnormal and a concept clearly evident in their religions and mythologies (Garland, 1995).

Similarly, laws in the American colonies, which today may seem excessively harsh, reflect social conditions in times when settlers focused their energies on the struggle for survival (President's Committee on Employment of the Handicapped, 1976). During the eugenic period of the early part of this century, the eradication of "feeble-mindedness" through sterilization was thought humane and considered an enlightened effort to produce a better society (White, 1993). Thus, every era's approach to persons with disabilities was a product and reflection of its social environment. Teachers must consider such social contexts of the times, not to provide a justification or rationalization for such behavior, but to help provide some understanding for the thinking behind it.

Influencing Factors

As early as 1970, Safilios-Rothschild listed the seven basic factors that influenced the direction and degree of prejudice and discrimination toward persons with disabilities within each society:

1. the degree of a country's socioeconomic development and its rate of unemployment;

2. the prevailing notions about the origins of poverty and unemployment and socio-political beliefs concerning the proper role of the government in alleviating social problems;

3. the prevailing notions about the etiology of illness and the degree of individual responsibility involved in falling ill and remaining disabled;

4. the cultural values or stigmata attached to different physical conditions or characteristics;

5. such disability-connected factors as (a) the visibility of the disability, (b) whether or not the disability is contagious, (c) the part of the body affected, (d) the nature and pervasiveness of the disability (for example, mental or physical), (e) the severity of the functional impairment and (f) the degree of predictability of its course;

6. the effectiveness of the public relations groups representing the interests of a specific disability and the dramatic-sensational image attached to it (for example, muscular dystrophy); and

7. the degree of importance for the nation's welfare, economy, and security os such high-disability-risk undertakings as modern warfare and industrial work (pp. 4-5).

Segregation by Extermination

Primitive Society

Throughout recorded history people with disabilities have been part of our community. Archaeologists constantly uncover evidence of persons with disabilities dating back to the Neanderthal Period (Mackelprang & Salsgiver, 1996). Most primitive societies followed the custom that individuals with disabilities had to be sacrificed for the good of the group (Funk, 1987). Early humans were hunters and foragers. They were also generally frail, living only to their early twenties. Life was hard, dangerous and short. People slept on the cold ground and faced daily starvation, stress, trauma and fear (Scheerenberger, 1983). The harshness of the environment made survival dependent on group coop-eration. With the reality of hunger ever-present, each individual was vital to the band for hunting, gathering and collective defense (Bowe, 1978; Ross, 1979; Scheerenberger, 1983; and Gallagher, 1995). As Morgan (1987) stated, "Children born with physical, sensory, or mental handicaps were definite liabilities to primitive societies. Not only were they unable to contribute to group efforts of providing shelter, or hunt-ing, gathering, and farming food, their requirements for individual care would remove from the work force some able-bodied person needed for those survival tasks (p. 16).

As early humans leading nomadic existences were forced to pursue their prey, they could tolerate no form of weakness and those unable to assume their share of the work or keep up were left behind to die. The elimination of the incapacitated, old, or feeble was not only accepted but also expected. Although such indifference seems callous by today's standards, primitive humans had no alternative. The life of the band, which was of primary importance, had to be ensured. As Morgan (1987) stressed,

> If children were born with conditions so disabling that they required
> life-long care by someone in the group, then those children were seen
> as a liability to the society. Harsh environment conditions of those
> ancient times placed great demands on human beings to be strong and
> fit so that they were able to take care of themselves and contribute to
> the daily living needs of the group. Simple living, in primitive times,
> was laborious and spirit-killing, causing people to behave in ways,
> that by today's standards, would be considered ruthless, and bar-
> barous (p. 16).

For early humans, the severity of the conditions made every phys-ical disability an environmental handicap. Survival of the hardiest was a demanding reality and an individual unable to see, hear or walk pre-sented a threat to the daily existence of the entire band. The severity of the living conditions of the times—the environment—chiefly account-ed for early deaths of those with physical disabilities, not innate cruel-ty (Ross, 1979). Meanwhile, children with disabilities were more vul-nerable to disease and the elements because of their impairments, and they were killed or left to die for this reason (Bowe, 1978). In most cases, those exterminated by infanticide were killed shortly after birth and were disposed of in various ways, including being buried alive or even eaten (Ross, 1979). According to Morgan (1987), "Put into per-spective of the times, these child murders were all considered rather unremarkable events" (p. 17).

Early Civilization
The environment became more accommodating to individuals with disabilities around 12,000 B.C. when humans passed from the age of itinerant hunting to growing crops, reasoning symbolically, communi-cating verbally and living in communities (Scheerenberger, 1983). Although no longer exclusively nomadic with the attendant need to hunt or keep up with the group, people of early civilizations continued to destroy those with severe physical or mental disabilities as a result of superstition and demonology even though they now had the time and ability to care for their disabled friends and relatives.

Primitive society believed in animism—the existence of spirits that incite or perform evil. According to Scheerenberger (1983), the treat-ment of physical and mental disorders were entrusted to the shaman or medicine man, thereby establishing the shamanistic legacy of the med-ical model. A striking difference or a disability was usually perceived as evil, ominous or unlucky, with a strong "demonological conception of a power that controlled behavior" (Ross, 1979, p. 8). According to Charkins (1996), for example, "Throughout the world, there is docu-mentation that children born with facial difference (and often their par-ents, too) were treated with hostility and accused of being evil" (p. 38).

Similarly, the ancient Assyrians assumed that children with dis-abilities or physical differences were omens of evil. Among their recorded beliefs are these four:

1. If a woman gives birth to a "cripple," her house should be destroyed.

2. If a woman gives birth to a boy with six fingers on the left hand, he will vanquish an enemy.

3. If a woman gives birth to a child with two heads, the nation will be torn asunder.

4. If a woman gives birth to twins joined at the spine, the gods will forsake the people and the king must abdicate his throne (Monestier, 1978, p. 13).

Ancient Babylonians practiced customs like fetomancy (prophesying by examining fetuses) and teratoscopy (divination based on examination of "abnormal" births). Another common custom was trephining—cutting holes in the skulls of those with a physical disabilities or epilepsy to allow the evil spirits to escape. According to Thompson (1994) Babylonian fetomancy included the following eight prognostics from "monstrous births":

1. If a woman should give birth to an infant that has the ears of a lion, there will be a powerful king in the land.

2. If a woman should give birth to an infant whose right ear is small, the father's house will be destroyed.

3. If a woman should give birth to an infant that has a bird's beak, the country will be peaceful.

4. If a woman should give birth to an infant that has no mouth, the mistress of the house will die.

5. If a woman should give birth to an infant that has no nostrils, the country will be in affliction and the house of the man will be ruined.

6. If a woman should give birth to an infant that has no right hand, the country will be convulsed by an earthquake.

7. If a woman should give birth to an infant that has six toes on each foot, the people of the world will be injured.

8. If a woman should give birth to an infant whose right foot is absent its father's house will be ruined and there will be abundance in the house of his neighbor.

The Concept of Monster

The term "monster" as currently used, refers to dangerous and repugnant creatures. But "monster" was once the standard medical term for individuals born with a demonstrable physical difference (Bogdan, Biklen, Shapiro and Spelkoman, 1982; Bogdan, 1988). The word "monster" is derived from either *moneo*, to warn, or *monstro*, to show. In either case, the word's Latin etymology strongly suggests that the birth of a child with a physical or mental anomaly was a dreaded omen—a sign of divine wrath and providence that presaged evil (Fiedler, 1978; Monestier, 1978; Bogdan, 1988; Thompson, 1994; and Garland, 1995).

As early as 1573, Paré also described monsters as foreboding evil and noted that, "such marvels often come from the pure will of God, to warn us of the misfortunes with which we are threatened, of some great disorder, and also the ordinary course of Nature seems to be twisted in [producing] such unfortunate offspring" (p. 6). He stated that monsters, marvels and maimed persons, were against Nature:

> Monsters are things that appear outside the course of Nature (and are usually signs of some forthcoming misfortune), such as a child who is born with one arm, another who will have two heads, and additional members over and above the ordinary. Marvels are things which happen that are completely against Nature as when a woman gives birth to a serpent or dog or some other thing that is totally against Nature. Maimed persons include the blind, the one-eyed, the hump-backed, those who limp, or [those] having six digits on the hand or on the feet, or else having less than five, or [having them] fused together; or having arms too short, or the nose too sunken, as do the very flat-nosed; or those who have thick, inverted lips or a closure of the genitals in girls, because of the hymen; or because of a more than natural amount of flesh, or because they are hermaphrodites; or those having spots or warts or wens, or any other thing that is against Nature (in Pallister, trans. 1982, p. 3).

Moreover, teratology, (the study of congenital "defects") comes from the Greek word for monster (Ingstad & Whyte, 1995).

Infanticide

Disabilities, so widely often feared, motivated extreme practices like infanticide. In some extreme cultures, the custom was so severe that the mother was killed along with her "malformed" child (Scheerenberger, 1983). The precise rituals varied. Some, like the ancient Melanesians, buried their disabled children alive. Others, like the ancient Indians, cast their deformed babies into the sacred river Ganges (James, 1975; Van Riper & Emerick, 1984).

Most early Egyptians tolerated physically different children and appear not to have condoned infanticide. In fact, it was later banned by decree (Moores, 1996). Before its prohibition, however, those parents who chose to practice infanticide were forced to hug their dead child continually for three days and three nights to express the appropriate remorse (Scheerenberger, 1983).

The early Egyptians represented one of the most humane societies of the time and were the first to display an interest in both the causes and cures of handicapping conditions as well as the personal and social well-being of individuals with disabilities, especially those with visual impairments. According to Moores (1996), "The priests of Karnak trained the blind in music, the arts and massage. Blind people participated in religious ceremonies and, during some periods, represented a large proportion of the poets and musicians of ancient Egypt" (p. 32).

Customs in Africa varied according to tribe. The South African Kaffir tribe clubbed their sickly or deformed children to death (Van Ripper & Emerick, 1984). The East African Wanika tribe destroyed both deformed infants as well as those believed to be unusually precocious because they were viewed as ominous forecasters of trouble for the tribe. Albinism was considered a severe disability in the Bakongo tribe because it was believed to cause "humpback and rheumatism" (Ross, 1979). The early Mesopotamians viewed diseases and mental disorders as punishment from God or as possession by the devil or evil spirits. Mental and physical diseases were considered "afflictions"— impure, taboo, and the result of sin, a belief still widespread today.

Native Americans in the New World also had rituals that varied by tribe. For example, the beliefs and practices of the Aztec culture were particularly harsh for those with physical impairments. Often believed to possess magic powers, "deformed" individuals were favored for sacrifice by priests who cut out their beating hearts during times of famine to mark the death of a leader (Van Ripper & Emerick, 1984).

Most Native American cultures valued rather than devalued those with physical and mental differences and many Native American tribes venerated those with physical disabilities and blindness. The Zuni, for example, believed that those with severe mental retardation had intimacy with good spirits and often regarded their words and sayings as divine (Ross, 1979). Similarly, among the North American plains tribes, youngsters with deafness were often admired because of their skillful use of sign language (Moores, 1996).

Greek and Roman Attitudes

Both the Greek and Roman cultures sought the perpetuation of physical perfection, beauty and health. According to Edwards (1996), Herodotus (5th century B.C.), the father of history, listed at the top of his criteria for happiness, "freedom from deformity" (p. 30). Thus, the social response to disability and difference was partially determined by religion, with beauty and wholeness favored by the gods and deformity interpreted as divine wrath. For example, persons with facial differences were created by the gods for their own amusement and sent here "to warn, admonish or threaten mankind," (Charkins, 1996, p. 38). In fact, "the birth of a deformed child was interpreted by the Greeks as a punishment inflicted upon its parents by the gods" (Garland, 1995, p. 13). Children with disabilities were often segregated so as to limit severely their chances for survival. Most infants born with physical disabilities were immediately killed by "exposure" or were allowed to die of their conditions shortly after birth. For example, in Sparta, around 800 B.C., "mentally and physically defective children were left on mountain sides or in pits to fend for themselves. Even enlightened Athenians put deaf children to death" (Burgdorf & Burgdorf, 1976, p. 884).

The practice of destroying newborn babies with impairments reportedly had the full approval of Plato and Aristotle (James, 1975; Burgdorf & Burgdorf, 1976). In fact, in *The Republic*, Plato stated that persons with mental retardation or weakness had little place in society. He advised the examiners to inspect newly born offspring to make sure they were not deceived by a "lifeless phantom not worth rearing" (cited in Garland, 1995, p. 15). Plato further wrote, "And those of the worst, and any others born deformed, they will hide away in an unspeakable and unseen place, as is seemly" (Bloom, trans., 1968, p. 139). Plato's plan for the "ideal state" included betterment of the race, improved breeding and exposing "malformed" children as a "rudimentary form of eugenics" (Despart, 1965). Similarly, in his *Politics,* Aristotle wrote, "With regard to the choice between abandoning an infant or rearing it, let there be a law that no crippled child be reared" (Sinclair, trans., 1992, p. 443).

Greece's city-state of Sparta exemplified the philosophy of "rugged individualism" and "a sound mind in a sound body." The laws of Sparta viewed those with disabilities as burdens to be eliminated for the betterment of their militant warlike society. Edwards (1996), however, found that the boundaries of who was considered disabled were not as well-defined as in today's society. A soldier with an impairment—for example, a limp or the loss of an eye or even a more serious condition—but who could still fight or be of service to the military, was not considered disabled. Artemon, a man with a physical disability, served in the role of military advisor and designed siege-engines. He was known by the name of "Periphoretus," which means "Carried-Around" because he could not walk. "Artemon was not considered less than a man because he was on the front lines, in fact, he was a man of ability and high prestige" (p. 30).

In ancient Greece, however, infanticide, not considered at all barbaric, was a legal right invoked by paternal decision. Within the first week of its existence, each infant faced the father's right to terminate its life. But, the same infant was also brought to a place called *Lesche*, before a state council of inspectors (The Committee of Hygiene or The State Health Committee), where it was carefully examined by "triers" or elders of the tribe to which the child belonged. Any child that appeared to be or was suspected of being defective was thrown from a cliff of Mount Taygetus onto the jagged rocks below, or was left to die exposed to the elements (James, 1975; Preen, 1976; and Scheerenberger, 1983). Despart (1965) wrote, "There was no indication that the baby was eased into death through some humane form of euthanasia, and the plain fact is that it was abandoned to be destroyed, probably by wild animals, while 'alive and kicking'" (pp. 45-46).

Although Athenian parents showed more affection for their children than the Spartans, they also practiced infanticide on their weak or deformed children. It was thought to be a necessary social practice. The Athenian child was examined at birth, not by a state committee, but by the father alone (Despert, 1965). Any infanticide decision had to be made shortly after birth. First the father had to perform "The Ceremony of the Hearth," sometimes referred to as the *Amphidromia*. Five days after its birth, the father would take the child in his arms and walk around the hearth, carefully studying the child's physical condition. The significance of the hearth reflected the Athenian belief that it was the altar of the goddess Hestia, who would help a father decide rightly the destiny of his child. But in reality "the Athenians upheld the right of the father to make the final decision" (Preen, 1976, p. 15). If not destroyed before the age of ten days, the infant received the father's name and his protection (Scheerenberger, 1983).

Preen (1976) believed infanticide by exposure was more humane in Athens than Sparta. For Athenians, it often became a heartbreaking family experience entailing almost enough careful planning to ensure the infant's survival rather than its death (p. 11). Each baby was placed in a large earthen jar set by a temple with the hope someone might want it (Scheerenberger, 1983). Such infants were regularly left at well-traveled areas at the most appropriate times of the day, to be rescued by childless couples or other interested parties. A watch was sometimes kept on the child or the place revisited to ascertain the infant's fate (Preen, 1976).

Our appraisal of such harsh treatment as infanticide must take into consideration the beliefs and social environment of the times. Greek religious beliefs emphasized that individuals with disabilities had immortal souls, so that their elimination from this life probably meant a more prompt reincarnation—a pleasant prospect than lives of hardship as disabled and stigmatized individuals. This belief encouraged many parents to accept the custom as a blessing, or "at least the best possible course of action as regards their handicapped children" (Preen, 1976, p. 14).

The treatment of disabled persons in Rome varied over the broad span of the Empire's history, roughly from 800 B.C. to approximately 500 A.D. According to Charkins (1996), the Romans often placated their gods by sacrificing children with facial differences seen as an evil. They often sacrificed the mother as well.

Like the Spartans, the Romans sought to establish a military state dependent on a physically strong population and believed in killing unsuitable children. For example, Seneca the Elder, an influential teacher and theoretician in the early Roman Empire, compared the drowning of deformed children to the "killing of unwanted dogs or unhealthy cattle" (Ross, 1979, p. 9).

Under the principle of *patria potestas* the laws of Rome gave the father extensive authority over the person and property of his family and descendants. Such power included the right to sell, mutilate or even kill his children. Despart (1965) observed, "The father's *patria potestas* was absolute and extended well into the adulthood of the son's and daughter's married lives. He had the right of life and death over his children" (p. 53).

But although the laws were harsh, children with disabilities had some rights. For example, during one Roman period, a child could be exposed only for the first eight days of life (Scheerenberger, 1983). Later, a child was exposed only after it was inspected by male members of five neighboring families who unanimously decided the child was unworthy to live. If the decision was less than unanimous, the father could not expose it at any other time during its life (Preen, 1976).

Meanwhile, Roman emperors had absolute, unrestrained, autocratic power to deform their subjects either as a punishment or just "for the purpose of their own idle amusement" (Garland, 1995, p. 51). For example, Augustus ordered the legs of a slave broken as punishment for accepting a bribe. Hadrian stabbed a slave in the eye in a fit of rage. Perhaps the emperor cruelest to his subjects with disabilities was Commodus (A.D. 161-192), who nicknamed his subjects "one-footed" or "one-eyed" after breaking their legs or gouging out their eyes (Garland, 1995). Under his direct order, those with physical impairments were brought to Rome for his use as moving targets for archery practice (Scheerenberger, 1983). One of his favorite pastimes was to reenact mythical battles by taking physically disabled subjects unable to walk, covering their legs from the knees down "in wraps and bandages to resemble serpents, and then slaying them with arrows" (Garland, 1995, p. 52). Once he sliced an obese subject down the middle to see his intestines splatter. No wonder the people rejoiced when he was choked to death by his wrestling coach by order of the Praetorian Guard!

Later Forms of Extermination
Withhold the hope that extermination of disabled people ended with the Greeks and Romans. During the 13th century, for example, Philip the Fair of France, concerned with the spread of leprosy in his kingdom, made this suggestion for its control: "Let us collect in one place all of the lepers and burn them, and so often as more appear, let us burn them also, until the disease is eradicated" (Haggard, 1932, p. 25). Similarly, this Prussian law of 1230 survives in the literature:

> Be a man laden with sick women, children, sisters, or domestics, or
> be he sick himself, then let them be where they lie, and we praise him
> too if he would burn himself or the feeble person (Despart, 1965, p. 67).

In France, the Edict of 1556 provided severe penalties for infanticide of the newborn, found to be sharply on the increase. Unfortunately, the extermination of persons with disabilities has continued into contemporary times, as witness the "euthanasia" killing program in Nazi Germany and the "summary resolution" killing program in contemporary China which will be discussed in detail later.

Early Religious Attitudes

Early religions traditionally considered congenital disability and differentness as "an example of the capacity of the divine to violate natural law" (Garland, 1995, p. 59). The birth of a disabled or deformed child was treated as retribution against the tribe or parents for angering the gods, and although seen as an innocent victim of its parents' sinfulness, the child served as a reminder of general human evilness. Gallagher (1995), concluded that most people continue to view disability as a moral judgment and punishment since society, in a sense, finds it difficult to tolerate a world where punishment is dispensed "with an even hand" to both the guilty and innocent alike.

Early religions, thus became highly influential in shaping attitudes toward persons with disabilities (Garland, 1995). UNESCO (1995) reported that "religious teachings have provided some of the most negative attitudes towards disabled people" (p. 32). Because of the huge influence the major religions Judaism, Christianity, and Islam have had on the forming of attitudes toward persons with disabilities, they warrant some extended examination.

THE VIEWS OF JUDAISM: A new awareness and compassion of persons with disabilities developed with the coming of Judaism. Although the early Egyptians and Indians initiated the idea of charity by giving alms, it was the early Hebrews who made the practice religious requirement. Trattner (1994) wrote of the ancient Jewish doctrines that taught not only the duty of giving, but also the right of those in need to receive:

> Throughout the Old Testament, the ancient Hebrew collection of historical books, laws, proverbs, psalms, and prophetic writings that go as far back in time as the late eleventh century B.C., one finds commandments to be charitable to the unfortunate—the sick, the old, the handicapped, and the poor. Moreover, such "charity should be given with a friendly countenance, with joy, and with a good heart" (p. 2).

Thus, between 400 and 500 B.C., as the Hebrews began codifying their laws, they explicitly forbade taking advantage of an individual's disability for sadistic, economic or other reasons. As the Torah, for example, specifically stated:

> Thou shalt not curse the deaf, nor put a stumbling block before the blind (Leviticus 14:14).

> Cursed be he that maketh the blind to wander out of the way (Deuteronomy 27:18).

> Ye shall not afflict any widow or fatherless child (Exodus 22:22).

> If there be among you a poor man of one of thy brethren within thy gates in thy land which the Lord thy God giveth thee, thou shalt not harden thine heart, nor shut thine hand from any poor brother: but thou shalt open thine hand wide unto him, and shalt surely lend him sufficient for his need, in that which he wanteth (Deuteronomy 15:7-8).

Baskin and Harris (1977), stressed that "lameness" as a sign of disfavor was a common belief of early people. For example, Mackelprang and Salsgiver (1996) found that the

> Judeo-Christian tradition, prevalent among Europeans during and after the Middle Ages, taught that people with disabilities were expressions of God's displeasure. Disability signified "sinner" to the ancient Hebrews, and people with disabilities were thought to be possessed by evil demons (p. 8).

Although the laws of the early Hebrews displayed sensitivity toward those with disabilities by forbidding their exploitation or humiliation, certain common presuppositions associating one's purity with one's outer appearance nevertheless arose, producing restricted religious and social roles. Such restrictions resemble those imposed by the early Greeks who had a propensity for physical perfection in their religious ceremonies: "Not only did the victims which were offered in sacrifice have to be without blemish, but the priests, too, were required to be physically perfect" (Garland, 1995, p. 64). The Romans, as well, prohibited men with disabilities from the priesthood of their pagan temples, "a practice embraced by the Roman Catholic Church, which continued until recently, to bar disabled men from its priesthood" (Gallagher, 1995, p. 248). Both the ancient Hebrews and early Christians associated physical disability and sin (Safilios-Rothschild, 1970). Disability was believed to be inflicted on those being punished by God.

The Hebrews required their practicing priests (Koheins) to be without blemish. The book of Leviticus specifically lists the physical attributes that disqualify a Kohein from performing the priestly functions:

> Speak to Aaron and say: No man of your offspring throughout the ages who has a defect shall be qualified to offer the food of his God; no man who is blind, or lame, or has a limb too short or too long; no man who has a broken leg or a broken arm; or he who is a hunchback, or a dwarf, or who has a growth in his eye, or who has a boil-scar, or scurvy, or crushed testes. No man among the offspring of Aaron the priest who has a defect shall be qualified to offer the Lord's offerings by fire; having a defect, he shall not be qualified to offer the food of his God (Leviticus 21:17-21).

A commentary by Rabbi Magriso in 1753 analyzed this rule:

> One could take an example from the behavior of men of flesh and blood. If a person wishes to bring a gift to a pasha or any other great leader, he does not send it with a blind man or a cripple. If he did so, the recipient would certainly be angry. It would be considered an insult to send it through a person with a physical defect. This is all the more true when one wishes to send a gift to the King of kings, the Lord of the universe. Certainly one should not send a gift through a "cripple" or maimed agent (trans. Kaplan, 1982, p. 105).

Although a physical disability did not cost a Kohein his priestly status, it did disqualify him from performing his public duties of the priesthood. Koheins with physical disabilities shared the priestly meals and lodging and were even given domestic jobs like deworming the kindling wood in a special area set aside for that purpose (Astor, 1985). But, a blemished priest was forbidden to enter the sanctuary or approach the altar under the penalty of flogging (Kaplan, 1882). Such limitations were based on the belief that the work of the priesthood was sacred and pure and that a noticeable physical difference would distract worshipers during the special prayers and blessings.

Disabilities were often used by the biblical prophets as a symbol of moral imperfection and evidence of a need to pray for a perfected world:

In that day, the deaf shall hear even written words,
And the eyes of the blind shall see even in darkness and obscurity
(Isaiah 29:18).

Then the eyes of the blind shall be opened,
And the ears of the deaf shall be unstopped.
Then the lame shall leap like a deer,
And the tongue of the dumb shout aloud;
For the waters shall burst forth in the desert,
Streams in the wilderness (Isaiah 35: 5-6).

I will bring them in from the northland,
Gather them from the ends of the earth—
The blind and the lame among them (Jeremiah 31:8).

Meanwhile, most early Hebrews viewed madness as retribution afflicted by an angry God. They believed "madness" to be supernaturally inflicted on those who sinned. For example, the first book of Samuel describes the details of King Saul's paranoia. As early as the 7th century B.C., Moses told his people in the book of Deuteronomy (28:15,28) "[I]f you do not obey the Lord your God and do not carefully follow all his commands and decrees. . . the Lord will afflict you with madness, blindness and confusion of the mind" (Bullock & Mahon, 1997, p. 32).

Although the criteria for determining madness was the display of impulsive, uncontrollable behavior, not everyone who displayed such behavior was considered "mad." The behavior of the prophets, for example, was often perceived as strange, peculiar and bizarre. It was written that Ezekiel often clapped his hands, stamped his feet, screamed inarticulately, swung around his sword, experienced trances and visions and once even ate the papyrus scroll containing a written message of grief and mourning he was about to deliver (Conrad & Schneider, 1992). Because of his exalted role of "prophet," his behavior was not considered a form of "deviance" or "mental illness" but one of "prophecy" and "revelation."

> The Hebrew verb to "behave like a prophet" also means to rave or to act like one is beside oneself. Both were attributed to divine intervention and socially ascribed individuals. Although the mad person and the prophet alike engaged in peculiar and extreme behavior, the prophet's was attributed to divine inspiration and the mad person's to

divine retribution. Prophecy was an explanation available to the Hebrews for certain types of extreme behavior and an available social role for some deviants. It is interesting to speculate where the prophets are today, when we no longer attribute hearing voices to God, but to mental illness (Conrad & Schneider, 1992, p. 39).

THE RESPONSE OF EARLY CHRISTIANITY: The preaching of Jesus includes several references to persons with disabilities. He stressed the notion of showing charity, sympathy and pity to those with physical and mental impairments and recognizing them as children of God (Preen, 1976). This view helped establish the image of persons with disabilities as holy innocents and pitiable. Jesus, who preached a way of life based on love and mercy, seemed particularly concerned with the well-being of children (Scheerenberger, 1983). However, Jesus' mission demonstrated concern for far more than just the "spiritual" welfare of disabled individuals. He cured their impairments by miraculous healing, drawing upon their faith to achieve the exorcism of demonic influences (Scheerenberger, 1983). As Mackelprang and Salsgiver (1996) noted, "In the New Testament, people with mental disorders were believed to be possessed. It was thought that people with disabilities had them because of their own or their parents' sins" (p. 8). For instance, Haggard (1932) recalled a disciple's question to the man with blindness brought before Jesus, "Who has sinned, this man or his parents, that he was born blind?" (p. 14). According to Paré, "And Jesus Christ answered them [saying] that neither he nor his father nor his mother sinned, but that it was in order that the works of God might be magnified in him" (Pallister, trans., 1982, p. 4). Thus, the healing acts Jesus performed sometimes served as object lessons to glorify God or to vilify the unbelievers. In this incident described in John 9, the restoration of sight to the man with blindness is contrasted with the so called "blindness of the Jews" during Jesus' time who refused to "see" in him "God's healing purpose for them" (Ken, Hanawalt, Lindberg, Seban & Noll, 1991, p. 66).

In Christianity, the parables are all based on disability as sin and the concept that if you have enough faith you will be cured. Obversely, as a nondisabled person, you are more likely to go to heaven if you are good to a disabled person (the Parable of the Good Samaritan), (UNESCO, 1995, p, 33).

Included among the specific examples of Jesus' cures included in the New Testament are:

- The healing of a "dumb" man (Matthew 9);

- The healing of a "paralyzed" man (Matthew 9);

- The restoration of sight to two "blind" men (Matthew 10);

- The healing of a man with a "withered" hand (Matthew 12);

- The cleansing of a "leper" (Mark 1);

- The cure of an "insane" man (Mark 5);

- The healing of a "deaf" man with a "speech impediment" (Mark 7);

- The mass healing of the sick at Capernaum (Matthew 8);

- The healing of a "lame" man at the Pool of Bethesda (John 5).

Underlying these healing miracles was an assumption that disability symbolized impurity and evidenced a soul to be saved (Bowe, 1978; and Ross, 1979). Scheerenberger (1983) noticed that the healing miracles of Jesus, with evil spirits and the Devil as the antagonists had an enormous influence on future attitudes.

One result of associating spiritual purity and physique is that persons with disabilities become demonic influences and evil spirits themselves, conspiring with the Devil, and therefore, requiring exorcism. The stereotype of disabled persons as "evil sinners afflicted in retribution" derives from such beliefs. As Charkins (1996) wrote,

> In European folklore, children with physical deformities or mental retardation were thought of as the offspring of fairies, elves, or other sub-human beings, or as beings who had been substituted for non-disabled children. In most areas, the child was treated cruelly so that the elves would be coerced into returning the "stolen" child. . . . A later myth was that the devil had performed the exchange as retribution for the sins of the parents (pp. 38-39).

Despite the tenet of Christianity to protect and provide for disabled individuals, religious leaders of the Reformation often promulgated strong convictions about the linkage of sin and disability. Both Luther and Calvin, for instance, considered persons with mental retardation to be essentially evil, possessed and filled with Satan. Luther referred to a twelve-year-old boy with mental retardation as godless and advocated his drowning. He further declared that "cripples," "cretins," and other "deviants" were "miracles," unfit to live, and in fact, he believed that it would please God to see them destroyed because as miracles, they were just a mass of flesh with no soul. He believed that "the Devil sits in such changelings where their soul should have been" (Scheerenberger, 1983, p. 32). Luther believed that such babies had surely been substituted by a diabolical mother of the deformed child and advised that "such disabled children should be severely beaten in the hope that the evil mother would be forced to return with the healthy child" (Gallagher, 1995, p. 249).

According to Monestier (1978), beliefs like Luther's were based on early Christianity's strict notions of good and evil and its interpretation of natural phenomena as attributable to the intervention of either God or Satan. Good and evil were thought to be in constant conflict. Since, according to the Scriptures, God created man in His own image, monsters and "the deformed" had to be creations of the Devil. Similarly, the basic theological attitude toward individuals with mental illness was that such persons were possessed by demons, dangerously inferior, and, therefore, not deserving of Christian charity. Burgdorf and Burgdorf (1976) noted that

[T]he ravings of many persons suggested a sinister background. Such individuals might be "possessed" of a devil, or in communion with Satan himself. Since Christian theology stressed the freedom of human will, it was assumed witches or wizards who had abandoned themselves to these evil contacts had done so of their own consent and were therefore deserving of the most severe punishment (pp. 884-885).

The most common treatments for mental disorders were torture on the rack and death at the stake or gallows (Burgdorf & Burgdorf, 1976). As Monestier (1978) recalled,

[T]he mute baby's tongue had doubtless been wrenched from his head by infernal tongs, so that it would not reveal the secrets of the netherworld, while a deaf child was thought to be receptive only to the mur-

murings of the Beast, and the blind baby's eyes had surely been seared by the red-hot coals of Hell, while the club-footed and the lame were crippled not only physically, but spiritually as well. The hunchback no doubt bore the weight of a horrible curse on his back; could one not detect, when he passed by at night laboring under the weight of his Satanic master, a distinct odor of sulphur which permeated the soul and clothes of passers by? (p. 4).

Another enormous influence Jesus had on attitudes toward persons with disabilities was the creation of the provider-receiver relationship typified by charitable causes today. Early Christian philosophy, based on Judaism, preached sympathy and pity; and as the church assumed the role of provider for the less fortunate by furnishing food, protection and shelter, it awarded itself a position of superiority and control. It based this control on the belief that disability was an indication of impurity and "evidence of a soul that needed to be saved." As Bowe (1978) stated, "The question of whether a man was helped when control of his destiny was removed from his hands appeared little to concern the early Christians in their zeal to perform good works" (p. 7). The same may be said of many of today's charity drives and telethons.

Finally, Astor (1985) concluded that although specific examples can be cited connecting physical imperfections and divine displeasure, "[I]n general the biblical attitude toward the disabled seems to be one of acceptance and protectiveness" (p. 40).

THE TEACHINGS OF ISLAM: Mohammed (569-622 A.D.) composed the Qur'an (Koran) with 114 chapters (Suras) that proclaim one God who is both powerful and merciful. The Koran views infanticide as a sin: "Kill not the old man who can not fight, nor the young children nor the women." It also considers persons with mental retardation and mental illness as God's innocents:

Give not unto those who are weak of understanding the substance which God hath appointed you to preserve for them; but maintain them there out, and clothe them, and speak kindly to them.

Haj (1970) noted that visual impairments are by far the most common type of disability mentioned in the Koran. In fact, it gives special consideration to individuals with blindness because education was based on oral ability thereby making it possible for motivated blind students to succeed, even at universities (cited in Moores, 1996, p. 37). But UNESCO (1995) reported that

> The laws of some Muslim countries inflict physically disabling punishments to fit a particular crime, such as amputation of a hand for stealing, which reinforced the supposed link between punishment and disability (UNESCO, 1995, p. 33).

According to Scheerenberger (1983), Arab culture, in many respects, was reportedly more humane and socially advanced in the treatment of the mentally "deviant" than early western Europe.

EASTERN RELIGIONS: A comparison of the treatment of persons with disabilities in eastern cultures to treatment under the Greeks and Romans reveals a wide variety of differing philosophies. As early as 850 A.D., Japan reserved membership in masseuse guilds for individuals with blindness. But as UNESCO reported,

> The Shinto concept of purity leads to contempt for disabled people. Under this practice, all worldly sources of defilement such as contact with death, sickness, childbirth and menstruation were avoided. Disabled people came to be included in the category of *hin-nin* or "non-people" (UNESCO, 1995, p. 33).

In China, persons with blindness often received special training as fortune tellers (French, 1932). Confucius (551-479 B.C.) taught that fundamental to a just and peaceful world was the decent behavior of the individual. His beliefs were rooted in the concept of a moral sense of responsibility toward others which included kindness, gentleness, and service to those of weak mind (Scheerenberger, 1983). Confucius taught that the "weak minded" had a claim on society which had a responsibility to care for those who could not care for themselves (L'Abate and Curtis, 1975). Family loyalty was an important value and "Everyone calls his son his son, whether he has talents or not." Every individual was regarded as an integral member of the family even if he or she differed mentally or physically (Ross & Freelander, 1977).

Miles (1995), citing the lack of studies available in European languages regarding disabilities in South Asia and China over the past 4,000 years, expressed appreciation for the new translations that are beginning to provide important glimpses of Asian disability history. For example, stories recently translated tell of Confucius's respectful and kind treatment of a music master with blindness; how the princess Gandhari permanently blindfolded herself out of respect for her bridegroom who could not see; and of Buddha's incarnation as a baby prince, who chose deafness, muteness and immobility because he could not condone unethical behavior (Miles, 1995, pp. 27-28).

Buddhism, founded in approximately 400 B.C., taught that all other forms of righteousness "are not worth the sixteenth part of the emancipation of the heart through charity" (Trattner, 1994, p. 1). Buddha taught that love was expressed through helpfulness, charity, and generosity (Scheerenberger, 1983). A result of that philosophy was the early establishment of a ministry, in approximately 200 B.C. by Asoka, a Buddhist monk, for the care and treatment of persons with disabilities which included appointed officials to oversee "charitable works" (Van Riper & Emerick, 1984, p. 19).

Segregation by Ridicule

Another historical role persons with disabilities filled was providing entertainment by inviting mockery and humiliation. Superstition, witchcraft, myths and monsters were part of the common lives of illiterate people and persons with physical differences were seen as living reminders of the elves, giants and goblins who populated medieval myths and horror stories.

Although the real "Era of Ridicule" burgeoned during the Middle Ages, its roots were planted firmly in early Egyptian, Greek and Roman cultures where the role of persons with disabilities as buffoons or jesters began. Aristotle asserted that persons with physical differences were *lusus naturae* or "jokes of nature," which made them appropriate sources of amusement or pets in the households of the wealthy (Fiedler, 1978). As early as 1000 B.C. disabled individuals were used to provide entertainment and amusement. As Van Ripper and Emerick (1984) recounted, "Cages along the Appian way held various grotesque human disabilities, including Balbus Blaesus 'the stutterer,' who would attempt to talk when a coin was flung through the bars" (p. 19).

According to Thompson (1994), "[T]he Romans, especially under the first Emperors, placed dwarfs among the objects of their luxury and ostentation" (p. 187). Among those who owned dwarfs were Augustus, Tiberius and Mark Antony. As Thompson (1994) explained,

These dwarfs in Roman times, who became the pets of emperors and great ladies, commonly went naked, and richly decked with jewels and festooned with hands studded with precious stones (p. 187).

The Spaniards under Cortez, invading Mexico in 1519, entered the city of Tenochtitlan (now Mexico City), where they were shown the Aztec Emperor Montezuma's extensive royal zoo. The Spaniards were amazed to see that alongside the many rare wild animals on display, were persons with dwarfism or albinism, bearded women and other "deformed" humans (Van Ripper & Emerick, 1984). Wolfensberger (1972) noted, "At times (apparently especially at meal time), some of these persons played the role of jesters amusing Montezuma and his court, who might feed them left-overs from his table" (p. 71). Lest one believe that such attitudes were only found in ancient times, however, Garland (1995) noted the case of Ota Benga, an African pygmy, who was exhibited to the public in a cage in the Bronx Zoo in 1906. [His] cage was also occupied by a chimpanzee. The Pygmy's filed teeth were erroneously believed to be a sign of cannibalism (p. xiii).

During the Hellenistic Period, persons with dwarfism were highly prized as pets and often given as gifts. Frequently, they were forced to exhibit themselves at banquets and celebrations naked, adorned only with jewelry. Others provided special entertainment by fighting one another or wild beasts in the arena (Fiedler, 1978). Such entertainment may be likened, in many ways, to the current so-called sports of "dwarf-tossing," and "midget wrestling."

By the second century A.D., persons with mental retardation or physical differences were commonly found in homes of wealthy Romans to provide household entertainment. Garland (1995) noted,

[I]t would almost seem as if no fashionable household was complete without a generous sprinkling of dwarfs, mutes, cretins, eunuchs and hunchbacks, whose principal duty appears to have been to undergo degrading and painful humiliation in order to provide amusement at dinner parties and other festive occasions (p. 46).

The fool or buffoon became a part of entertainment and feasts—making the guests laugh with his so-called "idiocy" or "deformity." "The popularity of statuettes and vase-paintings depicting deformed dwarfs, hunchbacks and obese women strongly suggests that people of this sort were in high demand as singers, dancers, musicians, jugglers and clowns" (Garland, 1995, pp. 32-33). The strong desire to possess such entertainment was described by Tietze-Conrat (1957), who related Plutarch's telling of, "the buyers in the Roman markets passing over the most beautiful slave girls and boys, concerned only with hideous cripples and freaks" (p. 14). In fact, the Romans established a special market where legless and armless humans could be purchased along with giants, dwarfs and hermaphrodites (Durant, 1944). According to Garland (1995), this "monster market" was called "*teraton agora*" and its merchandise was described to include "persons who have no calves, or who are weasel-armed, or who have three eyes, or who are ostrich-headed" (p. 47).

The Middle Ages

The "Era of Ridicule" continued apace during the Middle Ages as small independent kingdoms developed in Europe and the treatment of persons with disabilities changed with the needs of the culture. In general, the inhumane and discriminatory practices of earlier times persisted. Most individuals with physical or mental disabilities found themselves imprisoned or driven from cities into the rural areas to fend for themselves:

> Western society for the most part has refused to treat handicapped persons differently from criminals, drunkards or slaves. Prisons have, in the past, confined hardcore criminals with handicapped persons whose only crime was their inability to support themselves (Burgdorf & Burgdorf, 1976, p. 884).

Also during this period, some individuals with disabilities or with physical or mental "deviances," that were later considered fortunate, were provided security and safety by the nobility in return for being jesters and the objects of ridicule (Kolstoe & Frey, 1965). As Tietze-Conrat (1957) reported, "The idiot was not only prized for his idiocy, but for the bodily abnormalities that accompanied or conditioned his absurdity" (p. 14). In their roles as fools, court dwarfs and other jesters became the playthings of princes and aristocracies. In France they were known as *fous* or *bouffons*, in Germany as *hofnarren* (Fiedler, 1978). Irish court jesters were termed *miclach*, *mer*, and *faindelach*, all denoting not only idiocy but also men who were regarded as "disreputables and in a state of semi-outlawry" (Bullock & Mahon, 1997, p. 32).

During the twelfth century, English kings began to make the care and treatment of "idiots" a matter of royal concern and, therefore, their wards. Charles V of France gave exclusive rights to the province of Champagne to supply his court with fools. Philip IV of Spain gathered persons with retardation into his court where they were well fed and well clothed and had the freedom to do as they pleased.

In 1490, King James IV of Scotland, brought to his court the Scottish Brothers, twins joined in the upper part of the body and having four arms and two legs. The king ordered that the brothers be carefully raised and well educated. Under his patronization and protection, the brothers learned to play musical instruments, sing in harmony (treble and tenor) and read Latin, French, Italian, Spanish, Dutch, Danish and Irish (Thompson, 1968, 1994): Thompson (1994) continued,

> The custom of keeping dwarfs as dependents in noble families survived, and later, in the Middle Ages, they were to be found attached to nearly every Court and the lively dwarf, with his quips and cranks, frequently played the part of the jester. They were given unlimited license of speech, and often became the pets and favorites of their Royal or Court ladies of the time (p. 188).

Among the nobility, the number of dwarfs owned was an important measure of personal wealth. King Sigismund-Augustus of Poland owned nine, Catherine de Medicis owned six (Fiedler, 1978). Cardinal Vitelli had 34 dwarfs, mostly all "deformed," to serve at his banquets in Rome (Tietze-Conrat, 1957; Thompson, 1994). In addition, Charles IX had nine dwarfs, and Catherine de' Medici owned six (three couples) at one time and in 1579 was reported to own five "pygmies" named Merlin, Mandricart, Pelavine, Rodomont and Majowski (Thompson, 1994).

In Russia, dwarfs were also highly valued. During the time of Peter the Great, both dwarfs and giants were much prized throughout Europe as wondrous ornaments in royal and noble households. As in the Greco-Roman period, dwarfs were regarded as lavish gifts, especially when given in pairs and were extremely valued "household pets." An example of such an attitude can be seen in a 1708 letter sent by Russian Prince Menshikov to his wife introducing his gift to her of two female dwarfs:

> I send you a present of two girls, one of whom is very small and can serve as a parrot. She is more talkative than is usual among such little people and can make you gayer than if she were a real parrot (Massie, 1980, p. 617).

Ownership of dwarfs was a high status symbol among the Russian aristocracy and competition among the nobility for their possession was intense. The birth of a dwarf was considered good luck, so certain members of the Russian aristocracy forced their dwarfs to marry with the hope of producing dwarf children to add to their collection (Massie, 1980).

Often, in the role of providing amusement, court dwarfs and other jesters were treated with extreme cruelty, particularly in Russia. Peter the Great, for example, loved to celebrate occasions by using all types of "physically deformed" individuals as entertainment. He had so many "fools" in his court that he had them classified according to the occasions in which they would be displayed (Van Riper & Emerick, 1984). One of Peter's favorite pastimes was to watch his dwarfs pop out of pies into which he was cutting. At a mock wedding held for of one of his tutors, who was then 84, Peter made four persons with severe stammers serve as the official invitors. He chose for the stewards and waiters, old, feeble men unable to walk or stand. In addition, "There were four running footmen, the most unwieldy of fellows, who had been troubled with gout most of their lifetime, and were so fat and bulky they needed others to lead them" (Massie, 1980, p. 619). On another occasion honoring the marriage of his favorite dwarf, Valakoff, to the dwarf of the Princess Prescovie Theodorovna, Peter assembled 72 male and female dwarfs to form the bridal party (Thompson, 1994).

Dmytryshyn (1977) described the way Empress Anne, Peter's niece, treated the dwarfs of her court:

> Sadistic, cruel, haughty, and highly suspicious by temperament, she surrounded herself with dwarfs, cripples, and animals of all kinds. Perhaps the most bizarre of these entertainments was the wedding of two crippled dwarfs, who, to amuse the empress and the court, were ordered to consummate the marriage then and there on a bed made of ice (p. 272).

Hibbert (1975) depicted a similar sadistic account at the dinner table of Pope Leo X:

> The Pope's own dinners were noted for their rare delicacies and for their jocularity, for such surprises as nightingales flying out of pies or little, naked children emerging from puddings. Buffoons and jesters were nearly always to be found at his table where the guests were encouraged to laugh at their antics and the cruel jokes which were played on them—as when, for instance, some half-witted hungry

dwarf was seen guzzling a plate of carrion covered in a strong sauce under the impression that he was being privileged to consume the finest fare (pp. 225-226).

Throughout Europe, cruelty became conspicuous in the selection of court jesters recruited mostly from groups of persons with misshapen bodies or mental retardation (Kanner, 1964). In fact, many jesters were selected because their disabilities included spastic movements, particularly cerebral palsy or epilepsy. Spasms and seizures caused the required bells on their costumes to jingle thereby adding to everyone's amusement and delight.

Fiedler (1978) noted, by contrast, that some court dwarfs worked themselves into positions of great power. Some gained charge over the master's treasury, under the assumption that a dwarf would be easier to find and catch should he attempt to abscond with the funds. In fact, several court dwarfs became quite influential and found themselves in positions of total trust within the court and noble households. Many were known for their wit and cleverness. Once trusted by a king or noble, they often proved capable of moving up from the status of joker to counselor. The Emperor Augustus, for example, always had his court dwarf by his side for consultation on matters of state. In the late Middle ages, Bertholde, a court dwarf known for his cleverness, became the King of Lombardy's prime minister.

Tietze-Conrat (1957) related an incident when a court dwarf at the table of the Emperor Tiberius dared to interpose a remark regarding the Emperor's politics. "The Emperor rebuked his impudence, but acted in accordance with the wishes of the dwarf" (p. 15).

One of the few known Jewish dwarfs, Jacof Ris, became an ex-officio counselor to the Imperial court of The Emperor Charles VI of Vienna. Interestingly, Ris was one of the few known Jews at the time to possess a visible physical difference. As Abrahams (1958) noted,

> The number of Jewish cripples and confirmed invalids cannot have been great, for we occasionally find in medieval records individuals described by such titles as "Moses the Invalid" or "Samuel the Cripple." These epithets would hardly have been distinctive had there been many to whom they would be applicable (p. 310).

Because Church offices were also within the power of the court, dwarfs were often elevated to high ecclesiastical positions as well.

Godeau, an individual with dwarfism, was appointed Archbishop of Grasse in 1672, by Richelieu (Fiedler, 1978).

Creating Deformity

Persons with disabilities without the opportunity to perform as jesters for the nobility would sometimes perform as beggars for the lower classes. The art of begging, highly lucrative and remunerative, often resulted in children being purposefully deformed for the purpose. Youngsters were sometimes locked up in chests to hinder their growth. Hugo related the practice in Spain, whereby young children were purposefully deformed by "muzzling," having their features distorted. They also had their growth stunted, by *comprachicos* or "buyers of children" who then sold their creations to traveling carnivals and collectors of human oddities (Drimmer, 1973).

According to Abrahams (1958), the Talmud alluded to a regular class of early Jewish professional beggars who practiced self-mutilation in order to arouse sympathy, but were regarded with contempt and aversion and disappeared as a class before the Middle Ages. In fact, the practice of deliberately maiming the young for entertainment purposes dates at least to the early Romans who apparently produced stunted children by dietary deprivation which produced rickets (Fiedler, 1978). As Thompson (1994) stated, "The Romans were credited with the knowledge of making children dwarfs by giving them insufficient food when young, but they soon became rachitic and many perished" (p. 186).

During the first century A.D., many unwanted infants in Rome were traditionally placed at the base of the *Columna Lactaria*, where the government provided wet nurses to feed and save them. Many who were adopted were then mutilated to increase their value as beggars. As Morgan (1987) noted,

> Professional beggars frequently took abandoned children and, if not already handicapped, deliberately maimed them so that they could be sent to beg for money, food or other necessities. In this way they could be made useful for some utilitarian purpose; their differences, however, were still something to be despised" (p. 17).

According to James (1975),

> Seneca wrote of the common practice of beggars taking children exposed by their mothers and maiming them so that they would have

shortened limbs, club feet, broken joints, and other grotesque features. The beggars then used the children to gain sympathy—and coins-from the compassionate (p. 28).

Similarly, Garland (1995) related Senaca's horror story of the

vile racketeer who deliberately deformed children and then sent them out to beg in order that he could live off their earnings. The latter's technique included smashing legs, cutting off arms, tearing out tongues and eyes, and beating shoulder blades into a hump (p. 39).

According to Morgan (1987):

Sexual abuse and mutilation of children also has a long history; during the Greek and Roman periods many young boys were kept in bordellos and sold for sexual pleasures. A young, castrated boy could command high prices for sexual favors, so it was not extremely uncommon for some parents to castrate their children and collect large sums of money. This practice was a definite case of children who were made handicapped through abuse (p. 16).

In fact, the mutilation of children for the practice of begging continued for many centuries (Scheerenberger, 1983). Thompson (1994) described how beggars stole children from "good and honest citizens who have charitably relieved them," and then

have broken or dislocated their arms and legs, have cut out their tongues, have depressed their chests or whole breast that with these as their own children begging up and down the country they may get more relief, pitifully complaining that they came by this mischance by thunder or lightning or some other strange accident (pp. 96-97).

The images of such children nourished attitudes of pity and repugnance. Van Ripper and Emerick (1984) also recalled how,

Legs and backs of little children were broken and twisted by their exploiters. Soon the commercialization of pity became so universal that it became a community nuisance. Alms became a conventional gesture to buy relief from the piteous whining that dominated every public place. True pity was lost in revulsion (p. 20).

Scheerenberger (1983) explained that although mutilating exposed slave children to make them objects of charity was a great abuse at the time, it was justified by the philosophers as "better than letting them die" (p. 19).

The practice of producing "human oddities" made to order was not just a Western phenomenon. The practice existed in China as well. Fiedler (1978) described a method used during the nineteenth century:

> Young children are bought or stolen at a tender age and placed in a *Ch'ing*, or vase with a narrow neck, and having in this case a movable bottom. In this receptacle the unfortunate little wretches are kept for years in a sitting posture their heads outside being all the while carefully tended and fed. When the child reached the age of twenty or over, he or she is taken away to some distant place and *discovered* in the woods as a wild man or woman (*China Mail*, May 15, 1878, cited in Fiedler, 1978, p. 50).

Hugo elaborated on this practice in *The Man Who Laughs Last*:

> Chinese dealers who took a small child and put him in a grotesquely shaped porcelain vase without a top or a bottom. At night they laid the vase on its side, so the child could sleep; in the morning they set it upright again. They kept the child in it for years, while his flesh and bones grew according to its shape. Then they smashed the vase. "The child comes out-and, behold there is a man in the shape of a mug!" cited in Drimmer, 1973, p. xi.

Thompson (1994) related how a man from Shanghai begged for charity by

> exposing to view the mutilated stumps of his legs while the feet that belonged to them were slung around his neck. . . . When questioned how he had lost his feet, he admitted that he had performed the amputations himself, starting about a year previously. He had commenced by fastening cords round his ankles, drawing them as tightly as he could bear, and them increased the pressure every two or three days. . . . At the end of six weeks he was able to remove his feet by partly snapping and partly cutting the dry bone, and so successfully feigned the appearance of them having been severed by an accident. The pair of feet are now preserved in the Museum of the Royal College of Surgeons (p. 98).

Of course, not all beggars mutilated themselves or children, but still went to great lengths to create devious methods of getting alms for pity. As Thompson (1994) stated,

> In ancient times the maimed, the halt and the blind frequented the gates of the cities to excite compassion and collect alms from those who passed by, and among them no doubt fraudulent rogues were to be found who, by feigning some deformity, were easily able to make a living (p. 96).

If caught, they usually faced harsh penalties. Paré related the following incident:

> I have a recollection, being in Angers, in 1525, that a wicked scoundrel [and beggar] had cut off a hanged man's arm—already stinking and infected—which he had tied to his vest, letting it lean on a small fork against his side, and he hid his natural arm behind his back, covered with his cloak, so that people would think that the hanged man's arm was his own; and he shouted at the temple [Protestant church?] door so that people should give him alms for Saint Anthony's sake. One Good Friday, the people seeing his rotted arm, gave him alms, thinking it was real. The beggar having wiggled this arm around for a long time, finally it came loose and fell to the ground, where as he was trying to pick it up, he was perceived by some to have two good arms, not counting that of the hanged man; thereupon he was led off as a prisoner, then condemned to get the whip, by order of the magistrate, with the rotted arm hung around his neck, in front of his stomach, and [to be] banished forever from the country (in Pallister, trans. 1982, p. 74).

Feigning a disability to receive charity became a large social problem. Laws like the one passed by the English Parliament in 1531 provided for stiff punishments for able-bodied beggars. Such beggars, when caught, were to be brought to the market place and "there to be tyed to the end of a carte naked and be beten with whyppes throughe out tyll [their bodies] be blody by reason of such whypping" (Trattner, 1994, p. 8). While laws like the 1536 *Act for the Punishment of Sturdy Vagabonds and Beggars* provided for such punishments as branding, enslavement, and executions for repeated offenders, they also ordered public officials to "obtain resources, through voluntary contributions collected in churches, to care for the poor, the lame, the sick and the aged" (Trattner, 1994, p. 9).

Medical Curiosities and Freak Shows
Throughout history, the medical community had a huge influence on how persons with disabilities were treated. During the Middle Ages, physical and mental differences caused interest amid a renewed pursuit in anatomical study leading to the development of surgery and medical care, though extremely primitive and still based on the use of divinity, witchcraft, spells and amulets (Scheerenberger, 1983).

Epilepsy, in particular, received a lot of medical study and the wide range of treatments included,

> the consumption of the brain of a mountain goat drawn through a golden ring;
> the dust of a burnt prickly pig;
> *theriaca magna* (substances, chief of which was the flesh of poisonous snakes), mixed with women's milk with a touch of sugar of rose;
> the gall still warm from a dog who should have been killed the moment the epileptic fell into the fit (Scheerenberger, 1983, pp. 30-31).

Writing of the historical medical cures for stuttering, Bobrick (1995) noted that in the early Christian era, the Roman physician Cornelius Celsus recommended

> gargling with concoctions of pennyroyal, hyssop, and thyme; chewing mustard, garlic, and onions (as stimulants); rubbing the tongue with lazerwort; and (to help relax the articulators) massaging the head, neck, mouth, and chin. As the therapeutic coup de grace, the patient was "to immerse his head in cold water, eat horseradish, and vomit" (p. 52).

As late as 1810, the noted English physician Joseph Frank regarded stuttering "a depraved habit" and recommended as therapy regular beatings. Other documented medical remedies included "ingesting a Finnish insect repellent normally rubbed on cows, bleeding the lips with leeches, and eating the feces of goats!" (Bobrick, 1995, p. 87).

By the late 1800s, persons with physical and mental differences began to be viewed as medical anomalies subject to scientific study and classification rather than as evil omens, the results of witchcraft, or parental punishments for past sins (Bogdan, 1988). Heightened medical interest helped to increase and reinforce the public's curiosity about those perceived to have deviant or deformed physiques helping to develop into a form of ridicule based on fascination and curiosity-the freak show. Bogdan (1988), defined the freak show as,

> the formally organized exhibition for amusement and profit of people with physical, mental or behavioral anomalies, both alleged and real (p. 2).

He further added that between 1840 and 1940 "Freak Shows were an accepted part of American life and were called by variety of terms including: "Sideshow," "Ten in One," "Kid Show," "Pit Show," "Odditorium," "Congress of the Oddities," "Congress of Human Wonders," "Museum of Nature's Mistakes" (pp. 2-3).

> The fact that reputable scientists were interested in such things legitimized the public's interest in curiosities. When physicians and natural scientists visited freaks, as they often did, their comments served to fan widespread interest and debates as to the nature and origin of these creatures. [Moreover] scientists and medical practitioners aided and abetted such displays by visiting, examining, and commenting on exhibits. "Human curiosities" were the specimens for scientist's speculations, and the manner in which they were explained to the public often paralleled scientific theories about human variation (Bogdan, 1986, p. 120; 1988, p. 27).

Bogdan (1988) also explained that the term "freak" is not a quality that belongs to the person on display, but a created perspective, "a set of practices—a social construction" (p. xi). For instance, Clyde Ingalls, manager of the Ringling Brothers sideshow, once reportedly approached an extremely tall man and asked him if he had any interest in becoming a giant (pp. 2-3).

Segregation by Asylum and Institutionalization

Total Institutions
A most successful method used to banish and segregate individuals with mental illness or mental retardation was simply to keep them in dungeons with keepers, instead of protectors, who tended to use extremely

cruel forms of treatment. Although these places were referred to as "schools" or "hospitals," in reality they were "total institutions."

Goffman (1961) defined a total institution as, "[A] place of residence and work where a large number of like-situated individuals, cut off from the wider society for an appreciable period of time, together lead an enclosed and formally administered round of life" (p. xiii). He further explained how such institutional living constitutes an unnatural existence, primarily because it negates the basic social arrangement in modern society of an individual sleeping, playing and working in different places, with different co-participants, under different authorities, and without an overall rational plan. The central characteristic of a total institution can be described as a breakdown of the barriers ordinarily separating these three distinct areas of one's life.

To begin with, in a total institution, all aspects of life are conducted in the same location and under a single control. Next, each activity of an individual's daily life occurs in the company of others, all of whom are treated similarly and are required to do the same thing together. Then, all phases of the individual's daily activities are strictly structured, each leading at a prearranged time into the next. In addition, the entire scope of one's program is imposed from above by a system of explicit formal rulings and a body of officials. Finally, the activities forced upon the residents are infused into a single rational plan purportedly designed to fulfill the official aims of the institution (p. 6). As Trattner (1994) explained,

> The institution itself, rather than inmates' or patients' needs, is the crucial determinant of life within its walls: the administrators' desire to maintain order and insure a smooth daily routine, and to economize on costs, is at odds with the therapeutic goals that supposedly justify operation of the facility, yet the former always takes precedence (p. 63).

Goffman (1961) emphasized that individuals in total institutions are moved in blocks by personnel whose chief responsibility is surveillance. Similarly, Flynn and Nitch (1980) concluded that

> On the whole, people usually live in one place, work or attend school in another, and find their leisure time activities in a variety of settings. It seems, therefore, wrong that a retarded person should have his training, his special therapies and his recreational activities in the same building that serve as home (p. 37).

The principle of normalization suggests that the three sets of experiences—home, work, and leisure—cannot be satisfactorily expressed or experienced in an institutional setting—that is to say, following the same daily routines with the same people. Only through gaining new experiences from various social situations and their accompanying roles can one expand one's horizons and gain self confidence. The people you live with are generally not the people with whom you work or spend most of your leisure time. Therefore, by their very inhibiting nature, institutions force their *patients* or *inmates* to live in an unreal restrictive world.

Early Asylums

As the Renaissance began, the Roman Catholic Church initiated the "Era of Asylum" by accepting persons with disabilities into its segregated monasteries and asylums for protection and care as wards of the church, thereby removing them from society. Disabilities remained hidden, the prevailing attitude being "out of sight—out of mind."

> Mentally retarded and mentally ill persons in need of residential protection were tended in one of a wide variety of institutions—monasteries, hospitals, charitable facilities, prisons, almshouses, pesthouses, workhouses, warehouses, and other buildings most of which lost their original usefulness (Scheerenberger, 1983, p. 34).

These asylums themselves soon became, however, places of horror. Esquirol (1848) described the atrocities he encountered upon inspecting the French asylums of the time:

> I have seen them naked, or covered with rags, and protected only by straw from the cold damp pavement upon which they were lying. I have seen them coarsely fed, deprived of fresh air, or water to quench their thirst, and the most necessary things for life. I have seen them delivered and abandoned to the brutal supervision of veritable jailers. I have seen them in squalid, stinking little hovels, without air or light, chained in caves where wild beasts would not have been confined. These unfortunate beings, like the criminals of the state, are cast into dungeons or into dark cells into which the eye of humanity never penetrates. There they remain to waste away in their own filth under the weight of chains which lacerate their bodies. Their faces are pale and emaciated; they wait only for the moment which will end their misery and conceal our disgrace. They are exhibited to the public gaze by

greedy keepers who make them appear as rare beasts. They are hud-
dled together in a disorderly manner with no known means of maintaining order among them, except terror. Whips, chains and dungeons
are the only means of persuasion employed by the keepers who are as
barbarous as they are ignorant (p. 221).

During the eighteenth century, "insanity" was perceived as "the
absence of reason" with its "purpose of treatment" to "return reason to
the patient." The foundation of such a return to reason was the "purification" and "awakening" of the patient's body which, in practice, took
on "overly cruel and inhuman forms of treatment." Purification often
consisted of "burning and cauterizing to produce the effect of relieving
the body of infection through the newly made open wounds." A resident
physician at the Middlesex Asylum described a form of purification used
in some continental asylums whereby, "[T]he patients were chained in a
well and the water gradually allowed to ascend, in order to terrify the
patient with the prospect of inevitable death" (Arieno, 1989, p. 68).

In addition to those for "purification of the body," there were treatments for the "awakening of the body" which often included the use of
chains and whips. Arieno, (1989) related one method used in 1777 on
patients who were experiencing "convulsions" at a madhouse in
Haarlem:

When an epidemic of convulsions occurred and anti-spasmodics were
unable to alleviate the symptoms, Dr. Boerhaave, the medical director, had stoves filled with burning coals ready to heat hot irons, which
he announced, were ready to burn to the bone the arm of any convul-
sive who refused to return to a reasonable state on his own initiative
(p. 68).

A typical example of the horrors of asylums emerges from the history
of Bethlehem Hospital in London. From the 14th to the 17th centuries,
the average citizen of London amused himself or herself by attending
cockfights, bare knuckle boxing matches, public hangings or shows displaying the "antics of the lunatics" at Bethlehem Hospital, better known
later as "Bedlam." There the keepers exhibited the patients like animals
for an admission price that reached 10 shillings. If the patients happened
to be docile on a particular day, the keepers would beat, prod and agi-
tate them with clubs or sticks to ensure the visitors a good show.
Wolfensberger (1972) stated, "[T]he curious public in the 1700's would

pay their coins to go and stare and laugh at the writhing and screaming of the chained inmates" (p. 71). In 1891, Tiffany described Bedlam's role as a primary form of entertainment in London society:

> Up to so late a date as 1770, this famous hospital was still regarded as the rare show of the city, superior even, in the attractions it offered the pleasure-seeker, to a bull baiting or a dog fight. No more diverting entertainment could be devised by the average citizen for guests visiting him from the country than to take them for a hearty laugh to Bedlam, to see the madmen cursing, raving, and fighting. There was to be had on show St. Paul or Julius Caesar chained to the wall, or Semiramis or Joan of Arc ironed to the floor, while the general throng, left more at liberty, were guarded by brutal keepers, ready on the slightest provocation to knock them senseless with heavy clubs. The annual fees derived from this public entertainment amounted to several hundred pounds. No one seems to have felt any pity for the poor wretches. The abyss which opened between them and ordinary humanity was too deep and wide for any sympathetic imagination to span. A madhouse was a menagerie, nothing more; and it was legitimate to look through the bars at one class of wild beasts as another (cited in Wolfensberger, 1972, p. 71).

Bedlam was founded in 1247, when the sheriff of London gave his estate and land to the Bishop and Church of Bethlehem for the purpose of building a hospital for persons associated with the Order of St. Mary of Bethlehem. It did not accept "lunatics" until 1377, at which time a few patients with mental illness were transferred there from a storehouse thought to be too close to the royal palace (Scheerenberger, 1983). Bethlehem, at first, was not a large institution. In 1403 there were only six mad patients. Toward the end of Elizabeth I's reign, the last years of the 16th century, Bethlehem had about 20 "lunatics" (Metcalf, 1818). An equipment inventory made at Bedlam in 1398, included four pairs of manacles, eleven chains of iron, six locks and keys, and two pairs of stocks (Scheerenberger, 1983). In 1547, King Henry VIII gave the hospital to the City of London as a hospital for "poor lunatics" (Arieno, 1989, pp. 16-17).

The more docile patients were allowed to beg on the streets to help pay for their upkeep at the hospital. At one time, many were given official badges, easily recognizable by the public. Such badges had value because they permitted the wearers to seek alms legally. Before long, a group of rogues and thieves known as "Toms of Bedlam" faked mental illness in order to obtain them. But their numbers grew so large that in 1675, the Governor's of Bedlam were forced to issue a proclamation stating that no patients were to be discharged with a license to beg. In fact, a public fear of unqualified individuals receiving charity is a strong recurring feeling throughout history:

> The concept of the false beggar, tricking innocent people into giving them alms, has been the source of much derision and fear. Many laws have been passed designed to punish such miscreants. For example, a royal decree of 1750 in France specified that infirm beggars be confined to hospitals and nondisabled beggars sentenced to five years at sea in the galleys (Gallagher, 1995, p. 250).

Patients in Bedlam were medically treated by "routing," "bleeding," "vomiting" then "purging." An investigation in 1815 found that the patients were often chained and manacled to the walls. One female patient was chained without release for eight years (Metcalf, 1818). Scull (1979) described the conditions under which a Bedlam inmate named Norris had been kept night and day, for twelve to fourteen years:

> Norris was found to be restrained by a specially constructed piece of apparatus; an iron cage encased his body, from the neck down, and this in turn was attached by a short chain to an iron bar from the floor to the ceiling of the cell. The degree of confinement was such that he could lie only on his back, and could advance no more than twelve inches away from the bar to which he was attached (p. 66).

Metcalf witnessed firsthand, as a patient, the abuses toward Norris and others in Bethlehem Hospital: "Part of the time, I occupied the room next to that occupied by the truly unhappy Norris, whose case is already before the public. The iron bar to which he was fastened stood at the foot of my bed. O what a disgrace!" (p. 78). It is interesting to note that at an official inquiry of Norris' treatment, the Governors conceded that the facts in the case were accurate but, contended that the confinement was kind and merciful rather than cruel and brutal. They even expressed their undiminished confidence in the asylum's medical officers (Scull, 1979, p. 66; Metcalf, 1818, p. 74). Metcalf (1818) also described the filth of Bedlam's basement:

> It is observed that the basement is appropriated for those patients who are not cleanly in their persons, and who, on that account have no

beds, and lie on straw with blankets and a rug; but I am sorry to say, it is too often made a place of punishment, to gratify the unbounded cruelties of the keepers (p. 76).

Yet another typical institution of the time was the York Asylum. Godfrey Higgins, a Yorkshire magistrate, heard of the mistreatment of a pauper he committed there and after paying 20 pounds to become an Asylum Governor, Higgins forced an official investigation into conditions at the institution. As a result, he found

evidence of wrongdoing on a massive scale; maltreatment of patients extending to rape and murder; forging of records to hide deaths among inmates; an extraordinarily widespread use of chains and other forms of mechanical restraint, massive embezzlement of funds; and conditions of utter filth and neglect (cited in Scull, 1979, p. 73).

During his investigation, Higgins discovered a series of cells whose entrance had been deliberately hidden from view. He described them this way:

When the door was opened, I went into the passage, and I found four cells, I think, of about eight feet square in every horrid and filthy situation; the straw appeared to be almost saturated with urine and excrement; there were some bedding laid upon the straw in one cell, in the others only loose straw. A man (a keeper) was in the passage doing something, but what I do not know. The walls were daubed with excrement; the airholes, of which there was one in each cell, were partly filled with it. In one cell there were two pewter chamber-pots, loose. I asked the keeper if these cells were inhabited by patients and was told they were at night. I then desired him to take me upstairs, and shew me the place of the women who came out of those cells in that morning. I then went up stairs, and he shewed me into a room, which I caused him to measure, and the size of which was twelve feet by seven feet ten inches; and in which there were thirteen women, who, he told me, had all come out of those cells that morning. . . . I became very sick, and could not remain any longer in the room. I vomited (*Report of the Select Committee on Madhouses*, 1815).

Early American Attitudes and
the Rise of Almshouses and Institutions

During the American Colonial Period, the British Parliament through a series of laws, authorized the shipping to America of thousands of rogues, convicts, political prisoners, beggars, vagrants, orphans, unemployed laborers and other "undesirable" individuals. Although many did not survive the trip, those who did were sick and infirm, forcing each colony to deal with the problem of caring for "the poor, the aged, the blind, the sick, the lame, the mentally ill, the lazy, and the destitute of all kinds" (Trattner, 1994, pp. 16-17).

The American colonists also brought with them from Europe many extreme religious customs, ideas and attitudes. The prejudices toward persons with physical and mental disabilities which existed in Europe followed settlers to colonial America. As Grob (1994) stated,

> Most individuals who migrated to the New World brought with them the beliefs, traditions, and practices common in England as well as on the continent. . . . Those who settled in America were the heirs of Elizabethan thought, and brought with them the intellectual and cultural perceptions of the homeland. . . the boundaries between magic, religion, medicine, and science were virtually nonexistent" (pp. 8-9).

Scheerenberger (1983), for example, pointed out that in the colonies the birth of a child with a congenital deformity or mental deviation was always suspected of being the devil's work. As a matter of policy, both Governors Braddock and Winthrop of the Massachusetts Bay Colony had the bodies of still-born children examined for evidence of witchcraft (p. 93).

Child rearing similarly was based on rigid religious beliefs, foremost among them was the concept of total submission to the wishes of one's parents. Children classified today as emotionally disturbed or learning disabled would have received little allowance for their handicaps in the colonies. A good example is the following item from the *Plymouth Colony Records* of 1679 cited by Scheerenberger (1983):

> Edward Bumpus for striking and abusing his parents, was whipt at the post: his punishment was alleviated in regard hee was crasey brained, otherwise hee had bine put to death or otherwise sharply punished (p. 93).

In the colonies, the practice of medicine was crude, often based on folklore and astrology. For example, "Madness was a term that conjured up supernatural, religious, astrological, scientific, and medical elements" (Grob, 1994, p. 8). In the absence of physicians, medical decisions were frequently prescribed by religious leaders, barbers, or persons in authority like civil office holders, plantation owners and women. An example of the medical sophistication of the time can be judged by some of cures brought from Europe. For example, individuals with epilepsy were generally treated with:

> the moss from the skull of an unburied dead man who died violently, leeches for blood letting, thirty drops of spirits, the pulverized brains of a young man, the administration of *hellebore* (a toxic form of the buttercup plant), or forced starvation (Scheerenberger, 1983, p. 94).

During the 17th and 18th centuries, the American colonists devoted their energies to surviving, which left little time or desire to administer to the needs of those with disabilities. Community ethics stressed physical stamina, moral worthiness, and material success "as guarantees for a better tomorrow" (The President's Committee on Employment of the Handicapped, 1977, p. 1). Idleness and indolence were viewed as the prime sources of poverty. Because disabilities were seen as chronic medical conditions, persons who had them were consigned to the role of permanent pauper.

The colonists never really questioned the connection between poverty and mental disability (Ferguson, 1994). As Grob (1994) stated, "[C]oncern was focused largely on the nature rather than the treatment of mental disorders" (p. 7). Persons with disabilities, particularly strangers, were simply incapable of becoming independent and self supporting and disability was synonymous with chronic dependency. That common social perception led many colonists with disabilities, themselves, to believe that even attempting to become self-reliant and independent was futile (United States Commission on Civil Rights, 1983). As Ferguson (1994) observed, "For the disabled population, poor or not, there was often little optimism about improving their condition" (p. 28). Funk (1987) related how such a view of persons with disabilities resulted in discriminatory social policies and practices that, in turn, affected all disabled people in practically every aspect of their lives:

> Thus, a societal attitude developed that this class of person, viewed as unhealthy, defective, and deviant, required special institutions, services, care, and attention in order to survive. This social construct has been supported by national welfare policies to care for the deserving poor, charitable programs to help the unfortunate, the continued

application of the medical model to disability, and rehabilitation services provided in a manner that undermines self-initiative and self-respect and perpetuates stereotypical education and employment avenues. This has resulted in discriminatory programs, policies, and laws designed to deny disabled people's participation in organized society (p. 9).

Although acceptance and survival were difficult for many American colonists with disabilities, some nevertheless broke the stereotype and proved they were more than helpless dependents to be labeled and cared for by society. Peter Stuyvesant, for example, the last Dutch director-general of New Amsterdam, governed until 1664 without being handicapped by the loss of his leg, a war injury he acquired while fighting the Portuguese in the West Indies. Also, not handicapped by a leg amputation was Gouverneur Morris, who wore a "rough stick" which he called his "handsome leg" (President's Committee on Employment of the Handicapped, 1977). One individual with an impairment gained an unusual place in American history. John Coode, a famous "malcontent," reportedly took part in five major movements against authority. One such action appears in history books as "Coode's Rebellion" (President's Committee on Employment of the Handicapped, 1977). Jordan (1975) noted that Coode's "unusual appearance helped shape his rebellious personalty" (p. 2). He was described in the 1689 proclamation for his arrest as "deformed and club-footed with a face resembling that of a baboon or monkey" (cited in The President's Committee on Employment of the Handicapped, 1977, p. 12).

Although some colonists with disabilities managed to overcome handicaps engendered by a harsh environment and society, they formed a minuscule minority. For the most part, limitations of intelligence and physical ability became stigmatic and degrading. "Feeblemindedness," "lameness," and "insanity" began to epitomize an inability to function in society and "compete for the good things in life." Successful and flourishing colonists came to believe that one's lack of success in a land of such abundance could be attributable only to one's unworthiness. Although given preferential treatment in the distribution of relief, persons with disabilities remained stigmatized as inadequate (Presidents Committee On Employment of the Handicapped, 1977, p. 18).

According to Ferguson (1994), the major concern within the colonies focused more on dependency than disability. "Insanity," for example, was above all a problem involving the individual's dependency on his or her family. As Grob, 1994, explained, "Throughout the seventeenth and eighteenth centuries, most cases involving the 'insane' were not initiated over behavior, but out of the inability of the distracted individuals to support themselves" (p. 6):

> Whether it was because you could not walk or talk, or were old or orphaned, widowed or homeless, the etiology of your indigence was seldom an urgent question. What mattered to the community was, first, whether you were a resident or not; second, who would care for you; and third, how the provisions for care were to be handled (Ferguson, 1994, p. 24).

During the colonial period, persons with mental illness (referred to as "lunatics" or "distracted persons") were seen to cause social and economic rather than medical problems. "Insanity" had not yet come under medical jurisdiction:

> The care of the insane remained a family responsibility; so long as its members could provide the basic necessities of life for afflicted relatives, no other arrangements were required (Grob, 1994, p. 6).

Bowe (1978) wrote of the time when the idea of education and rehabilitation for disabled persons was largely unknown. In fact, as Grob (1994) stressed, essentially none of the early legislation addressed the medical treatment of the insane but rather focused "strictly upon the social and economic consequences of mental disorders" (p. 7). Unfortunately, the existence of a disability "became reason enough to deny a person the opportunity to participate in community life" (Bowe, p. 8).

For colonists with disabilities, "the family was the first line of relief" (Ferguson, 1994, p. 25). Mental illness (lunacy), for example, was "perceived to be an individual problem, to be handled by the family of the disordered person and not by the state" (Grob, 1994, p. 5). It was the custom of colonial families with means to care for their own members with disabilities—often out of concern for the preservation of the individual's property rights. But for the most part, treatment at the time was unsympathetic, oppressive, and achieved mostly through humiliation, banishment or confinement. "[S]ome communities forced the town paupers to wear brightly colored badges on their shirts, emblazoned with the letter 'P'" (Ferguson, 1994, p. 25).

Perhaps the starkest examples of persons with disabilities being treated as useless burdens occurred in the slave trade where the only criterion for survival was the ability to work. During the 18th century, for example, a Dutch slave trader wrote of branding slaves aboard his ship after throwing overboard "The Invalides and Maimed" (McPherson, 1995).

Since disability and dependency were closely related, the care of persons with impairments remained a family responsibility, so long as family members could provide the basic necessities for life. If, however, the effects of the disability spilled outside the family, care of the individual fell under the jurisdiction of the local community, which, in turn, was required to assist the individual or his or her family.

Laws and codes were, however, gradually enacted regarding the care and treatment of persons with physical and mental disabilities. The first such law enacted by the Massachusetts legislature in 1614 contained several references to "Children, Idiots, Distracted persons and all that are strangers or newcomers to our plantation" (cited in Grobe, 1994, p. 7). Thus the colonies began to enact "Poor Laws" and "Ugly Laws" patterned after those in England, as well as accompanying "Settlement Laws," which required an individual to live and work for a period of three months to one year before legal residence could be established. Determining the residency of a pauper was important because residency created a responsibility for his or her care. A stranger who could not support himself or herself was banished, unless a resident of good financial standing assumed responsibility for his or her custody, guardianship, and supervision (Bowe, 1976; Rothman, 1990; Trattner, 1994). Every colony was concerned about needy strangers and tied their poor laws to settlement requirements. As Rothman (1990), wrote,

> The statutes established qualifications for residence and instructed municipalities on enforcement procedures. The succession of laws in New York, for example, exemplified both the concern and results of the legislative actions. The first province-wide code of 1683, "An Act for Maintaining the Poor and Preventing Vagabonds," announced in its very title the goals for the next hundred years of poor-law legislation: to relieve the needy resident while cutting off and excluding the dependent outsider (p. 20).

The southern colonies adopted similar laws. For example, in 1741 the Delaware Assembly passed "An Act for the Relief of the Poor" with the stated dual purposes of providing for "the better relief of the poor, [and] the prevention of straggling and indigent persons from coming into and being chargeable to the inhabitants" (cited in Rothman, 1990, p. 24).

Disabled colonists without families or those whose families could not or would not support them were "placed out" or "farmed out" to other families who received public assistance for providing them with room, board, shelter and care. Many times, the agreement included indentured service akin to slavery. In fact, many communities "auctioned off" those with physical or mental disabilities to whomever made the lowest bid, and was then free to demand manual labor services from the persons bought during their period of retention, support, room and board (Obermann, 1965; Baumeister, 1970; Funk, 1987, Trattnor, 1994). This auctioning system lasted until the latter half of the 19th century when public outrage over scandalized abuses led to reform. Among the recorded instances were those where "care providers collected their fees and then locked their charges in the attic to starve or freeze to death" (United States Commission on Civil Rights, 1983, p. 18).

Persons with mental and physical disabilities who were new to the community and not perceived as a threat to public safety were often afforded the opportunity to work. Colonial newcomers with disabilities, not seen as dangerous, but having the potential of becoming public charges, were treated as minor criminals and often "warned out" of their communities. "Warning out" was a practice

> based on the proposition that towns had the right to exclude strangers.
> Legal residency during the colonial period was not an inherent right,
> but rather a privilege granted by existing residents. The distrust of
> strangers reflected both the relative absence of formal mechanisms of
> control to deal with behavior that might menace public order and a
> desire to absolve towns of any financial liability for the support of ill
> or unemployed strangers. Hence it was not uncommon for local
> officials to force the return of insane persons to the community in
> which they were legal residents (Grob, 1994, p. 16).

Strangers with disabilities were told that the town would not be responsible for their misfortunes, neither then nor in the future (Scheerenberger, 1983). The New York Assembly when tightening its regulations in 1721, stated that "several idle and necessitous come, or are brought into this province from neighboring colonies who have either fled from thence for fear of punishment for their crimes, or being slothful and unwilling to work'" (cited in Rothman, 1990, p. 21). Under the New York law, those transported out who did return faced corporal punishment like the one imposed by the New York law prescribing "36 lashes on the bare back of a man and 25 for a woman" (Burgdorf & Burgdorf, 1976, p. 885; Rothman, 1990, p. 21).

Similarly, in Rhode Island, a statute of 1727 was written "Enabling the Town Council to receive or reject any persons from becoming inhabitants" [and preventing] "diverse vagrant and indigent persons" from entering its towns and being sheltered by negligent residents (Rothman, 1990, p. 23).

Officials of Boston, the largest town in New England, often had to return "insane," "crippled" and "feebleminded" individuals to the communities in which they were thought to be legal residents. Sometimes they were returned with a warning to their home town:

> When sending Edward XI to Ipswich, the Boston selectmen noted that he was "disposed to wander" and requested Ipswich officials to "take care to prevent his returning to us, which if he should will occasion a charge to your Town (cited in Grob, 1994, p. 16).

In addition to warning out, many colonial communities resolved their disabled problem by "passing on." This practice consisted of kidnapping their own "feebleminded" and "insane" inhabitants at night and leaving them on the outskirts of strange, far away towns, with the hope that their inability to communicate would effectively preclude their return (Burgdorf & Burgdorf, 1976). Klebaner (1976) reported that "Onondaga County in upstate New York commonly smuggled paupers into a neighboring county in a conspiracy between justices of the peace and overseers of the poor" (cited in Ferguson, 1994, p. 27).

The colonial period had few systematic approaches to dealing with mentally retarded (feebleminded) or mentally ill (insane) citizens, particularly those perceived as being medically incurable, economically useless, morally intractable, or aesthetically offensive (Ferguson, 1994, p. 21). Care and treatment was largely up to local officials, who then decided the most convenient way to control them. Colonists with disabilities considered able to work were sent to workhouses or almshouses where they could be rehabilitated into hardworking, useful citizens. In addition to the almshouses (as provided for in European poor laws), residential facilities also included jails and insane asylums (Baumeister, 1970; Crissey, 1986; Rothman, 1990; Ferguson, 1994).

The choice of residential placement usually depended on how the individual with the disability became known to the colonial authorities. For instance, when people with mental retardation or mental illness came to the attention of the government simply as public charges, they were sent to almshouses; if they exhibited behavior identifiable as disturbed, they were sent to hospitals for the insane; and if caught breaking the law, they were sent to prison (Crissey, 1986).

In time, a level of specialization occurred with the establishment of institutions for specific categories of disability (Funk, 1987). Residential programs for persons with blindness, deafness and insanity were established in America long before those for persons with feeblemindedness (Baumeister, 1970; United States Commission on Civil Rights, 1983). The Massachusetts Asylum for the Blind (later the Perkins Institute) has been serving residents since 1832. The American Asylum for the Deaf was established in Hartford, Connecticut, by Thomas Gallaudet as early as 1817, followed by the New York Institution for the Deaf and Dumb in 1818. Public programs for deaf individuals followed in Kentucky (1823), Ohio (1829), Virginia (1838), Indiana (1844), Tennessee (1845), Georgia (1846), and California (1864). Three years later Gallaudet College was founded in Washington, D.C. and is still regarded as a model for "deaf" higher education (J. Shapiro, 1993; United States Commission on Civil Rights, 1983).

As early as 1773, the Eastern State Hospital at Williamsburg, Virginia undertook the treatment of the mentally ill. But, the first institution solely for the mentally ill and mentally retarded began in 1766 when Governor Fauquier of the Virginia Colony suggested that, "a legal Confinement and proper Provision ought to be appointed for these miserable Objects who can not help themselves" (Scheerenberger, 1983, p. 95). However, according to Scheerenberger (1983), it was not until 1769 that the legislature finally passed an act providing for the "Support and Maintenance of Idiots, Lunatics, and other persons of unsound minds" (p. 95).

As Ferguson (1994) emphasized, "The institutionalization of mentally retarded people in America began with the almshouses in the eighteenth and early nineteenth centuries, not with the first idiot asylums of the 1850's and 1860's" (p. 24). The first almshouse was built in Boston in 1660 and the first workhouse and first poorhouse in Philadelphia in 1771 and 1773 respectively (Scheerenberger, 1983; Rothman, 1990; Grob, 1994). By 1830, almost every state encouraged and or mandated an almshouse to shelter the poor, sick, or insane, resulting in a rapid growth of the system. In Massachusetts alone, the number grew from 83 almshouses in 1834, to 180 only fifteen years later (Rothman, 1990; Trattner, 1994). By the time the Civil War ended, four out of five persons receiving extended relief in Massachusetts lived in an institution. Similar growth in institutional care occurred throughout the country (President's Committee on Employment of the Handicapped, 1977, pp. 19-20).

The colonists brought with them from England and Holland the idea of storing almost all of their unwanted in almshouses and poorhouses, a practice dating back to the tenth century and perhaps even earlier (James, 1975). For example the first house of corrections established in Connecticut in 1727 included,

> all rogues, vagabonds and idle persons going about in town or country begging, runaways, common drunkards, common nightwalkers, pilferers, wanton and lascivious persons, common railers and brawlers [and] persons under distraction and unfit to go at large, whose friends do not take care for their safe confinement (Scheerenberger, 1983, p. 95).

Unfortunately, more often than not, persons with disabilities were confined with juvenile delinquents, prostitutes, and elderly and poor people. Generally, the poor, the sick, the feeble-minded, and the insane were all grouped together under the stigmatizing label of "pauper" (James, 1975; Scheerenberger, 1983, Trattner, 1994). As early as 1729, officials in Boston sought authorization for a separate facility to keep "Distracted Persons Separate from the Poor." It never happened. In 1764, Thomas Hancock, a wealthy Bostonian and the uncle of John, bequested £600 for the establishment of a facility exclusively for insane persons. The bequest, which included a three year limit and a requirement that the town raise supplementary funds, was never used for the purpose. In fact, the establishment of a separate facility exclusively for persons with mental illness would not be reality for more than half a century (Grob, 1994).

Ferguson (1994) observed, "The almshouse started an American tradition of formalized custodialism in its more vicious forms that tied economic failure and social deviance to moral categories and individual inadequacy" (p. 24). Although special care institutions and poor farms appeared to be a step up from total indifference to some recognition for minimum care, residential placement in them usually resulted in physical and mental abuse and torture. "The institutions charged with custodial care became known more for the horrors they committed against the inmates than for the extent of care" (Funk, 1987, p. 9).

Rothman (1990), compared the almshouse to its sister institutions the penitentiary and the mental hospital:

> The almshouse-workhouse, like the other institutions, tried to impose a regularity on inmates' lives to counteract the influences promoting and perpetuating idleness and vice. Unlike wardens and medical supervisors, however, almshouse managers were not very consistent. The routine of the almshouse lacked the quasi-military tone of the penitentiary or the less coercive but still regulatory quality of the insane asylum. It crossed the two, but not very effectively. Like mental hospitals it eschewed the lockstep, armed guards, and striped uniforms; but like the prison it established strict punishments for anyone violating the rules and was not at all loath to enforce obedience through physical coercion. [The almshouse managers] referred to their charges as inmates—a term midway between patient and prisoner—who lived in cells, not rooms. But attendants, not guards, supervised them (pp. 192-193).

Similarly, Trattner (1994) stated,

> While for the most part the public accepted its responsibility for erecting such institutions, oftentimes little or no regard was paid to the type of care provided within their walls. Into many were herded the old and the young, the sick and the well, the sane and the insane, the epileptic and the feebleminded, the blind and the alcoholic, the juvenile delinquent and the hardened criminal, male and female, all thrown together in haphazard fashion. Nakedness and filth, hunger and vice, and other abuses such as beatings by cruel keepers were not uncommon in many of those wretched places, vile catchalls for everyone in need, defined by one contemporary as "living tombs" and another as "social cemeteries" (pp. 61-62).

Most almshouses were filthy, unsanitary, and overcrowded by any standard. Persons with mental retardation were frequently found in tiny unheated cells and maintained like "dogs in a kennel" (Obermann, 1965). Ferguson (1994) especially wrote of the notorious *crazy cellars* or dungeons which "held these poor souls: naked, chained, without heat or light" (p. 21).

Because of the common belief that the insane were oblivious of their physical environment, persons with mental illness were frequently abused in almshouses. A common form of mistreatment was forcing them to stand naked outside in the winter snow for long periods (Burgdorf & Burgdorf, 1976, p. 885). Apparently, it was not much warmer inside. For example, a dilapidated building housing 65 inmates at the Clinton County House in upstate New York, was described as having no ventilation system "and so many cracks and crevices in the walls that in the winter snow blowing through the crevices [formed] banks" (Report of Select Committee, 1857, cited in Ferguson, 1994, p. 37). Other conditions found in almshouses described by The Senate Report included the forcing of inmates to eat without knives or forks; providing a diet solely of pea and bran soup, Indian pudding, and sweetened water; restraining inmates by ball and chains; chaining inmates to the floor; and severe whippings. Specifically, the Select Committee (1857) stated,

> The treatment of lunatics and idiots in these houses is frequently abusive. The cells and sheds where they are confined are wretched abodes, often wholly unprovided with bedding. In most cases, female lunatics had none but male attendants. Instances were testified to of the whipping of male and female idiots and lunatics, and of confining the latter in loathsome cells, and binding them with chains. . . . In some poor houses, the committee found lunatics, both male and female, in cells, in a state of nudity. The cells were intolerably offensive, littered with the long accumulated filth of the occupants, and with straw reduced to chaff by long use as bedding, portions of which, mingled with the filth, adhered to the persons of the inmates and formed the only covering they had (cited in Ferguson, 1994, p. 36).

Concern over the appalling conditions found in the almshouse system aroused reformers like Dorothea Dix and Samuel Gridley Howe to crusade for state supervision of institutionalized facilities and for the establishment of state institutions that would provide specialization of care (United States Commission on Civil Rights, 1983). While teaching a Sunday school program in the East Cambridge House of Corrections, Dix found conditions there abominable—for example, insane women kept in unheated rooms. This discovery inspired her to visit, for the next two years, almshouses, jails, and houses of correction throughout Massachusetts, "recording lengthy lists of observations and grievances in her ever-handy notebook" (Scheerenberger, 1983, p. 105). Dix confronted many of what she called "helpless, forgotten, insane and idiotic men and women rotting in jails or almshouses" (cited in the President's Committee on Employment of the Handicapped, p. 20). She observed first hand, individuals with mental illness and mental retardation in cages, closets, cellars, stalls and pens. She also saw them chained, naked, beaten with rods, and lashed into obedience (cited in J. Shapiro, 1993, p. 59). She described, with eloquence, the squalid accommodations she observed for "a gibbering idiot, or cowering imbecile, or perhaps a murmuring half demented creature" (Dix, 1844, cited in Ferguson, 1994, p. 22).

Although normally quiet and dignified, Dorothea Dix argued her case to state and federal legislators with great passion and zeal:

> In the province of God, I am the voice of the maniac whose piercing cries from the dreary dungeons of your jails penetrate not your Halls of Legislation. I am the Hope of the poor crazed beings who pine in the cells, and stalls, and cages, and waste rooms of your poor houses. I am the Revelation of hundreds of wailing, suffering creatures, hidden in your private dwellings and in pens and cabins—shut off, cut off from all healing influences, from all mind-restoring cares (cited in Scheerenberger, 1983, p. 107).

Dix agitated for State supervision of institutional facilities as well as for specialized care—for example—mental hospitals that serve patients with mental illness, epilepsy and mental retardation. Her enormous influence, based on her dynamic appeals, excellent documentation and "vignettes of horror," resulted in a growth of state mental hospitals and the improvement of existing ones over the next forty years (Burgdorf & Burgdorf, 1976; President's Committee on the Employment of the Handicapped, 1977; United States Commission on Civil Rights, 1983; Scheerenberger, 1983; J. Shapiro, 1993; Ferguson, 1994).

Responding to the influence of reformers like Dix, State Legislative Committees began to attack the almshouse relief system as inefficient, wasteful, and ineffective. They began pressing for a shift of public programs for poor and disabled people to those providing more structure and organization with indoor institutional care. In 1846, Massachusetts enacted the first legislation providing for a public facility for persons with feeblemindedness. The bill required the governor to appoint a commission "to inquire into the condition of the idiots on the commonwealth [and] to ascertain their number and whether anything could be done for their relief" (Baumeister, 1970, p. 5). Dr. Samuel Gridley Howe, director of the Perkins Institute and Massachusetts School for Blind was appointed head of the commission. Howe, who supported Dix in her crusade, argued for the rights of various groups including persons with blindness, persons with deafness, persons with mental retardation, slaves, and the politically persecuted in several nations of Europe (President's Committee on Employment of the Handicapped, 1977).

Like Dix, Howe, too, was an interesting historical figure. Although he came from a wealthy family, he championed causes of those who had no privilege, including slaves. While attending a private school for youngsters of wealthy businessmen, he so irritated the other students with his "liberal" attitudes and remarks, that he was physically thrown down a flight of stairs. He was frequently disciplined in school for his mischievous behavior, and on one occasion was suspended for leading the president's horse up to the fourth floor of the school (Scheerenberger, 1983, p. 102). In spite of his conduct, Howe graduated and entered the Harvard Medical School in 1821. According to Scheerenberger (1983), Howe and his fellow students would occasionally resort to grave robbing to procure a cadaver (p. 102).

Upon his graduation from Harvard Medical School in 1824, Howe volunteered for six years as a surgeon in the Greek revolt against the Turks (Kanner, 1964; President's Committee on Employment on the Handicapped, 1977; Scheerenberger, 1983). When he returned to Boston in 1831, a colleague, Dr. John Fisher, asked him to help finalize plans for an asylum for blind individuals and to assume the role of its first administrator. Howe agreed with the stipulation that he be allowed to tour Europe visiting schools for blind individuals in order to observe the latest methods of teaching such youngsters (Kanner, 1964; Scheerenberger, 1983).

While in Europe, Howe was temporarily diverted from his mission when asked by Lafayette to carry relief funds to the Polish refugees across the Prussian frontier. When Howe publicly complained about their situation, he was captured and placed into the solitary confinement unit of a Berlin prison. After his release, five weeks later, he continued on his tour and returned home determined to apply the new ideas and teaching methods he had learned.

Many of the new concepts he wanted to implement challenged the traditional belief that blindness was a permanently disabling "affliction" that routinely precluded learning, independent living, and self-sufficiency. Unfortunately, at that time, individuals with blindness automatically became charity cases, being attended to by their families or receiving some form of public relief. The almshouses in America provided shelter to many blind children and adults, but those who ran them had little awareness that anything could be done to better the lot of those visually impaired (President's Committee on Employment on the Handicapped, 1977, p. 23).

Colonel Thomas H. Perkins was so impressed with Howe's work, that he offered his own estate and gardens as a permanent facility for the school if Howe could raise fifty thousand dollars as its base support. Howe raised the money, then transferred the program to the Perkins Estate. The school was officially named the Perkins Institute and Massachusetts School for the Blind. Howe became its first director, a post he held for 44 years until his death (Kanner, 1964; President's Committee on Employment of the Handicapped, 1977; Scheerenberger, 1983). Howe based the school on five premises:

1. The blind child must be treated as an individual and trained according to personal ability and job opportunities in the community;

2. The curriculum should correspond to that of the common schools except for providing more music and crafts;

3. Blind youths were to be educated to participate in the economic and social life of their home communities (President's Committee on the Employment of the Handicapped);

4. The school's sole concern be with education during the best learning years;

5. The school's primary goal is to return its students to their families (President's Committee on Mental Retardation, 1977, p. 4).

In 1839, Howe had success in educating a "blind idiot," whom he accepted into the school. His later further success with two more students with similar impairments, combined with his genuine concern for mentally retarded people, encouraged him to recommend that a specialized facility for their training be established (Scheerenberger, 1983, p. 103). He reasoned that, if so much could be done for idiots who are blind, still more could be done for "idiots who were not blind" (cited in Kanner, 1964, p. 43).

Thus, in 1848 the commission headed by Howe submitted its report to the Massachusetts Legislature, which was extremely impressed with both its thoroughness and its "eloquent appeal for compassion, understanding and action" (Baumeister, 1970, p. 6). Said the report,

> The benefits to be derived from the establishment of a school for this class of persons, upon humane and scientific principles would be very great. Not only would all the idiots who should be received into it be improved in their bodily and mental condition, but all the others in the State and the country would be indirectly benefited. The school, if conducted by persons of skill and ability, would be a model for others. Valuable information would be disseminated through the country; it would be demonstrated that no idiot need be confined or restrained by force; that the young can be trained for industry, order, and self-respect; that they can be redeemed from odious and filthy habits, and there is not one of any age who may not be made more of a man and less of a brute by patience and kindness directed by energy and skill (cited in Scheerenberger, 1983, pp. 103-104).

Howe's commission specifically challenged the state of Massachusetts:

> Will she longer neglect the poor idiots—the most wretched of all who are born to her—those who are usually abandoned by their fellows—who can never, of themselves, step upon the platform of humanity—will she leave them to their dreadful fate, to a life of brutishness, without an effort on their behalf?(cited in Baumeister, 1970, p. 6).

Though skeptical, the Massachusetts legislature provided twenty-five hundred dollars per annum to establish an experimental school for the feebleminded.

Thus, on October 1, 1848, the first permanent institution in the United States was opened for ten feebleminded children placed together in a wing of Perkins Institute under the responsibility of James J. Richards, a teacher later known for his pioneering work in Pennsylvania (Kanner, 1964; Baumeister, 1970). Three years later, having been declared a huge success, the school was incorporated by the state and officially named the Massachusetts' School for Idiotic and Feebleminded Youth. Now located in Waltham it is called the Fernald State School, after one its most influential superintendents (Kanner,

1964; Baumeister, 1970; President's Committee on the Employment of the Handicapped, 1977).

The successful efforts of Dix, Howe, and others, resulted in the proliferation of residential institutions for mentally retarded individuals throughout the United States. It is important to remember, however, that the founders of these early institutions saw as the primary goal of their education and treatment programs, the ultimate return of persons with mental retardation to their own homes and communities (United States Commission on Civil Rights, 1983, p. 19).

In a sense, mental retardation came to be perceived as a simple lag in the development of intelligence. It was believed that with proper perseverance, persistence, and skill, such minds might be trained. Howe fought to have each new institution considered a school with education its primary function, rather than as an asylum, with implications of custody being primary. A basic belief urged upon the public with these new institutions were schools with the same responsibilities as other schools in the community and a place within part of the common school system (Baumeister, 1970). To enhance their success, these first institutions accepted very few students and only those who offered a reasonable prognosis for achievement. Howe, for example, excluded youngsters with hydrocephaly, epilepsy or mental illness (Baumeister, 1970).

Although these early institutions achieved some success, they began to be replaced, between 1870 and 1890, by larger facilities whose primary aim was protecting persons with disabilities from society. These institutions viewed themselves as "benevolent shelters." The result was the development of many large institutions housing great numbers of disabled people far from population centers, and unfortunately, they provided no training that might enable their residents to return home. It became obvious that in many early hospitals for the "insane," the function of custody took precedence over therapy, and many were perceived as well-kept prisons (Grob, 1994). Some residents were taught some basic skills like farming and gardening but only to help defray institutional costs (United States Commission on Civil Rights, 1983, p. 19).

Unfortunately too, as these custodial institutions began to grow, they often became "places of abuse, isolation, and segregation" (J. Shapiro, 1993, p. 61). The view of the institution as a school with educational programs began to fade. The function of the institution was extended beyond that of relatively short-term training to the inclusion

of comprehensive care for the individual for long periods of time—
sometimes even for life (Baumeister, 1970, p. 9).

Burgdorf and Burgdorf (1976) traced this change from the progressive ideal to rigid and anachronistic:

> The custodial concept—simply providing food, clothing, and shelter—
> became dominant. All too often the motivation was philanthropic
> rather than scientific, and this sentimental humanitarianism resulted in
> an unproductive stasis. The institution began to be conceived as an end
> in itself, a universal solution to the problem of dealing with mentally
> and physically handicapped persons. Construction of institutions took
> precedence over any concern for operating them according to scientific
> or medical principles (p. 886).

Regarding the influence of the Social Darwinism of the late 19th
century, the United States Commission on Civil Rights (1983) added,

> Ironically, the protective isolation model, premised upon the belief
> that handicapped persons needed to be protected from the hardships
> incident to normal society, was replaced in the late 1800's and early
> 1900's by a growing sentiment that society needed protection from
> handicapped people (p. 19).

It is interesting to note that Howe, later in life, became aware of the
dangers of institutionalization, especially as its role changed from educational to custodial, resulting in segregation. As early as 1857, he
wrote to the governor of Massachusetts,

> In almost all public, charitable and penal institutions with which I am
> familiar, serious evils arise from the violation of the principle that we
> should separate not congregate (President's Committee on Mental
> Retardation, 1977, p. 5).

As his hostility toward institutions grew, Howe became increasingly vocal on the subject. In 1866, in a speech at the cornerstone lay-
ing ceremony of a new institution for blind persons in Batavia, New
York, he had the courage to question the utility of the school.

> Society, moved by pity for some special form of suffering, hastens to
> build up establishments which sometimes increase the very evil
> which it wished to lessen. . . . Our people have rather a passion for

public institutions, and when their attention is attracted to any suffering class, they make haste to organize one for its benefit. All great
establishments in the nature of boarding schools, where the sexes
must be separated; where there must be boarding in common, and
sleeping in congregate dormitories; where there must be routine and
formality, and restraint, and repression of individuality; where chores
and refining influences of the true family relation cannot be had, all
such institutions are unnatural, undesirable, and very liable to abuse.
We should have as few of them as possible, and those few should be
kept as small as possible. The human family is the unit of society
(President's Committee on Mental Retardation, 1977. p. 5).

Incredibly, Howe envisioned the importance of concepts like least
restrictive environment, integration and normalization as early as 1874
when he wrote,

Now the danger of misdirection in this pious and benevolent work is
that two false principles may be incorporated with the projected institutions which will be as rotten piles in the foundations and make the
future establishments deplorably defective and mischievous. These
are, first, close congregation; and, second, the life-long association of
a large number of idiots; whereas, the true, sound principles are: sep-
aration of idiots from each other; and then diffusion among the normal population. . . . For these and other reasons it is unwise to organize establishments for teaching and training idiotic children, upon
such principles as will tend to make them become asylums for life. . . .
Even idiots have rights which should be carefully considered!
(President's Committee on Mental Retardation, 1977, p. 5).

The first hospital for the "insane" was established in the mid 18th
century in Philadelphia by Dr. Thomas Bond. Greatly impressed with
what he saw at Bethlehem Hospital during his trip to London, he hoped
to reproduce the care he saw given there to the mentally ill patients. He
and Benjamin Franklin raised funds and applied to the Assembly with
the following declaration:

THAT with the Numbers of Lunaticks, or Persons distempere'd
in Mind, and deprived of their rational Faculties, hath greatly increased in this Province.
THAT some of them going at large, are a Terror to their
Neighbours, who are daily apprehensive of the Violences they may
commit; and others are continually waisting their Substance, to the

great injury of themselves and Families, ill disposed Persons wicked-
ly taking Advantage of their unhappy Condition, and drawing them
into unreasonable Bargains. . . (cited in Gober, 1994, p. 19).

Another public hospital devoted exclusively to the care and treatment of the "insane" was established as early as 1769 in the Colony of
Virginia which based its treatment on the Poor Laws of England. Gober
(1994) cited the wording of the act "to make provision of the support
and maintenance of idiots, lunatics, and other persons of unsound
minds" (p. 20).

Another important issue that needs to be considered was the way
laws could be used for control. With psychiatry yet to be established as
a branch of medicine, the decision to commit someone to an insane asylum came from the individual's family, and many abuses occurred. The
landmark case *Packard v Packard* (1864), attacked legal incarceration
and challenged the subordination of women to their husbands. Elizabeth
Packard challenged her husband for falsely incarcerating her although
at that time, an Illinois law allowed a husband to hospitalize his wife for
insanity with the approval of the superintendent of the institution.
Elizabeth claimed she had been denied due process, and that no legal or
medical procedures had been taken to protect her. She was a vibrant,
bright girl who had married Theophilus Packard, a Protestant minister
19 years older than she. She was described as "a preacher's dutiful
daughter another preacher's dutiful wife, and a devoted mother of five"
(Sapinsley, 1991, p. 3). But, she and her husband had sharp differences
regarding religion. While she believed in a liberal interpretation of the
Bible, her husband was a devout Calvinist who believed in the total
depravity of humanity. When Elizabeth challenged him philosophically
and refused to be the totally obedient wife he wanted, he had her committed in 1860 to the Illinois State Hospital for the Insane in
Jacksonville where she languished for three years.

Upon her release, her husband confined Elizabeth to a locked room
with the doors and windows nailed shut. After her friends failed to see
her, they secured a writ of *habeas corpus*. Declared sane by the courts
after her widely publicized trial, she was left destitute by her husband.
Undaunted, she campaigned over the next two decades for personal liberty laws that would protect individuals, and particularly married
women, from wrongful commitment to and retention in asylums. She
wrote books, gave lectures and lobbied in thirty-one states for legislative reform. Because of her work, attitudes have changed toward per-

sons with mental illness, and it is, of course, now unlawful to incarcerate anyone without due process (Sapinsley, 1991).

The Beginning of Education for Persons with Disabilities

In the 1500's the desperate plight of individuals with disabilities, particularly those with deafness and blindness, improved as society began to understand that they could be educated and accept more productive roles.

Education of Children with Deafness

Although the education of individuals with deafness had been studied by such early thinkers as Socrates, Aristotle and St. Augustine, it was not until the 16th century that any systematic instructional methods appeared (Winefield, 1987). During the 1500s, the education of aristocratic deaf children was first began in Spain, reflecting the results of Iberian cultural practices. At the height of its power and wealth gained from its exploration of the new world, Spain was still strictly feudal and stratified. Aristocratic exclusivity led to frequent intermarriages and inbreeding, which often produced congenitally deaf children. More than occasionally, these offspring were the heirs to great estates (D. Wright, 1969). Most deaf Catholics were prohibited from receiving communion because of their inability to confess their sins and only those who had given confession were permitted to inherit property or titles (Solomon, 1994; Moores, 1996). If the individual were considered deaf and mute, his estate and title would pass on to his next of kin. But if the "deaf-mute heir" could be taught to speak, his legal disability was lifted, a powerful incentive for parents to encourage any method of oral education for their deaf children (D. Wright, 1969; Solomon, 1994).

A Spanish monk, Ponce de León (1520-1584), is considered to be the first systematic instructor of children with deafness (D. Wright, 1969; Winefield, 1987; Moores, 1996). While serving in a Benedictine monastery in San Salvador, Ponce de León met a man who had been denied ordination as a monk because of his deafness. Although little is known of his techniques, he was able to teach the man to read and speak well enough to be accepted as a postulant. Because the Benedictine monks at Ponce de León's monastery assumed vows of silence, the sign language they used probably formed the basis of his teaching methods (Moores, 1996). Later, Ponce de León established a school near Madrid where he taught the deaf children of the nobility. His students included two deaf and mute brothers, Francisco and Pedro de Velasco, who learned to speak well enough to inherit their lands and titles, serve in the military, pray, offer confessions, and even assist in the mass. Ponce de León's work, deeply appreciated by the Spanish aristocracy, continued after his death in Spain and later throughout all of Europe (D. Wright, 1969; Winefield, 1987).

Unfortunately, commoners with deaf children would have to wait more than 200 years for their children to receive comparable instruction. The Abbe de l'Epee learned the manual language developed for the Spanish nobility and brought it to France to teach written French to poor Parisians with deafness. Thus, "it was the Abbe's charitable example that did most to implant the idea that something should be done for all deaf mutes, that from now on it was no longer permissible for society to neglect and forget prisoners of silence" (D. Wright, 1969, p. 160).

Soon, different concepts for teaching persons with deafness began to emerge and influence the field of deaf education. Some of these various views aroused controversy and still cause dissension among educators of deaf persons and among persons with deafness themselves. From the time of Ponce de León to the present, a primary issue consistently dividing educators of deaf persons is the use of sign language. The philosophical debate on this matter, reflecting two distinct attitudes toward deafness, reached its height during the nineteenth century. In the United States, the controversy engaged two well-known figures, Alexander Graham Bell and Edward Miner Gallaudet. While Bell led the fight against the teaching of sign language, Gallaudet fiercely advocated its use (Winefield, 1987). The confrontation between the "oralists" and "combinists" became extremely heated at times with intolerance displayed on both sides, and remnants of that extend into the present (Winefield, 1987).

Bell's oral proponents founded their convictions on the premise that almost everyone processes language auditorialy. They believed that persons with deafness must be prepared to live as much like hearing people as possible, and claimed that sign language limited a deaf person's ability to communicate with the hearing world. Because American Sign Language (ASL), the language used by most adults with deafness who sign, has a different grammatical structure from English, a number of educators found it difficult to use while simultaneously speaking (Winefield, 1987). In addition, the use of ASL was viewed as abnormal or deviant and, therefore, impermissible. Youngsters in oral programs were to be instructed in communication through the use of speech, lipreading, and observation of facial movements. The use of residual hearing supplemented with hearing aids was strictly prohibited (Winefield, 1987). As J. Roth, an advocate with deafness recalled, "I got my hands rapped if I signed" (cited in Solomon, 1994, p. 41).

The manual proponents, led by Gallaudet, believed that lip reading did not work well enough as a means of communication for large numbers of children with deafness. Although the early proponents of manualism advocated a sign-language-only approach, under the leadership of Gallaudet they later changed to include speech development as an essential element of their philosophy. This method later became known as "the combined method" or "total communication," and included the use of sign language, finger spelling, speech or lip reading, residual hearing, and anything else that might help an individual communicate. Today, the Deaf community generally views deafness as a civil rights issue and takes pride in a distinct Deaf culture (Solomon, 1994). A civil rights activist with deafness, M. J. Bienvenu stated, "When I communicate in A.S.L., my native language, I am living in my culture. I don't define myself in terms of 'not hearing' or of 'not anything else'" (cited in Solomon, 1994, p. 42).

Education of Children with Blindness
As with deaf education, the systematic education programs for children with blindness did not develop until the mid-eighteenth century. Although some talented individuals with blindness managed, like the poet Homer, to educate themselves. Up to that time, such education was spasmodic, uncoordinated and primarily focused instruction on helping youngsters with blindness express their thoughts rather than on developing reading skills.

The first organized school for blind individuals, the *Institution des Jeunes Aveugles* (Institution for Blind Youth), was founded in Paris in 1784 by Valentin Haüy. Several profound personal experiences greatly influenced Haüy's career as a dedicated teacher of blind persons. One occurred in 1771, while strolling down a Paris street, the Place Louis-le-Grande where Haüy's attention was drawn to the shouting and laughing of a crowd coming from the Cafe Saint Omde. He encountered the following scene:

> Mounted on a high platform in the cafe were ten blind men scraping crude bows on rough stringed instruments. Huge pasteboard spectacles, devoid of lenses, emphasized the emptiness of the sightless eyes. Lighted candles set to illuminate the sheets of music only revealed

their uselessness, for the notation was turned towards the audience. Grotesque robes and dunce caps with ass's ears added insult to the ridicule to which the men were subjected. For some two months these poor beggars attracted business to the cafe by the discord they thumped out on the false instruments as they moaned a monotonous chant. And in this burlesque, at the expense of handicapped human beings, the Parisians of the time found amusement (G. Farrell, cited in Preen, 1976, p. 25).

The scene was so offensive, sorrowful, and revolting to Haüy that he decided then and there to devote his life to teaching sightless persons to read so they could earn a living in more dignified ways (Preen, 1976; Roberts, 1986).

Another of Haüy's personal experiences involved an honest beggar who received a coin from him which was larger than usual. The beggar questioned the size of the donation, suggesting Haüy had given him a coin more valuable than intended. Impressed by the man's honesty, Haüy was also impressed by his ability to perceive so quickly by his sense of touch. Thus, Haüy decided to use the tactile sense to educate persons with blindness. "Haüy had come to realize that the blind might be made to see through their hands" (Preen, 1976, p. 25).

Enrollment at Haüy's school grew rapidly as he arranged for demonstrations of his students' accomplishments throughout France. Haüy allowed no pity for his students but he, himself, often demonstrated great admiration for their accomplishments. The school's curriculum included the teaching of vocational skills, writing, the performance of music and reading through the use of embossed print:

> Haüy and his first student noticed that the reverse sides of printed pages had tactually legible characters. At that time printers routinely used wet paper for printing; thus the paper itself took on the forms of the letters to some extent. Haüy had letters cast in reverse so that when printed on wet paper they left tactile impressions in correct position and order. Subsequently he modified the letters somewhat to make them easier to read. For writing, his students used a metal pen with a rounded tip to produce raised letters in reverse on the back of heavy paper (Roberts, 1986, p. 8).

The school and its methods soon became a model for blind education and Haüy later accepted requests from other countries, including Russia, to establish others based on his model (Roberts, 1986).

Another major contribution to the development of educating blind children came from Louis Braille, who was himself blind. As a former student and then member of the faculty at the Royal Institution for Blind Youth in Paris, Braille perfected, in 1829, a code of raised dots, which he first used for music notation. He based his dot system on the work of an army artillery officer who developed a similar code which could be read by touch during night maneuvers (Roberts, 1986).

Based on the work of individuals like Haüy, Braille, and later Samuel Gridley Howe, Anne Sullivan and Laura Bridgman, teaching blind students became a widely recognized and respected educational pursuit. Both residential and day programs grew throughout the world, and individuals with blindness won their rights to be educated in public schools along with their sighted peers. Their education was still based, however, on the medical model and included sight conservation and sight saving classes following the faulty premise that to use residual vision was to lose it. The concept is analogous to not exercising because of fear of using up one's muscles. The role of teachers in such classes was to provide an education which entailed no reading or other visual tasks (Roberts, 1986, p. 10).

The Rise of Eugenics

Blatt (1987) called the eugenics movement the dark side of mental retardation with sterilization and institutionalization as the consequences (p. 46). The concept of eugenics greatly influenced the lives (and deaths) of millions of individuals, it's basic principle being that "portions of the human race are inherently and genetically inferior, and that this status is not modifiable" (Smith, 1985, p. 2). According to Friedlander (1995), the eugenics movement had two basic policies:

> First, it sponsored research to investigate the transmission of social traits, especially undesirable ones, and undertook to classify individuals, groups, and nations on a scale of human worth. Second, it proposed biological solutions to social problems and lobbied for their implementation (p. 5).

Francis Galton, a cousin of Charles Darwin, introduced the term "eugenics" and defined it as the science that would deal with all of the influences that could improve the inborn qualities of a race (Jefferis & Nichols, 1928; Smith 1985; and Pfeiffer, 1989). Davenport later defined it as "the science of the improvement of the human race by better breeding" (1911, p. 1). Later, in 1928, "negative eugenics" was defined by Jefferis and Nichols (1928) as

> simply preventing the unfit from bringing children into the world, and [it] lets the positive improvement of the race take care of itself. The difficulty of drawing a line definitely between the fit and the unfit is at once apparent. But by common consent there are certain classes who are not fit for parenthood, namely, the feeble minded, the epileptic, the insane, the syphilitic, etc. By one means or another the unfit must be prevented from propagating their kind if we ever hope to improve humanity to any great extent (p. 12).

The primary aim of the eugenics movement was "the translation of scientific information into social policies that would lead to the prevention of human stock prone to degeneracy" (Trent, p. 136). The concept was based on the assumption that biology, or any physical or psychological variation, predetermined an individual's social status. Also intrinsic to this notion was the belief that the biological progress of mankind required the elimination of those considered hereditarily unfit. Davis (1997), for example, stated, "In 1883, the same year that the term *eugenics* was coined by Galton, [Alexander Graham] Bell delivered his eugenicist speech *Memoir upon the Formation of a Deaf Variety of the Human Race,* warning of the 'tendency among deaf-mutes to select deaf-mutes as their partners in marriage with the dire consequence that a race of deaf people might be created (p. 15).

As Friedlander (1995) suggested, "Eugenic research was designed to isolate and record individuals with inferior intelligence and other social disabilities. Eugenicists claimed that their research on individuals and families proved the inferiority of entire groups" (p. 5). Darwin, himself, laid the foundation:

> We civilized men, on the other hand, do our utmost to check the process of elimination; we build asylums for the imbecile, the maimed, and the sick; we institute poor laws; and our medical men exert their utmost skill to save the life of every one to the last moment. . . . Thus the weak members of civilized societies propagate their kind. No one who has attended the breeding of domestic animals will doubt that this must be highly injurious to the race of man (cited in Haller, 1963, p. 4).

The huge rise of institutionalization in the United States largely resulted from the influence of the eugenics movement and its notion of the "moron as a menace." Manni, Winikur and Keller (1984) observed that "feeblemindedness became associated with not just social incompetence, but also social irresponsibility (p. 90). As Friedlander (1995) wrote,

> Eugenicists focused attention on the feebleminded—labeled as idiots, imbeciles, or morons—and argued that their findings proved the existence of a relationship between low intelligence and both immorality and crime. They saw the cause of the social problems of their times, such as alcoholism and prostitution, as inherited feeblemindedness and viewed the manifestations of poverty, such as intermittent unemployment and chronic illness, as hereditary degeneracy (p. 6).

Thus, mental retardation (feeblemindedness) became closely linked with poverty, crime and illegitimacy. Trent (1994) stated that persons with mental retardation were perceived as having, "a disorder of the senses, a moral flaw, a medical disease, a mental deficiency so as to make them a menace to the social fabric (p. 2). It was widely accepted that mental and physical impairment was the root of most social problems and that "the occurrence of such disabilities was increasing rapidly in modern civilization" (Burgdorf & Burgdorf, 1977, p. 997). A leading eugenicist, Stoddard (1922) stated, "[T]he uncontrolled reproduction among families and the intermingling of defective and normal human stock was resulting in the 'twilight of the American mind,' the 'dusk of mankind'" (p. 94, and cited in Smith, 1985, p. 3). Those advocating race purification underscored the idea that through the prevention of inferior stock and the reproduction of good stock, "problems that had always plagued human beings—poverty, crime and vice, unwanted children, insanity, and feeblemindedness—could be eliminated" (Trent, 1994, p. 136).

During the early 1900s pamphlets and enactments incorporating the principles of eugenics began to appear in states throughout the nation. In Pennsylvania, for example, the pamphlet, *The Menace of the Feebleminded in Pennsylvania* (1913), which influenced the establishment of the Pennhurst institution sought

> A comprehensive plan for the lifelong segregation of these unfortunates. . . on state lands of no great value, far from dangerous contact

with communities or transportation (cited in Testimony of Thomas
Gilhool, 1995, pp. 6-7).

Similar documents appeared in many states including, *The Menace of
the Feeble minded in Connecticut* (1915), *The Burden of the Feeble-
Minded* (1912) in Massachusetts, and *The Feeble-Minded, Or, The Hub
to Our Wheel of Vice* (1913) in Ohio (cited in Testimony of Thomas
Gilhool, 1995, pp. 6-7).

Goddard's Moron as a Menace
In 1912, Henry Herbert Goddard, then Director of research at the
Training School for Feeble-Minded Girls and Boys in Vineland, New
Jersey, published his famous study, *The Kallikak Family: A Study in the
Heredity of Feeble-Mindedness*. As Pfeiffer (1989) noted, "In this work,
Goddard ascribed almost all social ills to a particular class, the feeble-
minded" (p. 10). Goddard began his study with the admission of an
eight year old girl to the institution, who was born in an almshouse. He
gave her the fictitious name of Kallikak derived from the Greek words
kallos (beauty) and *kakos* (bad), two symbolic hereditary influences
which he believed resulted in her "feeble-minded" condition. He also
gave her his new label *moron*, a word he coined from the Greek word
for foolish. (Smith, 1985).

Goddard's term "moron" became widely accepted for those considered to be "high grade defectives." Morons were not retarded seriously enough to be obvious to the casual observer nor were they impaired by such adventitious means as brain injury, disease or other
injury. Morons evinced the typical characteristics of intellectual dense-
ness, social dullness and inadequacy and moral deficiency. From the
beginning, Goddard tried to prove that these traits were hereditary. As
Smith (1985) observed, "He was of the opinion that reproduction
among people with these traits posed a threat to the social order and the
advancement of civilization" (p. 12).

Goddard conducted his study by having his assistants trace
Deborah's ancestry back to her great-great-great-grandfather, Martin,
Sr., who as a soldier during the Revolutionary War, had an affair with a
local barmaid believed to be feeble-minded. This liaison resulted in the
birth of an illegitimate son, Martin Kallikak, Jr, who himself had 408
direct descendants. Goddard claimed to have proof that of these, 143
were feebleminded, 36 were illegitimate, 36 were sexually immoral
(mostly prostitutes), 24 were confirmed alcoholics, 3 were epileptics, 82

died in infancy, 3 were convicted criminals, 78 kept houses of prostitution, and, only 46 were found to be normal (Scheerenberger, p. 149).

Goddard also discovered that Martin Kallikak, Sr., who came from a "good family" and had "normal" intelligence, married a woman from a similar background after the War. From this union, Goddard traced 496 descendants none of whom could be called feeble-minded and only, one insane. The descendants of this union were primarily socially prominent citizens and included judges, physicians, lawyers educators, and land owners. Goddard found no epileptics, illegitimate children, prostitutes or criminals. From this data Goddard concluded that

> [F]eeble-mindedness is largely responsible for these social sores.
> Feeble-mindedness is hereditary and transmitted as surely as any other
> character. We cannot successfully cope with those conditions until we
> recognize feeble-mindedness and its hereditary nature, recognize it
> early, and take care of it (cited in Scheerenberger, 1983, p. 150).

Goddard recommended that solutions to the problem include compulsory sterilization and institutionalization (Smith, 1985). Goddard's study had an enormous influence on the care and treatment of persons with mental retardation for many years, even though its methodology later proved invalid (Scheerenberger, 1983; Smith, 1985). As Gould (1981) observed, "Goddard's study is little more than guesswork rooted in conclusions set from the start" (p. 168).

However inaccurate, Goddard's Kallikak study received excellent reviews and great acclaim, and one of its strongest promoters was Fernald who, in 1912, wrote:

> The feebleminded are a parasitic, predatory class, never capable of
> self-support or of managing their own affairs. The great majority ulti-
> mately become public charges in some form. . . . It has been truly said
> that feeblemindedness is highly hereditary. . . . No feebleminded per-
> son should be allowed to marry or become a parent. . . . Certain fam-
> ilies should become extinct. Parenthood is not for all (cited in Pfeiffer,
> 1989, p. 11).

Goddard's Kallikak book became such a best seller that he was asked to sell the dramatic rights, and it quickly received world wide acclaim, especially in Germany (Smith, 1985):

A simplistic explanation that social ills like poverty, prostitution, crime, and alcoholism were the result of feeblemindedness—especially of the high-grade moron type—was appealing to the spirit of the time. To improve society, the "menace of the feebleminded" must be recognized and controlled (p. 61).

Trent (1994) observed that the view of "mental defectives" changed in between 1910 and 1920 from being merely associated with social vices to being their fundamental cause. He noted that "mental defectives became a menace, the control of which was an urgent necessity for existing and future generations" (p. 141).

Haller (1963) wrote earlier that from 1910 to 1920 a myth of the "menace of the feeble-minded" became a major force in American social thought (p. 95). Goddard's conception of the moron as a feebleminded menace would grow and flourish for many years (Smith, 1985). Trent stressed that this was more than just a shift of labels. The term "moron" carried a new meaning calling for a new social response (p. 141).

Controlling Feeblemindedness and the Unfit

The early eugenic aim of eliminating unwanted inherited disorders from human populations by selective marriage practices soon encompassed the promotion of laws enforcing compulsory sterilization, restricted immigration, restricted marriage, and custodial care (institutionalization) to halt the increasing burden of mental disease and delinquency.

The expanding interest in genetics, at the beginning of the century, led to the establishment of the first organization of the eugenics movement, the American Breeders' Association. Organized in 1903 by leading agricultural breeders, renowned university biologists, and others including Dr. Charles Davenport of Harvard and Alexander Graham Bell, the organization established in 1906 several committees to research specific breeding problems. One of their primary committees, the Committee on Eugenics set out "to investigate and report on heredity in the human race" [and] "to emphasize the value of superior blood and the menace to society of inferior blood" (Haller, 1963, p. 62).

In 1911, the American Breeders Association, wanting to "purge from the blood of the race innately defective strains," recommended the following procedures: selective scientific breeding to remove defective traits, restrictive marriage laws, euthanasia, sterilization and life segregation for all handicapped persons (Burgdorf & Burgdorf, 1976,

p. 887). Two years later, the Association defined as socially unfit "the feebleminded," "paupers," "criminaloids," "epileptics," "the insane," "the constitutionally weak," "those predisposed to specific diseases," "the congenitally deformed" and "those having defective sense organs." They further advocated that such humans should, if possible, be eliminated from the human stock if we would maintain or raise the level of quality essential to the progress of the nation and our race (cited in Scheerenberger, 1983, p. 154). According to Pfeiffer (1989), "Extermination was hinted, but not openly used" (p. 11).

Thus, eugenicists, while pretending to use precise science, saw fit to lump all of "the unfit" into one category grouping criminals (including the delinquent and wayward); prostitutes; persons with paralysis, mental retardation and mental illness (including the psychopathic); epilepsy; blindness; deafness; physical differences (including dwarfism); any other congenital differences; and the dependent (including orphans, ne'er-do-wells, the homeless, tramps and paupers) (Pfeiffer, 1989; Gallagher, 1995). All were seen as weak, degenerate and unfit. "These were people with weak genes. The degeneracy of their character, as well as the flawed nature of their bodies was seen to be inherited. There was no point in attempting to train them" (Gallagher, 1995, p. 50). Society would have to be saved from the burdens imposed upon it by these defectives by such methods as marriage restriction, sexual sterilization and permanent institutionalization.

Already by the mid-1890s approximately half of the states had passed laws declaring null and void the marriages of insane or feebleminded persons on the grounds that such persons were not capable of making contracts (Haller, 1963). Burgdorf and Burgdorf (1977) noted that by the late 1970s, most states carried statutory prohibitions of marriages where one of the partners was mentally ill or mentally retarded. In addition, while some states restricted marriage among persons considered physically handicapped, at least 17 extended such prohibitions to persons with epilepsy.

The theory of eugenics soon spread through out the world. Stone (1996), for example, cites Kang Youwe, a Chinese reformer who, at the end of the nineteenth century included the following measures in his One-World Philosophy:

> The insane will be placed on special islands. They will not be allowed to procreate their kind. They will be taught agriculture and other work and half of whatever they can earn will be given to them. However,

there will not be such people in this age, since they will not be allowed
to have children. Persons with malformed bodies, harelips, and so
forth, will not be permitted to marry and propagate their kind. They
may receive official permission to have sexual intercourse if they have
such a desire, however, at this time, there will be 'mechanical persons'
to substitute for real persons for sexual relief (pp. 469-483)

As late as 1975, a number of states also restricted or denied the
right of persons with mental retardation and those considered "deaf
mutes" from entering into any sort of legal contract. Such restrictions
also served to control marriages among such persons, marriage being
considered a contractual agreement at law. In fact, "deaf mutes" earned
the right to enter into contracts only by litigation. For example, *Alexier
v Matzke*, 151 Mich.36, 115 N.W. 251 (1908) specifically held that "the
doctrine that deafness and dumbness were the same no longer prevails
and that 'deaf mutes' could enter into contracts" (Burgdorf & Burgdorf,
1977, p. 861-862).

Sterilization

The eugenics movement, based as we have seen, on research like that of
Goddard, raised the fear that the prevalence of congenital physical disability and feeble-mindedness would undermine society (Smith, 1985).
The public became afraid that the occurrence of such disabilities was
increasing rapidly in modern civilization and that "the spreading of
handicapping conditions through heredity was the single most important problem facing American Society" (Burgdorf & Burgdorf, 1977, p.
998). To illustrate the pervasiveness of such convictions, Burgdorf and
Burgdorf (1977) cited the language used in a Temple University Law
Review note discussing 1934 sterilization statute:

> Since time immemorial, the criminal and defective have been the "can-
> cer of society." Strong, intelligent, useful families are becoming small-
> er and smaller; while irresponsible, diseased defective families are
> becoming larger. The result can only be race degeneration. To prevent
> this race suicide we must prevent the socially inadequate persons from
> propagating their kind, i.e., the feebleminded, epileptic, insane crimi-
> nal, diseased, and others (cited in Burgdorf & Burgdorf, 1977, p. 998).

According to Burgdorf and Burgdorf (1977), the author further declared
the United States to be a pioneer in the movement for sterilization with
Germany eagerly following America's lead in this field. Smith (1985)

later emphasized that the eugenics movement had, in its time, the spirit of a religious crusade.

Compulsory sterilization became practically feasible in the late nineteenth century when safe, effective and morally acceptable surgical methods were developed. Up to the 1890s the only surgical procedure available for producing sterility was castration, considered extremely radical because it was medically dangerous, caused undesirable changes in secondary sexual characteristics and was widely considered morally unacceptable. Such thoughts, however, did not stop some institution administrators. During the 1890s, Dr. F. Pilcher, Superintendent of the Kansas State Asylum for Idiotic and Imbecile Youth, castrated 44 older boys and men for masturbating (Trent, 1994, p. 193). Pilcher had 44 boys castrated and 14 girls clitorectomized until public outrage forced him to stop (Burgdorf & Burgdorf, 1977, p. 999). Martin Barr, a contemporary of Pilcher's, stated in an 1899 journal article, that one of the benefits of castration was the fact that "some nice male soprano voices could be obtained for the institutional choir" (cited in Baumeister, 1970, p. 12)

By the end of the nineteenth century, the vasectomy (severing the vas deferens) for men and the salpingectomy (the cutting or removing of the fallopian tubes) for women, were developed. Seen as safe and morally acceptable surgical procedures, sterilizations of mentally retarded increased, especially in institutions, despite the fact that no state had enacted legislation authorizing them (Burgdorf & Burgdorf, 1977).

Although Goddard believed that sterilization was a more undesirable solution to controlling "moronity" than segregation and institutionalization, other of his eugenicist colleagues disagreed. H. Laughlin, for example, of the Eugenics Record Office, dedicated himself to the drafting of state laws requiring sterilization of hereditary defectives, a classification in which he included paupers, the diseased, tramps, beggars, alcoholics, criminals, the feebleminded, the insane, epileptics, the physically deformed, the blind, the deaf and even orphans and ne'er do wells (Smith, 1985, p. 138; Haller, 1963, p. 133). His influence and that of the other eugenicists led to a rapid increase in such legislation.

In 1907, Indiana passed the nation's first sterilization law, which applied to "inmates of state institutions who were confirmed criminals, idiots, imbeciles, or rapists" (Burgdorf & Burgdorf, 1977, p. 1000). By 1930, 28 states had enacted compulsory laws that authorized the sterilization of "inmates of mental institutions, persons convicted more than once of sex crimes, those deemed to be feebleminded by IQ tests, 'moral degenerate persons' and epileptics" (Friedlander, 1995, p. 8). By 1938, more than 27,000 forced sterilizations had been performed in the United States (Smith, 1985).

Burgdorf and Burgdorf (1976) noted that the majority of American states had statutes providing for the involuntary sterilization of mentally handicapped and certain physically handicapped persons. For instance, a 1977 statute permitted Mississippi to sterilize those "afflicted with hereditary forms of insanity that are recurrent, idiocy, imbecility, feeblemindedness, or epilepsy." In fact, at one time in the late 1950s, of the 28 states with sterilization statutes, 17 specifically included persons with epilepsy, as well as those with mental illness and mental retardation (p. 861).

The flood of state statutes authorizing eugenic sterilizations met occasional obstacles in those courts that found such procedures unconstitutional, until 1925 when the Supreme Court of Virginia made its ruling in the landmark case of *Buck v. Bell* reenforcing the state's right to force unwanted sterilizations. In 1924, Carrie Buck had been committed to the State Colony for Epileptics and Feebleminded at Lynchberg. Under the authority of the *Virginia Sterilization Act* (1924), which provided for the sterilization of "mental defectives" confined to state institutions when, in the judgment of the superintendents of those institutions, "the best interests of the patients and society would be served by their being rendered incapable of producing offspring" (White, 1993, p. 404). The superintendent presented to the Colony's Board of Directors, a petition for an order to sterilize Carrie by salpingectomy, alleging that she had the mind of nine-year-old, was the mother of a mentally defective child and was the daughter of a woman previously committed to that same institution. The *Virginia Sterilization Act* (1924) stated in part,

> Whereas the Commonwealth has in custodial care and is now supporting in various State institutions many defective persons who if now discharged or paroled would likely become by the propagation of their kind a menace to society but who if capable or procreating might properly and safely be discharged or paroled and become self-supporting with benefit to themselves and society, and
>
> Whereas, human experience has demonstrated that heredity plays an important part in the transmission of insanity, idiocy, imbecility, epilepsy and crime, now, theretofore. . . Be it enacted by the general assembly of Virginia, That whenever the superintendent of the Western State Hospital, or of the Eastern State Hospital, or of the

Southwestern State Hospital, or of the State Colony for Epileptics and
Feeble-Minded shall be of the opinion that it is for the best interests
of the patients and of society that any inmate of the institution under
his care should be sexually sterilized, such superintendent is hereby
authorized to perform, or caused to be performed by some capable
physician or surgeon, the operation of sterilization on any such patient
confined in such institution afflicted with hereditary forms of insanity that are recurrent, idiocy, imbecility, feeble- mindedness or epilepsy; provided that such superintendent shall have first complied with
the requirements of this act (*The Virginia Sterilization Act, 1924, Va.
Acts 569-71* [repealed 1968]).

Carrie's state appointed guardian appealed the decision up to the
United States Supreme Court (Burgdorf & Burgdorf, 1977, pp. 1000-
1005). Justice Oliver Wendell Holmes, writing for the eight-man majority of the Court (which included respected names like Louis Brandeis,
William Howard Taft and Harlan Stone) held that the Virginia Statute
was legal and did not violate Carrie's rights under Due Process or the
Equal Protection Clause of the Fourteenth Amendment (Friedlander, p.
8). Thus, the Court endorsed the eugenic justifications for the state's
sterilizing the unfit and the often quoted excerpts of Holmes' opinion
entered the language:

It is better for all the world, if instead of waiting to execute degenerate offspring for crime, or to let them starve for their imbecility, society can prevent those who are manifestly unfit from continuing their
kind. The principle that sustains compulsory vaccination is broad
enough to cover cutting the fallopian tubes. . . . Three generations of
imbeciles are enough (cited in Burgdorf & Burgdorf, 1977, p. 1004).

Though Justice Holmes likened the sterilizations of defectives to compulsory small pox vaccinations, White (1993), in his biography of
Holmes, questioned the comparison of the two situations. He noted that
compulsory vaccination had two purposes, "to prevent disease in the
individual and to prevent the spread of disease within the population"
(p. 406). He further noted that while compulsory vaccination had no
substantial adverse effects on the person vaccinated, compulsory sterilization deprived a person of the right to procreate and provided no
beneficial effects for the person sterilized. The only purpose of compulsive sterilization was to prevent the individual from reproducing:

The genetic unpredictability of mental disability and the difficulty in diagnosing mental illness-witnessed by Virginia's lumping together the feeble-minded and epileptics in the same state facilities—made it much less likely that sterilization of inmates would result in fewer criminals or starving imbeciles than vaccination would result in fewer cases of small pox. In short, the principle of vaccination cases seemed distorted when applied as a rationale to justify compulsory sterilization (p. 406).

Although based on faulty logic, Holmes' decision, opened the floodgates for sterilizations in the United States. In 1927, Carrie Buck was sterilized and Smith (1994) estimated conservatively, that 50,000 people have been sterilized in the United States under that authority. More than 4,000 have been sterilized at the Lynchburg Training School alone (*Trenton Times*, 1989).

It is also ironic, as Smith (1994) emphasized, that the eugenic evidence in Carrie's case was fallacious and inaccurate. "Carrie's child, alleged to represent a 'third generation of imbeciles,' actually grew to be an honor student" (p. 234). In fact, Carrie herself left the institution after she was sterilized, married a deputy sheriff and lived a modest, productive and respectable life. It was later proven that she did not have mental retardation, and careful examination of her family tree would have revealed she was actually descended from a prominent Virginia family (Smith, 1994).

Unfortunately, Goddard's faulty study had vast repercussions for years to come. According to Kuhl (1994), Goddard's book, originally published in 1914, was republished in Germany in November of 1933, as was Dugdale's earlier prominent family study of the Jukes, supposedly the first to prove the hereditary character of inferiority. The Nazis eagerly adopted the accounts of the Jukes and Kallikaks to legitimize their own sterilization program. The Nazis formulated their sterilization laws only after carefully studying those of California where nearly half of all sterilizations in the United States were performed (Kuhl, 1994):

The example of California reveals the critical role that the transfer of knowledge about medical, scientific, and political aspects of sterilization played in the formulation of Nazi sterilization legislation (p. 45).

Worldwide repercussions of Goddard's study and California's lead continue into the present. In Japan today, for example, "There is a law left over from Nazi times 50 years ago, which allows sterilization of people with disabilities" (Harkins, 1995, p. 31).

Nazi Medicalization of Killing

Having carefully studied American sterilization and institutionalization laws, the National Socialists based much of their philosophy on the "science of eugenics" (Bowe, 1978; Kuhl, 1994; Friedlander, 1995; Pernick, 1996). As Davis (1997) noted, "We have largely forgotten that what Hitler did in developing a hideous policy of eugenics was just to implement the theories of the British and American eugenicists" (p. 19). With much of its rationale grounded in the American eugenics movement, the Nazis attempted to combine ethnic and eugenic racism into a comprehensive program of race improvement. Kuhl (1994) defined eugenic racism as "The demarcation of certain elements within a particular race, followed by attempts to reduce these elements through discriminatory policies" (p. 71).

Race purification and improvement as a cornerstone of Nazi ideology appeared as early as 1924, when Hitler characterized the German state in *Mein Kampf*:

> It must set race in the center of all life. It must take care to keep it pure. It must declare the child to be the most precious treasure of the people. It must see to it that only the healthy beget children. . . . It must declare unfit for propagation all who are in any way visibly sick or who have inherited a disease and can therefore pass it on. . . . Those who are physically and mentally unhealthy and unworthy must not perpetuate their suffering in the body of their children. . . It must act in this sense without regard to understanding or lack of understanding, approval or disapproval (Manheim, trans., 1971, pp. 403-404).

He also stated that,

> The right of personal freedom recedes before the duty to preserve the race. There must be no half measures. It is a half measure to let incurably sick people steadily contaminate the remaining healthy ones. . . . If necessary, the incurably sick will be pitilessly segregated—a barbaric measure for the unfortunate who is struck by it, but a blessing for his fellow men and posterity (p. 205).

Hitler wrote in 1928 of his strong admiration for the Spartans and their policy of killing newborn weaklings and associated such selective killing with Spartan military prowess required to wage a successful war (Weindling, 1981). Hitler said of the Spartans,

> The exposure of the sick, weak, deformed children, in short their destruction, was more decent and in truth more humane than the wretched insanity of our day which seeks to preserve the most pathological subjects (cited in Gallagher, 1995, pp. 21-22).

Under the Nazis, the goals of medicine changed. In 1930, the Nazi Party's National Socialist German Medical Association proclaimed the "primacy of national biology over national economics" (Bleuel, 1973, p. 191). As Pernick (1996) stated,

> By the 1930s racial hygiene, eugenics, and euthanasia played a complex but central role in the evolution of Nazi ideology and in the legitimation of Nazi genocide. Depicting their intended victims as carriers of racial "diseases" constituted a key feature of Nazi propaganda and justified the power of the Nazi state as necessary to protect the public health from such contamination. Programs for killing incurably ill institutional patients. . . pioneered the machinery and trained the medical personnel who were then transferred to run death camps for the "racially diseased" (p. 164).

As early as July, 1933, immediately upon Hitler's assumption of power, the Nazis established special Health Courts to implement their newly enacted law requiring sterilization of those with hereditary diseases, and Smith (1994) has noted that the American legal precedent for the sterilization of defective individuals helped the Nazis to justify their own sterilization programs. As Smith noted earlier, "In 1933, the statute enacted by Virginia, and under which Carrie was sterilized became law in Germany" (1985, p. 234).

The Nazi definition of the hereditarily sick included those with congenital mental deficiency, schizophrenia, manic-depressive insanity, inherited epilepsy, Huntington's chorea, inherited deafness or blindness or "grave physical defect." The law, which forbade the sterilization of "normal persons," was ultimately responsible for the sterilization of approximately 300,000 persons perceived as defective by the state (Lifton, 1986; Finger, 1992). Gallagher (1995) reported a higher estimate of 375,000 persons sterilized by the Nazis broken down into the following nine categories:

1.	Congenital feeblemindedness	203,250
2.	Schizophrenia	73,125
3.	Epilepsy	57,750
4.	Acute alcoholism	28,500
5.	Manic-depressive insanity	6,000
6.	Hereditary deafness	2,625
7.	Severe hereditary physical deformity	1,875
8.	Hereditary blindness	1,125
9.	St. Vitus' dance	750

But, sterilization under the Nazis was just the beginning. As Bleul (1973) explained,

> In the Third Reich, with its fanatical allegiance to national health and purity of blood, wholesome popular sentiment and racial laws, the door to despotism was flung wide. The inexorable consequence of such ideas was that the very existence of the congenitally sick seemed a threat, and that mentally ill and incurable people in need of care were seen as an unnecessary charge on the nation as a whole (p. 192).

"Euthanasia" and Life Unworthy of Life

The Nazi policy of sterilization quickly led to a much more comprehensive and vigorous eugenics program that soon included "euthanasia" (their own euphemistic term) and the medical killing of approximately 200,000 disabled men, women and children (Burleigh, 1994; *Handicapped*, n.d.). The Nazi program of killing persons considered by the state to be "unworthy of life" was in a direct line of succession from the law requiring sterilization (Bleul, 1973, p. 192). The "euthanasia" policy of the Nazis amounted, in fact, to a throwback to the Era of Extermination of the early Greeks and Romans.

Friedlander (1995) explained that the common usage of the term "euthanasia"—"the act of painlessly putting to death a person suffering from a terminal and incurable disease"—does not reflect how the Nazis used the term:

> The Nazis used the term "euthanasia" and also "mercy death" as a euphemism to disguise their murder of the handicapped. They killed them for racial and eugenic reasons, not to ease the suffering of the individuals. Their killing operation was a secret government program and not an act of individual mercy. It was not applied against persons suffering from common physical diseases like cancer but only against those considered "life unworthy of life." The Nazi's victims did not suffer from diseases that were terminal or from disabilities that were necessarily incurable. And their deaths were not painless (p. xxi).

By camouflaging their program of mass murder under a medical guise and euphemistically labeling their killing policy "euthanasia," the Nazis presented it as a form of relief for the terminally ill (Weindling, 1981). Their concept of eugenics became "racial hygiene." As Finger (1992) observed, "From the outset, a link was made between physical disability, moral degeneracy and other deviations from the norm, propped up by quasi-scientific notions and language" (p. 24). Lifton (1990) discussed the euphemistic term "euthanasia" as used by the Nazis:

> Euthanasia is what the Nazis called their project, but in my previous writings about it, I always put quotations around it no matter how often I used the word. It was not genuine euthanasia. Euthanasia really means helping the dying to die, the idea that a person should be allowed to have a good death or a dignified death. Under the guise or cloak of euthanasia, the Nazis murdered a hundred thousand people, mostly mental patients (p. 222).

"Euthanasia" was an authorized medical program of murder to protect the *Volksgemeinschaft*—the Aryan racial community. Those considered non-Aryans were perceived as potential threats to the purity and health of German blood and had to be removed like a "cancer" or "infection." The aim of the Nazi "euthanasia" program was to "exterminate the mentally ill and the handicapped, thus 'cleansing' the Aryan race of persons considered genetically defective and a financial burden to society" (*Handicapped,* n.d., p. 8). The "euthanasia" program reestablished the old principle of the early Greeks and Romans that exterminating persons with disabilities was the legitimate business of government.

The Nazis justified their policy of direct medical killing on the simple principle of *lebensunwertes Leben* or "life unworthy of life," a concept they did not originate but one, as Lifton (1986) wrote, they carried to its "ultimate biological, racial, and 'therapeutic' extreme" (p. 21).

The Nazis perceived persons with disabilities, illnesses or differences as less than human and therefore worth less than "whole human beings." The party line stressed that "[A] healthy Reich could not afford sick people because they were too expensive" (Bleuel, 1973, p. 192), particularly in time of war. The Nazi rationale for such killing was to provide beds for wounded soldiers and civilians in "total war" by emptying mental hospitals, foster homes and institutions for persons with disabilities (Pross, 1992). Therefore, forcible "euthanasia" was also based on the needs of a wartime economy, or on what Proctor (1992) called "a preemptive triage to free up beds" (p. 35). The medical establishment became obsessed with how much food and resources could be saved with the killing of each defective person. As Burleigh (1994) noted, "Psychiatrists put much mental energy into working out what asylums could save in the context of the 'battle for food'" (p. 49).

Hitler knew he could take advantage of a war to accomplish goals that would never be tolerated during peace time. He was fully aware, for example, that during World War I, approximately one third to one half of all German psychiatric patients had been starved to death, some 45,000 in Prussia alone, because "they were simply too low on the list to receive rations" (Proctor, 1992, p. 35). As Caplan (1992a) stated,

> In 1917, patients in psychiatric hospitals in Germany were given low priority for food under government wartime rationing schemes. The government decided that the mentally ill should be excluded from scarce rations, since they were not making a productive contribution to the well-being of the nation (p. 271).

Still, the mass elimination of persons perceived as "defective" was not uniquely a Nazi philosophy (Wolfensberger, 1981; Smith, 1985; Müller, 1991; J. Shapiro, 1993; Kuhl, 1994, Gallagher, 1995; Friedlander, 1995). Wolfensberger (1980; 1981) revealed that much of the Nazi genetic philosophy was based on the 1920 book, *Die Freigabe de Vernichtung lebersunwertend Lebens; ihr Mass und ihre Form*, (*The Release of the Destruction of Life Devoid of Value*) by Binding and Hoche, distinguished professors of law and psychiatry respectively. The work stressed the economic and social costs to society by "defective" individuals and argued, in a scientific-scholarly style, that unworthy life included children with mental retardation, mental illness, and physical "deformities." The Binding-Hoche book professionalized and medicalized "euthanasia" by stressing its therapeutic aspect and proposing the destruction of life unworthy of life as a healing process (Lifton, 1986, p. 46). The authors further pictured "euthanasia" as kind, compassionate, reasonable, moral and economical (Wolfensberger, 1980). Binding argued that "euthanasia" was a compassionate way to dispose of the "empty human husks that fill our psychiatric institutions" (Bayman, 1989, p. 582). Furthermore, Binding and Hoche,

> developed the perception of the weak, poor, and handicapped as "useless eaters" and "superfluous" people. The message was that there should be a social obligation to find and eliminate the "misfits" and the "unfit" (Smith, 1985, p. 165).

Although written 13 years before Hitler came to power and twenty years before the Nazi "euthanasia" policy began, Binding and Hoche's book,

> became the intellectual, social, legal, medical, and moral basis for the widespread advocacy for the destruction of handicapped and enfeebled people during the early years of World War II (Wolfensberger, 1981, p. 2).

Of course, as we have seen, beliefs like those Binding and Hoche advocated were held by many other respected eugenicists around the world. In 1933, Gould, an American physician, proposed in the *Journal of the American Institute of Homeopathy* that euthanasia helped resolve economic difficulties, citing with approval, the "elimination of the unfit" in ancient Sparta (Gould, 1933, p. 82, cited in Proctor, 1988).

Similarly, in 1941, American psychiatrist Foster Kennedy, professor of neurology at Cornell Medical College, delineated a proposal to the American Psychiatric Association for killing "defective" and "hopelessly unfit" children, whom he labeled "those helpless ones who should never have been born—Nature's mistakes" (Kennedy, 1941; Proctor, 1988; Hollander, 1989; J. Shapiro, 1993; Gallagher, 1995):

> When a "defective" child turned five, Kennedy suggested, the parents or guardians should be allowed to ask a panel of doctors that the child "be relieved of the burden of living." Kennedy compared this to the "solace given a stricken horse." If the panel found the child to have "no future nor hope of one," Kennedy wrote, "than I believe it is a merciful and kindly thing to relieve that defective—often tortured and convulsed, grotesque and absurd, useless and foolish, and entirely undesirable—of the agony of living" (Kennedy, 1941, cited in J. Shapiro, 1993, p. 272).

Hollander (1989) reported that the editorial board of the *American Journal of Psychiatry* reviewed Kennedy's proposal with sympathy and "characterized the issue of euthanasia as 'a live one' worthy of serious consideration and debate" (p. 53).

Like Binding and Hoche, and later Kennedy, Hitler and the Nazis "medicalized" the issue of "euthanasia" for persons with disabilities, thereby giving it "scientific legitimacy." Doctors became "the guardians of national hereditary health" (Burleigh, 1994, p. 191). Once medically legitimized, "euthanasia" was then quickly and efficiently implemented by physicians, nurses, aides, technicians and others seen as healers, who willingly dealt out death by starvation, gas, injections and poison believed they were doing it for the "health" of their country (Wolfensberger, 1980) with "doctors [as] the highest echelon of those directly or indirectly involved in mass murder" (Burleigh, 1994, p. 154). Hitler Nazified the medical profession by redefining its goal as the "promotion and perfection of the health of the German people to ensure that the people realize the full potential of their racial and genetic endowment' (Lifton, 1986, p. 30). Hitler let the Medical establishment know in no uncertain terms that he considered it proper that the "life unworthy of life" of severely mentally ill persons be eliminated by "actions that bring about death" (Lifton, 1986, p. 62).

The role of medicine, then, was to protect the state from unwanted citizens thought to be contaminating it. The worthiness of the goal justified any means to attain it. Hitler allowed physicians, and especially psychiatrists, to pronounce value judgments both on individuals on medical grounds and on entire groups on medical-sociological grounds (Wertham, 1978). As Weindling (1989) observed, "The transition from medicine as care for the individual to the welfare of society and future generations attained the most extreme and brutal realization in the killing of the sick and disabled" (pp. 542-543).

While Hitler and the Nazi regime legitimized killing persons with disabilities, the medical experts assumed the crucial administrative role (Weindling, 1989). The German medical community proved itself shockingly amenable to the eradication of whole groups of people whom it first stigmatized and euphemistically labeled. Terms like, "the incurable," "lives unworthy of life," "creatures of no value," "weaklings," "useless eaters," "burdensome ballast" or "the mentally dead" came to describe Europeans with disabilities, and the psychiatrists, in particular, gradually assumed a central roll in what became the Holocaust. As Szasz (1970), observed,

> It should be recalled that psychiatrists in Nazi Germany played a leading role in developing the gas chambers whose first victims were mental patients. Even in occupied territories, where soldiers were used for the mass murder of civilian populations, the inmates of mental hospitals—in Kiev, for example—were killed by doctors (p. 214).

Gallagher (1995) suggested that the reason that the doctors were so willing to comply was their own arrogance, "bred of a confidence in science and the prestige of the medical profession" (p. xvii). Part of that arrogance was based fundamentally on the medical model of viewing persons with disabilities as sick people who never get well. Such a view challenged those doctors who viewed "failure" as a personal affront. Disabled patients were seen as "refractory cases," the term used by the German physicians of the thirties for their patients "who refused to respond to therapy":

> [I]t has been said that physicians are often frustrated by their inability to cure their chronic patients. If this is so, in the Germany of the thirties doctors sought to eliminate this frustration by eliminating the source—their patients (Gallagher, 1995, p. xv).

Thus, Hitler had no difficulty finding doctors, nurses and hospital workers to carry out his goals (Conot, 1983). In fact, as Gallagher (1995) noted, "The program's sponsors and senior participants were the leading medical professors and psychiatrists of Germany, men of international reputation" (p. xv). Kater (1989) observed that "physicians

became Nazified more thoroughly and much sooner than any other profession, and as Nazis they did more in the service of the nefarious
regime than any of their professional peers" (pp. 4-5). Falstein (1963)
went so far as to write that in no other area of professional life had the
Nazi force of destruction "demonstrated greater power for evil than in
the medical profession" (p. 267), and Lifton (1986) elaborated on the
extent to which German physicians, as a profession, offered their services to the Nazis: "So did most other professions; but with doctors, that
gift included using their intellectual authority to justify and carry out
medicalized killing, which meant practicing therapy via mass murder"
(pp. 43-44). Under the assumption that its desire to perfect the human
race justified killing, the medical profession used eugenics, genetics,
and biology to provide a "rationale" for it actions (Gallagher, 1995).
According to Proctor (1992), finding a "scientific" basis as part of the
Nazi, doctors found themselves strongly attracted:

> Doctors in fact joined the Nazi Party earlier and in greater numbers
> than any other professional group. By 1942, more than 38,000 doctors
> had joined the Nazi Party, nearly half of all doctors in the country. In
> 1937, doctors were represented in the SS seven times more often than
> was the average for the employed male population; doctors assumed
> leading positions in German government and universities (p. 27).

Lifton (1986) too described the German medical profession's
eagerness to comply with the goals of the Nazis: "Prior to Auschwitz
and the other death camps, the Nazis established a policy of direct medical killing, that is, killing arranged within medical channels, by means
of medical decisions, and carried out by doctors and their assistants"
(p. 23). Gallagher (1995) added that "[although] this program was
authorized by Hitler and carried out under the auspices of the National
Socialist government of the Third Reich, it would be a mistake to call it
a Nazi program. It was not. The program was conceived by physicians
and operated by them. They did the killing" (p. xv). And, according to
Goldhagen (1996), the medical community killed its victims in a
detached, unemotional way:

> Coldly uninvolved were the Germans who killed the mentally ill and
> the severely handicapped in the so-called euthanasia program. Most
> of them were physicians and nurses who dispatched their victims in
> the dispassionate manner of surgeons, who excise from the body
> some hideous and hindering excrescence (p. 398).

One should note, however, that not all German doctors had a direct hand in the Holocaust. Individual physicians did oppose the regime in various ways, even though open opposition meant certain death (Kater, 1989). Weindling (1981) stressed that not all Nazi doctors who favored sterilization, favored medical killing, and such doctors became passive onlookers rather than active participators of medical murder (p. 546).

One should also note that the medicine was not the only profession to legitimize the mass murder of disabled children. As Müller (1991) stated, "Although responsibility for this mass murder of the physically and mentally handicapped and 'asocial types' lay primarily with the medical profession, the legal profession was associated with it in a variety of ways" (p. 126). For example, in 1941 when Hitler gave instructions that all criminal charges filed in connection with the "euthanasia" program be classified as matters outside the jurisdiction of the courts and referred directly to the Ministry of Justice, the judges and public prosecutors who appeared at the meeting in their Nazi party uniforms stood in silence. Those present included numerous high officials of the Ministry of Justice, the president of the Supreme Court, the president of the People's Court, the public prosecutors assigned to those courts, the presidents of all 34 Courts of Appeals, and all 34 chief public prosecutors. Not one questioned "how such a directive was to be reconciled with the principle that all crimes were to be prosecuted, with the laws on murder, and with the prohibitions against perversion of justice and aiding and abetting a crime" (Müller, 1991, p. 128).

With the legal complications out of the way, the Nazis could use racial science to define social ills and prescribe cures. The medical community willingly complied by helping to sell the public on the idea that Germany's "ills" were not economic or political, but were threats to the "folkish body" from the increasing number of humans who were perceived as "genetically unworthy" and "inferior." According to Müller (1991), those condemned by the government were described as "ballast to society." By making social problems medical, scientific, and genetic, the Nazis gave them an "untreatable hopeless biological cause" that justified a cure of segregation and elimination. Racial hygiene became both science and social policy governing inferiority and disability (Proctor, 1988). According to Szasz (1970), "[T]he Nazis even perfected a fresh rhetoric of hygiene to justify their programs" (p. 214). As a medical model, it could explain, categorize, and prescribe. The science of racial hygiene allowed the Nazis to determine the value of human beings first by mental and physical characteristics, then later by racial and social ones. For example, psychiatrists segregated those youth thought by the state to exhibit poor social behavior. Under Himmler's orders, youth camps like Moringen were established for certain young-sters (for example the "swing youth") who did not exemplify the behav-ior the state expected. On arrival at the camps, the youngsters were rel-egated to blocks as subjects for racial and biological research. S Block, the trouble-makers' block, accommodated

> pupils who are difficult, deviant in character, suffering from emotion-al inadequacies, hyperactive, excitable, discontented in disposition, bad-tempered, incorrigible mischief-makers or determined petty criminals—pupils who are continually at odds with the community.

D Block, the persistent failures block, accommodated

> pupils with personality weaknesses, who are unsettled and lacking in drive, who cannot pass any of the proficiency tests and have an unfail-ing tendency to aberrancy.

G Block, the occasional failures block accommodated

> pupils who are primarily unstable, irresponsible or lacking in in-dependence, who are severely at risk and liable to do recidivism (cited in Peukert, 1987, p. 206).

When these youngsters reached the age of majority, most moved on to a mental institution where they became victims of "euthanasia." Thus the medical community, and especially the psychiatrists, exterminated not only the physically and mentally unfit but the socially unfit as well.

At first the "euthanasia" program remained small and secret. It officially began by killing "defective" newborns, then children up to three, and finally adolescents. From its inception, it selected those con-sidered to be "disabled" and "retarded" along with other, more "nor-mal" candidates:

> The inmates of orphan asylums, juvenile homes, and foster care were appraised; and many healthy children who were thought to be trouble-makers went to their death. So did children of mixed races, children with adolescent pimples, and even those who may have annoyed a staff member for one reason or another (Gallagher, 1995, p. 9).

Justification for killing some of the children in the early program was often based on recruited requests from parents of youngsters with severe disabilities for "the granting of a mercy killing" (Lifton, 1986, p. 50).

Those first killed in Germany were physically disabled children in a hospital near Wurthberg operated by the Samaritan Brothers. The SS appropriated the hospital under the state's policy of taking over of church-controlled asylums (Weindling, 1981). The youngsters, already victims of institutionalization and sterilization, were killed by drug overdoses (usually Luminal, a barbiturate) hidden in their food. Those who refused to eat received forced injections or suppositories filled with the poison (Conot, 1983; Smith, 1985).

Prominent academic administrative doctors sympathetic to the regime and used by the Reich to maintain the medicalized structure administered this death-dealing protocol (Lifton, 1986). The bureaucracy established to implement the killing was called the Reich Committee for the Scientific Registration of Serious Hereditary and Congenital Diseases (Lifton, 1986; Proctor, 1988, Friedlander, 1995). The purpose of such a bureaucratic organizational structure was to diffuse individual responsibility and allow those involved in the killing to distance themselves from their deeds.

On August 18, 1939, the "Committee" began its work by requiring midwives, medical officers, and doctors to register all children born with serious hereditary diseases particularly "idiocy" and "mongolism" (especially when associated with blindness and deafness); microcephaly; hydrocephaly; malformations of limbs, head, and spinal column; and paralysis, including spastic conditions (Lifton, 1986, p. 52).

The children selected were sent to one of Germany's 28 most respected children's institutions and hospitals newly equipped for implementing exterminations (Proctor, 1988). The medical units where the actual killing took place were in areas of institutions where the children marked for death could be dispersed among the ordinary pediatric patients (Lifton, 1986).

Burleigh and Wippermann (1991) revealed the terror many of the children faced as the program grew and the children were transferred to the killing centers. At first, the children being transferred were happy to be going on a ride, with the officials getting some complaints from those left behind. However, this mood

> soon gave way to terror at the regular arrival of the vans which never
> brought patients back. . . . Long-term residents were severely trauma-

tized by being removed from their accustomed habitat; others tried to cling to nursing staff they knew and trusted or uttered a few words of resignation; some had to be put in strait-jackets or handcuffs to get them into the vans (p. 149).

Upon their arrival at the centers, children were killed in various ways including: lethal injections of Luminal or morphine-scopolamine tablets, and gassing with cyanide or chemical warfare agents (Proctor, 1988; J. Shapiro, 1993; Friedlander, 1995). The poisons were commonly administered slowly, over several days or weeks, so that the cause of death could be disguised as pneumonia, bronchitis, or some other complication. Some medical superintendents left their institutions without heat causing the children to die of exposure, which could then be rationalized as "letting nature take its course" (Proctor, 1988, p. 187).

Finger (1987) stated that the parents of the children selected for death were told that their children would receive "special treatments," which were in reality large doses of pneumonia-causing sedatives. Once induced, the pneumonia went untreated (cited in Johnson, 1986, p. 24). Parents were then informed by a standardized letter used at all institutions that their child had died suddenly and unexpectedly of brain edema, appendicitis, or some other fabricated cause, and that owing to the danger of an epidemic, their child's body required immediate cremation (Proctor, 1988). The condolence letters and death certificates were frequently accompanied with an urn containing ashes (Berenbaum, 1993).

Scheerenberger (1983), Conot (1983), Lifton (1986), Burleigh, (1994) and Friedlander (1995), described some of the occurring bureaucratic administrative blunders—for example, parents receiving two letters and two urns containing the remains of the same child; parents being informed that their child died of appendicitis when the child's appendix had been removed years before; hairpins found among the ashes of male children; or parents being informed their child had died before he or she had even left home.

Most of the children died horrifying deaths. It was often institutional policy to starve child inmates with mental retardation or mental illness to death (Scheerenberger, 1983; Lifton, 1986; Proctor, 1988), and "Deliberate starvation based upon differential diets was practiced in asylums throughout the length and breadth of Germany" (Burleigh, 1994, p. 242). In 1939, for example, the medical director of the institution in Eglfing-Haar, a psychiatrist named Dr. Hermann Pfannmuller, instituted a policy of starving designated children to death rather than "squandering" medication or food on them. As a non-medical visitor to Pfannmuller's institution recalled,

> I remember the gist of the following general remarks by Pfannmuller: "We do not kill. . . with poison, injections, etc. . . . No, our method is much simpler and more natural, as you see." With these words, he pulled, with the help of a nurse, a child from its little bed. While he then exhibited the child like a dead rabbit, he asserted with a knowing expression and a cynical grin, "For this one it will take two or three more days." The picture of this fat, grinning man, in his fleshy hand the whimpering skeleton, surrounded by other starving children, is still vivid in my mind. The murderer explained further then that sudden withdrawal of food was not employed, rather a gradual decrease of the rations (Lifton, 1986, p. 62; Friedlander, 1995, p. 50).

Pfannmuller justified his actions by stating,

> The idea is unbearable to me that the best, the flower of our youth must lose its life at the front in order that feebleminded and irresponsible asocial elements can have a secure existence in the asylum (Lifton, 1986, p. 63).

At the Nuremberg Doctor's Trial in 1946 and 1947, Pfannmuller was accused of killing hundreds of mentally and physically disabled individuals, and his American interrogators were shocked that he had lost count of the many children he had killed (Friedlander, 1995). He pleaded in his defense that the exterminations were "just as legal as the regulation for transmission of hereditary disease and infection in marriage. These laws were passed during the National Socialist regime. But the ideas from which they arose are centuries old" (Kuhl, p. 101). Pfannmeuler's defense worked. At the War's end, he received only a five-year sentence for his part in the Nazi extermination program (*The New York Times*, 1951).

Remak (1969) reported that the full official implementation of the "euthanasia" program began with Hitler's 1939 memorandum authorizing the extension of "the responsibilities of physicians still to be named in such a manner that patients whose illness, according to the most critical application of human judgment, is incurable can be granted release by euthanasia" (pp. 133-134). The signature was backdated to coincide with the invasion of Poland, and basically the beginning of

World War II. A war economy sanctioned the Nazis' killing of life unworthy of life. After bombing attacks, for instance, psychiatric institutes and homes for the elderly were regularly emptied (their patients murdered) to make up for lost bed space (Proctor, 1992).

The program labeled "Aktion T-4" (named for Berlin Chancellery Tiergarten 4, which directed it) focused on chronic adult patients and "involved virtually the entire German psychiatric community and related portions of the general medical community" (Lifton, 1986, p. 65). Aktion T-4 extended the "euthanasia" project to include adults and called for the identification of all patients with more severe disabilities including schizophrenia, epilepsy, encephalitis, chronic illness, cerebral palsy, delinquency, perversion, alcoholism, antisocial behavior and a number of others (Wolfensberger, 1981; Scheerenberger, 1983; Lifton, 1986; Proctor, 1988; Rogasky, 1988; Gallagher, 1995; Friedlander, 1995).

The first gassing of mental patients occurred 45 days later at Posen, in Poland. In Germany, itself, "euthanasia" quickly "became part of normal hospital routine" (Proctor, 1992, p. 35). Like the killing of disabled children, the killing of disabled adults was carried out by neat and economical methods including, mass gassing of from 15 to 20 people in a chamber disguised as a shower; oral poison given with meals or as medicine; injections into the bloodstream of naphtha, morphine, barbiturates or air; starvation; withholding of medical care; and exposure to cold, wet or stress coupled with the withholding of food and medical care (Wolfensberger, 1981, p. 3). Such methods were considered "neat" by the Nazis because without blood and violence, "the sensibilities of the people involved in the executions were protected. Indeed, it was this very 'neatness' that enabled many of the perpetrators to later disclaim both wrong-doing and guilt" (Wolfensberger, 1981, p. 3).

Hollander (1989) noted the ease with which the program was implemented attributable in large part, to the cooperation of the "service providers" (p. 53). Proctor (1988) stressed that physicians were never ordered to murder psychiatric patients or children with disabilities; they were only empowered and permitted to do so:

> [And they] fulfilled their task without protest, often on their own initiative. Hitler's original memo of October 1939 was not an order (*Befell*), but an empowerment (*Vollmacht*), granting physicians permission to act. In the abortive "euthanasia" trial at Limberg in 1964, Hefelmann testified that "[N]o doctor was ever ordered to participate

in the euthanasia program; they came of their own volition." Himmler himself noted that the operations undertaken in psychiatric hospitals were administered solely by medical personnel (p. 193).

Friedlander pointed out that at the killing centers,

> The physician-in-charge absolutely controlled three areas. He was in charge of the actual gassing of the patients. He was also responsible for maintaining all medical records, including the determination of the cause of death. Finally, he officially represented the killing center, masquerading as a hospital, to the outside world (p. 99).

Wolfensberger (1981), also, stressed the vital participatory role played by physicians, especially psychiatrists, in the killing of disabled individuals. It was often the psychiatrist—rather than a technician—who turned on the gas "probably as another neat, noble, sensitive gesture" (p. 4). Wolfensberger described the fervor and zeal with which the task was implemented:

> [P]articipation was not only voluntary but even enthusiastic and committed! For instance, upon the extermination of the ten thousandth mental patient at the Hadamar psychiatric institution in 1941, a big celebration was held in which all psychiatrists, nurses, attendants and secretaries participated and free drinks were poured (p. 4).

Gallagher (1995) described this incident in more detail:

> Accordingly, doctors, nurses, orderlies, even grounds attendants gathered in the lobby of the right wing in the evening. Beer and wine were served, and then all present filed downstairs to the crematorium in the basement. . . . The room had been decorated, and the oven itself was bedecked with fresh flowers. On a gurney in front of the oven was the naked body of a dead man—the actual ten-thousandth victim. The body was adorned with flowers and small flags with the swastika emblem. . . . Standing with his back to the oven door, Dr. Brenner gave a short, inspirational talk about the importance of the work that was being done at Hadamar and his pride at being part of such a dedicated and hard-working team. With a nod from Brenner, the body was placed in a trough-like structure and shoved into the oven. . . . And then it was time for the fun. Mr. Merkle, the hospital bookkeeper, came out. He turned his collar about, put his coat on backwards and intoned a burlesque eulogy of the deceased insane person. The

audience howled with laughter. . . . Music was provided by a local
polka band; much more beer was served. There was dancing and
laughter; and later, a drunken march around the sanitorium grounds
with lots of singing and shouting (pp. 12-13).

Because of the early success of the "euthanasia" program, it soon
spread to include those less severely disabled, those physically different
but not disabled (for example, persons with dwarfism), those reported
as having behavior problems, those suspected of being racially or genetically tainted and those who were devalued entirely for their social identities (for example, Gypsies, homosexuals, Polish prisoners of war). As
Friedlander (1995) stated,

> Although most Reich Committee children were obviously not suffer-
> ing from painful or terminal diseases, the killers defended their
> actions on the grounds that their afflictions were disabling and incur-
> able. The disabilities that had to be reported were indeed physical ail-
> ments. They included neurological disorders and physical deformities
> considered incurable and hereditary by the standards of medical
> knowledge at that time. But even this criterion for killing-that a dis-
> ease should be incurable though not necessarily terminal—remained
> only a theory (p. 57).

Once the death-making apparatus had been developed, structured
and refined, it required more victims. In July of 1941, Goring com-
manded Heydrich, as chief of security services, criminal police and
Gestapo, to oversee the "final solution of the Jewish problem." Heydrich, in turn, transferred the thoroughly tested "euthanasia" technology to the killing of Jews by transferring Aktion T-4 specialists to the
Belzec, Sobibor and Treblinka concentration camps to set up the gas
chambers (Weindling, 1981). Although Hitler ostensibly ordered the
"euthanasia" program against persons with disabilities to be stopped in
August of 1941 in response to public outcry and the legal objection of
the Bishop of Munster and other advocates, it continued more subtly
and discreetly with many mentally ill and mentally retarded continuing
to be killed by injection. At the same time, a new program, Aktion
14F13 authorized the killing of approximately 20,000 more mentally
retarded, mentally ill, physically disabled and other socially unacceptable and undesirable concentration camp inmates. Under this program,
Jews, who were previously considered unworthy of euthanasia, were

included, and as Scheerenberger (1983) noted, "Thus began the Holocaust" (p. 211).

"Racial hygiene" as practiced by the medical community implied that persons with mental and physical disabilities were a threat to the "body" of Germany. "These flawed people were thought to have infected the collective body of the German people, and they were to be dealt with the way a physician would deal with a pathogenic infection of an individual body—by isolation and disinfection" (Gallagher, 1995, p. 29). Hitler medically justified the Holocaust in the same way by espousing the idea that a Jewish "infection" was causing the Aryan race to be "weak and ill." The only cure was to rid the body of the infection, the Jews. The patient was neither the Jews nor the Gypsies nor any other group; it was the Aryan Race. "The way of curing the Aryan Race was to get rid of whatever had made it ill" (Lifton, 1990, p. 225). Kater (1989), in fact, emphasized that the Nazis saw Auschwitz as a racial "clinic" and the medically logical extension of sterilization and "euthanasia" (p. 182). As Reichsfuhrer Himmler stated, "Antisemitism is exactly the same as delousing. Getting rid of lice is not a question of ideology. It is a matter of cleanliness" (cited in Szasz, 1970, p. 214). According to Proctor (1996),

> Hitler was celebrated as the "great doctor" of German society and as the "Robert Koch of politics" (Koch was a 19th century pioneer in studying the bacterial origin of diseases). The seductive power of National Socialism for many physicians lay in its promise to cleanse German society of its corrupting elements—not just communism and Jews, but also metallic lead and addictive tobacco, along with homosexuality and the "burdensome" mentally ill. [Moreover] Jews and Gypsies were considered "diseased races," tumors in the German body politic. Nazi medical crimes simply don't make sense without this conception of healthy and diseased races, lives worthy and unworthy of living (pp. 32, 34).

As Hubbard (1997) stressed,

> There is a direct link between this campaign of "selection and eradication" and the subsequent genocide of Jews, gypsies, communists, homosexuals and other "undesirables." Early on these people were described as "diseased" and their presence, as an infection or a cancer in the body of the *Volk*. Proctor (1988, p. 194) calls this rationalization

"the medicalization of "antisemitism." . . . [N]othing came easier than
a medical metaphor: Jews as cancer, Jews as disease (pp. 194-195).

Once Jewishness became a malignant medical problem, the step
from the "euthanasia" program to the "final solution" became an acceptable progression. In fact, according to Goldhagen (1996), the Jews were
regarded as a much more dangerous medical threat to the Nazis than
were individuals with disabilities:

> It is highly implausible to maintain that Hitler and those who imple-
> mented the so-called "Euthanasia" program set out to kill, by the tens
> of thousands, non-Jewish Germans with mental illness but did not
> consider, let alone believe with religious-like certitude that the
> Jews—conceived of as being far more malignant and dangerous—
> ought to share this fate. Those whom the Nazis marked for slaughter
> in the "Euthanasia" program (aside from the small percentage of Jews
> among the victims), if conceived of as being "life unworthy of liv-
> ing," were nevertheless thought to be far less of a threat to Germany
> than were the Jews. The congenitally infirm and insane imperiled the
> health of the nation in two ways: first, by their potential for passing
> on their maladies to new generations through propagation and second,
> by consuming food and other resources. But this was child's play
> compared to the putative threat of the Jews, who—unlike the
> "Euthanasia" program's victims—were considered to be willfully
> malignant, powerful, bent upon and perhaps capable of destroying the
> German people *in toto*. Until the Jews were stamped out, Germany
> would be afflicted by their plague. As Hitler put it, "Countless ill-
> nesses are caused by one bacillus: the Jews!" To believe that Hitler
> and other Nazi leaders would have undertaken the "Euthanasia" pro-
> gram and not want to have done the same to the Jews is to believe that
> the same person who would kill a bedbug would prefer not to kill the
> black widow, but to let it continue to live somewhere in his house
> (p. 143).

"Euthanasia" as a prototype for the "Final Solution"
The "Euthanasia" medical killing program served, then, as a pilot
scheme and training model for those who would later implement the
Holocaust (Weindling, 1981). Through its medical killing program the
Nazis learned detached, efficient assembly-line ways to kill huge numbers of persons and how to dispose of their bodies. The euthanasia program also taught them how to perfect the use of gas chambers—methods later adapted and refined by Adolph Eichmann upon his

appointment as head of the Jewish Deportation Department. As Wolfensberger (1981) observed, "[T]he killing of the Jews evolved out of the desensitization, legitimization, personnel preparation and equipment development associated with the killing of handicapped persons" (1981, p. 3). Conot (1983) termed the euthanasia program a "prototype" for the extermination of millions that was to follow. In short, the euthanasia program demonstrated to the Nazis how to fashion a medically based murder machine (p. 210).

Berenbaum (1993) also recognized that the euthanasia program designed to kill disabled persons "prefigured" the Holocaust:

> The killing centers to which the handicapped were transported were the antecedents of the death camps. The organized transportation of the handicapped foreshadowed mass deportation. . . . Gas chambers were first developed at the handicapped killing centers. So was the use of burning to dispose of the dead bodies. . . . Some of the physicians who became specialists in the technology of cold-blooded murder in the late 1930's later staffed the death camps (p. 65).

Proctor (1992) came to the same conclusion:

> The ultimate decision to gas Jews emerged from the fact that the technical apparatus already existed for the destruction of the mentally ill. In the fall of 1941, with the completion of the bulk of the euthanasia operation, the gas chambers at psychiatric hospitals were dismantled and shipped east, where they were reinstalled at Majdanek, Auschwitz, and Treblinka. The same doctors, technicians, and nurses often followed the equipment (p. 37).

An example on point is Dr. Irmfried Eberl, who began his career by learning how to operate the gassing mechanism in the T-4 program at Brandenberg. Eberl later became the commandant of Treblinka, where "killing of a magnitude as yet unimagined" would take place (Lifton, 1986, p. 65). One can judge his cruelty by the fact that he kept huge dogs at Treblinka trained to snap off the genitals of male inmates (Kater, 1989). The euthanasia program taught Eberl the basics of his craft, like the importance of the presence of a physician in a white coat at killing sites (for example, the gas chambers) "to calm the mentally ill and camouflage the killing process" (Lifton, 1986, p. 64). Berenbaum (1993) noted that by 1942, during the fourteen months when Treblinka served as a death camp, between 750,000 and 870,000 Jews were murdered by a staff of 150, some thirty of whom were SS personnel—all veterans of the "euthanasia" program in Germany. They were supported in their work by 120 collaborating Ukrainians (p. 123).

Similarly, Gustav Wagner, the Austrian deputy commandant of the Sobibor extermination camp, trained before the war at Schloss-Hartheim euthanasia institution, where he studiously learned the basics of cold-blooded murder. The euthanasia program taught him well. Wagner learned how to gas large numbers of humans with carbon monoxide fumes from a captured Russian tank. He also learned cruelty. He enjoyed killing inmates with his own hands, sometimes using an ax, shovel or whip (Bower, 1981). In Sobibor, Wagner was known as the "Angel of Death."

Another Angel of Death who served his apprenticeship in the euthanasia program was Dr. Joseph Mengele at Auschwitz. Mengele thought of himself as a "biomedical scientist" participating in a broad program of racial research (Proctor, 1988). During the Holocaust itself, Mengele and many other Nazi physicians used thousands of concentration camp inmates with disabilities and "deformities" as subjects for their biomedical racial "research" (Lifton, 1986; Posner and Ware, 1986; Proctor, 1988; Müller, 1991).

Mengele held both an M.D. degree in medicine and a Ph.D. in anthropology. He had studied under the leading exponents of the "life unworthy of living theory" and it greatly influenced his thinking and behavior. As Posner and Ware (1986) speculated, "The notion that some lives were not worth living, soon to become academically respectable, may explain why ten years later Mengele experimented on concentration camp inmates as though they were laboratory rats" (p. 9).

Mengele was known for conducting crude surgery and painful tests often without anesthetics. Mozes-Kor (1992), a victim of Mengele's experiments related horror stories of operations, including castrations, conducted in the attempt to "make boys into girls and girls into boys. Mengele also attempted to connect the urinary tract of a 7-year old girl to her own colon. Many experiments were performed on the male and female genitals" (p. 57). During his bizarre experiments on twins (his specialty), he performed needless amputations, lumbar punctures and typhus injections, and he deliberately infected wounds for comparison purposes. In one such experiment, he wanted to interchange a pair of identical twins' blood supply. A witness provided this graphic description:

One day Mengele brought chocolate and special clothes. The next day, SS men came and took two children away. They were two of my pets, Tito and Nino. One of them was a hunchback. Two or three days later, an SS man brought them back in a terrible state. They had been cut. The hunchback was sewn to the other child, back to back, their wrists back to back too. There was a terrible smell of gangrene. The cuts were dirty and the children cried every night (cited in Posner & Ware, 1986, p. 37).

Posner and Ware (1986) also described Mengele's cold medical detachment from his victims:

After spotting a "hunchbacked" father standing next to his fifteen-year-old son, who had a deformed right foot, he was impatient to learn if there were further common abnormalities. He selected them from the ramp and gave them a last meal, which they ate ravenously, unaware that they were soon to die. . . . Half an hour later, Mengele had them shot and ordered their skeletons to be prepared by boiling their bodies in water so the flesh could be easily stripped from the bones. The skeletons were then immersed in a bath of petrol to make them dry, odorless, and white (p. 41).

A witness to the incident described how Mengele was so pleased he brought in several officers to inspect the bones:

They pompously examined parts of the skeletons and launched into high-sounding scientific terms, talking as if the two victims represented an extremely rare medical phenomenon. They abandoned themselves completely to their pseudo-science (Nyiszli, cited in Posner & Ware, 1986, p. 41).

Besides twins, Mengele's other medical fascination for study were persons, particularly Jews, with such medical differences as scoliosis, mental retardation, hermaphroditism, extreme height and dwarfism. Under Hitler and Mengele, the Nazis practiced a most frightening form of "heightism". As Hitler himself wrote in *Mein Kampf,*

Any crossing of two beings not at exactly the same level produces a medium between the level of the two parents. This means: the off-spring will probably stand higher than the racially lower parent, but not as high as the higher one. Consequently, it will later succumb in the struggle against the higher level. Such mating is contrary to the will of Nature for a higher breeding of all life (p. 285).

According to Gillis (1982),

The single most important physical feature of the so-called Nordic race, which Hitler claimed to be superior, was height. Blond hair and blue eyes were also part of his ideal type, but height was more essential because the Nazi doctrine centered upon the principle of conquest through brute force and intimidation (p. 11).

Most of the time, those with dwarfism and other "abnormal" physical development were selected upon arrival at Auschwitz and carefully measured and recorded by inmate doctors. Each was then shot by an SS non-commissioned officer, who then turned the body over to an inmate doctor for dissection and further medical recording. The corpses were then treated with calcium chloride, with the bones carefully wrapped and sent to the institute at Berlin-Dahlem for study (Lifton, 1986).

Mengele was so thrilled upon discovering inmates, particularly Jews, with physical differences, that he was described as beside himself with joy upon discovering an entire circus family of Romanian Jews with dwarfism arriving at Auschwitz (Lifton, 1986, p. 360, Posner and Ware, 1986, p. 54). To focus Himmler's attention on his work,

[He] set up a sideshow of his most treasured set of dwarfs, all seven of them, before an audience of one senior bureaucrat and 2,000 SS Men. . . . Mengele stripped the family naked and triumphantly paraded them on stage, complete with a family tree to illustrate his point that they were the offspring of "degenerate" Jewish forebears (Posner & Ware, p. 55).

So devoted to his work was Mengele that he continued until the end of the war when it was certain that Nazi Germany would lose. As late as December 5, 1944, before Auschwitz could be destroyed and dismantled, Mengele experimented on sixteen females with dwarfism. Only five survived.

One of Mengele's colleagues at Auschwitz was Dr. Horst Schumann, the leading sterilization experimenter. Earlier, Schumann had been predictably the head of one of the euthanasia projects and had been a prominent figure in the program (Lifton, 1990, p. 225).

The Nazi doctors involved all learned important lessons from their apprenticeship in the euthanasia program designed to eradicate persons with disabilities. In particular, the Nazis learned that by adopting a model based on medical authority and calling it a healing process, they could build a murder machine to exterminate millions. They were relished by the medical efficiency implemented in completing the important task of killing those people they considered useless social ballast. Lifton and Markusen (1988) summarized this monstrous rationale:

> A kind of apocalyptic biology led, perhaps inevitably, to a vision and practice of killing to heal. The Nazi cure was as literal as it was murderous and consisted of ridding the world of *life* unworthy of life by means of five identifiable steps: coercive sterilization, the killing of impaired children, the killing of impaired adults (these latter two steps erroneously called "euthanasia"), the selection and killing of impaired inmates of concentration camps, and finally the mass killings of Jews in the extermination camps them-selves. . . . They were all expressions of biological purification, of destroying bad genes and bad racial elements in order to revitalize the Nordic race and the world at large (p. 57).

Proctor (1992) added that "there were both theoretical and practical continuities between the destruction of the 'lives not worth living' in Germany's hospitals and the destruction of Germany's ethnic and social minorities" (p. 37). It all was based on the medical model. As Dr. Andrew Ivy, who helped prosecute the Nazi physicians at Nuremburg concluded, "Had the profession taken a strong stand again the mass killing of sick Germans before the war, it is conceivable that the entire idea and technique of death factories for genocide would not have materialized" (cited in Gallagher, 1995, pp. 31-32). Gallagher added that "had the doctors acted differently, had they said no, things would have been different. An early link in the chain of events leading to the Holocaust would have been broken" (p. 32). As Fiedler (1996) wrote of the "euthanasia-final solution" link: "It is a development which should make us aware of just how dangerous enforced physiological normality is when the definition of its parameters falls into the hands of politicians and bureaucrats" (p. 150).

Unfortunately, because the victims of the euthanasia (Aktion T4 and the later Aktion 14F13) were "defective" and thought to be subhuman, the German courts tended to tolerate the perpetrators. According to Müller (1991), the Supreme Court of Germany decided that although Dr. Kurt Borm, a former SS officer, had killed 6,652 disabled individuals, he was found not guilty because the mass murders were seen as "chiefly an act of humanitarianism" (cited in Müller, 1991, p. 255). The Supreme Court viewed the physicians of the euthanasia program as acting out of "considerations of an ethical nature" (cited in Müller, 1991, p. 255). Müller (1991) stated,

> In 1949, for example, a trial took place involving the staff of Grafeneck "asylum" where about 10,000 victims were first "disinfected" and then disposed of by burning. On July 5, the Tübingen County Court found that the determining factor in the behavior of psychiatrist Dr. Valentin Falthauser had been "pity, one of the noblest motives for human action." And on October 24, 1951, the Cologne County Court acquitted the neurologist Dr. Lau because he had been moved to participate in the euthanasia program "out of idealism." He had, in the words of the court, "seen the inmates of the asylum as creatures still human and deserving of pity," as was proven "by the concern he showed in procuring the coffins necessary to bury" them (pp. 255-256).

Disablist (handicapist) attitudes toward survivors with disabilities is extremely evident in the German governmental policy on reparations for those persecuted by the Nazis. The Federal Reparations Law of 1953 limited itself only to those who suffered discrimination or injury "because of their opposition to National Socialism or because of their race, creed, or ideology" (cited in Müller, 1991, p. 263):

> The wording of the law thus excluded large groups of victims from the very start, including the 350,000 people who had undergone sterilization and the families of all those murdered in the course of the euthanasia program. Applications for reparation payments filed by the former group were regularly turned down "because sterilization was not a form of persecution but was performed purely for medical reasons," and because "the Law for Prevention of Hereditary Diseases was not unconstitutional as such" (p. 263).

Contributions of Americans with Disabilities to the War Effort
As an interesting historical sidelight, while the Nazis killed their citizens with disabilities, Americans with disabilities served their country as workers and soldiers in the war effort. Wolfe (1995) described how

they regularly filled in for ablebodied young men fighting in the armed forces. With the massive war mobilization, citizens with deafness, blindness, physical disabilities and mental retardation worked in weapons and clothing factories. For some, physical difference provided an advantage rather than a disadvantage. For example, air raid wardens with blindness teamed with sighted partners because it was believed their heightened auditory acuity helped them hear planes approach more quickly, and factory workers with dwarfism in airplane plants could squirm into the wings and other tight places that required welding or riveting. Just as the manpower shortage gave working opportunities to Blacks and women like the wartime heroine, "Rosie the Riveter," it gave similar opportunities to persons with disabilities. For instance, workers with blindness sewed uniforms and gun covers and over 1,000 workers with deafness worked in rubber factories in Ohio. As Wolfe (1995) noted, young men with mental retardation even served in the armed forces. One hundred young men with mental retardation from the Wayne State School in Michigan had joined the service by 1943. Eighty-eight successfully adjusted to military life and thirty-one per cent even received promotions. At the time, these soldiers with mental retardation could die for their country but could not get married or obtain an education or job in most of the states that made up the country they were defending (Wolfe, 1995). "They were real-life Forrest Gumps" (J. Shapiro, 1995, p. 29). It is also a sad commentary that as soon as the war ended, almost all of those with disabilities who had contributed to the war effort lost their jobs because their country no longer needed them for uniforms or weapons, and returning veterans needed the work (Wolfe, 1995).

Japanese Medical Atrocities
Meanwhile, the Nazis' Axis partners, the Japanese, also practiced medical killing. In fact, American, Russian and Chinese prisoners of war were subjected to horrific experiments by the Japanese Imperial Army's Unit 731, with the participation of Kyushu University. The horrors perpetrated by the Japanese physicians on American prisoners included these documented five:

1.   shooting them in the stomach to give Japanese surgeons practice extracting bullets,

2. performing needless amputations and dissections while the victims were awake,

3. removing parts of livers to see if the patient would survive and giving intravenous injections of sea water to determine its ability to serve as a sterile saline solution,

4. removing part of the brain to control epilepsy, and

5. performing vivisection.

Like the work of the Nazi doctors, the Japanese proceeded in the name of science and medicine. Like the Nazis, many got away with it. Of the 30 Japanese doctors brought to trial, 23 were found guilty of various charges and all were set free by 1958 (A Nightmare Amid the Horrors of War, 1995, p. A-18).

A Comparison of Institutional to Concentration Camp Living
Nazi concentration camps, with their roots and rationale in the medical model and many state institutions for persons with mental retardation or illness in the United States, bear some disturbing social-process similarities. But, as Caplan (1992a) stressed, "Analogies to the Holocaust must be carefully constructed and justified" (p. 273). Glib claims of moral equivalence distort the monstrosity of the Holocaust crimes. Nevertheless, lessons can be learned by examining certain analogous social processes and mechanisms. As Orlans (1948) wrote,

> I [do not] assert that there is an identity between the American asylum and the German Death camp. I am, instead, interested in certain similarities of social process in both institutions, and my thesis is that the American asylum manifests, in embryo, some of the social mechanisms which in Germany matured into death camps (cited in Szasz, 1970, p. 216).

And Ellis (1995), an advocate with cerebral palsy, noted,

> I remember that the same eugenics movement that went haywire in Nazi Germany led this country to throw a lot of people with mental retardation and other developmental disabilities into institutions just to get us out of sight. That same inhumanity led to the castration and sterilization of thousands of us during the first half of this century.

That same inhumanity led to scientific experiments that fed hundreds more of us radioactive materials in the 1940s and 1950s. That same inhumanity still produces countless acts of cruelty in our institutions today. . . . [W]e have come across reports of several instances of coerced homosexuality, a woman being tortured with a hot curling iron, and several men and women being raped, one with a garden hose (pp. 2-3).

State institutions for persons with mental retardation and illness and Nazi concentration camps were both examples of what Goffman (1962) called "total institutions." As such, they shared much in common. For example, when reading interviews and personal accounts of survivors of both concentration camps and institutions, one commonly comes across the theme, "I survived to tell my story." Of course, institutional inmates were not terrorized by daily threats of slaughter, and whatever atrocities they did face were, on balance, overall far less barbaric and heinous. In addition, some institutions operated in a humane manner. Still, similarities exist beyond the "I survived" theme. For example, inmates of concentration camps and institutions both had to live under a system that dictated the entire scope of their lives from above by explicit rulings devised by medical officials. Moreover, both faced incarceration not for what they did but for who they were. As a result, inmates of concentration camps and inmates of institutions were dehumanized, robbed of their person-hood, officially perceived as genetically inferior and seen as a threat to society. Both types of inmates were segregated by sex; victimized by medical abuse, (for example, being sterilized without their consent); forced to work against their will; forced to live in a caste system under the rule of other inmates; often victimized by physical abuse, (often rape); provided inadequate diets and cheap, ill-fitting clothing from a common pool; forced to sleep in large groups in cramped, sparsely furnished, dormitory barracks; treated and moved in blocks; and forced to live all phases of their lives under a structured system with its rules imposed for the purpose of meeting the needs of the state and institution.

The daily routines of both institutions were humiliating and dehumanizing. As J. Shapiro (1993) stated, "As late as the 1960s it remained common for inmates at state hospitals to be bathed by stripping off their clothes, forming them into a line, and spraying them with water from a garden hose" (p. 160). In addition, institutionalized persons with disabilities and concentration camp inmates were both forced to live in filthy, squalid conditions.

Additionally, inmates in concentration camps and institutions were subject to often intrusive medical experimentation. Of course, the experiments conducted on institutionalized inmates were less hideous than those conducted by Mengele and his cohorts. Still, they were conducted without the knowledge or permission of the subjects and their families, and without any prospect of direct medical benefit to the subjects or society (Advisory Committee on Human Radiation Experiments [ACHRE], 1994, 1996). At the Fernald School, during the 1950s, government-sponsored research was conducted on children with mental retardation, and as ACHRE reported, "The Fernald School experiments were tracer studies using radioactive calcium in a population that included institutionalized mentally compromised children" (p. 16). These government experiments whose researchers also involved Harvard University and the Massachusetts Institute of Technology helped feed approximately 120 of the school's students oatmeal breakfasts with small doses of radioactive isotopes. The ingredients, given in milk and cereal, hoped to ascertain if a chemical in oatmeal would interfere with the body's ability to absorb iron and calcium. The students were told they were participating in a "science club activity." Those studies now receive criticism for being conducted without the full consent from the participants or their guardians, for providing no benefit to the participants, and for using persons in a vulnerable population without protecting them (ACHRE, 1994; Retarded school alumni told they consumed radiation with their oatmeal, (Newark, NJ) *The Star Ledger*, January 14, 1994, p. 27; Burns, 1995; Hoversten, 1995; Clinton apologizes to all wronged by radiation testing, *The Trenton Times*, October 4, 1995, p. A10; ACHRE, 1996). Such experimentation on "vulnerable populations" occurred between World War II and the mid-1970s nationally on over 16,000 humans with the Atomic Energy Commission's express approval or financial support. For example, during the 1960s at the University of Arkansas Medical Center in Little Rock, children with mental retardation (some as young as 13) who were wards of the Arkansas Children's Colony, a state institution, received "iodine-131" in a thyroid study. In a similar University of Arkansas study experiments involved infants as young as nine months. A study completed at the University of Washington between 1954 and 1958 used "mental patients" from the Northern State Hospital in Sedro-Woolley as unknowing subjects (Burns, 1995; Hoversten, 1995a, 1995b). As ACHRE (1996) reported,

> in some nontherapeutic tracer studies involving children, radioisotope exposures were associated with increases in the potential lifetime risk for developing thyroid cancer that would be considered unacceptable today (pp. 10-11).

ACHRE (1996) found that little attention had been paid, during the 1940s and 1950s, to issues of fairness in the selection of subjects for radiation studies it reported:

> The Committee then selected for particular consideration radioisotope research that used children as subjects. We determined to focus on children for several reasons. First, at low levels of radiation exposure, children are at greater risk of harm than adults. Second, children were the most appropriate group in which to pursue the Committee's mandate with respect to notification of former subjects for medical reasons. They are the group most likely to have been harmed by their participation in research, and they are more likely than other former subjects still to be alive. Third, when the Committee considered how best to study subject populations it chose the ones that were most likely to be exploited because of their relative dependency or powerlessness (p. 27).

Obviously, as ACHRE concluded, the groups considered powerless and dependent included, infants, children, minorities, the terminally ill, persons with cognitive disabilities and the institutionalized (1994, pp. 4-5).

More similarities between the living conditions of death camp inmates and state institution patients include environmental deprivation through isolation enforced by such devices as locked living units, barred windows and fences (often reinforced with barbed wire) and constant surveillance. Blatt (1970, 1981), while observing four state institutions for persons with mental retardation in four Eastern states during the Christmas season of 1965, was appalled by the high priority accorded to security:

> Sometimes there are fences, once in a while with barbed wire. Very frequently, the buildings impress [the visitor] with their sheer massiveness and impenetrability. I have observed bars on windows and locks—many locks-on inside as well as outside doors. . . . Many

of the doors are made of heavy gauge metal or thick wood. It is routine, and second nature, for attendants to pass from room to room with a key chain in hand locking doors as they pass (pp. 142-143).

At the four state institutions, Blatt found remarkably similar conditions to those described by Higgins and Metcalf over 150 years earlier in the Bedlam and York asylums. He related the following first hand account:

> As I entered this dormitory, housing severely mentally retarded adolescents and adults. . . an overwhelming stench enveloped me. It was the sickening, suffocating smell of feces and urine, decay, dirt and filth, of such strength as to hang in the air and, I thought then and still am not dissuaded, solid enough to be cut or shoveled away. But, as things turned out, the odors were among the gentlest assaults on our sensibilities. I was soon to learn about the decaying humanity that caused them (1981, p. 142).

Like Higgins and Metcalf at the Bedlam and York asylums, Blatt encountered filth, as well as cruel, inhuman treatment, including the common use of restraints and solitary confinement:

> Many dormitories for the severely and moderately retarded ambulatory residents have solitary confinement cells or what is officially referred to, and is jokingly called by many attendants, "therapeutic isolation." Therapeutic isolation means solitary confinement—in its most punitive and inhumane form. These cells are located on an upper floor, off to the side and away from the casual or official visitor's scrutiny. . . . Isolation cells are generally tiny rooms, approximately seven feet by seven feet (p. 143-144).

Blatt found in one such therapeutic isolation cell a young boy, 13 or 14 years old, completely nude, lying on his own urine and feces. Apparently, the youth had been in solitary confinement for several days for using abusive language to an attendant. Blatt also found, at several institutions, youngsters in solitary confinement for infractions like breaking windows, or supposedly striking attendants. By ironic contrast, in one dormitory Blatt saw another young man who had been merely sent to bed early because he had bitten off the ear of a patient:

Apparently, it is infinitely more serious to strike an attendant (and it should not be misunderstood that I condone this) than to bite off the ear of another resident (p. 143).

Other conditions Blatt found included a young man who was glaring at him through the screen of a door in a solitary cell splattered with feces around the opening, and the use of restraints on children whose hands were tied, legs bound or waists secured (pp. 143-144).

The conditions Blatt reported from 1965 sound a lot like those found by Biklen (1977) and a group of special educators who observed in six state institutions and five state hospitals as part of the 1970 and 1971 *Workshop on Human Abuse, Protection, and Policy* at Syracuse University. Biklen's group was warned in advance of conditions within the institutions "almost to the point where we thought only the worst hell could compare with the horrible conditions we would find. As it turned out nothing could have prepared us for what we experienced" (p. 31). Here are four of the conditions Biklen and his colleagues described:

1. Twenty severely retarded boys, clothed in short gray pants or naked, locked in a large, barren room with nothing to do;

2. A man batting his head against the locked steel doors of a ward;

3. A young girl in a locked ward who ate a shoelace, a television knob, and her own excrement while the attendants went on a coffee break; and

4. Young children in isolation cells, old women tied to benches, and youngsters "who sit in locked wards staring into space or at television sets (both on and off)" (pp. 31-33).

The horrible conditions Blatt, Biklen, and others found, (for example at Willowbrook and Pennhurst), reflect society's paradigm of an institution and its role. Again, change comes, not from replacing the medical and administrative personnel, but from viewing the problem as a matter of the civil rights of the patients.

Biklen (1977) stressed the importance of maintaining a political and social perspective and examining the broader issues of deviance and social control so as to understand institutional life. He concluded, "[I]nstitutions are products primarily of society, not of individuals and the effects of institutionalization can best be understood as originating from social rather than individual forces" (p. 35). Sarason and Doris (1979) similarly stated, "Let us not scapegoat institutions which, after all, exist as an expression of attitudes and policies of the larger society" (p. 93).

Braginsky and Braginsky (1971) found that institutions functioned "primarily as catchment areas which facilitate the 'social sanitation' process of society" (p. vi). They noted, "The only large scale facilities available for the collection of discarded, unneeded children are the institutions for the mentally retarded" (p. vi).

The Continued Legacy: Some Worldwide Examples
Abuse and sanctioned killing of persons with disabilities can be found throughout the world. Six of the more blatant reported examples follow here:

China: The Sanctioned Killing of Disabled Children in Orphanages
One would have thought that the horror of government sanctioned killing of disabled children with the full complicity of the medical establishment had ended with the Nazis. But such government sanctioned policies continue into the present. Thousands of babies with disabilities have been systematically starved to death or killed through prolonged neglect and abuse in Chinese orphanages (China's orphanages of death, 1996; Orphanage denies human rights claims, 1996; Report: Chinese orphanages starve babies, 1996; Human Rights Watch/ Asia, 1996). In 1989, the death rate in some of the orphanages in various Chinese provinces ran as high as 72.5 percent. Abandoned children, mostly female or disabled, "were being neglected as a deliberate policy to kill them" (Fletcher, 1996, p. 1). Thousands of babies have been systematically starved to keep the Chinese orphanage population stable.

As with the Nazi "euthanasia" program and much of the Holocaust, the current policy of deliberate murder reflects the application of medical practices for the "good of the state." Like the death-making of the Nazis, the Chinese methods of eliminating unwanted children proceeds with intentional neglect and extreme cruelty. As Human Rights Watch/Asia (1996) found:

> medical records and testimony show that deaths at the Shanghai orphanage were in many cases deliberate and cruel. Child-care workers reportedly selected unwanted infants and children for death by

intentional deprivation of food and water—a process known among the workers as "summary resolution" of children's alleged medical problems. When an orphan chosen in this manner was visibly on the point of death from starvation or medical neglect, orphanage doctors were then asked to perform medical "consultations" which served as a ritual marking the child for subsequent termination of care, nutrition, and other life-saving intervention. Deaths from acute malnutrition were then, in many cases, falsely recorded as having resulted from other causes, often entirely spurious or irrelevant conditions such as "mental deficiency" and "cleft-palate" (p. 5).

As with the Nazi "euthanasia" program, unwanted children were systematically eliminated with senior medical staffs playing a central role within a medical model. Human Rights Watch/Asia reported that unwanted girls are being labeled as being physically or mentally disabled and,

doctors then used these supposed disabilities as justification for eliminating unwanted infants through starvation and medical neglect. Such unconscionable behavior by doctors in China's most advanced and cosmopolitan city points to an ethical crisis of immense proportions in the country's medical profession (p. 6).

In addition, China's current policy toward persons with disabilities, like that of the Nazis, is based on notions of "Racial Purity and Eugenics." As Human Rights Watch/Asia further explained,

In order to address this issue properly, we must consider China's contemporary theory and practice in the realm of birth science—a literal English rendering of the Chinese term *youshengxue,* which is the original translation (and the only term found) in Chinese for the word "eugenics." A set of quasi-medical concepts and theories deriving largely from social Darwinism notions of competitive national evolution, eugenisism held that certain types of people, particularly the mentally disabled and those with various congenital physical defects, represented a blemish on human society which could be gradually removed by the adoption of various new and orthodox medical interventions. By common consensus, eugenics remains a highly dangerous field of human endeavor, and one especially susceptible to political manipulation (p. 208).

Again, attitudes and paradigms provide the basis of negative social policy. For example, in 1988, the Province of Gansu passed legislation entitled, "Regulations Prohibiting Idiots, Imbeciles and Morons from Having Children." These regulations state that upon medical discovery,

> feeble-minded persons are prohibited from having children; feeble-minded persons must undergo surgical sterilization as a prerequisite of receiving permission to marry; and feeble-minded persons who are already pregnant must undergo termination of pregnancy and surgical sterilization (cited in *Death by Default*, p. 209).

Human Rights Watch/Asia (1996) documented some of the cruel, inhuman, or degrading treatment toward children in the orphanages. Such abuse included improper feeding practices, tying of limbs, improper medication, beatings, torture and physical abuse.

1. IMPROPER FEEDING PRACTICES LEADING TO SEVERE MALNUTRITION OR DEATH: Human Watch Rights/Asia (1996) found that although the diet provided the children at one orphanage, The Children's Institute, was "far from ideal, containing inadequate levels of protein and vitamins," it was the feeding method itself that forced babies to die. Infants at the orphanage were bottle-fed cow's milk. However, for administrative convenience, the hospital staff did not directly feed the babies. Instead, the child care workers placed the bottles in the cribs wrapped in a cloth diaper for infants to nurse unattended. This act of administrative convenience proved fatal to many children, especially the large number with cleft palate (a failure of the two halves of the palate to grow together during the embryological period) waiting for the relatively simple operation to correct the problem. Human Rights Watch/Asia (1996) observed, "Since infants with cleft palates cannot bottle-feed without assistance this usually led to starvation and death long before surgery could be arranged" (p. 258). In addition, Human Rights Watch/Asia found that many unattended children choked to death from being tied to their beds. Others died during these unattended bottle feedings because they lost their grip on the nipple and consumed only a portion of the allotted meal. When this occurred, the child care workers routinely would not provide further nourishment. Undernourishment led to malnutrition which led to death from pneumonia and other contagious diseases. Children were often allowed to choke to death with no attempt at

intervention by the child care staff. When a child's death occurred, it was reported at the end of feeding time.

2. TYING OF CHILDREN'S LIMBS: According to Human Rights Watch/ Asia, many witnesses reported that before 1993, "infants and children at the Child Welfare Institute were routinely tied to cribs, beds and chairs, chiefly as another means of reducing the staff workload" (p. 259). One witness reported seeing close to 200 infants and young children lying in bed with their hands tied to the bed frames with gauze. During the winter of 1991, during a period of extremely cold weather in Shanghai, at least fifteen children died at the orphanage over a four-day period. An investigative team subsequently found that

> large numbers of children were being tied to their beds. The team also discovered several small children tied to their chairs, often wearing only thin clothing with no shoes or socks, and able to relieve themselves only through holes in the chair seats into chamberpots placed underneath. A number of these children had developed blue-black discolorations on their skin, apparently a symptom of advanced hypothermia aggravated by the immobilization of their limbs (p. 259).

One institute official denied that the children were suffering from frostbite and told the investigators that the marks and bruises were caused by a "platelet disorder" (Human Rights Watch/Asia, 1996).

3. IMPROPER MEDICATION: Before 1993, many children at the Children's Welfare Institute were forced to take powerful, addicting, and medically inappropriate drugs—again, for administrative convenience. The purpose of these drugs, given to older orphans in the Disabled Section (*Shangcanbu*), was to keep children with severe disabilities calm, sedated and confined to their beds. Drugs most routinely used for this purpose were phenobarbital, chlorpromazine (a tranquilizer used in the treatment of schizophrenia) and dilantin (a muscle relaxant and anticonvulsant used to treat seizure disorders). In addition, girls at the orphanage who reached puberty were routinely placed on contraceptives, "not to prevent unwanted pregnancies but simply to suppress menstruation and avoid the associated inconvenience to orphanage staff" (Human Rights Watch/ Asia, 1996, p. 260).

4. BEATINGS, TORTURE, AND PHYSICAL ABUSE BY STAFF: It was reported that all older orphans at the Children's Welfare Institute suffered violent physical abuse, amounting to torture, by the hands of the staff, for minor disciplinary infractions or just at the whim of the child care workers. Violent attacks on children were so common, that many smaller children would instinctively duck and put up their hands for protection when an adult came near. Human Rights Watch/Asia listed some of the most common disciplinary methods:

- forcing children to assume the "airplane" and "motorcycle" positions for long periods of time (respectively, bent forward horizontally at the waist with arms held vertically upward, and sitting unsupported at half-squat with arms stretched forward horizontally). In some cases, these techniques were supplemented by forcing children to balance bowls of hot water, so that scalding occurred when the child fell;

- forcing children to kneel on ridged washboards for long periods of time;

- hanging children upside down with their heads submerged in water, until nosebleeds and near-suffocation ensued. This technique, known as *qiang shui* ("choking on water"), was reportedly the one most feared by children (p. 260).

Other less sophisticated disciplinary methods included,

- giving blows to the head and face with wooden poles and heavy plastic slippers (resulting in cuts and bruises that most often went medically unattended, in turn, resulting in infections and death from untreated septicemia);

- locking a child in a hot tin shed with very little food or water;

- hanging a six-year-old child, with a disfiguring birthmark, out of a high dormitory window and forcing her to step on tiptoe while she got beaten;

- forcing a child with partially disabled legs to swallow a number of small magnets;

- forcing youngsters with disabilities into slave labor;

- tying up a fourteen-year-old boy with mild mental retardation, in a standing position where he was then stabbed in his genitals repeatedly with a *yacha* (a metal fork attached to a bamboo pole, used to hang and remove clothes hangers from a clothesline or drying rack). The youngster was also tied up and ordered to jump up and down as his classmates were ordered to pull out his pubic hair.

In addition, a large number of orphan girls with mental retardation at the Shanghai Children's Institute claimed to have been regularly raped and sexually abused by the male staff, including the director (Human Rights Watch/Asia, 1996, pp. 260-265).

Viet Nam
Frightful conditions can be found in institutions throughout the world, and Justin Dart, Jr., a disabilities rights activist who contracted polio as a child in 1948, described conditions he found in Saigon that clearly demonstrate the "subhuman status" assigned to those with disabilities like this. He likened them to conditions found in concentration camps. Dart, in his wheelchair, entered a large metal shed with a concrete floor:

> One hundred young children had been brought into this flimsy shed, left to die and be buried in an unmarked grave outside. . . . The children had been left on the floor "with bloated bellies and matchstick arms and legs like you see in pictures from Dachau and Auschwitz, with their eyes bugging out, lying in their own feces and urine and their bodies covered with flies." Once in a while, someone would bring a suffering child a bowl of maggoty rice (J. Shapiro, 1993, p. 109-110).

North Korea
As Kristof (1994) reported,

> There are no mentally retarded or handicapped people in the North Korean capital, Pyongyang, a rare beauty of a city in a continent where capitals tend to be cluttered and chaotic. It is impossible to prove, of course, but it appears that the Government has exiled disabled people to other cities for fear that foreigners might see them and get a bad impression. North Korean officials deny this, saying that disabled people have voluntarily moved to other parts of the country (p. 6E).

Japan

A similar pattern of embarrassment, avoidance, and denial appears in Japan, where, "Physical and mental disabilities seem to arouse powerful feelings of shame" (Kristof, 1996, p. 3). As Naotaka Kumeta, a wheelchair user from Shizoka, stated,

> Japanese consider someone different an outcast, a source of shame. People think it shameful that I go out and about. They say, "Remember, you're handicapped." . . . People say that Japan is a very developed society. But for the handicapped it is very backward, decades behind the United States. Look how people are staring at me—it's like that all the time (cited in Kristoff, 1996, p. 3).

Because Japanese culture emphasizes conformity, those who look or act different are often stigmatized and excluded. According to Kumeta (1996), "The exclusion usually means that the disabled are often discouraged from working, from marrying, from going to movie theaters or restaurants" (cited in Kristoff. 1996, p. 3). Such ostracism is more severe in Japan because the social group is "far more cohesive, far more important and less tolerant of individuality than in America" (WuDunn, 1996, p. 3E).

Such stigmatizing extended even to those children who, in 1966, were infected with E. coli 0157:H7 food poisoning acquired in their school cafeterias. The children who fell ill became outcasts at school and were so severely bullied (*ijime*) by their uninfected classmates that some committed suicide (WuDunn, 1996). Infected children were teased by being called, "You germ!" "You're 0157!" According to WuDunn,

> In traditional Japanese belief, infectious diseases were less a medical phenomenon than a superstitious one in which the victim's ancestors were thought to have done something bad, or at least deviated from the social standards. The term also brings back images of past horrors like smallpox and leprosy. And so many people mistakenly concluded that E. coli 0157 victims should be avoided like the plague (p. 3E).

Another indicator of official Japanese attitude is the government's refusal to offer apologies or pay compensation for a program that forcibly sterilized more than 16,000 women with disabilities for over 5 decades (ending in 1996), because "the program was legal at the time"

(*Japan Says Forced Sterilizations Merit No Payments, No Apologies,* 1977, p. A12).

Germany

According to Fletcher (1993), "Since 1989, a vicious campaign of violence and intimidation against disabled people in Germany has gathered force, in parallel with attacks on other minority groups" (p. 23). Fletcher cited these examples:

•   fire-bombing residential institutions for disabled people;

•   chasing of disabled individuals from North Sea beaches;

•   banning disabled children from school trips;

•   the brutal beating of an elderly man with visual impairment, who died on the way to the hospital;

•   the brutal beating of children with hearing-impairments by skinheads offended by their use of sign language;

•   brutally beating and spitting upon wheelchair users;

•   driving a wheelchair user to suicide with insults like "under Hitler, people like you would have been gassed long ago." (Fletcher, 1993, Disabled Germans feeling echoes of Nazism, 1992).

Perhaps, one of the most revealing recent examples of continued negative hostility in Germany involved a judge in the city of Flensburg who granted a couple on tour, a ten-percent refund on their travel costs, "on the grounds that their holiday enjoyment was compromised since they had to eat their meals in a hotel restaurant where a group of disabled people also ate" (Fletcher, 1993, p. 24). According to Wolfe (1993), the judge ruled that "the unavoidable sight of disabled people reminded the appellants in an unusually intensive way of the possibilities of human suffering. Such experiences are not expected on a typical holiday" (p. 12).

El Salvador

Fletcher (1993) revealed that in May of 1993, security police in San Salvador

> opened fire with automatic rifles on a group of 5,000 disabled people who were demonstrating for medical care and other benefits. Three disabled people were killed and another ten to fifteen disabled people were injured. About thirty people were arrested, including two wheelchair users who were dragged along the ground by police (p. 23).

Era of Civil Rights

Funk (1987) noted that by the end of the 1950s disability policy began to effect a civil right orientation and one could detect an increasing humanization of a certain class of disabled people based on qualities of deservedness, normality and employability, and a move from total societal indifference to a recognition that the remaining unfortunates must receive some minimum level of care (p. 14).

Funk described the attitudes before then as tolerant of retaining persons with disabilities in a caste status and assuming that most would always require segregated care and protection. With charity and medical professionals in charge, better services would be provided to individuals who would, "retain their childlike dependent status in perpetuity" (p. 14).

After World War II, as the world became aware of the atrocities of the Holocaust with its roots in "race purification," as well as the horrors in institutions, concepts like eugenics began to wane in acceptance and influence.

In addition, such advocacy and parent organizations as the Association for Retarded Children (now Citizens), and the United Cerebral Palsy Association began to fight for deinstitionalization and the public education of their children. They successfully lobbied Congress to establish a federal bureau for "handicapped children" and to provide funds for training special education teachers and developing appropriate curricula (J. Shapiro, 1993).

By the 1960's, the United States entered a civil rights era, a time when formal organizations and coalitions of persons with disabilities could, by analogy to other oppressed groups, cut across medically based disability differences and focus their efforts on civil rights issues rather than on the advancement of a particular small constituency. Demands for equal rights, options, opportunities, inclusion in society, and access arose in the wake of such civil rights demands as those of Black Americans and a revitalized feminist movement (Scotch, 1987; Funk, 1987). Funk (1987) described the influence of this social and political activity on the disability rights movement:

> The pressures of history coalesced in mounting demands for equality of opportunity for a major segment of the population who were disenfranchised and disadvantaged because of discrimination based on poverty, racial, or ethnic background or gender. . . . Disabled people began to question the tradition of limited options, exclusions, and dependency (p. 14).

The first civil rights act for persons with disabilities, *Section 504 of the Rehabilitation Act Amendments of 1973, (PL 93-112),* was really a legislative afterthought, but its influence was soon well established (Scotch, 1984; J. Shapiro, 1993). Before the more all encompassing *Americans With Disabilities Act, (PL 101-336), Section 504* provided the most comprehensive civil rights protection to persons with disabilities. Basically, the law stated that recipients of federal funds could not discriminate against any individual in the provision of services, regardless of handicap. More specifically, *Section 504* stated that

> No otherwise qualified handicapped individual in the United States, as defined by section 7(6), shall, solely by reason of his handicap, be excluded from the participation in, be denied the benefits of, or be subjected to discrimination under any program or activity receiving Federal financial assistance (U.S. Congress, 1973).

The wording in *Section 504* matched the *Civil Rights Act of 1964*, which abolished discrimination in federally funded programs on the basis of race, color or national origin. Regarding youngsters classified as handicapped, *Section 504* guaranteed that they receive educational services and opportunities equal to those provided to nonhandicapped children (Shore, 1986). For example, a school district may not shorten the school year for its classified students only. Similarly, if a student classified as "learning disabled" needs a calculator to succeed in a mathematics class, denying him or her to use of that calculator is a civil rights violation. The calculator becomes a sort of "prothesis" the student needs to overcome an environmental handicap. *Section 504* also prohibits a district from excluding a student with a physical disability from an appropriate program, curriculum or school simply because the building is not accessible (Shore, 1986). Non compliance with *Section 504* can result in a cutoff of federal support to that organization, agency or school (Yohalem and Dinsmore, 1978).

In 1975, Congress passed legislation that guaranteed a free and appropriate education for *all* of the nation's approximately eight million children with disabilities—namely, *Public Law 94-142*, better known as the *Education for All Handicapped Children Act* (recently amended and renamed *IDEA* or the *Individuals with Disabilities Education Act*). The act has six major provisions to ensure disabled youngsters an education appropriate to their individual special education needs:

1. ZERO REJECT: requires that all educationally handicapped children receive a free, appropriate education. No child may be denied an education because of the severity of his or her disability.

2. A NONDISCRIMINATORY EVALUATION: means that the required assessment of a youngster's handicap is conducted by a multidisciplinary team, is not culturally biased and is individually administered (no group testing).

3. AN INDIVIDUALIZED EDUCATION PROGRAM (IEP): ensures that the educational program is tailored individually to meet the needs of one child and includes documentation of that child's current level of educational performance, annual goals, short term objectives, special education and related services (for example, counseling, speech services and occupational and physical therapy), the extent of time the youngster will spend in regular education programs, projected dates for the initiation and duration of the services and appropriate objective evaluative criteria for determining mastery of the annual goals and objectives.

4. PARENT AND STUDENT PARTICIPATION: means that parents and the students themselves, where appropriate, receive opportunities to make decisions regarding the youngster's educational program.

5. LEAST RESTRICTIVE ENVIRONMENT: means that the educational placement of children classified as handicapped will take place to the maximum extent possible with children who are not handicapped. The removal of handicapped children to special classes and separate facilities should occur only when the nature or severity of the handicap pre-

vents the child from successfully being educated with the use of supplementary aids and services in regular classes.

6. DUE PROCESS: means that an enacted procedure ensures the fairness of educational decisions and the accountability of both parents and professionals in making these decisions. "Due process can be viewed as a system of checks and balances concerning the identification, evaluation, and provision of services regarding handicapped students" (Turnbull, Strickland and Brantley, 1982, p. 10).

As late as 1985, some United States Government officials still resisted all assistance to persons with disabilities, and advocated the repeal of *PL 94-142* based on stereotyped ideology. Then Secretary of Education William J. Bennett, appointed as a special assistant for the Office of Educational Philosophy and Practice, Eileen Marie Gardner, who had written for the American Heritage Foundation that "the handicapped constituency displays a strange lack of concern for the effects of their regulations upon the welfare of the general population" and that regulations enacted to aid children with disabilities "probably weakened the quality of teaching and falsely labeled normal children" (cited in Friedberg, Mullins & Sukiennik, 1992, p. 10). Gardner is also quoted as stating that,

> They [handicapped children] and their parents are "selfish." They are draining badly needed resources from the normal school population [to the extent of $1.2-billion]. . . . Children and all who suffer affliction were made that way to help them grow toward spiritual perfection and that we are violating the "order of the universe" by trying to help these people (p. 10).

In response to opposition, Gardner resigned in 1985 and in 1986, Congress enacted further amendments to *PL 94-142* enlarging the responsibilities of states and school districts regarding the education of children with disabilities.

Although *Section 504* and PL 94-142 provided rights for persons with disabilities, it would take a new comprehensive law to ensure their full civil rights. The legislation, *The Americans with Disabilities Act (PL 101-336)*, was signed by President Bush on July 26, 1990. An examination of the *Americans With Disabilities Act* (ADA) reveals a comprehensive approach to ensuring the civil rights of persons with disabilities. Each part of the law was designed to end discrimination toward persons with disabilities and is thought to be the most significant piece of federal civil rights legislation since the *Civil Rights Act of 1964*. It provides protection to 43 million Americans who have been the consistent recipients of serious and pervasive discrimination, prejudice, paternalism, and labeling based on perceived physical or mental differences (Mackelprang & Salsgiver, 1996). It prohibits discrimination in both the private and public sectors in employment, public services, transportation, and communication. It also provides a comprehensive mandate to bring persons with disabilities into the economic and social mainstream of American life. Unlike *Section 504,* the ADA does not require the receipt of federal funding for coverage. The ADA contains strong standards and ensures that the Federal government plays a central role in their enforcement. Basically, the law prohibits discrimination on the basis of a handicap and provides civil rights protection similar to that guaranteed to individuals on the basis of race, sex, national origin, age and religion. The legislation answers to these five persistent questions:

1. WHO IS CONSIDERED DISABLED? A firm definition of "disability" underlies the authority of the ADA, which defines "individual with a disability" rather broadly. A person may be considered disabled if he or she (a) has a physical or mental condition that substantially limits one or more of the major life functions, (b) has a record of such impairment, or (c) is perceived as having such an impairment. Even if the impairment is no longer present, the individual may still be considered disabled. Therefore, if an employer fails to hire an

> individual who was once known to have alcoholism, cancer, or mental illness, or may still have a severe disfigurement, that employer may be guilty of discrimination. Not covered under the definition are those with minor, non-chronic conditions that last a short time like sprains, infections or broken limbs.

2. HOW ARE PUBLIC ACCOMMODATIONS AFFECTED? ADA's public accommodations requirements which became effective on January 26, 1992, define public accommodations as "private entities that affect commerce." Thus, the requirements extend to hotels, restaurants, theaters (how many times have you seen wheelchair users at the movies?), doctors' offices, pharmacies, retail stores, museums, libraries, parks, private schools and day care centers. Not covered under the ADA are private

clubs and religious organizations including churches, mosques and syn-agogues.

The ADA also affects ways in which public accommodations deter-mine who may receive their services. For example, a business that requires a driver's license as the only acceptable identification for cash-ing a check, could be considered discriminatory toward persons with blindness. In addition, the ADA requires appropriate auxiliary aids and services to ensure effective communication with those with hearing and visual impairments. These may include qualified interpreters, assistive listening devices, note takers, large print or Braille materials or taped texts. The law does not require such aids if they cause an undue burden or basic alteration in the nature of the goods and services provided. The public accommodation must still provide an alternative auxiliary aid. For example, restaurants are not required to have Brailled menus if waiters or other employees are available to read the menu to a customer with blindness. Similarly, stores need not provide Braille price tags if such information is available orally from sales personnel on request. They need not provide sign language interpreters if their sales employ-ees are willing to communicate in writing when necessary. Physical bar-riers need to be removed only when it is "readily achievable,"—that is, carried out without much difficulty or expense. Examples of readily achievable modifications include providing ramps, lowered telephones and urinals, or spaces for wheelchair users in theaters.

3. HOW ARE TRANSPORTATION SERVICES AFFECTED? The ADA requires the Department of Transportation to issue regulations mandating acces-sible public transit vehicles and facilities, and all public transit buses and rail cars ordered after August 26, 1990, must be accessible to indi-viduals with disabilities, including wheelchair users. In addition, transit authorities must provide comparable paratransit or other special trans-portation services. As of July 26, 1993, all existing rail systems must have one accessible car per train and all new bus and train stations must be accessible. Finally, all existing Amtrak stations will be accessible by July 26, 2010.

4. HOW ARE COMMUNICATIONS AFFECTED? Companies offering tele-phone services to the general public must offer telephone relay services to people who use telecommunications devices for deaf persons (TDD's) or similar devices.

5. How is Employment affected? The ADA employment provisions apply to private employers, state and local governments, employment agencies, and labor unions. Specifically, the ADA prohibits discrimination in all employment practices including job application procedures, hiring, firing, advancement, compensation, training, and other terms, conditions and privileges of employment. It applies to recruitment advertising, tenure, layoff and leave procedures, fringe benefits, and all other job activities (U.S. Congress, 1990).

Conclusion

It has been a long difficult trek from the time persons with disabilities were left to die or thrown off cliffs as babies, to the *Americans with Disabilities Act*. This historical examination of the treatment and segregation of persons with disabilities has provided insight and perspective for understanding the origins of our more familiar current common attitudes. This chapter reveals an evolutionary progression suggesting of how far our society has come in its acceptance, treatment, and integration of persons with disabilities. It also reminds one of how far it has to go. Although we are in the "Era of Civil Rights," disabled persons continue to be segregated, particularly in education. The stigma of disability remains a common reality. Students must recognize that persons with disabilities continue to be denied equal opportunity as a result of stereotyped and prejudiced images based on myths and earlier attitudes. Now that we have examined the source of these attitudes, we turn to understand a discussion of specific disabilities and sensible, humane responses to them.

CHAPTER FIVE

Disabilities and Common Sense Approaches

For integration to reach all handicapped students, teachers need to know and provide basic and accurate information about the commoner disabilities and convey common sense approaches to dealing with them. Empathy develops only when typical children gain an understanding of the causes, origins, handicapping effects and consequences of disabilities and feel comfortable interacting with those who have them. Moreover, youngsters can easily become accustomed to providing their handicapped friends with a more "user friendly" environment. As Cohen (1974/1977) stated, "A very simple way to make people feel less uncomfortable with the disabled is to teach them how to behave in the presence of a person with an impairment" (p. 13).

Since teachers generally set the example for their classes, their response patterns will prompt similar response patterns in their students. This chapter provides this basic information on various disabling conditions as well as those common sense approaches for interacting with persons who have disabilities. When introducing each disability type, a teacher can select basic books, films, videocassettes, and other materials (listed in the appendix) appropriate for the grade level.

Important Basic Considerations
When introducing curricula on disability awareness, teachers need to stress the following five points:

1. DIFFERENT IS NOT ABNORMAL: All students should be encouraged to let their peers with disabilities know they are accepted rather than abnormal or inferior. It is important for the teacher and classmates to accept the youngster with a disability positively, no matter how severe the impairment (unless other reasons exist for not doing so). When a student with any disability is included (or "mainstreamed") in a regular class, the teacher should help the class understand that although the stu-

dent may accomplish the work in a different way, he or she can participate in most activities and can achieve the overall goals. "Sameness"
should be emphasized over differentness. Typical students need to
understand that whatever differences may appear, they are differences
in degree, not in kind. Children with disabilities are more alike than different from their peers. A teacher should address questions from normally achieving peers openly, honestly, accurately and objectively.
Non-disabled children tend to be less cruel and more receptive when
they understand another's problem. The student with a disability should
be involved in as many class activities as practical without command-
ing special treatment or attracting undue attention to the disability. He
or she should be treated like anyone else, free from pampering, pity and
overprotection. Pity and sympathy are out; empathy and sensitivity
always help. Eliminating teasing, name calling and rejection become
the responsibility of everyone in class. For example, the teacher can
work cooperatively with all of the students to develop reasonable standards of behavior.

2. SELF-ESTEEM IS IMPORTANT: In addition, students need to realize that
many of their class mates with disabilities are seen in negative ways that
cause them to feel inferior and socially inadequate. Labeled students
often have poor self concepts and see themselves as low status failures.
As Rogers (1994) noted, "The greatest loss that we all have to deal with
is the loss of the image of ourself as a perfect person" (p. 8). Thus, all
students should examine their own attitudes toward their peers with disabilities and become alert to the importance of significant others (in this
case themselves) in forming self-images. They also need to know that
their attitudes will exert a great influence on the success and self image
of their classmates with disabilities. How the youngster perceives himself or herself will influence every experience he or she has, and students with disabilities need respect and acceptance as much as anyone
else in the class. A student with a disability should be encouraged to
take leadership positions just as other children do. In fact, classroom
duties, discipline, and privileges should be the same for all students.
Teachers should include all children when assigning room chores and
responsibilities and hold all students responsible for work production.
Opportunities for the student with a disability should include participation in subjects like home economics and industrial arts. Students with
disabilities are likelier to succeed in classrooms with realistic and positive expectations. The utilization of structured teaching methods,

including peer tutoring and cooperative learning, can ensure that they and their normally achieving peers enjoy regular opportunities to work together. Each day, the teacher should find some aspect of the lesson being taught in which the student with a disability can succeed in the presence of his or her classmates to create a pattern of success for that student. The most critical contribution in helping the student overcome a handicap is a strong and positive self image. The youngster with a disability may have a fragile self concept. However, with an understanding environment, honest praise and tasks that invite success and progress, that youngster can gain confidence and reach toward new goals and horizons.

3. CLASSROOM ATMOSPHERE IS IMPORTANT: The teacher and typical students should maintain a relaxed and natural atmosphere so that the child with a disability can develop in a natural relaxed way. Perhaps the most important response to disability a teacher can model is an acceptance of the physical and mental aspects of the youngsters' disability. As Derman-Sparks (1989) noted, "Anti-bias teaching about disabilities requires that teachers become aware of their own deep-seated attitudes" (p. 40).

In the classroom, desks should be arranged so that students with disabilities can interact with their non-disabled peers easily. The room should reflect positive images of disability. As Derman- Sparkes (1989) noted, "Children with disabilities need to see themselves reflected in the world around them, in pictures, in toys, in books, in role models" (p. 39). (See Appendix I, Resources.)

The teacher can create a positive climate by communicating individually with all students, showing respect for all students, making expectations clear and reflecting a gentle sense of humor. Humor can help reduce a youngster's anxiety. Meeting a challenge with humor, helps a teacher retain leadership while allaying the tension that created the defiance—as long, that is, as the humor is pleasant and cordial, never ridiculing or sarcastic. While students with disabilities need as much positive reinforcement as possible, their super-sensitivity, often leads them to draw inward at the first sign of disrespect.

4. IT IS ALWAYS APPROPRIATE TO OFFER HELP: Typical students need to know that it is always appropriate to offer help to a classmate with a disability. But, the offer should come in two questions: "Can I help you?" And if the answer is "yes," the second question should be "*How* can I

help?" The student with the disability is the expert on his or her situation and knows what specifically needs to be done. Because some students hesitate to call attention to their disability, they will accept assistance only when absolutely necessary. Classmates should never insist on helping if their offers are declined and should not feel offended or be surprised if help is refused. If help is needed, it should always be rendered in a way that keeps the youngster's dignity intact. One of the most common frustrations persons with disabilities face is so-called "stigma spread," like being treated as a non-person. One form of stigma spread considered extremely rude is speaking about a classmate with disability as if he or she were not present.

5. STUDENTS ARE INDIVIDUALS NOT LABELS: Students should be thought of and addressed by their names, not as an EMR or LD. Remember that two children with almost identical disabilities may function quite differently and should not be lumped into one category. They must be motivated, taught, and challenged according to their ability to function as individuals. Social maturity, family background and adaptive behavior vary widely among children with disabilities. Any combination of these and other factors (like how and when the disability occurred) may be more important than the youngster's specific impairment in determining his or her ability to learn or adapt to the environment. A youngster with an IQ of 75 may have better adaptive skills than a youngster with an IQ of 95. Moreover, every youngster's special capabilities and interests should be encouraged in the classroom. All youngster's should come to feel that they excel in something. As Rogers (1994) noted, "We all need to feel that we have gifts that are acceptable and valued" (p. 5).

Basic Information on
Specific Disabilities for Building Empathy

Three important criteria society uses to judge individuals are physique, intelligence and speech. Some basic factual information on the causes, effects, and issues regarding differences in these areas can help increase an understanding of and building empathy for people with disabilities.

About Physical Disabilities and Differences

Students with physical disabilities include, of course, those whose physical limitations or health problems interfere with school attendance or learning to such an extent that they require special services, special education, special equipment, materials or facilities (Hallahan & Kauffman,

1994). Sometimes these youngsters have other disabilities as well like blindness, deafness, mental retardation or learning disabilities. Because of the serious medical nature of their disabilities they often require related services including occupational therapy, physical therapy, speech and language therapy, rehabilitation, special transportation or adaptive physical education. The nature of their disabilities may also require the use of such devices as standing tables, wheelchairs, head sticks, protheses (devices designed to replace, partially or completely, parts of the body) and orthoses (devices designed to restore, partially or completely, a lost function of the body, such as crutches or braces). Thus, interdisciplinary cooperation between professionals providing education and medical services is essential. Of primary importance is the idea that "children's reactions to their own physical disabilities are largely a reflection of the way they have been treated by others. Shame and guilt are learned responses" (Hallahan & Kauffman, 1994, p. 416). Something less than 0.5 percent of our school population is classified physically or orthopedically impaired. Important factors affecting the education of these comparatively few students include the age of the child (adolescence being most critical), when and how the disability came about (congenital or adventitious), and whether the disability is episodic or progressive.

The most common and apparent of these conditions found in school include cerebral palsy, arthritis, epilepsy, scoliosis, muscular dystrophy, multiple sclerosis, poliomyelitis, spina bifida, spinal cord injury, head injury, amputation and dwarfism. In order to meet the classroom needs of youngsters with these impairments and to answer questions about these conditions as the questions arise, teachers should ideally understand their implications and acquire a basic awareness of disability and its resulting handicaps (Hanna & Graff, 1977). Teachers can find more specific information on these disabilities in books listed in Appendix I, Resources.

CEREBRAL PALSY actually refers to a group of disabling conditions often characterized by paralysis, weakness, incoordination and motor dysfunction. Approximately 50 percent of the youngsters classified as "physically impaired" have this condition (Hallahan & Kauffman, 1994). It is a central nervous system developmental disability caused by damage to the brain before or during birth attributable to several possible causes. Cerebral palsy is neither contagious, nor progressive. It often results in physical impairment of combinations of the limbs— most commonly, hemiplegia (an upper and lower extremity on the same side), paraplegia (legs only), and quadriplegia (all four extremities). Regarding the attitudes of others, Gething, Leonard and O'Loughlin (1986) observed that

> Cerebral palsy in its more severe forms is obvious to any observer. However, for acceptance and self-confidence to develop, the person needs to be acknowledged as more important than the disability. Feelings of frustration come from the experience of not being treated in this way. . . it is often the attitude of other people that makes cerebral palsy (and any other form of physical or intellectual impairment) a handicap in social, emotional and environmental terms (p. 35).

ARTHRITIS is a rheumatic disease of the skeletal joints which causes motor impairment, can occur at any age and affects each person differently. Swelling may occur in just one joint or in many. The amount of swelling can also vary from day to day. Teachers and student peers need to know that a classmate with arthritis is often in extreme pain and requires medication. Gething, Leonard and O'Loughlin (1986) stated that others may not fully understand or appreciate the severity of the pain associated with arthritis. The tendency to dismiss arthritis as not being disabling derives from the widespread superficial impressions of its milder forms in persons as they age.

EPILEPSY Seizure Disorder (formerly called epilepsy) is a symptom of a neurologic problem that affects the brain. Basically it is an invisible medical condition that often results in visible, recurring seizures, which are actually irregular discharges of electrical energy in particular brain cells often generated by stress, poor eating habits, or lack of sleep. The former and still more familiar term "epilepsy" comes from a Greek word that means "to possess seize, or hold." It is not considered a disease. Moreover, seizure disorders are treatable most of the time (Moshe, Pellock & Salon, 1993). Seizures related to epilepsy have been traditionally classified as "grand mal" (now called "generalized tonic-clonic"), "petit mal" (now called "absence seizures") and "psychomotor" (now called "complex partial"). The symptoms of a generalized tonic-clonic seizure include slumping or falling, with the muscles becoming rigid and then beginning to jerk spasmodically. There may be breathing difficulty and frothy saliva may collect in the mouth and run from the lips. The student may also lose bladder control. Although vigorous, the seizure will be brief with the youngster becoming drowsy or sleepy after it occurs. After a brief rest, the youngster will usually be able to continue with the school day.

An "absence seizure" (once called "petit mal") consists of a momentary loss of consciousness. The student may appear to be self-absorbed or day dreaming with a blank or vacant look. Ordinarily, the entire seizure lasts only five or ten seconds, and ends abruptly, the youngster having no memory of the episode. If untreated, however absence seizures may occur up to 200 times a day leading teachers and peers to consider the student a "daydreamer." Complex partial seizures (once called "psychomotor") are characterized by behaviors lasting from a few minutes to an hour that include smacking the lips loudly, wandering aimlessly, getting undressed, displaying irrelevant movements, exhibiting disturbances in communication, swallowing or chewing movements, or other behaviors that appear unmotivated. Complex partial seizures may start with the child experiencing hallucinations, distortions of the environment, or strange odors, tastes, and sensations sometimes called "an aura." No wonder that seizures related to epilepsy, particularly those with convulsions, were commonly thought to be caused by demonic possession, the only explanation unenlightened people could think of for such unusual behavior.

MULTIPLE SCLEROSIS is a progressive disease that affects the central nervous system and involves sensory and motor systems (Hanna & Graff, 1977). It appears when the covering (myelin) that protects the brain and spinal cord becomes scarred so that messages have difficulty passing from the brain to other parts of the body. Any part of the body may be affected including speech. Multiple sclerosis usually occurs between the ages of 15 and 50, and hopeful scientists still search for both its cause and cure. It is important to know that multiple sclerosis is rarely fatal, is neither contagious nor congenital (inherited) and often includes intervals of spontaneous and apparently complete or partial recovery. The name derives from multiple or many and sclerosis which means scars.

MUSCULAR DYSTROPHY is primarily a central nervous system disease that affects skeletal and respiratory functions. It is slowly progressive and occurs most often in males. Its symptoms are generally discovered between three and five years of age. It progresses with muscle weakness, wasting and contracture in the pelvic and shoulder areas. In most cases, the calf muscles display a false enlargement (pseudohypertrophy). Generally, a loss of ambulation occurs by the ages of nine to eleven. By the time the youngster reaches adolescence, he experiences a slow generalized weakness and curvature of the spine. By the time he reaches thirty, respiratory failure usually takes hold (Umbreit, 1983).

SPINA BIFIDA is a congenital disorder of the spinal column (the bony arch of the vertebrae) that affects motor coordination and other body functions (Hanna & Graff, 1977). "Bifida" means split in two. More specifically, spina bifida refers to the malformation of a few vertebrae usually in the low spine, and occurs when the flexible casings or covers of the spinal cord (the meninges) escape through the malformation in a developing fetus. The infant is then born with a protruding sac (a meningocele) which may or may not be covered by skin. Severe neurological consequences occur when the sac contains a portion of the spinal cord or nerve roots. Most commonly, the leg muscles are paralyzed with the degree of paralysis depending on the location of the lesion in the spinal cord. In addition to orthopedic problems, the youngster may develop difficulties with bones, joints, and muscles, including those that control the bowels and bladder (Umbreit, 1983).

POLIOMYELITIS (Polio) is an infectious viral disease that attacks the nerves in the spinal cord or brain and often causes paralysis. It is also known as "infantile paralysis."

SPINAL CORD INJURY is an insult to the body that produces an impairment of the spinal column resulting in the sensory or motor loss of two or more functional abilities. The effect depends on the nerves involved as well as the location of the injury. The injured areas may interrupt messages from the brain to those parts of the body below the area of damage. The higher the damage on the spinal cord, the greater the affected area, with varying degrees and amounts of paralysis and weakness. With the paralysis, sensory loss in the ability to feel touch, pain or temperature may occur. The individual may also experience difficulties with bladder or bowel control.

AMPUTATION of course, refers to the surgical removal of a limb or body part. The losses range from the absence of a single finger or toe to the absence of all four limbs. Amputations occur as a result of accidents or diseases like bone cancer. Because amputations are acquired disabilities, a person with one needs to come to terms with the loss. The amount of time needed to adjust varies widely among individuals and is based on such factors as age, gender, family support, education and the extent of the amputation. Again, other children's attitudes in the classroom help determine how a youngster adjusts to and copes with an amputation. If singled out as different and treated differently, the youngster's self-image can plummet (Gething, Leonard & O'Loughlin, 1986).

DWARFISM is an inherited disorder of the skeleton resulting in short stature. In the past, the term "dwarf" referred to persons of disproportionate short stature and the term "midget" referred to those of proportionate short stature. While "midget" has become pejorative, "dwarf" is still accepted, along with the preferred terms "short," "little," "small" or "persons of short stature." Under current use, the term "dwarf" includes little persons who are "proportionate" and "disproportionate." Because of the differences in their body stature, little persons often attract the curious stares of persons in the general population. According to Ablon (1982), "Dwarfs carry with them the historical and cultural baggage of special and even magical status much more than do persons with various other physical differences" (p. 6). She further asserted that

> [A]lthough dwarfism is a dramatic, physically distinctive, and immediately identifiable condition, dwarfs are usually not physically disabled or handicapped in the general sense of these terms. The body parts are all present, with each part fitting into a harmonic, although different whole (p. 6).

For the most part, little people see themselves as "normal," with their bodies just "packaged differently." The most important issues regarding the education of youngsters with dwarfism include introducing the child smoothly into the school, such logistical problems as high fountains, urinals, blackboards, the attitudes of classmates and faculty and problems encountered in sports and other school activities. Most little people, however, believe that the greatest handicaps they face are prejudice and discrimination from the general population. In a word it is the attitudes of others toward a person with short stature that turns that difference into a social and emotional handicap. Teachers should stress the need to avoid a patronizing or protective attitude towards persons of short stature.

EXPERIENCING A PHYSICAL DISABILITY—Describing his own thoughts on having a disability Long (1985/1990) included the following:

1. The frustration you feel when you're the guest of honor at he "Handicapped Person of the Year" award luncheon but the rest room doors are too narrow for the wheelchair and you have to urinate in a broom closet.

2. The rage you feel when someone says to you, "Oh, you have muscular dystrophy? If that happened to me, I'd kill myself."

3. The annoyance that comes from not being able to turn the radio on or the television off.

4. The indignity of having to see everything from about four feet off the ground. (How'd you like to go to a cocktail party where all you can see are rear ends at eye level?)

5. The indignity of having to ask, all the time.

6. The restlessness of having to sit in one place for 9 hours and then to go home and sit in a different chair for 7 hours.

7. The frustration of feeling violence and anger and having absolutely no strong physical way of expressing it (p. 81).

COMMON SENSE RESPONSES—Accommodating a classmate with a physical disability becomes easier if the other students keep in mind the following 18 precepts:

1. In the classroom, desks should be arranged so that students with physical disabilities can interact with their non-disabled peers comfortably.

2. Classmates should be aware of the wheelchair-using student's reach limits. Shelves and display racks in the classroom should be within their grasp, and paths leading to them should be clear.

3. If the school has different routes through it, signs directing wheelchair-using students to the most accessible ways around the building should be evident.

4. If the nearest student restroom is not readily accessible, students with disabilities should be allowed to use the faculty restroom.

5. Students should never push a classmate's wheelchair without the occupant's permission. Two persons trying to control the same chair could cause a serious accident. Similarly, when pushing a wheelchair, never let go of the chair without first asking the occupant, especially on a hill.

6. Students who use manual wheelchairs may appreciate some help on difficult terrain—for example, steep uphill or downhill grades, dirt or stone paths, high pile carpeting, pot holes, or curbs.

7. Non-disabled students should become familiar with their disabled peers' wheelchairs and how they work. "Persons accustomed to pushing shopping carts tend not to realize that wheelchairs are less steady and that hitting even a small bump in the ground can send the occupant face down on the pavement" (Maloff & Wood, 1988, p. 11). Students pushing an occupied wheelchair for the first time need to become familiar with the experience slowly and cautiously. Wheelchairs are heavy and can gain quick momentum on a hill. In addition, students should become familiar with the dimensions of the chair—for example, with how far the foot plates protrude out the sides. Maloff & Wood (1988) cited the thoughts of one wheelchair user:

> I hate being pushed in malls. The person pushing me always underestimates how far my feet stick out and my foot plates mash people in the ankles. I spend the whole time getting looks and saying, "I'm sorry, I'm sorry, excuse me, I'm sorry." It's embarrassing (pp. 11-12).

8. Students who assist their mobility impaired classmates by pushing their wheelchairs, should remember to ask the occupant where he or she wants to go.

9. Maloff and Wood (1988) advised the following procedure for helping a wheelchair user who encounters steps:

Going up the step, lean the chair back to raise the front wheels, and push the chair frontward. When going down, ask whether the person prefers to go frontwards or backwards. Either way, raise the front wheels and keep them up until the entire chair is down the step. The occupant should always be tilted towards the back against the back instead of towards the front where there is no support (p. 12).

10. When planning school events like class trips to unfamiliar places, make sure that the transportation and buildings at the destination are barrier free, especially parking lots, walks, ramps, entrances and exits, doors and doorways, steps and stairs, floor surfaces, restrooms, water fountains, telephones, elevators, switches and - controls.

11. When planning a recreational or social event (for example, a ski trip) classmates who use wheelchairs should be invited. They may not accept but they will appreciate the choice. Advance notice is also appreciated.

12. In the school cafeteria, in a restaurant, or at a party, it may be difficult for a mobility impaired classmate to eat or manage certain foods because of difficulty moving his or her arms or hands. Once help is accepted, the meal becomes more manageable if the meat is pre-cut and put back and re-shaped, corn is sliced from the cob, or fruit is separated from its rind (Maloof & Wood, 1988).

13. Non-disabled classmates should learn that wheelchairs, crutches, and other orthotics are personal items and should not be touched without their owner's consent. Putting an item like food or a book on the arm of wheelchair is an invasion of the user's privacy.

14. If a non-disabled student is unsure how to behave with a disabled classmate, he or she should ask.

15. Non-disabled students should refrain from asking their disabled classmate about amputations or other physical disabilities until they are well acquainted.

16. Non-disabled students should not make assumptions about, for example, the degree of pain associated with their classmates' impairments.

17. Non-disabled classmates may need to learn how to communicate in different ways with their disabled classmates by using an alphabet board, sign language, or other methods.

18. If a student with a seizure disorder should experience an episode in the classroom the following procedures should be followed:

    a. Above all else, keep calm. Ease the youngster to the floor and loosen his or her clothing, especially the collar. Because the seizure cannot be stopped, it should be allowed to run its course. Although a seizure may seem intense, it does not hurt the student experiencing it.

    b. Remove nearby hard or sharp objects that may cause injury but do not interfere with the youngster's movements. Keep him or her clear of radiators or other hot objects.

    c. Turn the youngster on his or her side so the saliva can flow out of the mouth. Place something soft under his or her head.

    d. Do not force anything between the child's clenched teeth and never place a finger in the mouth.

    e. When the movements stop and youngster regains consciousness and is relaxed, he or she should be allowed to rest in a quiet place.

    f. Both the school nurse and the youngster's parents should be notified.

    g. The teacher must remember that how the class reacts to seizures depends on how he or she reacts.

A teacher can use the occurrence of a seizure, especially one with convulsions, to teach acceptance. His or her calm, adept approach can normalize the situation to the point where fears and questions can be discussed and important information conveyed—for example, how to react in an emergency. Provided with the right attitude, the class is like-lier to accept seizures (even those with convulsions) as just another nor-mal classroom occurrence. If handled poorly, however, a seizure could be a tense and frightening experience for its observers.

About Blindness

The topic of blindness can be both frightening and fascinating for youngsters, who often draw upon images of dark glasses, a white cane, a tin cup, a guide dog and perhaps a sad life of hopelessness and eternal darkness to form attitudes. In fact, blindness is currently the third most feared condition, following cancer and AIDS (Hallahan & Kauffman, 1994). Blindness makes many people ill at ease because of the impor-tant role the eyes play in our social interaction. "We seem to rely a great deal on the expressiveness of people's eyes to judge how they are responding to what we are saying" (Hallahan & Kauffman, 1994, p. 342). As Hine (1993) observed,

> The eye is certainly the most remarkable seat of the senses. It encom-passes the distant and the immediate; it is the most maneuverable; it swivels and turns; it closes off completely simply by shutting its lids; it changes and blurs as we squint; it includes clever protective mech-anisms of tearing and blinking. To lose it is to lose a truly extraordi-nary instrument (p. 173).

The thought of becoming blind may frighten youngsters particular-ly because of their familiar experiences of stumbling and groping for articles in the dark or perhaps wearing a blindfold—experiences lead-ing to the assumption that blind persons live in a dreary, black world. But, in reality, only about ten percent of all persons labeled as blind are totally without sight (Scholl, 1986). As Hallihan and Kauffman (1994) stressed, "The majority of people who are blind can actually see" (p. 342).

Moreover blindness occurs rarely in children—in fact, in less than .10 percent of the population between the ages of 6 through 17. Thus, the chances are high that a student with blindness will be the only one in his or her school or even community with that disability. The low incidence of blindness in the young can isolate that student, and encourage stereotyped misconceptions on the part of others. As one student with blindness urged, "I want you to know you shouldn't overreact when you see people who are blind, but just treat them like anyone else" (Westridge Young Writers, 1994, p. 88).

"Blindness" carries many various definitions. Odom and Clark (1982) advised that educators use a definition of blind or visually impaired developed for legal and funding purposes with little educational relevance. Legal blindness refers to visual acuity of 20/200 or less in the better eye after correction, or peripheral vision no greater than 20 degrees. This means that what the visually impaired person sees at 20 feet the person with regular vision sees at 200 feet. An individual considered to be partially sighted or having low-vision has 20/70 vision. Such acuity numbers have, however, little meaning for an educator who needs to know what the student "has," not what he or she "does not have." Therefore, educators tend to label students with visual impairments by how they read and acquire information. Students with blindness are generally taught with Braille or talking books because they may learn best through their tactile or auditory senses. Such students are usually able to distinguish the presence or absence of light, and any partial vision may be used effectively for learning mobility and orientation as well as other tasks. Students considered to be partially sighted or with low vision may be able to see objects near at hand under modified conditions—for example magnification, or have limited functional vision under average circumstances (Hunt & Marshall, 1994, p. 389).

In any event, before the youngster with a visual problem can be fully integrated into a classroom, the common myths should be discussed. As Odom and Clark (1882) stated, "Over a period of time these myths have surrounded the blind and in certain situations may have impeded the progress of integrating children in the regular classroom" (p. 55). Such common myths include the notions that persons with blindness cannot see at all, are all alike; have exceptional musical ability and hearing, live a sad and melancholy life, are dependent and helpless, are led around by their guide dogs, need to be taught Braille and have become blind as punishment for past sins. Because these myths inaccurately describe persons with blindness and other visual impairments, they need to be dispelled.

Students need to understand that most persons with blindness do not live in worlds of total darkness; their disability usually allows them to respond to some visual stimulation like light and dark, or shadows or moving objects, providing them with some useful residual functional vision.

Obviously some persons with blindness have natural musical talent, and some develop a musical talent, but a lot do not. Because music is a career in which persons with blindness can achieve success, many blind people choose it. In addition, those persons with blindness who use guide dogs are not taken where they want to go by their dogs. The individual with blindness determines the destination, using the dog as a prothesis and protection against unsafe areas or obstacles.

The belief that most persons with blindness need Braille to read is also inaccurate. Hunt and Marshall (1994) stated that only ten percent of legally blind students use Braille as their primary learning medium; the majority of youngsters with visual impairments can read either regular or enlarged print.

Few persons with blindness are beggars; the large majority are not. In fact, most are independent, earn a living and live quite normal lives as spouses, parents, and neighbors. As a group, persons with blindness are quite diverse; some are rich, some are poor; some are educated, some are uneducated; some are talented, some are not; some are old, some are young; some are heavy, some are thin; some are tall; some are short; some are fun-loving, some are grouchy. As Scholl (1986) pointed out, "[T]hey have all of the characteristics found in any group of people. They possess no characteristics specific to themselves as blind persons, and they show no typical reaction to being blind" (p. 24). Patton et al. (1987) made the same point:

> As a group, people who are visually impaired comprise a normal range of personalities, interests and abilities. Some visually impaired people are gifted, some are retarded, and many intellectually normal. There are those who are emotionally disturbed and others with learning disabilities. We have visually impaired athletes as well as scholars. There are those who are socially adept, delinquent, prolific, dull, fascinating, obnoxious, or anything else (p. 120).

Much earlier, Bowe (1978) said, "There is no conclusive evidence that blind individuals differ from sighted persons in language use, personality, intelligence, auditory acuity, musical ability, or academic achievement" (p. 50). Nor does such a thing exist as a "blind culture."

As with most disabilities, the effect of blindness on an individual's activities and interactions with others relies on several factors like whether the disability is congenital, adventitious, stable, progressive, hidden or visible. Of most importance is when and how the blindness occurred. For example, a youngster with congenital blindness or with blindness from early childhood may have difficulty forming accurate self perceptions and perceptions of the world. He or she might misinterpret the feelings or intentions of others by relying on their voices and speech rather than on gestures, facial expressions and posture (Bowe, 1976). A simple act like not being able to see and respond to a smile or a wink carries a large penalty. As Hull (1991) explained,

> Nearly every time I smile. I am conscious of it. I am aware of the muscular effort; not that my smiles have become forced, as if I were pretending, but it has become a more or less conscious effort. Why is this? It must be because there is no reinforcement. There is no returning smile, I am no longer dazzled by a brilliant smile. I no longer find that the face of a stranger break into sudden beauty—and friendliness. I never seem to get anything for my efforts. Most smiling is responsive. You smile spontaneously when you receive a smile. For me, it is like sending off dead letters. Have they been received or acknowledged? Was I even smiling in the right direction? In any case, how could my sighted friend make acknowledgment? (p. 34).

The inability to see may also hinder a youngster's ability to learn and acquire skill through the simple imitation of visual cues, which can leave learning gaps and distortions. Blindness affects cognitive development by restricting the number and variety of experiences thereby leaving the youngster's *gestalt* less definite (Hunt & Marshall, 1994). For example, how he or she perceives another person's face will be much less precise.

Blindness also forces an individual to perceive in a different way. Hull (1990) made the following entry in his diary:

> For me, the wind has taken the place of the sun, and a nice day is a day when there is a mild breeze. This brings into life all the sounds of my environment. The leaves are rustling, bits of paper are blowing along the pavement, the walls and corners of the large buildings stand out under the impact of the wind, which I feel in my hair and on my face, in my clothes. . . . The sound of the wind creates trees; one is surrounded by trees whereas before there was nothing. . . . The misunderstanding between me and the sighted arises when it is a mild

day, even warm, with a light breeze but overcast. To the sighted, this would not be a nice day, because the sky is not blue (p. 16).

As Milligan (1995) stated,

[B]lind people are missing a very great deal as compared with sighted people; and what we are deprived of is not only an important range of practical abilities in coping with the world of things, and an enormous amount of information that it would be interesting and helpful to have (including many clues to the character, condition and stream of thoughts and feelings of fellow human beings, and a capacity to take in a relatively large amount of information about our immediate surroundings in a short time); but we are also denied a range of experiences of a specific kind, some of which are to some of those who have them intensely pleasurable (Magee & Milligan, 1995, p. 37).

Hull (1990) also wrote about the person with blindness as having the unique experience of an "illusion of privacy":

It refers to the difficulty of remembering all the time, when you are blind, that you can be seen. It is hard always to bear in mind the astonishing range of this faculty which other people are said to have. The blind person has to remind himself all the time, when he is tempted to scratch his bum, that he is visible. . . . That is not the case when hearing is lost. . . . Sight is reciprocal, but hearing is sequential (p. 59).

Because language necessarily mediates much of the information a youngster with congenital blindness learns, many of the child's conceptions will be approximate and taught through "verbalism," the use of words without concrete firsthand knowledge of their meanings. An example of verbalism is using a cold ice cube to teach the concept of blue or using something hot to teach red. As early as 1951, Cutsforth discussed his concerns of teaching through verbalism, which he believed conveyed an unrealistic view of the world to a youngster born with blindness:

A congenitally blind person's discussion of the theory of color mixture is not a whit more verbal than a college students's opinion on the labor question when he has never worked a day in his life. The factual content in each case is derived from the experience of others. The adolescent college student knows no more about the un-idealistic aspects of love and marriage than a man born blind knows about the hue, tint, and chroma of colors (p. 49).

Cutsforth (1951) also believed that the use of verbalism would help a child with blindness develop a desire to use a visual adjective "in lieu of one which is infinitely more meaningful to him" (p. 69). He theorized for a congenitally blind youngster, a preferred realistic description of coal would be "hard" rather than "black," a realistic description of blood would be "sticky" rather than "red," and a realistic description of a rabbit would be "furry" rather than gray. He stressed that such youngsters should be taught about the world through the real sensory qualities they experienced rather than abstract qualities—for example, "[A] robin is much more of a singer than it is either red-breasted or bold" (p. 69).

Cutsforth's ideas regarding the education of congenitally blind students raised some interesting arguments that are still debated today. Whether one agrees with him or not, educators generally agree that youngsters born with blindness experience their environments in a more vicarious manner requiring a highly structured learning environment during their early years.

Moreover, it makes an important difference whether the blindness is congenital or adventitious. A child born with a visual impairment will usually have less difficulty adjusting to the disability than the child who becomes blind. Gershe (1969) depicted this issue of adjustment in his play *Butterflies are Free:*

Jill: You're so adjusted.

Don: No I'm not. I never had to adjust. I was born blind. It might be different if I'd been able to see and then went blind. For me, blindness is normal. I was six years old before I found out everyone else wasn't blind. By that time it didn't make much difference (p. 15).

Such an opinion of blindness differs from that of the person who acquires blindness later in life and must learn to adjust to a self-concept different from the one before the onset of the impairment. A child born with blindness will have to be taught skills that a sighted child may learn through simple observational learning, for example, eating, dressing, toileting and playing with games and toys.

The ability of any individual with blindness to deal with his or her environment is affected in many various ways. Because blindness restricts one's ability to read print, maneuver in unfamiliar places, perceive one's surroundings as sighted people do, and understand such social cues as a wave, a wink, a smile or other type of body language, the youngster with blindness may be perceived as lacking animation.

Because one's motor development depends highly on one's sight, youngsters born with blindness or a visual impairment will generally have difficulty with both gross and fine motor performance. Their physical skill and coordination deficiencies are generally attributable to environmental factors—for example, seldom being encouraged to participate in physical activities or being unable to see small objects and thereby lacking practice in picking them up. Blindness may also cause a youngster difficulty in understanding abstract concepts, for example, speed (one hundred miles per hour), size (the height of the Empire State Building), or distance (one hundred feet away).

Karuth (1985/1990) compared having legal blindness with a small amount of residual vision to:

> living in a bizarre fun house where what you see is not necessarily what you get. . . . Being blind with residual vision means that you "see" your relatives and friends on the Boston trolleys and busses even though those relatives never left Buffalo. It means looking both ways before crossing the street and then walking out into the side of a school bus. It means entering an unfamiliar room and being visually bombarded by confusing patterns of light and dark. It means getting so accustomed to familiar places that your friends accuse you of being able to see, or worse, they forget to warn you about newly placed obstacles. Being blind means not knowing Aunt Trudy has lost weight, or that cousin Carol is eight months pregnant (until you embrace them). . . . It means being confused by cars making right and left turns on red. It means spending too much time looking for house keys, dark glasses, the checkbook or the vegetable steamer. And it means knowing how to take notes into exams by a method so wonderfully clever that I will not reveal it here (p. 14).

COMMON SENSE RESPONSES—In order to interact with persons with blindness in positive and meaningful ways should learn and discuss the following 19 common sense approaches:

1. When introducing a student with blindness to a sighted student, the sighted student should verbally offer to shake hands, saying for example, "Shake hands, friend." The child should be introduced in the same way as all other children are introduced. When classmates raise questions about the child's blindness, the visually impaired youngster himself or herself should answer them. Of course, the teacher may help if it seems appropriate.

2. When greeting a student with blindness, it is important to identify oneself and anyone else present—for example, "On my left is Joe Smith." It is especially important to identify oneself when entering a room if a student with blindness is present alone, especially if the person entering the room is wearing sneakers. In addition, it is rude to leave an individual with blindness standing alone without telling him or her. One should not just walk away.

3. Students need to know it is never bad manners to offer to help a student with blindness.

4. Students and teachers need to recognize that speaking about a classmate with blindness as if he or she were not present is a form of "stigma spread" and is considered extremely rude. One should speak directly to the student, not to a companion or guide dog. Consider these examples Dickman (1972) described:

> A teacher from North Dakota with blindness stated, "If I'm in a cafe with friends, sometimes a waitress will ask them 'Does she want anything?' as if I weren't even there" (p. 4).

Another woman with blindness from Iowa explained why she became furious with a clerk one day "because I went shopping with a friend and the clerk kept asking my friend what I wanted. No matter how many times *I* answered her she kept referring to me as 'she'" (p. 4). Dickman's third example presents an extreme case of the "non-personness" individuals with blindness can experience:

> Not long ago I visited the dentist with my guide dog, Amber. A receptionist showed us into the waiting room, and the three of us were alone. "And what my dear," said the receptionist, turning to Amber, "is the gentleman's name?" (p. 4).

5. Students need to feel comfortable using common words like "look" and "see." These words are part of everyone's vocabulary, and is perfectly allowable to ask a student with blindness if he or she saw a television show or bumped into so-and-so at the mall. Expressions like, "I'll see you later" are also perfectly acceptable.

6. Students with visual impairments should be oriented into the classroom and made aware of classroom settings and where landmarks like student desks, the teacher's desk, bookshelves, permanent cabinets, lockers, wastebaskets, windows, pencil sharpener, doorways, windows, bathrooms, chalkboards and bulletin boards are situated. Wastebaskets and other movable items should be made stationary or kept in the same place. The student should be told of any changes in a familiar furniture arrangement.

7. Sighted students should practice being relaxed and smooth in leading a classmate with blindness. The proper "sighted guide" method involves the student with blindness taking the other's elbow. This enables the sighted student to guide, rather than propel or lead. It becomes similar to dancing; from the motion of the guide's body the student with blindness learns to tell when curbs, steps or turns are encountered. To avoid surprises, the student with blindness may want to walk a half step behind the classmate guide. The sighted student should use specific directions and numbers like "on the right two yards" or "seven steps including the landing," not "over there" or "go straight up and to the left." When facing a classmate with blindness a sighted student using directions like right or left should specify whose right or left. Pointing is of no help. One must be given accurate useful information. When offering seating to a student with blindness, place his or her hand on the back of the seat and state which way it is facing.

8. Students should be reminded that a guide dog is a "prothesis"—that is a working dog responsible for the safety of its master. Such a dog is not a pet and should not be petted without the consent of its master, especially while it is working. Also, when accompanying a student using a guide dog, walk on the opposite side from the dog.

9. A visually impaired student may bring such adaptive aids to the classroom as bookstands, braille writers, large print books, a cane,

raised line paper, templets, writing guides, talking books and talking calculators. The other students may be interested in these devices as well as other topics related to visual impairment, and the teacher can usefully incorporate these topics into class lessons—for example, in science units discussing light, vision and blindness.

10. Sighted students should remember that their fellow classmate has blindness, not deafness. Shouting at a person with blindness is another rude form of stigma spread.

11. In the school cafeteria or any other public eating place, the sighted student should guide the student with blindness into the shortest line. If there is a menu, the sighted companion should offer to read the menu and the prices and report what is on the table—for example, a vase of flowers, rolls, butter, water and so forth. Helping to locate the food and condiments on the table should be based on such common sense gestures as guiding his or her hand to the different items on the table. Another method is to use "clock directions" to explain where objects are—for example, your hamburger is at six o'clock in front of you, your fries are at eight o'clock, your drink at twelve o'clock, and so forth. In a restaurant, when the meal is brought by a waiter or waitress, the friend with a visual impairment should be told about any decorative items on the food that he or she would not want to eat. In addition, it is helpful to accompany a visually impaired friend to salad bar or buffet table to describe what is there and even put the food on the plate if so desired.

12. In the rest room, the student with a visual disability should be guided to the location of the toilets, urinals, sinks, towel dispenser or hand dryer, especially if he or she is in a public facility like a restaurant.

13. A visually impaired student may sometimes be unaware of events in the classroom, and sighted student seated nearby might inform him or her of helpful, verbal cues like a smile, a facial expression, a nod or a beckoning arm movement. A conversation may not always make sense to someone who cannot read the expression on the speaker's face.

14. Sometimes, youngsters with visual impairments may exhibit certain mannerisms mistakenly called "blindisms," for example, head rolling, eye poking, rocking. Blindism is a poor name because children without blindness often do not develop such mannerisms. The teacher may help the student overcome these mannerisms.

15. On a school bus it is helpful to a classmate with blindness to be told, "There's an empty seat two rows back." It keeps him from having to feel around every seat to see if it is empty.

16. Sighted students who want to make after school plans with a classmate with a visual impairment should give advanced notice so that transportation can be arranged. Transportation is a key issue for persons with visual problems.

17. When planning an after school activity that may require vision, the sighted student should not assume that a visually impaired classmate would not want to participate. As Maloff and Wood (1988) recommended, "[I]f you are planning a certain activity and you would enjoy having a visually impaired friend along, invite her" (p. 79). Persons with visual impairments surprisingly enjoy a wide variety of recreational activities including bowling, movies and the theater. At the movies and theater, the sighted friend can quietly describe some of the purely visual like the opening scene, costumes and special effects.

18. Students need to remember that it is considered extremely rude to gesture about a classmate with blindness to someone else who may be present. Persons with blindness often become aware of such gestures and usually feel that they are "being talked about behind their backs."

19. If a sighted student invites a classmate with a visual impairment home, he or she should survey the house for any possible hazards, for example, an open basement door, a roller skate on the floor, a cabinet door ajar, and so forth. It is also a good idea to take the friend with the visual impairment on a brief tour of the house to familiarize him or her with the surroundings, particularly the bathroom, stairs, room dividers and low lamps. It is also a good idea to let the person know if there is a pet in the house. (Halliday, 1971;

Dickman, 1972; Interrelated Teacher Education Project, 1980; Aiello, 1984; Corn & Martinez, 1985; Maloff & Wood, 1988; Hunt & Marshall, 1994, Lessen, 1994; J. Cohen, n.d.).

About Deafness

Dealing with deafness down through the years, has always inspired ignorant assumptions in persons with hearing, from the monks who placed their deaf charges into institutions for the feebleminded to Mayor Carty Finkbeiner of Toledo, Ohio who recently suggested that the city provide housing for persons with deafness near the Express Airport. The agency that operates the airport was purchasing the nearby homes because the noise from the jets exceeded government standards. The Mayor observed that "deaf people [would] not be as bothered by the noise and raised the possibility of offering them homes that others are fleeing" (Mayor claims deaf idea, 1994, p. 69).

The issue of inclusion is greatly sensitive to persons with deafness. Hearing impaired students present unique challenges regarding inclusion in education programs designed for non-handicapped students. Within the Deaf community one can find several opinions on what is the most educationally appropriate and least restrictive environment for students with deafness.

Youngsters with severe hearing impairment may have difficulties processing information, conceptualizing ideas and especially developing language. Because one acquires language by imitating sounds heard in one's early environment, the youngster with a severe hearing impairment is handicapped in learning communication skills because of not being able to hear them much less imitate them. The severity of the difficulty depends on many factors including the degree of hearing loss, the age of its onset, and early intervention procedures adopted (Odom & Clark, 1982).

Approximately .12 percent of the students in public schools from ages six to seventeen years are estimated to have impaired hearing and approximately 16 million Americans, of all ages, from newborns to the elderly, have a hearing impairment (Hallihan & Kauffman, 1994). Both the disability of hearing impairment and its handicapping consequences range from mild to severe. Of the 16 million, over two million are considered to have deafness, the definition of which includes those who cannot hear sounds at or above a certain intensity level (90dB), and those who have enough hearing loss to hinder an ability to speak and develop language The *Individuals with Disabilities Education Act (IDEA)* defines deafness as

> Hearing impairment that is so severe that the child is impaired in processing linguistic information through hearing, with or without amplification, that adversely affects a child's educational performance (42 U.S.C., Secs. 1400 et seq.).

IDEA further defines "hearing impairment" as

> An impairment in hearing whether permanent or fluctuating, that adversely affects a child"s educational performance but which is not included under the section of deafness in this section (42 U.S.C., Secs. 1400 et seq.).

According to Hallihan and Kauffman (1994), "Hearing impairment [is a] generic term indicating a hearing disability that may range in severity from mild to profound; it includes the subsets of deaf and hard of hearing" (p. 304). They go on to define a deaf person as "one whose hearing disability precludes successful processing of linguistic information through audition, with or without a hearing aid. A hard of hearing person "[I]s one who, generally with the use of a hearing aid, has residual hearing sufficient to enable successful processing of linguistic information through audition" (p. 304). In other words, having deafness means that one's hearing loss is so severe that the student can not understand speech through the ear, with or without a hearing aid. Having a hearing impairment or a classification of "hard of hearing" means that one can understand speech through the ear, with or without the use of hearing aids (Turnbull, Turnbull, Shank & Leal, 1995).

Odom and Clark (1982) added these four important definitions:

1. "Congenitally deaf" means born deaf;

2. "Adventitiously deaf" means became deaf after birth because of illness or accident;

3. "Pre-lingually deaf" refers to the child who was deaf before developing language; and

4. "Post-lingually deaf" refers to the child who became deaf, or was "deafened," after he or she had developed language by hearing it spoken (p. 58).

In addition, these are several types of hearing loss, each of which can raise different obstacles and different prospects for dealing with both disabilities and handicaps. Hearing losses can, for example, be classified according to the location of the problem within the hearing mechanism. Hallihan and Kauffman (1994) classified them accordingly:

1. A "conductive loss" means a loss that interferes with the transfer of sound along the conductive pathway of the middle or outer ear to the auditory nerve for processing;

2. A "sensorineural impairment" involves a problem in the inner ear; either the cochlea or the auditory nerve itself is not functional; and

3. A "mixed hearing impairment" involves a combination of the two.

The primary handicap deafness causes is to interrupt communication. In the United States, persons with deafness use at least seven communication methods to cope with this handicap:

1. AMERICAN SIGN LANGUAGE (ASL) is a language with its own grammar and syntax. Its signs designate words and things both abstract and concrete. One makes the signs by using either one or both hands to make distinctive shapes and movements in specific locations. Its grammar includes the use of spatial relations, orientation, direction, hand movements, facial expressions, and body shifts.

2. FINGER SPELLING is a manual alphabet with hand shapes and positions that correspond to the letters of the alphabet. Finger spelling is literally writing in the air; individuals actually spell out their entire conversation.

3. MANUAL COMMUNICATION uses a combination of sign language (ASL) and finger spelling for both expressive and receptive communication.

4. ORAL COMMUNICATION uses speech and speech reading as the primary means for communicating with persons with deafness. It is often called "lip reading." According to Kisor (1990), the biggest problem with lipreading is that many sounds look identical:

> *M, p,* and *b* are made by bringing the lips together. *T, d,* and *l* all take shape with the tongue on the roof of the mouth just behind the teeth. As a result, the words *bat, bad, ban, mat, mad, man, pat, pad,* and *pan* all look exactly alike. To the eye there is no difference between *s* and *z*. Sounds formed in the back of the throat are impossible to distinguish from one another. *Cat* and *hat* cannot be told apart, let alone *mamma* and *papa* (p. xii).

Kisor provided a further illustration in the title of his book, *What's that Pig Outdoors*, which he once misread when his son said, "What's that big loud noise?" (p. xvi). In addition, lip reading may be difficult because the meaning of a sentence can appear to change when the speaker stresses its different words.

5. CUED SPEECH is a system of communication in which eight hand movements supplement what is being spoken. In sign language the signs represent words; in cued speech the signs represent sounds. Cued speech is not really a form of sign language. Rather, the hand cue indicates visually the exact pronunciation of the syllable being spoken. Its goal is to lessen the guesswork in lipreading.

6. SIMULTANEOUS COMMUNICATION means the combined use of speech and ASL.

7. TOTAL COMMUNICATION is the philosophy which implies the acceptance, understanding and use of all methods including ASL, finger spelling, speech reading, cued speech, and any other ways that aid communication.

COMMON SENSE RESPONSES—When accommodating a classmate with deafness, try to keep the following 16 principles in mind:

1. When communicating with a student with deafness or a hearing impairment, remember there are many ways of expressing yourself. The most important thing is to create a situation conducive to

understanding and feel free to use whatever methods work best: pantomiming, pointing, writing notes, using facial expressions and such gestures, as wiping your brow to say, "That was a close call!" Over-exaggerated gestures are, however, inappropriate in public places where they attract unwanted attention to the conversation. Natural, not exaggerated gestures, supplement oral conversation best. When referring to an object in the room, the teacher or hearing student should point to it, nod in its direction, look at it, or go over and touch it.

2. Positioning can be helpful. Where a teacher or classmates position themselves can make the difference between being understood or not. For example, a teacher should avoid standing directly in front of a light source like a window because it darkens and obscures a face in front of the bright light. The principal light source should be behind the students and the teacher. When communicating with a deaf or hearing impaired student it is best to face the person directly. Get as close as possible, face the person squarely and either stand or sit at his or her level. Common sense dictates that a teacher or other students not turn their backs to the hearing impaired student while speaking, (for example, while writing on the chalkboard), but try also to keep your head stationary. The best position is two to five feet away. Farther away and the lips become more difficult to read. Closer and the student may have a hard time focusing on the mouth, or may get a neck pain from the angle.

3. Remember that a student with a hearing impairment can usually comprehend the teacher or other students with partial hearing, speech reading or a combination of the two. Accordingly, the speaker's mouth should be easily seen. When speaking to a student with a hearing impairment, a teacher or other classmates should not eat, chew gum, play with eye glasses place a book or papers or hands in front of the mouth. When the teacher or other students read orally, keep the book down.

4. A male teacher with a moustache or beard needs to know that facial hair often obscures the mouth, making lip reading difficult. As Holcomb (1985) observed, "Little do people realize that lip reading a person with a moustache is like hearing half a conversation"

(p. 37). That is not to suggest that a teacher must be clean shaven, but that he pay closer attention to making himself understood.

5. Students with hearing impairments or deafness appreciate their hearing classmates learning some basic sign language and finger spelling. It is also helpful for the teacher to discuss the hearing impaired child's problem with the class so they gain understand and empathy.

6. A teacher and classmates should work to speak and project their voices clearly. It is best to speak moderately without shouting. Shouting contorts lip movements. Teachers and hearing classmates should also avoid dropping their voices at the end of a sentence, and enunciate the last words in a sentence, those often being most important words. Remember also, that negatives like *not* or *no* should be clear since their absence reverses the meaning. It is better for a hearing impaired student if the teacher and other students speak a little slower than normal, pronouncing every syllable, and stopping for a pause at the end of a sentence to allow the thought to "sink in." An extra pause is helpful when the topic of conversation changes. Students with hearing impairments should be spoken to in full sentences in preference to single words and fragments. It is easier to grasp a word's content or meaning in context than in isolation.

7. Fuller explanations and rephrasing the same concepts in different and redundant ways can help the student with a hearing impairment. Synonyms can improve communication. It is particularly helpful to use examples to help make a point. If the message is long, the speaker should look for intermediate responses to make sure he or she is conveying the message. It is also important to remember that long complex sentences can be hard for a student with a hearing impairment to understand. In addition, key words, expressions, or phrases should appear on the chalkboard or on a projector image. Moreover, speech reading or using sign language may be tiring for a student with a hearing impairment. If the student puts his or her head down on the desk, that is not necessarily a sign of boredom or non interest. He or she may just need to rest.

8. In classrooms (and other rooms too), try to reduce unwanted sounds. Students with hearing impairments can hear better away

from telephones, radios, and other noise sources. The best place to converse with a person with a hearing impairment is in a quiet room with good acoustics. Sounds that vary, like music, interfere the most. Students without hearing impairments should reduce the general noise level when a hearing impaired classmate receives instructions or listens to a conversation. Because a hearing aid amplifies all sounds equally, it can put its wearer at a disadvantage under noisy conditions. Similarly, students with hearing impairments must sometimes be reminded if they are unknowingly making noise.

9. If you shout to a deaf or hearing impaired student from across a room or from another room be prepared to be ignored.

10. Students who need them should be encouraged to wear their hearing aids. The teacher and hearing students should speak toward the ear with the hearing aid. Remember, if a student has hearing impairments in both ears and wears one hearing aid, it probably serves the "better" ear. In addition, especially with younger children, hearing aids need to be checked from time to time to ensure they are working.

11. It is harder for a student with a hearing impairment to understand the teacher or classmates if they walk and talk at the same time. A teacher should try to stay in one place when giving a test or notes.

12. The teacher with a hearing impaired child should use as many visual aids as possible. Captioned films are preferred and when showing slides leave enough light in the area to let the youngster see faces clearly when the narrator makes comments.

13. Remember that students with hearing impairments cannot take notes while they watch faces. If notes must be taken, all students should receive the notes or arrangements should be made for two students with hearing to take the notes (for example, with carbon paper) for the student with the hearing impairment. Two students taking the notes will miss less material.

14. Inclusion implies that students with hearing impairments will learn from their classmates any special vogue words or expressions chil-

dren use in the class or neighborhood. The same holds true for social skills and rituals.

15. Students with hearing impairments and their parents should be provided with classroom topics to be covered or discussed in the next day, week or month.

16. Most important of all, remember that hearing youngsters quickly emulate their teacher's attitudes and will treat their hearing-impaired classmates as they see their teacher treat them. A good teacher will seize every opportunity to turn a child's handicap into an asset. Units in science on sound or communication may provide the key to changing negative attitudes into positive behavior.

About Communication and Speech Handicaps

Van Riper and Emerick (1984) defined speech as "defective" when "it deviates so far from the speech of other people that it calls attention to itself, interferes with communication, or causes the speaker or his listeners to be distressed" (p. 34). In other words, they consider speech defective when it is conspicuous, unintelligible, or unpleasant. Addressing the social handicapping of students with speech problems is especially important because communication disorders constitute the largest handicapping disability of all and statistics indicate that as many as 20 million Americans have a speech, language, or hearing impairment.

The problem with having a speech impairment is less about having difficulty communicating than society's stigmatizing attitudes toward what it considers to be unacceptable speech. When a person with a stutter, for example, says "h-h-h-hello," the listener usually understands. The problem usually arises because the delivery embarrasses the speaker, the listener, or both.

Language is the complicated, extraordinary means by which humans communicate. It allows us to share our brain activity. Thus, communication and language are the essence of life. Accordingly, along with such attributes as physique and intelligence, we prize highly and reward the ability to communicate verbally (Odom & Clark, 1982). In fact, "effective speech in society is of the utmost importance if one is to gain and maintain membership or to get status and material possessions, which are constantly held up to us as goals to be desired" (Van Riper and Emerick, 1984, p. 4).

Because verbal skills are valuable, language judged deviant is quickly disparaged. Negative societal attitudes have an enormous influence on an individual with so-called "deviant" speech. In fact, Hertz (1996) reported that a person who stutters is often stereotyped as lacking in social adjustment and self-confidence. Moreover, the standard stereotype of the person who stutters as inferior in social adjustment and self-esteem has also been revealed in studies that compare attitudes toward people with communication impairments and, specifically, people-who-stutter, with attitudes toward people with other disabilities. . . . By inference, people who stutter were being considered more intellectually impaired, less educable, and less competent—all three harsh judgments of mental functioning—than people who are blind or deaf, or those who have mobility impairments (p. 36). Hertz (1996) concluded that

> language is so crucial an instrument for the species may explain, in a most profound manner, the stigmatizing perception that people who stutter are suffering not only from social maladjustment, but also from extreme mental impairment. People who stutter, especially those who stutter severely, may be perceived as slow, or even unable to think to themselves and to convey those thoughts to others (p. 38).

Thus, a listener can threaten their very humanness.

Possessing speech deemed "defective" (for example, stuttering or lisping) becomes a part of one's personal identity and sense of self (Odom & Clark, 1982; Van Riper & Emerick, 1984). A young child in the process of developing a personal self-image will factor in society's reactions to a stutter or a lisp. How much influence such reactions have depends on many factors including the child's family, friends, social environment, and above all that self image.

Noting the influence negative speech has on self image, Rollin (1987) stated, "Our clinical experiences with stuttering children and adults tell us of the domination stuttering has over all else in terms of how they see themselves and what they can and cannot do in life" (p. 125). Van Riper and Emerick (1984) earlier observed that

> Not only do we use [speech] in thinking and in the sending and receiving of messages, we also build our very sense of self out of word stuff. Indeed, language infiltrates every aspect of our lives; even the way in which we view the world is molded by the symbols we use (p. 4).

Youngsters with a speech difference often grow increasingly frustrated with their communication problems and develop feelings of rejection and self-doubt when trying to connect and communicate with other human beings. A stigma of the child's communicative behavior cannot avoid helping to shape his or her perception of self (Rollin, 1987). Van Riper and Emerick (1984) described how an individual who stutters becomes a victim of blame:

> These people have been hurt deeply and repeatedly because they did not and could not conform to the speech standards of our society. The tragedy lies in the fact that they "could not." They were not responsible for their defective speech, but those who hurt them acted as though they were, as though they had a choice. This assumption is at the core of the problem not only of the person with a speech disorder but also of the poor, the insane, and most other kinds of deviancy (p. 5).

Although almost all individuals have experienced problems interacting verbally with others at one time or another, few have felt the "overwhelming emotions that accompany severe difficulties in oral communication" (Patton, Payne, Kauffman, Brown & Payne, 1987, p. 143). Most human beings without speech problems fail to understand how difficult it is to live in our culture without "acceptable" speech. They underestimate the handicap that results from even a minor speech deviation. In addition, those without speech problems tend, consciously or subconsciously to "blame the victim" when they deal with unfamiliar speech sounds or patterns:

> We find it relatively easy to form an empathic relationship with an individual who has an obvious physical, emotional, or mental disorder, but we tend to feel that the individual with a speech disorder suffers no lasting penalty and could easily overcome the difficultly with a little determination (Patton et al., 1987, p. 143).

Another problem arises when a person without a speech problem is unsure how to behave toward the person with one. As Carlisle (1985) observed,

> The average person may know, more or less, how to deal with a deaf person, a paraplegic, an amputee, or someone who is mentally handicapped; but very few people know what to do when faced by a stutterer. Do you help the guy begin his word? Do you look at him or look

away as he struggles to speak? Do you smile encouragingly or sit there like a stuffed dummy? Most people look away, fidget, and think of ways to escape; or if they happen to be holding a cup of coffee, stir it as though their lives depended upon it. Many just flee in alarm as the stutterer battles his way to the next word. Few know what to do, and uncertainty breeds fear with its attendant tension, rudeness, hostility, and anger. To make matters worse, stutterers' own attitudes vary; some welcome help and others do not. All stutterers welcome a little patience (p. xi).

Rollin (1987) stated,

Although experimental literature cannot confirm a negative self-image that is distinctive to those who stutter, few therapists would deny that the stuttering individual in time develops feelings of frustration, rejection and self-doubt while attempting to communicate (p. 124).

Van Riper and Emerick (1984) coined the acronym PFAGH to explain the emotional components of "defective speech." The letters stand for penalty, frustration, anxiety, guilt and hostility.

A penalty is the price one often pays for using deviant speech. The penalties include quick rejection, imitative behavior, ridicule, curiosity, nicknaming, humorous responses, embarrassed withdrawal, brutal attacks, impatience, exclusion, overprotection, pity, misinterpretation and condescension. As Van Riper and Emerick, (1988) noted, the severity and type of penalty one must pay for speech deviance depends on four basic factors:

1. the vividness or peculiarity of the speech difference;

2. the person's attitude toward his own difference;

3. the sensitivities, maladjustments, or preconceived attitudes of the people who react; and,

4. the presence of other personality assets (p. 7).

Bowe (1978) stressed that

The effects of speech disabilities are largely social and personal. Others may find the speech unpleasant and may avoid the disabled individual, who may in turn lower his or her self concept. Difficulties in speaking may lead a person to withdraw from social interaction and may negatively affect his or her motivation to learn and to work with others (p. 67).

Carlisle (1985) related the following incident which occurred while he accompanied a young man with a severe stutter into a store to try out his newly learned speech techniques while buying a pack of cigarettes:

> On the second word he blocked badly. Instead of using the speech techniques, he panicked and tried to push through the word with quivering, pursed lips. The eyes of the woman behind the counter went blank. She shrugged, walked away to serve another customer, and never returned (p. 8).

Carlisle acknowledged that some people consider a severe stutter not to be a true disability like a physical impairment, deafness or blindness. But, "very severe stuttering can be as disabling as many major problems of limb control, hearing, and even sight" (p. 154). When asked hypothetically to choose between a severe stutter or blindness, Carlisle chose blindness because,

> [S]ociety to some extent accepts blind people and allows for their disability. Sightless people, although they miss a great deal, can communicate effectively and participate in society in many ways. A person who stutters very severely is denied effective communication most of the time, and the attitudes of society limit his social activities unless he is very determined indeed. He can all too easily be forced to live in the dark, lonely cave of his own mind (p. 154).

Van Riper and Emerick (1984) reported the experience as cited by a client with a stutter:

> Most people are shocked when I open my mouth and stutter. But once they get past the initial surprise, they react in various ways: almost all of them look away from me; a lot of them supply words I am trying to say; a few smile or laugh nervously. . . . One of the worst things about having a speech defect, though, is it becomes so hard to have an ordinary conversation or conclude a simple transaction (p. 21).

Another client reported this experience:

> I hate to stutter in restaurants because the waitress ignores me and then talks to my companions. I feel like a nonperson. And when they do talk to me, they speak too loudly, slowly, in a patronizing manner; and they never, ever look at me (p. 7).

Maloff and Wood (1988) reported the experience of yet another person with a severe stutter:

> If a person looks directly at me, if he has a smile on his face or a warm look in his eye, then that encourages me to keep on talking. But if he looks at me strangely or looks away, I feel I should keep it short (p. 104).

One of the worst penalties endured by people with speech differences is becoming the object of ridicule, like Balbus Blaesius in his cage along Rome's Appian Way. Today's mass media actually encourage children to laugh at someone who speaks differently. They learn early to laugh at Porky Pig's "comical" stutter, Elmer Fudd's reversals, Tweetybird's lisps or Dopey Dwarf's muteness. The film portrayals that raised the greatest protest recently were Michael Palin's stuttering role in *A Fish Called Wanda,* and the stuttering defense attorney in *My Cousin Vinnie.* Not long ago, Van Riper and Emerick (1984) found a, nationally distributed poster linking venereal disease and stuttering. Printed beneath a silhouette of a male and female embracing on a park bench was this slogan, "Talking about VD can be the first step toward preventing it. . . unless you stutter" (p. 21).

From a stutter, others often infer foolishness, mental retardation or psychopathy. In many movies evil characters stutter to illustrate psychopathic tendencies reflecting an unhappy childhood—like Michael Palin in *A Fish Called Wanda.* The media portray most of those who stutter as weak, stupid and unreliable—typically as cowards, wimps, or dangerous criminals—and viewers begin to get the idea that this is the way things are (Carlisle, 1986, p. 189).

Frustration, the feeling of being thwarted in the satisfaction of a goal like communicating, occurs when human potential is blocked. Ruch (1967) listed three types of frustration: environmental, personal and conflict. An individual with a speech impairment often experiences all three.

Among the frustrations found in the environment are those provided by one's social surroundings. A handicap is environmental. When the person who endures social frustration caused by prejudices aroused by his or her speech difference becomes a casualty of disablism. As Carlisle (1985) said, "Rebuffs and rejection are as much a part of stuttering as the speech blockages and interruptions" (p. 5).

One suffers personal frustration when he or she is, in Ruch's words, "prevented from realizing his or her ambitions by some personal limitation—either real or imagined. Personal frustration frequently builds up 'feelings of inferiority' and a lack of personal worth which, in turn, serve to increase the frustration" (1967, p. 462-462).

"Conflict frustration" occurs when an individual has both positive and negative feelings about a particular goal or must choose one of two goals. As an example of conflict frustration individuals with speech "defects" must often choose between being quiet or being seen as "abnormal." Many psychologists tend to believe that the primitive, natural reaction to frustration is aggressive behavior usually accompanied by hate for the person or situation perceived as the source (Harriman, 1947, p. 143). Frustration generates anger and aggression, and people, as Van Riper and Emerick (1984) observed, who have severe speech problems are constantly frustrated:

> Those who cannot talk normally are constantly thwarted [and] even when the listener can understand the words, he finds himself distracted by the odd contortions of the spastic's or stutterer's face, the twitching of the cleft-palate case's nostrils; and he forgets what has been said and asks that it be repeated. This is frustration too (pp. 10-11).

The individual needs speech for self-fulfillment:

> The good things of life must be asked for, must be earned by the mouth as well as the hands. The fun of companionship, the satisfaction of earning a good living, the winning of a mate, the pride of self-respect and appreciation, these things come hard to the person who cannot talk. Often he must settle for less than his potential might provide, were it not for his tangled tongue. Speech is the "Open Sesame," the magical power. When it is distorted, there is small magic in it-and much frustration (p. 11).

A speech impairment often puts such a large strain on the process of communicating that the disorder itself becomes the core of the interaction. Our speech, in a sense, is a "safety valve" for our emotions. When we use it to verbalize our anger or grief it decreases our fear and distress. "A fear coded into words and shared by a companion seems less distressing. A guilt confessed brings absolution" (p. 11).

Van Riper and Emerick also believed the inability to use speech as an expression of self to be among the most frustrating of all aspects of having a speech problem. One of the hardest words for a person with a stutter to say is his or her own name. Most people, after all, talk about themselves most of the time and the most used word in the English language is "I." Talk about oneself is "egocentric speech," extremely important in the development of one's personality. Speaking this way reassures the speaker that all is well, and he or she exists and belongs. The individual with a severe speech problem lacks this reassurance when speaking. Instead, that person exposes himself or herself as little as possible, producing self-denial and frustration. "Speech" wrote Van Riper and Emerick (1984), "is the vital prerequisite for human interaction. It is the bond that unites us. When it is impaired, that bonding is disrupted" (p. 12).

Ruch (1967) defined "anxiety" as "generalized feelings of apprehension" (p. 720). It is easy to understand why people who meet rejection, pity, or mockery would become anxious, especially when one endures punishment for recurring behavior. Van Riper and Emerick (1984) noted that for a person who stutters, anxiety becomes at once a way of life, and a contagious and destructive challenge to the individual's self esteem.

"Guilt" as defined by Harriman (1965) is "a pervasive and disruptive feeling of having failed to meet some high expectation or standard [and] a moral anxiety" (p. 77). Like anxiety, guilt often exacerbates a speech problem. Because youngsters are taught early in life that guilty persons get punished, they may not understand that its converse need not necessarily be true—namely, that those who get punished need not be guilty. Van Riper and Emerick (1984) noted that both youngsters with speech problems and their parents often ask "What have I done to *deserve* this evil?"

"Hostility" is the expression of anger. As Van Riper and Emerick (1984) observed, "Both penalty and frustration generate anger and aggression. We who are frustrated, rage "(p. 16). Carlisle (1985) noted, "If the boy with the stutter is handy with his fists he won't have too much trouble from kids his own age, although there are always a few bigger boys who will beat him up and continue to taunt" (p. 157). Some speculate that Mike Tyson's speech problems explain his ascendancy to the boxing Heavyweight Championship of the World.

Speech handicaps, like all other handicaps result from environmental barriers, and by changing the environment, educators can reduce or eliminate the handicap. This does not mean that an individual who stutters can always stop, but a pressure-free environment that invites an individual to flourish can surely help. The pressure to communicate can worsen stuttering. Many believe that social pressure causes stuttering. Johnson (1956) went so far to assert that "The diagnosis of stuttering is one of the causes of stuttering, and apparently one of the most potent causes" (p. 2). Jonah (1977) stated that a child starts to stutter because he or she becomes too acutely aware of the need to use the correct word and the correct accent while trying to coordinate his or her articulation, cerebration, respiration, phonation, resonation, and so on. Those who believe in this theory note that several Native American tribes in the Midwest—among them the Utes and the Bannocks—have virtually no members who stutter. Coincidentally, these tribes also have an exceptionally permissive attitude toward their children's speech. By contrast, the Cowichans, who expect their children to take part at an early age in complicated rituals under the close scrutiny of the tribal elders and who place a premium on verbal skills, have a high incidence of stuttering.

COMMON SENSE RESPONSES—To help make the environment more comfortable for students with speech impairments problems, teachers can create "user friendly" classrooms by implementing a dozen basic common sense strategies while teaching their students to interact with their peers with speech problems:

1. A student with a speech problem may speak slower than usual, and it will put this speaker more at ease if classmates simply accept the fact that the conversation will proceed more slowly and that there is no need to rush it. Students and teachers should remain calm and relaxed, listen attentively and become the kind of people with whom those classmates with speech problems like to converse.

2. Face the student speaking and maintain eye contact. He or she needs to know the listener is willing to give the conversation his or her full attention.

3. Because surrounding noise may force the student with a speech problem to raise his or her voice and put extra stress on the conversation, it is useful to sit closer. It is also difficult for the student

with the speech problem to communicate from a distance or another room. Find or secure a quiet place for a talk.

4. Youngsters with typical speech should be taught that it is always good manners to pause for a moment after a classmate with a speech problem speaks to be sure he or she has finished. Nor should others should finish the sentence even if the speaker has difficulty though the listener knows what the end of the thought will be. Avoid any prompting.

5. It is perfectly permissible to ask the student to repeat himself or herself if you do not understand what he or she said. It is a good idea to repeat aloud such important information as names, addresses and phone numbers to make sure your understanding is correct.

6. During the conversation, nod once in a while and ask questions so that the student with the speech problem knows that you are listening and understand.

7. Take turns speaking. A conversation implies both participants speaking and listening.

8. In fact, most students with speech problems prefer one-on-one conversations over group discussions, so implement these conversations in your teaching.

9. Instead of trying to stop the student from stuttering, encourage him or her to stutter naturally. Avoid offering unsolicited advice.

10. Resist the temptation to label a student a "stutterer."

11. Always shield the student with a speech problem from ridicule.

12. Typical students and their teachers should know that the way they respond to a classmate with a stutter will affect his or her speech. Always use good manners, hear the person out, and avoid finding excuses to leave. Most persons with speech problems, especially those with stutters, dislike it intensely when others switch them off or walk away to hide their own discomfort (Johnson et. al. 1956; Carlisle, 1986; Maloff & Wood, 1988; Lesse, 1994).

About Learning Disabilities

Learning disabilities are permanent disorders that affect the manner in which individuals with average or above average intelligence receive, retain and express information. Messages traveling between the eyes, ears or skin and the brain seem to "cross wires" or become scrambled. The resulting problem involves perception rather than acuity. A youngster with a visual perceptual problem, for example, may have perfect vision but cannot discriminate between the foreground and background on a photograph. He or she may see it but be unable to perceive or interpret it.

Most definitions of learning disabilities are negative—that is, they tend to describe what the youngster does not have. A child is considered learning disabled if he or she has a learning difficulty attributable to some impairment in perception, conceptualization, language, memory, attention or motor control that is often unexplainable but is not caused by hearing impairment, visual impairment, mental retardation or cultural factors (Harwell, 1989). Basically, learning disabilities are characterized by significant differences in the youngster's achievement and intelligence.

The term "learning disabilities" emerged in the 1960s. Earlier terms used to label youngsters exhibiting a wide variety of the now-familiar symptoms included "Minimal brain dysfunctioned," "brain-injured," "minimal cerebral dysfunctioned," "neurologically impaired," "perceptually impaired," "Strauss syndrome," "attention deficit disordered," (to name only seven). Because youngsters with learning disabilities exhibit problems in various areas, each has its own set of "medical" terms. Consider, for example, the following six general problems with some of the medical conditions they include:

1.   reading comprehension and spelling: *dyslexia, alexia;*

2.   written expression: *dysgraphia, dysphasia, agitographia;*

3.   mathematical computation: *dyscalcula, acalcuia;*

4.   coordination: *dyskinesia, apraxia, ataxia;*

5.   memory and recall: *dysnomia, aphasia, anomia;* and

6.   oral language skills—for example, *aphonia, dysarthria;*

Some of the estimates of the number of persons with learning disabilities reach as high as 20 percent of the population. According to Hallahan and Kauffman (1994), "In 1976-1977 about 23 percent of all students identified for special education were learning disabled. Today, that figure stands at about 50 percent" (p. 167). The general classification referred to as learning disabilities is the fastest growing educational disability category, to the extent that the growing numbers have forced the federal government to place a ceiling on the percentage of children school districts and states can so classify. The numbers of learning disabled students can, of course, vary depending on who does the counting and who is counted. As with most handicapping conditions, learning disabilities range from mild to severe. In fact, most of us have or exhibit some of following 23 characteristics commonly associated with learning disabilities:

1. deficits in visual discrimination: including problems matching sizes, shapes and colors and problems with reversals like distinguishing a *b* from a *d* or a *p* from a *q* or inversions like a *w* and an *m*;

2. deficits in visual memory: including problems finding one's way to and from frequently used areas in the school or problems writing one's name from memory;

3. deficits in visual sequencing: including problems reproducing a visual pattern of colors, shapes, objects and pictures; problems with using a dictionary or finding the right page or writing or reading saw for was, or on for no;

4. deficits in visual figure ground perception: including problems staying within the lines when drawing, finding hidden figures, completing a partially drawn figure, finding little words in big words, or completing material on a crowded page;

5. deficits in visual motor coordination: including problems with coordination that may affect writing skills (such as mirrored writing), or the ability to catch a ball, follow an outline while cutting, tie one's shoes, button one's clothes, reproduce a motor pattern, or skip, hop, dance or run;

6. deficits in auditory discrimination: including problems discriminating between two sounds like horns or whistles, between different musical instruments or letter sounds, such as ch and sh (chose and shows), the inability to tell where a sound is coming from, the inability to follow oral directions and the inability to discriminate between sincere and sarcastic comments or other subtle changes in tone of voice;

7. deficits in auditory figure ground perception: including problems with filtering sound like hearing the clock and the teacher as equally loud or becoming overwhelmed by loud noises in the cafeteria;

8. deficits in auditory memory: including problems with oral instructions or forgetting what was learned the day before;

9. deficits in auditory sequencing: including problems learning one's telephone number, address, the alphabet, the days of the week or the months of the year;

10. deficits in auditory association: including problems understanding the answer to a riddle, the punch line to a joke, the real meaning of an idiom or figure of speech or the moral of a fable;

11. deficits in time concepts: including problems relating one's schedule and the time of day, telling time, monitoring one's time or understanding a "deadline";

12. problems with spoken language: including speech and language delays, discrepancies in listening and speaking and speech disorders;

13. perseveration: including the repetition of the same response over and over and difficulty in transitioning from one task to another often caused by undue attention to minor details or fear of being in a new situation;

14. unusual scatter on psychological and achievement tests: including a marked variability in educational skills like average or above language skills but poor number concepts;

15. compulsive tendencies: including a need for order and routine and poor adjustment to environmental changes;

16. deficits in directional sense: including confusion with concepts like right and left, up and down, over and under or above and below;

17. deficits in spatial sense: including a tendency to write off the end of the page, bump into things, "clumsy" body movements, an inability to keep columns straight in mathematics or exhibiting a distorted concept of body image;

18. mixed laterality and dominance: including being "right sided" but left handed;

19. attention deficit disorder: including hyperactivity, frustration, fidgety movement, impulsive behavior, disorganized thinking, an easily distracted temperament, difficulty with concentrating, poor organizational skills, poor short-term or long-term memory, excessive variations in mood or noticeably good and bad days;

20. deficits in social judgment: including an inability to "read" people or social situations, behavior often inappropriate for the situation, an overly gullible nature, difficulty making decisions or an inability to see the consequences of one's actions;

21. serious emotional overlay: including an explosive, unpredictable, socially withdrawn, fearful, anxious, tense, frustrated or uncommunicative nature;

22. poor self image: including insecurity, a tendency to describe oneself as dumb, a tendency to resist criticism or reprimands, a tendency to "act out" or perform as class clown and learned helplessness; and

23. difficulty with abstract reasoning: including with problem solving difficulties and abstract and concrete and thought processes and difficulty in organizing and integrating thoughts.

No one person would exhibit all of these problems and all of us exhibit at least a couple of them to some degree. But we generally learn to compensate for them. It is less the number of problems a youngster has that determines whether the disability is mild or severe, than the degree to which each exhibits itself and how they cluster.

These symptoms can work together to bring on disablism—that is the negative attitudes of those around a youngster who exhibits them. Youngsters with learning disabilities may well be the most routinely discriminated against by parents, family, friends, and especially the school. For example, the research on non-exceptional peer attitudes toward learning disabled students overwhelmingly indicates that those with learning disabilities are perceived negatively. After an extensive review of the research, Reid (1984) concluded that

> Regular classroom teachers associate the label "learning disability" with a negative stereotype. LD children have significantly lower social status than their non exceptional peers. . . . Regular classroom teachers and non-exceptional peers behave more negatively toward LD children than their normal peers (p. 167).

Because a youngster with a learning disability has what Kranes (1980) called a "hidden handicap" and may even display superior ability in selected subjects, he or she may be misjudged as lazy, stubborn, or "dumb" by teachers and classmates, especially when his or her performance is noticeably deficient in other areas (Shapiro & Margolis, 1988/89). In essence they may be blamed for their handicaps. Brown (1983) compared the criticism received by those with hidden handicaps to the praise received by persons with physical disabilities:

> We admire the person in a wheelchair who travels around the country in a motorized van. . . . On the other hand, people with invisible handicaps are expected to attain the norm without effort. They rarely receive credit for their attempts; they are criticized for having trouble in the first place (p. 15).

The handicap of a hidden learning disability also concerned Harwell (1989):

> People with learning disabilities do not look handicapped—they wear no prosthesis to assist them. The fact that they have no visible handicap has led to this condition being referred to as the "invisible handicap." Because their difficulties are not obvious, learning disabled persons are often misunderstood and maligned. They are accused of not

listening, of being lazy, of being clumsy, or of being weird. Not understanding their own problem, they often experience loss of self-esteem and feelings of worthlessness (p. 3).

Scheiber (1982) characterized that derogatory and devastating labels like "dumb," "lazy," "spoiled" and "hopeless" when applied to young-sters with learning disabilities, often produced feelings of low self-esteem and rejection.

Unfortunately, youngsters with learning disabilities often lack the social understanding and skills to combat these labels and attitudes and to go on to form interpersonal relationships (Shapiro & Margolis, 1988). As Long (1988) wrote,

The learning disabled youngster has trouble reading gestures and ex-pressions, sizing up social situations, and relating to, connecting with, and tuning into other people's feelings. Problems with relationships plague learning-disabled students throughout their adult lives, leading to feelings of loneliness and low self-esteem and affecting their pro-ductivity (p. 23).

Because it is a hidden handicap, only the consequences of the learn-ing disability, rather than the disability itself, become apparent. This gap between cause and effect provokes, in turn, prejudices based on lack of information, understanding, and tolerance for the difficulties posed in the classroom (Shapiro & Margolis, 1988). For example, Smith (1988) specified 70 problems typical of learning disabled youngsters. Those unfamiliar with learning disabilities might well consider these problems (like a distracted nature, avoidance of writing, erratic and inconsistent behavior, tardiness and losing homework) to be intentional.

The negative attention associated with learning disabilities coupled with the rise of prejudice and discrimination in the schools makes it imperative for teachers to address directly such negative attitudes. Failure to do so may place the youngster with the learning disability in a situation that may prove threatening to his or her well-being.

COMMON SENSE RESPONSES— In order to create a "user friendly" school environment for students with learning disabilities a teacher should adopt the following 14 strategies:

1. Both teachers and students should use visual aids, simulations, role playing, guest speakers, discussions and other methods to learn about learning disabilities and their consequences;

2. The physical classroom should provide a utilitarian and attractive environment geared to the learning disabled student's needs. It should be clean, well organized and free of outside distractions or excessive visual stimuli (for example, loud wall colors or teacher wearing apparel) and auditory stimuli (like a ticking clock or sounds from the band room);

3. Student with learning disabilities should ideally work within a comparatively small space like a cubicle or desk with a carrel. The student with a learning disability should be placed in the classroom so that the unavoidable distractions are behind him or her. Keep stimulating materials unrelated to the current lesson away from the teaching area so the student will not be distracted.

4. Both learning disabled students and their normally achieving peers should have generous opportunities to work together by the use of structured teaching methods including peer tutoring and cooperative learning.

5. Teachers should create a positive climate in their classrooms by communicating on a personal level with all students, showing respect for all students, making expectations clear, and reflecting a sense of humor. Students with learning disabilities need as much positive reinforcement as possible. On the other hand, their super sensitivity can turn them off at the first sign of disrespect. As one student with a learning disability wrote, "I hope that people learn not to make fun of others with dyslexia and other learning problems. I want people to treat everyone who has disabilities with respect" (in Westridge Young Writers Workshop, 1994, p. 29).

6. All students should be held responsible for work production, and students with learning disabilities can succeed in classrooms with realistic and positive expectations.

7. A teacher should address questions like these from normally achieving peers openly, honestly and correctly:

How come he's lazy and doesn't pay attention?

How come he's so clumsy?

How come she is allowed to use a calculator in math and we can't?

How come we get more homework than she does?

How come he gets good grades with such sloppy writing?

As you can see, these questions give the class a chance to discuss the issue of fairness as embodied in the concepts of equality and equity. "Equality" means everyone gets treated alike; "equity" means everyone gets what he or she needs.

8. Students with learning disabilities learn better if they can read a ditto sheet listing the three or four major points to be covered that day with room for developing those points. Whenever possible, they should also receive a written outline of each unit. In addition, a teacher should try to assign one project of high interest at a time, lessons that allow the student to apply newly learned skills in other areas, and realistic daily assignments. Assignment sheets and tests should be clear and free of clutter. A teacher should make an assignment both orally and in written form. It is also a good idea to provide study questions for exams that demonstrate the format as well as the content of the test. Teachers should explain what constitutes a good answer and why.

9. Each day, the teacher should find some aspect of the lesson in which the student with a learning disability can succeed in the presence of his or her classmates.

10. Teachers should permit the use of different kinds of devices for studying and taking notes or examinations. For a learning disabled student, a calculator or tape recorder is a prothesis.

11. In addition, the class should be tested in ways that allow the student with a learning disability to demonstrate progress within the class structure.

12. One of the greatest aids a student with a learning disability can have is time—for example, extra time to complete an assignment or test.

13. A teacher should ensure that the entire class is sensitive to the needs of their learning disabled peers and should avoid making them feel different.

14. Above all, the teacher should create a pattern of success for the student with a learning disability. The most critical element in helping the child with a learning disability overcome his or her handicap is a strong, positive self image. For the youngster with a learning disability that self concept may be exceedingly fragile. But, with an understanding environment, honest praise, and tasks that invite success and progress, the youngster with a learning disability can gain confidence and stretch toward new goals and horizons. The wide variety of those who succeeded despite a learning disability include Leonardo da Vinci, Woodrow Wilson, Nelson Rockefeller, Albert Einstein, Winston Churchill, Hans Christian Anderson, Agatha Christie, Thomas Edison, Tom Cruise, Bruce Jenner and Cher.

About Mental Retardation.

Like "learning disabled" the definition of "mental retardation" has evolved gradually over many years. As early as the first century A.D. a Roman aristocrat, Aurelius Cornelius Celsus, used the term *imbecillus* to denote a general weakness or any form of impairment. The term *idios*, the original Greek form described a private person—that is, one who did not engage in public life. Both terms became descriptors of forms of mental retardation much later in the Renaissance (Scheerenberger, 1983).

During the early fourteenth through sixteenth centuries, the term *ideocy* began to be replaced by "dunce," a term that had its origins with the activities of John Duns Scotus, a Scot who, in 1303, argued against the King of France's proposal to tax the Roman Catholic Church to finance a war with England. In response, the Pope excommunicated the French King, who in return banished Scotus from France. Two hundred years later, Renaissance humanists and Reformation leaders hostile to Duns Scotus's defense of the Papacy began to call any follower of his teachings as a "Duns man" or "dunce"—hence, a dull-witted person (Scheerenberger, 1983).

The definitions changed several more times. As early as 1846, Samuel Gridley Howe defined persons with "feeble-mindedness" as those who ranged in level of incapacity from those with "reason enough for simple individual guidance plus normal powers of locomotion and animal action" to those who were "mere organisms." In 1914, Goddard subdivided the classification of feeblemindedness into the subcategories of "morons," "imbeciles," and "idiots" (President's Committee on Mental Retardation, 1975, p. 2).

In 1941, Egdar Doll defined the term "mental deficiency" as "(1) social incompetence, (2) due to mental subnormality, (3) which has been developmentally arrested, (4) which obtains at maturity, (5) is of constitutional origin and (6) is essentially incurable" (President's Committee on Mental Retardation, 1975, p. 2).

Perhaps the past definition of mental retardation that received the widest use was developed by Heber in 1959 for the American Association on Mental Deficiency (now the American Association on Mental Retardation): "Mental retardation refers to subaverage general intellectual functioning which originates during the developmental period and is associated with impairment in adaptive behavior." He went on to define subaverage intelligence to mean anyone who tested more than one standard deviation below the so called normal, or having an IQ of approximately 84 or below. Heber's definition also labeled degrees of impairment as "mild,""moderate," "severe" and "profound" (President's Committee on Mental Retardation, 1975, p. 2).

Mercer (1973) defined mental retardation from a social system perspective rather than a clinical perspective. Instead of viewing intelligence as an entity that exists independent of the cultural setting, she saw intelligence as existing relative to the requirements of the particular social system. She believed mental retardation to be a fluid condition and that an individual could be mentally retarded in certain situations and not mentally retarded in others—for example, in school or family life. She further believed that one can become mentally retarded only by being labeled that way in a particular setting. In addition, the number of persons labeled "retarded" in a given area is determined by the social structure of that area—that is to say, what is expected of persons or how much or how well the difference is tolerated. Thus, Mercer's definition began to shift the focus to the handicap aspect of mental retardation rather than its disability aspect.

Most present definitions of mental retardation include the concept of one's adaptation (or lack of it) to one's surroundings, particularly the ability to respond effectively to the many social and environmental demands of life. The response to such social and environmental demands is called "adaptive behavior" which is defined as "the effectiveness or degree with which individuals meet the standards of personal independence and social responsibility expected for age and cultural group" (Grossman, 1983, p. 1). The current definition of mental retardation incorporates

> substantial limitations in present functioning. It is characterized by significantly subaverage intellectual functioning existing concurrently with related limitations in two or more of the following adaptive skill areas: communication, self-care, home living social skills, community use, self-direction, health and safety, functional academics, leisure, and work. Mental retardation manifests before age 18 (American Association on Mental Retardation, 1992a).

The American Association on Mental Retardation, 1993b, stresses that mental retardation is not a personal trait like one's stature or weight, nor is it a medical or mental disorder. It is a "particular state of functioning that begins in childhood and is characterized by limitations in both intelligence and adaptive skills. . . . Mental retardation, is short, reflects the "fit" between the capabilities of individuals and the structure and expectations of their environment" (p. 1).

Adaptive behavior problems vary at different ages. For example, during the school years, the main demands arise in academic, reasoning, judgment and social skill areas. During one's adolescent and adult years, vocational and social adjustments become the main adaptive behavior criteria. What ever the developmental stage, however, the idea persists that an individual can be considered to have mental retardation only when he or she is deficient in both intelligence and adaptive behavior. An individual who scores a 50 on a standardized intelligence test, but functions adequately in his or her environment would not be considered mentally retarded.

The phrase "significantly subaverage intellectual functioning" is defined as an IQ score of 75 or below, which equates to more than two standard deviations below the mean, based on an assessment that includes one or more individually administered standardized general intelligence tests (for example, the Wechsler). Note the change from the earlier definition that used the 84 IQ and one standard deviation below the mean. In the earlier definition, individuals with IQ's of 75 to 84 were considered "borderline" mentally retarded. The more or less arbitrary change of definition greatly reduced the number of individuals considered to be mentally retarded which demonstrates how current attitudes can shape the definitions that categorizes real people.

As with most handicapping conditions, mental retardation ranges from mild to profound and its severity is approximately determined by the following IQ scores:

1. mild (IQ's of 55 to 69)—in schools often called "educable";

2. moderate (IQ's of 40 to 54)—in schools often called "trainable";

3. severe (IQ's of 25 to 39); and

4. profound (IQs of 24 and below).

Teachers and the peers of students with low IQ scores should remember that intelligence tests do not measure innate intelligence, IQ scores can change, intelligence tests provide only imperfectly reliable scores, and they never measure all one needs to know about a person's intelligence. Not even a battery of tests can provide a complete personal profile. Meanwhile, seven general characteristics commonly related to mental retardation follow:

1. personal and social skill deficits—for example, immature behavior, poor interpersonal skills, preference for interaction and play with younger children, inability to handle conflict and inability to interpret social cues or body language;

2. deficits in general academic performance—for example, significant deficits in the areas of reading and mathematics, learning at a slower rate than peers, often having difficulty applying learned information to new situations;

3. delayed speech and language development—for example, articulation problems, stuttering problems, limited breadth and depth of vocabulary and single-word responses, inability to use complex

syntax, limited understanding of the nuances of meaning and inability to understand directions or express needs;

4. intellectual deficits—for example, inability to grasp abstract con-
    cepts, need for instruction that is concrete and practical and a low
    fund of information;

5. memory deficits—for example, especially in short term memory,
    information stored only for a few seconds to a few hours, difficulty
    focusing on relevant stimuli in learning situations and deficient
    meta-cognitive processes;

6. poor self image—for example, feelings of unworthiness, self deval-
    uation, and preference for low level tasks; and

7. frustration proneness—for example, gives up easily.

Unfortunately, persons with mental retardation often become stereotyped as anxious, volatile, impulsive, dangerous, extremely strong
without realizing their strength, peculiar, delinquent, oversexed, or possessing other contemptuous characteristics.

The causes of mental retardation tend to be characterized as
biomedical, cultural-familial or psychological. Biomedical causes
include over 200 identified central nervous system pathologies including phenylketonuria (PKU), hydrocephalus, microcephalus, and Down
syndrome. Between 10 and 25 percent of persons with mental retardation fall into this category.

Cultural familial causes include poor nutrition, poor physical health,
and lack of sensory stimulation. A youngster with cultural-familial mental retardation exhibits no evidence of biological or organic conditions.

Some individuals are misclassified mentally retarded as a result of
temporary psychological problems, and to perceive these individuals as
truly mentally retarded or intellectually limited is to underestimate and
limit their potential.

Although prevalence figures vary, approximately 3 percent of the
United States population has mental retardation (Beirne-Smith, Patton
& Ittenbach, 1994). By far, the majority (89 percent) of those estimated
to have mental retardation fall into the mild category. The estimated
prevalence of mental retardation, based on the IQ scores of 210 million
Americans, breaks down this way:

IQ SCORE	POPULATION
0-20	105,000
20-25	420,000
50-70	6,330,000

Because intelligence occurs on a continuum, many professionals challenge the practice of placing individuals into a delimited category based on IQ scores and labeling them mentally retarded. For example, Sarason and Doris (1979) observed that mental retardation as a concept had been created to serve two purposes: to separate a group of people; and to justify social action in regard to those who are set apart (p. 11). Similarly, Blatt (1981) felt that the treatment of persons with mental retardation is inherently abusive because mental retardation is an invented concept:

> Mental retardation is an invented disease, an untrue and unnecessary story about a large group of people. In some families, old age is an invented disease, while in other families it is an honored state of being. . . . But "always," mental retardation is an invented disease [and] mental retardation, itself, can't be appreciated by a study of marbles and holes or neurons and dendrites. Mental retardation, itself, requires the study of our prejudiced inventions about certain people who have wires loose or who read poorly. Illiteracy is real. Blindness is real. However non-revealing and misinforming it may be, the 50 IQ is real. The chronological age of 80 is the truth about the octogenarian. But mental retardation is an invention, an untrue story. And as nothing good obtains from such untrue stories, the treatments for mental retardation are neccessarily inventions, and, consequently, are always abuses (pp. 118-119).

Bogdan and Taylor (1994) similarly concluded that mental retardation as a concept is not real but "exists in the minds of those who use it as a term to describe the cognitive states of other people" (p. 7).

COMMON SENSE RESPONSES—Accordingly, a teacher can usefully consider the following 14 accommodations for students with mental retardation:

1. Typical peers of students with mental retardation need to know that one does not measure a person's worth by an IQ score;

2. Typical students need to understand that their classmates with mental retardation differ in degree rather than kind. Intelligence occurs on a slippery continuum from low to high, and those at either end of the scale are more alike than different from their average peers.

3. All students need to understand that mental retardation is a "person-made" concept and its definition constantly changes.

4. Students need to know that most persons labeled mentally retarded are mildly affected and can lead successful lives within the community with proper education and training.

5. Persons labeled mentally retarded do not have a unique "retarded personality" different from a hypothetical "normal personality." Students need to become aware of personality characteristic stereotypes that unfairly imply persons with mental retardation as being dangerous, unmotivated, happy, socially inadequate, impulsive, and in need of constant supervision.

6. Students need to recognize that the label "mental retardation" reflects only the current status of an individual and can certainly change as that individual acquires adaptive behaviors. An individual's level of mental functioning does not necessarily remain unchangeable, especially those labeled mildly retarded or educable.

7. Students need to understand that persons with mental retardation have been historically victimized by unequal and unfair treatment— for example, sterilization, institutionalization and segregation. Only recently, since the passage of *PL 94-142* in 1975 have students with mental retardation had the right to a public education in every state.

8. Students should realize that their peers labeled mentally retarded may require more repetition, practice, reinforcement and patience in order to learn.

9. Students with mental retardation need encouragement to overcome their problems with short attention span, poor memory and frustration. One can improve their abilities to handle cognitive tasks by carefully sequencing materials and proceeding from the simple to the complex.

10. Students with mental retardation may have difficulty thinking and reasoning abstractly. They may need more details when receiving instructions and assignments. They may also benefit from practical experiences, "over-learning," and transferring their learning from one activity to another.

11. Students should talk to a person with mental retardation as they would speak with anyone else, but with more specificity. Also, they should never "talk down" to a person with mental retardation nor treat him or her as a child. But remember, when speaking with a person with mental retardation, avoid abstractions and speak in concrete terms. It is helpful to demonstrate (show and explain) what needs to be done—for example, specifying exactly what "away" means when told to put his or her books away. It is also helpful to ask the student with mental retardation to repeat directions to make sure they are fully understood.

12. The youngster with mental retardation should be introduced to the rest of the class, and a non retarded student identified as a buddy to be available to answer questions as they arise.

13. Students and teachers need to take extra care and time to explain to classmates with mental retardation where to find the school office, school nurse, lockers, cafeteria, art room, music room and lavatories. The student with mental retardation should also become familiar with school schedules and routines and be told where to report each day and where to go at the end of the day for transportation home.

14. Students need to realize that many of their classmates with mental retardation have been mocked or teased or picked on in ways that cause them to feel inferior and socially inadequate. They need to examine their own attitudes toward their peers with mental retardation. These attitudes can strongly influence the success and self

images of classmates classified with mental retardation. These students need affection and acceptance as much as anyone else in the class. The elimination of teasing, name calling and rejection should involve everyone in the class. All students deserve respect and have the right to be treated as equals.

About Autism

A developmental disability, autism occurs in between 5 and 15 of every 10,000 births and is usually diagnosed during the first three years of life. It occurs in every race, ethnic group but is four times more prevalent in boys than in girls. Children and adults with autism usually exhibit deficits in both verbal and non-verbal communication, socialization and appropriate leisure or play activities. Common behaviors include repeating body movements like rocking or flapping hands, unusual responses to the world around them, and insistence on following strict routines. In some cases, individuals with autism may display aggressive or such self-injurious behavior as head banging or finger biting. Individuals with autism may also exhibit various combinations of some or all of these 17 signs and symptoms:

1.   resistance to conventional methods of teaching,

2.   laughing or crying for no apparent reason,

3.   little or no apparent fear of real dangers,

4.   insensitivity to pain,

5.   aversion to being hugged or cuddled,

6.   sustained odd play,

7.   little or no eye contact,

8.   preference to be alone,

9.   communication of needs by gesturing,

10. inappropriate attachment to objects,

11. lack of speech,

12. behaving as if he or she lacks hearing,

13. obsession with spinning objects,

14. resistance to change in routine,

15. difficulty in interacting with other children,

16. uneven development of skills, and

17. marked physical over-activity or extreme passivity.

Although the specific cause of autism remains an unknown, research suggests that it is neurologically or biologically based and is not a product of psychological factors in the child's environment. Autism is not caused by parental neglect or abuse. Rather, it appears to be associated with other disorders affecting the function of the brain, including metabolic disturbances, infections, mental retardation, epilepsy, and such genetic disorders as "Fragile X Syndrome." From one-quarter to one-third of all those who have autism develop seizure disorders. In addition, research indicates that approximately two-thirds of those with autism exhibit some degree of mental retardation. Conversely, about one-third function within the average or above-average range of intelligence. Accurately assessing the cognitive skills of individuals with autism can, however be difficult, especially younger children and individuals with significant communication impairment. Because there are no current medical tests to detect autism, its diagnosis must rest with observations of the child's behavior by a trained diagnostician, usually a psychologist or neurodevelopmental pediatrician. Ideally, a child should be evaluated by an interdisciplinary study team (which may include a neurologist or other medical doctor, psychologist, speech and language therapist, learning consultant, social worker or other professional). It is important to distinguish autism from mental retardation, developmental delay and other disorders, since an accurate diagnosis can facilitate referral to the most appropriate and effective education and treatment programs.

Many parents first suspect "something is wrong" when their child fails to reach such traditional developmental milestones, as speaking his or her first words. But, unlike individuals with mental retardation who typically show developmental delay in all areas, individuals with autism may acquire skills in one area and reveal delays or skill deficiencies in another area. For example, a child may be unable to imitate waving "bye-bye," yet may complete a jigsaw puzzle with ease. Children and adults with autism may have distinct skills in some areas like music or rote memory, but perform poorly in other areas like reading comprehension or gross motor skills. One of the hallmarks of autism is a verbal language deficit. A common form of communication—particularly with autistic children—is called "leading" whereby the child physically leads an adult to a desired object or activity.

Individuals with autism do develop speech to various levels of proficiency. Their common speech problems include echolalia (immediate or delayed repeating of information), unconventional word use, and such other peculiar traits as unusual tones, pitches and inflections. Even when they acquire more complex speech, individuals with autism usually have poor conversational skills. Although some children with autism fail to develop functional speech many of these learn to communicate with sign language, picture boards, computers and other augmentative devices.

COMMON SENSE RESPONSES—In short, students with autism have special requirements their teachers and fellow students should learn and accommodate. Six common sense approaches to students with autism follow here:

1.   Students and teachers need to be aware that their classmates with autism may respond differently to sensory stimuli. For example, youngsters with autism may overreact or under react to simulation from one or more of the senses (sight, smell, hearing, taste, touch). For instance, their classmates need to realize that youngsters with autism may appear to be fearful of the soft buzz of an alarm clock but may enjoy the loud noise of a car horn. Also, some children and adults with autism show an exceptionally high threshold of pain.

2.   Youngsters need to understand that a classmate with autism may relate to people, objects, and events in unexpected ways. Often, young children with autism initially have difficulty interacting with adults and other children at all. Many become more responsive to

others as they learn to communicate and understand the world around them. That is why they are in class.

3. Youngsters need to realize that their classmates with autism may react in ways that they do not understand. For example, individuals with autism may form strong attachments to objects, or engage in peculiar, sustained play activities. The child may spin the wheels on a toy car rather than put it on the floor and push it, or find one shoestring and continually dangle it in front of his or her eyes.

4. Teachers and classmates need to realize that youngsters with autism often resist changes in their routines. This dependence on objects or routines can be difficult for a class that looks forward to a break in routine but faces an upset classmate.

5. Both the teacher and non-disabled students should learn about applied behavior analysis, which has been proven effective in remediating many of the skill deficits and behavior problems youngsters with autism exhibit.

6. A youngster with autism should receive a structured individualized program delivered in a consistent comprehensive and coordinated manner. The time spent in the regular classroom has to be initiated in increments and thoroughly planned.

About Emotional Disturbance

Emotional disturbances or behavior disorders involve inappropriate social interactions between an individual and his or her environment as perceived by those in authority. Hence, we confront here the special education problem likeliest to lead teachers and schools to "blame the victim." For example, they see the youngster "being emotionally disturbed" instead of "exhibiting disturbing behavior in particular environments."

Although definitions differ, Hallahan and Kauffman (1994) specified three behavioral conditions need to be present for the behavior to be considered disturbed or disordered: (1) the behavior is extreme, (2) the behavior is unacceptable because of social or cultural expectations, and (3) the behavior is chronic.

Who becomes categorized as "emotionally disturbed" depends generally on many confusing factors. Society sets standards for acceptable behavior and expectations for both children and adults, and such conditions as the individual's age, the characteristics of the surrounding society, and the conditions under which the behavior occurs all influence how society judges the appropriateness of the behavior (Smith & Luckasson, 1995). In addition, a wide variation of legal definitions of the terms "emotional disturbance" and "behavior disorder" exist. For example, IDEA (1990) defined emotional disturbance as a condition exhibiting one or more of the following five characteristics, displayed over a long time and to a marked degree that adversely affects a student's educational performance:

1. an inability to learn that cannot be explained by intellectual, sensory, of other health factors;

2. an inability to build or maintain satisfactory interpersonal relationships with peers and teachers;

3. inappropriate types of behavior or feelings under normal circumstances;

4. a general pervasive mood of unhappiness or depression; or

5. a tendency to develop physical symptoms or fears associated with personal or school problems.

The term includes children who are "schizophrenic" but not children who are "socially maladjusted," unless they are seriously emotionally disturbed [*15, 20 U.S.C., 1401*]. It is, however, up to each state to provide its own definition of the term. For example, in New Jersey,

> "Emotionally Disturbed" means the exhibiting of seriously disordered behavior over an extended period of time which adversely affects educational performance and may be characterized by i. or ii. below.:
>
> i. An inability to build or maintain satisfactory interpersonal relationships;
>
> ii. Behaviors inappropriate to the circumstances, such as a general pervasive mood of depression or the development of physical symptoms or irrational fears (*NJAC: 6:28*, [3.5, (d), 5], pp. 26-27).

Turnbull, et al. (1995) found that many professionals consider such definitions ambiguous because they invite various interpretations which, in turn, make identification difficult. In fact, "disturbing behavior to one teacher may be viewed as independence and creativity by another" (Odom and Clark, 1982, p. 76). Such definitions assume that "seriously disordered behavior" is demonstrably inappropriate for the time and place in which it occurred. "Over an extended period of time" implies that both the force of the behavior and its rate must receive consideration.

But, terms like "seriously disordered behavior" and "over an extended period of time" are actually vague and ambiguous and encourage subjective conclusions. Is an extended period of time a day, a week, a month, or a year? How is seriously disordered behavior measured? One can measure visual acuity loss, hearing decibel loss, range of motion loss, and intelligence; but how does one measure the seriousness of behavior precisely? The many differing professional conceptual frameworks psychologists, social workers, special educators, psychiatrists, and lawyers adopt, leave no clear-cut, agreed-upon definition of mental health.

In addition, terms like "emotional disturbance" and "behavior disorder" are hard to define because we tend to describe them in terms of deviance from cultural norms that are themselves variable. What may appear to be "emotional disturbed behavior" in one setting may appear to be "normal behavior" in another. For example, one might ask, "Can it ever be considered normal behavior to remain in a constant state of severe depression?" If one were a concentration camp detainee at Auschwitz during World War II, deep depression would have been normal and cheerfulness, abnormal. Similarly, in Germany, during World War II, individuals not adhering to Nazi beliefs and party line were considered to be exhibiting deviant, inappropriate, disturbed behavior. Today, neo-Nazis, who admire and yearn for the discipline of the Third Reich are considered deviant and disturbed. Hallahan and Kauffman (1994) listed five factors that make defining emotional or behavioral disorders difficult:

1. We lack a precise definition of mental health;

2. Differences in conceptual models abound;

3. It is difficult to measure emotions;

4. Relationships often exist among emotional or behavior disorders and other disabilities; and

5. Different professionals categorize and serve people in the emotionally disturbed category (pp. 206-207).

We often find "emotional disturbance" classified into two subgroups consisting of externalized and internalized behaviors, commonly referred to as "fight" or "flight." Typically, externalized or "acting out" behaviors are characterized by impulsive, anti-social, hostile, or aggressive actions directed toward others. Boys exhibit this type of behavior much more than girls and, therefore, have a higher identification, referral and classification rate. Internalized behaviors, much more prevalent in girls, are often characterized by social withdrawal, fear, immaturity, shyness, depression, an excessive craving for control and the development of self-directed symptoms like bulimia and anorexia. Internalized disturbed behaviors inherently mask a youngster's problems (Mullen & Gearheart, 1993; Hunt & Marshall, 1994; Smith & Luckasson, 1995).

Because of the subjective identification criteria and the varied and vague definitions of "emotional disturbance," prevalence estimates also vary widely. Hallahan and Kauffman (1994) estimated that from six to ten percent of the school aged population have emotional or behavior disorders. According to Turnbull et al. (1995) from three to five percent of children and adolescents have emotional or behavioral disorders. During the 1990-91 school year the number of children classified as emotionally disturbed or behaviorally disordered under IDEA was 356,050 or 8.5 percent of the entire special education population, leading many professionals to conclude that students with needs in this area may be greatly underserved.

Students who exhibit behavior disorders need assistance and guidance designed to help them learn how to cope with their environments by establishing positive interpersonal relationships. "The overall goal," wrote Brolin (1995), "is to provide an environment that will modify or help the student control the behavior problem, that will enhance the student's feeling of self-worth, and that will help the student's self-control so that appropriate learning can occur" (p. 254). According to Kirk and Gallagher (1989), students seen as exhibiting emotionally disturbed behaviors need to be included in the mainstream of education for three important reasons: (1) to give them a chance to interact with youngsters who are not handicapped, (2) to provide constructive role models for behavior, and (3) to keep up academically.

COMMON SENSE RESPONSES—Toward these ends, a teacher should become familiar with the following 15 common sense approaches to accommodating the youngster classified emotionally disturbed:

1. Provide a "user-friendly environment." Youngsters have a right to be placed into a classroom where they are fully accepted, they have opportunities for positive interactions with their teacher and classmates and they are provided ample opportunities for academic progress and appropriate behavior development.

2. The teacher and all of the students should cooperatively develop appropriate classroom procedures and standards of classroom behavior. The student with the behavior problem should be asked directly what the class and teacher can do to make his or her program work. Also, establishing classroom routines helps a student who exhibits disturbing behaviors know what is expected. All students should be held responsible for demonstrating an understanding of the standards and procedures. Rules for managing student behavior need to be appropriate, stated positively, applied fairly, and clearly posted. Consequences for inappropriate behavior should be clear to all students. In addition, the consequences should be implemented in an educationally, respectful, prompt and consistent way. The teacher should use the word "no" when required. An outright "no," when used cautiously and sparingly, can actually reassure a child that someone cares enough to put limits on his or her behavior.

3. The seating arrangement should be suitable for the students and conducive to the attainment of the program goals. Students who sometimes exhibit disturbing behaviors should be positioned for optimum interaction with their teachers and those peers who are appropriate role models. In addition, students should be provided enough space to feel comfortable. Additional space between youngsters helps eliminate pushing, shoving, or other contact that may lead to aggression or retaliatory behavior. Sometimes, youngsters who exhibit disturbing behaviors do not distinguish between accidental and purposeful actions of others.

4. Some youngsters who exhibit disturbing behaviors function better if their inclusion in a regular classroom is phased in gradually. Others may function perfectly well on a full-time basis. Students are individuals, and one should determine their placements according to their individual needs.

5. A teacher should provide an appropriate, challenging and interesting program. Busy, interested students rarely cause trouble. Tasks and schedules should provide variety and diversity, be both active and passive, and take place individually, in small groups and with the whole class. Varied teaching techniques, sports and other extra curricular activities, and interesting materials and resources, like computers, help arouse and retain student interest. When a student becomes restless, the teacher can avoid problems by changing the nature of the activity or redirecting the interest of the class. In addition, the instructional program should be appropriate to the student's need, skill level, and learning style. It is also important that all subject matter be relevant to the student's life and that he or she understands the relationship.

6. Provide a program that allows students to "let off steam" in acceptable ways. Learning activities should provide relief from tension and exhaustion, which may provoke unwanted behaviors. A student who exhibits disturbing behaviors needs opportunities to drain off anger and frustrations in order to regain self-control. The youngster should have an opportunity to express his or her personal feelings openly to classmates or teachers.

7. Some negative behaviors are best ignored. By purposely avoiding eye contact and overlooking the student's behavior, the teacher may discourage the behavior rather than fuel it. The misbehaving student may be testing the teacher. By ignoring the behavior, the teacher gives the student time and a chance to reduce anxiety or anger. Of course, the application of the strategy of "planful ignoring" always depends on the situation. Never ignore behavior if the student is liable to harm himself or others.

8. Initiate a "signal system." Many teachers use a prearranged signal to alert a student or the entire class to unwanted or unacceptable behavior. Such signals may include turning the classroom lights off

and on, raising a hand, sitting down in one's chair, putting a finger to the lips, or using other gestures to indicate a need to control undesirable behavior. But, remember that signals are usually most effective during the early stages of misconduct to keep small incidents from growing.

9. Provide direct teaching and support. Sometimes problems arise in the classroom because a youngster cannot cope with some aspects of the program. If this occurs, specific help—for example working on the assignment directly with the student—may make what he or she thinks difficult easy. The teacher's focus should be on teaching the child to overcome the learning problem at hand, rather than on the student's misconduct.

10. Provide "teacher proximity." Teachers tend to sense potential problems, and a teacher's physical nearness at such times may help a student control his or her behavior. A teacher may avert an outburst in a stressful situation if the student draws reassurance from the teacher's nearness and support. The teacher can provide the student with a model of self control, self concept reinforcement, and on-the-spot encouragement.

11. A teacher can usefully anticipate and allow for changes in the environment. If the youngster is exhibiting a problem in his or her environment, it may be helpful to change that environment until self-control returns. The emphasis should be on ameliorating the unruly behavior and helping the child "get over it."

12. Reinforce and reward positive behavior. Rewards can help build positive self concepts.

13. Avoid threats and blame. Some youngsters who exhibit disturbing behaviors interpret blame as rejection. Always keep the behavior and the individual separate:"I don't like what you are doing but I still like you." But a teacher who states firmly the consequences of an action may help the child retain self-control. "Positive affirmation" of desirable student behavior builds positive self-concepts. Teachers who call attention to positive peer behaviors promote appropriate role modeling.

14. Teachers should be especially aware of and sensitive to the needs of youngsters who exhibit anxious and withdrawn behavior. Such youngsters need as much help as the "acting out" youngster.

15. Implement an ongoing "classroom management plan." The successful inclusion and education of students who exhibit disturbing behaviors require the committed support of collaborative teams that include the teacher, students, administration, parents, and pupil personnel support staff. The basis of the plan should be to instill in each youngster a sense of self-worth and self-control.

About Severe and Multiple Impairments

Children with severe or multiple impairments form the classification most diverse with regard to the types and combinations of impairments a teacher must address. It is hard to define "severe and multiple disabilities" because as Turnbull et al. (1995) aptly stated, "[N]o one definition covers all the conditions that special educators associate with it" (p. 286). The terms often cause confusion, because most states placed such children in segregated special classes often labeled "severe *and* multiply handicapped" as if the two groups constituted one group. Thus, they became linked within an all-encompassing classification reserved mostly for youngsters with mental retardation and other impairments like severe physical disabilities or severe language problems (Turnbull et al., 1995).

Kirk, Gallagher and Anastasiow (1993) estimated more than 70,000 children with severe and multiple handicaps are currently enrolled in special education programs in the United States. Approximately 150,000 children are born each year in the United States with congenital dysfunctions and disabilities, and the prevalence of severe and multiple disabilities is between 1 percent and 1.9 percent (Turnbull et al., 1995). In the not too distant past, these youngsters found themselves largely excluded from the public schools and denied access to society (Patton, Payne, Kauffman, Brown & Payne, 1987).

The Individuals with Disabilities Education Act (IDEA) uses separate definitions for multiple disabilities and severe disabilities. In the IDEA definition, "multiple disabilities" means concomitant impairments (such as mental retardation and blindness; mental retardation and orthopedic impairment), the combination of which causes such severe educational problems that the child cannot be accommodated in special education programs solely for one of the impairments. Those who are "deaf-blind" comprise a separate category (34 C.F.R.,Part 300, Sec. 300.7).

In the IDEA definition, children with "severe disabilities" refers to children with disabilities who, because of the intensity of their physical, mental, or emotional problems, need highly specialized education, social, psychological and medical services in order to maximize their full potential for useful and meaningful participation in society and for self-fulfillment. The term includes those children with disabilities who exhibit severe disturbance (including schizophrenia), autism, severe and profound mental retardation, and those who have two or more serious disabilities such as mental retardation and blindness, and cerebral palsy and deafness:

> Children with severe disabilities may experience severe speech, language and/or perceptual-cognitive deprivations, and evidence abnormal behaviors such as failure to respond to pronounced social stimuli, self-mutilation, self-stimulation, manifestation of intense and prolonged temper tantrums, and absence of rudimentary forms of verbal control; and may also have intensely fragile physiological conditions (34 C.E.R., Part 300, Sec. 315.4[d]).

Other conditions found in the population include these five:

1. attention deficits in the ability to respond to social stimuli;

2. the inability to speak, imitate, follow directions, play or control one's behavior;

3. being passive, hyperactive, impulsive, rigid, suggestible, withdrawn, and develop mentally immature;

4. being susceptible to seizures or extremely threatening medical conditions; and

5. having a limited ability to learn without direct intervention. (For such children, the lack of mobility can greatly limit their early exploration of the environment and sensory experimentation.

As Baken (1977) stated,

As a result of his multiplicity of handicaps (both primary and secondary) it might be well said that the severely handicapped child is faced with an inconsistent confusing environment to which he cannot respond and which he is very likely to soon ignore (p. 5).

One of the most complex and volatile issues disability groups face is the resurgence of both the public and private debate over the issue of infant euthanasia—that is withholding medical treatment from newborns with severe and multiple disabilities. According to Cohen (1981) it is common practice for physicians not to treat infants with severe disabilities. Lusthaus (1985) noted that even though many perceive it to be murder, practicing euthanasia on babies with severe handicaps enjoys a great deal of support among ethicists, physicians, and even theologians. Among them, one finds considerable agreement that withholding treatment from infants with severe disabilities, with the intention of letting them die, is a legitimate form of medical intervention (p. 87). Remembering the roots of the Holocaust, this issue should continually engage educators.

Basically, euthanasia means "a good death" and is thought of as ending life painlessly. Hardman and Drew (1978) placed euthanasia into one of four classifications based on two criteria, who does it and who wants it done:

1. DIRECT AND VOLUNTARY—Death is chosen and implemented by the person himself or herself. Basically the death is a suicide carried out by a person in pain;

2. INDIRECT AND VOLUNTARY—Death is chosen by the person himself or herself. However, physically unable to carry out the act, the person exacts from a friend or relative in advance the promise to carry out the act for the person suffering;

3. DIRECT AND INVOLUNTARY–This is often termed simply "mercy killing";

4. INDIRECT AND INVOLUNTARY—Treatment is withheld in order to allow the patient to die. The Nazis tried to cover their murders of persons with severe disabilities by calling the practice euthanasia, but of course, they took direct action to see that the infant patients

would die, for example, by reducing rations or putting the babies into unheated rooms to freeze or to die of pneumonia.

Some ethicists like Kuhse and Singer (1985) consider it permissible in some cases involving children with severe disabilities to withhold treatment and allow a baby to die. Some believe it is even permissible to take direct action to kill the child. Kuhse and Singer, for example, also accept the premise that some lives are not worth living. It follows, that if not all human lives are equally worth living, it may be in the best interest of those who are severely disabled to help them avoid their "doomed" lives. Letting disabled infants deteriorate until "nature takes its course" appears to replace the moral responsibility of action with cruel inaction. Therefore, according to this reasoning, the infant should be put to death as quickly and painlessly as possible.

On the other hand, some like Weir (1984) believe that the contemporary practice of selectively withholding treatment from severely disabled newborns simply continues the historical practice of infanticide that dates back to the Spartans and before. Observed Orelove and Sobsey (1987), "Rather than parents engaging in physical abandonment, drowning, or smothering—to name just a few of the past methods of infanticide—today's decisions to treat or withhold treatment are usually made in neonatal intensive care units" (pp. 339-340). As Hollander (1989) stated,

> Today, what shocks our ideas of propriety, or what does *not* shock our ideas of propriety, *still* gives abundant reason to fear that science may, in the end, conquer sentiment. . . . It is all too clear that the idea, and the reality, of killing people with mental retardation is still in the wind in the latter decades of this century, as it was in the latter decades of the 19th century. The final chapter to this story is not yet written. It could end in tragedy if enough voices are not raised in protest (p. 60).

The issues surrounding youngsters with severe and multiple disabilities go beyond those controversies regarding the right to life to involve the right to an education, an appropriate curriculum and placement in the least restrictive environment possible. The concept of inclusion presupposes that such youngsters spend at least part of their school day in regular classrooms with non-handicapped peers. Such placements can be most beneficial to all of the youngsters in the room if it is carefully planned.

COMMON SENSE RESPONSES—The following ten ideas can help teachers accommodate youngsters with severe and multiple disabilities:

1. Non-handicapped peers should be reminded that each student in class is an integral part of the whole student body. The student with severe or multiple disabilities must be welcomed as a valued member. No student should be excluded because he or she is considered too different.

2. The teacher should use instructional methods that encourage pupil interactions, provide opportunities for forming friendships, and allow students to spend time together. Such methods include cooperative learning groups, group discussions, the practice of pairing students to work on assignments, and finding common areas for discussion.

3. Teachers should use group facilitation skills to acquaint the class with the severely or multiply handicapped classmate and his or her needs. Questions regarding the student's disabilities should be discussed openly, and all students should be encouraged to help make the classroom environment "user friendly" for their classmate with a disability.

4. A student with severe or multiple disabilities should have a schedule as similar to the schedule other students follow as possible. For example, he or she should enter and exit the classroom at the same time as the other students and engage in classroom activities and make transitions at the same time as his or her classmates.

5. A student with severe or multiple disabilities should be positioned so that he or she can participate to the fullest extent possible. The teacher and other students should be able to interact with him or her easily as part of the class, not in isolation. The student with severe or multiple disabilities should be actively involved in classroom activities, asking and responding to questions whenever appropriate.

6. A student with severe or multiple disabilities should be encouraged to follow all the classroom and social rules—for example, hugging others only when appropriate, paying attention to instruction and remaining seated.

7. A student with severe or multiple disabilities should receive assistance only when necessary and as briefly as possible. Classmates should be encouraged to offer a disabled classmate help (and to ask for help or advice from them when appropriate.)

8. As much as possible, a student with severe or multiple disabilities should use the same or similar materials during classroom activities.

9. Both the student with a disability and his or her non-disabled peers need to be taught how to communicate with each other. If the student with a disability uses an alternative communication system, the teacher and the other students should know how it works and how to use it.

10. A student with severe or multiple disabilities should dress like his or her non-disabled peers, and should be encouraged to attend to his or her appearance and be neatly groomed. This nicety includes having one's hair combed, hands and clothing clean, and body odor free. It also also includes keeping one's equipment (even the wheelchair) clean as well (Stainback and Stainback, 1990; Stainback and Stainback, 1992; Stainback, Stainback and Forest, 1989).

Conclusion

The information on disabilities this chapter provides can begin and guide the appropriate discussions. More detailed information on specific disabilities appears in such current special education textbooks as J. Cohen (n.d.), Gearheart, Mullen and Gearheart (1993); Kirk, Gallagher and Anastasiow (1993); Hardman, Drew, Egan and Wolf (1993); Hallahan and Kauffman (1994); Haring, McCormick and Haring (1984); Hunt and Marshall (1994); Smith and Luckasson (1995); and Turnbull, Turnbull, Shank and Leal (1995). Now we have explored *what* to teach we can focus on *how* to use critical education practices to change negative attitudes.

CHAPTER SIX

Critical Educational Practices
for Changing Negative Attitudes

Published Curriculum Guides and Activity Books

With the passage of P.L. 94-142, the Education for All Handicapped Children Act in 1975, children with disabilities suddenly enjoyed the right to be placed in least restrictive educational settings. This mandate, in turn, presented the need to prepare non-disabled students for such processes as mainstreaming and inclusion. Accordingly various activity compendia, curriculum guides and disability awareness bulletins appeared in the system from pre-school through college. These materials described a wide variety of methods for changing negative attitudes toward students with disabilities. (Appendix I presents a bibliography of curriculum guides and activity books on disability awareness and prejudice reduction). All of these resources contain activities for classroom use and help guide curriculum building.

For example, Getskow and Konczal (1996), provide both information and activities to promote awareness and understanding of youngsters with special needs. Cohen, Koelher and Grand developed an earlier series of guides on accepting individual differences including an overview (1977a), and an analysis of motor impairment (1977b) and visual impairment (1977c). They also wrote a comprehensive secondary curriculum guide that included a staff orientation manual (1981a), and information on disabled persons in society (1981b), disabled persons in literature (1981c) and science and health perspectives on disability (1981c). Bliss and Schwartz (1979) developed a guide for exploring attitudes toward women with disabilities. Shaver and Curtis (1981) focused their guide on teaching about disability awareness and handicapism in the social studies. McCahill, Nicholls, Peterson, Hines, Leonard and Cassell (1987) developed a booklet to help Scouts earn a merit badge in Handicap Awareness, and J. Cohen (1998) on disability etiquette and tips on interacting with people with disabilities for the Eastern Paralyzed Veterans Association.

Additional helpful resources were published by organizations and agencies including: The President's Committee on Employment of the Handicapped (Jones & Stevens, 1979), the New Jersey Department of Education (Schnitzler & Rappaport, 1983), the Council for Exceptional Children (Ward, Arkell, Dahl & Wise, 1979), the Children's Museum of Boston (Kamien, Jennes, Porter & Shortreed, 1978), the Center on Human Policy (Barnes, Berrigan & Biklen, 1978), the National Easter Seals Society (Cumblad & Strickman, 1990) and Paraquad (n.d.). The guide published by Kids Come in Special Flavors edited by Cashdollar and Martin (1981), was written entirely by parents of youngsters with disabilities.

An early childhood curriculum about disability was developed by Froschol, Colon, Rubin and Sprung (1984). Bookbinder's (1978) curriculum focused on teaching about disabilities in grades one to four. The Newton (Massachusetts) schools' (1979) disability awareness curriculum, developed for fourth graders, was updated in 1994. Another curriculum guide for third, fourth and fifth grade students was developed by Paraquad (n.d.).

Ross and Freelander (1977) developed a comprehensive curriculum that contained activities for the elementary, middle school and high school levels. Masters and Stevens (1987) focused their curriculum for grades Kindergarten through eight. Other excellent curriculum and activity guides that can serve as bases for curriculum building include those by Cleary (1976), White (1979), Shields (1980), Commings, London, Moore, Raschke, Schwartz and Tofty (1981), Shields, Christmas, Deitchman, Langford, Newingham, O'Daniel, Yeker and Goodridge (1981), Konczal and Pesetski, (1983), Hague and Engstrom (1984). Getskow and Konczal (1996).

In addition, Schniedwind and Davidson (1998) wrote a sourcebook of learning activities to affirm diversity and promote equity, and Derman-Sparks (1993 ed.) wrote an anti-bias curriculum. Other sourcebooks on teaching for equity, justice and tolerance by Fleming et al. (1997) and Bigelow et al. (1994) can also be used for curriculum building. Two books for older children are, *Lets talk about disabled people,* by Sanders (1992) and *Coping with special needs classmates,* by McCarthy-Tucker (1993). A publication edited by Hey and Zola (1995) contained course syllabi, instructional materials and experiential learning activities for teaching about disability on the college level. Although these guides varied in style, technique and extensiveness, they all stressed a *multi dimensional experiential approach* requiring active participation on the part of the students.

Strategies for Changing Negative Attitudes Toward Persons with Disabilities

When students possess and display negative attitudes toward individuals whom they consider different, a teacher can employ a variety of attitude change strategies to provide information that counter stereotypic views and reduce resistance (Conway & Gow, 1988; Donaldson, 1980).

Schroedel (1979), Donaldson (1980), and Watts (1984), all found that the most effective of these techniques include social gaming (for example, role-playing, behavior rehearsing, and simulation activities, always followed by discussion); value confrontation and learning about inference; interaction with persons with disabilities (including cooperative learning with disabled peers and exposure to guest speakers with disabilities); the provision of basic information on disabilities by exposure to books, articles, and a wide variety of audio-visual media, including films, slides, audio and videotapes, and compact discs; and exposure to adaptive devices, aids and appliances known professionally as "assistive technology." (An extensive list of these resources appears in Appendix I.)

Basic Goals of A Disability Awareness Program

From the literature on disability awareness, one can adduce the following 23 principles for a comprehensive disability awareness program:

1. One's value as a human being need not be deserved.

2. People are more alike than different.

3. Differences can be seen as both positive and negative. Different does not imply one is better or worse than another person. Differentness need not be stigmatized.

4. All persons benefit from a diverse population.

5. Although people are different, an overall transcending humanness unites us all.

6. All persons are educable and can learn to grow.

7. Disabilities are normal.

8. People are unique individuals, not labels. Everyone has a right to be judged on individual merit, not prejudged by group membership.

9. People have a right to be different.

10. It is hurtful to judge someone by something that can not - be changed.

11. Feelings are important. A caring person avoids hurting others.

12. Self-esteem helps an individual grow.

13. Language is a critical ingredient in framing our thoughts and attitudes.

14. Handicapping conditions, as opposed to disabilities per se, are situational and environmental and therefore can be eliminated.

15. Those who have disabilities have basic rights that must be safeguarded for everyone's benefit.

16. Positive attitudes and understanding help us all develop empathy and achieve true integration.

17. Developing empathy, understanding, compassion, and concern for others enhances our own growth. Cruelty to others hinders personal growth.

18. We gain much more insight into ourselves and others by concentrating on our abilities rather then our disabilities. In defining ourselves, what we can do is more important than what we can not do.

19. Each disability group is unique, special and significant, as is each individual member of that group. We can learn valuable lessons from each disability group and each disabled individual.

20. Persons with disabilities deserve empathy rather than sympathy or pity, and exercise of empathy is a valuable and compassionate skill.

21. Negative attitudes toward persons with disabilities is deeply ingrained in our culture, language, media and history.

22. Negative attitudes lead to negative social policy.

23. Integration is preferable to segregation.

Getskow and Konczal (1996) centered their disability awareness curriculum on the following five developmental themes:

1. Children notice and ask questions about disabilities.

2. Children are able to see their shared abilities and similarities.

3. Children need information, words, and support for handling questions about their disabilities.

4. Children are curious about the equipment and devices people use for specific disabilities.

5. Children may be confused about what a child with a particular disability can and cannot do (p. 8).

Three Basic Considerations for Implementing Disability Awareness Programs

Yuker and Block (1979) found that a comprehensive disability awareness program should stress goals that facilitate integration by establishing a classroom climate in which students with disabilities can find acceptance and respect as their peers learn about the benefits, advantages and opportunities of living in a diverse and pluralistic society. To support and promote integration and inclusion, one can usefully consider these three:

1. EMPHASIS ON SAMENESS RATHER THAN DIFFERENTNESS—When teaching about disability awareness, continually emphasize sameness over differentness. For example, when teaching about persons with mobility impairments emphasize the commonalities in people. We may do some things differently, but we do the same things. Although some people get

around with the use of a wheelchair, we all need transportation. Some people communicate with sign language, but we all need to communicate. In fact, although we are all different, we are also all the same and more alike than unlike. When teaching about a particular disability, raise questions that invite this kind of thinking. For example, discussion questions on blindness may include, "What could you still do if you became blind? What couldn't you do? What could you still do but have to do differently or with help? Would you still be you?" When introducing examples of differing disabilities at the younger grade levels reinforce the concept of sameness by proceeding from the least to the most severe. Also, present disabling conditions most familiar to the students, like blindness, earliest (Bookbinder 1978).

2. EMPHASIS ON APPRECIATING INDIVIDUAL DIFFERENCES—Another important basic theme in a disability awareness program is the appreciation for all individual differences, not just disabilities. Educators need to emphasize the idea that people are individuals who represent themselves, not a group, and each has a right to be different. Lessons and activities should reflect an appreciation for differences and diversity and avoid stereotypes and stigmatizing. Information included should stress how every individual contributes to the culture and classroom, and every student is equally worthy. Students, in turn, need to become equipped with a positive way to express their curiosity, concern, and acceptance of those who appear different. Whatever the disability, the classroom discussion should encompass and emphasize individual differences and an appreciation of uniqueness. Similarly, when a guest with a disability comes to class, remind the students that her or she speaks only for himself or herself, not for all disabled people.

3. EMPHASIS ON INVOLVEMENT—Students should, of course, become aware of the enormous impact public attitudes have on the potential for acceptance and inclusion of persons with disabilities into community life and how negative impressions lead to prejudice, discrimination and segregation persons with disabilities encounter every day. When students begin to understand the issues that affect their classmates and others with disabilities, they will be likelier to support social policies and programs that promote inclusion and independence. As Yuker and Block (1979) found,

> In order to change attitudes you typically have to get people to do something. You seldom change attitudes by lectures or written mate-

rial. They may have a long-range effect, but the only real way of changing attitudes is by getting people to actively participate (p. 55).

This is precisely why cooperative techniques like conducting a media watch or accessibility study can be productive and enriching.

General Conditions for Changing Attitudes

Attitude change often comes in the aftermath of targeting an abundance of messages upon an intended audience—for instance, school children. On any given day most people confront a multiplicity of information and impressions, often to the point of "sensory overload." A common technique for coping with so much information is to address first general categories of perceptions, then the specific details. Most people form attitudes through this process of mental categorization or labeling. Because labels are examples of "characterized" attitudes, they become extremely important ingredients in the formation of children's impressions of persons with disabilities. For example, "regular education" teachers tend to refer to exceptional children by the assigned label. The child becomes the label and is perceived as *being* mentally retarded rather than *having* mental retardation.

Basic Considerations for Changing Attitudes

According to Golin (1970) and Goldstein and Blackman (1975) the following three considerations require careful thought when setting out to change attitudes:

1. THE NATURE OF THE INFORMATION PROVIDED—can create either a positive or negative attitude (raising money for "Jerry's Kids" does not guarantee a favorable attitude toward persons with muscular dystrophy);

2. THE INDIVIDUAL'S INTENSITY OF COMMITMENT TO AN ATTITUDINAL POSITION—can influence the susceptibility to change (extreme attitudes are often more difficult to modify than moderate attitudes);

3. THE CREDIBILITY AND COMPETENCE OF THE CHANGE AGENT—is crucial to redirecting attitudes.

Yuker and Block (1979) discussed the effects of education and information on attitude change and stressed the importance of the nature of the actual contact between disabled and non-disabled students. Their discussion included the following five general principles:

1. THE INTERACTION OF NON-DISABLED STUDENTS AND THEIR PEERS WITH DISABILITIES SHOULD RELY ON COLLABORATING RATHER THAN HELPING— This orientation must be taught. Because of physical segregation, many students both with and without disabilities simply lack the necessary skills to interact with each other. Thus, a teacher needs the instructional skills to teach this collaboration. But such an effort can end the perception that the student with a disability has a lowered status because he or she must be helped.

2. THE INTERACTIONS OF NON-DISABLED STUDENTS WITH THEIR DISABLED PEERS SHOULD BE COOPERATIVE RATHER THAN COMPETITIVE—As Yuker and Block (1979) observed, "If people engage in cooperative behavior it leads to increased *positiveness* in attitudes; if they engage in competitive behavior it does not. You get to like people more when you cooperate with them than when you compete" (p. 53). It follows therefore, that all planned activities should allow for the individualization of instruction emphasizing cooperation rather than competition. Techniques like cooperative learning that emphasize group accomplishment and de-emphasize competition nurture self-esteem by building confidence and inviting students to achieve their potential. As Slavin (1990) stated,

> Because cooperative learning methods are social interventions, they should provide social effects. The criteria for positive intergroup relations are similar to the widely accepted antecedents of friendship formation or cohesion. . . . These include contact; perceived similarity; engaging in pleasant activities; and, once again, cooperation where individuals who work toward the same goal come to see one another as providers of rewards. Cooperative learning increases contact between students, gives them a shared basis of similarity (group membership), engages them in pleasant activities together, and has them work toward common goals. As such, it can clearly be hypothesized that they would increase positive affect among students (p. 49).

3. THE INTERACTIONS OF NON-DISABLED STUDENTS WITH THEIR DISABLED CLASSMATES SHOULD BE INTIMATE RATHER THAN CASUAL—As Yuker and Block (1979) said, "The closer the contact, the more people are likely

to help one another and, therefore, develop positive attitudes. Casual contact will have relatively little effect" (p. 53).

4. THE INTERACTIONS OF NON-DISABLED STUDENTS WITH THEIR DISABLED CLASSMATES SHOULD BE FREQUENT RATHER THAN OCCASIONAL— "[F]requency of contact makes a great deal of difference; the more frequent the contact, the more likely it will be positive" (p. 53). Thus, inclusion is preferable to mainstreaming and both are preferable to segregation.

5. THE INTERACTIONS OF NON-DISABLED STUDENTS AND THEIR CLASSMATES WITH DISABILITIES SHOULD TAKE PLACE ON SETTINGS THAT MAKE THEM EQUALS—Students with disabilities should not be treated as "guests" who earned their way into the mainstream, but as students who belong in that classroom as much as any other student. We all belong in only one "stream." Donaldson (1980) found an "equal status relationship" to be an essential factor in successful attitude change strategies, and such a relationship is based on the premise that both parties view each other as having equal social, educational or vocational status. As Albright et al. (1989) wrote,

> For over 100 years we have spent billions of tax dollars serving people with severe intellectual disabilities in homogenized environments such as "institutions for the retarded," segregated schools, segregated classes in regular schools, and segregated art, music, and physical education classes. Now we realize that the logic and economics of homogeneity and the associated segregated service systems that accrue from them are no longer acceptable. Heterogeneity or integration is now the rule of the day. We now know that students with and without disabilities must be physically next to each other as much as possible if both are to flourish (p. 64).

Curricular Options

Depending on various factors like the age and grade level of the students, disability awareness can enter the curriculum either as a separate unit or as integrated experiences infused into other subject areas. Separate units are usually more appropriate for younger students. Teachers will have already accepted such important basics as all students, regardless of grade level, should be included. All age groups can be taught about disablism provided a teacher presents the material in a meaningful and appropriate way. Every planned activity should be educational and enjoyable. When designing a curriculum, one should take into account feelings. Remember that many teachers and students experience discomfort at first upon encountering persons with disabilities. Fear, curiosity and guilt need to be discussed openly. Because youngsters rarely express their inner feelings when meeting persons who appear to be different, discussions between teachers and students regarding these experiences should be promoted.

Basic Guidelines for Developing Separate Units on Disability Awareness
When introducing a separate unit on disablism or disability awareness, the teacher should keep a definite sequence in mind. Background information should include the meanings of the terms "handicap," "disability," "stereotype," "prejudice," "discrimination," "stigma" and "special education" (see the Chapter II discussion of the issues surrounding language and terminology). The history of disablism should explore the treatment of disabled persons in different eras and cultures (Chapter IV Early Attitudes and Their Legacies discusses this history). Current events discussions should include the disabilities rights movement and laws like *The Education for All Handicapped Children's Act*, *Section 504 of the Rehabilitation Act* and *The Americans With Disabilities Act*. (Resource materials and disability units suitable for various grade levels appear in Appendix I, Resources, Curriculum Guides and Activity Books on Disability Awareness and Prejudice Reduction.)

Curricular Infusion
Disability awareness topics can enhance many subject areas in the curriculum. "Curricular infusion" refers to a new topic of interest introduced as a continuing component of the curriculum. When infusing information about disabilities, the teacher should include references at appropriate points within the general education curriculum rather than altering the focus of the curriculum just to accommodate disability-related issues. Such subject areas may include (but not be limited to) science, reading and language arts, music, art, drama, journalism, social studies, and history. As Biklen, Ford and Ferguson (1989) stated, "Secondary school can make disability a topic of investigation and discussion in the same way that some schools explore the issues of sexism and racism" (p. 256). Teachers can challenge those negative, inaccurate images of persons with disabilities perpetuated by newspapers, magazines, television programs, films and other mass media by

1. identifying and discussing current examples of distortion, inaccuracy, or misdirected attention and using instructional techniques that help students examine their own thoughts, thought processes, and attributions to help students discover in a safe way the personal biases and beliefs they were unaware of;

2. inviting persons from disability rights and news organizations to discuss the issues of media coverage;

3. organizing instructional units that analyze and evaluate newspaper and magazine coverage and compare findings to explicit criteria (for example, Does this story ignore major issues facing persons with disabilities? Does the story accurately reflect the person's abilities as well as his or her disabilities?), and reviewing magazines concerned with disabled persons can add a unique perspective to the unit (see Appendix I—and its section on Magazines Relating to Persons with Disabilities); and

4. using sensitivity simulations and role paying (for example, blindfolding students; having peers do everything for volunteer students, depriving them of all opportunities to act independently). Shaver and Curtis (1981) and Barnes, Berrigan and Biklen (1978) provide excellent compendiums of sensitivity simulations for social studies teachers. Additional resources appear in Appendix I—Curriculum Guides and Activity Books on Disability Awareness.

Assessing Existing Attitudes

Shaw and Wright (1967), concluded that one cannot predict complex behaviors without prior knowledge of the person's attitudes. Therefore, teachers must assess class members' general knowledge of and attitudes toward persons with disabilities. Specifically, they need to assess their students' current attitudes, common assumptions and misconceptions before they can respond effectively and attempt to induce change. What myths do students believe to be truth? Yuker and Block (1979) called this technique "attitudinal self-examination" and it can be an especially effective introductory strategy for helping youngsters reflect on their feelings toward persons with disabilities. The teacher should avoid using the answers to attitudinal self-examinations to determine grades. They serve only as analytical tools to determine the beginning point of instruction. Such information should be considered a "ruler for attitudes."

Before teachers can attempt to change negative attitudes, they must know how their students truly feel. What are their beliefs? What paradigms regarding disability do they have? What attitudes the teachers themselves hold might be handicapist? For example, does the student or teacher regard stuttering as amusing? Does he or she believe that persons with mental retardation are dangerous or that persons with disabilities can never be happy? Does he or she consider it foolish to take an individual with blindness to an art museum? What is his or her belief regarding integration and segregation? For example, should children with disabilities go to separate schools and if so, why? Does he or she regard persons with disabilities as a homogeneous group of persons who lead lives quite different from those of the rest of society? Does he or she associate physical disability with evilness or retribution? Such self-examination should be as intense as possible and should always include discussion. Those who actively participate are far likelier to change attitudes while no change is likely to occur in those who remain passive.

Four effective basic techniques successfully used for assessing student attitudes toward disabilities are direct observation, student "opinionnaires," sentence completion techniques and drawings. All four encourage youngsters to reflect on their attitudes and thoughts toward persons with disabilities and then convey them to the teacher.

DIRECT OBSERVATION—Salend (1994), who wrote that direct observation of the interaction between disabled and non-disabled students in integrated settings can be an excellent way of assessing acceptance of individual differences. He recommended that teachers focus on:

1. the frequency students with disabilities interact with their peers;

2. the nature of the interactions;

3. the initiators of the interactions;

4. the number of non-disabled students who interact with their peers;

5. the circumstances that seem to promote interactions;

6. the circumstances that seem to limit interactions;

7. the skills needed by the youngsters with disabilities to interact successfully; and

8. the outcomes of the interactions.

STUDENT OPINIONNAIRES—*The Measurement of Attitudes Toward People With Disabilities,* by Antonak and Livneh (1988), includes opinionnaires on all levels for assessing pertinent information. Most of these opinionnaires use a Likert rating scale that include the familiar range of answers: *strongly agree, agree, undecided, disagree,* and *strongly disagree.* Administered as a pre-test and post-test this type of assessment can also help a teacher evaluate the degree of the impact at the end of the school year. The opinionnaire may also prompt discussions of issues related to disabilities. If students believe, for example, that classmates with disabilities should be educated separately in segregated settings, or that villainy and physical disability are related, a discussion might focus on the origin of that idea. The opinionnaire can also serve to introduce such concepts as stereotype, discrimination and prejudice.

The opinionnaires scales Antonak and Livneh (1988) included are standardized measures having validity and reliability. The authors discourage the creation of similar "Likert-format scales" for measuring attitudes toward persons with disabilities, especially in formal research projects. They suggest that existing scales should be refined rather than new ones created (p. 274).

Nevertheless, simply as tools for guiding curriculum development with their limited purposes kept foremost in mind, these opinionnaires can be quite useful. They should be used only for "instructional" purposes, not "comparative" or "normative" ones. Teachers may want to develop opinionnaires that include items appropriate for the level of the students they teach and based on the curricular material they teach. In addition, they may want to adapt an existing opinionnaire for younger students who require explanations of language and terms. Teachers may want to rephrase, explain, or simplify questions, or even change them to a true and false format (Antonak and Livneh, 1988).

The following non-standardized opinionnaire lacks validity or reliability and appears only as a model, based on material included in this book. Although the publications listed at the end of the questionnaire served as sources for some of the ideas, no direct items came from them. Notice that items 11, 41, 89, 92, 93, 95, 96, and 100 are reverse items, where *strongly agree* is the preferred answer.

A QUESTIONNAIRE ON DISABILITY AWARENESS

The following list of 100 statements focuses on persons with disabilities. In order to teach about disability awareness, we need a sense of what our students believe, feel, fear and know. Please read the statements below. After carefully reading each sentence circle on the right whether you strongly agree (SA), agree (A), are undecided (U), disagree (D), or strongly disagree (SD) with it. We realize that you are being asked to reveal your feelings on very sensitive issues and may have some reluctance to expose your true feelings, but try to answer each question honestly. Only through this type of assessment can we accurately determine what areas of the curriculum should be developed and stressed. This questionnaire is for that purpose only and is not judgmental in any way. Thank you.

1. I generally don't like to be with people who are different; they make me ill at ease. (SA) (A) (U) (D) (SD)

2. If I had a sister or brother with mental retardation or cerebral palsy, I would rather not tell anyone. (SA) (A) (U) (D) (SD)

3. Seeing a person in a wheelchair often upsets me.
    (SA) (A) (U) (D) (SD)

4. I really would not want a person with mental retardation living in my neighborhood. (SA) (A) (U) (D) (SD)

5. Watching a severely disabled person eat makes me nauseous.
    (SA) (A) (U) (D) (SD)

6. Dwarfs makes me laugh. (SA) (A) (U) (D) (SD)

7. People with deafness live in a sad, silent world.
    (SA) (A) (U) (D) (SD)

8. Thank God I'm not mentally retarded or physically disabled.
    (SA) (A) (U) (D) (SD)

9. I would rather die than become blind, deaf or physically disabled.
    (SA) (A) (U) (D) (SD)

10. I can't help but adore children with Down Syndrome.
(SA) (A) (U) (D) (SD)

11. Women with disabilities often face extreme discrimination.
(SA) (A) (U) (D) (SD)

12. I fear people with mental illness because they are often unpredictable and dangerous. (SA) (A) (U) (D) (SD)

13. Stuttering is funny. (SA) (A) (U) (D) (SD)

14. Most persons with physical disabilities feel resentment and envy toward able-bodied persons. (SA) (A) (U) (D) (SD)

15. Most people in wheelchairs are sick or chronically ill.
(SA) (A) (U) (D) (SD)

16. Most people with disabilities are naturally inferior.
(SA) (A) (U) (D) (SD)

17. People with disabilities are different in "kind" rather than "degree."
(SA) (A) (U) (D) (SD)

18. People with disabilities are more comfortable with "their own kind." (SA) (A) (U) (D) (SD)

19. There is a distinct type of "disability personality."
(SA) (A) (U) (D) (SD)

20. People with blindness are often sad and acquire a sixth sense like improved hearings. (SA) (A) (U) (D) (SD)

21. Most people with deafness are naturally suspicious of others.
(SA) (A) (U) (D) (SD)

22. Most people with mental retardation are unpredictable and cannot control their sexual urges. (SA) (A) (U) (D) (SD)

23. People with disabilities should be pitied. (SA) (A) (U) (D) (SD)

24. People with disabilities are abnormal. (SA) (A) (U) (D) (SD)

25. People with disabilities are brave and courageous.
    (SA) (A) (U) (D) (SD)

26. Most persons with deafness can read lips. (SA) (A) (U) (D) (SD)

27. Most people with disabilities lead lives that are very different from others without them. (SA) (A) (U) (D) (SD)

28. People who stutter think the way they talk. (SA) (A) (U) (D) (SD)

29. Most people with disabilities never really accept their conditions.
    (SA) (A) (U) (D) (SD)

30. It is really not a big deal to call someone a "retard" when he or she makes a mistake. (SA) (A) (U) (D) (SD)

31. I don't like students from special education sitting next to me on the school bus or on a class trip. (SA) (A) (U) (D) (SD)

32. It costs too much money to make schools and other buildings accessible to wheelchair users. (SA) (A) (U) (D) (SD)

33. On the whole, women with disabilities have an easier life than men with disabilities because they do not have to work.
    (SA) (A) (U) (D) (SD)

34. I never spend time with a fellow classmates with disabilities.
    (SA) (A) (U) (D) (SD)

35. I could never really become a good friend to someone who has mental retardation or a physical disability. (SA) (A) (U) (D) (SD)

36. Most persons with physical disabilities have an "attitude problem" and are difficult to get along with. (SA) (A) (U) (D) (SD)

37. The government should take care of persons with disabilities.
    (SA) (A) (U) (D) (SD)

38. We should learn to expect less from most persons with disabilities. (SA) (A) (U) (D) (SD)

39. Children with disabilities should be placed in their own special education schools. (SA) (A) (U) (D) (SD)

40. Persons with disabilities can never really be happy. (SA) (A) (U) (D) (SD)

41. Integration is preferable to segregation. (SA) (A) (U) (D) (SD)

42. Most disabled persons are basically different from non-disabled persons. (SA) (A) (U) (D) (SD)

43. Most persons with disabilities are "pushy." (SA) (A) (U) (D) (SD)

44. People with disabilities should date and marry each other, not able-bodied persons. (SA) (A) (U) (D) (SD)

45. Persons with disabilities need sympathy and special attention. (SA) (A) (U) (D) (SD)

46. A person's value as a human being does not have to be earned. (SA) (A) (U) (D) (SD)

47. Students with learning disabilities are really just lazy. (SA) (A) (U) (D) (SD)

48. People with severe facial scars are often evil. (SA) (A) (U) (D) (SD)

49. Students with disabilities need to earn the right to be educated with non-disabled students by exhibiting good behavior and the ability to do grade-level work. (SA) (A) (U) (D) (SD)

50. Non-disabled students have little to learn from their disabled classmates. (SA) (A) (U) (D) (SD)

51. Parents and teachers of youngsters with disabilities should be less strict then they are with non-disabled children. (SA) (A) (U) (D) (SD)

52. Wheelchairs are confining to their users. (SA) (A) (U) (D) (SD)

53. I would not hire a person with mental retardation or a physical disability. (SA) (A) (U) (D) (SD)

54. How or when an individual acquires a disability has little effect on that person's adjustment and education. (SA) (A) (U) (D) (SD)

55. All persons with disabilities are handicapped.
    (SA) (A) (U) (D) (SD)

56. Labels like "emotionally disturbed" or "learning disabled" tell us very little about an individual to whom they are given.
    (SA) (A) (U) (D) (SD)

57. Telethons enhance the self-images of persons with physical disabilities by giving them publicity. (SA) (A) (U) (D) (SD)

58. Some people are "afflicted" with disabilities by God as payment for their past sins or those of their parents. (SA) (A) (U) (D) (SD)

59. Persons with disabilities generally make poor employees.
    (SA) (A) (U) (D) (SD)

60. Persons with mental retardation are forever childlike.
    (SA) (A) (U) (D) (SD)

61. Mentally retarded adults have strong sex drives and should, therefore, be sterilized. (SA) (A) (U) (D) (SD)

62. Severely and multiply disabled persons are really "useless eaters."
    (SA) (A) (U) (D) (SD)

63. Most decisions regarding the lives of persons with disabilities are medical in nature and, therefore, are best made by physicians.
    (SA) (A) (U) (D) (SD)

64. All persons with epilepsy should barred from driving.
    (SA) (A) (U) (D) (SD)

65. The media—for example, TV, newspapers, and the movies—depict persons with disabilities in fair, positive and accurate images. (SA) (A) (U) (D) (SD)

66. Terms like "Mongoloid," "hunchback" and "cripple" are just words and can't really hurt anyone. (SA) (A) (U) (D) (SD)

67. Disabilities and other differences are looked down upon and stigmatized in all cultures. (SA) (A) (U) (D) (SD)

68. People described as disabled make up an extremely homogeneous group. (SA) (A) (U) (D) (SD)

69. Disabilities and handicaps are the same. (SA) (A) (U) (D) (SD)

70. Persons with disabilities are handicapped in all situations. (SA) (A) (U) (D) (SD)

71. Persons with disabilities are burdensome. (SA) (A) (U) (D) (SD)

72. It's never a good idea to offer help to persons with disabilities because you never know how they will react. (SA) (A) (U) (D) (SD)

73. The major problem of having a speech impairment—like a lisp or stutter—is not being able to be understood. (SA) (A) (U) (D) (SD)

74. If a person with a stutter has difficulty getting the words out, it is helpful to finish the sentence for him. (SA) (A) (U) (D) (SD)

75. Persons with blindness live in a totally dark world. (SA) (A) (U) (D) (SD)

76. It is bad manners to use words like "look" and "see" in the presence of a person with blindness. (SA) (A) (U) (D) (SD)

77. A person's basic worth can really be measured by his or her IQ score. (SA) (A) (U) (D) (SD)

78. Some human beings have more worth than others.
    (SA) (A) (U) (D) (SD)

79. Persons with mental retardation have a unique "retarded" personality. (SA) (A) (U) (D) (SD)

80. Institutions for the mentally retarded are needed in society.
    (SA) (A) (U) (D) (SD)

81. Using American Sign Language is really an "unnatural" way to communicate. (SA) (A) (U) (D) (SD)

82. Lipreading (speech-reading) is easy. (SA) (A) (U) (D) (SD)

83. Behavior considered "emotionally disturbed" is regarded so in all cultures and situations. (SA) (A) (U) (D) (SD)

84. Keeping severely disabled persons alive is scientifically unnatural and flies in the face of Darwin's notion of "survival of the fittest." (SA) (A) (U) (D) (SD)

85. The United States Constitution, the laws of the land, and the courts have always protected the rights of persons with disabilities. (SA) (A) (U) (D) (SD)

86. We have a responsibility to "do for" persons with disabilities. (SA) (A) (U) (D) (SD)

87. Students with learning disabilities are often just unmotivated. (SA) (A) (U) (D) (SD)

88. All disabilities are caused by diseases. (SA) (A) (U) (D) (SD)

89. All students, whether disabled or not can learn from each other in school. (SA) (A) (U) (D) (SD)

90. IQ tests give us a clear and accurate picture of a person's innate intelligence. (SA) (A) (U) (D) (SD)

91. People with severe mental retardation can not really benefit from an education. (SA) (A) (U) (D) (SD)

92. All children are normal and all children are special.
(SA) (A) (U) (D) (SD)

93. Our attitudes can have a strong effect on how a person with a disability sees himself or herself. (SA) (A) (U) (D) (SD)

94. It would be foolish to suggest taking a friend with blindness to an art museum. (SA) (A) (U) (D) (SD)

95. Persons with deafness can appreciate music. (SA) (A) (U) (D) (SD)

96. Wheelchair users can drive cars, dance, bowl, play tennis, and even learn martial arts. (SA) (A) (U) (D) (SD)

97. Because of the "sympathy factor," persons with disabilities can get employment easier than those who are able-bodied.
(SA) (A) (U) (D) (SD)

98. I would never consider dating a person with cerebral palsy.
(SA) (A) (U) (D) (SD)

99. I have a fear of becoming disabled. (SA) (A) (U) (D) (SD)

100. All people are precious and valuable to society.
(SA) (A) (U) (D) (SD)

The following publications were helpful sources of questionnaire items:

Cohen, S., Koehler, N. & Grand, C. (1981c). *A curriculum to foster understanding of people with disabilities: The handicapped in literature.* Albany, NY: University of the State of New York & The State Education Department, Office for Education of Children with Handicapping Conditions. pp. 36-37, 223-225.

Konczal, D. & Pesetski, L. (1983). *We all come in different packages: Activities to increase handicap* awareness. Santa Barbara, CA: The Learning Works, Inc. pp. 14-17.

Mortenson, R. (1980). *Prejudice project.* New York: Anti-Defamation League of B'nai B'rith & the University of Nebraska College of Education Curriculum Development Project. pp. 37-50.

Ross, E. & Freelander, I. (1977). *Handicapped people in society: A curriculum guide.* Burlington, VT: University of Vermont. pp. 5-8.

Shaver, J. & Curtis, C. (1981). *Handicapism and equal opportunity: Teaching about the disabled in social studies.* Reston, VA: The Foundation for Exceptional Children. pp. 12-13.

Shields, L., Christmas, D., Deitchman, L., Langford, T., Newingham, D., O'Daniel, L., Yeker, C. & Goodridge, J. (1981). *Project aware: A project to develop awareness of and empathy toward differences/handicaps.* Evansville, IN: Evansville-Vanderburgh School Corporation. p. 35. pp. 36-37, 223-224.

Voeltz, L. (1981). *Acceptance scale, secondary level B.* (Cited in R. Antonak & H. Livneh (1988). *The measurement of attitudes toward people with disabilities: Methods, psychometrics & scales.* Springfield IL: Charles C Thomas. pp. 130-133).

Yuker, H., Block, J. & Campbell, J. (1960). *A scale to measure attitudes toward disabled persons.* (Human Resources Study No. 5). Albertson, NY: Human Resources Center, cited in R. Antonak & H. Livneh (1988). *The measurement of attitudes toward people with disabilities: Methods, psychometrics and scales.* Springfield IL: Charles C Thomas. Publisher. pp. 138-139.

Yuker, H., Block, J. & Campbell, J. (1962). *Disability types and behavior.* Human Resources Study No. 6. Albertson, NY: Human Resources Center, cited in R. Antonak & H. Livneh (1988). *The measurement of attitudes toward people with disabilities: Methods, psychometrics and scales.* Springfield IL: Charles C Thomas. pp. 142-143.

STUDENT SENTENCE COMPLETION TECHNIQUES—Sentence completion provides another method for adducing feelings and attitudes of students. A student reads a series of open-ended statements to complete. Again, the teacher may want to develop additional or different sentences to match the level of the class and or a specific curriculum.

SENTENCE COMPLETION ON FEELINGS TOWARD DISABILITIES

1. If I had blindness, I would want other people especially not to ____
   _____

2. When I see a poster child I want to _____
   _____

3. I believe that children with severe mental retardation _____
   _____

4. Crutches and wheelchairs make me feel _____
   _____

5. When I see a person with dwarfism I feel _____
   _____

6. I consider persons with deafness to be _____
   _____

7. Persons with mental illness most often _____
   _____

8. If I acquired blindness, I would still be able to _____
   _____

9. When I see persons with physical disabilities it makes me feel ____
   _____

10. I believe people with severe stutters _____
    _____

11. Looking at a prosthetic arm or leg makes me feel _____
    _____

12. A child born without the use of his or her legs can still _____
    _____

13. Special education students _____
    _____

14. Having epilepsy (seizure disorder) _____
_____

15. "Empathy" means _____
_____

16. If others could not understand me when I spoke _____
_____

17. Having a classmate with mental retardation sitting next to me ___
_____

18. I do not think that persons with hearing impairments should ____
_____

19. Probably the most frustrating thing about having a disability is __
_____

20. People born with disabilities _____
_____

21. All children are special and all children are normal means that __
_____

22. Living in an institution means that _____
_____

23. The legal rights of disabled persons _____
_____

24. Women with disabilities _____
_____

25. Students with learning disabilities always _____
_____

26. "Mongoloid," "moron," "cripple," "idiot" and "hunchback" are
words that _____
_____

27. Historically people with disabilities _____

_____

28. Physical barriers _____

_____

29. Attitudes are important because _____

_____

30. When seeing a person with a physical disability, it is always
important to _____

_____

31. "Normalization" means _____

_____

32. My idea of a "whole" person means _____

_____

33. All people have a right to _____

_____

34. "Reasonable accommodation" means _____

_____

35. "Integration" means _____

_____

36. People are different in "degree" rather than "kind" means _____

_____

37. Telethons are _____

_____

38. When I think of the word "handicap," I think _____

_____

39. Schools just for special education students _____

_____

STUDENT DRAWINGS—Yet another valuable attitude assessment strategy is to ask younger students to draw a picture of a scene depicting persons with disabilities. For example, if the student draws a picture of a character with blindness, is the individual wearing dark glasses, holding a cane or tin cup or using a guide dog? What is the expression on the character's face? If the child draws a picture of a parent of a child with a disability, is the parent sad? If both a parent and a disabled child appear, where are they spaced in relation to each other? If possible, the teacher may want to sit with the child as he or draws. As DiLeo (1983) stated, "Articulate children are likely to talk as they draw. These comments should be noted as they may clarify what may or may not be visibly evident" (p. 4). In addition, to assess of the youngster's feelings accurately, a teacher should ask them to write a story explaining the picture (Salend, 1994).

TEACHING ABOUT THE CONCEPTS OF ATTITUDE, PREJUDICE, DISCRIMINATION, STEREOTYPE, LANGUAGE, DISABLEISM (HANDICAPISM), AND THE MEDICAL MODEL—Jones and Guskin (1984) concluded that before one can change attitudes toward persons with disabilities, one must understand the development and structure of those attitudes. In other words, to change attitudes, we must teach what they are. According to Oskamp (1977), the study of attitudes can also clarify the controversy surrounding the relative importance of heredity and environment in determining one's behavior. Attitudes may constitute bridging elements, formed by an interplay of both genetic factors and experiential learning, which influence an individual's behavior. Emphasizing the learning element, Shaw and Wright (1967) argued that since attitudes are acquired through experience, they represent the products of the socialization process and accordingly predispose one's responses to events and other people. Since the study of attitudes can promote an understanding of the socialization process, it can contribute to the understanding of the prejudices acquired by one's social group and assimilation of values held by one's parents and peers (Thomas, 1980).

As we have noted, Jones and Guskin (1984) found the most widely accepted assumption to be that attitudes toward children with disabilities are uni-dimensional and largely negative. In the rare instances where the possibility of negative attitudes toward disabled persons have been considered multidimensional, the greatest influences appear to be the degree and type of handicap, the nature of the interpersonal situation being responded to, and the personal characteristics of both the disabled and non-disabled persons (Jones, Gottfried and Owens, 1966; Effron and Effron, 1967; Gottlieb, Corman and Curci, 1984).

Once discerned, the mechanisms underlying the development and structure of attitudes may be used to alter reactions to various human behavior and characteristics, like those encountered in education. Consequently, the study of attitudes is particularly relevant in the field of special education. Knowledge of the development and structure of attitudes toward persons with disabilities precedes any attempt to change them and, thereby, increase the possibility of integration into the larger society (Jones and Guskin, 1984).

Yuker (1965) suggested that a knowledge of the attitudes of non-disabled people toward persons with disabilities promotes an understanding of the nature of the interaction of the two groups. Studies measuring these attitudes can, therefore, elucidate the components of negative attitudes (for example, avoidance and rejection) as well as positive attitudes (for example, friendliness and interaction) toward disabled persons.

In order to fully cover the important concepts in disability awareness, teachers should develop lessons based on the material covered in Chapter II: Terminological & Language Issues and Chapter III: The Minority Group and Medical Model Paradigms.

Literature and Attitudinal Development

Analyzing Fiction

According to Bunch (1996), "Skillful use of literature by thinking teachers can assist in the development of positive attitudes" (p. 5). Baskin (1975) believed that "literature can have both preparatory and sustaining functions in the process of providing knowledge and altering attitudes toward the handicapped" (p. 48). As Cohen, Grand, Koehler and Berman (1981) stressed, "[A]wareness of stereotypes, prejudices and fears—those which we already have and those to which we are continually exposed in literature—is a first step in overcoming these impediments to acceptance and integration of persons with disabilities" (p. 2).

Because books, and especially classics, forcefully inculcate values, teachers have both the opportunity and responsibility to address those negative stereotypical portrayals in literature that cause bias and intolerance toward disabled persons. A message in a classic receives respectability and even prestige, making it doubly difficult for those with disabilities to overcome deeply entrenched, complex prejudices

(Margolis & Shapiro, 1987). Beyond transmitting values, classical literature provides interpretation, teaches in the form of allegory, and provides models for identification and behavior (Baskin, 1975). It gives the reader ideas and situations to reflect upon and serves as a resource for society (Trautman, 1978). But, as Margolis and Shapiro (1987) emphasized,

> The issue is never that of banning or censoring but of discussing and explaining symbolism so that damaging messages are negated. When literature is taught without an explanation of the moralistic meaning assigned to disabilities, those with impairments may find it difficult to overcome deeply entrenched prejudices (p. 21).

Thus, instead of censoring the material that contains prejudiced ideas, teachers should use it as object lessons to offset stereotypes. When teaching about these literary devices in classical fiction, Margolis and Shapiro (1987) recommended the following seven exercises:

1. carefully examine excerpts that introduce and describe persons with disabilities;

2. explain how each adjective, phrase or expression influences their responses;

3. enumerate the number of positive and negative qualities the author attributes to the person with the disability;

4. read literature that realistically portrays the competency and abilities of persons with disabilities in a positive light;

5. assign research on the disability and its history as a term paper, project, or independent study (for example, when reviewing Steinbeck's *Of Mice and Men* assign research on "eugenics");

6. ask the students to rewrite the book with the disabled character no longer disabled, and have them discuss, "How does it affect the story?" (Students may also rewrite the story from the disabled character's point of view); and

7. ask high school students to analyze and review books with disabled characters for children in the lower grades.

The following basic questions can help guide discussion:

1. How would you describe the character's disability? Does the author specifically state it or is it implied (for example Lennie's mental retardation in Steinbeck's *Of Mice and Men*)? Was the disability congenital like Tiny Tim's or was it acquired like Captain Ahab's? Is it progressive or episodic?

2. What specific words does the author use to describe the character with the disability? How realistic is the description of the disabling condition?

3. What do you perceive to be the character's handicap?

4. When was this book written? Does it have dated ideas and use outdated language?

5. What stereotype(s) of disability are portrayed (for example is the character pitiable, evil, amusing, weak, burdensome)?

6. Are the characters with disabilities portrayed as people or as literary devices (for example, "the twisted mind in the twisted body" or "the foreteller of ominous events")?

7. Is the character with the disability portrayed as interacting in ways that are mutually beneficial? (Disabled individuals are often depicted in literature as pitiable "receivers" in their relationships with able-bodied characters.)

8. Are disabled characters depicted as functioning freely in least restrictive settings?

9. Why do you think the author chose to make this character disabled? (A frequent answer is "Because many people are afraid of those who are different, the author used the disability to create an atmosphere of fear.")

10. How do you think such depictions and descriptive passages influence the way you feel about people with disabilities?

11. How do you think such depictions and descriptive passages influence the way persons with disabilities feel about themselves?

12. What is the overall theme of the book? (For example, "suffering as payment for grace and enlightenment," "suffering of disabled persons for the benefit of others," "a search for self-identity," "suffering as a catalyst for the maturation of others" (Tiny Tim), or "faith leading to cure.")

Non-fiction and Bibliotherapy

Literature consistently proves itself a powerful means for providing information and influencing the attitudes and development of individuals, and according to Friedberg, Mullins and Sukiennik (1985),

> Nonfiction carries the unique power of verifiable authenticity, giving special effect to biography, autobiography, concept, and information books about people who are disabled. Children are born without prejudice toward disabilities, but as they meet those who differ from themselves in significant ways, they are affected by societal attitudes as well as by their own individual reactions. Books that sensitively and honestly depict persons with disabilities expand limited experience and can mitigate the uneasiness that stems from material that helps them deal with anxieties and suggests ways that problems can be solved and the good life lived, even in the face of imperfection and adversity (p. ix).

Thus, an excellent method of sensitizing youngsters to the issues of disability is to have them read and evaluate a book of non-fiction written by a person with a disability (or his or her parent, sibling or teacher) for its bibliotherapeutic value. Kokaska and Brolin (1985) defined bibliotherapy this way:

> [O]ne means of helping individuals with disabilities to understand their difficulties is by exposing them to works of literature in which characters with limitations confront and, in most instances, succeed in life's challenges. The key element to the process, aside from the physical act of reading the book, occurs when the individual identifies with the character or circumstance, transfers insights from the literature,

and applies them to his own situation. . . . Bibliotherapy has received expanded interest among teachers, counselors, and therapists who are attempting to broaden the individual's perspective of his situation and potential problem-solving behaviors that increase the student's self-confidence. This interest has been aided by the fact that a greater number of literary works by individuals with a disability have found their way into print (p. 136).

Grindler, Stratton and McKenna (1997) listed five research conclusions regarding the effects of bibliotherapy on children:

1. bibliotherapy can produce positive attitude change related to the reduction of children's fear,

2. listening and reading used in conjunction with discussion may change attitudes more than listening or reading alone,

3. positive changes in self-concept can be attributed to bibliotherapy,

4. bibliotherapy provides children with knowledge of strategies they might employ in particular situations, and

5. books can be useful in helping children solve problems and in helping children realize the usefulness of books for this purpose (p. 7).

As with a Black Studies or Women's Studies course, a reader can learn a great deal about the experience of being Black or a woman by reading the firsthand accounts of those who lived it. In the same way, autobiographies of persons with varying disabilities can also provide insight. For example, extremely moving accounts by Brown (1954), Zola (1982), Jewell (1984), Nolan (1987), Beisser (1989), Callahan (1989), Kriegel (1991), Hockenberry (1995) and Reave (1998) provide insight and therapeutic value for both persons with physical disabilities and those without them. One can learn much about living with deafness by reading the life experiences of Jacobs (1989), Kisor (1990), Sidransky (1990), D. Wright (1993) or Cohen (1994) or about the experience of having blindness by reading accounts by Sullivan (1975), Hull, 1990 or Neer (1994). Appendix I Resources: Personal Accounts of Disability by Individuals, Their Parents, and Their Teachers can be an excellent source for basic books lending themselves to bibliotherapeutic evaluation by students. Two excellent resources for younger students are the books by Friedberg, Mullins and Sukiennik, *Accept Me as I Am: Best Books of Juvenile Nonfiction on Impairments and Disabilities* (1986) and *Portraying Persons with Disabilities (nonfiction): An Annotated Bibliography of Nonfiction for Children and Teenagers* (1992).

Information on disability awareness needs to appear in both the elementary and secondary grades, and teachers should modify their activities and book assignments to suit the age levels of their students. When assigning a nonfiction book to be analyzed for its bibliotherapeutic value, teachers may want to consider the following 15 questions for inclusion and discussion:

1. What is the title of the book?

2. Who wrote the book? Was it a person with a disability, a parent, a sibling or a teacher?

3. When was the book written? Does it have dated ideas?

4. Why was the book written?

5. What was the nature of the disability of the individual and how did it occur?

6. What problems were encountered by the author as a result of the disability?

7. How did the disability affect the author's education, home life, friends and job?

8. What were the author's accomplishments, contributions, goals and hopes?

9. For whom was the book written—for example, children, persons without disabilities, other disabled persons, siblings or parents?

10. What is the message of the book—for example, "finding the meaning of life," "coping with a disability," "finding religion," "seeking

civil rights," "contributing information on disability awareness," "parenting a child with a disability" and so forth?

11. How would you evaluate the language and terminology used?

12. Did you find the book meaningful, relevant and realistic? Why or why not?

13. Do you believe that an individual in a situation like the author's would find this book bibliotherapeutically relevant? Why or why not?

14. What did you learn about the disability experience you were unaware of before?

15. What else would you like to say about this book?

A teacher might also ask students read two to three more books by different authors covering the same topic. The students might then make connections between them. (See Appendix I-Resources: Personal Accounts of Disability by Individuals, Their Parents and Their Teachers, divided by disability category.) The students can use these six questions to compare and contrast the authors' approaches, feelings, points of view and attitudes.

1. On what issues do they agree?

2. On what issues do they differ?

3. What views and what important issues do they have in common?

4. What experiences do they have in common?

5. What are their individual feelings toward the medical model?

6. What do they have to say about language and terminology?

The following is a brief list of familiar disabilities discussed as first-hand accounts by various writers:

- Living with cerebral palsy (Brown, 1954; Valens, 1966; Jewell, 1984; Nolan, 1987);

- Having dwarfism (Phifer, 1979; Gillis, 1982; Kuklin, 1986; Albon, 1988;Van Etten, 1988);

- Acquiring a physical disability (Kovic, 1976; Zola, 1982b; Beisser, 1989; Callahan, 1989; McDonald & McDonald, 1989; Kreigel, 1991; Hockenberry, 1995; Reave, 1998);

- Growing up as a hearing child in a deaf world (Walker, 1986; Glickfield, 1989; Sidransky, 1990; Preston, 1994);

- Raising and parenting a child with autism (Greenfield, 1972, 1978, 1986; Kaufman, 1976, 1981; Maurice, 1993);

- Being female with a disability (Hannaford, 1985, Miller, 1985; Brown, Connors, & Stern, 1985; Saxon & Howe, 1987; Rousso, 1988);

- Being a child with a disability (Goodman & Krauss. 1977; Exley, 1984).

- Having Blindness (Sullivan & Gill, 1975, Clark, 1977; Hocken, 1978; Hull, 1990; Hine, 1993; Neer, 1994);

- Having deafness (Spradley & Spradley, 1978; Lane & Pittle, 1981; Pittle &Rosen, 1984; Walker, 1985; Padden & Humphries, 1988; Jacobs, 1989; Sacks, 1989; Kisor, 1990; Wright, 1993; Cohen, 1994);

- Living with a speech problem (Tillis, 1984; Carlisle, 1985; Bobrick, 1995).

- Living with a severe disfigurement (Howell & Ford, 1989; Harmon, !982; Minahan, 1985; Rothenberg & White, 1985; Severo, 1985).

- Having mental retardation (Kaufman, 1988; O'Reilly, 1989; Schwier, 1990; Burke & McDaniel, 1991; Bogdan & Taylor, 1994; Kingsley & Levitz, 1994).

- Having learning disabilities (Simpson, 1979; Hampshire, 1982; Scotson, 1985; Maccracken, 1986; Callahan, 1987; Sacks, 1987);

- Living with severe and multiple disabilities (Keller, 1965; Brown, 1976; Yoken, 1979; Harris, 1983; Rosenberg, 1983).

Excellent resources for teaching about disabilities through literature and drama include:

Baskin, B. and Harris, K. (1977). *Notes from a different drummer: A guide to juvenile fiction portraying the handicapped.* New York: R. R. Bowker.

Baskin, B. and Harris, K. (1984). *More notes from a different drummer: A guide to juvenile fiction portraying the disabled.* New York: R. R. Bowker.

Batson, T. and Bergman, E. (1973). *Angels and outcasts: An anthology of deaf characters in literature.* Washington, DC: Gallaudet University Press.

Bower, E. (1980). *The handicapped in literature.* Denver, CO: Love Publishing Company.

Bunch, G. (1996). *Kids, disabilities and regular classes, An annotated bibliography of selected children's literature on disability.* Toronto, Canada: Inclusion Press.

Cohen, S., Grand, C., Koehler, N. and Berman, D. (1981). *A curriculum to foster understanding of people with disabilities: The handicapped in literature.* Albany, NY: University of the State of New York and The State Education Department.

Friedberg, J., Mullins, J. and Sukiennik, A. (1985). *Accept me as I am: Best books of juvenile nonfiction on impairments and disabilities.* New York: R. R. Bowker.

Friedberg, J., Mullins, J. and Sukiennik, A. (1992). *Portraying persons with disabilities: An annotated bibliography of nonfiction for children and teenagers.* New York: R. R. Bowker.

Landau, D., Epstein, S. and Stone, A. (1978). *The exceptional child through literature.* Englewood Cliffs, NJ: Prentice-Hall, Inc.

Miller, V. (ed.) (1985). *Despite this flesh: The disabled in stories and poems.* Austin, TX: University of Texas Press.

Quick, J. (1985). *Disability in modern children's fiction.* Cambridge, MA: Brookline Books.

Robertson, D. (1992). *Portraying persons with disabilities: An annotated bibliography of fiction for children and teenagers.* New Providence, NJ: R. R. Bowker.

Saxton, M. and Howe, F. (eds.)(1987). *With wings: An anthology of literature by and about women with disabilities.* New York: The Feminist Press at the City University of New York.

Disabilities on Stage

Plays, like books, convey values and ideas, and drama can teach about disability (Tomlinson, 1982). The students may see the play performed on stage or screen or they can read it in class. The same questions discussed for fiction are appropriate here. Some excellent current and classical plays for discussion include:

The Boys Next Door by Griffin (1986) (Mental Retardation)
Butterflies Are Free by Gershe (1969) (Blindness)
Children of a Lesser God by Medoff (1980) (Deafness)
The Elephant Man by Pomerance (1979) (Disfigurement, Neurofibromatosis)
The Fifth of July by Wilson (1978) (Physical disability)
The Glass Menagerie by Williams (1945) (Physical Disability)
The Miracle Worker by Gibson (1960) (Multiple Disabilities)
My Left Foot by Connaughton and Sheridan (1989) (Cerebral Palsy)
Richard III by Shakespeare (1597) (Physical Difference, Scoliosis)
Whose Life Is It Anyway by Clark (1974) (Quadraplegia)

Analyzing Quotations

As a special project, a teacher could ask students to read any of the quotations in this book and interpret in writing what the author is expressing. Students should be encouraged to include their feelings and conclusions about what they read. They may also compare what different persons wrote regarding the same topic. For example, compare what Davies (1987) and Kriegel (1991) each said about being called a "cripple" (in Chapter II Language and Terminological Issues). Which opinion is more reflective of your own?

Interacting with Persons with Disabilities

Cooperative Learning

Conard (1988) concluded that cooperative learning experiences can promote greater acceptance of differences and interpersonal attraction between students with disabilities and students without disabilities. Direct contact and interaction through cooperative experiences can move students beyond one dimensional prejudices to multidimensional views of one another. Conard, B. (1988) also suggested that teachers can help students reduce their prejudices by allowing them to learn cooperatively and encouraging them to value each other. Research supports the proposition that cooperative learning reduces prejudice. Practiced cooperation leads to spontaneous cooperation, the polar opposite of prejudice. Assigning students with disabilities to work cooperatively with their non-disabled peers creates a pattern of positive interaction in which there is

1. more direct face-to-face interaction between students with and without disabilities;

2. an expectation that one's peers weather disabled or not will facilitate one's learning;

3. more open-mindedness about peers with disabilities and willingness to be influenced by their ideas and information;

4. more reciprocal communication and fewer difficulties in communicating with each other; and

5. less hostility, verbal and physical, expressed towards peers perceived as different.

In addition, cooperative projects can create perceptions and feelings of

6. higher trust between students with and without disabilities;

7. more mutual concern and friendliness, more attentiveness, more feelings of obligation to and responsibility for classmates with disabilities, and a greater desire to win their respect;

8.   more positive responses to and reinforcement of each other;

9.   stronger beliefs that one is liked, supported, and accepted by other students, and that other students care about how much one learns;

10. less fear of failure and more psychological comfort;

11. higher valuing of classmates perceived to be different; and

12. greater feelings of success for all students.

Perhaps the most important psychological outcome of cooperative learning is the last in the list, the positive effect it can have on student self-esteem and self-confidence. The students' realization enables them to withstand life's disappointments, to be confident decision makers, and ultimately to be happy and productive individuals.

Because cooperative learning methods amount to social interventions, they should produce social effects. The criteria for positive intergroup relations Allport (1954) outlined resemble the widely accepted antecedents of friendship formation or cohesion, including contact, perceived similarity, engagement in pleasant activities, and once again, cooperation, where individuals who work toward the same goal come to see one another as reward providers. Cooperative learning increases contact between students, gives them a shared basis of similarity (group membership), engages them in pleasant activities together, and encourages them work toward common goals. As such, one can fairly hypothesize that they would increase positive effects among students. According to Allport (1954),

> Prejudice may be reduced by equal status contact between majority and minority groups in the pursuit of common goals. The effect is greatly enhanced if this contact is sanctioned by institutional supports and if it is of a sort that leads to the perception of common interests and common humanity between members of the two groups (p. 281).

In a cooperative learning situation, the teacher establishes a group goal and a criterion-referenced evaluation system. The group members receive rewards on the basis of their group performance. For example, a teacher may

1. assign students to small groups (each containing at least one student with a disability, perhaps a wheelchair user);

2. give them a problem or task to complete (for example, assessing the accessibility of a building);

3. provide them with an accessibility study;

4. detail the criteria that will be used to evaluate the group's work;

5. have the group report back to the class for further action;

6. have the class report on what awareness was acquired by doing the project.

The following Barrier Free Accessibility Compliance Checklist represents an example of a cooperative learning assignment to evaluate the accessibility of a public building.

BARRIER FREE ACCESSIBILITY COMPLIANCE CHECKLIST

(Circle Yes or No and make any comments you consider important.)

Evaluating the Parking Lot

1. Are parking spaces easily accessible to the facility and identified as reserved for use by individuals with physical disabilities by the international symbol of access logo?

. . . . Yes No

2. Are parking spaces open on one side, allowing at least a 12-foot minimum width for individuals using wheelchairs or braces and crutches to get in and out onto a level surface?

. . . . Yes No

3. Can individuals in wheelchairs or those using braces and crutches wheel or walk without having to go behind cars?

. . . . Yes No

4. Are at least two percent of the parking spaces reserved for use by persons with physical disabilities?

. . . . Yes No

5. Do curbcuts accommodate wheelchairs?

. . . . Yes No

Comments:

Evaluating Walkways

1. Are public walkways at least 48 inches wide?

. . . . Yes No

2. Are slopes, gradients, and ramps not slanted more than five percent

. . . . Yes No

3. Do the walkways have a continuing common surface uninterrupted by steps or sudden changes in level?

. . . . Yes No

4. Do walkways blend to a common level wherever they cross other walks, driveways, or parking lots?

. . . . Yes No

5. Do walks have a level platform at the top?

. . . . Yes No

6. Does the platform extend at least one foot beyond each side of the doorway?

. . . . Yes No

Comments:

Evaluating Ramps

1. Do ramps have a slope no greater than a one-foot rise in 12 feet?

. . . . Yes No

2. Do ramps have handrails on at least one side?

. . . . Yes No

3. Are the ramps 32 inches in height measured from the surfaces of the ramp?

. . . . Yes No

4. Are the surfaces on the ramp smooth?

. . . . Yes No

5. Do the surfaces extend one foot beyond the top and bottom of the ramp?

. . . . Yes No

6. Do ramps have a non-skid surface?

. . . . Yes No

7. Do ramps have at least six feet of straight clearance at the bottom?

.   .   .   .   Yes No

8. Do ramps have level platforms at 30-foot intervals for purposes of rest and safety, and wherever they turn?

.   .   .   .   Yes No

Comments:

Evaluating Entrances and Exits

1. Is at least one primary entrance to each building usable by individuals in wheelchairs? (All or most entrances and exits should be accessible to, and usable by, individuals who use wheelchairs or have other forms of physical disability.)

.   .   .   .   Yes No

2. Is at least one entrance usable by individuals in wheelchairs on a level that would make the elevators accessible?

.   .   .   .   Yes No

Comments:

Evaluating Doors and Doorways

1. Do doors have clears opening of no less than 32 inches?

.   .   .   .   Yes No

2. Are the doors operable with pressure or strength one could reasonably expect of disabled persons?

.   .   .   .   Yes No

3. Is the floor on the inside and outside of each doorway level?

.   .   .   .   Yes No

4. Are doorsills free of sharp inclines and abrupt changes in level?

.   .   .   .   Yes No

5. Do pressure door closers allow persons with physical disabilities to use the doors, and do they take at least three seconds to close?

.   .   .   .   Yes No

6. Are doorways wide enough to accommodate wheelchairs?

.   .   .   .   Yes No

7. Are furniture and other obstacles arranged so that persons with motor-impairment have enough room to maneuver in easily?

.   .   .   .   Yes No

8. On the pull side of each door, next to the handle, is there at least 18

inches of clear wall space so that a wheelchair-user can get near enough
to open the door?

.   .   .   .   Yes No

9. Are all door handles 48 inches high or less and able to be operated
without needing fingers?

.   .   .   .   Yes No

Comments:

Evaluating Stairs and Steps

1. Do steps avoid precipitous edges?

.   .   .   .   Yes No

2. Do stairs have handrails 32 inches high as measured from the tread
at the face of the riser?

.   .   .   .   Yes No

3. Do stairs have at least one handrail that extends at least 18 inches
beyond the top and bottom step?

.   .   .   .   Yes No

4. Does each step have a riser of seven inches or less?

.   .   .   .   Yes No

Comments:

Evaluating Elevators

1. Are elevators available to and usable by persons with physical
disabilities?

.   .   .   .   Yes No

2. Are the floor buttons labeled with braille or raised (or indented) letters beside them?

.   .   .   .   Yes No

3. Are the buttons easy to push or touch sensitive?

.   .   .   .   Yes No

4. Is the elevator cab at least five feet square?

.   .   .   .   Yes No

5. Does the elevator have bell and light signals to help riders with deafness or blindness?

.   .   .   .   Yes No

6. Are the elevator call buttons in the hallway no more than 42 inches from the floor to accommodate riders who are little people or wheelchair users?

.   .   .   .   Yes No

7. Is there a sign on the jamb at each floor identifying the floor in raised and braille letters?

.   .   .   .   Yes No

8. Does the emergency intercom depend entirely on voice communication?

.   .   .   .   Yes No

9. Are there braille and raised-letter instructions for the communication system?

.   .   .   .   Yes No

10. Are there ramps or elevators to all levels?

.   .   .   .   Yes No

11. Is there an accessible alternate route on each level if there are stairs between the entrance and/or the elevator and crucial public areas?

.   .   .   .   Yes No

Comments:

Evaluating Identification

1. Do raised (or recessed) letters or numbers identify rooms or offices?

.   .   .   .   Yes No

2. Is identification placed on the wall to the right or left of the door at a height between 4 1/2 and 5 1/2 feet measured from the floor?

.   .   .   .   Yes No

Comments:

Evaluating Drinking Fountains

1. Is there an appropriate number of water fountains?

.   .   .   .   Yes No

2. Are the fountains accessible to physically disabled persons?

.   .   .   .   Yes No

3. If fountains are inaccessible to people in wheelchairs, are paper cups and dispensers provided?

.   .   .   .   Yes No

4. Do water fountains or coolers have frontal spouts and controls?

.   .   .   .   Yes No

5. Does the fountain protrude no more than four inches into the circulation space?

. . . .   Yes No

6. If coolers are wall mounted, are they hand operated, with spouts 36 inches or less from the floor?

. . . .   Yes No

7. If there are floor mounted fountains, are spouts no higher than 30 inches?

. . . .   Yes No

8. Does at least one fountain have a clear floor space of at least 30 by 48 inches in front?

. . . .   Yes No

9. Are controls mounted on the front or on the side near the front edge, and usable with needing fingers fist?

. . . .   Yes No

Comments:

Evaluating Warning Signals

1. Are audible warning signals accompanied by simultaneous visual signals for use by individuals with hearing or sight disabilities?

. . . .   Yes No

2. Are fire alarms low enough for persons in wheelchairs or little people?

. . . .   Yes No

Comments:

Evaluating Public Telephones

1. Is there an appropriate number of public telephones accessible to persons with physical disabilities?

. . . .   Yes No

2. Is there a clear floor space of at least 30 by 48 inches in front of at least one public telephone?

. . . .   Yes No

3. Is the highest operable part of the phone (typically the coin slot) no higher than 48 inches from the floor?

. . . .   Yes No

4. Does the telephone protrude no more than four inches into the public area?

. . . .   Yes No

5. Does the telephone have push-button controls?

. . . . Yes No

6. Does at least one public telephone have enlarged numbers for partially-sighted persons?

. . . . Yes No

7. Is at least one public telephone hearing-aid compatible?

. . . . Yes No

8. Is at least one public telephone adapted with volume control?

. . . . Yes No

9. Is at least one public telephone equipped with a text telephone (TT or TDD) for persons with hearing impairments?

. . . . Yes No

10. Is the location of the text telephone clearly identified by accessible signs bearing the International TDD Symbol?

. . . . Yes No

Comments:

Evaluating Controls

1. Can wheelchair users easily use the switches and controls for light, heat, ventilation, windows, and fire alarms?

. . . . Yes No

Comments:

Evaluating Restrooms

1. If lavatories are available to the public, is at least one rest room (either one for each sex, or a unisex facility) fully accessible?

. . . . Yes No

2. Are inaccessible restrooms marked with signs that provide directions to those that are accessible?

. . . . Yes No

3. Are restrooms marked with a tactile (for example, in braille) sign identifying them?

. . . . Yes No

4. Are the restrooms marked with the international access symbol ?

. . . . Yes No

5. Is the doorway of each accessible lavatory at least 32 inches wide to allow a wheelchair easy access?

. . . . Yes No

6. Are lavatory doors 48 inches high or less and equipped with accessible handles (usable with a closed fist)?

. . . .   Yes No

7. Can a wheelchair user open all doors easily?

. . . .   Yes No

8. Do wheelchair users have enough space to maneuver upon entering the rest room? (Wheelchair users need at least 36 inches of clear width for forward movement, and a five foot diameter of clear space or a T-shaped space to make turns. In addition, a minimum distance of 48 inches, clear of the door swing is needed between the two doors of an entry vestibule.)

. . . .   Yes No

9. Is the path to all fixtures at least 36 inches wide?

. . . .   Yes No

10. Are the doors usable with a closed fist both into and out of the toilet stalls?

. . . .   Yes No

11. Is at least one toilet stall wide enough to accommodate a wheelchair?

. . . .   Yes No

12. Are grab bars placed behind and on the side wall nearest to the toilet?

. . . .   Yes No

13. Is the toilet seat between 17 and 19 inches high?

. . . .   Yes No

14. Does one toilet have a clear space in front at least 30 by 48 inches?

. . . .   Yes No

15. Are the sinks and paper towels at a height that can be reached easily by a person in a wheelchair?

. . . .   Yes No

16. Can the faucet be used with a closed fist?

. . . .   Yes No

17. Are the soap and other dispensers and hand dryers less than 48 inches high and usable with one closed fist?

. . . .   Yes No

18. Can a person in a wheelchair see himself or herself in the mirror?

. . . .   Yes No

Comments:

Evaluating Hazards

1. Are all open excavations sites barricaded on all open sides at least eight feet from the hazard, with warning devices installed?

. . . . Yes No

2. Is the area free from low-hanging signs, ceiling lights, fixtures or similar objects that may protrude into corridors or traffic ways? (They should be at least seven feet from the floor)

. . . . Yes No

3. Is the lighting on ramps and other walkways adequate?

. . . . Yes No

4. Are exit signs easily identifiable to persons with all types of disabilities?

. . . . Yes No

Comments:

What is your conclusion regarding the overall accessibility of this building? Did you become more sensitive to the needs of persons with disabilities by completing this accessibility study? Explain how.

The following publications were helpful sources of accessibility checklist items:

American national standard specifications for making buildings and facilities accessible to, and usable by the physically handicapped. (1961). New York: American National Standards Institute. pp. 6-11, cited in *A curriculum to foster understanding of people with disabilities: The handicapped in society.* (1981). Albany, NY: The University of the State of New York and The State Education Department, Office for Children With Handicapping Conditions. pp. 32-37.

The Americans with Disabilities Act checklist for readily achievable barrier removal. (1992). Washington, DC: Adaptive Environments Center and Barrier Free Environments. pp. 6-12.

Barnes, E., Berrigan, C. and Biklen, D. (1978), *What's the difference? Teaching positive attitudes toward people with disabilities.* Syracuse, NY: Human Policy Press. pp. 81-83.

Bookbinder, S. (1978). *Mainstreaming: What every child needs to know about disabilities.* Providence, RI: Rhode Island Easter Seal Society. p. 16.

Getskow, V. and Konczal, D. (1996). *Kids with special needs: Information and activities to promote awareness and understanding.* Santa Barbara, CA: The Learning Works, Inc. p. 34.

Hanna, R. and Graff, D. (1977), *The physically handicapped child: Facilitating regular classroom adjustment.* Hingham, MA: Teaching Resources Corporation. pp. 114-119.

Lifchez, R., Williams, D., Yip, C., Larson and M. Taylor, J. (1979). *Getting there: A guide to accessibility for your facility.* Sacramento, CA: California Department of Rehabilitation. pp. 8-40.

McCahill, W., Nicholls, M., Peterson, R. Hines, F., Leonard, E. and Cassell, R. (1987). *Handicap awareness.* Irving, TX: Boy Scouts of America.pp. 27-30.

Shaver, J. and Curtis, C. (1981). *Handicapism and equal opportunity: Teaching about the disabled in social studies.* Reston, VA: The Foundation for Exceptional Children. pp. 43-46.

Understanding Handicaps, Inc. (1994) *Understanding handicaps: A disability awareness curriculum.* Newtonville, MA: Author.

Analyzing the News Media

Another lively project that lends itself to cooperative learning is analyzing the news media. Individuals and organizations involved with disability rights have become increasingly critical about the biased way the media cover disability issues and stories. Prominent among these complaints are demeaning language, inaccuracy, bias, and ethical lapses. Organizations of persons with disabilities increasingly recognize biased reporting patterns they consider in Johnson and Elkins (1974) words "long on inspiration and short on issues":

> Disability advocates believe reporters feel pity for them or think they are brave and inspiring. They want reporters to use them as legitimate sources for story ideas, disability issues, problems disabled people face, physical barriers, discrimination, societal attitudes. Disability advocates claim too many reporters don't know there are such things as disability issues (p. 1).

Moreover, as Margolis, Shapiro and Anderson (1990) stated,

> Journalists frequently strive to capture and keep the public's attention through headlines and human-interest stories. Human-interest stories constitute one of the more common newspaper and magazine genres.

They sell newspapers by evoking emotions about issues that have no direct influence on readers' lives. In their quest to engage readers' emotions, journalists often trivialize important social issues that warrant sensitive, informed, balanced reporting. Their biases and need to capture attention are revealed in both tone and language. . . . Other than to capture attention and evoke pity, there seems little reason to include the words "quadriplegic" and "crippled," which in these cases totally define the people involved by their physical disability (p. 28).

Biklen (1986) described how the tone of a story may already be set in the reporter's mind long before the reporter sits down at the word processor:

Besides the specific conscious content relevant to a story (for example, a person's age, the level of disability, the ethical questions being raised), the media set a story's tone (for example, exciting, a drama, a tragedy, a contest, or entertainment). And usually, news writers have more or less "stock" ways of presenting a particular issue. Disability, for example, is typically cast in terms of tragedy, of charity and its attendant emotion, pity, or of struggle and accomplishment. When reporters approach any story, they bring with them one or a combination of such standard "frames" for presenting to the readers (p. 46).

Margolis, Shapiro and Anderson (1990) continued:

Unfortunately, newspapers and magazines often reinforce the negative, inaccurate images of persons with disabilities that make their ongoing struggle for equality and understanding ever more difficult. Inasmuch as children tend to adopt negative or enfeebling attitudes promulgated by authoritative sources like newspapers and books, their negative and inaccurate stories need to be chal-lenged. . . . The problem of combating stereotypes seems especially acute when we realize that some research indicates that "by age twelve, children have already developed a complete set of stereotypes about every ethnic, racial, and religious group in society" (Sonnenschein, 1988, p. 265). And, since the primary print media in our society, newspapers and magazines, appear to be promoting stereotypes, the teacher is waging a constant battle against the reinforcement of stereotypical thinking. Certainly, undoing stereotypical thinking is much more difficult than preventing it (pp. 28-29).

Teachers at the junior or senior high school levels consistently confront prejudices already embedded in their students' minds, and examining the beliefs students already hold is the first step in unmasking stereotypes. Next comes organizing instructional units that analyze and evaluate newspaper, magazine, and television coverage of disabled persons that requires students to compare their findings with explicit criteria. Combating stereotypes of the disabled in newspapers and magazines can be different at each schooling level, but in every case combating stereotypes means examining assumptions, discussing issues, and critically responding to societal injustices. For example, a teacher can use the following nine questions as beginning criteria for analyzing news stories:

1. Does this story ignore major issues facing persons with disabilities?

2. Does the story accurately reflect persons' abilities as well as disabilities?

3. Does it use the proper terminology?

4. Does it use person first language? (Are people described as "voters with disabilities" rather than "disabled voters?")

5. Is disability being portrayed in a positive sense rather than as a fate worse than death? (Do words like "tragedy," "sufferer" and "afflicted" appear?)

6. Does disability appear in the story unnecessarily? (Is the person's disability referred to even though it has no relevance to the story?)

7. Is the disabled individual described in sentimental or pop terms? (Are words like "courageous," "heroic," "inspiring," "special" or "brave" used?)

8. Is disability portrayed as overcoming barriers and a challenge? (Are terms like "in spite of his handicap," "overcame her disability" used?)

9. Is the terminology accurate? (Are terms like "Down's Syndrome," "handicapped parking," and "disabled seating" used rather than

"Down Syndrome," "parking for disabled persons" and "accessible seating?")

Organizing a Media Watch

Few cooperative learning instructional techniques engage students at any level quicker than a media watch campaign. These campaigns can help students cooperatively correct misconceptions about persons with disabilities newspapers and magazines inadvertently perpetuated and thus increase understanding. The concomitant benefits of these campaigns include the development of critical reading and thinking skills and improved attitudes toward persons with disabilities. Because media images of persons with disabilities are often superficial or biased, they provide teachers with continual examples of negative language, prejudice and stereotypes.

A media watch campaign is a planned method of monitoring the media and then providing reporters, newscasters, editors and producers with responses, often in the form of personal letters that commend appropriate disability terminology and portrayals or suggest positive, constructive alternatives when problems appear. In addition, a media watch campaign teaches about prejudice by encouraging students to challenge biased coverage of disabilities, especially in news reports and human-interest stories. As a cooperative educational technique, such a campaign can help students learn how to analyze critically what they read and view about persons with disabilities. It also provides, of course, an excellent opportunity for implementing cooperative learning experiences. A media watch campaign can easily include various cooperative learning groups, each assigned to a different newspaper, television or radio station, with follow-up responsibilities for the whole class.

A media watch campaign allows students cooperatively to exert a direct impact on improving public attitudes toward persons with disabilities and exposing disablism in the media. Students personally and directly become involved in the media's ability to communicate, influence, and shape social values in our society. The class gains the experience of becoming involved through direct interaction with media professionals who have often been criticized for creating and perpetuating stereotypes through inaccurate or sensationalized portrayals of persons with disabilities. Such interaction challenges those image makers who consider themselves responsible and responsive to their audience. Even a small segment of that audience, if vocal and persistent, can effect change. As Elkins, Jones and Ulicny (1987) wrote,

Inaccurate and inappropriate media portrayals may persist because journalists want to write about issues they believe to be of interest to the public. Unfortunately, the public's interest in disabilities is often limited to a fascination with the unusual or grotesque. Of course, one has to ask whether public attitude shapes what journalists write about or, more likely, journalists shape public attitude (p. 3).

Media watch campaigns also provide a way for students to encourage positive media portrayals by communicating constructively with the media when their story or article is well-written.

Establishing a media watch campaign takes a lot of work and commitment on the part of both the teacher and the class. The class must understand the purposes and structure of the cooperative campaign assignment. The first step is to decide what particular goals the class hopes to accomplish so it can focus on exactly what it wants to do. Letters and phone calls to the media must reflect clear goals to be attained. The class may have several possible purposes or goals. It may want to focus, for example, on any or all of these five purposes:

1.   improving images in the media of persons with disability;

2.   correcting the terminology used by the media;

3.   increasing the frequency of news features about people with disabilities;

4.   encouraging the media to include features or present information for the benefit of disabled persons in the community (for example, encouraging restaurant critics to provide accessibility information in their restaurant reviews, or encouraging chambers of commerce to promote accessible community activities in their promotional brochures); or

5.   promoting coverage of policy decisions that affect persons with disabilities, (for example, broad coverage of how a recent mass transit decisions affects disabled persons).

The next step in establishing a media watch campaign is to set the scope of activities. Once the goals of the project are established, the class must then cooperatively decide on the scope of its activities.

Possible activities include monitoring, taking action, and evaluating what it does. Many questions need to be answered. For example, monitoring procedures need to be clearly established. The class will need to decide which media sources will be monitored, whether to monitor several newspapers or one, and whether to monitor local or national magazines, and television and radio stations (see Appendix I- Resources for Networks and Cable Stations).The class should, of course, limit its activities to what it can realistically handle. When setting goals, the class should consider monitoring comparatively few media sources regularly. It will need to discuss other important issues relating to its goals as well. For example, if the class decides to monitor newspapers, on what items will it focus? According to Elkins, Jones and Ulicny (1987), the possibilities include, local, national and international news stories; regional features; sports and entertainment; editorials; business items and advertisements; and even comics and political cartoons

The class must also decide how long to conduct its campaign. Will it monitor news features for a day, a week or a month? Elkins, Jones, and Ulicny (1987) found that daily monitoring is best. But, once the class sets the schedule, it must be followed. Only a regular monitoring schedule can measure the project's effects accurately; success depends on the consistency of the classes' monitoring and response letters. The class needs to agree on how long the campaign will last and at what intervals will it decide whether to continue—say a whole school year, a half year or less?

The next step in the process is deciding on appropriate action. Having decided what and when to monitor, the class must then decide what specific kinds of action it intends to take. If a student monitor brings in an article with an obvious handicapist bias what will be the follow up? It is critical that the entire class discuss the handicapist aspects of the article and then vote on an appropriate action? Elkins, Jones, and Ulicny (1987) mentioned the following four options:

1. "EDUCATING" THE MEDIA PROFESSIONALS—Such education may include sending a brochure to the media (for example, *Beyond the AP Stylebook in Reporting and Writing About People With Disabilities,* by the Advocado Press, 1987). In addition, the class could invite a media professional to speak to the class or it could appoint a representative to meet personally with media professionals, or with an editorial board of a targeted paper or station. The more personal contacts the class makes, the better its chance of establishing a positive relationship with the

media. Personal meetings increase the class's credibility and its opportunity to bring about change.

2. REWARDING POSITIVE ARTICLES—The class may send a personal letter to a reporter or editor complimenting a story.

3. PROVIDING CORRECTIVE RESPONSES TO NEGATIVE OR UNDESIRABLE ARTICLES—The class may send letters to a reporter or editor mentioning problems with a particular story or feature, identifying negative aspects (for example, unacceptable portrayals and language) and then suggesting suitable alternatives. In addition, the class may want to quantify the problems and let the editor or reporter know how often such problems have occurred in the past.

4. PROVIDING CORRECTIVE ACTIVITIES FOR UNCOOPERATIVE MEDIA PROFESSIONALS—The class must also decide how it will deal with media professionals who remain uncooperative and insensitive to disability issues. The class, for example, may opt to contact an agency, organization, or individual with the influence or power to make change—like an editor, a publisher, a sponsor who buys lots of advertising or even the Federal Communications Commission.

The next step in developing a media watch campaign is to choose a structure and procedures. Once the class has cooperatively developed its media watch goals and functions, its structure includes, establishing review procedures, deciding what circumstances warrant what kinds of action (for example, when to write positive or corrective letters or make telephone calls), and detailing monitoring activities. A coordinator appointed or elected for each cooperative monitoring group should be responsible for meeting the group goals and taking appropriate follow-up actions. The teacher, who may serve as the overall coordinator of the project should make sure that all students know what they are doing and that the entire project is runs smoothly.

Students need to understand that the project requires a clear time commitment, much of it after school hours. The teacher must declare forthrightly how much time will be needed and when. Student monitors must understand that they are committed to the project and cannot skip a day of monitoring simply because they feel too tired or would rather visit the mall. In addition, be agreed upon by the entire class and the teacher will have to explain fully the monitoring procedures to the class and carefully conduct spot checks to be sure monitoring is accurate and consistent.

Because of the wide variety of emphases possible, the class must decide cooperatively where to focus its efforts. What disability groups will it include? Does the class want to include stories only about persons with physical, sensory, or mental disabilities, or will it include features on alcoholism, drug dependency, AIDS, mental illness, aging and so on? As the students discuss which groups to include, they must consider to what extent their class can "accurately" speak for these groups.

Another cooperative decision can focus on whether or not the class monitors reports on the funding of programs that affect persons with disabilities. After a discussion on how social policy often reflects attitudes, should the class take a stand on Medicaid cuts, or state cutbacks for supervised apartments, or reduced supported employment for persons with developmental disabilities?

Although a feature may relate only indirectly to disability issues, the class may want to respond to a particular point or segment. In addition, the class may want to monitor other features ostensibly unrelated to disability. For example, as Elkins, Jones and Ulicny (1987) suggest, does the class want the local restaurant or theater critics to include accessibility information in their reviews?

The monitoring process is, of course, at the heart of the media watch campaign, which is why each media source must be monitored exactly according to schedule, and materials and forms must be returned promptly for group and class discussion. Consistency is essential to the process. Because monitoring takes time, cooperative learning groups should be large enough to keep students from becoming overwhelmed by the monitoring assignment. Several students in each group provides enough flexibility for a student to take over for others who may be unable to help at certain times.

Each student is assigned to read a daily newspaper or watch a nightly news broadcast or TV program, carefully looking for issues or features related to disabilities. Elkins, Jones, and Ulicny (1987) suggest that monitors consider the following questions:

1. What type of disability does the article cover? (The disabilities discussed probably include those covered in Chapter Five.)

2. What terminology, both positive and negative, are used to describe the disability or person with the disability? (Review the terminology discussed in Chapter Two.)

3. How is the person with a disability or the disability issue portrayed? (Review the stereotypes in Chapter Three as well as the medical model versus the handicapism model paradigms.)

Having discovered an appropriate item, the student should cut it out carefully noting the source, date and page. He or she should review the article and identify the terminology and issues and rate each one as acceptable or unacceptable and why. The groups should make copies of each article for the entire class and its own files.

If the student is assigned to monitor television newscasts or features, a videotape is the best way to capture the issue for the entire class. The procedure should be similar for written news but a videotape helps the discussion come alive. At least once a week each group should present its findings and then decide what action to take. Students may open a discussion of the issue or report, write letters, role play taking turns between advocate and reporter (or editor), or even rewrite the story in a more acceptable manner.

These periodic reports constitute an integral part of the cooperative monitoring procedure. Each monitoring review should include a reference (source, date, title, author, page number); the topic and a review of its major points; a statement of the relationship to disability; and a rating of the appropriateness of the article. The student monitors in their groups can then present the feature to the class for discussion and action. Having the monitored issue presented to it, the class should first decide if it requires action. According to If so, Elkins, Jones, and Ulicny (1987) suggest the monitors consider the following four issues:

1. What is the origin of the feature? Is it local or from a wire service?

2. Whom should the class contact? Is there a byline on the story? Should a secondary source be contacted like the editor or an advertiser?

3. Can the class identify the specific type of portrayals (for example, the stereotypes discussed in Chapter Three) and negative terminology (for example, the negative terms as discussed in Chapter Two)?

4. How important and persistent is the issue? The principal criterion for determining its importance is the daily impact it has on the lives of persons with disabilities. The class must also decide if it will treat a "repeat offender" different from one with a past record for covering disability issues fairly?

Upon considering all of the important issues, the class must then decide whether or what type of action is required for each feature or story. Elkins, Jones, and Ulicny (1987) suggest that any action in response to a media report be taken as quickly as possible. Persons who work in the media focus on current stories and quickly forget items published in the past. Thus, each group must take follow-up action is taken with specific assignments—for example, who will write letters to whom, who will make telephone calls, and so forth. (on this point see Appendix One, Resources: Networks and Cable Stations).

According to Elkins, Jones and Ulicny (1987), the last step in establishing a media watch campaign is assessment. To determine whether or not the campaign has reached its goals, the class needs to develop cooperatively a method of evaluating outcomes. A flow chart that tracks group reports can be helpful; it can, perhaps measure whether negative portrayals, language and terminology has decreased, increased, or remained unchanged. Established base lines for the number of acceptable and unacceptable terms and the frequency of disability features need to be established for comparison purposes at the end of the project. To accomplish this work, media reports need to be examined over a specified period for trends and then documented in a class or group journal containing the features addressed, follow-up actions taken, and outcomes. The class must judge whether the media are changing their portrayals and terminology over time. Thus, both the teacher and students must monitor the monitors for accuracy and consistency.

Encountering Guests with Disabilities
Another way to encourage students to interact with persons with disabilities is to invite guests with disabilities to speak to the class. Few adults, much less youngsters, know how to relate to someone with a disability as a person first, and as an individual with an exceptionality second. Because youngsters learn best from actual experiences, introducing persons with disabilities into the daily classroom routine provides an ideal first-hand learning opportunity. Speakers with different disabilities provide additional information on the topic of disability

and can relate its academic aspects to the real world. They offer students a chance to have personal contact, to observe, and above all, to interact with an individual who at first may seem to be different, but in actuality is much like themselves. The experience gives the youngsters an opportunity to learn how persons with impairments accommodate their disabilities and accomplish what non-disabled persons do only differently. They get the chance to see persons with disabilities as individuals, each with their particular personalities, lifestyles, interests, jobs, problems, and ideas. A variety of speakers might address different disability areas.

When preparing their presentations, speakers may want to broach such topics as the environmental and social problems they encounter as well as those they experienced when they were the same age as the students. The speakers could discuss their school experiences, hobbies and interests, families, employment, future plans and even what a typical day is like. They should also be prepared to speak of the disability itself including its causes and how they use adaptive devices and what adaptations they require. Speakers should be encouraged to use short anecdotes and humorous stories that portray positive episodes of their lives.

Classroom encounters with guests with disabilities should be well planned and the next pages present ten preparatory considerations:

1. SELECTING A GUEST SPEAKER—For the encounter to be meaningful, teachers should be cautious in the identification, selection, and preparation of guest speakers. A teacher can rely on a number of ways to identify potential speakers. Guests with special needs can be located through local branches of national agencies like the Association for Retarded Citizens (ARC) and the United Cerebral Palsy Association (UCP). Appendix I, Resources: Disability Organizations and Self-Help Groups, presents a list of national agencies to be contacted for this purpose. These national agencies can provide teachers with the list of local affiliates who, in turn, will provide the names of persons with disabilities who may be available for classroom visits. In addition, every state has a Developmental Disabilities Council, and most publish directories of agencies and services within that state. Local agencies are also listed in the Yellow Pages under *Human Service Organizations* or *Social Service Organizations*.

2. SELECTING THE NUMBER OF GUESTS—Teachers sometimes conclude that the experience will be more valuable if they invite several guests

with similar disabilities at the same time. They feel one visitor may be more comfortable with others. But, this decision should be considered carefully. Although it may seem to be a good idea for the students to get more than one viewpoint, having more than one guest at a time can cause confusion. For example, guests expounding conflicting philosophies may raise feelings that cause confusion and misunderstanding among younger children. Inviting several guests works only if the guests complement one another.

3. ADDRESSING FEELINGS—Be sure to allow opportunities for both the guest and children to express their feelings about being with each other. Such a visit may be the first experience youngsters have had to interact with a person with a disability. If the experience is positive, open and natural, it will influence the way the youngsters may approach others with disabilities when they meet them. It is better to talk openly in front of most guests than talk about them after they have left. Persons with disabilities live with a need to express their feelings, and teachers should understand that individuals with disabilities are more comfortable with questions than non-disabled adults realize. In fact, the conclusion that persons with disabilities avoid talking about their impairments or are ashamed of them is, itself, a form of prejudiced thinking. Moreover discussing people now out of sight encourages shyness in children.

4. SCREENING POTENTIAL GUESTS—Having identified potential guest speakers, a teacher should interview them informally. Call the potential speaker, introducing yourself, and explain that your class is learning about disabilities and you are drawing up a list of potential speakers for a program on "Disability Awareness." Briefly describe the program and ask if the potential speaker wants to know more about it. If the response is favorable, describe the project in detail and explain what preparation the students will have before the visit. Explain as well what you expect in a guest speaker, to help the potential guest speaker decide whether he or she would be comfortable participating in the program. You might also ask the potential guest if he or she would be interested in helping to develop the curriculum. Here are eleven sample questions to generate a conversation:

• Would you please tell me about yourself?

- How do you spend your time? Are you working or going to school?

- Do you live alone? If not, with whom do you live?

- How or when did you become disabled?

- What special problems did you encounter in growing up?

- What things in your life do you particularly need help with?

- What do you do for recreation?

- Have you ever worked with children? What was your experience with them like?

- What do you believe children should know about your particular disability?

- What do you believe would be most helpful for students to experience or learn in their studies of disabilities?

- Have you ever spoken to groups of people about your disability?

From this initial conversation, you could gain some principles to include in the curriculum, more important this telephone conversation should help you get an idea of the person's personality, lifestyle, comfort with speaking of his or her disability, ability to communicate, independence, warmth, sense of humor, and ability to answer questions. Based on the way a person responds, you can get a good idea of how he or she would speak to the class. Keep the initial interview over the telephone as friendly and informal as possible. Share something personal of your own.

5. IMPORTANT CHARACTERISTICS TO LOOK FOR IN A SPEAKER—If the guest speaker comes from an organization he or she will probably be accustomed to public speaking. The teacher needs to be sure only that the guest will speak effectively before the class's age group. If the speaker is an ordinary citizen with a disability, or the parent of a child with a disability, he or she may be a less experienced speaker. Potential speakers need to know ahead of time that they may be asked personal questions.

Therefore, guest speakers should be at ease with themselves and with their disabilities and be prepared to discuss them openly and respond to naive or blunt questions.

Because the lesson stresses the importance of diversity, a teacher should include guests who not only have both differing disabilities and different ages and races. All guests should be warm, open, interesting people, unafraid to express their feelings. They should all live active lives, show positive attitudes and display an acceptance of their disabilities. Other important characteristics to look for include an affection for children and a desire to break down prejudice and attitudinal barriers.

Remember that most individuals with disabilities are glad and even eager to share their knowledge, feelings and experiences if they can see a positive purpose in it—for example, combatting negative attitudes. Because such willingness often reflects to varying degrees of an individual's self-acceptance, the teacher should try to understand the guest's point of view and motivation ahead of time. For example, some guests may want to address the class because they want the world to be a better place for others with similar problems. Thus they may relate how they feel when they are helped or hindered. Other speakers may need to discuss the social and environmental barriers they encounter for their own growth, satisfaction, and acceptance. A teacher needs to establish ahead of time which motivation exists. Although such screening may seem time-consuming, it can help in many ways. For example, once discovered, most good speakers like the experience and return for future classes.

6. PREPARING THE SPEAKER—Teachers should keep foremost in their minds the importance of planning and preparation. Each speaker should know ahead of time what the class expects. Teachers should tell speakers what the students should experience or learn, and speakers need to know how long a presentation should be (an hour is usually about right), how much of the hour to allow for questions, and what kinds of questions will be asked. They need to know, for example, that questions may involve their childhood, family, occupation, special talents, recreational activities and schooling. Questions may also focus on coping with daily problems, how people seem to treat them, what they believe to be the major issues their disability raises. Speakers should also be prepared to talk about what it feels like to have a disability and what friends, special equipment sustains them. Teachers should also prepare their guests to relate real life anecdotes that will have personal meaning for the students.

7. PREPARING THE STUDENTS—Inviting guests with disabilities should be part of an inclusive, multidimensional classroom experience. Therefore, the students will already have engaged in such experiences as role playing, simulations, seeing movies and slides and reading books on the specific disability. If students know something about the disability before the guest speaker's visit, their interest will be heightened and they will tend to ask more meaningful questions. The more knowledge, experiences, understanding, and perception the students attained about the disability before the visit, the more effective the presentation will be. In addition to the various programmed experiences, a teacher should

- center a classroom discussion on the students' feelings or fears about disabilities;

- discuss the idea of inviting a guest speaker with a disability before making the invitation;

- discuss specific rules regarding the use of guide dogs or interpreters;

- review with the students what questions that may be impolite to ask for example, personal questions regarding bodily functions;

- review what language is acceptable or unacceptable during the guest's visit;

- let the students know that the speaker will be willing to talk about his or her disability and its effects, and that almost any tasteful question, will be allowed;

- let the students know that the speaker has a right to decline any question;

- let the students know that the general tone of the session will be informal; and

- review with the class specific questions that may be asked including any of the following:

What are the suitable terms to describe your disability?

By what term would you like people to refer to your disability?

When did you first become disabled?

How did you feel then?

How do you feel today?

What caused your disability?

Could it have been prevented then, now?

Do you ever hope for a medical or technical advance that will "fix" your disability?

Do you use a prosthesis, aid or other equipment?

Do you belong to any disability organizations? Which ones? Why?

How do you feel about charities and telethons?

Do you think that people react to you according to stereotypes based on your disability? If so, what sort of incidents have you experienced?

How should non-disabled persons act when they are introduced to persons with disabilities?

Are any rooms in your house or apartment specially designed for you?

Do your clothes have special features?

What do you particularly need help with? Who provides this help?

Can you get emergency help if you need it?

Were you educated in a special school or class, or in a regular classroom?

Which would you have preferred and why?

What particular problems did you have in school? Did you overcome these problems, and, if so, how?

Do you work? What do you do? How did you get your present job?

Do you like your job? Why or why not?

Do you need special equipment to do your job?

Are most of your friends disabled or non-disabled?

Are you married? Is your husband or wife disabled?

What do you enjoy doing for recreation?

What are you good at doing?

Do you participate in any sports? Which ones? How?

Do you take vacations away from home?

Are there special considerations in deciding where you will vacation?

Do you drive a car? Does it require special equipment in order to drive?

Do you have problems with public transportation? If so, what problems? Could these problems be solved?

In addition, the teacher and students may want to discuss questions for specific disabilities. For example, the following questions are appropriate for a guest with blindness:

How do you pick your clothes out each morning, and how do you tell their colors?

How do you tell the difference between bills in your wallet?

How do you select canned food in your house?

Were you born blind?

How do you pour a cup of coffee without it spilling over?

What is it like to be blind?

Is the world dark or black to a blind person?

What do persons born with blindness see in their dreams?

Why do persons with blindness wear dark glasses?

When playing a game, how do you know the other person isn't cheating?

How do persons with blindness shop, read, travel, work and go to school?

Besides hearing speakers with disabilities, a class should be able to meet and interact with parents of disabled children. Parents can often share important experiences with the class. Questions for parents could include these:

How has family life been affected by having a disabled child?

What was your initial reaction when you found out your child was disabled?

How do you feel about it now?

Did your child's disability present special problems while he or she was an infant?

How do you describe your child when people inquire about him or her?

If you have other children, what is the relationship between your child with a disability and the siblings?

Do problems develop between your child with a disability and the other children? If so, how do you deal with them?

What concerns do you have about your disabled child as an adult?

What advice would you give the parents of a child with a similar disability?

8. MAKING PHYSICAL ARRANGEMENTS—The teacher should, of course, call a speaker and make both the invitation and arrangements. Schedule a precise date and time, and allow between 45 minutes and an hour for the session. Make arrangements, as well, for transportation or parking, if necessary. Ask the speaker to bring along any special aids or appliances that might interest youngsters—for example, a talking clock, a Brailler, or a communication device. Follow the verbal invitation with a letter of confirmation and information, to provide the speaker with a clear understanding of all that you discussed.

If a speaker has blindness the teacher should ascertain what mobility aid he or she uses. For example, if a guide dog is present, what specific instructions do the students need to know about it. Also, the dog's needs need to be known. Transportation may be provided by the school district or a parent, and if a driver is involved, he or she could be invited to attend the session. Both the teacher and driver should know how to guide the person. Upon his or her arrival, the speaker should receive any information he or she may need about the students and the room including a description of the physical layout, exhibits, displays, pets, plants, what the students are currently studying and where they are in the room.

If the speaker has deafness the teacher should make the initial contact by letter and be as specific and detailed as possible. Ask the potential speaker if there is a way to communicate by telephone. Arrange an in-person interview. Ask the speaker if he or she will need an interpreter. If so, specify who will make those arrangements, and find out if the school will pay for one.

If the speaker has an orthopedic impairment, the teacher should make sure the aisles, parking spaces, bathrooms and so forth are accessible. When the teacher makes arrangements, he or she should keep in mind that many wheelchair users drive their own vans. But, some do not. The speaker needs to be asked what his or her transportation needs are. (If the speaker brings his or her own van, perhaps a tour of the van outside, with its lifts and special hand controls could become part of the presentation.) Whatever the speaker's transportation needs may be they should be met. Ask the speaker, as well, if he or she needs help getting in or out of the vehicle.

If parents are to be the speakers, have them bring slides and or photos of their children at different ages up to the present.

9. MAKING THE VISITOR FEEL AT HOME—Because the teacher sets the classroom tone, he or she should provide an informal setting for the visit. It is better and more informal if the speaker sits rather than stands. It also adds to the informal climate if the students sit around a speaker in chairs or in front on the floor. The teacher should then introduce the speaker to the class. Next the speaker should talk to the students for approximately five or ten minutes, providing them with some personal information about his or her disability, work, family, hobbies and so forth. The teacher should then invite the youngsters to ask their questions, but to keep their hands down while speaker responds so they can listen closely to the answers. On occasion the teacher may need to stimulate questions by asking students to remember their reactions when they studied the disability under discussion. If the questions are inappropriate or off the subject, the teacher will need to refocus the questions or encourage the youngsters to ask others. If the guest has blindness, the teacher will have to call on the youngsters by name. The youngsters should be encouraged to state their names before asking their questions so that the guest with blindness can get to know their voices and locations.

If the speaker has deafness he or she and the interpreter should take the time to decide where they want to sit in relation to each other and the class. Such background noises as phonographs or fans, should be eliminated. The teacher should remind the students not to speak to the interpreter but direct all questions and comments to the speaker.

If the speaker is a parent of a youngster with a disability, he or she should emphasize what the child can do, how the child gets along in the community, where the child goes to school, and how the child reacts when being teased or picked on. The parent should include some specific anecdotes of positive interactions of neighborhood children with his or her child.

If the exchanges between the speaker and the class have been natural and cordial, the youngsters' attitudes toward persons with disabilities will be more empathetic. The youngsters will feel more comfortable around persons with disabilities at school and in the community. The next time they encounter a person with blindness they may forget Mr. Magoo and think, instead, of how a person they now know interacts with the environment to overcome the handicap of lessened mobility. The teacher should end the session by allowing five minutes or so to tell the speaker their feelings, to express what they have learned, and to say "thank you."

10. FOLLOW-UP ACTIVITIES—The best follow-up is to invite the children to write thank-you letters to your speaker. This experience provides the youngsters with a chance to ask more questions and to comment on some of what the speaker told them. They should be encouraged to write their ideas and draw pictures. The two crucial follow-up steps are for the teacher and the students to send the speaker thank you notes (if the speaker has blindness they can use an audio tape) and for the class to discuss the presentation. A suggested classroom discussion follows:

If our class were to get a new student tomorrow and that student had the same disability as the speaker has, what could I do as the teacher to make this classroom more user-friendly and accommodating? What would you do as classmates? How do you think he or she would fit into the class? What way would you act and what accommodations would you make? The teacher should encourage specific answers and discuss the long term consequences of having a student with that disability in the room. The students can then make a display in the room of the visit and their responses to the discussion.

Providing Information On Prejudice and Discrimination

Learning About Stereotypes and Discrimination
To create and maintain truly inclusive schools and communities, children and teachers must see themselves as change agents, willing and able to confront and challenge stereotypes and oppressive, discriminatory behavior. At different ages, students reach different levels of social activism, but even young children can recognize and respond to stereotypes and prejudice.

Teachers of very young children may, for example, explain the difference between a "dislike" and a "prejudice." The children may be allowed to express a dislike for something—that is, have a negative reaction to a food, or an activity after they have had extensive experience with it. But they should resist prejudging people without sufficient experience. Children need to learn to discriminate legitimate dislikes ("I decided I don't like spinach after I tasted it" or, "Jerry pushes smaller kids and I don't want to play with him") from prejudices ("I don't want to taste that, it looks yucky" or, "Children with only one leg are mean"). The children may look at and then taste a lemon. The teacher can then raise the question, do all fruits that have a yellow outside taste sour? What about a banana?

Or, the teacher might bring in two boxes similar in size but one wrapped in a ripped, stained paper bag, and the other in gift wrap. The students are then told that the teacher has brought some presents or cookies for the class in one box and put garbage in the other. The class then decides which one to open and which one to throw away? In most instances, the will choose the gift-wrapped one to open. But the gift-wrapped box contains the trash and the other the gifts or cookies. The teacher can then raise inferential questions about judging by exteriors.

Questionnaire On Stereotyping and Evaluating on Incomplete Information

A teacher can usefully point out that most people stereotype without realizing it. Youngsters may be unaware that they have developed pre-conceived notions about people with disabilities. The exercise that follows helps students detect stereotyping behavior in their own class. This is only a sample exercise, teachers may want to develop their own based on other disabilities and their assumed traits. The three goals of this exercise are

1. to detect stereotypes that may be held by class members;

2. to introduce and discuss the concept of stereotyping; and

3. to help students realize that they may unconsciously stereotype and base judgments about others on incomplete information.

Half the class receives form A and the other half form B of each of the two exercises, but the students should think everyone received the same form. Students should also know that their responses are confidential and that they need not put their names on the forms. After students complete the questionnaires, the results should be tabulated. As usual, the key is the discussion that takes place at the end. In this exercise, the students need to know that their attitudes are being discussed. Sample questions may include these seven:

1. Were you surprised at the results? Why or why not?

2. What are stereotypes and how do they develop?

3. How do stereotypes affect both the person who is being judged and the person doing the judging?

4. What are some of the other prevalent stereotypes in our society?

5. Is a stereotype ever valid?

6. Would the results of this questionnaire be different if administered to the entire school or community?

7. Have you or someone you know ever been the victim of stereotyping or prejudice?

The following exercise is based on: Sawyer, D. and Green, H. (1984). *The Native Education Services Associates (NASA) activities handbook for native and multi-cultural classrooms (Volume 1).* Vancouver, BC: Canada, Tillacum Library, pp. 49-54.

Exercise 1 FORM A
Jerry Armstrong is seventeen years old and is a Junior at Westville High School. He is on the soccer team and delivers papers after school. Jerry probably is

Trustworthy	1	2	3	4	5	Untrustworthy
Motivated	1	2	3	4	5	Un-motivated
Happy	1	2	3	4	5	Unhappy
Friendly	1	2	3	4	5	Unfriendly
Interesting	1	2	3	4	5	Boring
Easy-going	1	2	3	4	5	Hot-tempered
Verbal	1	2	3	4	5	Non-verbal
Predictable	1	2	3	4	5	Impulsive
Patient	1	2	3	4	5	Frustration-prone
Considerate	1	2	3	4	5	Thoughtless

Exercise 1 FORM B
Jerry Armstrong is seventeen years old and is a Junior at Westville High School. He is classified as Educable Mentally Retarded. He is on the soccer team and delivers papers after
school. Jerry probably is

Trustworthy	1	2	3	4	5	Untrustworthy
Motivated	1	2	3	4	5	Un-motivated

Happy	1	2	3	4	5	Unhappy
Friendly	1	2	3	4	5	Unfriendly
Interesting	1	2	3	4	5	Boring
Easy-going	1	2	3	4	5	Hot-tempered
Verbal	1	2	3	4	5	Non-verbal
Predictable	1	2	3	4	5	Impulsive
Patient	1	2	3	4	5	Frustration-prone
Considerate	1	2	3	4	5	Thoughtless

Exercise 2 FORM A

Mary Barton is a senior at Westville High School. She is on the student council and President of the Poetry Club. Mary is probably

Happy	1	2	3	4	5	Sad
Talented	1	2	3	4	5	Not Talented
Musical	1	2	3	4	5	Not Musically Inclined
Easy-going	1	2	3	4	5	Hot-tempered
Self-assured	1	2	3	4	5	Poor Self-Esteem
Friendly	1	2	3	4	5	Unfriendly
Interesting	1	2	3	4	5	Boring
Joyful	1	2	3	4	5	Melancholy
Enviable	1	2	3	4	5	Pitiable
Adroit	1	2	3	4	5	Bumbling/Inept

Exercise 2 FORM B

Mary Barton is a senior at Westville High School. She has been blind since birth and gets around with the use of a guide dog and cane. She is on the student council and President of the Poetry Club. Mary is probably

Happy	1	2	3	4	5	Sad
Talented	1	2	3	4	5	Not Talented
Musical	1	2	3	4	5	Not Musically Inclined
Easy-going	1	2	3	4	5	Hot-tempered
Self-assured	1	2	3	4	5	Poor Self-Esteem
Friendly	1	2	3	4	5	Unfriendly
Interesting	1	2	3	4	5	Boring
Joyful	1	2	3	4	5	Melancholy
Enviable	1	2	3	4	5	Pitiable
Adroit	1	2	3	4	5	Bumbling/Inept

Behavior Rehearsing

Students can learn from acting out situations that give them a chance to try out new roles without real life consequences or to test how they might handle a certain situation. Role playing is helpful in having students consider opinions other than their own. It is a good way to show alternatives to situations. All students may participate in this activity.

Role Playing

Role playing offers an effective technique for changing attitudes. For example, Watts (1984) concluded that active participation, such as role playing provides the most effective approach to changing attitudes toward persons with disabilities. The proven effectiveness of these methods reinforce his recommendation and, more important, conclude the resulting changes appear to be relatively permanent. Clore and Jeffrey (1972) conducted a relevant study that focused on the attitudinal effects of role playing. They demonstrated the dramatic effects of emotional role playing upon individuals' attitudes.

When initiating a role-playing situation, the teacher should emphasize that role-playing includes no "right or wrong" judgment. The students should know that everyone is acting. The goal is to act out a situation and to talk about the results. It is important for the teacher to state the goal of and the reason for using the technique. For example, "By role-playing and acting out this situation, you will have a chance to observe and express some of the behaviors we have been discussing in class."

To begin the role-playing activity, the teacher should describe the situation to be enacted clearly and in detail, and never force a student to assume a role. While the role-players are provided with written or verbal descriptions of their roles, the observers should be provided with such specific tasks as watching the verbal and nonverbal responses of particular characters. Once the role-playing begins it should continue until enough has happened to stimulate discussion, the situation has been adequately illustrated, or the action has become dull or repetitive to the point of diminishing its impact. After the role-playing situation is stopped, the class should debrief both the actors and the observers. All actors should describe their experiences and responses to particular behaviors and feelings. Asking actors for their feelings before discussing the role play with the group lessens their anxiety about criticism. In addition, observers should report on what happened and be encouraged to ask questions, discuss what happened in the role play, why it turned out the way it did, and whether they are satisfied with the way it turned out (Salend, 1994).

Most of the following 61 exercises reflect real life situations:

ROLE PLAYING EXERCISES

1. You are sitting with a group of friends at a fast food restaurant. One of your friends has cerebral palsy and is a wheelchair user. The manager approaches and asks if your group can finish eating and leave as quickly as possible because some young children having a birthday party nearby are upset about seeing your friend in the wheelchair. How do you react?

2. You see a woman you know sitting in a wheelchair drinking a cup of coffee. As a stranger passes he throws a quarter into her cup and keeps walking. How do you react?

3. You are at a mall with friends and see some severely mentally retarded individuals. A friend says, "Look at those retards. Don't they make you sick?" How do you respond?

4. A family friend gives birth to a child with Down Syndrome. Well-meaning friends ask you to add your name to a sympathy card they plan to send. How do you react?

5. A classmate classified as educable mentally retarded seems to be accepted in class but not on the playground or at lunch where he is constantly ignored. How would you handle this?

6. A friend's parent is upset because her child's third grade class includes a youngster with blindness whom, she believes, upsets her daughter to the point of coming home sick every day, and slows the academic pace of the rest of the class. How would you respond?

7. You are at a store with a friend who slips into a seizure. The sales person becomes frightened and begins to scream for help. How do you handle the situation?

8. You can just about make it on time to a class where the teacher gets irked when students are late. As you race around a corner in the hallway you run into a student, knocking the pile of books she's carrying onto the floor. You then recognize her as a classmate who has cerebral palsy. How do you react?

9. You are a class officer. At a planning meeting for your three-day out-of-town class trip your principal gives your committee the option of excluding "the special ed kids." How do you respond?

10. A person you are seriously dating tells you in an almost apologetic way that he or she has a brother with severe mental retardation living at home. How would you react?

11. You are at a party. You extend your hand while being introduced to another guest and realize she has blindness and is unaware you want to shake hands. What do you do?

12. You visit a friend at the hospital who just gave birth. You find out the child has dwarfism and the doctor told the mother she "unfortunately" gave birth to "a circus freak." You see the doctor in the hall. What, if anything, would you say to him?

13. Your mother does not like to have animals in the house, especially dogs. You are planning a party and want to include a friend with blindness who uses a guide dog. How would you handle the situation? What would you say to your mother?

14. You see a policeman yelling at a man you know who has deafness. Do you get involved? If so, how do you handle it?

15. You visit a friend at the hospital who just gave birth. You find out the child has Down syndrome and the doctor told the mother she has given birth to a "Mongolian idiot" and she "should have the child institutionalized before you begin to bond with it." You see the doctor in the hall. What, if anything, would you say?

16. While standing next to a bank of pay telephones, you notice that a woman with dwarfism can not reach high enough to dial what appears to be an important call. Would you offer help? Why or why not?

17. A wheelchair user parked nearby accidently falls out of his chair while transferring from his van. You want to help him. Would you get involved? If so, how?

18. As you get into your car in a crowded parking lot you notice a car pull into a "handicapped" parking spot without "handicapped" license plates or a special permit in the window. The driver, obviously not disabled, sees your annoyed look and says, "I'm in a rush! It's only for a few minutes." How would you react? Would you say something even if the driver did not address you?

19. You are at a store and the customer ahead of you is speaking with a severe stutter to the salesperson who abruptly walks away in the middle of a sentence and asks if you need help. How would you react?

20. You invite a person with blindness to a party at your house. You have a valuable collection of figurines and other delicate objects on your tables and shelves. Would you put them away before the party?

21. Your sister is asked to go out on a date by a boy you know and like but is classified as "emotionally disturbed" by your school system. Do you tell her or your parents? Why or why not?

22. A friend asks you to raise money for *Jerry's Kids* by taking part in a bed race. Knowing that many persons with physical disabilities have negative feelings toward such fund raising activities would you participate or decline? What would you say?

23. You are at a restaurant with a friend with blindness. The waiter points to your friend and asks you, "What does he want?" How do you respond?

24. On the trip home your school bus stops for a traffic light. A group of boys on the bus notice out the back window that the driver of the car behind the bus has cerebral palsy and displays spastic movements. They laugh and begin to mock and imitate him through the window. How would you handle the situation?

25. Your parents and their friends are discussing the high taxes they pay. One of your parents' friends says that severely physically disabled

and retarded persons are "vegetables' with no real lives and should, therefore, be allowed to die to save the taxpayers money. How do you respond?

26. Your school is playing a basketball game against a team from a school for youngsters with deafness. A number of your schoolmates begin to mock and make fun of the obviously different speech patterns of the other team members and cheerleaders. What do you do?

27. A friend makes the statement to you that "retarded people are dangerous." How do you respond?

28. A classmate with cerebral palsy wants to join the Chess Club with you at school. You know him to be a brilliant player who consistently beats you. However, the teacher assigned to serve as club advisor discourages him from joining because "his spastic movements will knock the pieces over." How would you respond?

29. Your good friend, a wheelchair user, is the best trumpet player in the school. He tells you that the bandmaster refused to allow him to join the band "because he will mess up the formations when they march in parades." How would you respond?

30. Your social studies teacher remarks that the American colonists were extremely heartless and cruel to their fellow colonists with disabilities. How do you respond?

31. A doctor tries to convince your family that it would be a good idea to have your brother, who has been labeled mildly mentally retarded, sterilized. What do you say?

32. A person with whom you are having a conversation has a communication handicap and you can't quite understand what he is saying. How do you respond?

33. A student with blindness trips over a wastebasket in your classroom. A number of students laugh and call him Mr. Magoo. How do you handle the situation?

34. A number of students with deafness and their parents are petitioning your school board to have American Sign Language taught at your school for foreign language credit. You are at the board meeting. Do you address the board in support of their request? Why or why not?

35. You notice that your parents and siblings refer to a neighborhood child as "that retarded kid down the block." Knowing that no malice is intended what would you say to them?

36. You and a group of friends have been looking forward to seeing a new movie. One member of your group is a wheelchair user. When you call to get the starting time of the picture you also learn that the theater is not wheelchair accessible. What do you do?

37. A classmate complains that it is unfair that a student with learning disabilities had only half the number of problems for homework. How would you respond?

38. A friend who is congenitally blind asks, "What kind of a night is it?" How do you describe the beautiful starry night with its full moon?

39. A friend remarks that it's a shame wheelchair users with physical disabilities are not whole persons. How do you respond?

40. You are in the store with a friend who has a severe stutter. The salesperson chastises him by stating that he would be much better understood if only he would speak slower and not be so nervous. Do you respond? If so what would you say?

41. A friend with blindness has a big food stain on her blouse. Do you tell her? What would you say?

42. A classmate expresses a feeling of discrimination because a fellow student with a learning disability is the only one in the class with permission to use a calculator during a math exam. How do you respond?

43. You and a friend with congenital blindness go up to the observation tower of the Empire State Building. Upon being asked, how would you describe the view?

44. A teacher calls a classmate with learning disabilities clumsy. How do you respond?

45. You and a group of friends are going to movie. Do you invite a friend with blindness along? What if you are going skiing?

46. You hear your father say, "Institutions for the mentally retarded are important because the retarded prefer to be with their own kind." How would you respond?

47. A friend expresses the view that "dwarfs are funny looking." How do you respond?

48. You and a group of friends are planning to go to a rock concert. Do you ask a friend with deafness to join you? Why or why not?

49. A friend expresses the view that mentally retarded people should not be allowed to marry or vote. What is your response?

50. You and a friend with blindness are in a store making a purchase. Your friend wants to pay with a check but the store manager will accept only a driver's license as required identification. How do you respond?

51. A classmate has an accident resulting in paraplegia. You know she comes from a wealthy family with complete medical coverage. Some well-meaning students in your school asks you to help organize a drive to raise money for her by putting canisters with her picture in most of the local stores. What is your reaction? How do you handle it?

52. While in the city, you and a friend, who is a wheelchair user, are stopped by a religious evangelist who tells your friend to "repent and ask forgiveness" if he wants to walk again. What is your response?

53. You are being introduced to a person with no right hand. How do you shake hands?

54. A friend of your family, who happens to be the personnel director of a large company, remarks how much more important it is to provide employment for men with disabilities than women with disabilities. How do you respond?

55. A number of your neighbors are holding a meeting to express their anger at the state for wanting to open a group home for eight young adults with autism in your community. Among their fears are the safety of their children and lowered property values. You have an opportunity to address the meeting. What do you say?

56. You visit a friend for the first time since his accident in which he lost his legs. Role play both a "sympathetic" and an "empathetic" reaction to his physical impairment.

57. Role play a "stigma spread" reaction to a physical disability.

58. A young boy who uses a wheelchair moves next door to you. You like him. As your families get to know each other the boy's mother confides in you that her son has a difficult time making friends with youngsters his own age. She asks if you would introduce him to the youngsters in the neighborhood and ease the transition for him. You and he see a group of youngsters from the neighborhood playing the next day. Role play what you would do and say.

59. Martin Luther said that persons with mental retardation were "changelings" born in the image of Satan. He also said that it would please God to see them dead. If you could meet Martin Luther today, what would you say to him about those beliefs?

60. Your friend's father has cerebral palsy and is president of a bank. He takes a group, including you, to a fancy restaurant. The waiter comes over to take the drink orders. When your friend's father orders a Scotch and soda, the waiter looks at the rest of you and says, "Is it okay for him to have it?" Role play what should happen next.

61. You are invited to a Halloween party where each of the male guests is supposed to come in a costume based on a disabled character in a novel—for example, Captain Hook, Captain Ahab, Long John Silver, Quasimodo, Tiny Tim. Would you do it? What, if anything, would you say to the host?

Simulations
Experiencing simulations is much like role playing. Both are forms of social gaming. Learning takes place by creating circumstances (for

example, temporary handicapping conditions) and working out solutions to problems that naturally arise in those circumstances. Broadbelt (1969) described a simulation as a means of allowing the student to live vicariously. "Furthermore, the simulation has the desirable quality of enabling the teacher to manipulate various courses of action and their consequences without the student suffering physically for the wrong choices" (p. 176).

As Margolis and Shapiro (1988) stated, "[T]he purpose of a simulation is to allow the learner to experience essential aspects of a situation through active participation which generates insight into the real world" (p. 139). In addition, by raising consciousness, simulations show students there is a range of severity in each disability and that each individual reacts differently. Teachers should stress that although simulations convey some idea of being environmentally handicapped, they can not provide the total experience—particularly that of negative attitudes and active discrimination.

Simulations give non-disabled students opportunities to feel what it is like to be handicapped by the environment and why children with certain disabilities behave, communicate, transport themselves, or progress the way they do (Shapiro and Margolis, 1988). A simulation of blindness may, for example, help a student realize why children with blindness may avoid running and why they resent the bumbling antics of Mr. Magoo. Non-disabled students can gain a direct sense of the serious, practical reasons for the way students with disabilities behave as they do. These simulated experiences can help make a student more fully aware of the consequences of negative attitudes like ridicule, and therefore help them develop empathy. Ideally, able-bodied classmates learn to see beyond the disability, that people are people and that a disability is not the essence of personhood (Bookbinder, 1978).

Teachers should be aware, however, that simulation as a tool for effecting attitude change among non-disabled students has some limitations. As Cohen, Koehler, and Grand (1981) stated,

> Although we can never completely duplicate the condition of being disabled through simulation, we can get a glimmer of some of the difficulties and differences in living engendered by a disability through simulation of that disability (p. 10).

In fact, some activists with disabilities have misgivings about the use of simulations as a teaching tool. Wright (1987) quoted Laura Raucher, a disability rights advocate with a physical impairment:

> I don't encourage simulations because I think they're based on a false assumption that fifteen minutes, or two hours, or two weeks in a wheelchair or walking around blindfolded could give someone any idea what it's like to be disabled. . . . What a simulation approximates is not the reality of being disabled, but the trauma of *becoming* disabled—the awkwardness, humiliation, and fear of confronting a world that isn't set up for you and frankly looks down on you, with tools you haven't yet mastered. . . . The point we are missing, in the terrifying blackness behind the blindfold or the sweaty confusion of our first bout with double doors, is that people learn to manage, and manage well with disabilities (p. 4).

But the author among many others believes that such issues and concerns can usefully become part of the discussion that must always follow a simulation. With their accompanying discussions, simulations can help change negative attitudes if they are a part of a comprehensive program that includes a variety of approaches: face to face integration, personal involvement, role playing, media and audio-visual presentations, guest speakers with disabilities, demystifying aids, appliances and assistive devices used by persons with disabilities, and so forth. In fact, Donaldson (1989) suggested that empathy developed as a result of simulation activities may become a driving force to ameliorate negative attitudes. The understanding developed in taking the place of a disabled person may contribute to the formation of more positive attitudes. In addition, simulations provide a youngster with some appreciation of the difficulties disabled persons may face and exposes them to methods of adaptation used by persons with disabilities (Jones, Sowell, Jones, and Butler, 1981). Ideally, they then learn to infer how the removal of certain barriers also reduces the handicap.

In fact, the longer the simulation experience the more effective it becomes. Sitting in a wheel chair for an entire day, rather than for just an hour, conveys a more realistic idea of the problems involved in maneuvering the wheelchair. Having to face stairs and curbing for a whole day can quickly raise one's consciousness. The longer this activity goes on the better.

Of course, the teacher must understand that the effectiveness of using simulations is less the activities themselves, than in the "discussion" of the students' feelings and reactions to their experiences. Youngsters should always be encouraged to express their feelings regarding the simulated "frustrating" activity. It is also important to stress the students' "similarity of feelings," despite the nature of the handicapping conditions. In general, youngsters will view a person with a disability differently after they have learned first-hand about the nature of the condition and the skills needed to overcome its handicaps.

Please note that the simulations suggested here represent only a small sample. They are also presented in several forms. Teachers may want to use a plan they find particularly suitable for the age-level of the children in their class. To explore the many available disability simulation ideas they can refer to those contained in the guides listed in Appendix I, Resources: Curriculum Guides and Activity Books on Disability Awareness and Prejudice Reduction.

SOME REPRESENTATIVE SIMULATION EXERCISES AND ACTIVITIES

Experiencing Blindness
The Primary Objectives of this simulation are:

1. to help students develop some understanding of how it feels to be unable to enjoy full mobility;

2. to provide experiences like walking, drinking from a fountain, dressing, and washing when one is unable to see;

3. to compel students to rely on other senses to compensate for the loss of sight;

4. to help students experience a dependency on other persons for mobility;

5. to demonstrate how to assist a person who has blindness;

6. to encourage an awareness that people who cannot see are more like us than different; and

7. to gain empathy for a person with blindness.

Students may do this exercise for at least several class periods or one-half day if possible. The longer, the better.

Materials needed are blindfolds for half the group. An easy way of making blindfolds is to take a "Lone Ranger" type mask and put opaque tape across both sides of the eye slits. Now follow this procedure:

1. Divide the group into pairs of students with the same gender.

2. In each pair, one person will be the sighted leader and the other the person with blindness. The exercise will be repeated reversing roles.

3. The teacher should demonstrate how to guide a person with blindness in situations like walking, going through a doorway, sitting in a chair, taking a drink from a fountain, and so forth.

    a. The person with blindness holds the sighted leader's arm above the elbow. The sighted leader walks slightly ahead of the blind partner to allow warning time for obstacles.

    b. The teacher should emphasize that the sighted guide should never leave the partner with blindness alone.

    c. It is important to provide specific directions and numbers like "two yards to the left," when giving directions to the person with blindness. The person with blindness may get confused if the sighted leader uses expressions like "over there." Also, when facing a classmate with blindness, a sighted student should specify whose right and whose left. The sighted leader should explain the environment, including information regarding doors, narrow passages and steps. When encountering steps it is important to tell the partner with blindness how many steps (including the landing) and whether they go up or down. The leader should constantly remind himself or herself that the person being led can not see.

    d. When encountering a chair or fountain, the sighted leader should place the hand of the person being led on them. The students with blindness, however, should always be encouraged to do as much for themselves as possible.

4. Before beginning the "blind walk" students should be instructed to be aware of their feelings throughout the activity.

5. Students should be given the following directions:

    a. Go out of the room to another part of the building. If the school has more than one story, go up or down a flight of stairs.

    b. Go to a lavatory and wash and then dry your hands with a paper towel.

    c. Go to a fountain and take a drink of water.

    d. Return to your room and sit at a student desk.

    e. Reverse roles.

    f. If the simulation is to last for at least half a day, students may get to eat lunch in the cafeteria.

    g. When starting the "blind walk" it is a good idea to have some of the pairs start at different points, (for example, at the fountain or in the lavatory) so that not all students are doing the same task at the same time.

6. The teacher should help the pairs of students get started, so that they stay on task, and provide verbal support as needed. Again, students should be encouraged to talk to each other about their experiences and feelings as the simulations proceed. For younger groups, it may be a good idea to allow some students to serve as "spotters" or "monitors" in the hallways to help ensure safety. Any student expressing fear of the exercise should be excused without penalty.

7. Before it takes place, the teachers who assist should experience the simulation on their own so that they can give verbal support to their students by using expressions like, "That was scary to me too when I couldn't see!"

8. After all of the students return to the classroom the teacher should allow for at least a one hour discussion. Some questions that may be discussed include:

   a. How did it feel to have blindness?

   b. How did you use your hearing and other senses differently? Did you listen more carefully?

   c. What was scariest to you?

   d. What kind of information did you need to feel comfortable?

   e. What were you able to do the same as always?

   f. What were you able to do on your own without help from your guide?

   g. What problems did you encounter? How did you work them out?

   h. If we did this simulation every day do you think it would become easier with practice? Do you think persons who become blind find it easier with experience?

   i. What was the most comfortable way for you and your leader to work together?

   j. What fears might a child with blindness have that would make him or her hesitate to run? How could a child with blindness learn to run?

   k. Did others make fun of you? How would you feel if you really had blindness and someone made fun of you?

   l. How do you feel about cartoon characters like Mr. Magoo that make fun of a person with blindness and their troubles getting around?

   m. Did others talk louder to you?

n. If you were to acquire blindness, what activities that require sight would you be unable to do? What would you still be able to do?

o. If a child with blindness joined our class tomorrow, what could we do to make our environment more user friendly and comfortable?

9. The teacher should briefly summarize the students' discussion. Emphasis should be placed on sameness and that a person with blindness can do many of the things sighted persons do, only they may do them a bit differently.

Experiencing a Visual Discrimination Learning Disability

The object of this simulation is to give youngsters a sense of what it is like to have a visual discrimination problem affect reading. In such situations letters may be reversed, or rotated. For example, a student may confuse the letters *p, q, b,* and *d.* An *n* and an *h* or a *u* may also get confused as may a *w* and *m.* Some letters may appear backwards. There may be spaces between words. The student with a visual discrimination problem has to decode and decipher the words being read.

Here is a passage from *Johnny Tremain* as it might appear to a person with a visual-perceptual learning disability. Students should be asked to read it quickly and then explain it to the class:

* * *

Jouhhy layin the 'birt hand deatn roow.' Th iswas narply woretham a clo set mith a tiuy mihpom of fthe ki tcheu, nseq for st orage exceqt in tiwes of sickhess. His haud had deen bone np in a liuseep donltice. The swell of the liuseepd mas stifling and hom, on the seconp pay, the daiu nap re ally pegnu. Hisarm thropped to the shonlper.

* * *

Johnny lay in the 'birth and death room.' This was hardly more than a closet with a tiny window off the kitchen, used for storage except in times of sickness. His hand had been done up in linseed oultice. The smell of the linseed was stifling, and now, on the second day, the pain had really begun. His arm throbbed to the shoulder.

* * *

An exercise like this can stimulate discussion about the problems by students with visual- perceptual learning disabilities experience. The discussion should also include how students with such disabilities are treated, how the class can be most helpful, and the importance of equity—that is, everyone being treated according to his or her individual needs. The students should be encouraged to discuss their feelings when trying to read the passage and to describe how it might feel always to perceive written language this way. Variations of this simulation include having students attempt to read a passage from a textbook turned upside down or to read a printed passage from a page reflected in a mirror.

Experiencing a Spatial Orientation Problem
Invite students to play a few rounds of "Simon Says," then give the directions slowly and clearly. When the students are comfortable with the game and having fun, begin the game again with the following rule changes: *down* means *up*, *up* means *down*; *left* means *right*, *right* means *left*. Play the game faster than before until a winner emerges. The class discussion following the exercise should emphasize that certain learning disabled students have problems with spatial orientation—for example, recognizing the difference between left and right, up and down, over and under. For some learning disabled students, ordinary statements of rules may be more complicated than the second set of "Simon Says" rules was for them. The discussion should also cover how the second game could have been made easier to learn and how the students might help a classmate with a learning disability who constantly faces with such a problem.

Experiencing a Communication Problem
The teacher should explain to the youngsters that some people who have cerebral palsy have a hard time speaking and communicating, not because they are slow-witted, but because the muscles in their faces have been affected by a form of brain damage.

Call each child to the front of the room, one at a time. Then give the child a nursery rhyme to read or a passage of a book to read. Stipulate, however, that the child may not move his or her lips or tongue. Each child may have a different reaction: some will attempt to vocalize, some will giggle or laugh nervously, and some may just stand there not knowing what to do. Here are six useful follow-up questions for this exercise:

1. How did it feel to have something to tell everyone but not being able to express it?

2. Why couldn't you talk?

3. In what way did you have the ability?

4. In what ways did you have the disability?

5. Does that mean that if a person is not talkative he or she may have this very same problem?

6. How could a person with this problem communicate?

Discuss how a person may feel if he or she has a lot to say but has difficulty speaking.

Experiencing Extra Weight

Children who wear braces or artificial limbs are carrying around a great deal of extra weight. To give a sense of how tiring this can be, have the children walk about with sandbags hung from their wrists. You can borrow special sandbags from a physical therapist, or make your own by getting a small bag of sand and attaching a strip of material so you can hang it from a wrist. The children must hold their arms straight out and walk around the room this way two or three times. Young children find this exercise exhausting. You can also strap rulers or rolled up newspapers to the children's legs and have them walk around the room with their legs stiffened in this awkward way. Another simulation for older students is to tape a two or three-pound weight around the student's dominant wrist or lower forearm. Using that arm, the students should try to copy one or two pages of written material, dial a telephone, comb his or her hair (or put on lipstick), clean the blackboard, or any other chore he or she wants to attempt.

After these activities, talk with the class about how much patience a person must have to keep working at activities that are, for others, automatic activities like walking, keeping balance and sitting up straight. Ask them how they would feel if they were working their hardest to walk and others teased them or imitated them. You might ask your class to think about why people tease other children who look different. Mention that it is natural to feel strange, or curious, or a little afraid when you first see someone who looks so different, and ask them whom they might talk to when they have these feelings.

Experiencing an Auditory Memory Problem
The teacher should explain that some students with learning disabilities
or mental retardation find it confusing to follow even a few simple
directions. Telling such a child, "Go get a ball, a bat and your glove, and
I'll meet you at the ball field in ten minutes" might be too much information to take in at time. This simulation activity is designed to show
just how frustrating it is to receive too many directions at once.

Call on two students to come to the front of the room and sit in
chairs back to back. Have a prepared list of ten or fifteen simple directions: "Stand up," "Put your hands on your hips," "Touch your nose,"
"Say your zip code," "Spell your first name backwards," "Retie your
shoe laces," "Hop on one leg," "Shake hands with a classmate," and
then ,"Pull your earlobe." Explain to the two children that you will read
the list through once, then you want them to follow the directions in
order. Then ask a few other pairs of children to try the exercise but make
sure you read the list in a different order each time. In the discussion
that follows, invite the students to discuss how they felt trying to
remember everything. How would they feel to be this overwhelmed
whenever most people spoke to them? How could they talk to another
youngster with this problem so that he or she would feel comfortable
and would understand rather than feel confused?

Experiencing the Use of a Wheelchair
Borrow a wheelchair from a local first aid squad or from a local affiliate
of a national organization for persons with disabilities (see Appendix I,
Resources, for a list of such National Organizations). Select one student
to be the wheelchair user with a physical disability. A second student
can help by wheeling the chair or walking at its side. Students should
then leave the room and move about the corridors, take a drink from a
water fountain, use an elevator, use the restroom, use a public phone, eat
a meal in the cafeteria, and attempt any other activities they choose.
After at least an hour, they should then reverse roles. Again, remember
that the longer the time spent in the wheelchair the more effective the
simulation.

Experiencing the Use of Crutches
Obtain a pair of crutches and ask one student to play a person with a
physical disability requiring the crutches. Another student, approximately the same size, should be paired up with the person using the
crutches for safety reasons. Be sure the crutches are adjustable and fitted

to each user's size. Each student should practice using the crutches before leaving the room. Students should move about the building, attempting to visit another floor at some point. Reverse the roles after at least one hour.

Experiencing Fine Motor Coordination Problems
The teacher should explain to the class that some disabilities cause some youngsters to lose fine motor coordination which can cause great frustration. In this exercise, provide students with pairs of heavy ski mittens or work gloves. To add to the frustration, the teacher may cut a tongue depressor to fit into the thumb. Beforehand, the teacher should gather some everyday objects like a rubber band, a paper clip, a button, a key, a playing card, an envelope, a small soft-covered book, some pieces of a puzzle, a wallet with play money in it, and a big shirt with buttons. Ask a student to put on the gloves and

- pick up the small objects and place them in the envelope;

- turn the pages of a book;

- complete part of a puzzle;

- take a bill out of the wallet; and

- button and unbutton the shirt.

As the student attempts these tasks, invite the rest of the class to mock the effort with remarks like "Can't you go any faster?" "You're holding us up!" "You're such a slowpoke!" The focus of the discussion following the simulation should be on the question, "What could we have done to have made it easier for the person?" (for example provide encouragement or allow more time).

Experiencing an Auditory Disability
The teacher should obtain a hair dryer with a bonnet attached and then ask a student to place the bonnet over his or her head and ears, and turn the dryer on to the "high." Ask another student to sit down opposite the student with the hair dryer, and challenge them to carry on at least a ten-minute conversation. After ten minutes, the students should then reverse roles. Again, the discussion following the simulation should focus on

improving communication, feelings of being unable to hear, and what makes auditory disabilities different from other types of disabilities.

Experiencing Deafness

Another interesting simulation of an auditory disability is to have students see an unfamiliar movie or taped television show with a plot with the sound turned off. After watching the show or film, the students can take a short quiz centered on the plot. The students, of course, will provide a wide variety of answers. Note that some television shows, like reruns of *I Love Lucy* and *Laverne and Shirley*, contain more visual humor than shows like soap operas and are, therefore, easier to enjoy without sound. Others, like mysteries or action films, lose some of their impact without the accompaniment of background music. After discussing the students' answers, show the film or tape again, this time with the sound on. Then have the students answer the quiz again and compare their answers with the first ones.

Here are eight productive follow-up questions:

1. What did you miss most by not being able to hear?

2. What did you understand although you could not hear?

3. What helped you to understand (for example, body language, facial expressions)?

4. How did you feel watching the story without sound (tired, bored, frustrated)?

5. What sounds did you miss the most (for example, background music, water running, animal sounds, variations of voice)?

6. What everyday problems might you incur if you had deafness (for example, answering a telephone, hearing an alarm clock, hearing a siren, communicating)?

7. How do telephones with TDY's, closed-captioned television programs, and American Sign Language help persons with deafness function like the rest of us in a hearing world?

8. What do you think life would be like if you could not hear? (Stress *differentness* rather than *worse*.)

Classroom Discussions

All classroom activities—including simulations, role playing and entering guests with disabilities—should include thorough discussions.

QUESTIONS FOR CLASSROOM DISCUSSION

When presenting any information on disability awareness, teachers may find any one or all of the following ninety questions helpful for promoting classroom discussions. These questions lend themselves nicely to writing assignments:

1. Why are all people more alike than different?

2. How are differences seen as both positive and negative?

3. What is meant by the statement, "All persons have value and can learn to grow"?

4. Why are disabilities, and those who have them, normal?

5. Why is it important to see people as individuals, not labels?

6. Why do people have a right to be different?

7. How do our feelings influence our attitudes and behavior?

8. How does our language reflect our attitudes?

9. What is meant by the statement, "Handicaps are situational?"

10. Why must the basic rights of persons with disabilities be safeguarded for everyone's benefit?

11. How do our negative attitudes lead to negative social policy and laws?

12. Why do most persons with disabilities want us to "empathize" with them rather than "sympathize" with them?

13. How are negative attitudes toward persons with disabilities deeply ingrained in our culture, language and history?

14. What is meant by the statement, "A disability is a characteristic of a person; a handicap is a characteristic of the environment"?

15. Is any life "unworthy of life"? Why or why not?

16. Why is it wrong to judge someone by something he or she cannot change?

17. In what ways is cooperation better than competition?

18. What are the differences and similarities between the concepts of disablism (handicapism) and racism and sexism?

19. Why are all children *normal* and all children *special*?

20. How do labels become stereotypes? What other negative effects do labels have?

21. Should *all* children with disabilities be *included* into regular classrooms?

22. What is meant by the statement, "People are different in *degree* rather than *kind*"?

23. How do labels affect self-image?

24. In your own words, how are handicaps different from disabilities?

25. Why do many people with physical disabilities view telethons and similar fund-raising methods as demeaning?

26. Why do fiction writers often give their villains a disability?

27. What is the difference between "laughing at" people and "laughing with" them?

28. How did early Greek and Roman attitudes toward their citizens with disabilities differ from those of Nazi Germany? How were they similar?

29. Does any government ever have the right to sterilize its citizens against their wills? Why or why not?

30. Why is "inclusion" important for students both with and without disabilities?

31. How did the Nazi "euthanasia" program serve as the prototype for the "final solution" of the Holocaust?

32. Although mutilating exposed slave children to make them objects of charity and pity for begging purposes was a great abuse in early Greek and Roman times, some philosophers justified it as "better than letting them die." What is your response to this position?

33. Why is living in a "total institution" an unnatural way to exist?

34. During the time of early humans why was every disability a handicap?

35. Why is integration preferable to segregation?

36. What are the different effects of being born with a disability and acquiring one later in life?

37. What is the difference between "prejudice" and "dislike"?

38. How are handicaps defined by community and culture? Give examples.

39. Why do you think many people with disabilities describe themselves as "ordinary" and wonder why others do not see them in the same way?

40. How does a disability become an "all-defining" characteristic?

41. In what ways was living in an institution for persons with mental retardation similar to living in a Nazi concentration camp? In what ways was it different?

42. How do our paradigms shape our attitudes?

43. How do cartoon characters like Porky Pig, Tweetybird, Elmer Fudd and Sylvester endorse a youngster's right to laugh at a real person's speech impairment?

44. How can you become handicapped without changing your characteristics, only your environment?

45. Why is "segregation" unfair and "inclusion" a right?

46. How does culture determine handicap?

47. What is a "stigma"? How does it affect how we think about someone?

48. What is the origin of the word "handicap"? How did it develop into its current meaning?

49. What are the differences between "equity" and "equality"?

50. What causes peer cruelty? Why do we tend to laugh at something or someone who is different? Is it right to do so?

51. How can a disability obstruct people's views of each other?

52. In what ways were people with disabilities once treated as animals?

53. What does it mean to have mental retardation?

54. What three major things would you have to do differently if you became blind? What three major things would you still do the same way?

55. What three major things would you have to do differently if you became deaf? What three major things would you still do the same way?

56. What three major things would you have to do differently if you acquired paraplegia? What three things would you still do the same way?

57. What are some of the major consequences of having a disability that is "progressive"? How is it different from having a disability that is not "progressive"?

58. What are some of the major consequences of having a disability that is "episodic" like a seizure disorder? In what areas of life does it have no effects?

59. Why do you think many people with disabilities describe themselves as "ordinary" and wonder why others do not see them in the same way?

60. Why is it wrong to base judgments of others on appearances?

61. How might you respond to the argument that "residential institutions evolved probably less to serve persons with disabilities than to protect non-disabled persons from having to associate with them"?

62. How similar are the current Chinese program of allowing orphans with "so-called" disabilities to starve to death and the Nazi "euthanasia" program?

63. What is wrong about believing that individuals who teach special education or work with persons with disabilities do so with "patience" out of a martyr-like dedication?

64. How can a segregated placement affect a student's feelings of self-worth?

65. How are the attitudes of an adult greatly influenced by socialization experiences he or she encountered during childhood years?

66. What is the meaning of the adage, "Beauty is in the eye of the beholder"?

67. What is a "stigma spread"?

68. How important are first impressions?

69. How are segregated special education classes restrictive?

70. What is a "self-fulfilling prophecy," and how does it affect one's self-image?

71. How does the "medical" paradigm of disability differ from the "civil rights" paradigm?

72. What are the major barriers persons with disabilities face? How can they be overcome?

73. How does the "medical model" of disability affect the perceptions of non-disabled people?

74. Is there anything humorous about disability?

75. What does the term "pride" really mean as it relates to one's self-esteem and one's people?

76. Discuss the differences between prejudice and discrimination, especially as they relate to persons with disabilities.

77. What are the implications of calling someone a "vegetable"?

78. What are the implications of viewing disability as an "affliction"?

79. What do the concepts of "monster" and "freak" imply?

80. What are the implications for persons with disabilities regarding beliefs like "social Darwinism," "eugenics" and "racial hygiene"?

81. How does religion influence perceptions of disability and disabled persons?

82. How are prisons, public mental hospitals, institutions, and public schools alike? How are they different?

83. What is wrong with the statement, "Persons with disabilities lead very different lives from the rest of society"?

84. Discuss the implications of having a "congenital" disability rather than an "adventitious" disability?

85. Why is integration both "a matter of right" and "a matter of rights"?

86. What is meant by the statement, "Maybe we should see persons with disabilities as *differently*-abled rather than as *"dis*-abled"?

87. Why is important to treat all persons as individuals?

88. Why is it wrong and unfair to judge a disability as a form of punishment?

89. How does viewing disability through the medical model affect charities?

90. How does the medical model affect the use and implementation of adaptive technology?

Interactive Puppets, Dolls, and Games

According to Matiella (1991), "Dolls and puppets provide a way for children to act out roles and get into others shoes. They fit well into a range of activities, and commercial dolls are beginning to reflect more diversity" (p. 41). (See Appendix I, Resources: Puppets, Dolls, and Games for sources.)

Puppets and Dolls

One of the oldest and perhaps best known puppet program is *The Kids on the Block*, which originated as a troupe of educational puppets designed to teach children about disabilities and differences. Currently 37 different programs address various disabilities, educational and medical differences like diabetes, and social concerns like aging, divorce, teen pregnancy, child and substance abuse, and cultural diversity. Each topic is thoroughly researched and field tested before becoming available to school districts, community service organizations, hospitals and special service groups. *The Kids on the Block* curriculum includes puppets, props, scripts, audio cassettes, follow-up materials like stickers and posters, resource suggestions, a training guide, and ongoing technical support and counsel from the national company. The many programs available address autism, blindness, cerebral palsy, deafness, mental retardation, spina bifida, emotionally disturbance, the gifted and talented, learning disabilities, AIDS, arthritis, epilepsy, leukemia, and being the sibling of a child with a disability. The puppets portray students with disabilities in real-life situations, and the vignettes encourage students to express their feelings toward individuals with disabilities and ask questions about specific disabilities.

Another effective program for teaching disability awareness is *Adaptive Equipment for Dolls with Disabilities,* which includes a teacher's guide, doll equipment including a wheelchair, a protective helmet, a guide dog harness and cane, two leg braces, two forearm crutches, a walker with an accessory bag, two hearing aids and two pairs of eyeglasses. Another program, *Block Play People with Differing Abilities* includes a set of four dolls with differing abilities, one wheelchair user, one person with blindness, an individual with forearm crutches, and one with leg braces. Yet another, *People of Every Stripe*, comes with a set of 20-inch dolls, a miniature wheelchair, a leg brace made of heavy metal and Velcro, a youngster with Down syndrome, a child with a prosthesis, a child with crutches, and several dolls with visual impairments and amputations.

Gaming

According to Matiella (1991), "Games provide a high-interest vehicle to teach about diversity" (p. 42). Games can offer students the chance to practice, reinforce, or apply a concept, and they provide a welcome break from routine class activities. They also serve as excellent motivators and learning tools. An example of a published game is EMPATHY, where students role-play in the fantasy-styled land of Multicappia. The class is divided into four teams and is commissioned by the Elders of Empathopia to travel through Multicappia while under the influence of certain induced impairments. To win they must gain empathy points by learning to understand the problems involved in having various types of disabilities by experiencing such disabilities as blindness, deaf-muteness, and physical impairments through simulations. Varied activities are provided throughout the simulation to amplify the students' experiences.

Demystifying Aids, Appliances and Adaptive Technology

Many included students require support devices, aids, materials, and appliances to function successfully in the regular classroom. These materials include talking books, hearing aids, speech synthesizers, wheelchairs, Braille and adaptive technology devices. Since regular students need to feel comfortable with these aids and devices, a program to prepare regular students for their entry should be an integral part of the inclusion process (Aiello, 1979; Bookbinder, 1978).

When meeting any person with a physical impairment, children with little or no exposure to disabilities, are often fascinated by all the "gear," including aids, appliances, prosthetics and adaptive technology. Because their fascination focuses on the equipment, they sometimes seem unaware of the person using it. In other words, people often concentrate more on the wheelchair than its user. A large aspect of the stigma of disability lies in the mystification of its accompanying equipment—like wheelchairs, crutches, braces, and walkers—to the extent that people may be afraid to touch these objects, as if they might "catch" the disability. Unfortunately, charity drives reinforce these attitudes. In their quest to make their disability the most debilitating so the public will donate, they often use aids and appliances in a shocking way in their advertising. For example, to dissuade teenagers from drinking and driving, a Blue Cross and Blue Shield of Pennsylvania ad featured an empty wheelchair with the caption, "Is this the set of wheels you've been saving for?" Another ad shows a wheelchair with the caption, "Thousands of youngsters are sentenced to the chair each year." The message is plain to see, Living your life in a wheelchair is the worst thing in the world. An ad for the Muscular Dystrophy Association shows a glass-box like terrarium with a child's leg brace in it. The top has a slit like a bank to collect money. A sign on the box reads, "Help Jerry's Kids bury the brace." If such campaigns must convey their points in a negative way, they should focus on what causes the handicap and disability, not what helps the individual overcome it. Such ads make it imperative that teachers, introducing a unit on physical disabilities or sensory impairments, show protheses and wheelchairs as positive objects that help people deal with environmental barriers and handicaps.

Recently, various juvenile books have been written that familiarize children with different kinds of equipment (see Appendix I—Resources, Juvenile Books on Disability). In addition, various magazines, targeted for persons with disabilities, that carry ads and information on adaptive equipment (see Appendix I—Resources, Magazines Relating to Persons with Disabilities). Teachers may have their students read them to learn about adaptive equipment.

Such equipment may be shown in a light-hearted context (for example, electric wheelchairs go quite fast, much faster than a person on foot, and can be pictured in races or tag games) to counteract the link between this equipment and injury, death, disease, and vulnerability. Having "practiced" with the equipment, children are less likely to find it strange or frightening. When something is overwhelming, children sometimes react with fear or aggression—in order to make themselves feel more secure. Relieved of their resistance or fear, they can learn to take the paraphernalia for granted and recognize the persons using it. Teachers can introduce these devices in interesting ways that help youngsters develop an appreciation for their purpose, to liberate persons with disabilities.

Inventors, engineers, designers, therapists and imaginative lay people have devised a wide range of ingenious aids to help disabled people in all phases of their lives—for example, at home, traveling, at work, at recreation. From a simple homemade reacher that retrieves dropped articles, to a sophisticated breath-controlled switch that operates a typewriter, these devices help persons with disabilities live more independently. Aids can simplify eating, grooming, dressing—in fact, almost all the basic tasks of daily living. A few specialized gadgets can make household chores like cleaning, cooking and laundering easier. Among the more sophisticated adaptive apparatuses are electronic systems, telephones, reading and writing contrivances and alternative and augmentative communication devices. Automobile adaptations, special controls, and transfer aids make driving possible. Wheelchairs, walkers, hoists, lifts and ramps increase outdoor and indoor mobility.

The literally thousands of these devices and aids range from expensive equipment obtainable only from specialists to simple gadgets illustrated in a variety of mail order catalogs and magazines catering to the need of persons with physical disabilities. The large number and wide variety of these products make it impossible to mention every one. For example, just in the area of automobile transportation, automated controls help a physically disabled person drive his or her own car. These include parking brake extensions, left-foot accelerators, built-up brake and gas pedals, left-hand shift levers and light-weight folding van ramps.

Similarly, a wide assortment of kitchen and cooking aids include a safety cutting fork with the cutting edge along one side designed specifically for either the right or left hand. For those with limited arm range, an angle handled utensil of stainless steel with a plastic handle is available. Also obtainable are slip-on or large handled utensils. An inner-lip or suction cup dinner plate keeps food from sliding. Microwave ovens come with tactile touchpads, tactile dials, and Braille kits for the controls. A talking bread and dough maker comes with an optional voice feature that can be activated to guide users through all phases of the baking process.

There are also non-slip special jar openers, capscrew openers, plastic sack openers, milk carton holders, tactile measuring spoons, tab grabbers. Special dinnerware includes sectioned plates with raised sides to push a fork or spoon against. An arthritis mug features two handles with thumb rests. A variety of aids for dressing and other daily living needs includes an elongated no-stoop shoehorn, elastic shoe laces that permit shoes to be slipped on or off without tying or untying, zipper pull rings or a long reach zipper pulls with 18-inch plastic cords and metal hooks and rings. A one-handed dental flosser with features floss storage and tension control in one handle.

For the wheelchair user, an aluminum E-Z reach can be extremely helpful. Weighing only 9 ounces, it combines a powerful grip with delicate sensitivity. It handles objects up to two pounds, yet can pick up a dime or hold a paper cup without crushing it. Also, a number of bathroom and shower aids includes a shower or tub chair of heavy duty nickel and chrome steel construction, with a perforated molded polypropylene seat and back. A bathtub seat has been designed for someone with a more severe condition. It is adjustable with easy push buttons to fit any standard tub. For those who can stand and shower, bathtub guard rails or wall-mounted grab bars are made from heavy-walled anodized aluminum.

Thus, any disability awareness program should introduce students to aids, appliances and assistive technology, and they should have plenty of time to examine and try out the devices that persons with disabilities use. In their own classrooms they can learn to write in Braille and to use finger spelling and some sign language. They learn to operate and take care of hearing aids. They use wheelchairs, walkers, and crutches.

They can examine braces, artificial legs and other prostheses. Schools may borrow the aids and appliances from local agencies, or special schools in the area. (see Appendix I, Resources for *Disability Organizations and Self-Help Groups*). Students may even design adaptive equipment as science projects.

Leaders of the disability civil rights movement believe that technology will be the equalizer of the twenty-first century. Technology already enhances our independence and productivity, whether or not we have disabilities. When a person with a disability uses a technology application, it is commonly referred to as "assistive technology." Assistive technology may be high or low tech; it may be an item available at a local department store, like a large-key telephone, or a specially designed product, like an electric wheelchair equipped with a sip-and-puff control.

In the next decade, this technological "liberation" is likely to free more and more of our citizens with disabilities. Combined with civil rights, improved access and education, assistive technology can help us transcend the myths and prejudices that have limited persons with disabilities for so many years and usher in a new age of inclusion for those so labeled.

Teachers may want to take their students on a class trip to one of the Rehabilitation Technology Services and Resource Centers in their state (see Appendix One, Resources for a list of these state assistive technology centers). The services a technology center provides include on-site equipment modification, design and fabrication; as well as general consultation and assessments for consumers, parents and rehabilitation professionals. Assistive technology devices are available for examinations and assessments, and the centers usually offer hands-on tours, equipment loans and educational seminars. Information and referral about the latest trends in assistive technology, including product literature and computerized databases, are also available. Rehabilitation technologists provide services related to the following assistive technology: adapted toys, mobility, seating and positioning systems, augmentative communication, computer access and environmental controls. If such a class trip is not possible, a teacher may arrange for a speaker from the center to address the class and bring along devices for demonstration.

Teachers can also assign students to review catalogs from the companies manufacturing the equipment. Lessons in subjects like science and art can be easily developed from such material. In addition, speakers from the State Commission for the Blind may come to classes and demonstrate equipment like specialized canes, Braille alphabet cards, guide dogs, slates, styluses, Braille paper and special glasses that simulate different kinds of visual impairments. If possible, the class should borrow the equipment so that after the presentation, the children can practice using it and become familiar and comfortable with it.

Wherever possible, it would be best for students with the disabilities using adaptive equipment to introduce and explain the aids and devices they use themselves. They can show their classmates the devices and allow them to touch and experiment with the equipment. For example, a student with a hearing impairment could explain the parts and maintenance of the hearing aid, and then invite other students to use a hearing aid briefly. If the student with the disability feels uncomfortable explaining the aids he or she uses, a physical therapist, teacher, guidance counselor, or parent might do so. Aiello (1979) proposed that adaptive devices be obtained from a variety of sources and placed in a central location within the room. Students could then examine and experiment with the devices at different times during the school day.

Such alternative communication systems, such as Braille, sign language and finger spelling can be introduced to students in a variety of ways that simultaneously promote academic skills. Teachers can teach students the manual alphabet, then have them practice their spelling words by spelling them manually. Teachers can include hand signs for numbers as part of a math assignment. For example, rather than writing the numbers of a division computation on the board, the teacher could present the problem with numerical hand signs. Teachers could introduce the students to basic signs and then use them to give directions and assignments. Students who have learned Braille might be assigned the task of reading Braille books, and writing their names or compositions in Braille.

Field Trips

Class trips help make student learning more enjoyable, meaningful and relevant. They provide first-hand experiences and teachers often use them as a culminating activity for a unit or subject. Some possible field trips complementing a unit on disabilities follows:

- a rehabilitation technology center,

- a state library for blind and disabled persons,

- a school where children with disabilities are included,

- a state institution,

- a group home,

- a private school for children with a specific disability (for example autism),

- a workday with a supported employment program,

- an occupational training center (sheltered workshop),

- the State Commission for the Blind

- a day training center for severely or multiply disabled children, and

- a preschool handicapped program.

Conclusion to this Chapter

The experiential (active participation) techniques presented here in this chapter included social gaming (especially role-playing, behavior rehearsing and simulation activities always followed by discussion); value confrontation and learning about inference; interaction with persons with disabilities (especially cooperative learning with disabled peers and exposure to guest speakers with disabilities). It also provided basic information on disabilities (including the roles of its paradigms, history, culture, the media and language) by exposure to books, articles, and a wide variety of audio-visual media (including films, slides, audio and videotapes, and compact disks),as well as exposure to adaptive devices, aids and appliances (assistive technology). All of these activities and efforts have proven themselves effective for changing attitudes. The more varied the experiences provided, the likelier the attitude change.

Some Final Thoughts About this Book

This is a book for all teachers. Attitudes toward persons with disabilities affect everyone. Nearly two decades ago, after compiling exhaustive research on "Attitudes Toward Disabled Persons," Schroedel concluded that "modifying attitudes toward and among Americans who are disabled is an important business. The thoughts and feelings which compose attitudes influence the behaviors of both those who perceive and are perceived" (p. 15). One of the great lessons of the Holocaust is that no individual's rights are secure until everyone's rights are secure. As persons with disabilities enter the "Era of Inclusion" concepts like "the medical model" and "segregation" need to be fully examined as well as the sources of our paradigms, like the media and our culture.

As stated in Chapter One, "Schools have a responsibility for encouraging diversity and tolerance, eliminating discrimination, increasing among youngsters an understanding of those perceived to be different, and respecting and protecting the rights of all diverse populations within our pluralistic society. Each individual child is the responsibility of the school and has a right to attend without having to feel inferior." As Rogers (1994) stated, "One of the universal fears of childhood is the fear of not having value in the eyes of the people whom we admire so much" (p. 35).

Educators need to recognize their responsibility to confront bigotry in all its *ism* forms. As stated in Chapter One, "schools can reduce harmful attitudes by instilling helpful ones, and make disability a topic of investigation and discussion in the same way that some schools explore the issues of sexism and racism" (Biklen, Ford & Ferguson, 1989, p. 257). Teaching teachers how to present students with various experiential techniques and information about disabilities will positively affect these students' attitudes toward persons who have them. As Bookbinder (1979) stated,

> When ordinary children understand the causes, visible effects, and
> consequences of disabilities, they will try to treat disabled children as
> they would anyone else (p. 3).

Attitudes can be changed by developing the cognitive sophistication achieved through planned intervention based on an understanding
of important established learning principles. Schools have the responsibility both to prepare youngsters with disabilities to enter the mainstream of school and society and to prepare the schools and society to
accept youngsters with disabilities without handicapping them through
prejudicial attitudes.

The central beliefs regarding persons with disabilities that inspire
and serve as a basis for this book are that "all people are valuable,"
"people are people with wide variations," and "negative attitudes can be
changed."

Blatt (1987) stressed that the conquest of mental retardation—that
is, its elimination—will not be achieved until youngsters learn to live
with each other, until segregation of all forms (especially that which
occurs in our schools) is eliminated, and until schools both believe and
teach that all human beings are precious and valuable to society (p. 6).
His insights ring true for all children who face prejudice, discrimination, stigmatization and segregation.

Resources

Curriculum Guides and Activity Books on Disability Awareness and Prejudice Reduction

Barnes, E. Berrigan, C. & Biklen, D. (1978). *What's the difference? Teaching positive attitudes toward people with disabilities.* Syracuse, NY: Human Policy Press.

Berry, J. (1987). *Every kid's guide to overcoming prejudice and discrimination.* Chicago, IL: Childrens Press.

Berry, J. (1990). *Good answers to tough questions: About physical disabilities.* Chicago, IL: Childrens Press.

Bigelow, B. et al., (eds.) (1995). *Rethinking our classrooms: Teaching for equity and justice.* Montgomery, AL: Rethinking Schools Limited.

Bliss, M. & Schwartz, A. (1979). *Exploring attitudes toward women with disabilities: A curriculum guide for employers and educators.* New York: New York City Commission on the Status of Women.

Bookbinder, S. (1978). *Mainstreaming: What every child needs to know about disabilities.* Providence, RI: Rhode Island Easter Seal Society.

Bunch, G. (1996). *Kids, disabilities and regular classrooms: An annotated bibliography of selected children's literature on disability.* Toronto, Ontario, Canada. Inclusion Press.

Byrnes, D. (1987). *Teacher they called me a _____!* New York: The Anti-Defamation League of B'nai B'rith.

Cashdollar, P. & Martin, J. (1977). *Kids come in special flavors: Understanding handicaps.* Dayton, OH: The Kids Come in Special Flavors Co.

Cleary, M. (1976). *Please know me as I am: A guide to helping children understand the child with special needs.* Sudbury, MA: The Jerry Cleary Company.

Cohen, J. (1998) *Disability etiquette: Tips on interacting with people with disabilities.* New York: Eastern Paralyzed Veterans Association.

Cohen, S., Koehler, N., & Grand, C. (1977a). *Accepting individual differences: Overview.* Niles, IL: Developmental Learning Materials.

Cohen, S., Koehler, N., & Grand, C. (1977b). *Accepting individual differences: Mental retardation and learning disabilities.* Niles, IL: Developmental Learning Materials.

Cohen, S., Koehler, N., & Grand, C. (1977c). *Accepting individual differences: Motor impairment.* Niles, IL: Developmental Learning Materials.

Cohen, S., Koehler, N., & Grand, C. (1977d). *Accepting individual differences: Visual impairment.* Niles, IL: Developmental Learning Materials.

Cohen, S., Koehler, N., & Grand, C. (1981a). *A curriculum to foster understanding of people with disabilities: Staff orientation manual.* Albany, NY: University of the State of New York and The State Education Department.

Cohen, S., Koehler, N., & Grand, C. (1981b). *A curriculum to foster understanding of people with disabilities: The handicapped in society.* Albany, NY: University of the State of New York and The State Education Department.

Cohen, S., Koehler, N., & Grand, C. (1981c). *A curriculum to foster understanding of people with disabilities: The handicapped in literature.* Albany, NY: University of the State of New York and The State Education Department.

Cohen, S., Koehler, N., & Grand, C. (1981d). *A curriculum to foster understanding of people with disabilities: Science health education perspectives on the handicapped.* Albany, NY: University of the State of New York and The State Education Department.

Cumblad, C., & Strickman, D. (1990). *Friends who care: A disability awareness program for elementary students (Teacher's guide).* Chicago, IL: National Easter Seals Society.

Cummings, M., London, K., Moore, L., Raschke, D., Schwartz, P., & Tofty, J. (1981). *Individual differences: An educator's handbook for a course of studies about people.* Madison, WI: Madison Public Schools.

Derman-Sparks, L., et al. (eds.) (1993). *Anti-bias curriculum: Tools for empowering young people.* Washington, D.C.: National Association for the Education of Young Children.

Epilepsy Foundation of America (1991). *Issues and answers: A guide for teens and young adults with epilepsy.* Landover, MD: Author.

Epilepsy Foundation of America (1992). *Issues and answers: Exploring your possibilities—A guide for teens and young adults with epilepsy.* Landover, MD: Author.

Epilepsy Foundation of America (1992). *Brothers and sisters: A guide for families of children with epilepsy.* Landover, MD: Author.

Fleming, M., et al (eds.). (1991). *Starting small: Teaching tolerance in preschool and the early grades.* Montgomery, AL: Teaching Tolerance, A Project of the Southern Poverty Law Center.

Froschl, M., Colon, L., Rubin, E., & Sprung, B. (1984). *Including all of us: An early childhood curriculum about disability.* New York: Educational Equity Concepts, Inc.

Getskow, V. & Konczal, D. (1996). *Kids with special needs: Information and activities to promote awareness and understanding.* Santa Barbara, CA: The Learning Works, Inc.

Hague, P. & Engstrom, C. (1984). *Responding to disability: A question of attitude.* St. Paul MN: Minnesota State Council for the Handicapped.

Hannibal, M. (1996). *Disability awareness manual: A hands-on program for exploring individual abilities and differences.* Carson, CA: Lakeshore Learning Materials.

Jenness, A. (1978). *Some ways the same, some ways different.* Weston, MA: Burt Harrison and Company.

Jones, M. & Stevens, M. (1979). *People just like you: About handicaps and handicapped people (An activity guide).* Washington, DC: The President's Committee on Employment of the Handicapped.

Kamien, E., Jenness, A., Porter, S. and Shortreed, A. (1978a). *What if you couldn't. . . ?: An elementary school program about handicaps developed by the Museum of Boston with WGBH Boston. Teacher's guide: Opening unit.* Weston, MA: Burt Harrison and Company.

Kamien, E., Jenness, A., Porter, S. and Shortreed, A. (1978b). *What if you couldn't. . . ?: An elementary school program about handicaps developed by the Museum of Boston with WGBH Boston. Teacher's guide: Mental retardation unit.* Weston, MA: Burt Harrison and Company.

Kamien, E., Jenness, A., Porter, S. and Shortreed, A. (1978c). *What if you couldn't. . . ?: An elementary school program about handicaps developed by the Museum of Boston with WGBH Boston. Teacher's guide: Orthopedic handicaps unit.* Weston, MA: Burt Harrison and Company.

Kamien, E., Jenness, A., Porter, S. and Shortreed, A. (1978d). *What if you couldn't. . . ?: An elementary school program about handicaps developed by the Museum of Boston with WGBH Boston. Teacher's guide: Hearing impairment unit.* Weston, MA: Burt Harrison and Company.

Kamien, E., Jenness, A., Porter, S. and Shortreed, A. (1978e). *What if you couldn't. . . ?: An elementary school program about handicaps developed by the Museum of Boston with WGBH Boston. Teacher's guide: Emotional problems unit.* Weston, MA: Burt Harrison and Company.

Kamien, E., Jenness, A., Porter, S. and Shortreed, A. (1978f). *What if you couldn't. . . ?: An elementary school program about handicaps developed by the Museum of Boston with WGBH Boston. Teacher's guide: Visual impairment unit.* Weston, MA: Burt Harrison and Company.

Kamien, E., Jenness, A., Porter, S. and Shortreed, A. (1978g). *What if you couldn't. . . ?: An elementary school program about handicaps developed by the Museum of Boston with WGBH Boston. Teacher's guide: Learning disabilities unit.* Weston, MA: Burt Harrison and Company.

Konczal, D. & Pesetski, P. (1983), *We all come in different packages: Activities to increase handicap awareness.* Santa Barbara, CA: The Learning Works, Inc.

Matiella, A. (1991). *Positively different: Creating a bias-free environment for young children.* Santa Cruz, CA: ETR Associates.

Mortenson, R. (1980). *Prejudice project.* New York: Anti-Defamation League and The University of Nebraska at Omaha, College of Education Curriculum Development Project.

Rehabilitation Services of Shriners Hospital for Children (1994). *Peer awareness and community education: An educational program to increase awareness and acceptance of people with different abilities.* Philadelphia, PA: Author.

Schniedewind, N., & Davidson, E. (1998). *Open minds to equality: A sourcebook of learning activities to affirm diversity and promote equity* (2nd ed.). Boston, MA: Allyn and Bacon.

Schnitzler, C. & Rappaport, K. (1983). *More alike than different: An activities book for handicap awareness.* Trenton, NJ: New Jersey Department of Education.

Shaver, J. & Curtis, C. (1981). *Handicapism and equal opportunity: Teaching about the disabled in social studies.* Reston, VA: Foundation for Exceptional Children.

Shields, L., Christmas, D., Deitchman, L., Langford, T., Newingham, D., O'Daniel, L., Yeker, C., and Goodridge, J. (1981). *Project aware: A project to develop awareness of and empathy toward differences and handicaps.* Evansville, IN: Evansville-Vanderburgh School Corporation.

Stevens, M. & Masters, S. (1987). *Being aware shows you care: School wide disability awareness program.* Portland, OR: Ednick Communications, Inc.

Thomson, B. (1993). *Words can hurt you: Beginning a program of anti-bias education.* Menlo Park, CA: Addison-Wesley Publishing Company.

Trappe, T. (n.d.). *After the kids: A follow-up for teachers.* Trenton, NJ: New Jersey Department of Human Services, Division of Developmental Disabilities.

Understanding Handicaps, Inc. (1994 ed.) *Understanding handicaps: A disability awareness curriculum.* Newtonville, MA: Author.

Ward, M., Arkell, R., Dahl, H., & Wise, J. (1979). *Everybody counts: A workshop manual to increase awareness of handicapped people.* Reston, VA: The Council for Exceptional Children.

White, B. (1979). *Understanding people with disabilities.* Lincoln, NE: Lincoln Public Schools.

Curriculum Kits on Disability
Awareness and Prejudice Reduction

AHEAD (Association for Higher Education and Disability) *In-service Education Kit.* Kit contains audio tape and materials for an Auditory Processing Test; an In-service Training Video; Information on Attitudinal Barriers: Suggestions for Helping Individuals with Visual Impairments, Auditory Impairments, Mobility Impairments and Learning Disabilities; a Mobility Quiz, An Unfair Spelling Test, a Celebrity Quiz and various simulation materials. Available from AHEAD, PO Box 21192, Columbus, OH. 43221.

Differing Abilities Book Set. Set contains six hardcover books containing stories about children with disabilities. Available from Lakeshore Learning Materials, 2695 East Dominguez St. Carson, CA. 90749. 1(800)421-5354.

Disability Awareness Kit. Kit contains over 30 pieces including, a 26 page manual full of lessons for pre-K through second grade that deals with various disabilities and includes colorful posters, flannel figures of children with disabilities, a book *(Just Because You're Different)*, Braille signs, a sign language poster, and assorted materials that help youngsters to understand vision impairment, hearing loss and muscular impairments. Available from Lakeshore Learning Materials, 2695 East Dominguez St. Carson, CA. 90749. 1(800)421-5354.

Friends Who Care: An Elementary Disability Awareness Program. Kit contains posters, worksheets, simulations, "Helpful Hints When Meeting Friends With Disabilities" handouts, and a 45-minute video. Available from National Easter Seal Society, 70 East Lake Street, Chicago, IL. 60601.

Hello Everybody: The Most Widely Used Mainstreaming Program in America. This program is designed to aid the mainstreaming and inclusion process by preparing students to accept others with disabilities through effective positive role models. The program consists of a Teacher's Guide and six videos or filmstrips:

> *An Introduction to Hearing and Speech Impairments*
> *An Introduction to Visual Impairment*
> *An Introduction to Orthopedic Handicaps*
> *An Introduction to Developmental Disabilities*
> *An Introduction to Learning Disabilities*
> *An Introduction to Behavior Disorders*

Available from James Stanfield Company, Inc. Drawer 66, PO Box 41058, Santa Barbara, CA: 93140. 1(800)421-6534.

Just Like Me and You: A Disability Awareness Curriculum. This curriculum was developed for Third, Fourth and Fifth Grade Students and addresses such questions as "What is a disability?", "How do I talk to someone with a disability?", and "What kinds of things can people with disabilities do?" The nine lesson plans, three per grade level, are designed to increase awareness about persons with disabilities. In addition to the nine lesson plans, the curriculum package includes an open caption video, two videotapes and six student worksheets. Available from Paraquad, Inc., 311 North Lindburg, St. Louis, MO: (314)567 1588.

Self-Advocacy for Persons with Developmental Disabilities (n.d.). This program, which illustrates the philosophy and practices of self advocacy and the *People First Movement*, consists of a Teacher's Guide and five videos:

> *Speaking for Ourselves: Self-Advocacy in Action*
> *Starting a Self-Advocacy Group*
> *The Role of the Advisor in Self-Advocacy*
> *Officer Training*
> *Organizing a Convention*

Available from James Stanfield Company, Inc. Drawer 66, PO Box 41058, Santa Barbara, CA: 93140.

Small Differences: A Children's Disability Awareness Production. (1997). (20 minutes). This video was produced mostly by children to help other children and adults feel comfortable around people with disabilities, and comes with a four page resource guide. Available from Program Development Associates, Suite B, Cicero, NY: 13039. #SD779.

Shaking Off Stereotypes (1997). (16 minutes). This video, about a woman wheelchair user who discovers her own self-worth despite the stereotypes she encounters on a daily basis, includes a Facilitator's Guide, participatory exercises, action plans, overhead masters, ten participant packages (each with a 24 page workbook) certificates of completion, buttons, posters and name tags. Available from Program Development Associates, Suite B, Cicero, NY: 13039. #SOS619.

Audio Visual Resources for Teaching Disability Awareness

Videocassettes

Able to Laugh (n.d.). Michael Dugan. (27 minutes). The world of disability as interpreted by six comedians who have them. ISBN 1-57295-105-2. Available from Fanlight Productions, 47 Halifax Street, Boston, MA 02130. Cat. # BQ-105.

A Day at a Time (1992). By William Garcia and Charles Schultz. (58 minutes). This video shows a portrait of a family with twin daughters who have cerebral palsy. Available from Filmakers Library, 124 East 40 St., New York, NY.

A Full Stride: Overcoming the Challenges of Amputation (n.d.). (24 minutes). Focusing on three very different people, this program shows the many sides of what is often a generic label: disabled or amputee. Available from Films for the Humanities and Sciences, Princeton, NJ 8543. #ALT6059.

And Then Came John. (1988). Produced by Scott Andrews and Stephen Olson. (36 minutes). This video, through the life of one individual with Down Syndrome, challenges stereotypes and shows how the attitudes of society can encourage or destroy a person with a disability. Available from Filmakers Library, 124 East 40 St., New York, NY.

Children Learn Differently (n.d.). (30 minutes). This video illustrates the characteristics of youngsters with learning disabilities. Available from Academic Therapy Publications, Novato, CA. 94949-6191. 1(800)422-7249.

Close Encounters of the Disabling Kind (1997). (22 minutes). This close-captioned video educates, in a light-hearted way, individuals in disability-related etiquette, and comes with printed resources. Available from Program Development Associates, Suite B, Cicero, NY: 13039. #CEDK700.

Dancing From the Inside Out (n.d.). By Thais Mazur and Sarah Shockley. (28 minutes.) This video examines the lives and work of three members of the acclaimed AXIS Dance Troupe which includes both disabled and non-disabled dancers. ISBN 1-57295-152-4. Available from Fanlight Productions, 47 Halifax Street, Boston, MA 02130. Cat.# BQ-152.

Deaf Like Me (n.d.). (24 minutes). This video explores the physical, emotional and communication difficulties of persons with deafness. Available from Clearvue, 6465 North Avondale Avenue, Chicago, IL: 60631-1996.

Disability and Motherhood (n.d). (25 minutes). This video examines the experiences of three mothers with disabilities and public attitudes toward them. Available from Films for the Humanities and Sciences. PO Box 2053, Princeton, NJ 08543. #ACN5407.

Dwarfism: Born to Be Small (n.d.). (51 minutes). This video follows four families impacted by achondroplasia, a form of dwarfism. Available from Films for the Humanities and Sciences, PO Box 2053, Princeton, NJ. #BGH7094

Educating Peter (1992). (30 minutes). This Academy Award Winning documentary on inclusion shows how a child with Down Syndrome was successfully included in a regular third grade class. Available with accompanying Discussion Guide from Insight Media, 2162 Broadway, New York, NY 10024. #TP406.

Everybody's Different (n.d.). (14 minutes). This video (with song lyrics) stresses that "Everybody's different, so one is quite the same," and the specialness of individual differences. It helps children (grades pre-k to 2) understand that everyone is different in some way but differentness is both good and interesting. Package comes with cassette, 7 worksheets, an audiocassette, and a teacher's guide. Available from Sunburst Communications, 39 Washington Ave. PO Box 40, Pleasantville, NY, 10570, # 2481-SE.

Given the Opportunity: A Guide to Interaction in the Workplace (Disability Awareness). (n.d.). (24 minutes). This video examines the situations of persons with physical disabilities and dispels common misconceptions. Viewers learn ways to approach and communicate with persons with disabilities and learn that successful interaction benefits everyone. Available from Guidance Associates, PO Box 1000, Mount Kisco, NY, #60613-439.

How Difficult Can This Be? (FAT City workshop) (1990). (70 minutes). Greater Washington Educational Telecommunications Association. This video allows the viewer to experience life in the way a student with a learning disability does. FAT stands for frustration, anxiety, and tension. Available with accompanying 13 page Discussion Guide from PBS VIDEO 1320 Braddock Place, Alexandria, VA 22314.

Kids in Wheelchairs (n.d.). (12 minutes). This video portrays children in wheelchairs in full inclusion settings, playgrounds, and classrooms. Children who use wheelchairs explain why they use the wheelchair and how the chair works. Most important, non-disabled children ask questions and address some of the feelings and fears they have about their peers who use wheelchairs. Available from Learner Managed Designs, Inc. P.O. Box 747, Lawrence, KS 66044 and from Program Development Associates, Suite B, Cicero, NY: 13039. #KIW710.

Little People (1985). Produced by Jill Kravitz and Michael Ott. (58 minutes). This video is a documentary on having dwarfism in an average-sized world. New York: Available from Filmakers Library, 124 East 4th St. New York, NY 10016

Living with Facial Disfigurement (n.d.). (25 minutes). This video is a documentary on the problems persons with disfigurements encounter when dealing with the public. Available from Films for the Humanities and Sciences, PO Box 2053, Princeton, NJ 08543. #ACN5404.

Look Who's Laughing (n.d.). (56 minutes). This video is a documentary about the lives, experiences, and humor of six working comedians who have various disabilities. Available from Program Development Associates, 7588 Fitzpatrick Drive. Liverpool, NY 13088. #LWL101.

Media Portrayals of People With Disabilities. (1997). (30 minutes). This video examines how the news media and the entertainment industry perpetuate negative stereotypes of persons with disabilities. Available from Program Development Associates, Suite B, Cicero, NY: 13039. #RLMP649.

Mistreating the Mentally Ill (n.d.) (56 minutes). This video is a documentary that examines how the differing cultures of the U.S., Japan, India, and Egypt each perceives mental illness and how each treats the "less accepted." Available from Films for the Humanities and Sciences, PO Box 2053, Princeton, NJ 08543. #AFH 5069.

People in Motion: A Three-Part Innovation Mini-Series. (Part 1) (1995):

> *Ways to Move* (50 Minutes). This video contains three stories which explore the medical model and the independence/ handicapism model.

> *Ready to Live* (53 Minutes). This video looks at ways adaptive technologies help persons with disabilities live independently.

> *Redesigning the Human Machine* (52 Minutes). This video explores the uses of technological advances, including virtual reality, robotics, and cochlear implants.

> Available with accompanying Viewer's Guide from New York: WNET Thirteen, Educational Resources Center, 356 West 58th St. New York, NY 10019.

People In Motion: A Three-Part Innovation Mini-Series. (Part 2) (1996):

> *A New Sense of Place* (56 Minutes). This video profiles individuals who have found a way to "ramp" their way into the world—in front of orchestras, in the glare of news cameras, on the walls of galleries, and in the workplace.

> *Breaking the Silence Barrier,* (56 minutes). This video reports on creative technologies that are being used to help people with autism, traumatic brain injuries, and learning and speech difficulties.

> *Without Barriers or Borders* (56 minutes).This video explores the burgeoning global movement for independent living and how people with disabilities are reshaping the world in which they live.

> Available with accompanying Viewer's Guide from New York: WNET Thirteen, Educational Resources Center, 356 West 58th St. New York, NY 10019.

Regular Lives (1989) (30 minutes). A documentary that shows the lives of children and adults with disabilities in various activities with non-disabled people. Available with Companion/Utilization Guide from Program Development Associates 7855 Fitzpatrick Drive, Liverpool, NY 13088. #RL105 and from Program Development Associates, Suite B, Cicero, NY: 13039. #RL105.

Responding to the Handicapped (n.d.). (26 minutes). Persons with disabilities have to deal not only with their disabilities, but also with the people who respond to them with fear, embarrassment or condescension. This video does not attempt to present one correct way to interact with individuals with disabilities; instead, it focuses on awareness that can lead the viewer to respond more easily with persons with impairments. Available from Films for the Humanities and Sciences, Princeton, NJ 8543. #ALT2361.

Rolling Along: Children in Wheelchairs at School (n.d.). (40 minutes). This video, which presents information on assisting children in wheelchairs throughout the day in educational settings, addresses proper positioning of the youngster in the chair, transferring techniques, and most important, a discussion of accessibility and psychosocial issues. It comes with a manual and test packet. Available from Learner Managed Designs, Inc. P.O. Box 747, Lawrence, KS 66044. #1000.

The Ten Commandments of Communicating with People with Disabilities (n.d.). (26 minutes). Produced by Irene Ward and Associates. This video uses light-hearted vignettes to teach individuals how to communicate respectfully with persons with all types of disabilities. Available with 11 pages of additional resource material from Program Development Associates, 7855 Fitzpatrick Drive, Liverpool, NY 13088. #TC103.

Understanding Hearing Loss (n.d.). (17 minutes). This video includes realistic simulations of what speech sounds like with different kinds of hearing loss. Available from Films for the Humanities and Sciences, PO Box 2053, Princeton, NJ 08543. #ACR4362.

Unfinished Business: The Diversity of Disabilities (n.d.). (32 minutes). This video, with the help of old film clips and other media portrayals, gives a review of how people with disabilities are currently as well as historically treated. The video comes with a 38 page camera resource kit. Available from Program Development Associates, 7855 Fitzpatrick Drive, Liverpool, NY 13088. #UB617.

A Video Guide to Disability Awareness (n.d.). (25 minutes). This video presents an orientation to the human side of the Americans with Disabilities Act. Includes Available with Employer's Manual and Study Guides and Open captioning from Fanlight Productions, 47 Halifax Street, Boston, MA 02130. #BQ-106 or Guidance Associates, PO Box 1000, Mount Kisco, NY 10549 (914)666-4100 or 1(800)431-1242.

What Do You Do When You See a Blind Person? (n.d.). (20 minutes). This video presents, in a humorous way, what seeing individuals need to know in order to interact comfortably with individuals with blindness. It dispels stereotypes. Phoenix Films, New York, NY.

Without Pity: A Film about Abilities (n.d.). (50 minutes). This documentary, narrated by Christopher Reeve, describes the efforts of persons with disabilities to live full productive lives with a determination to be independent and self-sufficient. It focuses on the lives of a young woman with cerebral palsy attempting to care for her baby, a man with cerebral palsy deinstitutionalized after 40 years, a six year old student without arms and legs, a computer expert with blindness, a professor of disability studies with polio and a man who recently became quadriplegic trying to get on with his life. The film, which won an Emmy Award, is available from Films for the Humanities and Sciences, PO Box 2053, Princeton, NJ. #BGH6981.

Withstanding Ovation (n.d.). 24 minutes. This video details the lives of two teenagers born with severe congenital limb anomalies, and how they came to lead productive and creative lives. Available from Fanlight Productions, 47 Halifax Street, Boston, MA 02130. ISBN 1-57295-107-9.

Film Strips

The Disabled: No Longer Handicapped (1978). Current Affairs Films, A Division of Key Productions, Inc. PO Box 398, 24 Danbury Road, Wilton, CT. Kit comes with booklet of the filmstrip's dialogue and a complete explanation.

Slide Shows

The Family Album: Views of Residential Settings for Mentally Retarded People (1978) Explores the reality behind institutional life in America. Contrasting views of individuals living in communities in the 1970's, it illustrates the degradation of institutions and how they are both unconscionable and unnecessary. Packet includes 160 slides and a script. Available from the Human Policy Press, PO Box 127, University Station, Syracuse, New York 13210. Order # HPP-17.

Our Voice is New: All About Self-Advocacy (1986). Explains what self-advocacy is, its importance, what its major issues are, and what self-advocates can do on their own behalf. This slide show can be used as a training device for developmentally disabled individuals who want to learn about self-advocacy as well as for support staff. Packet includes 114 slides and a script. Available from the Human Policy Press, PO Box 127, University Station, Syracuse, New York 13210. Order # HPP-21.

Compact Discs

Moyer, J. (1995). *We're People First: A Celebration of Diversity.* Cambridge, MA: Brookline Books. This CD contains a collection of songs that celebrate the inclusion philosophy and dignity of all people. The songs are categorized into two volumes relevant to youngsters from pre school to teenage years. Volume two is for older teenagers and adults. The CD also has the songs in an *accompaniment only* (Karaoke) format so they can be performed by the children, themselves. The CD also has an accompanying workbook, *We're People First: A Celebration of Diversity*, published by Brookline Books (1995), which contains background and explanatory materials for each song as well as suggestions for incorporation into the classroom.

Moyer, J. (1995). *Special Ed Ranger: Jeff Moyer in Concert.* Cambridge MA: Brookline Books. This CD is composed of Jeff Moyer's personal appearances where he sang his top of the list inspirational and entertainment songs on disability and the philosophy of inclusion. [Both CDs and accompanying materials are available from Brookline Books, PO Box 1047, Cambridge, MA: 02238-1047. (617)868-0360.

Audio Cassettes

Hull, J. (1991). *Touching the Rock: An Experience of Blindness.* Read by David Purdham. Known for its paradoxical acuteness of observation, *Touching the Rock* is a powerful, poignant memoir of what it is like to become blind and live one's life as a person with blindness. New York: Random House Sound Editions. Two cassettes: Total playing time 3 hours.

Moyer, J. (1988). *Do You See Me as an Equal: Songs of Disability Rights.* Music From the Heart, 670 Radford Drive, Cleveland, OH: 44691. Available from Prentke Romich Corporation, 81022 Heyl Road, Woosteer, OH: 44961.

Documentary Photo Aids and Posters

What It's Like to Be Me. Written and Illustrated by Disabled Children. (n.d.) Eleven posters with two illustrations and writing for each poster. The set comes with editor's explanatory notes and a Teacher's Resource Guide. May be ordered from DPA TalkAbout Information Poster, What It's Like to Be Me, Documentary Photo Aids, PO Box 956, Mt. Dora, FL. 32757.

What Do These People Have in Common Poster Set (1992) A series of three posters listing 40 famous individuals with disabilities. Accompanied by a two-page explanation. Association on Higher Education and Disability, PO Box 21102, Columbus, OH. 43221-0192.

If Someone Like. . . Poster Set (1991). A series of five posters asking if someone like Stevie Wonder, Franklin D. Roosevelt, Mary Tyler Moore, Agatha Chrisitie or Beethoven came to work in this office would he or she fit in? Association on Higher Education and Disability, PO Box 21102, Columbus, OH. 43221-0192.

> *Celebrate Community*
>
> *Label Jars Not People*
>
> *Not Being Able to Speak is Not the Same as Not Having Anything to Say*
>
> *I Am Blind Yet I See*
>
> *Don't Think That We Don't Think*
>
> *Our Voice Is New*
>
> *You Gave Us Your Dimes: Now We Want Our Rights*
>
> *How Often Have You Heard Recognize Resistance to Change and Fight It*
>
> *We Must Evacuate the Institutions for the Mentally Retarded People—Our Community's Most Natural Resource*
>
> *If You Thought the Wheel Was a Good Idea, You'll Love the Ramp*
>
> *Sticks and Stones Can Break MY Bones, But Names Will Really Hurt Me*

All Available from the Human Policy Press, PO Box 127, University Station, Syracuse, New York 13210.

Puppets and Dolls

Adaptive Equipment for Dolls with Disabilities. Kit contains a teacher's guide and doll equipment including a wheelchair, a protective helmet, a guide dog harness and cane, two leg braces, two forearm crutches, a walker with an accessory bag, two hearing aids and two pairs of eyeglasses. Available from Lakeshore Learning Materials, 2695 Domingues St. Carson, CA. 90749. 1(800)421-5354.

Block Play People with Differing Abilities. Kit contains a set of four dolls with differing abilities, including one wheelchair user, one person with blindness, an individual with forearm crutches, and one who uses leg braces. Available from Lakeshore Learning Materials, 2695 Domingues St. Carson, CA. 90749. 1(800)421-5354.

American Girl in a Wheelchair. The wheelchair has fully adjustable footrests and a side pocket. Available from Pleasant Company, 8400 Fairway Place, P.O. Box 620190, Middleton WI: 53562-0190.

Share a Smile Becky. "Barbie's friend in a wheelchair." The manufacturer states that Becky breaks down barriers and facilitates understanding between children with and children without disabilities, showing that they are more alike than different and creates an opportunity for children to ask questions and learn about people with disabilities. (Mattel is currently redesigning its standard Barbie House because it was found to be embarrassingly inaccessible to Becky). Mattel Corporation. Available at most toy stores.

Differing Abilities Book Set. Set contains six hardcover books containing stories about children with disabilities. Available from Lakeshore Learning Materials, 2695 East Dominguez St. Carson, CA. 90749. 1(800)421-5354.

The Kids on the Block. The Kids on the Block originated as a troupe of educational puppets designed to teach children about disabilities and differences. Currently 37 different programs address various disabilities, educational and medical differences, and various social concerns. Each topic is thoroughly researched and field tested before it becomes available to school districts, community service organizations, hospitals and special service groups. Each Kids on the Block curriculum includes puppets, props, scripts, audio cassettes, follow-up materials, resource suggestions, a training guide, and on-going technical support and counsel from the national company. The many programs available include autism, blindness, cerebral palsy, deafness, mental retardation, spina bifida, emotionally disturbance, gifted and talented, learning disabilities, AIDS, arthritis, epilepsy, leukemia, and being the sibling of a child with a disability. Available through The Kids on the Block, Inc., 9385-C. Gerwig Lane, Columbia, MD. (410)290-9358 or 1-800-368 KIDS.

People of Every Stripe. A set of twenty inch dolls, which includes a miniature wheelchair, a leg brace made out of heavy metal and Velcro, a youngster with Down Syndrome, a child with a prosthesis, a child with crutches, a range of dolls with visual impairments and amputations. Available from People of Every Stripe, PO BOX 12505, Portland OR. 97212. (503)282-0612.

Games

Empathy: A simulation of what it's like to be physically handicapped. In EMPATHY students role-play in the fantasy-styled land of Multicappia. The class is divided into four teams and is commissioned by the Elders of Empathopia to travel through Multicappia while under the influence of certain induced impairments. To win they must gain empathy points by learning to understand the problems involved in having various types of disabilities by experiencing the disabilities of blindness, deaf-muteness, and physical impairments through simulations. Varied activities are provided throughout the simulation to amplify the students' experiences. Booklets and Teacher Guide available from Interact, PO Box 997, Lakeside, CA: 92040.

In My Shoes: Friendmaking. This field-tested board game for two or more players stresses the importance of friendmaking and how it relates to persons with disabilities. The game comes with directions, a facilitator manual, suggestions for use, 7 exercises, and a certificate of commitment. Available from Program Development Associates, 7588 Fitzpatrick Drive, Liverpool, New York. 1(800)543-2110, Resource #FMIMS114.

Disability Organizations and Self-Help Groups

AIDS Action Council, 2033 M St., N.W., Ste. 801, Washington, DC 20036, (202)293-2437

Alexander Graham Bell Association for the Deaf, 3417 Volta Place, N.W. Washington, DC, 20007 (202)337-5220

Allergy Foundation of America 801 Second Avenue New York, NY 10017, (212)876-8875

American Foundation for the Blind, 15 West 11th Street, New York, NY 10011, (212)924-0420

American Juvenile Arthritis Organization Arthritis Foundation, 1314 Spring St. NW Atlanta, GA 30309, (404)872-7100

American Speech, Language and Hearing Association, 1801 Rockville Pike, Rockville, MD 20852, (301)897-5700

Amyotrophic Lateral Sclerosis Association, 21021 Ventura Blvd. Suite 321, Woodland Hills, CA 91364, 1(800)782-4747 (818)990-2151

Association for Children and Adults with Learning Disabilities (ACLD), 4156 Library Road, Pittsburgh, PA 15234, (412)881-1191

Association for Children with Down Syndrome, 2616 Martin Ave. Bellmore, NY 11710, (516)221-4700

Association for Persons With Severe Handicaps (TASH), 7010 Roosevelt Way, N.E., Seattle, WA 98115, (206)361-8870

Association of Birth Defect Children, Orlando Executive Park, 5400 Diplomat Circle, Suite 270, Orlando, FL 32810, (407)629-1466

Asthma & Allergy Foundation of America, 1717 Massachusetts Ave. NW, Ste. 305, Washington, DC 20036, (202)265-0265

Autism Society of America, 8601 Georgia Ave., Ste. 503, Silver Spring, MD 20910, (301)565-0433

Canine Companions for Independence, Northeast Regional Training Center, PO Box 205, Farmingdale, NY 11735-0205, (516)694-6938

C.H.A.D.D. National (Attention Deficit Disorders), 499 NW 70th Ave., Ste. 308, Plantation, Fl. 33317, (305)587-3700

Cleft Palate Foundation, 1218 Grandview Ave., Pittsburgh, PA 15211, 1 800/24-CLEFT (412)481-1376

Closer Look, Box 1942, Washington, DC 20013, (202)833-4160

Cystic Fibrosis Foundation, 6931 Arlington Rd., Bethesda, MD 20814, 1(800)FIGHT CF (301)951-4422

Epilepsy Foundation of America (EFA), 4351 Garden City Dr., Landover, MD 20785, 1(800)EFA-1000 (301)459-3700

Families of Children Under Stress (FOCUS), P.O. Box 1058, Conyers, GA 30207, (404)483-9845

Handicapped Organized Women, Inc., PO Box 35481, Charlotte, NC 28235, (704)376-4735

International Craniofacial Foundation, 10210 N. Central Expy., Ste. 230, LB37, Dallas, TX, 75231, 1(800)535-3643 (214)368-3590

Learning Disability Association, Library Rd., Pittsburgh, PA 15234, (412)341-1515 4156

Let's Face It, P.O. Box 711, Concord, MA 01742, (508)371-3186

Little People of America, Inc., Post Office Box 633, San Bruno, CA 04066

March of Dimes Birth Defects Foundation, 1275 Mamaroneck Ave., White Plains, NY 10605, (914)428-7100

Mental Health Association National Headquarters, 1800 North Kent Street, Arlington, VA 22209, (703)524-3352, (703)524-4230

Mental Health Law Project, 1101 15th St., N.W., Ste. 1212, Washington, DC 20005, (202)467-5730

National Amputation Foundation, 12-45 150th St., Whitestone, NY 11357, (718)767-0596

National Association for the Cranidfacially Handicapped (FACES), P.O. Box 11 082, Chattanooga, TN 37401, (615)266-1632

National Association Developmental Disabilities Councils, 1234 Massachusetts Ave., N.W., Ste., 103, (202)347-1234

National Association for Retarded Citizens—The Arc, 2709 Avenue E East PO Box 1047, Arlington, TX 76004, 1(800)433-5255 (817)261-4961

National Association for Visually Handicapped, 305 East 24th Street, New York, NY 10010, (212)889-3141

National Autism Hotline/Autism Services Center, Prichard Building, 605 Ninth St., P.O. Box 507, Huntington, WV 25701-0507, (304)525-8014

National Center for Learning Disabilities, 99 Park Ave., New York, NY 10016, (212)687-7211

National Council on Disability, 800 Independence Ave., S.W., Ste. 814, Washington, DC 20591, (202)267-3846 TDD (202)267-32322

National Down Syndrome Congress, 1800 Dempster St., Park Ridge, IL 60068-1146, 1(800)232-6372 (708)823-7550

National Down Syndrome Society, 666 Broadway, Suite 810, New York, NY 10012, 1(800)221-4602 (212)460-9330

National Easter Seal Society, 2023 West Ogden Avenue, Chicago, IL 60612, (312)243-8400

National Foundation for Facial Reconstruction, 317 East 34th St. 9th Floor, New York, NY 10016, (212)263-6656

National Hemophilia Foundation, 25 West 39th Street, New York, NY 10018, (212)869-9740

National Information Center for Children and Youth With Disabilities, 1(800)999-5599

National Information Center on Deafness, (202)651-5051 TDD (202)651-5052

National Organization for Albinism and Hypopigmentation (NOAH), 1500 Locust St., Ste. 1816, Philadelphia, PA 19102, 1(800)473-2310 (215)545-2322

National Organization for Rare Disorders, PO Box 8923, New Fairfield, CT 06812, (203)746-6518

National Organization on Disability, 910 16th St., N.W., Ste. 600, Washington, DC 20006, (202)293-5960

National Rehabilitation Information Center, 1(800)346-2742

National Society for Autistic Children, 169 Tampa Avenue, Albany, NY 12208, (518)489-7375

National Technical Institute for the Deaf, Rochester Institute of Technology, One Lomb Memorial Dr., Rochester, NY 14623, (716)475-6400

Orton Dyslexia Society, Chester Building, Suite 382, 8600 LaSalle Rd., Baltimore, MD 21204-6020, 1 800/ABCD123 (301)296-0232

Parents of Chronically Ill Children, 1527 Maryland St., Springfield, IL 62702, (217)522-6810

President's Committee on Employment of People With Disabilities, 1331 F St., N.W., Ste. 300, Washington, DC 20004-1107, (202)876-6200 TDD (202)376-6205

Spina Bifida Association of America, 343 S. Dearborn, Chicago, IL 60604, (312)662-1562

United Cerebral Palsy Association, 7 Penn Plaza Suite 804, New York, NY 10001, (212)260-9800

Books: Personal Accounts of Disability By Individuals, Parents and Teachers

Compilations (General)

Baum, D. (ed.) (1982). *The human side of exceptionality.* Austin, TX: Pro-Ed, Inc.

Bellarosa, J. (1989). *A problem of plumbing and other stories.* Santa Barbara, CA: John Daniel Company.

Bernstein, J., & Fireside, B. (1991). *Special parents, special children.* Morton Grove, IL: Albert Whitman and Company.

Bowe, F. (1978). *Handicapping America: Barriers to disabled people.* New York: Harper and Row, Publishers.

Brightman, A. (ed.) (1985/1990). *Ordinary moments: The disabled experience.* Syracuse, NY: Human Policy Press.

Fries, K. (ed.) (1997). *Staring back: The disability experience from the inside out.* New York: Penguin Books.

Gill, B. (1997). *Changed by a child: Companion notes for parents of a child with a disability.* New York: Doubleday.

Henrich, E. & Kriegel, L. (eds.) (1961). *Experiments in survival.* New York: Association for the Aid of Crippled Children.

Jones, R. (ed.) (1983). *Reflections on growing up disabled.* Reston, VA: Council for Exceptional Children.

Lessen, E. (1994). *Exceptional persons in society.* Needham Heights, MA: Simon and Schuster Custom Publishing.

Morris, J. (1991). *Pride against prejudice: Transforming attitudes to disability.* Philadelphia, PA: New Society Publishers.

Orlansky, M. & Heward, W. (eds.) (1981). *Voices: Interviews with handicapped people.* Columbus, OH: Charles E. Merrill Publishing Co. A Bell and Howell Company.

Sutherland, A. (1981). *Disabled we stand.* Bloomington, IN: Indiana University Press.

Weiner, F. (ed.) (1986). *No apologies: A guide to living with a disability, written by the real authorities-People with disabilities, their families and friends.* New York: St. Martin's Press.

Zola, I. (ed.) (1982). *Ordinary lives: Voices of disability and disease.* Cambridge, MA: Apple-wood Books.

Compilations (Children)

Exley, H. (ed.) (1984). *What it's like to be me: Written and illustrated entirely by disabled children.* New York: Friendship Press.

Goodman, R. & Krauss, B. (eds.) (1977). *An exceptional view of life: Written and illustrated by children with disabilities.* Los Angeles, CA: A Child's Point of View Publications.

Compilations (Women)

Browne, S., Connors, D. & Stern, N. (1985). *With the power of each breath: A disabled woman's anthology.* Pittsburgh, PA: Cleis Press, a Woman's Publishing Company.

Hannaford, S. (1985). *Living outside inside: A woman's experience towards a social and political perspective.* Berkeley, CA: Canterbury Press

Matthews, G. (1983). *Voices from the shadows: Women with disabilities speak out.* Toronto, Canada: The Women's Press.

Miller, V. (ed.) (1985). *Despite this flesh: The disabled in stories and poems.* Austin, TX: University of Texas Press.

Rousso, H. (1988). *Disabled, female, and proud: Stories of ten women with disabilities.* Boston, MA: Exceptional Parent Press.

Saxton, M. & Howe, F. (eds.) (1987). *With wings: An anthology of literature by and about women with disabilities.* New York: The Feminist Press at the City University of New York.

Autism

Gold, P. (1986). *Please don't say hello.* New York: Human Sciences Press.

Grandin, T. (1995). *Thinking in pictures and other reports from my life with autism.* New York: Doubleday.

Greenfeld, J. (1972). *A child called Noah: A family journey.* New York: Holt, Rinehart and Winston.

Greenfeld, J. (1978). *A place for Noah.* New York: Pocket Books/ Simon and Schuster.

Greenfeld, J. (1986). *A client called Noah.* New York: Henry Holt and Company.

Kaufman, B. (1976). *Son-rise.* New Warner Books.

Kaufman, B. (1981). *A miracle to believe in.* New York: Fawcett Crest Books.

Maurice, C. (1993). *Let me hear your voice; A family's triumph over autism.* New York: Alfred A. Knopf.

Rothenberg, M. (1987) (ed.). *Children with emerald eyes: Histories of extraordinary boys and girls.* New York: E. P. Dutton.

Stehli, A. (1991). *The sound of a miracle: A child's triumph over autism.* New York: Doubleday, a division of Bantam Doubleday Dell Publishing Company.

Thompson, M. (1992). *My brother Matthew.* Bethesda, MD: Woodbine House.

Thompson, M. (1996). *Andy and his yellow frisbee.* Bethesda, MD: Woobine House.

Watson, E. (1996). *Talking to angels.* San Diego, CA: Harcourt Brace and Company.

Williams, D. (1992). *Nobody nowhere: The extraordinary autobiography of an autistic.* New York: Avon Books.

Blindness

Alexander, S. (1990). *Mom can't see me*. New York: Macmillan Publishing Company.

Bergman, T. (1989). *Seeing in special ways: Children living with blindness*. Milwaukee, WI: Gareth Stevens Children's Books.

Bernstein, J. (1988). *Loving Rachel: A family's journey from grief*. Boston, MA: Little, Brown and Company.

Brock, J. & Gill, D. (1994). *More than meets the eye*. New York: Harper Collins Publishers.

Clark, E. (1977). *Eyes, Etc.: A memoir*. New York: Pocket Books/ Simon and Schuster.

Hine, R. (1993). *Second sight*. Berkely, CA: University of California Press.

Hocken, S. (1978). *Emma and I*. New York: E. P. Dutton.

Hull, J. (1990). *Touching the rock: An experience of blindness*. New York: Vintage Books, a division of Random House, Inc.

Kent, D. (1978). *Belonging*. Highland Park, IL: Dial Press, Inc.

Magee, B. & Milligan, M. (1995). *On Blindness*. New York: Oxford University Press.

Neer, F. (1994). *Dancing in the dark*. San Francisco, CA: Wildstar Publishing.

Sullivan, T. & Gill, D. (1975). *If you could see what I hear*. New York: Harper and Row, Publishers, Inc.

Sullivan, T. & Gill, D. (1976). *Tom Sullivan's adventures in darkness*. New York: McKay Publishers.

Weiss, M. (1976). *Seeing through the dark*. New York: Harcout, Brace, Jovanovich.

Cerebral Palsy

Jewell, G. (1984). *Geri*. New York: Ballentine Books.

Nolan, C. (1987). *Under the eye of the clock: The life story of Christopher Nolan*. New York: Dell Publishing a division of Bantam Doubleday Dell Publishing Group, Inc.

Cystic Fibrosis

Deford, F. (1983). *Alex: The life of a child*. Baltimore. MD: Cystic Fibrosis Foundation and New American Press.

Deafness

Benderly, B. (1980). *Dancing without music: Deafness in America.* New York: Double day Publishers.

Bove, L. (1980). *Sign language fun.* New York: Random House.

Cohen, L. (1994). *Train go sorry: Inside a deaf world.* New York: Houghton Mifflin Company.

Ferris, C. (1985). *A hug just isn't enough.* Washington, DC: Gallaudet University Press.

Forecki, M. (1985). *Speak to me.* Washington, DC: Gallaudet University Press.

Gannon, J. (1981). *Deaf heritage: A narrative history of deaf America.* Silver Spring MD: National Association of the Deaf.

Jacobs, L. (1989). *A deaf adult speaks out.* Washington, DC: Gallaudet University Press.

Kisor, H. (1990). *What's that pig outdoors: A memoir of deafness.* New York: Hill and Wang, a division of Farrar, Straus and Giroux.

Lane, L. & Pittle, I. (eds.) (1981). *A handful of stories: Thirty-seven stories by deaf storytellers.* Washington, DC: Gallaudet University Press.

Neisser, A. (1983). *The other side of silence: Sign language and the deaf community.* New York: Alfred A. Knopf.

Padden, C. & Humphries, T. (1988). *Deaf in America: Voices from a culture.* Cambridge, MA: Harvard University Press.

Pittle, I. & Rosen, R. (1984). *Another handful of stories: Thirty-seven stories by deaf storytellers.* Washington, DC: Gallaudet University Press.

Robinson, K. (1987). *Children of silence: The story of my daughters' triumph over deafness.* New York: Signet, Penguin Books.

Sacks, O. (1989). *Seeing voices: A journey into the world of the deaf.* Berkeley, CA: University of California Press.

Sidransky, R. (1990). *In silence: Growing up hearing in a deaf world.* New York: St Martin's Press.

Spradley, T., & Spradley, J. (1978). *Deaf like me.* Washington, DC: Gallaudet University Press.

Walker, L. (1985). *Amy: The story of a deaf child.* New York: E. P. Dutton.

Wright, D. (1993 ed.) *Deafness: An autobiography.* New York: Harper Collins Publishers, Inc.

Disfigurement

Harmon, L. (1982). *Why me?* New York: Stein and Day.

Howell, M. & Ford, P. (1980). *The true history of the Elephant Man.* New York: Schocken Books, Inc.

Minahan, J. (1985) *Mask.* New York: Berkley Books.

Rothenberg, M. & White, M. (1985). *David.* Old Tappan, NJ: Fleming H. Revell Company.

Severo, R. (1985). *Lisa H.: The true story of an extraordinary and courageous woman.* New York: Harper and Row, Publishers.

Dwarfism

Ablon, J. (1984). *Little people: The social dimensions of dwarfism.* New York: Praeger Publishers.

Albon, J. (1988). *Living with a difference: Families with dwarf children.* New York: Praeger Publishers.

Kuklin, S. (1986). *Thinking big: The story of a young dwarf.* New York: Lothrop, Lee, and Shepard Books.

Gillis, J. (1982). *Too tall too small.* Champaign, IL: Institute for Personality and Ability Testing.

Phifer, K. (1979). *Growing up small: A handbook for short people.* Middlebury, VT: Paul S. Eriksson, Publisher.

Van Etten, A. (1988). *Dwarfs don't live in doll houses.* Rochester, NY: Adaptive Living.

Emotional Disabilities

Axline, V. (1964). *Dibs: In search of self.* Boston, MA: Houghton Mifflin Company.

Bartocci, B. (1985). *My angry son: Sometimes love is not enough.* New York: Donald I. Fine, Inc.

Baruch, D. (1952). *One little boy.* New York: Dell Publishing Company.

Bograd, L. (1982). *Bad apple.* New York: Farrar Straus Giroux.

Craig, E. (1983). *If we could hear the grass grow.* New York: Signet Books/Simon and Schuster.

Jones, R. (1982). *Kids called crazy.* New York: Bantam Books.

Kaysen, S. (1993). *Girl, interrupted.* New York: Turtle Bay Books, a division of Random House.

MacCracken, M. (1973). *A circle of children.* Philadelphia, PA: J. B. Lippincott Com pany.

MacCracken, M. (1976). *Lovey: A very special child.* Philadelphia, PA: J. B. Lippincott Company.

Pinney, R. (1983). *Bobby: Breakthrough of a special child.* New York: McGraw Hill Paperbacks.

Sechehaye, M. (1951). *Autobiography of a schizophrenic girl.* New York: Grune and Stratton.

Wilson, L. (1968). *This stranger, my son.* New York: Signet Books.

Epilepsy (Seizure Disorder)

Gino, C. (1986). *Rusty's story.* Bantam Books, Inc.

Reese, R. (1988). *Healing fits: The curing of an epileptic.* Los Angeles, CA: Big Sky Press.

Fetal Alcohol Syndrome

Dorris, M. (1989). *The broken cord: A family's ongoing struggle with fetal alcohol syndrome.* New York: Harper and Row, Publishers.

Learning Disabilities

Callahan, M. (1987). *Fighting for Tony.* New York: Simon and Schuster, Inc.

Hampshire, S. (1982). *Susan's story: An autobiographical account of my struggle with dyslexia.* New York: St. Martin's Press.

MacCracken, M. (1986). *Turnabout children: Overcoming dyslexia and other learning disabilities.* Boston, MA: Little, Brown and Company.

Sacks, O. (1987). *The man who mistook his wife for a hat and other clinical tales.* New York: Harper and Row Publishers.

Scotson, L. (1985). *Doran.* New York: Signet/New American Library.

Simpson, E. (1979). *Reversals: A personal account of a victory over dyslexia.* New York: Washington Press books, Simon and Schuster.

Weiss, E. (1989). *Mothers talk about learning disabilities: Personal feelings, practical advice.* New York: Prentice Hall Press

Mental Retardation

Bogdan, R. & Taylor, S. (1994). *The social meaning of mental retardation: Two life stories.* New York: Teachers College Press, Columbia University.

Buck, P. (1992 ed.) *The child who never grew.* Rockville, MD: Woodbine House, Inc. (Original Publication Date 1950)

Burke, C. & McDaniel, J. (1991). *A special kind of hero: The star of "Life Goes On" tells his remarkable story.* New York: Doubleday, a division of Bantam Doubleday Dell Publishing group, Inc.

Cairo, S. (1985). *Our brother has Down's Syndrome*. Toronto, Canada: Annick Press Ltd.

Edwards, J. & Dawson, D. (1983). *My friend David: A source book about Down's Syndrome and a personal story about friendship*. Portland, OR: Ednick Communications, Inc.

Hunt, N. (1967). *The world of Nigel Hunt: The diary of a Mongoloid youth*. New York: Garrett Publications.

Kaufman, S. (1988). *Retarded isn't stupid, Mom*. Baltimore, MD: Paul H. Brookes Publishing Company, Inc.

Kinglsey, J. & Levitz, M. (1994).*Count us in: Growing up with Down Syndrome*. San Diego, CA: Harcourt Brace and Company.

MacDonald, W. & Oden, C. (1978). *Moose: A very special person*. Cambridge, MA: Brookline Books.

Meyers, R. (1978). *Like normal people*. New York: McGraw-Hill Book Company.

Noble, V. (1993). *Down is up for Aaron Eagle: A mother's spiritual journey with Down Syndrome*. San Francisco, CA: Harper Collins Publishers.

O'Reilly, D. (1989). *Retard*. Macomb, IL: Glenbridge Publishing Ltd.

Rabe, B. (1988). *Where's Chimpy?* Morton Grove, IL: Albert Whitman and Company.

Schwier, K. (1990). *Speakeasy: People with mental handicaps talk about their lives in institutions and in the community*. Austin, TX: Pro-ed, Inc.

Multiple Disabilities

Brown, H. (1976). *Yesterday's child*. New York: Signet Books.

Geraldi, C. and Burris, C. (1996). Camille's children. Kansas City, MO: Andrews and McMeel, A Universal Press Syndicate Company.

Harris, G. (1983). *Broken ears, wounded hearts: An intimate journey into the lives of a multihandicapped girl and her family*. Washington, DC: Gallaudet University Press.

Keller, H. (1965 ed.). *The story of my life*. New York: Airmont Publishing Company, Inc.

Rosenberg, M. (1983). *My friend Leslie: The story of a handicapped child*. New York: Lothrop, Lee and Shepard Books.

Tamler, J. (1993). *Perfect just the way I am*. Edina, MN: St. John's Publishing.

Yoken, C. (1979). *Living with deaf-blindness: Nine profiles*. Washington, DC: Gallaudet University Press.

Multiple Sclerosis

Mairs, N. (1989). *Remembering the bone house: An erotics of place and space.* New York: Harper and Row, Publishers.

Physical Disabilities

Beisser, A. (1989). *Flying without wings: Personal reflections on being disabled.* New York: Doubleday, a division of Bantam Doubleday Dell Publishing Group, Inc.

Bergman, T. (ed.) (1989). *On our own: Children living with physical disabilities.* Milwaukee, WI: Gareth Stevens Children's Books.

Brown, C. (1954). *My left foot.* London, GB. Octopus Publishing Group.

Callahan, J. (1989). *Don't worry, he won't get far on foot: The autobiography of a dangerous man.* New York: William Morrow and Company, Inc.

Camp, F. (1973). *Two wheelchairs and a family of three.* Wheaton, IL: Tyndale House Publishers.

Carson, M. (1971). *Ginny: A true story.* Garden City, NY: Doubleday and Company, Inc.

Gallagher, H. (1985). *FDR's splendid deception: The moving story of Roosevelt's massive disability-and the intense efforts to conceal it from the public.* New York: Dodd, Mead, and Company, Inc.

Havill, A. (1996). *Man of steel: The career and courage of Christopher Reeve.* New York: Penguin Books USA, Inc.

Hockenberry, J. (1995). *Moving violations: A memoir—war zones, wheelchairs, and decelerations of independence.* New York: Hyperion.

Jones, R. (1977). *The acorn people.* New York: Bantam Books.

Kenihan, K.(1985). *Quentin.* Ringwood, Victoria: Australia. Penguin Books of Australia.

Kovic, R. (1976). *Born on the Fourth of July: A true story of innocence lost and courage found.* New York: Pocket Books, a division of Simon and Schuster, Inc.

Kriegel, L. (1991). *Falling into life.* San Francisco, CA: North Point Press.

McDonald, S. & McDonald, P. (1989). *The Steven McDonald story.* New York: Donald I. Fine, Inc.

Milam, L. (1984). *The cripple liberation marching band blues.* San Diego, CA: Mho and Mho Works.

Pieper, E. (n.d.). *Sticks and stones: The story of a loving child.* Syracuse, NY: Human Policy Press.

Powers, M. (1986). *Our teacher's in a wheelchair*. Morton Grove, IL: Albert Whitman and Company.

Reeve, C. (1998). *Still me*. New York: Random House.

Sienkiewicz-Mercer, R. & Kaplan, S. (1989). *I raise my eyes to say yes: A memoir*. Boston, MA: Houghton Mifflin Co.

Smith, M. (1975). *Companions*. Denver, Co: Atlantis Community, Inc.

Valens, E. (1966). *The other side of the mountain*. New York: Warner Books.

Wolf, B. (1974). *Don't feel sorry for Paul*. Philadelphia, PA: J. B. Lippincott Company.

Zola, I. (1982). *Missing pieces: A chronicle of living with a disability*. Philadelphia, PA: Temple University Press.

Severe Allergies

Reisman, B. (1984). *Jared's story: A boy in a bubble and how his family saved his life*. New York: Crown Publishers, Inc.

Speech and Language Disabilities

Bobrick, B. (1995). *Knotted tongues: Stuttering in history and the quest for a cure*. New York: Simon and Schuster.

Carlisle, J. (1985). *Tangled tongue: Living with a stutter*. Toronto, Canada: University of Toronto Press.

Tillis, M. (1984). *Stutterin' boy: The autobiography of Mel Tillis*. New York: Dell Publishing Company, Inc.

Brain Injury

Cleland, M. (1989). *Strong at the broken places*. Atlanta, GA: Cherokee Publishing Company.

Connor, D. (1989). *I'm not Special: I'm just* me. Toronto, Canada: Dunal and Fortin.

Dickenson, M. (1987). *Thumbs up; The life and courageous comeback of White House press secretary Jim Brady*. New York, NY: William Morrow and Company.

Hughes, K. (1990). *God isn't finished with me yet*. Nashville, TN: Winston-Derek Publishers, Inc.

Krieg, M. (1994). *Awake again*. Waco, TX: WRS Publishing.

Kupfer, F. (1982). *Before and after Zachariah*. Chicago, IL: Academy Chicago Publish ers.

Lineberry, T. (1988) *Twice a champion: The Toney Lineberry story*. Manakin-Sabot, VA: Toney Lineberry.

Longenecker, S. (1984). *Crushed, but not destroyed: A true story of love and determination in the aftermath of tragedy.* Boring, OR: Sun Ray Publishing Co.

Mahanes, F. (1985). *A Child's courage, a doctor's devotion: Triumph over head trauma.* White Hall, VA: Frances F. Betterway Public

Mandrell, B. (1990). *Get to the heart: My story.* New York, NY: Bantam Books.

Oe, K. (1996). *A healing family.* New York: Kodansha International Ltd.

Pahler, C. (1985). *For Those Who Wait.* Winona, MN: Apollo Books.

Parker, J. (1992). *In His favor is life: The heartwarming story of a young man's struggle to survive and recover from a nearly fatal automobile accident.* Shippensburg, PA: Companion Press.

Pflug, J. (1995). *Miles to go Before I Sleep: My grateful journey back from the hijacking of Egyptian flight 648.* Center City, MN: Hazelden.

Richie, G. (1990). *Insights from a brain injury: Feelings as told by a survivor of traumatic brain injury.* Rice Lake, WI: Gary Richie.

Rickett, F. & McGraw, S. (1981). *Totaled.* New York, NY: William Morrow and Company, Inc.

Rife, J. (1993). *Injured mind, shattered dreams: Brian's journey from severe head injury to a new* dream. Cambridge, MA: Brookline Books.

Rimland, I. (1984). *The furies and the flame.* Novato, CA: Arena Press.

Taylor, J. (1992). *The Journey Back.* Dublin, Ireland: New Leaf.

Thompson, M. (1992). *My brother Matthew.*

Weiss, L. (1987). *I wasn't Finished with life.* Dallas, TX: E-Heart Press.

Juvenile Books on Disability

General

Adams, B. (1979). *Like it is: Facts and feelings about handicaps from kids who know.* New York: Walker and Company.

Bernstein, J., & Fireside, B. (1991). *Special parents, special children.* Morton Grove, IL: Albert Whitman and Company.

Biklen, D., & Sokoloff, M. (eds.) (1978). *What do you do when your wheelchair gets a flat tire?: Questions and answers about disabilities.* Syracuse, NY: Human Policy Press.

Dwight, L. (1992). *We can do it.* New York: Checkerboard Press.

Exley, H. (ed.) (1984). *What it's like to be me: Written and illustrated entirely by disabled children.* New York: Friendship Press.

Golant, M., & Crane, B. (1987). *It's o.k. to be different coloring book.* New York: Playmore Incorporated, Publishers and Waldman Publishing Corporation.

Golant, M., & Crane, B. (1988). *It's o.k. to be different!* New York: Tom Doherty Associates, Inc.

Goodman, R. & Krauss, B. (eds.) (1977). *An exceptional view of life: Written and illustrated by children with disabilities.* Los Angeles, CA: A Child's Point of View Publications.

McConnell, N. (1982). *Different and alike.* Colorado Springs, CO: Current, Inc.

Quinsey, M. (1986). *Why does that man have such a big nose?* Seattle, WA: Parenting Press, Inc.

Rosenberg, M. (1988). *Finding a way: Living with exceptional brothers and sisters.* New York: Lothrop, Lee, and Shepard Books.

Sanders, P. (1992). *Let's talk about disabled people.* New York: Gloucester Press.

Simon, N. (1976). *Why am I different?* Morton Grove, IL. Albert Whitman and Company.

Stein, S. (1974). *About handicaps: An open family book for parents and children together.* New York: Walker and Company.

Ward, B. (1988). *Overcoming* disability. New York: Franklin Watts, Publishers.

Westridge Young Writers Workshop. (1994). *Kids explore the gifts of children with special needs.* Santa Fe, MN: John Muir, Publications.

White, P. (1990). *Disabled people.* New York: Franklin Watts, Publishers.

Blindness

Aiello, B. & Shulman, J. (1988). *Business is looking up.* Frederick, MD: Twenty-First Century Books.

Alexander, S. (1990). *Mom can't see me.* New York: Macmillan Publishing Company.

Arnold, C. (1991). *A guide dog puppy grows up.* New York: Harcourt, Brace, Jovanovich.

Bergman, T. (1989). *Seeing in special ways: Children living with blindness.* Milwaukee, WI: Gareth Stevens Children's Books.

Blakeslee, M. (1991). *Hal.* Toronto, Ontario, Canada: Stoddart Publishing Co.

Brighton, C. (1984). *Maria.* London, UK: Farber and Farmer, Ltd.

Clifford, E. (1987). *The man who sang in the dark.* Boston, MA: Houghton Mifflin Co.

Corn, A. (1977). *Monocular Mac.* New York: National Association for the Visually Handicapped.

Dobson, D. (1990). *Woof, the Seeing-Eye Dog.* Dallas, TX: Word Publishing.

Eyerly, J. (1981). *The seeing summer.* New York: J. B. Lippincott.

Greig, D. & Brightman, A. (1978). *Laura.* New York: Scholastic Book Services.

Johnson, E. (1984). *Spring and the shadow man.* New York: Dodd, Mead, and Co.

Kroll, V. (1993). *Naomi knows it's springtime.* Honesdale, PA: Boyds Mills Press.

Litchfield, A. (1977). *A cane in her hand.* Chicago, IL: Albert Whitman and Company.

Marcus, J. (1979). *Cathy.* New York: National Association for the Visually Handicapped.

Marcus, J. (1979). *Larry.* New York: National Association for the Visually Handicapped.

Marcus, J. (1979). *Susan.* New York: National Association for the Visually Handicapped.

Marcus, R. (1981) *Being blind.* New York: Hastings.

Peterson, P. (1977). *Sally can't see.* New York: John Day Book Company.

Smith, E. (1987). *A guide dog goes to school.* New York: William Morrow and Co.

Thomas, W. (1980). *The new boy is blind.* New York: Gallein Messner.

Wapnick, S., & Kimmel, E. (1982). *Friends after all. . . First date.* Portland, OR: Ednick Communications, Inc.

Weiss, M. (1980). *Blindness.* New York: Franklin Watts.

Weiss, M. (1976). *Seeing through the dark: Blind and sighted—A vision shared.* New York: Harcourt.

Whelan, G. (1991). *Hannah. New York:* Alfred A. Knopf.

Wild, M. (1993). *All the better to see you with.* Morton Grove, IL: Albert Whitman and Company.

Physical Disability
Aiello, B. & Shulman, J. (1988). *It's your turn at bat.* Frederick, MD: Twenty-first Century Books.

Berger, G. (1979). *Physical disabilities.* New York: Franklin Watts.

Bergman, T. (1989). *On our own terms: Children living with physical disabilities.* Milwaukee, WI: Gareth Stevens, Inc.

Berry, J. (1990). *Good answers to tough questions: About physical disabilities.* Chicago, IL: Childrens Press.

Brightman, A. & Storey, K. (1978). *Hollis.* New York: Scholastic Book Services.

Brown, T. (1984). *Someone special just like you.* New York: Henry Holt and Company, Inc.

Burnett, F. (1986). *The secret garden.* New York: Penguin Books.

Carlson, N. (1990). *Arnie and the new kid.* New York: Puffin Books.

Curry, C. (1981). *Look at me.* Lawrence, KA: H and H Enterprises, Inc.

Ellis, K. (1992). *Maya.* Toronto, Ontario, Canada. James Lorimer and Company.

Emmert, M. (1989). *I'm the big sister now.* Chigago, IL: Albert Whitman and Company.

Fassler, J. (1975). *Howie helps himself.* Morton Grove, IL: Albert Whitman and Company.

Gerson, C. (1978). *Passing through.* New York: Dial Press.

Grealish, C. & Grealish, M. (1978). *Hackett McGee.* New York: Scholastic Book Services.

Holcomb, N. (1989). *Patrick and Emma Lou.* Exton, PA: Turtle Books/ Jason and Nordic Publishers.

Holcomb, N. (1989). *A smile from Andy.* Exton, PA: Turtle Books/Jason and Nordic Publishers.

Holcomb, N. (1989). *Andy finds a turtle.* Exton, PA: Turtle Books/ Jason and Nordic Publishers.

Klein, N. (1987). *My life as a body.* New York: Alfred A. Knopf.

Muldoon, K. (1989). *Princess Pooh.* Niles, IL: Albert Whitman and Company.

Osofsky, A. (1992). *My buddy.* New York: Henry Holt and Company.

Pettenuzzo, B. (1987). *I have spina bifida.* London, UK. Franklin Watts.

Pettenuzzo, B. (1988). *I have cystic fibrosis.* London, UK. Franklin Watts.

Powers, M. (1986). *Our teacher's in a wheelchair.* Morton Grove, IL: Albert Whitman and Company.

Rabe, B. (1981). *The balancing girl.* New York: Dutton Children's Books.

Rosenberg, M. (1983). *My friend Leslie: The story of a handicapped child.* New York: Lothrop, Lee, and Shepard Books.

Stewart, M., Shramuk, D., Burda, A. & Kodosky, C. (1991). *I can too!* Wheaton, IL: Marianjoy Rehabilitation Center.

Wapnick, S., & Kimmel, E. (1982). *Friends after all. . . Monster day.* Portland, OR: Ednick Communications, Inc.

Wapnick, S. & Kimmel, E. (1982). *Friends after all. . . Sloppy Joe.* Portland, OR: Ednick Communications, Inc.

Wolf, B. (1974). *Don't feel sorry for Paul.* Philadelphia, PA: J. B. Lippincott Company.

Deafness

Aseltine, L., Meuller, E., & Tait, N. (1986). *I'm deaf and it's okay.* Morton Grove, IL: Albert Whitman and Company.

Bove, L. (1985). *Sesame Street sign language ABC.* New York: Random House.

Brearley, S. (1996). *Talk to me.* London: A. and C. Black, Publishers Limited.

Ferris, C. (1980). *A hug just isn't enough.* Washington, DC: Gallaudet College Press.

Greenberg, J. (1985). *What's the sign for friend?* New York: Franklin Watts, Publishers.

LaMore, G. (1986). *Now I understand: A book about hearing* impairment. Washington, DC: Gallaudet College Press.

Levine, E. (1974). *Lisa and her soundless world.* New York: Human Sciences Press.

Peterson. J. (1977). *I have a sister-my sister is deaf.* New York: Harper and Row. New York: Lothrop, Lee, and Seppard Books.

Quinn, P. (1991). *Matthew Pinkowski's special summer.* Washington, DC: Kendall Green Publishers.

Rosenberg, M. (1983). *My friend Leslie: The story of a handicapped child.* New York:Lothrop, Lee, and Shepard Books.

Walker, L. (1985). *Amy: The story of a deaf child.* New York: E. P. Dutton.

Wapnick, S. & Kimmel, E. (1982). *Friends after all. . . the mystery at Paul's house.* Portland, OR: Ednick Communications, Inc.

Zelonky, J. (1980). *I can't always hear you.* Milwaukee, WI: Raintree Publishers, Inc.

Dwarfism

Brightman, A., Storey, K., & Benjamin, M. (1978). *Ginny.* New York: Scholastic Book Services.

Rudner, B. (1987). *The littlest tall fellow.* Louisville, KY: Art-Print Publishing Company.

Mental Retardation

Anders, R. (1976). *A look at mental retardation.* Minneapolis, MM: Lerner Publishers.

Braithwaite, A. (1987). *I have a mental handicap.* London, GB: Dinosaur Publications.

Burke, C. & McDaniel, J. (1991). *A special kind of hero: The star of "Life Goes On" tells his remarkable story.* New York: Doubleday, a division of Bantam Doubleday Dell Publishing Group, Inc.

Cairo, S. (1985). *Our brother has Down's Syndrome.* Toronto, Canada: Annick Press Ltd.

Edwards, J. & Dawson, D. (1983). *My friend David: A source book about Down's Syndrome and a personal story about friendship.* Portland, OR: Ednick Communications, Inc.

Fleming, V. (1993). *Be good to Eddie Lee.* New York: Philomel Books.

Kneeland, L. (1989). *Cookie.* Exton, PA: Turtle Books/Jason and Nordic Publishers.

Krementz, J. (1992). *How it feels to live with a physical disability.* New York: Simon and Schuster.

Rabe, B. (1988). *Where's Chimpy?* Niles, IL: Albert Whitman and Company.

Sanford, D. (1986). *Don't look at me: A child's book about being different.* Portland, OR: Multnomah Press.

Wapnick, S. & Kimmel, E. (1982). *Friends after all. . . Don't give up.* Portland, OR: Ednick Communications, Inc.

Learning Disabilities

Aiello, B. & Shulman, J. (1988). *Secrets aren't always for keeps.* Frederick, MD: Twenty-First Century Books.

Dunn, K. & Dunn, A. (1993). *Trouble with school: A family story about learning disabilities.* Rockville, MD: Woodbine House.

Dwyer, K. (1991). *What do you mean I have a learning disability?* New York: Walker and Company.

Gehret, J. (1995). *The don't-give-up kid and learning differences.* Fairport, NY: Verbal Images Press.

Janover, C. (1988). *Josh: A boy with dyslexia.* Burlington, VT: Waterfront Books.

Hall, D. (1993). *Living with learning disabilities: A guide for students.* Minneapolis, MN: Learner Publications Company.

Luks, P. (1985). *Me and Einstein.* New York: Human Sciences Press, Inc.

Parker, R. (1993). *Slam dunk: A young boy's struggle with attention deficit disorder.* Plantation, FL: Impact Publications, Inc.

Quinn, P. (1991). *Putting on the breaks: Young people's guide to understanding attention deficit hyperactivity disorder.* New York: Magination Press, an Imprent of Brunner/Mazel, Inc.

Root, A. & Gladden, L. (1995). *Charlie's challenge.* Temple, TX: U.S.A. Printmaster Press.

Stern, J. & Ben-Ami, U. (1996). *Many ways to learn: Young people's guide to learning disabilities.* New York: Magination Press.

Basic Books on Integrating Students With Disabilities

Beale, G., Brant, D., Clarke, B., Green, D., Heim, J., Kazminski, A., Keller, J., McCormick, L., Mollineux, B. & Richmond, B. (1990). *Project kidlink: Bringing together disabled and non-disabled preschoolers.* Tucson, AR: Communication Skill Builders.

Berres, M. & Knoblock, P. (eds.) (1987). *Program models for mainstreaming: Integrating students with moderate to severe disabilities.* Rockville, MD: Aspen Publishers, Inc.

Biklen, D. (1992). *Schooling without labels: Parents, educators, and inclusive education.* Philadelphia, PA: Temple University Press.

Biklen, D., Ferguson, D. & Ford, A. (eds.) (1989). *Schooling and disability.* Chicago, IL: Chicago University Press.

Blenk, K, & Fine, D. (1995). *Making school inclusion work: A guide to everyday practices.* Cambridge, MA: Brookline Books.

Bruininks, R. & Lakin, K. (1985). *Living and learning in the least restrictive environment.* Baltimore, MD: Paul H. Brookes.

Chalmers, L. (1992). *Modifying curriculum for the special needs students in the regular classroom.* Moorhead, MN: Practical Press.

Choat, J. (1993). *Successful mainstreaming: Proven ways to detect and correct special needs.* Boston, MA: Allyn and Bacon.

Cicchelli, T. & Ashby-Davis, C. (1986). *Teaching exceptional children and youth in the regular classroom.* Syracuse, NY: Syracuse University Press.

The Family Child Learning Center Children's Hospital Medical Center of Akron. (1991). *The preschool integration handbook: A day care provider's reference for inclusion of children with disabilities.* Tall-madge, OH: Author.

Gaylord-Ross, R. (1989). *Integration strategies for students with hand-icaps.* Baltimore, MD: Paul H. Brookes.

Giangreco, M., Cloninger, C. & Iverson, V. (1993). *Choosing options and accommodation for children (COACH): A guide to planning inclusive education.* Baltimore, MD: Paul H. Brookes.

Goodlad, J. & Lovitt, T. (1993). *Integrating general and special educa-tion.* New York: Merrill/Macmillan Publishers.

Granger, L. & Granger, B. (1986). *The magic feather: The truth about "special education."* New York: E. P. Dutton.

Lewis, R. & Doorlag, D. (1991). *Teaching special students in the main-stream* (3 rd. ed.). Columbus, OH: Merrill/Macmillan.

Lipsky, D.& Gartner, A. (1989). *Beyond separate education: Quality education for all.* Baltimore, MD: Paul H. Brookes.

Lloyd, J., Singh, N. & Repp, A. (1991). *The regular education initia-tive.* Sycamore, IL: Sycamore Publishers.

Mann, P., Suiter, P. & McClungm R. (1992). *A guide for educating mainstreamed students.* Boston, MA: Allyn & Bacon.

McCoy, K. (1995). *Teaching special learners in the general education classroom: Methods and techniques* (2nd ed.). Denver, CO: Love Publishing Company.

Meyen, E. & Skrtic, T. (eds.) (1995). *Special education and student dis-ability: Traditional, emerging, and alternative perspectives* (4th ed.). Denver, CO: Love Publishing Company.

Meyen, E., Vergason, G., & Whelan, R. (eds.) (1993). *Educating students with mild disabilities.* Denver, CO: Love Publishing Company.

Moore, L. (1996). *Inclusion: A practical guide for parents.* Minneton-ka, MN: Peytral Publications.

National Education Association. (1994). *Toward inclusive classrooms.* West Haven, CT: NEA Professional Library.

O'Brien, J., Forest, M., Snow, J., Pearpoint, J. & Hasbury, D. (1991/ 1993). *Action for inclusion: How to improve schools by welcoming children with special needs into regular classrooms.* Toronto, Ontario, Canada: Inclusion Press/Centre for Integrated Education.

Pearpoint, J., Forest, M. & Snow, J. (1992). *The inclusion papers: Strategies to make inclusion work.* Toronto, Ontario, Canada: Inclusion Press/Centre for Integrated Education.

Reynolds, M. & Birch, J. (1988). *Adaptive mainstreaming: A primer for teachers and principals (3rd ed.).* New York: Longman, Inc.

Sailor, W., Anderson, J., Halvorsen, A., Doering, K., Filler, J. & Goetz, L. (1989). *The comprehensive local school.* Baltimore, MD: Paul H. Brookes Publishing Company.

Salend, S. (1994). *Effective mainstreaming: Creating inclusive classrooms.* New York: Macmillan Publishing Company.

Schulz, J., Carpenter, D. & Turnbull, A. (1991). *Mainstreaming exceptional students: A guide for classroom teachers* (3rd ed.). Needham Heights, MA: Allyn and Bacon Company.

Schwartz, L. (1984). *Exceptional students in the mainstream.* Belmont, CA: Wadsworth Publishing Company.

Smith, T., Polloway, E., Patton, J. & Dowdy, C. (1995). *Teaching children with special needs in inclusive settings.* Needham Heights, MA: Allyn and Bacon Company.

Spodek, B., Saracho, O. & Lee, R. (1984). *Mainstreaming young children.* Belmont, CA: Wadsworth Publishing Company.

Stainback, S., & Stainback, W. (eds.) (1996). *Inclusion: A guide for educators.* Baltimore, MD: Paul H. Brookes.

Stainback, W., & Stainback, S. (1990). *Support networks for inclusive education: Interdependent integrated education.* Baltimore, MD: Paul H. Brookes.

Stainback, W. & and Stainback, S. (1991). *Curriculum considerations in inclusive classrooms.* Baltimore, MD: Paul H. Brookes.

Stainback, W. & Stainback, S. (1996). *Controversial issues confronting special education: Divergent perspectives* (2nd ed.). Needham Heights, MA: Allyn and Bacon Company.

Stainback, S., Stainback, W. & Forest, M. (1989). *Educating all students in the mainstream of regular education.* Baltimore, MD: Paul H. Brookes.

Thompson, B., Wickham, D., Wegner, J., Ault, M., Shanks, P. & Reinerston, B. (n.d.). *Handbook for the inclusion of young children with severe disabilities: Strategies for implementing exemplary full inclusion programs.* Lawrence, KA: Learner Managed Designs, Inc.

Turnbull, A., Turnbull, H., Shank, M. & Leal, D. (1995). *Exceptional lives: Special education in today's schools.* Englewood Cliffs, NJ: Prentice-Hall, Inc.

Villa, R., Thousand, J., Stainback, W. & Stainback, S. (1992). *Restructuring for caring and effective education: An administrative guide to creating heterogeneous schools.* Baltimore, MD: Paul H. Brookes.

Wood, J. (1993). *Mainstreaming: A practical approach for teachers (2nd ed.)*. New York: Merrill, an imprint of Macmillan.

Wortham, S. (1996). *The integrated classroom*. Englewood Cliffs, NJ: Prentice Hall, Inc.

Ysseldyke, J., Algozzine, B.,& Thurlow, M. (1992). *Critical issues in special education*. Boston, MA: Houghton Mifflin.

Magazines Relating to Persons with Disabilities

Ability magazine. 11349 Ganota Avenue, Granada Hills, CA 911344.

Accent on living. P.O. Box 700, Gillum Road and High Drive, Bloomington, IL 61702-0700.

Careers and the disabled: The career magazine for people with disabilities. Equal Opportunity Publications, Inc., 1160 East Jericho Turnpike, Suite 200, Huntington, NY 11743.

Disabled outdoors. 5223 South Lorel Avenue, Chicago, IL 60638.

Culture and disability. 97 Summers Street, Oyster bay, NY 11771.

Exceptional parent: Parenting your child with a disability. P.O. Box 3000, Dept. EP, Denville, NJ 07834.

The itinerary: The magazine for travelers with physical disabilities. P.O. Box 1084, Bayonne, NJ 07002-1084.

Kaleidoscope: International magazine of literature, fine arts and disability. Kaleidoscope Press, 326 Locust Street, Akron, OH 44310-0202.

Mainstream: Magazine of able-disabled. P.O. Box 370598, San Diego, CA 92137-0598.

New mobility: Disability lifestyle, culture and resources. Miramar Communications Inc., 23815 Stuart Ranch Road, P.O. Box 8987 Malibu, CA 90265.

New world for persons with disabilities. P.O. Box 1965, Reseda, CA 91335.

Paraplegia news. 5201 19th Avenue, Suite 111, Phoenix, AZ 85015.

Ragged edge: The disability experience in America. P.O. Box 145, Louisville, KY 40201.

Spinal cord injury life. National Spinal Cord Injury Association, 149 California Street, Newton, MA 02158.

Spinal network extra. P.O. Box 4162, Boulder, CO 80306.

Sports and spokes magazine. 5201 North 19th Avenue, Suite 111, Phoenix, AZ 85015.

TeamRehab report: For professionals in rehabilitation technology and services. Miramar Communications Inc., 23815 Stuart Ranch Road, P.O. Box 8987 Malibu, CA 90265.

Worklife: A publication on employment and persons with disabilities. The President's Committee on Employment of Persons with Disabilities, Suite 636, 1111 20th Street, N.W., Washington, DC 20036.

Networks and Cable Stations

WCBS-Channel 2, 524 W. 57th St., New York, NY, 10019 (212)975-4321.

WNBC-Channel 4, 30 Rockefeller Plaza, New York, NY, 10112, (212)664-4444.

WNYW-Channel 5, 205 East 67th St., New York, NY, 10021, (212)452-5555.

WABC-Channel 7, 7 Lincoln Square, New York, NY, 10023, (212)456-7777.

WWOR-Channel 9, 9 Broadcast Plaza, Secaucus, NJ, 07094, (201)348-0009.

WPIX-Channel 11, 11 WPIX Plaza, New York, NY, 10017, (212)949-1 100.

WNET-Channel 13, 356 W. 58th St., New York, NY, 10019, (212)560-2000.

NJN-The New Jersey Channel. Channels 23, 50, 52, 58, CN 777, Trenton, NJ, 08625, (609)777-5000.

WXTV-Channel 41/Univision, 24 Meadowland Pk., Secaucus, NJ, 07094, (201)348-4141.

WHSE-Channel 68 (Home Shopping Club), 390 W. Market St., Newark, NJ, 07107, (201)643-6800.

CBS Entertainment, 7800 Beverly Blvd., Los Angeles, CA, 90036, (213)852-2345.

NBC Entertainment, 3000 W. Alameda Ave., Burbank, CA, 91523, (818)840-4444.

ABC Entertainment, 2040 Avenue of the Stars, Century City, CA. W07, (213)557-7777.

PBS, 1320 Braddock Place, Alexandria, VA, 22314, (703)739-5000.

Fox Television Entertainment,10201 W. Pico Blvd., Los Angeles, CA, 90035, (213)203-3553.

American Movie Classics, 150 Crossway Park West, Woodbury, NY, 11797, (516)364-2222.

Arts and Entertainment (The History Channel), 235 E. 45th St., New York, NY, 10017, (212)661-4500.

Black Entertainment Television, 1899, 9th St. N.E., Washington, DC, 20018, (202)608-2800.

CNBC (America's Talking), 2200 Fletcher Ave., Fort Lee, NJ, 07024, (201)346-6777.

C-Span, 400 N. Capitol St. NW, Suite 650, Washington, DC, 20001, (202)737-3220.

CTN-Cable Television Network, of N.J. 124 W. State St., Trenton, NJ,. 08W8, (609)392-4360.

The Discovery Channel (The Learning Channel), 7700 Wisconsin Ave., Bethesda, MD,. 20814, (301)986-1999.

The Disney Channel, 3800 W. Alameda Ave., Burbank, CA, 91505, (818)569-7500.

ESPN (ESPN2) ESPN Plaza, Bristol, CN, 06010, (203)585-2000.

The Family Channel, 1000 Centerville Tpke., Virginia Beach, VA, 23463, (804)523-7300.

Home Box Office (Cinemax, Comedy Central, E), 1100 Sixth Ave., New York City, NY, 10036, (212)512-1000.

Lifetime, World Wide Plaza, 309 W.149th St., New York City, NY, 10019 (212)424-7000.

MSG, 2 Penn Plaza, New York, N.Y. 10121, (212)465-6000.

MTV (Nickelodeon, VH-I, Comedy Central), 1775 Broadway, New York, NY, 10019.

State Assistive Technology Programs

ALABAMA: Alabama Department of Education, Division of Rehabilitation Services, 2129 East South Blvd. Montgomery, AL 36111 (205)281-8780

ALASKA: Assistive Technologies of Alaska, 400 D St. Ste. 230, Anchorage, AK 99501, (907)274-0138 (Voice/TDD), (800)770-0138 (Voice/TDD), (907)274-1399 (FAX)

ARKANSAS: Arkansas Increasing Capabilities, Access Network, 2201 Braced, See 117, Little Rock, AR 72202 (501)666-8868 (Voice/TAD), (800)828-2799 (Arkansas Only), (501)666-5319 (FAX)

CALIFORNIA: Independent Living Division, California Dept of Rehabilitation, 830 K St Mall, 2nd A, Sacramento, CA 95814, (916)323-0595

COLORADO: Colorado Assistive Technology, Project Rocky Mountain Resource and Training Institute, 6355 Ward Rd, See. 310,

Arvada, CO 80004 (303)420-2942 (Voice/TAD), (303)420-8675 (FAX)

CONNECTICUT: Connecticut Assistive Technology Project, Bureau of Rehabilitation Services 10 Griffin Road N., Windsor, CT 06095 (203)298-2042, (203)298-9590 (FAX)

DELAWARE: Delaware Assistive Technology Initiative, Applied Science and Engineering Laboratories, University of Delaware, A.I. du Pont Institute, 1600 Rockland Rd, Rm 154, Wilmington, DE 19899 (302)651-6790 (302)651-6794 (TAD), (302)651-6793 (FAX)

DISTRICT OF COLUMBIA: RESNA Technical Assistance Project, 1101 Connecticut Ave NW, See. 700, Washington, DC 20036 (202)857-1140 (Voice/TAD) (202)223-4579 (FAX)

DC Partnership for AssistiveTechnology, National Rehabilitation Hospital, 102 Irving St NW Washington, DC 20010 (202)877-1498

FLORIDA: Florida Assistive Technology Project, Dept of Labor and Employment, Division of Vocational Rehabilitation, Bureau of Client Services, Rehabilitation Engineering Technology, 1709-A Mahan Dr, Tallahassee, FL 32399-0696 (904)488-8380, (904)488-6210 (FAX)

GEORGIA: Georgia Tools For Life, Division of Rehabilitation Services, 2 Peachtree St. NW, See 23-411, Atlanta, GA 30303 (800)726-9119, (404)894-4960, (404)657-3084, (404)657-3085 (TAD), (404)657-3086 (FAX)

HAWAII: Hawaii Assistive Technology System, 677 Ala Moana Blvd., See. 403, Honolulu, HI 96813, (808)532-7110 (Voice/TAD), (808)532-7120 (FAX)

IDAHO: Idaho Assistive Technology Project, 129 W Third St., Moscow, ID 83843, (208)885-9429, (208)885-6849, (208)885-9056 (FAX)

ILLINOIS: Illinois Assistive Technology Project, 110 ILES Park Pl., Springfield, IL 62718 (800)852 -5110 (Illinois Only-Voice/TAD), (217)522-7985 (Voice/TAD), (217)522-8067 (FAX)

INDIANA: Indiana Attain (Accessing Technology Through Awareness in Indiana) Project Indiana Family and Social Services Admin., Division of Aging and Rehabilitation Services 402 W Washington St., Rm. W453, PO Box 7083, Indianapolis, IN 46207-7083, (800)545-7763, (812)855-9396, (812)855-9630 (FAX)

IOWA: Iowa Program For Assistive Technology, Iowa Univ Affiliated Program, Univ Hospital School, Iowa City, IA 52242, (800)331-3027, (319)353-6386, (319)356-8284 (FAX)

KANSAS: Life Span Institute, Univ of Kansas, PO Box 738, Parsons, KS 67357, (316)421-6550, Ext. 1890/1854

KENTUCKY: Kentucky Assistive Technology Services Network Coordinating Center, 427 Versailles Rd., Frankfort, KY 40601, (502)564-4665 (Voice/TAD), (502)564-3976 (FAX)

LOUISIANA: Louisiana Technology Assistance Network, PO Box 3455, Bin #14, Baton Rouge, LA 70821-3455, (800)922-3425, (800)256-1633 (TAD), (504)342-2471 (Voice/TAD), (504)342-4419 (FAX)

MAINE: Maine Consumer Information and Technology, Training Exchange (Maine CITE), Maine CITE Coordinating Center, Univ of Maine at Augusta, University Heights, Augusta, ME 04330, (207)621-3195 (Voice/TAD), (207)621-3193 (FAX)

MARYLAND: Maryland Technology Assistance Program, Governor's Office for Handicapped Individuals, 300 W Lexington St., Box 10, Baltimore, MD 21201, (800)838-4827, (410)333-4975 (410)333-6674 (FAX)

MASSACHUSETTS: Massachusetts Assistive Technology Partnership Ctr., Children's Hospital 300 Longwood Ave., Boston, MA 02115, (617)727-5540, (617)345-9743 (TAD), (617)735-7820, (617)735-6345 (TAD), (617)735-6345 (FAX)

MICHIGAN: Michigan Assistive Technology Project, Michigan Dept of Education, Rehabilitation Services, PO Box 30010, Lansing, MI 48909, (517)373-4056, (517)373-4058 (FAX)

MINNESOTA: Minnesota Star Program, 300 Centennial Bldg., 658 Cedar St., St. Paul, MN 55155 (800)331-3027, (612)297-1554, (612)296-9962 (TAD), (612)297-7200 (FAX)

MISSISSIPPI: Mississippi Project Start, PO Box 1698, 300 Capers Ave., Bldg. 3, Jackson, MS 39215-1698, (601)354-6891 (Voice/TAD), (601)354-6080 (FAX)

MISSOURI: Missouri Assistive Technology Project, Univ of Missouri-Kansas City, Rm117, EDUC, 5100 Rockhill Rd., Kansas City, MO 64110-2499, (816)235-5342, (816)235-5339, (800)647-8558 (TAD), (816)235-5270 (FAX)

MONTANA: MonTECH, The Univ. of Montana. MUARID, MonTECH, 634 Eddy Ave., Missoula, MT 59812, (406)243-5676, (406)243-2349 (FAX)

NEBRASKA: Nebraska Assistive Technology Project, 301 Centennial Mail S, PO Box 94987, Lincoln, NE 68509-4987, (402)471-0734, (402)471-3647 (Voice/TAD), (402)471-0117 (FAX)

NEVADA: Nevada Assistive Technology Project, Rehabilitation Division, Community-Based Services Dept., 711 S Stewart St., Carson City, NV 89710, (702)687-4452, (702)687-3388 (TAD), (702)687-3292 (FAX)

NEW HAMPSHIRE: Now Hampshire Technology Partnership Project, Institute on Disability, 10 Ferry St., #14, The Concord Center, Concord, NH 03301, (603)224-0630 (Voice/TAD), (603)228-3270 (FAX)

NEW JERSEY: New Jersey Technology Assistive Resource Program, Labor Building, Room 806, CN 938, Trenton, NJ 08625, (609)292-7496, (609)292-7556, (609)292-4616 (FAX)

NEW MEXICO: New Mexico Technology Assistance Program, 435 St. Michael's Dr., Bldg. D, Santa Fe, NM 87503, (800)866-2253 (Voice/TAD), (505)827-3532 (Voice/TAD), (505)827-3746 (FAX)

NEW YORK: New York State Triad Project, Office of Advocate for the Disabled, One Empire State Plaza, Tenth Floor, Albany, NY 12223-0001, (518)474-2825, (818)473-4231 (TAD), (518)473-6005 (FAX)

NORTH CAROLINA: North Carolina Assistive Technology Project, Dept. of Human Resources, Division of Vocational Rehabilitation Services, 1110 Navaho Dr., See 101, Raleigh, NC 27609 (800)852-0042, (919)850-2787 (Voice/TAD), (919)850-2792 (FAX)

NORTH DAKOTA: Director of Rehabilitation, Office of Rehabilitation, 400 E Broadway, See 303, Bismarck, ND 58501, (701)224-3999

OHIO: Ohio Assistive Technology Project, 400 E Campus View Blvd., SW5F, Columbus, OH 43235-4604, (614)438-1450, (614)438-1257 (FAX)

OKLAHOMA: Oklahoma Assistive Technology Project, Dept. of Human Services, Rehabilitation Services Division, DHS, RS #24, PO Box 25352, Oklahoma City, OK 73125, (405)424-4311, (405)427-2753 (FAX)

OREGON: Oregon Technology Access For Life Needs Project, Chemeketa Community College, TALN Center, 4000 Lancaster Dr., NE, Bldg. 5, Rm. 103, PO Box 14007, Salem, OR 97309-7070, (503)399-6977, (503)378-2756 (FAX)

PENNSYLVANIA: Pennsylvania's Initiative on Assistive Technology, Institute on Disability/UAP, Ritter Hall Annex 433 (004-00), Philadelphia, PA 19122, (215)204-1356 (800)204-7428 (Voice/TAD), (215)204-6336 (FAX)

PUERTO RICO:Project Director, Box 22484, University of Puerto Rico, Station Rio Piedras, PR 00931, (809)754-8926

RHODE ISLAND: Office of Rehabilitation Services, 40 Fountain St., Providence, RI 02903, (401)421-7005

SAMOA: American Samoa Division of Vocational Rehabilitation, Dept. of Human Resources, Pago Pago, American Samoa 96799, (684)633-2336, (684)633-7183

SOUTH CAROLINA: South Carolina Assistive Technology Program, Vocational Rehabilitation Dept., PO Box 15, 141 O-C Boston Ave., West Columbia, SC 29171-0015, (803)822-5404 (Voice/ TAD), (803)822-4301 (FAX)

SOUTH DAKOTA: Dakota Link, 1925 Plaza Blvd., Rapid City, SD 57702, (800)645-0673 (Voice/TAD), (605)394-1876, (605)394-5315 (FAX)

TENNESSEE: Tennessee Technology Access Project, Office of Assistive Technology, Central Office, Doctor's Bldg., See 300, 706 Church St., Nashville, TN 37243-0675, (800)732-5059 (Tennessee Only), (615)741-7441, (615)741-0770 (FAX)

TEXAS: Texas Assistive Technology Project, The University of Texas at Austin, UAP of Texas, Dept. of Special Education, EDB 306, Austin, TX 78712, (512)471-7621

UTAH: Utah Assistive Technology Program, Center for Persons with Disabilities, UMC 6855, Logan, UT 84322, (800)333-8824, (801)750-1982, (801)750-2355 (FAX)

VERMONT: Vermont Assistive Technology Project, 103 S. Main St., Weeks I, Waterbury, VT 05671-2305, (802)241-2620 (Voice/ TAD), (802)241-3052 (FAX)

VIRGINIA: Virginia Assistive Technology System, 4900 Fitzhugh Ave., Richmond, VA 23230, (804)367-2442, (804)367-2445 (Voice/TAD), (804)367-2440 (FAX)

WASHINGTON: DSHS/DVR, PO Box 45340, Olympia, WA 98504-5340, (206)438-8049

WEST VIRGINIA: West Virginia Assistive Technology System, Division of Rehabilitation Services, Capital Complex, Charleston, WV 25305-0890, (800)841-8436, (304)766-4698, (304)293-7294 (FAX)

WISCONSIN: Division of Vocational Rehabilitation, PO Box 7852, 1 W. Wilson St., Rm 950, Madison, WI 53707-7852, (608)266-5395, (608)267-6720, (608)266-9599 (TAD)

WYOMING Program Consultant, Div. of Vocational Rehabilitation, 1100 Herschler Bldg., Cheyenne, WY 82002, (307)777-6841

Bibliography

Ablon, J. (1984). *Little people in America: The social dimensions of dwarfism.* New York: Praeger Publishers.

Ablon, J. (1988). *Living with a difference: Families with dwarf children.* New York: Praeger Publishers.

About being sensitive to people with disabilities. (1995). A Scriptographic Booklet, No. 49361B-93, South Deerfield, MA: Channing L. Bete Co., Inc.

Abrahams, I. (1958). *Jewish life in the Middle Ages.* New York: Meridian Books, Inc.

Adams, B. (1979). *Like it is: Facts and feelings about handicaps from kids who know.* New York: Walker & Company.

Advisory Committee on Human Radiation Experiments [ACHRE] (1994). *Interim report.* Washington, DC: U.S. Government Printing Office.

Advisory Committee on Human Radiation Experiments [ACHRE] (1996). *Executive summary and guide to final report.* Washington, DC: U.S. Government Printing Office.

Aiello, B. (1984). *The visually handicapped child in the regular class.* Washington, D.C.: The American Federation of Teachers. The Teachers' Network for the Education of the Handi capped.

Aiello, B., & Shulman, J. (1988). *Business is looking up.* Frederick, MD: Twenty-first Century Books.

Aiello, B., & Shulman, J. (1988). *It's your turn at bat.* Frederick, MD: Twenty-first Century Books.

Aiello, B., & Shulman, J. (1988). *Secrets aren't always for keeps.* Frederick, MD: Twenty-First Century Books.

Albright, K., Brown, L., Vandeventer, P. & Jorgensen, J. (1989). Characteristics of educational programs for students with severe intellectual disabilities, in D. Biklin, D. Ferguson & A. Ford (eds.)

Schooling and disability. Chicago, IL: University of Chicago Press, pp. 59-76.

Alexander, S. (1990). *Mom can't see me.* New York: Macmillan Publishing Company.

Alexier v. Matzke (1908). 151 Mich. 36, 115 N.W. 251.

Allport, G. (1958). *The nature of prejudice.* Garden City, NY: Doubleday & Company, Inc.

American Association on Mental Retardation (1992a). *Mental retardation: Definition, classification, and systems of supports.* Washington, DC: Author.

American Association on Mental Retardation (1992b). *Mental retardation: Definition, classification, and systems of supports* (Workbook). Washington, DC: Author.

American Psychiatric Association (1994). *Diagnostic and statistical manual of mental disorders (4th ed). (DSM-IV).* Washington, DC: Author.

American Psychiatric Association. (1994). *Quick reference to the diagnostic criteria from DSM- IV.* Washington, DC: Author.

Americans With Disabilities Act of 1990. PL. 101-336.

The Americans with Disabilities Act checklist for readily achievable barrier removal (1992). Washington, DC: Adaptive Environments Center & Barrier Free Environments. pp. 6-12. Author.

Anders, R. (1976). *A look at mental retardation.* Minneapolis, MM: Lerner Publishers.

Annas, G. & Grodin, M. (1992). *The Nazi doctors and the Nuremberg Code: Human Rights in Human Experimentation.* New York: Oxford University Press.

Antonak, R, and Livneh, H. (1988). *The measurement of attitudes toward people with disabilities: Methods, psychometrics and scales.* Springfield, IL: Charles C. Thomas, Publisher.

Antonak, R. and Livneh, H. (1990). The measurement of attitudes toward people with disabilities: Recommendations for researchers, In S. Hey, G. Kiger, B. Altman, and J. Scheer (eds.) (1990). *The social exploration of disability.* Salem, OR: The Society for Disability Studies and Willamette University. pp. 5-11.

Arieno, M. (1989). *Victorian lunatics: A social epidemiology of mental illness in mid-ninteenth century England.* Cranbury, NJ: Associated University Presses.

Asher, S., & Taylor, A. (1982). Social outcomes of mainstreaming: Sociometric assessment and beyond, in P. Strain (ed.) *Social devel-*

opment of exceptional children. Rockville, MD: Aspen Systems. pp. 1-18.

Astor, C. (1985). *Who makes people different: Jewish perspectives on the disabled.* New York: United Synagogue of America, Department of Youth Activities.

Baird, R. & Rosenbaum, S. (1989). *Euthanasia: The moral issues.* Buffalo, NY: Prometheus Books.

Baken, J. (1977). *Educational planning for the severely multiply handicapped.* Reston, VA: Council for Exceptional Children, Division on Physically Handicapped, Homebound & Hospitalized.

Barnes, E. (1975). Developing receptivity toward labeled children, in *Proceedings of the special study institute fostering positive attitudes toward the handicapped in school settings.* Rensselaerville, NY: The Division for Handicapped Children, New York State Education Department, A Project of the New York State Network of Special Education Instructional Material Centers. pp. 67-92.

Barnes, E., Berrigan, C., & Biklen, D. (1978). *What's the difference? Teaching positive attitudes toward people with disabilities.* Syracuse, NY: Human Policy Press.

Barr, M. (1899). The how, the why, and the wherefore of the training of feeble-minded children, *The Journal of Psycho-Asthenics,* Vol 4, In A. Baumeister, and E. Butterfield (eds.) (1970). *Residential facilities for the mentally retarded,* Chicago: Aldine Publishing Co. pp. 204-212.

Bart, D. (1984). The differential diagnosis of special education: Managing social pathology as individual disability, in Barton & Tomlinson (eds.). *Special education and social interests.* New York: Nichols Publishing Company, pp. 81-121.

Bartel, N. & Guskin, S. (1980). A handicap as a social phenomenon, in W. Cruickshank (ed.) *Psychology of exceptional children and youth.* Englewood Cliffs, NJ: Prentice-Hall. pp. 45-73.

Barton, L. (ed.) (1996). *Disability and society: Emerging issues and insights.* New York: Addison Wesley Longman.

Baskin, B. (1975). The handicapped in children's literature, in *Proceedings of the Special Study Institute, Fostering positive attitudes toward the handicapped in school settings.* Rensselaerville, NY: New York State Education Department. pp. 132-164.

Baskin, B. & Harris, K. (1977). *Notes from a different drummer: A guide to juvenile fiction portraying the handicapped.* New York R. R. Bowker Company.

Baskin, B. & Harris, K. (1984). *More notes from a different drummer: A guide to juvenile fiction portraying the disabled.* New York: R. R. Bowker Company.

Batson, T. and Bergman, E. (1973). *Angels and outcasts: An anthology of deaf characters in literature.* Washington, DC: Gallaudet University Press.

Bauer, C. (1985). Fostering positive attitudes toward the handicapped via literature. *Middle School Journal.* Vol. *16,* No. *5,* pp. 19-22.

Baum, D. (ed.) (1982). *The human side of exceptionality.* Austin, TX: Pro-Ed.

Baum, D. & Wells, C. (1985). Promoting handicap awareness in preschool children. *Teaching Exceptional Children,* Vol. *17,* No. *4,* pp. 282-287.

Baumeister, A. & Butterfield, E. (eds.) (1970). *Residential facilities for the mentally retarded.* Chicago, IL: Aldine Publishing Co.

Beattie v. Board of Education, 169 Wis. 231, 232, 172N.W. 153, 154, cited in L. Burrello & Sage (1979), *Leadership and change in special education,* p. 37.

Beirne-Smith, M., Patton, J., & Ittenbach, R. (1994). *Mental retardation.* (4th ed.). New York: Macmillan College Publishing Company, Inc.

Beisser, A. (1989). *Flying without wings: Personal reflections on being disabled.* New York: Doubleday.

Bell, C. &. Burgdorf, R. (1983). *Accommodating the spectrum of individual abilities.* (Clearinghouse Publication #81) Washington, DC: United States Commission on Civil Rights.

Bellarosa, J. (1989). *A problem of plumbing and other stories.* Santa Barbara, CA: John Daniel Company.

Benderly, B. (1980). *Dancing without music: Deafness in America.* New York: Doubleday Publishers.

Bennets, L. (1993, September). Jerry vs. the kids. *Vanity Fair.* pp. 82-98.

Berenbaum, M. (ed.) (1992). *A mosaic of victims: Non-Jews murdered by the nazis.* New York: New York University Press.

Berenbaum, M. (1993). *The world must know: The history of the Holocaust as told in the United States Holocaust Memorial Museum.* Boston: Little Brown & Co.

Bergantino, S. (1984). A person is a person. *Early Years.* Vol. *14,* No. *5,* pp. 40-41.

Berger, G. (1979). *Physical disabilities.* New York: Franklin Watts.

Bergman, T. (1989). *Seeing in special ways: Children living with blindness.* Milwaukee, WI: Gareth Stevens Children's Books.

Bergman, T. (1989). *On our own terms: Children living with physical disabilities.* Milwaukee, WI: Gareth Stevens, Inc.

Bernstein, J. & Fireside, B. (1991). *Special parents, special children.* Morton Grove, IL: Albert Whitman & Company.

Berry, J. (1987). *Every kid's guide to overcoming prejudice and discrimination.* Chicago, IL: Childrens Press.

Berry, J. (1990). *Good answers to tough questions: About physical disabilities.* Chicago, IL: Childrens Press.

Biklen, D. (1977). The politics of institutions, in Blatt, Biklen & Bogdan, R. (eds.). *An alternative textbook in special education,* pp. 29-84.

Biklen, D. (1989). Redefining schools, in D. Biklen, D. Ferguson & A. Ford (eds.) *Schooling and disability,* Chicago: National Society for the Study of Education. pp. 1-24.

Biklen, D. & Bogdan, R. (1977). Media portrayals of disabled people: A study in stereotypes, *Interracial Books of Children Bulletin,* 8, Nos. 6 & 7, pp. 4-9.

Biklen, D., Ferguson, D., & Ford, A. (eds.). (1989). *Schooling and disability.* Chicago: National Society for the Study of Education, University of Chicago Press.

Biklen, D. & Sokoloff, M. (eds.) (1978). *What do you do when your wheelchair gets a flat tire?: Questions and answers about disabilities.* Syracuse, NY: Human Policy Press.

Binding, K. & Hoche, A. (1975, originally published 1920). *The release of the destruction of life devoid of value.* R. Sassone (ed.) Santa Ana, CA: Life Quality Paperbacks.

Binkard, B. (1985). A successful handicap awareness program—Run by special parents. *Teaching Exceptional Children.* Vol *17.* pp. 12-16.

Blaska, J. (1993). The power of language: Speak and write "person first," *Perspectives on disability* (2nd ed). M. Nagler (ed.). Palo Alto, CA: Health Markets Research.

Blatt, B. (1970). *Exodus from pandemonium: Human abuse and a reformation of public policy.* Boston: Allyn & Bacon.

Blatt, B. (1981). *In and out of mental retardation: Essays on educability, disability, and human policy.* Baltimore, MD: University Park Press.

Blatt, B. (1987). *The conquest of mental retardation.* Austin, TX: Pro-Ed. Inc.

Blatt, B., Biklen, D. & Bogdan, R. (1977). *An alternative textbook in special education: People, schools and other institutions.* Denver, CO: Love Publishing Co.

Blatt, B. & Kaplan, F. (1966/1974). *Christmas in purgatory: A photographic essay on mental retardation.* Syracuse, NY: Human Policy Press.

Blatt, B., Ozolins, A. & McNally, J. (1979). *The family papers: A return to purgatory.* New York: Longman, Inc.

Bliss, M. & Schwartz, A. (1979). *Exploring attitudes toward women with disabilities: A curriculum guide for employers and educators.* New York: New York City Commission on the Status of Women.

Bloom, A. (trans.) *The republic of Plato* (1968 ed.). New York: Basic Books.

Bluel, H. (1973). *Sex and society in Nazi Germany.* Philadelphia, PA: J. B. Lippincott, Co.

Blumberg, L. (1991, October/November). On display: Your child is being humiliated. *Exceptional Parent,* Vol. *21,* No. *7,* pp. 25-26, 28, 30.

Bobrick, B. (1995). *Knotted tongues: Stuttering in history and the quest for a cure.* New York: Simon & Schuster.

Bogdan, R. (1986). Exhibiting mentally retarded people for amusement and profit, 1850-1940. *American Journal of Mental Deficiency.* Vol. *91,* No. *2,* pp. 120-126.

Bogdan, R. (1988). *Freak show: Presenting human oddities for amusement and profit.* Chicago, IL: University of Chicago Press.

Bogdan, R. & Biklen, D. (1977, March/April). Handicapism. *Social Policy,* 7, pp. 14-19.

Bogdan, R. & Knoll, J. (1988). The sociology of disability, in Meyen, E. & Skrtic, T. (eds.) *Exceptional children and youth: An introduction.* Denver, CO: Love Publishing Company. pp. 449-477.

Bogdan, R., Biklen, D., Shapiro, A. & Spelkoman, D. (1982, fall). The disabled: Media's monster. *Social Policy.* *13*, pp. 32-35.

Bogdan, R. & Taylor, S. (1994). *The social meaning of mental retardation: Two life stories.* New York: Teachers College Press, Columbia University.

Bookbinder, S. (1978). *Mainstreaming—what every child needs to know about disabilities.* Providence, RI: Rhode Island Easter Seal Society.

Bowe, F. (1978). *Handicapping America: Barriers to disabled people.* New York: Harper & Row.

Bower, E. (1980). *The handicapped in literature.* Denver, CO: Love Publishing Company.

Bower, T. (1981). *Blind eye to murder: Britain, America and the purging of Nazi Germany—a pledge betrayed.* London: Granada Publishing Ltd.

Braginsky, D. & Braginsky, B. (1971). *Hansels and Gretels: Studies of children in institutions for the mentally retarded.* New York: Holt, Rinehart & Winston, Inc.

Braithwaite, A. (1987). *I have a mental handicap.* London, GB: Dinosaur Publications.

Brand, D. (1988). This is the Selma of the deaf. *Time Magazine*, March 21, p. 6.

Brightman, A. (ed.) (1985/1990). *Ordinary moments: The disabled experience.* Syracuse, NY: Human Policy Press.

Brodbelt, S. (1969). Simulation in the social studies: An overview. *Social Education 33*, pp. 176-178.

Brodkin, M. & Coleman Advocates for Children & Youth (1993). *Every kid counts: 31 ways to save our children.* San Francisco, CA: Harper Collins Publishers.

Brolin, D. (1995). *Career education: A functional life skills approach.* Englewood Cliffs, NJ: Merrill/Prentice-Hall.

Brown, C. (1954). *My left foot.* London, GB. Octopus Publishing Group.

Brown, D. (1983). The handicap that had no name, in *Reflections on growing up disabled*, R. Jones (ed.). Reston, VA: Council for Exceptional Children. pp. 5-16.

Browne, S., Connors, D. & Stern, N. (eds.) (1985). With the power of each breath: A disabled women's anthology. Pittsburgh, PA: Cleis Press.

Buck v. Bell, 143 Va. 313, 130 S.E. 516, 517 (1925).

Bullock, C. & Mahon, M. (1997). *Introduction to recreation services for people with disabilities: A person-centered approach.* Champaign, IL: Sagamore Publishing.

Bunch, G. (1996). *Kids, disabilities and regular classrooms: An annotated bibliogtaphy of selected children's literature on disability.* Toronto, Ontario, Canada. Inclusion Press.

The Burden of the Feeble-Minded in Massachusetts, (1912), cited in testimony of Thomas Gilhool, 1995, p. 7.

Burgdorf, R. (1980). *The legal rights of handicapped persons: Cases, materials and text.* Baltimore, MD: Brookes Publishers.

Burgdorf, M. & Burgdorf, R. (1975). A history of unequal treatment: The qualifications of handicapped persons as a *Suspect Class* under the Equal Protection Clause, *Santa Clara Lawyer,* Vol *215,* No. *4,* pp. 855-910.

Burgdorf, R. & Burgdorf, M. (1977). The wicked witch is almost dead: "Buck v. Bell" and the sterilization of handicapped persons. Philadelphia, PA: reprinted from the *Temple Law Quarterly,* Vol. *50,* No. *4,* pp. 995-1034.

Burke, C. & McDaniel, J. (1991). *A special kind of hero: The star of "Life Goes On" tells his remarkable story.* New York: Doubleday, a division of Bantam Doubleday Dell Publishing Group, Inc.

Burleigh, M. (1994). *Death and deliverance: "Euthanasia" in Germany 1900-1945.* New York: Cambridge University Press.

Burleigh, M. & Wippermann, W. (1991). *The racial state: Germany 1933-1945.* Cambridge, Great Britain: Cambridge University Press.

Burns, R. (1995, August 18). 16,000 used in radiation experiments, *The Times,* (Trenton, N.J). p. 3B.

Burrello, L. & Sage, D. (1979). *Leadership and change in special education.* Englewood Cliffs, NJ: Prentice-Hall, Inc.

Buscaglia, L. (1983). *The disabled and their parents: A counseling challenge.* New York: Holt, Rinehart & Winston.

Buxton, W. (1985). *Talcott Parsons and the capitalist nation-state: Political sociology as a strategic vocation.* Toronto, Canada: University of Toronto Press.

Byman, B. (1989). Bitter fruit: The legacy of Nazi medical experiments, *Minnesota Medicine.* Vol. 72.

Byrnes, D. (1987). *Teacher they called me a _____!* New York: The Anti-Defamation League of B'nai B'rith.

Cairo, S. (1985). *Our brother has Down's syndrome.* Toronto, Canada: Annick Press Ltd.

Callahan, J. (1989). *Don't worry, he won't get far on foot: The autobiography of a dangerous man.* New York: William Morrow & Company, Inc.

Callahan, M. (1987). *Fighting for Tony.* New York: Simon & Schuster, Inc.

Caplan, A. (ed.) (1992). *When medicine went mad: Bioethics and the Holocaust.* Totowa, New Jersey: Humana Press.

Caplan, A. (1992a). The doctors' trial and analogies to the Holocaust in contemporary bioethical debates, in G. Annas & M. Grodin (1992), *The Nazi doctors and the Nuremberg code: Human rights in human experimentation,* New York: Oxford University Press, pp. 258-275.

Carlberg C. & Kavale, K. (1977). The efficacy of special versus regular class placement for exceptional children: A mega-analysis, *Journal of Special Education*, Vol. *14*, pp. 295-309.

Carlisle, J. (1985). *Tangled tongue: Living with a stutter*. Reading, MA: Addison-Wesley Publishing Company, Inc.

Cashdollar, P. & Martin, J. (1977). *Kids come in special flavors: Understanding handicaps*. Dayton, OH: Kids Come in Special Flavors Company.

Charkins, H. (1996). *Children with facial difference*. Bethesda, MD: Woodbine House.

Chicago, Illinois Mun. Code 36-34, 1966, repealed 1974, cited in M. Burgdorf & R. Burgdorf, A history of unequal treatment: The qualifications of handicapped persons as a "suspect class" under the equal protection clause, (1976) Santa Clara, CA: *Santa Clara Lawyer,* Vol. *15*, No. *4*, p. 863.

China's orphanages of death. (January 22,1966). *U.S. News and World Report, p. 14.*

Chinese orphanages are accused of abuses. (January 7, 1966). *The New York Times*, p. 2E.

Clark, K. (1954). Testimony in *Brown v. Board of Education,* cited in L. Weicker (1995). *Maverick: A life in politics*. Boston, MA: Little, Brown and Company.

Cleary, M. (1976). *Please know me as I am: A guide to helping children understand the child with special needs*. Sudbury, MA: Jerry Cleary Company.

Clinard, R. & Meier, R. (1979, 5th ed.). *Sociology of deviant behavior.* New York: Holt, Rinehart & Winston.

Clinton apologizes to all wronged by radiation testing. (Trenton, N.J.) *The Times*, October 4, 1995. p. A10.

Cohen, J. (1998) *Disability etiquette: Tips on interacting with people with disabilities*. New York: Eastern Paralyzed Veterans Association.

Cohen, J. (1996). *Monster theory.* Minneapolis: University of Minnesota Press.

Cohen, L. (1981). Ethical issues in withholding care from severely handicapped infants. *Journal of the Association for the Severely Handicapped*. Vol. *6*, pp. 65-67.

Cohen, L. (1994). *Train go sorry: Inside a deaf world*. New York: Houghton Mifflin Company.

Cohen, S. (1974/1977). *Special people*. Englewood Cliffs, NJ: Prentice-Hall, Inc.

Cohen, S., Grand, C., Koehler, N. & Berman, D. (1981). *A curriculum to foster understanding of people with disabilities: The handicapped in literature*. Albany, NY: University of the State of New York & The State Education Department.

Cohen, S. & Koehler, N. (1981). *A curriculum to foster understanding of people with disabilities: Science and health education perspectives on the handicapped*. Albany, NY: University of the State of New York & The State Education Department.

Cohen, S., Koehler, N. & Grand, C. (1977a). *Accepting individual differences: Overview*. Niles, IL: Developmental Learning Materials.

Cohen, S., Koehler, N. & Grand, C. (1977b). *Accepting individual differences: Mental Retardation and learning disabilities*. Niles, IL: Developmental Learning Materials.

Cohen, S., Koehler, N. & Grand, C. (1977c). *Accepting individual differences: Motor impairment*. Niles, IL: Developmental Learning Materials.

Cohen, S., Koehler, N. & Grand, C. (1977d). *Accepting individual differences: Visual impairment*. Niles, IL: Developmental Learning Materials.

Collins, T., Schneider, M. & Kroeger, S. (1995). (Dis)Abling images. *Radical Teacher*, No. 47, pp. 11-47.

Conard, B. (1988, April/May). Cooperative learning and prejudice reduction. *Social Education*. pp. 283-286.

Conot, R. (1983). *Justice at Nuremberg*. New York: Carroll & Graf Publishers.

Conrad, P. (1996). The medicalization of deviance in American Culture, in E. Rubington & M. Weinberg, (eds.) (1996). *Deviance: The interactionist perspective* (6th ed.) Boston, MA: Allyn & Bacon.

Conrad, P. & Schneider, J. (1992). *Deviance and medicalization: From badness to sickness*. Philadelphia, PA: Temple University Press.

Corn, A. (1977). *Monocular Mac*. New York: National Association for the Visually Handicapped.

Corn, I. & Martinez, I. (1985). *When you have a visually handicapped child in your classroom: Suggestions for teachers*. New York: American Foundation for the Blind.

Cox, S. (1989). *The Munchkins remember: The Wizard of Oz and beyond*. New York: E. P. Dutton.

Crissey, M. & Rosen, M. (1986). *Institutions for the mentally retarded: A changing role in changing times.* Austin, TX: Pro-Ed.

Crouch, B. (1987). *Dick Tracy: America's most famous detective.* New York: Citidel Press.

Cruickshank, W. (ed.) (1980). *Psychology of exceptional children and youth.* Englewood Cliffs, NJ: Prentice-Hall.

Cumblad, C. & Strickman, D. (1990). *Friends who care: A disability awareness program for elementary students (Teacher's guide).* Chicago, IL: National Easter Seals Society.

Cummings, M., London, K., Moore, L., Raschke, D., Schwartz, P. & Tofty, J. (1981). *Individual differences: An educator's handbook for a course of studies about people.* Madison, WI: Madison Public Schools.

Cutsforth, T. (1951). *The blind in school and society.* New York: American Foundation for the Blind.

Darwin, C. (1922). *The descent of man and selection in relation to sex,* (2nd. ed. rev.). New York: D. Appleton & Company.

Davenport, C. (1911). *Heredity in relation to eugenics.* New York: Henry Holt & Co.

Davies, J. (1987). Lame, in *With wings: An anthology of literature by and about women with disabilities,* M. Saxton, & F. Howe (eds.). New York: The Feminist Press. pp. 43-45.

Davis, L. (1995). *Enforcing normalcy: Disability, deafness and the body.* London, UK: Verso.

Davis, L. (ed.) (1997). *The disabilities studies reader. New York* Routledge.

Deegan, M. & Brooks, N. (eds.) (1985). *Women and disability: The double handicap.* New Brunswick, NJ: Transaction Books.

Derman-Sparks, L. (1989). *Anti-bias curriculum: Tools for empowering young people.* Washington, DC: National Association for the Education of Young Children.

Despert, L. (1965). *The emotionally disturbed child—then and now.* New York: Robert Brunner, Inc.

Developmental Disabilities Bill of Rights Act of 1978, PL 95-822.

Devlieger, P. (1994). Culture-based concepts and social life of disabled persons in sub-Saharan Africa: The case of the Deaf, in C. Erting, R. Johnson, D. Smith, & B. Snider, (eds). *The deaf way: Perspectives from the international conference on Deaf culture.* Washington, DC: Gallaudet University Press. pp. 85-93.

Dewar, R. (1982). Peer acceptance of handicapped students. *Teaching Exceptional Children*, Vol. *14*, No. *5*, pp. 188-193.

Dickman, I. (1972). *Living with blindness*. Public Affairs Pamphlet No. *473*, New York: Public Affairs Pamphlets.

DiLeo, J. (1983). *Interpreting children's drawings*. New York: Brunner/ Mazel Publishers.

Diodati, D. (1962). In *Experiments in survival*, E. Henrich & L. Kriegel (eds.). New York: Association for the Aid of Crippled Children, pp. 186-188.

Disabled Germans feeling echoes of Nazism. (1993, March/April). *The Disability Rag*, p. 13.

Disciplinary duo disdainfully dumps inept employee (1981, October 20), *Times Picayune/The States Item*, Sec. 1, p. 3. (cited in B. Baskin & K. Harris, 1984, *More notes from a different drummer: A guide to juvenile fiction portraying the disabled.* New York: R. R. Boker. p. 15.

Discover the possibilities (1988). PEAK Parent Center, Inc. Colorado Springs, CO: Author.

Dokecki, P. & Zaner, R. (1986). *Ethics of dealing with persons with severe handicaps: Toward a research agenda*. Baltimore, MD: Paul H. Brookes Publishing Co.

Dolson, F. (1988). How sweet it is for Massimino. *The Philadelphia Inquirer,* March 25, pp. 1C, 6C.

Donaldson, J. (1980). Changing attitudes toward handicapped persons: A review and analysis of research. *Exceptional Children*. *46*, (7), pp. 504-514.

Donaldson, J. (1981). The visibility and image of handicapped people on television. *Exceptional Children*. Vol. *47*, No. *6*, pp. 413-416.

Dmytryshyn, B. (1977). *A history of Russia*. Englewood Cliffs, NJ: Prentice-Hall, Inc.

Drake, R. (1996). Charities, authority, and disabled people: A qualitative study. *Disability and Society,* Vol. *11*, No. *1*, pp. 5-23.

Dr. H. Pfannmeuler gets 5 year sentence, Munich, for part in Nazi program (1951). *The New York Times,* March 16, p. 8.

Drimmer, F. (1973). *Very special people*. Secaucus, NJ: Citadel Press.

Dunn, T. (1993, October 29). Generally speaking: As I see things. *The Elizabeth Reporter*, p. 3.

Durant, W. (1944). *Caesar and Christ*. New York: Simon & Schuster.

Dwyer, K. (1991). *What do you mean I have a learning disability?* New York: Walker & Company.

Edwards, J. & Dawson, D. (1983). *My friend David: A source book about Down's syndrome and a personal story about friendship.* Portland, OR: Ednick Communications, Inc.

Edwards, M. (1996). Ability and disability in the Ancient Greek military community, in E. Makas and L. Schlesinger (eds.) (1996). *End results and starting points: Expanding the field of Disability Studies.* Portland ME: The Society for Disabilities Studies and The Muskie Institute of Public Affairs, pp. 29-33.

Efron, R. & Efron, H. (1967). Measurement of attitudes toward the retarded and an application with educators. *American Journal of Mental Deficiency.* Vol. *72*, pp. 100-106.

Elkins, S., Jones, M. & Ulicny, R. (1987). The media watch campaign manual. Lawrence, KA: The Research & Training Center on Independent Living, The University of Kansas.

Ellis, E. (1990). Why the disabled are always angry. Trenton, NJ: *The Times,* April 5, p. B-3.

Ellis, E. (1995, March). Comment: Listen. *People with Disabilities.* Vol. *5,* No. *1*, pp. 2-3.

English, W. (1977). Correlates of stigma towards physically disabled persons, in J. Stubbins (ed.) *Social and psychological aspects of disability: A handbook for practitioners.* Baltimore, MD: University Park Press. pp. 207-224.

Epilepsy Foundation of America (1992). *Brothers and sisters: A guide for families of children with epilepsy* Landover, MD: Author.

Enteman, W. (1996). Stereotyping, prejudice, and discrimination, in P. Lester (ed.) *Images that injure: Pictorial stereotypes in the media.* Westport, CT: Praeger, pp. 9-14.

Erting, C., Johnson, R., Smith, D. & Snider, B. (eds.) (1994). *The deaf way: Perspectives from the international conference on Deaf culture.* Washington, DC: Gallaudet University Press.

Esquirol, J. (1848). A village of lunatics. *American Journal of Insanity,* Vol. *4,* pp. 217-222.

European parliament condemns China (February, 1966), in *Life, Death and Rights, No. 5,* Disability Awareness in Action, London: p. 1.

The events, forces and issues that triggered enactment of the Education for All Handicapped Children Act of 1975, Joint Subcommittee Hearings (1995) (testimony of Thomas Gilhool).

Evans, J. H. (1976). Changing attitudes toward disabled persons: An experimental study, *Rehabilitation Counseling Bulletin,* Vol. *19*, pp. 527-579.

Exley, H. (ed.) (1984). *What it's like to be me: Written and illustrated entirely by disabled children.* New York: Friendship Press.

The Feeble-minded, or, the hub to our wheel of vice in Ohio (1913), cited in testimony of Thomas Gilhool, 1995, p. 7.

Feldman, S. (1975). The presentation of shortness in everyday life— Height and heightism in American society: Toward a sociology of stature, in S. Feldman & G. Thielbar, (eds.) *Life styles: Diversity in American society.* Boston, MA: Little, Brown.

Ferguson, P., Ferguson, D. & Taylor, S. (eds.) (1992). *Interpreting disability: A qualitative reader.* New York: Teachers College Press, Columbia University.

Fiedler, C., & Simpson, R. (1987). Modifying the attitudes of nonhandicapped high school students toward handicapped peers. *Exceptional Children*, Vol. *19*, pp. 342-349.

Fiedler, L. (1978). *Freaks: Myths and images of the secret self.* New York: Simon & Schuster.

Fiedler, L. (1996). *Tyranny of the normal: Essays on bioethics, theology, and myth.* New Brunswick, NJ: Rutgers University Press.

Fine, M. & Asch, A. (1985). Disabled women: Sexism without the pedestal, in M. Deegan, & N. Brooks, (eds.) (1985). *Women and disability: The double handicap.* New Brunswick, NJ: Transaction Books.

Fine, M. & Asch, A. (eds.) (1988). *Women with disabilities: Essays in psychology, culture, and politics.* Philadelphia, PA: Temple University Press.

Finger, A. (unpublished paper), Hitler's war on the disabled, in Johnson, (1987). Life unworthy of life. *Disability Rag*, Vol. *8*, No. *1*, January/February, pp. 24-26.

Finger, A. (1992). The idiot, the cretin and the cripple. *Disability Rag.* Vol. *13*, No. *6*, November/December, pp. 23-25.

Fletcher, A. (1992a). *Who and what we are—media information.* London, UK: Disability Awareness in Action.

Fletcher, A. (1992b). *Consultation and influence.* London, UK: Disability Awareness in Action.

Fletcher, A. (1992c). *Campaigns.* London, UK: Disability Awareness in Action.

Fletcher, A. (1992d). *Organisation-building.* London, UK: Disability Awareness in Action.

Fletcher, A. (1993). *Information kit to support the International Day of Disabled Persons,* London, UK: Disability Awareness in Action.

Fletcher, A. (1996). European parliament condemns China. *Life Death and Rights.* No. 5. London, UK.

Flynn, R. & Nitsch, K. (1980). *Normalization, social integration, and community services.* Austin, TX: Pro-Ed.

Forest, M. (1989). *It's about relationships.* Toronto, Ontario, Canada: Frontier College Press.

Fostering positive attitudes toward the handicapped in school settings: Proceedings of the special study institute (1975). Rensselaerville, NY: New York State Education Department, Division for Handicapped Children.

Francis, E. (November/December 1995). The faceless enemy. *The Disability Rag and Resource.* pp. 1,4-6).

Franks, B. (1996). Disability and fairy tales: An analysis, in E. Makas and L. Schlesinger (eds.) (1996). *End results and starting points: Expanding the field of Disability Studies.* Portland ME: The Society for Disabilities Studies and The Muskie Institute of Public Affairs, pp. 17-22.

Friedberg, J., Mullins, J. & Sukiennik, A. (1986). *Accept me as I am: Best books of juvenile nonfiction on impairments and disabilities.* New Providence, NJ: R. R. Bowker.

Friedberg, J., Mullins, J. & Sukiennik, A. (1992). *Portraying persons with disabilities (nonfiction): An annotated bibliography of nonfiction for children and teenagers.* New Providence, NJ: R. R. Bowker.

Friedlander, H. (1995). *The origins of Nazi genocide: From euthanasia to the final solution.* Chapel Hill, NC: The University of North Carolina Press.

Freidson, E. (1965). Disability as social deviance, in M. Sussman, (ed.) *Sociology and rehabilitation.* Washington, DC: American Sociological Association.

French, R. (1932). *From Homer to Helen Keller: A social and educational study of the blind.* New York: American Foundation of the Blind.

Fries, K. (ed.). (1997). *Staring back: The disability experience from the inside out.* New York: Penguin Books.

Froschl, M., Colon, L., Rubin, E. & Sprung, B. (1984). *Including all of us: An early childhood curriculum about disability.* New York: Educational Equity Concepts, Inc.

Funk, R. (1987). Disability rights: From caste to class in the context of civil rights, in Gartner & Joe (eds.) *Images of the disabled: disabling images.* New York: Praeger Publishers, pp. 7-30.

Gallagher, H. (1985). *FDR's splendid deception: The moving story of Roosevelt's massive disability and the intense efforts to conceal it from the public.* New York: Dodd, Mead & Company, Inc.

Gallagher, H. (1995). *By trust betrayed: Patients, physicians, and the license to kill in the Third Reich.* Arlington, VA: Vandamere Press.

Gannon, J. (1981). *Deaf heritage: A narrative history of Deaf America.* Silver Spring MD: National Association of the Deaf.

Garland, R. (1995). *The eye of the beholder: Deformity and disability in the Graeco-Roman world.* Ithaca, NY: Cornell University Press.

Gartner, A. & Joe, T. (eds.) (1987). *Images of the disabled: disabling images.* New York: Praeger Publishers.

Gartner, A., Lipsky, D. (1987). Beyond special education: Toward a quality system for all students. *Harvard Educational Review, 57* (*4*), pp. 367-395.

Gearheart, B. & Weishahn, M. (1984). *The exceptional student in the regular classroom.* St. Louis, MO: Times Mirror/College Publishing.

Gearheart, B., Mullen, R. & Gearheart, C. (1993). *Exceptional individuals: An introduction.* Belmont, CA: Brooks/Cole Publishing Company, A Division of Wadsworth, Inc.

Gerber, M. (1977). Awareness of handicapping conditions and socioeconomic status in a school setting. *Mental Retardation.* Vol. *15,* pp. 24-25.

Gershe, L. (1969). *Butterflies are free.* New York: Samuel French, Inc.

Gersten, I. & Bliss, B. (1974). *Ecidujerp/Prejudice: Either way it doesn't make sense.* New York: Franklin Watts, Inc.

Gething, L., Leonard, R. & O'Loughlin, K. (1986). *Person to person: community awareness of disability.* Sydney, Australia: Williams & Wilkins, Adis Pty. Limited.

Gill, B. (1997). *Changed by a child: Companion notes for parents of a child with a disability.* New York: Doubleday.

Gillis, J. (1982). *Too tall, too small.* Champaign. IL: Institute for Personality and Ability Testing, Inc.

Glickfield, C. (1989). *Useful gifts.* Athens, GA: University of Georgia Press.

Gliedman, J. (August, 1979). The wheelchair rebellion. *Psychology Today.* pp. 59, 60, 63, 64, 99, 101.

Gliedman, J. & Roth, W. (1980). *The unexpected minority: Handicapped children in America.* New York: Harcourt, Brace Jovanovich.

Goddard, H. (1912). *The Kallikak family: A study in the heredity of fee-ble-mindedness.* New York: Macmillan.

Goffman, E. (1961). *Asylums: Essays on the social situation of mental patients and other inmates.* Garden City, NY: Anchor Books, Dou-bleday & Co.

Goffman, E. (1963). *Stigma: Notes on the management of spoiled iden-tities.* Englewood Cliffs, NJ: Prentice-Hall.

Golan, A. (1970). Stimulus variables in the measurement of attitudes toward disability. *Rehabilitation Counseling Bulletin,* Vol. *14,* pp. 20-26.

Golant, M. & Crane, B. (1988). *It's o.k. to be different!* New York: Tom Doherty Associates, Inc.

Goldhagen, D. (1996). *Hitler's willing executioners: Ordinary Germans and the Holocaust.* New York: Alfred A. Knopf, Inc.

Goldstein, K. & Blackman, S. (1975). Generalizations regarding deviant groups. *Psychological Reports.* Vol. *37,* pp. 279-283, cited in R. Antonak & H. Livneh (1988). *The measurement of attitudes toward people with disabilities: Methods, psychometrics and scales.* Springfield, IL: Charles C. Thomas.

Golin, A. (1970). Stimulus variables in the measurement of attitudes toward disability. *Rehabilitation Counseling Bulletin.* Vol. *14,* pp. 20-26, cited in R. Antonak & H. Livneh (1988). *The measurement of attitudes toward people with disabilities: Methods, psychomet-rics and scales.* Springfield, IL: Charles C. Thomas.

Goode, D. (1994). *Quality of life issues for persons with disabilities: International perspectives and issues.* Cambridge, MA: Brookline Books.

Goodman, H., Gottlieb, J., & Harrison, R. (1977). Social acceptance of EMRs integrated into a non-graded elementary school, *American Journal of Mental Deficiency.* Vol. *76,* pp. 412- 417.

Goodman, R. & Krauss, B.(eds.) (1977). *An exceptional view of life: Written and illustrated by children with disabilities.* Los Angeles, CA: A Child's Point of View Publications.

Gottlieb, J. (1980, October). Improving attitudes toward retarded chil-dren by using group discussion. *Exceptional Children.* Vol. *47,* pp. 106-111.

Gottlieb, J., Corman, L. & Curci, R. (1984). Attitudes toward mentally retarded children, in R. Jones (ed.) *Attitude and Attitude Change in Special Education: Theory and Practice,* Reston, VA: Council for Exceptional Children. pp. 143-156.

Gould, S. (1981). *The mismeasurement of man.* New York: W. W. Norton & Company.

Gould, W. (1933). Euthanasia. *Journal of the Institute of Homeopathy.* Vol. *27,* p. 82.

Granger, L. & Granger, W. (1986). *The magic feather: The truth about special education.* New York: E. P. Dutton.

Greenfeld, J. (1972). *A child called Noah: A family journey.* New York: Holt, Rinehart & Winston.

Greenfeld, J. (1978). *A place for Noah.* New York: Pocket Books/ Simon & Schuster.

Greenfeld, J. (1986). *A client called Noah.* New York: Henry Holt & Company.

Grimms' Fairy Tales. (1995, rev. ed.). New York: Grosset & Dunlap, Publishers.

Grindler, M., Stratton, B. & McKenna, M. (1997). *The right book, The right time: Helping children cope.* Boston, MA: Allyn and Bacon.

Grob, G. (1994). *The mad among us: A history of the care of America's mentally ill.* New York: The Free Press.

Groce, N. (1985). *Everyone here spoke sign language: Hereditary deafness on Martha's Vineyard.* Cambridge, MA: Harvard University Press.

Grossman, H. (ed.) (1983). *Classification in mental retardation.* Washington, DC: American Association on Mental Retardation.

Grove, P. B. (ed.) (1981). *Webster's third new international dictionary.* Springfield, MA: Merriam Webster.

Gruenberger, R. (1971). *The 12-Year Reich.* New York: Holt, Rinehart, & Winston.

Guinagh, B. (1980). The social integration of handicapped children. *Phi Delta Kappan, 62,* (1), pp. 27-29.

Haggard, H. (1932). *The lame, the halt, and the blind.* New York: Blue Ribbon Books, Harper & Brothers.

Hague, P. & Engstrom, C. (1984). *Responding to disability: A question of attitude.* St. Paul, MN: Minnesota State Council for the Handicapped.

Hahn, H. (1987). Civil rights for disabled Americans: The foundation of a political agenda, in *Images of the disabled, disabling images.* Gartner, A. & Joe, T. (eds.) New York: Praeger Publishers, pp. 181-203.

Hahn, H. (1988). The politics of physical difference, in M. Nagler (ed.) (1990). *Perspectives on disability.* Palo Alto, CA: Health Markets Research.

Hahn, H. (1989). Mass production, consumption, imagery, and media: Disability and capitalism, in S. Hey, G. Kiger, and D. Evans (eds.) (1989), in *The changing world of impaired and disabled people in society.* Salem OR: The Society for Disability Studies and Willamette University. pp. 283-246).

Haj, F. (1970). *Disability in antiquity.* New York: Philosophical Library, cited in D. Moores (1996). *Educating the Deaf: Psychology, principles, and practices* (4th ed.). Boston, MA: Houghton Mifflin Co.

Hale, G. (ed.) (1979). *The source book for the disabled.* New York: Bantam Books, Inc.

Hallahan, D. and Kauffman, J. (1994). *Exceptional children: Introduction to special education* (6th ed.) Needham Heights, MA: Allyn & Bacon.

Haller, M. (1963). *Eugenics: Hereditarian attitudes in American Thought.* New Brunswick, NJ: Rutgers University Press.

Halliday, C. (1971). *The visually impaired child: Growth, learning, development infancy to school age.* Louisville, KY: American Printing House for the blind.

Hampshire, S. (1982). *Susan's story: An autobiographical account of my struggle with dyslexia.* New York: St. Martin's Press.

Handicapped (n.d.). Washington, DC: United States Holocaust Memorial Museum.

Hanna, R. & Graff, D. (1977). *The physically handicapped child: Facilitating regular classroom adjustment.* Hingham, MA: Teaching Resources Corporation.

Hannaford, S. (1985). *Living outside inside: A woman's experience towards a social and political perspective.* Berkeley, CA: Canterbury Press.

Hannibal, M. (1996). *Disability awareness manual: A hands-on program for exploring individual abilities and differences.* Carson, CA: Lakeshore.

Hardman, M. & Drew, C. (1978). Life management practices with the profoundly retarded: Issues of euthanasia and witholding treatment. *Mental Retardation,* Vol. *16,* pp. 390-396.

Hardman, M. Drew, C., Egan, M., & Wolf, B. (1993). *Human exceptionality: Society, school, and family (4th ed.)* Boston, MA: Allyn & Bacon.

Hardman, M., Drew, C. & Egan, M. (1996). *Human exceptionality: Society, school, and family (5th ed.).* Needham Heights, MA: Allyn & Bacon, Simon & Schuster Company.

Haring, N., McCormick, L. & Haring, T. (1994). *Exceptional Children and Youth* (6th ed.). New York: Macmillan College Publishing Co.

Harkins, S. (May/June, 1995). The state of disability in Japan. *The Disability Rag and Resources,* Vol. 16, No. 3, pp. 30-31.

Harmon, L. (1982). *Why me?* New York: Stein & Day.

Harriman, P. (1947). *The new dictionary of psychology.* New York: The Philosophical Library, Inc.

Harris, G. (1983). *Broken ears, wounded hearts: An intimate journey into the lives of a multihandicapped girl and her family.* Washington, DC: Gallaudet University Press.

Harwell, J. (1989). *Complete learning disabilities handbook: Ready-to-use-techniques for teaching learning handicapped students.* West Nyack, NY: The Center for Applied Research in Education.

Havill, A. (1996). *Man of steel: The career and courage of Christopher Reeve.* New York: Penguin Books USA, Inc.

Helping the disabled move up. (May 7,1995). *The New York Times*, pp. DC 6-7.

Henderson, H. & Bryan, W. (1997). *Psychosocial aspects of disability.* Springfield, IL: Charles C. Thomas.

Henrich, E. & Kriegel, L. (eds.) (1961). *Experiments in survival.* New York: Association for the Aid of Crippled Children.

Herbert, W. (February 9, 1998). Troubled at work: The courts are skeptical about mental disability claims. *U.S. News & World Report,* Vol. *124,* No. *5.* pp. 52-64.

Herrnstein, R. & Murray, C. (1994). *The bell curve: Intelligence and class structure in American life.* New York: Simon & Schuster, Inc.

Hershey, L. (1992). Remarks: Jerry Lewis in the 90's, in *Telethons: A Disability Rag reader.* Louisville, KY: *Disability Rag.*

Hertz, M. (1996). Stigmatization of people who stutter: Some reflections, in E. Makas and L. Schlesinger, (eds.) (1996). *End results and starting points: Expanding the field of disability studies.* Portland ME: The Society for Disabilities Studies and The Muskie Institute of Public Affairs, pp. 35-39.

Hevey, D. (1992). *The creatures time forgot: Photography and disability imagery.* New York & London: Routledge, division of Routledge, Chapman & Hall, Inc.

Hey, S., Kiger, G. Altman, B. & Scheer, J. (eds.) (1990). *The social exploration of disability.* Salem, OR: The Society for Disability Studies and Willamette University.

Hey, S. Kiger, G. & Evans, D. (eds.) (1989). *The changing world of impaired and disabled people in society.* Salem OR: The Society for Disability Studies and Willamette University.

Hey, S., Kiger, G.& Seidel, J. (eds.) (1987). *Impaired and disabled people in society: Structure, process and the individual.* Salem, OR: Society for Disability Studies and Willamette University.

Hey, S. and Zola, I. (eds.) (1995). *Course syllabi, experiential learning activities, and other instructional materials for teaching about disability.* Portland, ME: The Society for Disability Studies and the Edmund S. Muskie Institute of Public Affairs.

Hibbert, C. (1975). *The house of the Medicis.* New York: William Morrow.

Hine, R. (1993). *Second sight.* Berkeley, CA: University of California Press.

Hirsch, K. & Hirsch, J. (Fall, 1995). Self-defining narratives: Disability identity in the postmodern era. *Disabilities Studies Quarterly,* Vol. *15,* No.*4.* pp. 21-27.

Hockenberry, J. (1995). *Moving violations: A memoir of war zones, wheelchairs, and declarations of independence.* New York: Hyperion.

Holcomb, R. (1985). *Silence is golden, sometimes.* Berkeley, CA: Dawn Sign Press.

Hollander, R. (1989). Euthanasia and mental retardation: Suggesting the unthinkable. *Mental Retardation.* Vol. *27,* No. *2,* pp. 53-61.

Hourihan, J. (ed.) (1980) *Disability: The college's challenge.* New York: Project for Handicapped College Students, Teachers College, Columbia University.

Hoversten, P. (August 18, 1995a). Radiation test report: 16,000 were subjects, *USA Today,* p. 1A.

Hoversten, P. (August 18, 1995b). Hunting radiation records—and truth, *USA Today,* p. 3A.

Howard, P. (1994). *The death of common sense: How law is suffocating America.* New York: Random House, Inc.

Howell, M. & Ford, P. (1980). *The true history of the Elephant Man.* New York: Schocken Books, Inc.

Hubbard, R. (1997). Abortion and disability: Who should and who should not inhabit the world, in L. Davis (ed.) *The disabilities studies reader.* New York Routledge, pp. 187-215.

Hugo, V. (1831). *The hunchback of Notre Dame.* New York: Bantam Classics, (1986 ed.).

Hull, J. (1990). *Touching the rock: An experience of blindness.* New York: Vintage Press.

Human Rights Watch/Asia. (1966). *Death by default: A policy of fatal neglect in China's state orphanages.* New York: Author.

Hunt, N. & Marshall, K. (1994). *Exceptional children and youth: An introduction to special education.* Boston, MA: Houghton Mifflin Co.

In case you didn't know. (July 15-24, 1994). *Harper's Index, Time Off.* p. 2.

Individuals with Disabilities Education Act (IDEA). (1990). P.L. 101-47-642, U.S.C.

Ingstad, B. & Whyte, S. (eds.) (1995). *Disability and culture.* Berkeley, CA: University of California Press.

Institute on Community Integration (n.d.). *Integrated school communities for students with developmental disabilities: 10 reasons why.* Minneapolis, MI: University of Minnesota.

Interrelated Teacher Education Project (1980). *Billy: The visually impaired child in your classroom.* Daton, OH: Kids Come in Special Flavors Co.

Israelson, J. (1980). I'm special too: A classroom program promotes understanding and acceptance of handicaps. *Teaching Exceptional Children.* Vol. *13*, pp. 53-55.

Jacobs, L. (1989). *A deaf adult speaks out.* Washington, DC: Gallaudet University Press.

James, H. (1975). *The little victims: How America treats its children.* New York: David McKay Company, Inc.

Japan Says Forced Sterilizations Merit No Payments, No Apologies (September 18, 1977), *The New York Times,* p. A12.

Jefferis, B. & Nichols, J. (1928). *Safe counsel: Practical eugenics.* Chicago, IL: Franklin Publish ing Co. Reprinted by Intext Press, New York.

Jenness, A. (1978). *Some ways the same, some ways different.* Weston, MA: Burt Harrison & Company.

Jernigan, K. (1983). Blindness: Disability or nuisance. In *Reflections on growing up disabled*. R. Jones (ed.). Reston, VA: Council for Exceptional Children, pp. 58-67.

Jewell, G. (1984). *Geri.* New York: Ballantine Books.

Johnson, D., & Johnson, R. (1986). Mainstreaming and cooperative learning strategies. *Exceptional Children*, 52, 553-561.

Johnson, E. (January/February, 1987). Life unworthy of life, *Disability Rag*, Vol. 8, No. 1, pp. 24-26.

Johnson, M. (1994). Communicative action and its utility in disability research. *Insights and outlooks: Current trends in disability studies*. E. Makas & L. Schlesinger (eds.) Portland, ME: The Society for Disability Studies.

Johnson, M. & Elkins, S. (eds.) (1974). *Reporting on disability: Approaches and issues. (A sourcebook)*. Louisville, KY: Advocado Press, Inc.

Johnson, R. & Johnson, D. (1980). The social integration of handicapped students into the mainstream, in M. Reynolds (ed.). *Social environment of the schools*. Reston, VA: The Council for Exceptional Children (pp. 9-37).

Johnson, W. (1946). *People in quandaries*, cited in W. Rollin (1986) *The psychology of communication disorders in individuals and their families*. Englewood Cliffs, NJ: Prentice- Hall. Inc. p. 113.

Johnson, W. (1956). An open letter to the mother of a stuttering child, in W. Johnson, S. Brown, J. Curtis, C. Edney, & S. Keaster, (1959 ed.) *Speech handicapped school children*, New York: Harper & Bros. Reprinted by the National Society for Crippled Children and Adults.

Jones, M. & Stevens, M. (1979). *People just like you: About handicaps and handicapped people (An activity guide)*. Washington, DC: The President's Committee on Employment of the Handicapped.

Jones, R. (ed.) (1983). *Reflections on growing up disabled*. Reston, VA: Council for Exceptional Children.

Jones, R. (ed.) (1984). *Attitudes and attitude change in special education: Theory and practice*. Reston, VA: Council for Exceptional Children.

Jones, R. Gottfried, N. & Owens, A. (1966). The social distance of the exceptional: A study at the high school level. *Exceptional Children*, Vol. 32, pp. 551-556.

Jones, R. & Guskin, S. (1984). Attitude and attitude change in special education. In R. L. Jones (ed.) *Attitude and Attitude Change in Spe-*

cial Education: Theory and Practice. Reston, VA: Council for Exceptional Children. pp. 1-20.

Jones, T., Sowell, V., Jones, K. & Butler, G. (1981). Changing children's perceptions of handicapped people. *Exceptional Children, Vol. 47,* pp. 365-368.

Jordan, D. (1975). John Coode, perennial rebel. *Maryland Historical Magazine,* Vol. *20,* No. *1,* p. 2.

Kamien, E., Jenness, A., Porter, S. & Shortreed, A. (1978a). *What if you couldn't. . . ?: An elementary school program about handicaps developed by the Museum of Boston with WGBH Boston. Teacher's guide: Opening unit.* Weston, MA: Burt Harrison & Company.

Kamien, E., Jenness, A., Porter, S. & Shortreed, A. (1978b). *What if you couldn't. . . ?: An elementary school program about handicaps developed by the Museum of Boston with WGBH Boston. Teacher's guide: Mental retardation unit.* Weston, MA: Burt Harrison & Company.

Kamien, E., Jenness, A., Porter, S. & Shortreed, A. (1978c). *What if you couldn't. . . ?: An elementary school program about handicaps developed by the Museum of Boston with WGBH Boston. Teacher's guide: Orthopedic handicaps unit.* Weston, MA: Burt Harrison & Company.

Kamien, E., Jenness, A., Porter, S. & Shortreed, A. (1978d). *What if you couldn't. . . ?: An elementary school program about handicaps developed by the Museum of Boston with WGBH Boston. Teacher's guide: Hearing impairment unit.* Weston, MA: Burt Harrison & Company.

Kamien, E., Jenness, A., Porter, S. & Shortreed, A. (1978e). *What if you couldn't. . . ?: An elementary school program about handicaps developed by the Museum of Boston with WGBH Boston. Teacher's guide: Emotional problems unit.* Weston, MA: Burt Harrison & Company.

Kamien, E., Jenness, A., Porter, S. & Shortreed, A. (1978f). *What if you couldn't. . . ?: An elementary school program about handicaps developed by the Museum of Boston with WGBH Boston. Teacher's guide: Visual impairment unit.* Weston, MA: Burt Harrison & Company.

Kamien, E., Jenness, A., Porter, S. & Shortreed, A. (1978g). *What if you couldn't. . . ?: An elementary school program about handicaps developed by the Museum of Boston with WGBH Boston. Teacher's guide: Learning disabilities unit.* Weston, MA: Burt Harrison & Company.

Kanner, L. (1964). *A history of the care and study of the mentally retarded.* Springfield, IL: Charles C. Thomas.

Kaplan, A. (trans.) (1982 ed.). *The Torah Anthology (MeAm Lo'ez) Book 12—Holiness: The responsibilities of a Jew (Leviticus 19:1-27:34).* New York: Maznaim Publishing Corporation. Originally Published 1753 in Constantinople, Rabbi Y. Magriso (trans).

Karuth, D. (1985/1990). If I were a car, I'd be a lemon, in A. Brightman (ed.). *Ordinary moments: The disabled experience.* Syracuse, NY: Human Policy Press. pp. 9-31.

Kater, M. (1989). *Doctors under Hitler.* Chapel Hill, NC: The University of North Carolina Press.

Kaufman, B. (1976). *Son-rise.* New Warner Books.

Kaufman, B. (1981). *A miracle to believe in.* New York: Fawcett Crest Books.

Kauffman, J., Gottlieb, J. Agard, J. & Kukick, M. (1975). *Project PRIME: Mainstreaming toward an explication of the construct* (Project NO. IM-71-001). Washington, DC: U.S. Office of Education, Bureau of Education for the Handicapped, Intramural Research Program.

Kaufman, S. (1988). *Retarded isn't stupid, mom!* Baltimore, MD: Paul H. Brookes.

Kee, H., Hanawalt, E., Lindberg, C. Seban, J. & Noll, M. (1991 Publishing Company.). *Christianity: A social and cultural history.* New York: Macmillan.

Keller, H. (republished 1965). *The story of my life.* New York: Airmont Publishing Co. Inc.

Kelly, L. & Vergason, G. (1978). *Dictionary of special education and rehabilitation.* Denver, CO: Love Publishing Company.

Kemp, E. (September 3, 1981) Aiding the disabled: No pity, please, New York: *The New York Times.* Op Ed page.

Keniston, K. (1979). Foreword, in Gleidman & Roth (1980), *The unexpected minority: Handicapped children in America.* New York: Harcourt, Brace, Jovanovich. pp. xii-xvi.

Kennedy, D., Austin, D. & Smith, R. (1987). *Special recreation: Opportunities for persons with disabilities.* New York: CBS College Publishing.

Kennedy, F. (1942). The problem of social control of the congenital defective: Education, sterilization, euthanasia. *American Journal of Psychiatry*, Vol. *99,* pp. 13-16.

Kiger, G. (1989). Disability in film and social life: A dramaturgical perspective, in S. Hey, G. Kiger, and D. Evans (eds.) (1989). *The changing world of impaired and disabled people in society.* Salem OR: The Society for Disability Studies and Willamette University. pp. 149- 159.

Kiger, G. and Hey, S. (eds.) (1989). *Emerging issues in impairment and disability.* Salem, OR: The Society for Disability Studies and Willamette University.

Kilburn, J. (1984). Changing attitudes. *Teaching Exceptional Children.* Vol. *16,* pp. 124-127.

Kingsley, J. & Levitz, M. (1994).*Count us in: Growing up with Down Syndrome.* San Diego, CA: Harcourt Brace & Company.

Kirchner, C. (1996). Looking under the street lamp: Inappropriate uses of measures just because they are there. *Journal of Disability Policy Studies,* Vol. *7,* No. *1,* pp. 77-90.

Kirk, S., Gallagher, J. & Anastasiow (1993). *Educating exceptional children* (7th ed.) Boston, MA: Houghton Mifflin Company.

Kisor, H. (1990). *What's that pig outdoors? A memoir of deafness.* New York: Hill & Wang.

Klebaner, B. (1976). *Public relief in America: 1790-1860.* New York: Arno Press, cited in Ferguson, 1994, p. 27.

Klobas, L. (1988). *Disability drama in television and film.* Jefferson, NC: McFarland & Company, Inc.

Kokaska, C. & Brolin, D. (1985). *Career education for handicapped individuals* (2nd ed.) New York: Merrill, Macmillan Publishing Co.

Kolstoe, O. & Frey, R. (1965). *A high school work-study program for mentally subnormal students.* Carbondale, IL: Southern Illinois University Press.

Konczal, D. & Pesetski, L. (1983). *We all come in different packages: Activities to increase handicap awareness.* Santa Barbara, CA: The Learning Works, Inc.

Kovic, R. (1976). *Born on the Fourth of July: A true story of innocence lost and courage found.* New York: Pocket Books, a division of Simon & Schuster, Inc.

Kranes, J. (1980). *The hidden handicap.* New York: Simon & Schuster.

Krementz, J. (1992). *How it feels to live with a physical disability.* NY: Simon & Schuster.

Kriegel, L. (Fall, 1982). The wolf in the pit in the zoo. *Social Policy, 13,* pp. 16-23.

Kriegel, L. (1991). *Falling into life.* San Francisco, CA: North Point Press.

Kuhl, S. (1994). *The Nazi connection: Eugenics, American racism, and German national socialism.* New York: Oxford University Press.

Kuhse, H. & Singer, P. (1985). *Should the baby live? The problem of handicapped infants.* New York: Oxford University Press.

Kuklin, S. (1986). *Thinking big: The story of a young dwarf.* New York: Lothrop, Lee & Shepard Books.

L'Abate, L. & Curtis, L. (1975). *Teaching the exceptional child.* Philadelphia, PA: W. B. Saunders Co.

Lame & paraplegic. (March/April, 1987). *The Disability Rag,* p.17.

LaMore, G. (1986). *Now I understand: A book about hearing impairment.* Washington, DC: Gallaudet College Press.

Landau, D., Epstein, S. & Stone, A. (1978). *The exceptional child through literature.* Englewood Cliffs, NJ: Prentice-Hall, Inc.

Lane, H. (1992). *The mask of benevolence: Disabling the deaf community.* New York: Vintage Press.

Lane, L. & Pittle, I. (eds.). (1981). *A handful of stories: Thirty-seven stories by deaf storytellers.* Washington, DC: Gallaudet University Press.

Laplante, R. (1991). People with activity limitations in the U.S. *Disability Statistics Abstract,* prepared for the U.S. Department of Education, National Institute on Disability & Rehabilitation Research. San Francisco, CA: Disability Statistics Program, University of California.

Lathrop, L. (1990). Disabling conditions in art and myth, in S. Hey, G. Kiger, B. Altman, & J. Scheer (eds.) (1990). *The social exploration of disability.* Salem, OR: The Society for Disability Studies and Willamette University, pp. 173-180.

Leach, C. (1988, February 19). No hurdles for the handicapped on this campus. *Courier-Post* (Focus Section), pp. 1-2.

Lessen. E. (1994). *Exceptional persons in society.* Needham Heights, MA: Simon & Schuster.

Lester, p. (ed.) *Images that injure: Pictorial stereotypes in the media.* Westport, CT: Praeger.

Levine, E. (1974). *Lisa and her soundless world.* New York: Human Sciences Press.

Lewin, K. (1948). *Resolving Social Conflicts.* New York: Harper and Row.

Liachowitz, C. (1988). *Disability as a social construct: Legislative roots.* Philadelphia, PA: University of Pennsylvania Press.

Lickona, T. (1991). *Educating for character.* New York: Bantam Books.

Liebert, R. (1975), Television and attitudes toward the handicapped, in *Fostering positive attitudes toward the handicapped in school settings (Proceedings of the special study institute)* Rensselaerville, NY: New York State Education Department, Division for Handicapped Children) pp. 43-66.

Lifchez, R., Williams, D., Yip, C. Larson, M. & Taylor, J. (1979). *Getting there: A guide to accessibility for your facility.* Sacramento, CA: Sacramento, CA: Technical Assistance Project, California Department of Rehabilitation.

Lifton, R. (1986). *The Nazi doctors: Medical killing and the psychology of genocide.* New York: Basic Books.

Lifton, R. & Markusen, E. (1988). *The genocidal mentality: Nazi Holocaust and nuclear threat.* New York: Basic Books, Publishers.

Lifton, R. (1990). Sterilization and euthanasia, in M. Berenbaum, (ed.) (1992). *A Mosaic of Victims: Non-Jews Persecuted and Murdered by the Nazis.* New York: New York University Press, pp. 222-228.

Linton, S. (1998). *Claiming disability: Knowledge and identity.* New York: New York University Press.

Linton, S., Mello, S. & O'Neill, J. (1995). Disability studies: Expanding the parameters of diversity. *Radical Teacher*, Vol. *47*, pp. 4-10.

Litchfeld, A. (1977). *A cane in her hand.* Chicago, IL: Albert Whitman & Company.

Long, E. (1985/1990). Riding the iron worm, in A. Brightman (ed.). *Ordinary moments: The disabled experience.* Syracuse, NY: Human Policy Press. pp. 79-98.

Long, N. (1988). Introduction to Smith, Teaching the fourth R: Relationships. *The Pointer*, Vol. *32*, No. *3*, pp. 23-33.

Longmore, P. (1987). Screening stereotypes: Images of disabled people in television and motion pictures, in *Images of the disabled, disabling images* Gartner & Joe (eds.) New York: Praeger, pp. 65-78.

Lord, J. (1981). Opening doors, opening minds. *Recreation Canada*, in Kennedy, Austin & Smith, *Special recreation.* New York: CBS College Publishing.

Lusthaus, E. (1985). "Euthanasia" of persons with severe handicaps: Refuting the rationalizations. *Journal of the Association for Persons With Severe Handicaps.* Vol. *10*, pp. 87-94.

MacCracken, M. (1986). *Turnabout children: Overcoming dyslexia and other learning disabilities.* Boston, MA: Little, Brown & Company.

Macionis, J. (1989). *Sociology.* Englewood Cliffs, NJ: Prentice Hall, Inc.

Mackelprang, R. & Salsgiver, O. (January, 1996). People with disabilities and social work: Historical and contemporary issues. *Social Work.* Vol. *41,* No. *1.* pp. 7-14.

Mairs, N. (1994). On being a cripple, in E. Lessen *Exceptional persons in society.* Needham Heights, MA: Simon & Schuster. pp. 69-77.

Maisel, E. (1953). Meet a body. New York: Institute for the Crippled & Disabled. *Manuscript,* in B. Wright (1983). *Physical disability-A psychosocial approach.* New York: Harper & Row, Publishers, pp. 444-446.

Magee, B. & Milligan, M. (1995). *On blindness.* New York: Oxford University Press.

Makas, E. (1989). The relationship between contact with and attitudes toward people with disabilities: A question of theory or of method, in S. Hey, G. Kiger, & D. Evans (eds.) (1989). *The changing world of impaired and disabled people in society.* Salem OR: The Society for Disability Studies and Willamette University. pp. 18-25.

Makas, E. (1990) Positive attitudes toward disabled people: Disabled and nondisabled persons' perspectives, in M. Nagler, *Perspectives on Disability,* Palo Alto, CA: Health Markets Research, pp. 24-31.

Makas, E. (1990). Disabling sereotypes: The impact of contact with disabled persons on attitudes, in S. Hey, G. Kiger, B. Altman, & J. Scheer, (eds.) (1990). *The social exploration of disability.* Salem, OR: The Society for Disability Studies and Willamette University. pp. 13-20.

Makas, E. & Schlesinger, L. (eds.) (1996). *End results and starting points: Expanding the field of disability studies.* Portland ME: The Society for Disabilities Studies and The Muskie Institute of Public Affairs.

Maloff, C. & Wood, S. (1988). *Business and social etiquette with disabled people: A guide to getting along with persons who have impairments of mobility, vision, hearing, or speech.* Springfield, IL: Charles C. Thomas.

Manheim, R. (trans.) *Adolph Hitler: Mein Kampf* (1971 ed., originally published 1925). Boston: Houghton Mifflin Co.

Manni, J., Winikur, D. & Keller, M. (1984). *Intelligence, mental retardation and the culturally different child.* Springfield, IL: Charles C. Thomas.

March is women's month (March 21, 1988). *QC Quad*, p. 9.

Margolis, H. & Shapiro, A. (1987). Countering negative images of disability in classical literature. *The English Journal. 76, 3*, pp. 5-10.

Margolis, H., Shapiro, A. & Anderson, P. (1990). Reading, writing, and thinking about prejudice: Stereotyped images of disability in the popular press. *Social Education*, pp. 28-30.

Massie, R. (1980). Peter the Great: His Life and His World. New York: Wings Books.

Masters, S. & Stevens, M. (1987). *Being aware shows you care: School wide disability program.* Portland OR: Edmark Communications, Inc.

Matiella, A. (1991). *Positively different: Creating a bias-free environment for young children.* Santa Cruz, CA: ETR Associates.

Matthews, G. (1983). *Voices from the shadows: Women with disabilities speak out.* Toronto, Canada: The Women's Press.

Maurice, C. (1993). *Let me hear your voice: A family's triumph over autism.* New York: Alfred A. Knopf.

Mayor claims deaf idea isn't as dumb as it sounds. (November 6, 1994), *The Sunday* (Newark, NJ) *Star Ledger,* Sec. 1, P. 69.

McBee, F. (December, 1995). What they call us. *New Mobility, 6 (27)*, p. 51.

McCahill, W., Nicholls, M., Peterson, R. Hines, F., Leonard, E. & Cassell, R. (1987). *Handicap awareness.* Irving TX: Boy Scouts of America.

McCarthy-Tucker, S. (1993). *Coping with special needs classmates.* New York: Rosen Publishing Group, Inc.

McClean, V. E. (January 24,1988). How racism is embedded in the fabric of language. *The New York Times*, p. 26.

McConnell, N. (1982). *Different and alike.* Colorado Springs, CO: Current, Inc.

McDonald, S. & McDonald, P. (1989). *The Steven McDonald story.* New York: Donald I. Fine, Inc.

McGinn, C. (1997). *Ethics, evil, and fiction.* New York: Oxford University Press.

McPherson, J. (August 27, 1995). Involuntary immigrants. *The New York Times*, Section 7, p. 24.

Medgyesi, V. (May, 1996). Supercrip: Wanted? Needed? *New Mobility: Disability Lifestyle, Culture and Resources:* Vol. *7*, No. *32*, pp. 42-47, 74.

The Menace of the Feebleminded in Connecticut (1915), cited in testimony of Thomas Gilhool, 1995, p. 7.

The Menace of the Feebleminded in Pennsylvania (1913) cited in testimony of Thomas Gilhool, 1995, p. 7.

Mercer, J. (1973). *Labeling the mentally retarded.* Berkeley, CA: University of California Press.

Metaphors we could do without (March/April, 1992). *Disability Rag.* pp. 26-28.

Metcalf, U. (1818). The interior of Bethlehem Hospital, in D. Peterson (ed.) (1982). *A mad people's history of madness.* Pittsburgh, PA: University of Pittsburgh Press

Meyen, E. & Skrtic, T. (1988). *Exceptional children and youth: An introduction.* Denver, CO: Love Publishing Company.

Meyer, D. (Winter, 1995). Make 'em laugh: Comedians with disabilities get the chuckles—and understanding. *Careers and the disabled,* Vol. *10*, No. *2*, pp. 58-60.

Meyerowitz, J. (1962). Self-derogatives in young retardates and special class placement. *Child Development,* Vol.*33*, pp. 443-451, cited in Safford, 1978, *Teaching young children with special needs.* Saint Louis, MO: C.V. Mosby Co. p. 291.

Meyers, D. (1987). *Social psychology.* New York: McGraw-Hill Book Company.

Meyers, R. (1978). *Like normal people.* New York: McGraw-Hill Book Co.

Milam, L. (1984). *The cripple liberation marching band blues.* San Diego, CA: Mho & Mho Works.

Miles, M. (Summer, 1995). Disability studies among the Asian religions and philosophies. *Disability Studies Quarterly,* Vol. *15*, No. *3.* pp. 27-32.

Miller, V. (ed.) (1985). *Despite this flesh: The disabled in stories and poems.* Austin, TX: University of Texas Press.

Minahan, J. (1985) *Mask.* New York: Berkley Books.

Monestier, M. (1987). *Human oddities: A book of nature's anomalies.* Secaucus, NJ: Citadel Press.

Moores, D. (1996). *Educating the Deaf: Psychology, principles, and practices.* Boston, MA: Houghton Mifflin Co.

Morgan, S. (1987). *Abuse and neglect of handicapped children.* Boston, MA: Little, Brown and Company.

Morris, J. (1991). *Pride against prejudice: Transforming attitudes to disability.* Philadelphia, PA: New Society Publishers.

Morrison, J. & Ursprung, A. (1990). Children's attitudes toward people with disabilities; A review of the literature, in M. Nagler, *Perspectives on Disability*, Palo Alto, CA: Health Markets Research, pp. 158-164.

Mortenson, R. (1980). *Prejudice project.* New York: Anti-defamation League of B'nai B'rith & The University of Nebraska at Omah College of Education Curriculum Development Project. pp. 37-50.

Moshe, L., Pellock, J. & Salom, M. (1993). *The Parke-Davis manual on epilepsy.* New York: The KSF Group.

Moyer, J. (1995). *We're people first. . . a celebration of diversity.* Cambridge, MA: Brookline Books.

Mozes-Kor, E. (1992). The Mengele twins and human experimentation: A personal account, in G. Annas & M. Grodin (1992), *The Nazi doctors and the Nuremberg code: Human rights in human experimentation*, New YorkOxford University Press, pp. 53-59.

Mr. Snafoo, (December 21, 1997) *The New York Times*, Section 6, p. 21.

Mullens, J. (1979, June). Making language work to eliminate handicapism. *Education Unlimited,* Vol.*1*, pp. 20-24.

Müller, I. (1991). *Hitler's justice: The courts of the Third Reich.* Cambridge, MA: Harvard University Press.

Nagler, M. (ed.) (1990). *Perspectives on disability.* Palo Alto, CA: Health Markets Research.

Nagler, M. (ed.) (1993). *Perspectives on disability* (2nd ed.). Palo Alto, CA: Health Markets Research.

Nance, J. (1975). *The Gentle Tasaday.* New York: Harcourt, Brace Jovanovich, cited in D. Moores, 1996, *Educating the Deaf: Psychology, principles, and practices.* Boston, MA: Houghton Mifflin Co., p. 30.

Napier, G., Kappan, D., Tuttle, D., Schrotberger, W. & Dennison, A. (1981). *Handbook for teachers of the visually handicapped.* Louisville, KY: American Printing House for the Blind.

Neer, F. (1994). *Dancing in the dark.* San Francisco, CA: Wildstar Publishing.

New Jersey Administrative Code: Title 6 Education: Chapter 28, Special Education (1992). Trenton, NJ: New Jersey Department of Education.

New Jersey Developmental Disabilities Council (1988). Rag time. *Interface, 12* (2), pp. 8-9.

New Jersey Statutes Annotated, Title 15 A, 54:4-3.6.

New York Board of Regents Select Commission on Disability (1993). *Opportunity and independence: Meeting the needs of New Yorkers with disabilities.* New York: The University of the State of New York and the State Education Department.

A nightmare amid the horrors of war. (June 1,1995) (Trenton, N.J.) *The Times,* pp. A18-19.

Noddin, S. (1962), in E. Henrich & L. Kriegel (eds.) *Experiments in survival,* New York: Association for the Aid of Crippled Children, pp. 147-154.

Nolan, C. (1987). *Under the eye of the clock: The life story of Christopher Nolan.* New York: Dell Publishing a division of Bantam Doubleday Dell Publishing Group, Inc.

Norden, M. (1994). *The cinema of isolation: A history of physical disability in the movies.* New Brunswick, NJ: Rutgers University Press.

Norman, M. (February 3, 1988). Lessons. *The New York Times,* p. B4.

Obermann, C. (1965). *A history of vocational rehabilitation in America.* Minneapolis, MN: T. S. Denison.

Odom, M. & Clark, D. (1982). *The exceptional child in a regular classroom.* Manhattan, KA: The Master Teacher, Inc.

Ola, (Winter, 1995). Marketing your business to people with disabilities: A crash course. *Project Action Update,* pp. 10-11.

Oliver, M. (1990). *The politics of disablement: A sociological approach.* New York: St. Martin's Press.

Orelove, F. & Sobsey, D. (1987). *Educating children with multiple disabilities: A transdisciplinary approach.* Baltimore, MD: Paul H. Brookes.

O'Reilly, D. (1989). *Retard.* Macomb, IL: Glenbridge Publishing Ltd.

Orlansky, M. & Heward, W. (eds.) (1981). *Voices: Interviews with handicapped people.* Colombus, OH: Charles E. Merrill Publishing Co.

Orphanage denies human rights claims. (January 9,1996). (Trenton, NJ) *The Times,* p. A7.

Oskamp, S. (1977). *Attitudes and Opinions.* Englewood Cliffs, NJ: Prentice Hall.

Padden, C. & Humphries, T. (1988). *Deaf in America: Voices from a culture.* Cambridge, MA: Harvard University Press.

Padilla, R. (July/August, 1993). Lables can be harmful. *Exceptional Parent,* Vol. *23,* No. *6,* pp. 24-25.

Paré, A. (1982). *On monsters and marvels* (J. Pallister, trans.) Chicago, IL: University of Chicago Press. (translation based on the Malgaigne ed., 1840).

Parsons, T. (1951). *The social system.* Glencoe, IL: Free Press.

Parsons, T. (1958). Definitions of health and illness in the light of American values and social structure, in E. Jaco (ed.) *Patients, physicians and illness.* New York: Free Press of Glencoe.

Patton, J., Blackbourn, J. & Fad, K. (1996). *Exceptional individuals in focus* (6th ed.). Englewood Cliffs, NJ: Prentice Hall.

Patton, J., Payne, J., Kauffman, J., Brown, G. & Payne, R. (1987). *Exceptional children in focus.* (4th ed.). Columbus, OH: Merrill Publishing Company.

Pernick, M. (1996). *The black stork: Eugenics and the death of "defective" babies in American medicine and motion pictures since 1915.* New York: Oxford University Press.

Peters, A. (March/April, 1987). Victim's baggage. *The Disability Rag*

Peterson. J. (1977). *I have a sister—my sister is deaf.* New York: Harper & Row.

Peukert, D. (1987). *Inside Nazi Germany: Conformity, opposition and racism in everyday life.* New Haven, CT: Yale University Press.

Pfeiffer, D. (1989). Attitudes, disabled people and the law, in S. Hey, G. Kiger, and D. Evans (eds.) (1989). *The changing world of impaired and disabled people in society.* Salem OR: The Society for Disability Studies and Willamette University. pp. 5-17.

Pfeiffer, D. (1990). Student reaction to wheelchair use, in S. Hey, G. Kiger, B. Altman, & J. Scheer (eds.) (1990). *The social exploration of disability.* Salem, OR: The Society for Disability Studies and Willamette University. pp. 293-296.

Phifer, K. (1979). *Growing up small: A handbook for short people.* Middlebury, VT: Paul S. Eriksson, Publisher.

Pittle, I. & Rosen, R. (1984). *Another handful of stories: Thirty-seven stories by deaf storytellers.* Washington, DC: Gallaudet University Press.

Polak, M. (1988, August 21). The moron movie mogul. *The Philadelphia Inquirer Magazine*, pp. 9-10.

Pointon, A. & Davies, C. (eds.) (1997). *Framed: Interrogating disability in the media.* London: British Film Institute.

Pope, A. & Tarlov, A. (eds.) (1991). *Disability in America.* Washington, DC: Committee on a National Agenda for the Prevention of Disabilities, Division of Health Promotion and Disease Prevention, Institute of Medicine, National Academy Press.

Popp, R. (1983). Learning about disabilities, *Teaching Exceptional Children*, Vol. *15*, No. *2*, pp. 78-81.

Posner, G. & Ware, J. (1986). *Mengele: The complete story.* New York: McGraw-Hill Book Co.

Powers, M. (1986). *Our teacher's in a wheelchair.* Morton Grove, IL: Albert Whitman & Company.

Preen, B. (1976). *Schooling for the mentally retarded: A historical perspective.* New York: St. Martin's Press.

President's Committee on Employment of the Handicapped (1977). *Disabled Americans: A history.* Washington, DC: Author.

President's Committee on Mental Retardation (1975). *Mental retardation: The known and the unknown.* (DHEW Publication Nos. [OHD] 76-21008). Washington, DC:, U. S. Government Printing Office.

President's Committee on Mental Retardation (1977). *Mental retardation past and present.* Washington, DC:, U.S. Government Printing Office.

Preston, P. (1994). *Mother father deaf: Living between sound and silence.* Cambridge, MA: Harvard University Press.

The problem with challenge, [again]. (1992, January/February). *The Disability Rag.* p. 23.

Proctor, R. (1988). *Racial hygiene: Medicine under the Nazis.* Cambridge, MA: Harvard University Press.

Proctor, R. (1992). Nazi biomedical policies, in A. Caplan (ed.) (1992). *When medicine went mad: Bioethics and the Holocaust.* Totowa, NJ: Humana Press.

Proctor, R. (1996). Nazi medicine and public health policy. *Dimensions: A Journal of Hococaust Studies.* Vol. *10*, No. *2*. pp. 23-28.

Pross, C. (1992). Nazi doctors, German medicine, and historical truth, in G. Annas & M. Grodin (1992). *The Nazi doctors and the Nuremberg code: Human rights in human experimentation,* New York: Oxford University Press, pp. 32-59.

Quick, J. (1985). *Disability in modern children's fiction.* Cambridge MA: Brookline Books.

Raschke, D. & Dedrick, C. (1986). An experience in frustration: Simulations approximating learning difficulties. *Teaching Exceptional Children.* Vol. *18*, pp. 266-272.

Redl, F. (March, 1967). *Intervention Techniques.* Summary of presentation at the American Orthopsychiatric Association Conference.

Reeve, C. (1998). *Still me.* New York: Random House.

Reid, B. (1984). Attitudes toward the learning disabled in school and home, in *Attitude and attitude change in special education: Theory and practice.* R. Jones (ed.) Reston, VA: Council for Exceptional Children.

Reister, A. & Bessette, K. (1986). Preparing the peer group for mainstreaming exceptional children. *Pointer.* Vol. *3*, No. *1.* pp. 12-20.

Remak, J. (ed.) (1969). *The Nazi years.* Englewood Cliffs, NJ: Prentice Hall.

Report: Chinese orphanages starve babies. (January 6, 1996). (Trenton, NJ) *The Times,* p. A5.

Report of the special joint committee appointed to investigate the whole system of public charitable institutions supported by the State, & all city and county poor and work houses and jails (1857), in Ferguson, (1994), *Abandoned to their fate: Social policy and practice toward severely retarded people in America 1820-1920,* pp. 36-37.

Resources for people with developmental disabilities and their families. (1993). Trenton, NJ: New Jersey Developmental Disabilities Council.

Retarded school alumni told they consumed radiation with their oatmeal. (Newark, NJ) *The Star Ledger,* (January 14, 1994) p. 27.

Reynolds, M. & Birch, J. (1988) *Adaptive mainstreaming: A primer for teachers and principals.* White plains, NY: Longman Publishing Co.

Rioux, M. (1996). Services and supports in a human rights framework. *Disability Studies Quarterly.* Vol. *16*, No. *1.* pp. 4-10.

Roberts, F. (1986), in G. Scholl (ed.) (1986). *Foundations of education for blind and visually handicapped children and youth: Theory and practice.* New York: American Foundation for the Blind. pp. 1-18.

Robertson, D. (1992). *Portraying persons with disabilities: An annotated bibliography of fiction for children and teenagers.* New Providence, NJ: R. R. Bowker.

Rogasky, B. (1988). *Smoke and ashes: The story of the Holocaust.* New York: Holiday House.

Rogers, B. (October, 1978). Richard III: Shakespeare was quite wrong. *In Britain, 33*, pp. 31-35.

Rogers, C. (1951). *Client-centered therapy: Its current practice, implications, and theory.* Boston, MA: Houghton-Mifflin.

Rogers, F. (1994). *You are special.* New York Penguin Books.

Rollin, W. (1986) *The psychology of communication disorders in individuals and their families.* Englewood Cliffs, NJ: Prentice-Hall, Inc.

Rosenberg, M. (1983). *My friend Leslie: The story of a handicapped child.* New York: Lothrop, Lee & Shepard Books.

Rosenberg, M. (1988). *Finding a way: Living with exceptional brothers and sisters.* New York: Lothrop, Lee & Shepard Books.

Ross, R. (1978). Civilization's treatment of the handicapped, in *The handicapped experience: Some human perspectives.* G. McDevitt & L. McDevitt, L. (eds.) Baltimore, MD: University of Baltimore. pp. 7-13.

Ross, R. & Freelander, R. (1977). *Handicapped people in society: A curriculum guide.* Burlington, VT: University of Vermont.

Rothenberg, M. & White, M. (1985). *David.* Old Tappan, NJ: Fleming H. Revell Company.

Rothman, D. (ed.) (1990) The discovery of the asylum: *Social order and disorder in the new republic.* Boston, MA: Little Brown & Company.

Rousso, H. (1988). *Disabled, female, and proud: Stories of ten women with disabilities.* Boston, MA: Exceptional Parent Press.

Rowley-Kelly, F. & Reigel, D. (1993). *Teaching the student with spina bifida.* Baltimore, MD: Paul Brookes.

Rubenfeld, P. (1994). Special education: An institution whose time has come—and gone, in E. Makas & L. Schlesinger (eds.). *Insights and Outlooks: Current trends in disability studies.* Portland, ME: The Society for Disability Studies. pp. 235-238).

Rubington, E. & Weinberg, M. (eds.) (1996). *Deviance: The interactionist perspective* (6th ed.) Boston, MA: Allyn & Bacon.

Ruch, F. (1967). *Psychology and life* (7th ed.). Glenview, IL: Scott Foresman.

Ryan, W. (1971). *Blaming the victim.* New York: Vintage Books Random House.

Sacks, O. (1987). *The man who mistook his wife for a hat and other clinical tales.* New York: Harper & Row.

Sacks, O. (1989). *Seeing voices: A journey into the world of the deaf.* Berkeley, CA: University of California Press.

Sadker, M. & Sadker, D. (1992). *Teachers, schools, and society.* (2nd Ed.). New York: McGraw-Hill.

Safford, P. (1978). *Teaching young children with special needs.* St. Louis, MO: C.V. Mosby Co.

Safilios-Rothschild, C. (1970). *The sociology and social psychology of disability and rehabilitation.* New York: Random House.

Salend, S. (1994). *Effective mainstreaming: Creating inclusive classrooms* (2nd ed.). New York: Macmillan.

Sanders, P. (1992). *"Let's talk about" disabled people.* New York: Gloucester Press.

Sanford, D. (1986). *Don't look at me: A child's book about being different.* Portland, OR: Multnomah Press.

Sapinsley, B. (1991). *The private war of Mrs. Packard: The dramatic story of the 19th Century feminist who lobbied for laws to protect wives from husbands who could commit them to mental institutions without legitimate cause.* New York: Paragon House.

Sapon-Shevin, M. (1989). Mild disabilities: In and out of special education, in Biklen, Ferguson, & Ford (eds.) *Schooling and disability.* Chicago, IL: Chicago University Press. pp. 77-107.

Sarason, S. & Doris, J. (1979). *Educational handicap, public policy, and social history: A broadened perspective on mental retardation.* New York: The Free Press.

Saxton, M. & Howe, F. (eds.). (1987). *With wings: An anthology of literature by and about women with disabilities,* New York: The Feminist Press.

Scheerenberger, R. (1983). *A history of mental retardation.* Baltimore, MD: Paul H. Brookes.

Scheiber, B. (1982). *I can jump the rainbow.* Washington, DC: General Federation of Women's Clubs, President's Project, Learning Disabilities: An Invisible Handicap.

Schnitzler, C. & Rappaport, K. (1983). *More alike than different: An activities book for handicap awareness.* Trenton, NJ: New Jersey Department of Education.

Scholl, G. (ed.) (1986). *Foundations of education for blind and visually handicapped children and youth: Theory and practice.* New York: American Foundation for the Blind.

Schroedel, J. (ed.) (1979). *Attitudes toward persons with disabilities: A compendium of related literature.* Albertson, NY: National Center on Employment of the Handicapped at the Human Resource Center.

Schwartz, D., McKnight, J. & Kendrick, M. (eds.) (1988). *A story that I heard: A compendium of stories, essays, & poetry about people with disabilities and American life.* Harrisburg, PA: Pennsylvania Developmental Disabilities Planning Council.

Schwier, K. (1990). *Speakeasy: People with mental handicaps talk about their lives in institutions and the community.* Austin, TX: Pro Ed.

Scotch, R. (1984). *From good will to civil rights: Transforming federal disability policy.* Philadelphia, PA: Temple University Press.

Scotch, R. (1987). Disability as the basis for a social movement, in *Disabled people in society: Structure, process and the individual.* S. Hey, G. Kiger, & J. Seidel, (eds.). Salem, OR: Society for Disability Studies. pp. 252-261.

Scotson, L. (1985). *Doran.* New York: Signet/New American Library.

Scull, A. (1979). *Museums of madness: The social organization of insanity in 19th Century England.* London: Penguin Books.

Severo, R. (1985). *Lisa H.: The true story of an extraordinary and courageous woman.* New York: Harper & Row.

Seymour, E. (1990). Who am I when I'm sick? Lay responses to questions of identity, responsibility, and control in the experience of ordinary illness, in S. Hey, G. Kiger, B. Altman, and J. Scheer, (eds.) (1990). *The social exploration of disability.* Salem, OR: The Society for Disability Studies and Willamette University, pp. 29-44.

Shapiro, A. & Barton, E. (1991, Winter). Changing lives by eliminating handicapism. *New Jersey Journal of Lifelong Learning,* pp. 2-4.

Shapiro, A., Barton, E. & Barnhart, D. (1991). How the learning consultant can reduce handicapism. *The Learning Consultant Journal, 12,* pp. 5-10.

Shapiro, A. & Margolis, H. (December 7,1987), Labels should not be required for special education. New York: *The New York Times,* p. NJ46

Shapiro, A. & Spelkoman, D. (October 14, 1979), Why must we exploit them? *The New York Times,* p. NJ26.

Shapiro, J. (1993). *No pity: People with disabilities forging a new civil rights movement.* New York: Random House.

Shapiro, J. (September 24, 1995). They did their part, too. *U.S. News and World Report* Vol. *119,* No. *9,* p. 29.

Shaver, J. & Curtis, C. (1981). *Handicapism and equal opportunity: Teaching about the disabled in Social Studies.* Reston, VA: The Foundation for Exceptional Children.

Shaw, M. & Wright, J. (1967). *Scales for the Measurement of Attitudes.* New York: McGraw-Hill.

Shea, T. & Bauer, A. (1997). *An introduction to special education: A social systems perspective.* Madison, WI: Brown & Benchmark Publishers.

Shields, L., Christmas, D., Deitchman, L., Langford, T., Newingham, D., O'Daniel, L., Yeker, C. & Goodridge, J. (1981). *Project aware: A project to develop awareness of and empathy toward differences/ handicaps.* Evansville, IN: Evansville-Vanderburgh School Corporation.

Shindell, S. & Dunn, M. (1989). Disabling humor: Examples of visual media humor depicting people with disabilities, in G. Kiger and S. Hey (eds.) (1989). *Emerging issues in impairment and disability.* Salem, OR: The Society for Disability Studies and Willamette University, p. 7.

Shontz, F. (1975). *The psychological aspects of physical illness and disability.* New York: Macmillan.

Shore, K. (1986). *The special education handbook: A comprehensive guide for parents and educators.* New York: Teachers College Press.

Sidransky, R. (1990). *In silence: Growing up hearing in a deaf world.* New York: St Martin's Press.

Sienkiewicz-Mercer, R. & Kaplan, S. (1989). *I raise my eyes to say yes: A memoir.* Boston, MA: Houghton Mifflin Co.

Siller, J. (1979). Attitudes toward the physically disabled, in R. Jones (ed.). *Attitudes and Attitude Change in Special Education: Theory and Practice.* Reston, VA: Council for Exceptional Children, pp. 184-205.

Simons, C. (March, 1984). Costly cuisine, but it has a long life. *Smithsonian,* Vol. 7, p. 130, cited in B. Baskin & K. Harris, 1984, *More notes from a different drummer: A guide to juvenile fiction portraying the disabled.* New York: R. R. Boker. p. 15.

Simpson, E. (1979). *Reversals: A personal account of a victory over dyslexia.* New York: Washington Press books, Simon & Schuster.

Sinclair, T. (trans.) *Aristotle: The politics* (1992 ed.). London: Penguin Books.

Siperstein, G. & Bak, J. (1986). Understanding factors that affect children's attitudes toward mentally retarded peers, in J.Meisel (ed.). *Mainstreaming handicapped children: Outcomes, controversies, and new directions.* Hillsdale, NJ: Lawrence Erlbaum Associates, pp. 55-75.

Slavin, R. (1990). *Cooperative learning: Theory, research and practice.* Boston, MA: Allyn & Bacon.

Smith, D. & Luckasson, R. (1995). *Introduction to special education: Teaching in an age of challenge* (2nd ed.). Needham Height, MA: Allyn & Bacon, A Simon & Schuster.

Smith, J. (1985). *Minds made simple: The myth and legacy of the Kallikaks,* Austin, TX: Pro-Ed.

Smith, J.(1995). *Pieces of purgatory: Mental retardation in and out of institutions.* Belmont, CA: Brooks/Cole Publishing, a Division of Wadsworth.

Smith, R. & Neisworth, J. (1975). *The exceptional child: A functional approach.* New York: McGraw-Hill.

Smith, S. (1988). Typical academic problems of learning-disabled children. *The Pointer,* Vol. *32.* No *3.* pp. 8-10.

Solomon, A. (August 28,1994) Deaf is beautiful. New York: *New York Times Magazine,* Section 8, pp. 41-45, 62, 65-68.

Spradley, T. & Spradley, J. (1978). *Deaf like me.* Washington, DC: Gallaudet University Press.

Stacks, J. (March 21, 1988). Dwarf no more. *Time Magazine,* pp. 2-3.

Stainback, S. & Stainback, W. (1992). *Curriculum considerations in inclusive classrooms: Facilitating learning for all students.* Baltimore, MD: Paul H. Brookes.

Stainback, W. & Stainback, S. (1990). *Support networks for inclusive schooling: Independent integrated education.* Baltimore, MD: Paul H. Brookes.

Stainback, S., Stainback, W., & Forest, M. (1989). *Educating all students in the mainstream of regular education.* Baltimore, MD: Paul H. Brookes.

Starkloff, M. & Starkloff, C. (1992). Matters of control: An oral history. *New Mobility,* cited in M. Nagler, (1993), *Perspectives on disability* (2nd ed.). Palo Alto, CA: Health Markets Research, pp. 63-66.

Staron, R. (1996). Does contact influence boys' and girls' attitudes toward children with disabilities in E. Makas and L. Schleseinger (eds.) (1996). *End results and starting points: Expanding the field of Disability Studies.* Portland ME: The Society for Disabilities Studies and The Muskie Institute of Public Affairs, pp. 227-231.

Stein, J. (ed.) (1984). *The Random House College Dictionary* (revised ed.). New York: Random House.

Stein, J. (ed.) (1984a). *The Random House Thesaurus,* (college ed.). New York: Random House.

Stein, S. (1974). *About handicaps: An open family book for parents and children together.* New York: Walker & Company.

Steinbeck, J. (1937). *Of mice and men.* New York: Triangle Books.

Stevens, A. (1995). Changing attitudes to disabled people in the Scout Association in Britain (1908-1962): A contribution to a history of disability. *Disability and Society,* Vol. *10,* No. *3,* pp. 281-293.

Stevens, M. & Masters, S. (1987). *Being aware shows you care: School wide disability awareness program.* Portland, OR: Ednick Communications.

Stoddard, L. (1922). *The revolt against civilization.* New York Charles Scribner's Sons.

Stolberg, S. (August 23, 1996). Some see risk in Clinton's emphasis on teen smoking. *The Times,* Sec. B, p. 3.

Stone, E. (1996) A law to protect, a law to prevent: contextualizing disability legislation in China. *Disability & Society,* Vol. *11,* No. 4, pp. 469-483.

Stubbins, J. (ed.) (1977). *Social and Psychological aspects of disability: A handbook for practitioners.* Baltimore, MD: University Park Press.

Sullivan, T. & Gill, D. (1975). *If you could see what I hear.* New York: Harper & Row.

Sullivan, T. & Gill, D. (1976). *Tom Sullivan's adventures in darkness.* New York: McKay Publishers.

Sutherland, A. (1984). *Disabled we stand.* Bloomington, IN: Indiana University Press.

Szasz, T. (1970). *The manufacture of madness.* New York: Harper & Row.

Tessier, E. (1995), cited in *People in Motion: Viewers guide.* New York: Thirteen: WNET, p. 2.

Thirteen: WNET. *People in motion: Viewers guide.* (1995). New York: Author.

Thomas, D. (1980). *The Social Psychology of Childhood Disability,* New York, NY: Schoken Books.

Thomas, D., Miller, J., White, R., Nabokov, P. & Deloria, P. (1993). *The Native Americans: An illustrated history.* Atlanta, GA: Turner Publishing Company.

Thomson, B. (1993). *Words can hurt you: Beginning a program of anti-bias education.* Menlo Park, CA: Addison-Wesley Publishing Company.

Thomson, R. (1997). *Extraordinary bodies: Figuring physical disability in American culture and literature.* New York: Columbia University Press.

Thompson, C. (1968). *Giants, dwarfs and other oddities.* New York: Citadel Press.

Thompson, C. (1994). *The mystery and lore of monsters.* New York: Barnes & Nobel Books.

Thompson, D. (1985). Anger, in S. Browne, D. Connors, & N. Stern (eds.) (1985). *With the power of each breath: A disabled women's anthology.* Pittsburgh, PA: Cleis Press. pp. 78-85.

Thompson, L. (1958). *Ta T'ung Shu: The One-world philosophy of K'ang Yu-wei.* London: cited in E. Stone, 1996, A law to protect, A law to prevent: contextualizing disability legislation in China. *Disability & Society,* Vol. *11,* No. 4, pp. 469-483.

Thurer, S. (January/February, 1980). Disability and monstrosity: A look at literary distortions of handicapping conditions. *Rehabilitation Literature.* pp. 49-52.

Tietze-Conrat, E. (1957). *Dwarfs and jesters in art.* London: Phaidon Publishers, Inc.

Tiffany, F. (1891). *Life of Dorothea Dix.* Cambridge, MA: Riverside Press.

Tillis, M. (1984). *Stutterin' boy: The autobiography of Mel Tillis.* New York: Dell Publishing Company, Inc.

Tomlinson, R. (1982). *Disability, theatre and education.* Bloomington, IN: Indiana University Press.

Topics of the times. (October 16, 1994). *The New York Times,* p. E.

Trainer, M. (1991). *Differences in common: Straight talk on mental retardation, Down Syndrome, and life.* Rockville, MD: Woodbine House.

Trappe, T. (n.d.). *After the kids: A follow-up guide for teachers.* Trenton, NJ: State of New Jersey, Department of Human Services, Division of Developmental Disabilities.

Trattner, W. (1994). *From poor laws to welfare state: A history of social welfare in America.* New York: The Free Press, A Division of Simon & Schuster.

Trautman, J. (1978). Literary treatments of the handicapped, in G. McDevitt (ed). *The handicapped experience: Some humanistic approaches.* Baltimore, MD: University of Baltimore, pp. 17-23.

Trent, J. (1994). *Inventing the feeble mind: A history of mental retardation in the United States.* Berkeley, CA: University of California Press.

Turnbull, A., Strickland, B, & Brindle, J. (1982). *Developing and implementing individualized education programs* (2nd ed.) Colombus, OH: Charles E. Merrill Publishing Co.

Turnbull, A., Turnbull, H., Shank, M. & Leal, D. (1995). *Exceptional lives: Special education in today's schools.* Englewood Cliffs, NJ: Prentice-Hall, Inc. A Simon & Schuster Company.

Umbreit, J. (ed.) (1983). *Physical disabilities and health impairments: An introduction.* Columbus, OH: Charles E. Merrill Publishing Company.

Umbreit, J. & Baker, D. (1983). Reflections of disabled children, in R. Jones (ed.), *Reflections on growing up disabled,* Reston, VA: Council for Exceptional Children, pp. 1-4.

Understanding Handicaps, Inc. (1994 ed.) *Understanding handicaps: A disability awareness curriculum.* Newtonville, MA: Author.

UNESCO (1995). *Overcoming obstacles to the integration of disabled people.* (Report to The World Summit on Social Development). Copenhagen, Denmark: Author.

United States Congress (1973), *Public Law 93-112, Vocational Rehabilitation Act 1973, Section 504.*

United States Congress (1974), *Public Law 94-142, The Education for All Handicapped Children Act of 1975.*

United States Congress (1990), *Public Law 101-336, Americans With Disabilities Act of 1990.*

United States Congress (1990), *Public Law 101-476, Individuals with Disabilities Education Act of 1990.*

University of the State of New York. (1981a). *A curriculum to foster understanding of people with disabilities: Staff orientation manual.* Albany, NY: New York State Education Department. Office for Children with Handicapping Conditions.

University of the State of New York. (1981b). *A curriculum to foster understanding of people with disabilities: The handicapped in society.* Albany, NY: The State Education Department, Office for Children with Handicapping Conditions.

University of the State of New York. (1981c). *A curriculum to foster understanding of people with disabilities: The handicapped in literature.* Albany, NY: The State Education Department, Office for Children with Handicapping Conditions.

University of the State of New York. (1981d). *A curriculum to foster understanding of people with disabilities: Science and health education perspectives on the handicapped.* Albany, NY: New York State Education Department.

Va. hospital sterilized 4000: Tried to rid state of "misfits" for a pure race, records show. (February 22, 1980) (Trenton, N.J.) *The Times.*

Valens, E. (1966). *The other side of the mountain.* New York: Warner Books.

Van Etten, A. (1988). *Dwarfs don't live in doll houses.* Rochester, NY: Adaptive Living.

Van Riper, C. & Emerick, L. (1984). *Speech correction: An introduction to speech pathology and audiology.* Englewood Cliffs, NJ: Prentice-Hall, Inc.

Vash, C. (1981). *The psychology of disability.* New York: Springer Publishing Company.

Virginia Sterilization Act, Va. Acts 569-71. (1924, repealed 1968).

Voeltz, L. (1980). Children's attitudes toward handicapped peers. *American Journal of Mental Deficiency,* Vol. *84,* 455-464.

Voeltz, L. (1981). Acceptance scale, secondary level B, cited in R. Antonak & H. Livneh (1988). The measurement of attitudes toward people with disabilities: Methods, psychometrics and scales. Springfield IL: Charles C Thomas. Publisher. pp. 130-133.

Wahl, O. (1995). *Media madness: Public images of mental illness.* New Brunswick, NJ: Rutgers University Press.

Walker, L. (1985). *Amy: The story of a deaf child.* New York: E. P. Dutton.

Walker, L. (1986). A loss for words: *The story of deafness in a family.*

Walker, M. (August, 1991). Power of the people. *Guardian,* pp. 24-25, cited in A. Pointon, A. and C. Davies, C. (eds.) (1997). *Framed: Interrogating disability in the media.* London: British Film Institute.

Ward, B. (1988). *Overcoming* disability. New York: Franklin Watts, Publishers.

Ward, M., Arkell, R., Dahl, H. & Wise, J. (1979). *Everybody counts: A workshop manual to increase awareness of handicapped people.* Reston, VA: Council for Exceptional Children.

Watts, W. (1984). Attitude change: Theories and methods, in R. Jones, (ed.) *Attitudes and Attitude Change in Special Education.* Reston, VA: Council for Exceptional Children, pp. 41-69.

Waxman, B. (1991, May),. Hatred: The unacknowledged dimension in violence against disabled people, *Human Science Press*, pp. 185-199.

Waxman, B. (1992, May/June). Hate, *The Disability Rag*, Vol. *13*, No. *3*, pp 4-5, 7

We wish we wouldn't see. (March/April, 1996) *The Disability Rag and Resource*, Vol. *17*, No. *3*, p. 45.

Weicker, L. (1995). *Maverick: A life in politics*. Boston, MA: Little, Brown and Company.

Weinberg, N. & Santana, R. (1978). Comic books: Champions of the disabled stereotype. *Rehabilitation Literature*, Vol. *39*, pp. 327-331.

Weindling, P. (1981). *Health, race and German politics between national unification and Nazism, 1870-1945*. Cambridge, Great Britain: Cambridge University Press.

Weiner, F. (ed.) (1986). *No apologies: A guide to living with a disability, written by the real authorities—People with disabilities, their families, and friends*. New York: St. Martin's Press.

Weir, R. (1984). *Selective nontreatment of handicapped newborns*. New York: Oxford University Press.

Weiss, E. (1989). *Mothers talk about learning disabilities: Personal feelings, practical advice*. New York: Prentice Hall.

Weiss, M. (1976). *Seeing through the dark: Blind and sighted—A vision shared*. New York: Harcourt.

Weiss, M. (1980). *Blindness*. New York: Franklin Watts.

Wertham, F. (1980). *The German euthanasia program: Excerpts From "A sign from Cain"* Cincinnati, OH: Hayes Publishing Company, Inc.

Westridge Young Writers Workshop (1994). *Kids explore the gifts of children with special needs*. Santa Fe, NM: John Muir Publications.

Wetherow, D. (1992). *The whole community catalogue: Welcoming people with disabilities into the heart of community life*. Manchester, CT: Communitas, Inc.

White, B. (1979). *Understanding persons with disabilities*. Lincoln, NE: Lincoln Public Schools.

White, G. (1993). *Justice Oliver Wendell Holmes*. New York: Oxford University Press.

White, P. (1990). *Disabled people*. New York: Franklin Watts, Publishers.

Will there be a birthday card for Danny? (March 28,1981), (Trenton, N.J.) *The Times*, p. A-6.

Winefield, R. (1987). *Never the twain shall meet: Bell, Gallaudet, and the communications debate*. Washington, D.C.: Galladudet University Press.

Wolfe, K. (1993, November/December). Springtime for Hitler: A journal. *The Disability Rag*. pp. 11-13.

Wolfe, K. (August, 1995). War work. *Mainstream*. Vol. *19*, No. *10*, pp. 17-23.

Wolfensberger, W. (1975). *The origin and nature of our institutional models*. Syracuse, NY: Human Policy Press.

Wolfensberger, W. (1980). Extermination: Disabled people in Nazi Germany. *Polestar.* Vol. *1*, No. *9*, Developmental Disabilities Training Systems and Technical Research Center, Region III, New York.

Wolfensberger, W. (1981). The extermination of handicapped people in World War II Germany. *Mental Retardation*, Vol. *19*, (February). pp. 1-7

Wolfensberger, W. (1994). Let's hang up "Quality of Life" as a hopeless term, in D. Goode, *Quality of life issues for persons with disabilities: International perspectives and issues*. Cambridge, MA: Brookline Books. pp. 285-321.

Wolfensberger, W., Nirje, B., Olshansky, S., Perske, R. & Roos, P. (1972/1975). *Normalization: The principle of normalization in human services*. Toronto, Canada: National Institute on Mental Retardation.

Wood, J. (1993). *Mainstreaming: A practical approach for teachers* (2nd ed.). New York: Macmillan Publishing Co.

Wright, B. (1983). *Physical disability-A psychosocial approach*. New York: Harper & Row, Publishers.

Wright, D. (1993 ed.). *Deafness: An autobiography*. New York: Harper Collins Publishers, Inc.

Wright, P. (1987). Disabling attitudes. *Contact,* Vol. *XII,* No. *3*, pp. 4-9.

WuDunn, S. (September 8, 1996). For Japan's children, a Japanese torment. *The New York Times*, p. 3E).

Yohalem, D. & Dinsmore, J. (1978). *94-142 and 504: Numbers that add up to educational rights for handicapped children—A guide for parents and advocates*. Washington, DC: Children's Defense Fund of the Washington Project, Inc.

Yoken, C. (1979). *Living with deaf-blindness: Nine profiles*. Washington, DC: Gallaudet University Press.

Young, J. (1990). *Kokopelli, Canasanova of the Cliff Dwellers: The hunchbacked flute player.*Palmer Lake, CO: Filter Press

Youwei, K. trans. Thompson, 1958, p. 201-202, cited in E. Stone, 1996,
    A Law to Protect, A Law to Prevent: contextualizing disability leg-
    islation in China. *Disability & Society,* Vol. *11,* No. 4, pp. 469-483.
Yuker, H. (1965). Attitudes as determinants of behavior. *Journal of
    Rehabilitation,* Vol. *31,* pp. 15-16, cited in R. Antonak & H. Livneh
    (1988). *The measurement of attitudes toward people with disabili-
    ties: Methods, psychometrics and scales.* Springfield IL: Charles C
    Thomas. Publisher.
Yuker, H. (1979). Attitudes toward the disabled, in J. Hourihan, (ed.) *Dis-
    ability our challenge,* New York: Columbia University, pp. 33-51.
Yuker, H. & Block, J. (1979). *Challenging barriers to change: Attitudes
    toward the disabled.* Albertson, NY: National Center on the Em-
    ployment of the Handicapped at Human Resources Center.
Yuker, H., Block, J. & Campbell, J. (1960). *A scale to measure attitudes
    toward disabled persons.*(Human Resources Study No. 5). Albert-
    son, NY: Human Resources Center, cited in R. Antonak & H.
    Livneh (eds.) (1988). *The measurement of attitudes toward people
    with disabilities: Methods, psychometrics and scales.* Springfield
    IL: Charles C Thomas. Publisher. pp. 138-139.
Yuker, H., Block, J. & Campbell, J. (1962). *Disability types and behav-
    ior.* (Human Resources Study No. 6). Albertson, NY: Human
    Resources Center, cited in R. Antonak & H. Livneh (eds.) (1988).
    *The measurement of attitudes toward people with disabilities:
    Methods, psychometrics and scales.* Springfield IL: Charles C
    Thomas. Publisher. pp. 142-143.
Zimmerman, D. (1985/1990). The way I see myself, in A. Brightman,
    (ed.) *Ordinary moments: The disabled experience.* Syracuse, NY:
    Human Policy Press. pp. 33-49.
Zola, I. (ed.) (1982a). *Ordinary lives: Voices of disability and disease.*
    Cambridge, MA: Applewood Books.
Zola, I. (1982b). *Missing pieces: A chronicle of living with a disability.*
    Philadelphia, PA: Temple University Press.
Zola, I. (1986, Spring). Women and disability: Setting the agenda, *Dis-
    ability Studies Quarterly, 6, 2,* pp. 1-38.

Index

ABC Network, 118
able-bodied, 47; "passing", 143
Ablon, J., 275
Abnormall (see also normal), 46
Abrahams, I., 171-172
Academy Award nominees, 21
accessibility compliance checklist,
    379-387
ACHRE, 248
*Act for the Punishment of Sturdy
    Vagabonds and Beggars* (1536),
    175
activism, 126; against inhumane
    treatment, 194-195; Americans
    with disabilities, 243-244; dis-
    ability rights activists, 136;
    media watch ideas, 391-397;
    public outrage, 215;
affliction, 76-77
Africa, 59; African tribes, 58; cultur-
    al practices, 152; Egypt, 152
African Americans, 20
AIDS, 76, 280
Aiello, B., 443
Albright, K., Brown, L., Vandeven-
    ter, P., Jorgensen, J., 349
Alexier v. Matzke (1908), 214
Allport, G., 99-100, 102, 119, 121,
    139, 378
almshouses, 183, 190, 193-195, 210
Amazonian tribe, 58
American Association on Mental
    Deficiency, 317
American Association on Mental
    Retardation, 52
American Asylum for the Deaf, 191

American Breeders' Association, 212
American Journal of Psychiatry, 225
American Psychiatric Association,
    89, 224
Americans With Disabilities Act , 5,
    20, 31, 50-51, 144, 260, 262, 265
ancient cultures; ancient Assyrians,
    149; ancient Babylonians, 150;
    ancient Indians, 152; ancient
    Melanesians, 151; ancient Sparta
    and Spartans, 146, 154-155, 220,
    224, 337; diverse cultural prac-
    tices, 152-153; Spaniards, 167
Antonak, R. and Livneh, H., 353
Arieno, M., 180
Aristotle, 153, 166, 203
Asher, S. and Tailor, A., 30
Association for Retarded Children,
    259
Association for Retarded Citizens,
    398
Astor, C., 164
asylums, 177, 190, 202, 245; early
    asylums, 179-183
Atomic Energy Commission, 247
attention deficit disorder, 311, 335
attitudes, 5, 7, 86, 145, 162, 280,
    298; acquisition of 4; addressing
    of prior attitudes, 351-354; atti-
    tude change 10, 11, 26, 29, 31,
    347-349, 444; attitudinal devel-
    opment, 367; attitudinal preju-
    dice, 100; children's attitudes,
    104; cultural, 61; definitions of
    8-9; development and structure
    of, 366-367; handicapist, 37, 39,

51; negative attitudes, 9, 31, 87; of acceptance 14; of others, 57; origins of, 265; positive attitudes 6, 113; public, 103; religious attitudes, 157; social and personal, 53; societal, 185, 299; stigmatizing, 198; strategies for changing, 343; subliminal 18; understanding of 6

Baken, J., 335
Barnes, E., 64, 97, 108, 114
Barnes, E., Berrigan C. and Biklen, D., 351
Barr, Martin, 215
Bart, D., 91
Bartel, N. and Guskin, S., 54
Barton, L., 145
Baskin B. and Harris, K., 17, 27, 60, 74, 110, 158
Baskin, B., 367
Baum D. and Wells, C., 4
Beattie v. Board of Education (1919), 122
Bedlam asylum (Bethlehem Hospital), 180-182, 201, 249
Beisser, A., 115
Bell C. and Burgdorf, R., 16, 131
Bell, Alexander Graham, 204, 212
Bennetts, L., 134, 136
Berenbaum, M., 238
Bienvenu, M.J., 205
Bigelow et al., 342
Biklen, D., 66-67, 97, 250, 389
Biklen, D., Ford, A. and Ferguson, D., 4, 26, 27, 98, 350
Binding, K. and Hoche, A., 224-225
Blatt, B., 31, 146, 207, 248-250, 321, 446
Bleul, H., 221
blindness, 44-45, 117, 127, 130, 140, 161, 164, 196, 205; explained, 280-86
Bliss, M. and Schwartz, A., 341
Block, 346
Blumberg, L., 96
Bobrick, B., 176

Bogdan, R. and Biklen, D., 16, 99, 106, 110, 120
Bogdan, R. and Knoll, J., 100, 102, 119
Bogdan, R. and Taylor, S., 321
Bogdan, R., 177
Bookbinder, S., 34, 342, 445
Borm, Dr. Kurt, 243
Bowe, F., 9, 19, 29, 102, 131, 164, 187, 282, 301
Braginsky, D. and Braginsky, B., 64, 251
Broadbelt, S., 419
Brodkin, M., 4-5, 11
Brolin, D., 330
Brown, D., 312
Buck v. Bell, 216
Bunch, G., 367
Burgdorf, M. and Burgdorf, R., 163, 200, 213-214, 216
Burgdorf, R., 37, 46, 72
Burleigh, M. and Wippermann, W., 230
Burleigh, M., 223, 231
Buscaglia, L., 61, 77
Bush, President, 50, 262

Callahan, J., 131
Caplan, A., 223, 245
Carlisle, J., 118, 300, 302, 304-305
Cashdollar, P. and Martin, J., 342
censorship, 119
Center on Human Policy, 342
cerebral palsy, 140; defined, 271-272
charity, 133-134, 136-137, 157, 173, 182, 197
Charkins, H., 149, 155, 162
Child Welfare Institute, 254-255
Children's Museum of Boston, 342
children, 248; children's attitudes, 104; children with disabilities, 138; child rearing, 184; extermination of, 230-234
China, 58, 157, 165, 173; sanctioned killing in, 251-256
citizens, 15, 25, 43, 57, 69, 82, 173, 190, 243

City of New York's Commission on the Status of Women, 124
Civil Rights Act of 1964, 263
civil rights movements, 19, 442; of 1960's, 98
civil rights paradigm (see minority-independence-disablism paradigm)
civil rights, 25, 31, 44, 126, 128, 144, 146, 205, 250, 259, 262, 442
Clark, K., 121
Cleary, M., 342
Clinard, R. and Meier, R., 93
Cohen, J., 341
Cohen, S., 14, 63, 113, 129, 131-132, 267, 336
Cohen, S., Grand, C., Koehler, N. and Berman, D., 367
Cohen, S., Koelher, N. and Grand, C., 341, 419
Collins, T., Schneider, M. and Kroeger, S., 28
Commings, London, Moore, Raschke, Schwartz and Tofty, 342
common sense, 267, 276, 286, 294, 306, 313, 321, 326, 331, 338
community, 188
Conard, B., 377
concentration camps (see also extermination, eugenics, genocide), 235, 239, 245; killing centers, 230, 234
conformity, 258
Congolese tribe; The Bayaka, 58
Conot, R., 231, 238
Conrad, P. and Schneider, J., 58
Conrad, P., 89, 377
Coode, John, 186
Council for Exceptional Children, 342
Covey, 86
culture, 58, 87, 145; Deaf culture, 48; disability as a culture, 48; cultural customs, 150-161, 169; and IQ, 320
The Culture of Complaint, 40

CUNY Coalition of Students with Disabilities, 79
curriculum (see also teaching methods), 18, 26, 28, 206, 259, 261, 267, 337; activity books, 341; anti-bias curriculum, 342; curriculum for equity, 342; curriculum guides, 341; disability awareness curricular infusion, 350-351; disability awareness program, 27, 343-347; disability awareness questionnaire, 354-361; disability awareness separate units, 350; disability awareness with literature (see also Appendix), 367; early childhood curriculum, 342; fiction, 367-370; news media activities, 388-397; Newton Schools' disability awareness curriculum, 342; nonfiction and bibliotherapy, 370-372; supported integration, 27
Cutsforth, T., 285

Dart, Justin Jr., 256
Darwin, C., 208; Social Darwinism, 200
Davenport, C., 207
Davies, J., 38
Davis, L., 46-8, 70, 110, 208, 219
deafness, 38, 44-45, 49, 56, 203; Deaf culture, 48, 54, 205; Deaf person vs. person with deafness, 48; explained, 291-294; manual language, 204; language, 203-204, 293
Deegan, M. and Brooks, N., 124
deformity, 146, 167, 172, 239
democracy, 15
dependency, 188; culture of, 134
Derman-Sparks, L., 7, 269, 342
Despart, L., 155
Developmental Disabilities Bill of Rights Act (PL 95-822), 52
deviance, 89-90, 160, 204, 250, 299, 329
Devlieger, P., 59

Diagnostic and Statistical Manual of
   Mental Disorders (DSM-IV), 89
diagnostic-prescriptive medical
   model (see medical paradigm)
Dickens, Charles, 109
Dickman, I., 287
difference; appreciating, 346; cultural
   difference, 49; sameness, 345
dignity, 84, 91, 95-96, 114
DiLeo, J., 366
Diodati, D., 140
disabilities rights movements, 91,
   142, 442
Disabilities Studies, 144
disabilities, 51, 70; amputation, 274-
   275; arthritis, 272; as sins, 159;
   autism, 324-327; contextual definitions, 49-53; cultural repre-
   sentations of, 134; curricular
   experiencing, 425-431; definitions of, 44-46, 263; developmental disabilities, 52, 75, 87;
   diverse cultural/societal treatments of, 61-61; emotional disturbance, 327-334; epilepsy
   seizure disorder, 272-273, 279;
   feigning disabilities, 174-175;
   functional abilities, 52; historical
   treatment of, 145; images of,
   111; multiple sclerosis, 273;
   muscular dystrophy, 273-274;
   physical disabilities, 270-271;
   poliomyelitis, 274; sever and
   multiple impairments, 334-339;
   speech differences, 298-306,
   310; spina bifida, 274
disability awareness program (see
   curriculum)
Disability Rights Education and
   Defense Fund (DREDF), 106
Disability Statistics Abstract, 50
disablism (handicapism), 16, 18, 31-
   32, 75, 79, 82, 99, 102, 120, 123,
   126, 243, 304, 312; disablism
   movement, 128; handicapist attitudes, 37, 39, 51; toward women,
   124-125

discomfort; aesthetic anxiety, 131;
   feelings of, 130; negative feelings, 132
discrimination (see also prejudice),
   79, 81-83, 120, 122-126, 260,
   265; double discrimination, 126;
   influences of, 147; social policies, 185
discriminatory (oppressive) terminology, 18, 38, 41, 66, 68, 70-73,
   313; "moron", 209-210, 317;
   public usage of, 73-74
diversity, 16
Dix, Dorothy, 194-195
Dmystryshyn, B., 170
domestic violence, 126
Donaldson, J., 8, 11, 343, 349, 420
Drake, R., 137
due process (Equal Protection Clause
   of the Fourteenth Amendment),
   202-203, 217, 262
dwarfism, 37, 45, 47, 59, 115, 140,
   142, 171-172, 240-241; defined,
   275-276

E. coli, 257
Eberl, Dr. Irmfried, 238
*Education for All Handicapped Chil-
   dren Act* (PL 94-142) (see also
   *Individuals with Disabilities Edu-
   cation Act*), 5, 20, 22, 25, 261,
   341
education, 119, 164, 187, 199, 265;
   beginnings, 203; educational
   therapy, 92; mainstreamed, 120;
   unequal, 122
educators, 68, 75, 79, 97, 105, 114,
   123, 204
Edwards, M., 51, 153-154
Egyptians, 152
Eichmann, Adolph, 237
El Salvador; abuse in, 259
Elkins, S., Jones, M. and Ulicny, R.,
   391, 393, 395-397
Ellis, E., 18, 245
empathy, 267, 270, 300; empathy
   development, 31

employment, 123, 265; job discrimination, 123; unequal, 122
English, W., 102
Enteman, W., 103
epilepsy, 176
equality, 83, 128, 144, 315
equity, 128, 315
Esquirol, J., 179
eugenics (see also extermination; genocide; sterilization), 153, 207, 220-221, 227, 252; American eugenics movement, 219; Committee of Eugenics, 212; eugenic aims, 212;
eugenic period, 146; eugenics movements, 208-210; "negative eugenics", 208
Europe, 168, 171
euthanasia, 146, 157, 212, 221-224, 228-229, 232-233, 235-243, 336-337; infant euthanasia, 336; mercy killing, 230
Evans, J.H., 10
evil, 108, 162; animism, 149; omens, 176
extermination (see also eugenics; genocide; sterilization), 147, 156, 230; era of extermination, 222; Prussian law of 1230, 156

Falstein, 227
family, 188-189, 197, 208
Federal Equal Employment Opportunity Commission, 91
Federal Reparations Law of 1953, 243
Feldman, S., 71
Ferguson, 185-186, 191-193
Fernald, 211
fetomancy, 150
Fiedler, L., 39, 106-108, 110, 116, 174, 242
figurative language, 70
Fine, M. and Asch, A., 124-125
Finger, A., 222, 231
Fisher, Dr. John, 196

Fleming et al., 342
Fletcher, A., 258-259
Flynn, R. and Nitch, K., 178
Food and Drug Administration, 90
Francis, E., 40
Franks, B., 3
freak shows, 176
Freidson, E., 54
Friedberg, J., Mullins, J. and Sukiennik, A., 370
Friedlander, H., 207-209, 222, 231, 234-235
Froschol, M., Colon, L., Rubin, E. and Sprung, B., 37, 342
Funk, R., 146, 185, 259-260

Gallagher, H., 28-29, 53, 72, 76, 139, 157, 226-227, 134, 242
Gallaudet, Edwards Miner, 204
Gardner, Eileen Marie, 262, 262
Garland, R., 62, 145, 167-168, 173
Gartner, A. and Joe, T., 66, 84
Gartner, A. and Lipsky, D., 67
genocide (see also Nazis; eugenics; sterilization; institutionalization), 220, 227, 242
Gerber, M., 4
Germany, 211, 214, 218, 230, 233, 239, 241-242, 329; German physicians, 227-228; recent abuse in, 258
Gershe, L., 285
Gething, L., Leonard, R. and O'Loughlin, K., 272
Getskow and Konczal, 341, 345
Gillis, J., 71, 241
Glaton, Francis, 207
Glen Ridge case, 17, 21
Gliedman, J. and Roth, W., 102, 127
Gliedman, J., 94, 133
Gober, 202
Goddard, Henry Herbert, 210-212, 214-215, 218
Goffman, E., 138-139, 178, 246
Goldhagen, D., 237
Goldstein, K. and Blackman, S., 347

Golin, A., 347
Goodman, R., Gottlieb, J. and Harrison, R., 4
Gould, S., 224
Granger, L. and Granger, W., 65
Greece and Rome (see also ancient cultures), 158, 173; early attitudes, 153, 165; treatment of others, 146, 222-223; Greco-Roman world, 145, 169; Athenians, 154
Greece, 51, 154, 210
Gridley, Dr. Samuel, 196
Grindler, M., Stratton, B. and McKenna, M., 371
Grob, G., 184-5, 187
Groce, N., 56
group diversity, 49
Guinagh, B., 30
gypsies, 235-236

Haggard, H., 161
Hahn, H., 83, 85, 88, 120, 130-131, 144
Haj, F., 164
Hale, G., 46
Haller, M., 212
Hallihan and Kauffman, 280, 292-293, 309, 327, 329-330
handicap; contextual definitions of, 53-60; definitions of, 44-46; educational uses of, 66; environmental handicaps, 148; "hidden handicap", 312; origins of, 63; prejudicial attitudes as, 446; social construction of, 91;
handicapism (see disablism)
Hanna, R. and Graff, D., 139, 141, 143
Hardman, M. and Drew, C., 336
Hardman, M., Drew, C. and Egan, M., 87
Harriman, P., 305
Harwell, J., 312
Henderson, H. and Bryan, W., 100
Herbert, W., 90
Hershey, L., 134
Hertz, M., 299

Hevey, D., 89, 136
Hey, S. and Zola, I., 342
Hibbert, C., 170
Higgins and Metcalf, 249
Higgins, Godfrey, 183
Himmler, Reichsfuhrer, 236
Hine, R., 280
Hirsch, K. and Hirsch, J., 40, 88, 95, 98
Hitler, 219, 220, 223, 225-226, 236-237, 240
HIV positive, 50
Hockenberry, J., 120, 136
Holcomb, R., 295
Hollander, R., 225, 233, 337
Hollywood, 116-119
Holocaust (see also genocide, eugenics, extermination, Jews, Nazis), 238-239, 336, 445
homosexuals, 235-236, 246
Horne, 4
hospitals (see also asylums; institutions), 178; mental hospitals, 193
Hourihan, J., 64
Howe, 198, 200
Howe, Samuel Gridley, 194, 199
Hubbard, R., 236
Hughes, 40
Hugo, V., 174
Hull, J., 283-284
Human Rights Watch/Asia, 251, 253-256
human rights, 82
Hunt, N. and Marshall, K., 282

identity, 58, 92, 299; common identities, 127; group membership, 128
inclusion, 19, 20, 22, 29, 79, 259, 291, 332; "Era of Inclusion", 445; promotion of, 345; supports for, 27, 30
independence paradigm (see minority-independence-disablism paradigm)
individualized education program (IEP), 261
Individuals with Disabilities Educa-

tion Act (IDEA), 20, 261, 292, 334
infanticide, 149, 151-153, 156, 337
Ingstad, B. and Whyte, S., 44-45, 51, 58, 64
insanity (people classified as), 180, 186-187, 190; lunatics, 181; madness, 184
Institute on Community Integration, 24
institutions (see also almshouses, asylums, hospitals) 183; institutionalization, 22, 191, 200, 207, 209, 211, 230; special care institutions, 192
integration, 14, 22, 68, 201; as a moral issue, 30; social integration, 79
intelligence, 186, 199, 208, 322; as a eugenics instrument, 215; innate intelligence, 319; measures with IQ, 90, 319-321; standardized tests, 318
intolerance (see tolerance)
invalid, 77
isolation, 128
Itard, Jean-Marc-Gaspard, 96
Ivy, Dr. Andrew, 242

James, H., 5, 172
Japan, 165, 219; Japanese medical atrocities, 244-245; abuse in, 257-258
Jefferis, B. and Nichols, J., 208
Jeffrey, 411
Jernigan, K., 82, 103, 117-118, 141
Jerry Lewis, 116, 134; Jerry's Kids, 133
jesters, 167, 168, 170
Jews, 235-244
Johnson, D. and Johnson, R., 30
Johnson, E., 45, 65, 74, 306
Johnson, M. and Elkins, S., 388
Jonah, 306
Jones, R. and Guskin, S., 5-6, 10, 366
Jones, R., 18

Jordan, D., 186
juvenilization, 115

Kanner, L., 112
Karuth, D., 286
Kater, M., 226, 236
Kemp, E., 91, 135
Keniston, K., 47, 97
Kennedy, D., Austin, D. and Smith, R., 55
Kennedy, Foster, 224-225
Kids Come in Special Flavors, 342
Kiger, G., 109
King Henry VII of England, 63
Kirchner, C., 85
Kirk, S. and Gallagher, J., 330
Kirk, S., Gallagher, J. and Anastasiow, 334
Kisor, H., 294
Klebaner, B., 190
Koblas, L., 115
Kokaska, C. and Brolin, D., 370
Kranes, J., 312
Kriegel, L., 43, 111
Kristof, 256
Kuhl, S., 218-219
Kuhse, H. and Singer, P., 337
Kumeta, Naotaka, 257

labels (labeling), 14, 54, 65, 67, 73, 75, 77, 86, 90-93, 97, 212; educational labels, 64, 270, 308; legal labeling, 72; and stigmatization, 142
language; negative language, 79; and stereotypes, 37; and unconscious prejudice, 39
Laughlin, H., 215
laws (see legislation)
Learner, 128
learning disabilities, 50, 57, 66; explained, 308-313
learning, 24
least restrictive environment, 5, 19, 20, 22, 28, 201, 261, 341
legal profession, 228
legislation, 83, 143, 188, 264; equal

recognition before the law, 121;
    eugenics legislation, 213, 215;
    legislative committees, 195
Lewin, K., 10
Liachowitz, C., 94
Lickona, T., 17, 21
Liebert, R., 9
Life Goes On, 21
Lifton, R. and Markusen, E., 242
Lifton, R., 42, 222-223, 227, 231
Linton, S., Mello, S. and O'Neil, J.,
    90
Little People of America, 128
Long, E., 276
Long, N., 313
Longmore, P., 108, 113, 135-136
Lord, J., 54
Lusthaus, E., 336
Lynchburg Training School, 218

Macionis, J., 89
Mackelprang, R. and Salsgiver, O.,
    87, 95, 158, 161
Magriso, Rabbi, 159
mainstreaming, 6, 22, 23, 29, 34-35,
    79, 120, 330
Makas, E., 6, 29
Malaysia, 61
Maloff, C. and Wood, S., 277, 290,
    303
Manni, J., Winikur, D. and Keller,
    M., 209
Margolis, H. and Shapiro, A., 368,
    419
Margolis, H., Shapiro, A. and Ander-
    son, P., 388, 389
marriage, 126; restrictive laws, 212;
    selective marriage practices, 212
Martha's Vineyard, 56-57
Martiella, A., 437, 438
Massachusetts Asylum for the Blind,
    191
Masters and Stevens, 342
Mayen and Skrtic, 13
McBee, F., 38
McCahill, W., Nicholls, M., Peterson,

R., Hines, F., Leonard, E., and
    Cassell, R., 341
McCarthy-Tucker, S., 342
McGinn, C., 108
Measurement of Attitudes Toward
    People With Disabilities, 353
Medgyesi, V., 104
medical paradigm (medical model;
    diagnostic-prescriptive medical
    paradigm; medical functional-
    limitations model; medical view-
    point), 19, 31, 66, 82-98, 129,
    137, 143-144, 186, 207, 226,
    238, 242, 245, 445
medicalization, 89, 91; efficiency,
    237, 242; euphemistic terminolo-
    gy, 221, 225-226, 236; experi-
    mentation, 247; health, 225;
    medical community, 227, 229;
    medical conditions, 185; medical
    experts, 226; medical terms, 308;
    medicalization of disability, 90;
    medicalization of killing, 219-
    251; medicine, 184, 225; surgery,
    239; teratology, 151; the sick
    role, 93-95
Mein Kampf, 219, 240
melting pot, 127
Mengele, Dr. Joseph (see also medi-
    calization), 239, 247; medical
    detachment of, 240
mental retardation, 64, 165, 167, 177,
    191, 211; explained, 316-21; as a
    social construction, 321
Mercer, J., 317
Metcalf, U., 182
Meyerowitz, J., 12-13
Meyers, D., 103, 119-120
Miles, M., 165
Milligan, 284
minority group-independence-disab-
    lism paradigm (minority group
    paradigm; civil rights paradigm;
    independence view; social-civil
    rights paradigm), 31, 82-83, 86-
    87, 98-99, 143-144

Monestier, M., 163
monster, notion of, 151, 166; "monster market", 168
Montessori, Maria, 96
Moores, D., 152
Morgan, S., 148-149, 172-173
Morris, J., 13, 134
Morrison, J., and Urspring, A., 5, 8
Mortenson, R., 28
Mozes-Kor, E., 239
Mullens, J., 67, 78
Muller, I., 228, 243
Meyers, D., 100

Nance, J., 57
National Easter Seals Society, 342
National Federation of the Blind, 117
National Stuttering project, 119
Native Americans; cultures, 60; customs, 152; Papago, 58; Iroquis folk lore, 60; and speech, 306
nature, 151
Nazis, 218-220, 223, 225-227, 233, 237, 243, 329; Nazi doctors, 242, 245; Nazi extermination programs, 232; Nazi Germany, 157; Nazi Party's National Socialist German Medical Association, 220; racial purification, 112
New Guinea, 58
New Jersey Department of Education, 342
New York Institute for the Deaf and Dumb, 191
New York State of Regents, 28, 51, 105
Noddin, S., 140
non compliance, 261; accessibility compliance checklist, 379-387
Norden, M., 117
normal, 54, 115, 146, 211, 220, 229, 282, 329; different isn't abnormal, 267; language usage of, 46; normalization, 22, 23, 179, 201
North Korea; abuse in, 256

Odom, M. and Clark, D., 281, 292

Oliver, M., 84
oppression, 32, 83-84, 187; cruelty, 171; humiliation, 166; oppressive treatment; 146-147, 150
Orelove, F. and Sobsky, D.. 337
Orlans, 245
Oskamp, S., 366

Packard v. Packard (1864), 202
Padilla, R., 41
paradigms, 83, 85-86, 98, 144
Paraquad, 342
Pare, A., 151, 161, 175
Parsons, T., 93
patronization, 132; moral obligations of, 133
Patton, J., Blackbourn, J. and Fad, K., 45, 65, 124, 282
PEAK Parent Information Center, 24
peer cruelty, 17, 18
Perkins Institute and Massachusetts School for the Blind, 197; Colonel Thomas H. Perkins, 197
Pernick, M., 220
Peters, A., 75
Pfannmuller, Dr. Hermann, 231-232
Phifer, K., 71-72
Phiffer, D., 122, 210, 213
Philippine islands, 57
Pilcher, Dr. F., 215
pity, 105, 129, 132-135, 142, 164, 173-174, 206, 268
Plato, 153
Polish; prisoners of war, 235
political correctness, 39-40
Pope, A. and Tarlov, A., 85, 88
Posner, G. and Ware, J., 239-240
Preen, B., 155
preferential treatment, 84, 186
prejudice (see also discrimination), 5, 81, 83, 99, 102, 114, 112, 120, 124, 129, 184, 304; and curriculum, 407; curricular strategies against, 390-397; influences of, 147; overcategorization, 102; prejudicial attitudes, 28-29, 100; prejudicial beliefs, 101

President's Committee on Employment of the Handicapped, 342
President's Committee on Mental
Retardation, 112
pride, 127
privilege, 124, 196
Proctor, R., 223, 227, 233, 236, 238,
242
property rights, 187
psychiatry, 89, 202; psychiatric
patients, 223, 233; psychiatrists,
226
public accommodations, 263-264
public; public attitudes, 103; public
fear, 182; public outrage, 215;
public policy, 84, 146; public
programs, 195; public safety,
189;
purification, 180; race purification,
209, 219

racism, 99, 102, 126; notions of race,
153, 207; race "degeneration",
214; race "improvement", 219;
"racial hygiene", 222
reasonable accommodations, 5 5, 57,
128
recognition, 20
Rehabilitation Act, Section 504, 5
Rehabilitation Technology Services
and resource Centers, 442
rehabilitation, 187
Reid, B., 312
religion, 153, 184, 202; Christianity,
161-163; Eastern religions, 165-
166; faith, 161; Islam, 163-165;
Judaism, 157-161; moral imperfection, 159; religious attitudes,
157; religious leaders, 185; sin,
159
Remak, J., 232
reproduction (see also sterilization),
210; reproductive freedom, 126;
right to procreate, 217
respect, 21, 40
responsibility, 21

Richards, James J., 198
rights (see also civil rights, human
rights), 19, 82-83, 95, 156
Rioux, M., 81, 92, 93, 99, 132, 144
Rogers, C., 11
Rogers, F., 268, 270, 445
Rollin, W., 299-300
Ross, R. and Freelander, R., 342
Roth, J., 205
Rothman, D., 188, 193
Rubenfeld, P., 15, 26
Ruch, F., 303, 305
Russia, 169-170, 206
Ryan, W., 142

Safford, P., 57
Safilios-Rothchild, C., 147
Salend, S., 7, 19, 352
Sanders, P., 342
Sapon-Shevin, M., 98
Sarason, S. and Doris, J., 251, 321
Saxton, M. and Howe, F., 62
scapegoats, 79, 251
Scheerenberger, R., 149, 162, 165,
174, 184, 191, 196, 231, 236
Scheiber, B., 313
Schniedwind and Davidson, 342
Scholl, 53, 282
schools, 97, 105, 108, 113, 144, 199;
as total institutions, 178; classroom atmosphere, 269; classroom conditions, 347-349; public
schools, 207, 291; school environment, 6
Schroedel, 7, 18-19, 343, 445
Schumann, Dr. Horst, 241
science, 207, 213, 226, 245; racial
science, 228; scientific basis,
227; science of eugenics, 219;
scientific legitimacy, 225
Scull, S., 182
*Section 504 of the Rehabilitation Act
Amendments of 1973*, 260
segregation 13, 15, 31, 82, 113, 121,
144, 199-200, 445; adult imposed
18; by institutionalization, 177-

203, 215; by ridicule, 166-177; by sex, 246; in instructional settings 20, 24
self-concept (concept of self; self image), 11, 66, 74, 79, 268-269, 299, 311; interactions with others 12-15, 29; positive self image, 40
self-esteem (self confidence), 14, 39, 55, 132, 179
Senegal, 58
Sequin, Edouard, 96
sexism, 99, 102, 126
Shakespeare, 110-111
Shapiro, J., 49-50, 106, 135, 246
Shaver, J. and Curtis, C., 341, 351
Shaw, M. and Wright, J., 351, 366
Shea, T. and Bauer, A., 13, 45, 96, 122, 138, 142
Shields, L., 342
Shields, L., Christmas, D., Deitchman, L., Langford, T., Newingham, D., O'Daniel, L., Yeker, C. and Goodridge, J., 342
Shontz, F., 94
sin, 177; disability as sin, 159
Siperstein, G. and Bok, J., 104
slavery, 196; auctioning systems, 189; slave children, 173; slave labor, 256; slave trade, 188
Slavin, R., 348
Smith, J., 210, 214, 218, 220
Smith, R. and Neisworth, J., 67
Smith, S., 313
social distance scale 10
social liberation, 91
society, 95, 121; group cooperation, 148; social control, 250; social irresponsibility, 209; social judgment, 54; social order, 210; social pathology, 82; social policies, 83, 185; social relationships, 129; social responsibility, 318; social skills, 26; societal change, 76
South American tribes, 58
special education, 82, 86, 96, 270, 309, 334; field of, 65; labels in,

66; special educators, 250; textbooks, 339
Starkloff, M., 96
Staron, R., 29
Stein, J., 77
Steinbeck, J.,107
stereotypes, 31, 67-69, 78-79, 88, 98, 104, 113, 127, 129, 133, 186, 281, 322; and language, 42; and prejudice, 102; curricular strategies against, 350-351, 390-397; images of 16, 17; in children's literature 3; in classical literature, 110; in comic books, 4; in film, 117-119, 303; in literature, 106-113; in media, 107-110; internalization of, 109; of "the holy innocent", 114-116; of being subhuman, 107-108; of burden, 119-120; of comedy, 116-119; of dread, 113-114; of evil, 108-113; of pity, 105-107; stereotyping questionnaire, 408-410
sterilization, 146, 207, 211-19, 221, 241, 245-246; castration, 215
Stevens, A., 99
stigmas, 65, 138; stigma spread, 67, 130, 139, 270, 287, 289; stigmatization, 129; stigmatizing labels, 142
Stoddard, L., 209
Stone, E., 213
students; overprotection of, 114
stuttering, 299
Stuyvesant, Peter, 186
surveillance, 178
Sutherland, A., 40, 48, 52-53, 69, 104
sympathy (see also pity), 135, 137, 268
Szasz, T., 226, 228

teachers, 72, 79, 146, 198; preparation of 7, 30
teaching methods (see also curriculum), 8, 203, 206, 268, 314; active participation techniques,

444; addressing of prior knowledge, 351-354; anti-bias learning activities, 342; classroom discussion questions, 431-437; classroom guests, 397-407l; cooperative learning, 31, 269, 377-379; critical education practices, 339; disability awareness questionnaire, 354-361; experiencing disabilities, 425-431; field trips, 443-444; humor, 269; interactive activities, 437-439; interdisciplinary cooperation, 271; literature activities, 367-376; multi dimensional experiential approach, 343; role playing, 411-418; sentence completion activities, 362-365; simulations, 418-425; social gaming, 343; student involvement activities, 346; teaching strategies 7-8; technology, 439-443; value confrontation, 343

teratology, 151
teratoscopy, 150
terminology, 72
Tessier, E., 88
Third Reich, 221, 227; Reich Committee for the Scientific registration of Serious Hereditary and Congenital Diseases, 230
Thompson, C., 150, 166, 172-175
Thompson, D., 43
Tietze-Conrat, E., 168
Tiffany, F., 181
tolerance 15, 16, 313; intolerance, 81, 204
torture, 163
total institutions (see also asylums, institutionalization), 177-178
Trattner, W., 157, 178, 193
Trent, J., 209, 212
trephining, 150
Turnbull, A., Turnbull, H., Shank, M. and Leal, D., 329, 330, 334

Umbreit, J. and Baker, D., 12
UNESCO, 81, 157, 165
United Cerebral Palsy Association, 259
United Cerebral Palsy Association, 398
United Kingdom, 38, 137
United States Commission on Civil Rights, 16, 102, 138, 200
United States, 38, 199, 218, 320

values, 81
Van Etten, A., 17, 37, 115, 132
Van Ripper, C. and Emerick, L., 60, 166, 173, 298-301, 303-305
Vash, C., 37, 44, 55, 68, 70, 78, 121
victim, 75, 106, 142
Viet Nam; abuse in, 256
Virginia Sterilization Act (1924), 216

Wagner, Gustav, 239
Wahl, O., 13, 41, 68-69, 93, 107
Walt Disney Corporation, 116, 118
Watts, W., 7, 343, 411
Waxman, B., 82, 92, 134
Weicker, L., 121
Weinberg, N. and Santana, R., 4
Weindling, P., 225, 228
Weir, R., 337
wheelchair use, 87
White, B., 342
White, G., 217
whole person concept (person first language), 68; wholeness, 99
Wolfe, K., 243-244, 258
Wolfensberger, W., 22, 107-108, 133, 167, 180, 223, 234
Wolfensberger, W., Nirje, B., Olshansky, S., Perske, R. and Roos, P., 92, 105, 111, 113, 133
Wright, B., 46, 53, 58, 68-69
Wright, D., 45, 132, 139, 141, 420
WuDunn, S., 257

York asylum, 249, 183
Yuker, H. and Block, J., 345, 347-348

Yuker, H., 14, 46, 367

Zaire, Songye tribe of East Kasai, 59
Zimmerman, D., 44
Zola, I., 43, 78, 127, 130

Lecture Notes Computer Science

Edited by G. Goos and J. Hartmanis

4

J.
G.

S
D

M

RE
Ma
Pro

Springer-Verlag

Berlin Heidelberg New York London Paris Tokyo Hong Kong

CR Subject Classification (1987): F.3, D.1.3

ISBN 3-540-52559-9 Springer-Verlag Berlin Heidelberg New York
ISBN 0-387-52559-9 Springer-Verlag New York Berlin Heidelberg

Printing and binding: Druckhaus Beltz, Hemsbach/Bergstr.
2145/3140-543210 – Printed on acid-free paper